2009 03 11

Managing tourism in South Africa

Dedicated to Rohan

Managing tourism

in South Africa

Edited by RICHARD GEORGE

OXFORD

UNIVERSITY PRESS

Southern Africa

OXFORD
UNIVERSITY PRESS
Southern Africa

Oxford University Press Southern Africa (Pty) Ltd

Vasco Boulevard, Goodwood, Cape Town, Republic of South Africa
P O Box 12119, N1 City, 7463, Cape Town, Republic of South Africa

Oxford University Press Southern Africa (Pty) Ltd is a wholly-owned subsidiary of
Oxford University Press, Great Clarendon Street, Oxford OX2 6DP.

The Press, a department of the University of Oxford, furthers the University's objective of
excellence in research, scholarship, and education by publishing worldwide in

Oxford New York

Auckland Dar es Salaam Hong Kong Karachi
Kuala Lumpur Madrid Melbourne Mexico City Nairobi
New Delhi Shanghai Taipei Toronto

With offices in

Argentina Austria Brazil Chile Czech Republic France Greece
Guatemala Hungary Italy Japan Poland Portugal Singapore South Korea
Switzerland Turkey Ukraine Vietnam

Oxford is a registered trade mark of Oxford University Press
in the UK and in certain other countries

Published in South Africa
by Oxford University Press Southern Africa (Pty) Ltd, Cape Town

Managing Tourism in South Africa
ISBN 978 0 19 578913 3
Second impression 2008

© Oxford University Press Southern Africa (Pty) Ltd 2007

The moral rights of the author have been asserted
Database right Oxford University Press Southern Africa (Pty) Ltd (maker)

First published 2007

Publishing Manager: Alida Terblanche
Editor: Gavin Barfield
Project Manager: Marisa Montemarano
Designers: Marcus Bester, Sharna Sammy
Cover design: Sharna Sammy
Cartographer: John Hall
Indexer: Tanya Barben
Cover Photos: Photo Access, OUP Classet, Images of Africa

Set in Minion Pro 9.5pt on 12pt by Orchard Publishing
Printed and bound by ABC Press, Cape Town
108021

Contents

PART III: MANAGING TOURISM BUSINESSES 171

PART IV:
ISSUES IN TOURISM
MANAGEMENT   289

About the authors

Richard George (editor) Richard is a Senior Lecturer in Tourism Management and Services Marketing at the University of Cape Town (UCT). He holds a PhD in Marketing from UCT. His research interests include safety and security issues in tourism and tourism marketing. He is the author of several academic books and articles related to these topics, in particular *Marketing South African Tourism*, 2nd edition, Oxford University Press Southern Africa.

Tanya Barben Tanya is the Rare Books Librarian at the University of Cape Town libraries, with special responsibility as History and English subject librarian. Her current research interests include the importance of reading and writing in the development of a political consciousness, and the portrayal of South African history in juvenile fiction and literature.

Mark Boekstein Mark is the co-ordinator of the Tourism Programme in the Department of Geography, University of the Western Cape (UWC). He holds a MA in Geography and lectures in tourism planning, marketing, and development. He is the author of *Hot Spring Holidays: a tourist guide to hot springs and mineral spa resorts in southern Africa*.

Anton Brits Anton is Head of the Department of Transport Economics, Logistics, and Tourism at the University of South Africa (UNISA). He obtained a D.Com (Air Transport) at UNISA. His research interests in tourism are focused on the integrated nature of transport in the total tourism system, tourism's reliance on transport and the value which transport adds to tourism, with specific reference to the generation of foreign exchange through tourism as an export product.

Delano Caras Delano is a consultant to industry and a transaction advisor to government in the tourism and hospitality sectors, and a part-time Lecturer on the Postgraduate Diploma in Tourism Management Programme at the University of Cape Town. He is a Chartered Accountant, and holds a Masters degree in Business Administration from UCT.

Richard Chivaka Richard is an Associate Professor in the Department of Accounting at the University of Cape Town. He holds a PhD in Accounting from UCT, and is co-author of *Research Methodologies in Supply Chain Management* and *Handbook in Cost & Management Accounting*. His research interests include cost management, costing systems design, supply chain management and value chain analysis.

Scarlett Cornelissen Scarlett is a Senior Lecturer in Political Science at the University of Stellenbosch. She obtained her doctorate from the University of Glasgow. Currently her research interests focus on the international political economy of urban governance, and on the politics of sport mega-events.

Nicole Frey Nicole is a Lecturer in Marketing in the School of Management Studies at the University of Cape Town. She holds a Masters degree in Marketing from UCT. Her current research interests include Corporate Social Responsibility (CSR) and Social Marketing in the tourism industry.

Pieter Grobler Pieter is Professor of Human Resource Management in the Department of Human Resource Management at the University of South Africa. He holds a D.Com in Human Resource Management, and is the author of several books on the subject, in particular *Contemporary issues in human resource management*, 2nd edition, Oxford University Press Southern Africa.

Sabine Lehmann Sabine is the CEO of Table Mountain Aerial Cableway Company (TMACC), one of South Africa's premier tourist attractions. She holds a Masters degree in Business Administration from the University of Cape Town, and also runs a consultancy specialising in understanding and managing the visitor experience offered by visitor attractions.

Jennifer Nel Jennifer is a Lecturer in Tourism Management in the School of Economic and Management Sciences at the University of South Africa. She obtained an Honours degree (cum laude) in Tourism Management at the University of Pretoria, and worked in the tourism industry as Marketing Manager for a tour operator before following a career in education. Her research interests include marketing and customer service in the tourism industry.

Cecile Nieuwenhuizen Cecile is a Professor in the Department of Business Management at the University of South Africa. She holds a PhD in Entrepreneurship and Business Management. Cecile is author and editor of various books, including *Entrepreneurship: a South African perspective*. Her research focus is on entrepreneurship development and education, with a specific focus on opportunity and high-growth entrepreneurs.

Chris Saunders Chris is a Professor in the Department of Historical Studies at the University of Cape Town. He has a PhD in History from Oxford University, and has written extensively on all aspects of the history of southern Africa. Among his current interests is the way in which Namibia moved to independence in 1990, and the struggle for liberation in southern Africa.

Irene Thiede Irene is currently lecturing, tutoring and researching at the University of Cape Town, where she is registered for a PhD. She previously received her Masters in Economics at the same institution. Irene also holds degrees in Social Anthropology of Latin America and in Economics from the Free University of Berlin. She spent many years working in the German hotel and event management industries after doing a business degree in hotel management. Her research focuses on the economic impacts of tourism, particularly on poverty and income inequality.

Ciné van Zyl Ciné is an Associate Professor in Tourism Management in the Department of Transport Economics, Logistics and Tourism of the University of South Africa. She obtained an M.Phil in Tourism Management at the University of Pretoria, and a D.Com in Tourism Management at UNISA. Her research interests include the leisure and business tourism markets and, more specifically, the festival and events sectors of the South African tourism industry.

Gustav Visser Gustav is an Associate Professor in Human Geography in the Department of Geography at the University of the Free State. He holds a doctorate from the London School of Economics and Political Science, and has written extensively on the tourism and development nexus. His current research programme is focused on sexualised urban leisure spaces.

Patrick Vrancken Patrick is a Professor of Law and Head of the Department of International, Constitutional and Human Rights Law at the Nelson Mandela Metropolitan University. He holds LLM and LLD degrees from the University of Cape Town, and is the leading expert on tourism law in South Africa. He has published widely both in South Africa and abroad, and presently focuses on the legal aspects of international tourism.

Foreword

Over nine million international tourists visited South Africa in 2007 – a 8,3% increase on 2006 figures, faster than the global growth of 6% in tourist numbers. Looking back over a longer time period, you can clearly see how much we have achieved. In 1993, just 15 years ago, we had just over 3 million visitors. Attracting tourists from around the globe creates more jobs and economic opportunities, enabling us to meet the expectations created for the tourism industry in terms of the Accelerated and Shared Growth Initiative for South Africa (ASGISA). Over 947 500 people are directly and indirectly employed by the South African travel and tourism economy. Tourism contributed R141,86-billion or 8.3% of GDP in 2006.

Improved access to the country and the build-up to the FIFA World Cup in 2010 will accelerate South Africa's international competitiveness, further growing the country's tourism industry. However, one of the key issues is developing skills in the sector, especially in the high skills-levels band where there lies a shortage of management expertise. *Managing Tourism in South Africa* addresses this issue by linking the tourism industry and academic institutions through practice as well as theory. The book will be especially useful to new entrants into the industry and greatly assist in our goal of transforming the sector.

Managing Tourism in South Africa has unique application within the study of tourism management. The book begins by offering an overview of tourism, clarifying basic concepts for understanding the structure and interrelations of the South African tourism industry. It looks at the fascinating history of tourism in South Africa and then examines the various sub-sectors that comprise the industry. It examines an area that I consider absolutely important despite its absence in other works: the role of government in tourism. It is paramount to discuss tourism policy and how to implement it efficiently. The book then delves into fundamental management theory relating to tourism businesses, including marketing, financial management and human resource management. Finally, *Managing Tourism in South Africa* considers pertinent issues such as the management of the impacts of tourism and responsible tourism management, which can go some way to making our industry an environmentally sensitive one.

Managing Tourism in South Africa is equally useful for students and practitioners who work in and manage within the sector and who need an informed view of how the business of tourism works.

Marthinus van Schalkwyk
Minister, Environmental Affairs & Tourism
DEAT

environment & tourism

Department:
Environmental Affairs and Tourism
REPUBLIC OF SOUTH AFRICA

Preface

Since 1995, tourism has been the fastest growing sector in the South African economy. Tourist numbers – both international and domestic – are expected to continue growing in the coming years, as the country prepares to host the FIFA World Cup in 2010. Commensurate with this has been an increase in the study of tourism at all levels of the South African education system (from schools to FET colleges and universities). Organisations in both the public and private sectors are acting on the increasing importance of tourism. Travel and tourism companies, in particular, are seeking to recruit graduates who are in possession of relevant business skills, together with an understanding of tourism and the tourism industry. Notably, from my involvement with the industry, I realise that employers prefer to recruit students or graduates who have the business skills of marketing, human resource management, and financial savvy. Tourism, after all, is a business (and a complex one, at that), and management lies at the core of tourism businesses.

This book explores the issues of tourism management from a South African perspective. It is written in an easy-to-read, student-friendly style, yet is comprehensive in that it examines the management of tourism from the perspectives of all the components of the tourism industry, and discusses the challenges that managing tourism presents. While *Managing Tourism in South Africa* is aimed at first- and second-year undergraduate students, practitioners within the industry will find also find it a useful resource.

Academics and specialists from diverse disciplines have contributed to the book, thereby integrating the knowledge and skills-set of history, geography, sociology, economics, etc. within the context of tourism management. It is not possible, however, to include the entire range of approaches to tourism, given the nature of the book. Indeed, one of the greatest challenges faced in writing this book was to limit it to a suitable length, as each chapter could easily warrant a book in its own right, and, in certain cases, a topic within a chapter could be the focus of an entire book. This book does not aim to be a definitive textbook on tourism management, but nevertheless provides a comprehensive text on the principles of tourism management. Other texts dealing with the topics or subjects it covers can be found in the 'further reading' sections at the end of each chapter.

The book is presented in four parts: tourism overview, the tourism industry, managing tourism businesses, and issues in tourism management. Its structure follows a logical flow, so that lecturers and students can fit the chapters into the pattern of their course. All chapters are extensively referenced – combining theory with 'industry examples', which indicate best practice in tourism management in South Africa. Each chapter provides suggestions for further reading, and suggests useful websites. Vignettes (Example boxes) highlight the theory in practice. All chapters include a case study, applying the theory presented in the chapter to industry practice. Key words are highlighted throughout the text, and are explained in a glossary which appears at the end of the book.

Richard George

Acknowledgements

A number of people have contributed to this book. These include, first and foremost, Oxford University Press Southern Africa, who commissioned the book; in particular Marisa Montemarano for her enthusiastic involvement and meticulous management throughout the entire project, as well as my editor, Gavin Barfield, for his excellent editing.

I would like to thank several colleagues in the Department of Management at the University of Cape Town who made several useful suggestions to various topics in the book: Justin Beneke, Julian Hodson, Jacqui Kew, Alison Meadows, and Irene Thede.

I would also like to thank all the following individuals, some of whom acted as 'personal reviewers' and provided contemporary 'cross-over' experience from the industry, as well as a number of contributors who provided information for the case studies and the photographs and logos used throughout the text.

Anya Potgieter, 1Time Airlines
Carolyn Enzlin, Andrew Weir Shipping Company
Jacqui McKnight, Association for South African Travel Agents ASATA
Phenyo Marumo, The Big Hole
Juliet Browne, Blue Action Marketing
Melinda Swift, Cradle of Humankind & Dinokeng Blue IQ Projects
John Riddler, Cullinan Holdings
Riaan Aucamp, Department of Environmental Affairs and Tourism
Kate Rivett-Carnac, Department of Trade and Industry
Prabashni Reddy, Durban Africa
Rema van Niekerk, Federated Hospitality Association of South Africa
Amanda Hardy, Flight Centre Limited
Nigel Stoker, Harvey World Travel

Audrey D'Angelo, Independent Newspapers
Kealeboga Gift Mogapi, MO Happy People Travel & Tours
Garth Allen, Really Useful Knowledge Consultants
Palesa Tsiu, Regional Tourism Organisation of Southern Africa
Catherine Biggs, Singita Game Reserves
Samu Dube, South African Airways
Angeline Lue, Business Tourism Unit, South African Tourism
Marjorie Dean, Southern African Tourism Services Association
Liezl Gericke, STA Travel
Pamela Young, St Helena Tourist Office
Kerri McDonald, Strategic Business Partnerships
Gareth Haysom, Sustainability Institute and University of Stellenbosch
Lisa Paterson, Table Mountain Cableway Company Ltd.
Johann Strydom and Ania Ewan, Thompsons Tours
Sindiswa Nhlumayo, Tourism BEE Charter Council
Mmatšatši Marobe, Tourism Business Council of South Africa
Jane Msiska, Tourism, Hospitality, Education and Training Authority
Carrie Dangerfield, Tourism Grading Council of South Africa
Gail Lines, Tourvest
Hélder Tomás, United Nations World Tourism Organisation
Sarieu Caramba-Coker, World Travel & Tourism Council

Last, but not least, I would like to acknowledge the patience, understanding and hard work of all the highly respected authors who responded promptly to my editing requests and who helped to produce this book.

Abbreviations

AA	Automobile Association		ECPAT	End Child Prostitution and Trafficking
AAA	African Airlines Association		EC	European Commission
ACSA	Airports Company of South Africa		ECTB	Eastern Cape Tourism Board
ADS	Approved destination status		EIA	Environmental impact assessment
AIDS	Acquired immune deficiency syndrome		EMS	Environmental Management System
AITO	Association of Independent Tour Operators		ETC	European Travel Commission
AMPS	All media product survey		EU	European Union
ANC	African National Congress		FEDHASA	Federated Hospitality Association of South
APEX	Advance purchase excursion			Africa
ASGISA	Accelerated and shared growth initiative for		FET	Further education training
	South Africa		FFP	Frequent flyer programme
ASATA	Association for South African Travel Agents		FIFA	Fédération Internationale de Football
AU	African Union			Association
B2B	Business to business		FIT	Fully inclusive tour/independent tourist
B2C	Business to consumer		FSTA	Free State Tourism Authority
BA	British Airways		FTTSA	Fair Trade in Tourism South Africa
BARSA	Board of Airline Representatives of South		GAAP	Generally accepted accounting principles
	Africa		GDP	Gross domestic product
BABASA	Bed & Breakfast Association of South Africa		GDS	Global distribution system
B&B	Bed and breakfast		GNP	Gross national product
BEA	Break-even analysis		GOP	Gross operating profit
BEE	Black economic empowerment		GTA	Gauteng Tourism Authority
BEP	Break-even point		HDIs	Historically disadvantaged individuals
BSA	Backpacking South Africa		HR	Human resources
BT	Business Trust		HRIS	Human resource information system
C2C	Consumer to consumer		HRM	Human resources management
CAA	Civil Aviation Authority		IAAPA	International Association of Amusement
CBT	Computer-based tourism/training			Parks and Attractions
CEO	Chief executive officer		IATA	International Air Transport Association
CIPs	Critical incident points		IBTA	International Business Travel Association
CM	Contribution margin		ICCA	International Congress & Conventions
CoJ	City of Johannesburg			Association
CRM	Customer relationship management		ICT	Information and communication technologies
CRS	Central reservation system		IDTV	Interactive digital television
CSR	Corporate social responsibility		IH&RA	International Hotel & Restaurant Association
CT	Cultural tourism		IMC	International Marketing Council
CTC	Canadian Tourism Commission		IRR	Internal rate of return
CTRU	Cape Town Routes Unlimited		ITB	Internationale Tourismus-Börse
CTICC	Cape Town International Convention Centre		IUOTO	International Union of Official Travel
CVP	Cost-volume-profit			Organisations
DASLC	Domestic Air Services Licensing Council		JSE	Johannesburg Stock Exchange
DEAT	Department of Environmental Affairs &		JIPSA	Joint initiative on priority skills acquisition
	Tourism		KNP	Kruger National Park
DEDT	Department of Economic Development &		KZN	KwaZulu-Natal
	Tourism		LDC	Less developed countries
DMC	Destination management company		LSM	Living standards measure
DMO	Destination marketing organisation		LTA	Local tourism authority
DPE	Department of Public Enterprises		LTO	Local tourism organisation
DoT	Department of Transport		LTP	Limpopo Tourism & Parks
DPE	Department of Public Enterprises		MBO	Management by objectives
DTI	Department of Trade and Industry (dti)		MDGs	Millennium development goals
EAP	Employee assistance programme		MICE	Meeting, incentives, conferences, and
EBITDA	Earnings before interest, tax, depreciation, and			exhibitions
	amortisation		MIS	Management information system

MNCs	Multi-national corporations	SAT	South African Tourism
NAASA	National Accommodation Association of South Africa	SATOA	South African Tour Operators Association
NBG	National Botanical Garden	SATSA	Southern African Tourism Services Association
NBI	National Business Institute	SBP	Small Business Project
NCTA	Northern Cape Tourism Authority	SIT	Special interest tourism
NEPAD	New Partnership for Africa's Development	SMART	Specific, measurable, achievable, realistic and time
NGO	Non-governmental organisation	SMMEs	Small, medium and micro enterprises
NMA	National Heritage Resources	ST	Space tourism
NPA	National Ports Authority	SWOT	Strengths, weaknesses, opportunities and threats
NRTG	National Registrar of Tourist Guides	TALC	Tourism area life-cycle
NTO	National tourist/m organisation	TAP	Tourism action plan
NVP	Net present value	TBCSA	Tourism Business Council of South Africa
OAS	Organisation of American States	TDS	Total direct spend
OECD	Organisation for Economic Cooperation and Development	TEA	Total entrepreneurial activity
PATA	Pacific Asia Travel Association	TEP	Tourism Enterprise Programme
PLC	Product life-cycle	TGCSA	Tourism Grading Council of South Africa
POS	Point of sale	TGS	Tourism growth strategy
PPP	Public private partnership	THETA	Tourism, Hospitality and Sport Education and Training Authority
PPT	Pro-poor tourism	TIC	Tourist information centre
PR	Public relations	TISA	Timeshare institute of South Africa
PRISA	Public Relations Institute of South Africa	TIM	Tourism income multiplier
PSA	Proudly South African	TMACC	Table Mountain Aerial Cableway Company
PTA	Provincial tourism authority	TMNP	Table Mountain National Park
PR	Public relations	ToMA	Top of the mind awareness
QCS	Quality customer service	TOI	Tour operators initiative
RETOSA	Regional Tourism Organisation of Southern Africa	TOMSA	Tourism Marketing South Africa
ROI	Return on investment	TSA	Tourism satellite account
RTA	Responsible tourism awards	TTI	Tourism Training Institute
RTMSA	Responsible tourism manual for South Africa	UAE	United Arab Emirates
RTO	Regional tourism organisation	UN	United Nations
SAA	South African Airways	UNDP	United Nations Development Programme
SAACI	Southern African Association for the Conference Industry	UNEP	United Nations Environment Programme
SAARF	South African Advertising Research Foundation	UNESCO	United National Educational, Scientific & Cultural Organisation
SAATP	Southern African Association of Tourism Professionals	UNWTO	United Nations World Tourism Organisation
SABS	South African Bureau of Standards	USP	Unique selling proposition (or point)
SABOA	Southern African Bus Operators Association	VFM	Value for money
SABPP	South African Board for Personnel Practice	VFR	Visiting friends and relatives
SACAA	South African Civil Aviation Authority	VR	Virtual reality
SADC	Southern African Development Community	VTA	Virtual travel agency
SAHRA	South African Heritage Resources Agency	WBT	Web-based training
SAMSA	South African Maritime Safety Authority	WHO	World Health Organisation
SANParks	South African National Parks	WHS	World Heritage Site
SANRAL	South African National Roads Agency Limited	WOM	Word-of-mouth
SAPs	South African Police Services	WSSD	World Summit on Sustainable Development
SAR	South African Railways	WTM	World Travel Market
SARCC	South African Rail Commuter Corporation	WTO	World Trade Organisation
SARS	South African Revenue Services	WTTC	World Travel and Tourism Council
		WWW	World Wide Web
		ZTA	Zimbabwe Tourism Authority

PART I | Tourism overview

1

Introduction to tourism

Richard George

Promoting and encouraging domestic tourism in South Africa – the Sho't Left Fun Bus

Purpose

The purpose of this chapter is to introduce you to the business and academic subject of tourism management.

Learning outcomes

After reading this chapter, you should be able to:
- understand and describe the meaning of tourism
- appreciate the importance of tourism
- discuss the characteristics of tourism businesses
- identify the main international tourism flows
- understand the tourism system model
- describe how tourism is a multi-disciplinary subject
- understand the structure of the South African tourism industry.

Chapter overview

This chapter introduces the subject of tourism management. It begins with a debate surrounding various definitions of tourism. It outlines the importance of tourism as an economic activity, and discusses some of the key characteristics of tourism businesses, highlighting the difficulties in managing them. It then considers tourism and, more specifically, tourism management as a field of study. Finally, it introduces the concept of the tourism system model and discusses the model's interrelated elements, which provide a framework for the structure of the book.

The concluding case study illustrates how the theory contained in this chapter can be applied to a practical situation in the South African domestic tourism industry.

Introduction

Tourism is a global phenomenon. The world's largest and fastest-growing industry, it is a major economic, environmental, and sociocultural dynamic force. According to the World Travel and Tourism Council (WTTC), tourism 'directly and indirectly supports over 230-million jobs worldwide, and generates more than 10% of world gross domestic product' (2006: 2).

Tourism is characterised by constant change and development. Significant events over the last few years, such as the terrorist attacks of 9/11, the Iraq war, and avian flu have highlighted the vulnerability of the sector. Tourism is also one of the most dynamic of industries; offering new means of transport, innovative products, and new destinations every year – such as the world's largest cruise liner (*Freedom of the Seas*), which can accommodate over 5 500 passengers (see Chapter 5 – Managing transport for tourists); a pet hotel in New York, or the opening up of Chinese frontiers (see Chapter 17 – Future of tourism). Tourism, for business or pleasure, is a very competitive market – organisations and destinations compete to outdo each other. Tourism demands high standards of professional management, knowledge, and effective managers.

Some of the tasks involved in managing tourism are: understanding what tourism is, how it operates, its characteristics, its importance, and how it affects people. To begin with, what is meant by the term *tourism*?

Some basic definitions of tourism

This book is about **tourism management**, so it is important to establish what is meant by the concept of 'tourism'. 'Tourism' is perhaps one of the most widely used, yet least understood, words in the English language. Most people would agree that tourism is about travelling away from their home for recreational purposes. Many definitions of tourism have been put forward over the years. However, tourism remains an ambiguous term, and no definition of tourism is universally accepted. Indeed, one of the most frustrating aspects of studying tourism is lack of consistency in the use of the definition of *tourism*. Tourism is a very broad area to define, and debate has ensued ever since the League of Nations attempted in 1937 to define it as 'people travelling abroad for periods of more than 24 hours'.

Much of the argument has surrounded who should be included in the definition, such as 'visitors' and 'day visitors'. Tourism academics such as Cooper *et al.* (2005: 12) have tried to distinguish between demand-side and supply-side definitions of tourism.

Demand-side definitions of tourism

According to the United Nations World Tourism Organisation (UN-WTO), an intergovernmental body of **tourism**:

> '*Tourism is defined as the activities of persons travelling to, and staying in, places outside their usual environment for not more than one consecutive year for leisure, business and other purposes not related to the exercise of an activity remunerated from within the place visited*' (2004).

This conceptual definition of tourism, which is perhaps the most widely accepted and cited in academic literature, provides a view that tourism is a distinct activity, taking place away from the home area and for a period of 24 hours or more. Tourists who spend less than one night in a destination are defined by the UN-WTO as '**excursionists**' (also referred to as 'day visitors'). UN-WTO's definition suggests that tourism is about:

- the movement of people
- two key elements: the journey to and the stay at the destination
- the fact that it takes place outside the usual environment
- the fact that the movement to destinations is short-term and temporary
- the fact that destinations are visited for purposes other than taking up permanent residence or employment.

However, UN-WTO's definition of tourism is not immune from criticism. For example, it fails to refer to the purpose of the trip (it includes 'or other purposes'), thus providing the reader with a very broad definition. According to Gilbert (1990: 7), what makes tourism difficult to define is the very broad nature of both the concept, as well as the need for so many service inputs. Indeed, tourism involves many other sectors and industries. As Lickorish and Jenkins (1997: 1) point out, tourism is an activity which cuts across conventional sectors in the economy.

Supply-side definitions of tourism

As with the demand-side definitions of tourism, defining tourism from a supply perspective is also problematic. The word 'industry' implies that products may be categorised as being part of the industry, or not. However, this is practically impossible to do. For instance, how is a restaurant categorised that services both local residents and foreign tourists alike? Likewise, transport services often serve the needs of other consumers besides tourists. Indeed, Lickorish and Jenkins (1997: 1) question whether tourism can be described as an 'industry', as it does not have an output which can be physically quantified, unlike agriculture ('tonnes of wheat') or beverages ('litres of whisky'). Mill and Morrison (1992: xiii) are in agreement, and emphasise that tourism must be seen as a process rather than an industry.

Tourism may be viewed as a collective entity, which may or may not be described as an industry. Nevertheless, for the purpose of this book, tourism is referred to as both an 'industry' and as an 'activity' or 'process'. In view of these issues, let us now examine tourism's close relationship with other activities, such as *leisure* and *recreation*.

Interrelationships – tourism, leisure and recreation

Further adding to the ambiguity of what constitutes tourism is that it overlaps other concepts: recreation and leisure. In fact tourism, recreation, and leisure are all closely linked. Tourism, therefore, should not be considered as a distinct activity, but as one of a number of related activities; namely leisure and recreation.

What is meant by the term **leisure**? Like 'tourism', it, too, is problematic to define. Leisure means different things to different people. Some people consider it to be time when not working; others equate it with specific free-time activities, such as gardening, watching television, reading, or going to the cinema. Leisure is therefore associated with *leisure time* or *leisure activities*.

'Leisure' is defined as 'time spent in or free for relaxation or enjoyment' (Pearsall, 1999: 812). According to Torkildsen (2005: 175) the term is derived from the Latin *licere*, 'to be free or allowed'. However, all these definitions fail to take into account the many necessary functions that we have to perform in our daily lives, such as eating, sleeping, and carrying out domestic chores. Therefore, leisure might be more comprehensively defined as 'time left over after work, sleep and other basic needs have been met, for people to do as they please'. Gunter (1987: 116) found that leisure is characterised by 'a sense of separation from the everyday world, feelings of intense pleasure, freedom of choice, adventure...'.

Leisure also represents an opportunity for **recreation**. Recreation is the activities that happen during an individual's leisure time. Hobbies, games, sports activities – and tourism – are all types of recreation, and discretionary uses of our leisure time. The term is derived from the Latin word *recreatio*, meaning that which refreshes or restores. Recreation may be active or passive, and take place inside or outside the home. A game of golf in the local park would constitute recreation. As Mill and Morrison (1992: 9) note, there is no distance aspect to recreation. If a golfer were to drive 100 kilometres to a golf course for the weekend, the game of golf would be part of tourism and the golfer would be on a trip. Tourism can be seen as a type of recreation, but it is evidently not *all* recreation. It is also often described as an aspect of leisure, which does not account for business travel (see Figure 1.1 overleaf).

By considering the definitions above, we can help tourism managers and students alike to understand the range of needs that people seek to satisfy through their touristic behaviour.

Figure 1.1 Recreation, leisure and tourism

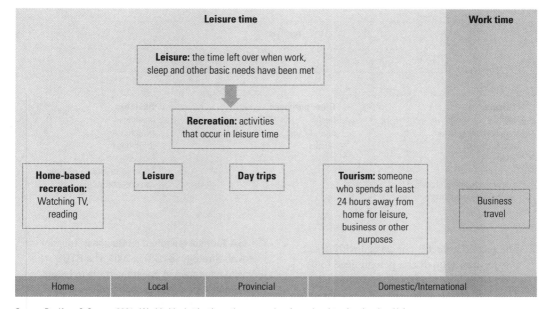

Source: Boniface & Cooper, 2001. *Worldwide destinations: the geography of travel and tourism.* London: Heinemann

Defining tourists

The problem of defining tourism can be overcome by defining and understanding the term *tourist*. A tourist is a person who travels outside their usual environment (see Figure 1.2 overleaf). More accurately, UN-WTO (2004) defines a **tourist** as 'a visitor whose visit is for at least 24 hours, and whose purpose of visit may be classified under one of the following three groups:

- leisure and holidays
- other tourism purposes – including studying or health reasons
- business and professional (a trip undertaken with the purpose of attending a conference, exhibition, event, or as part of an **incentive trip**)'.

Tourists may be further divided into the following categories:

- *domestic tourists* – residents taking holidays, short breaks, and trips within their own country

- *international tourists* – those who travel outside their country of residence
- *outbound tourists* – people who travel from their usual country of residence to visit another country. For example, the South African government would classify a tourist from South Africa who is going to Mauritius as an **outbound** tourist
- *inbound tourists* – those who travel from their own country to another to visit that country. For example, the government of Mauritius would classify the South African tourist visiting Mauritius as an **inbound** tourist.

It is generally accepted that there are four main aspects to what constitutes tourism as an activity:

1. A definition should take into account the *categories* that may or may not be counted as tourism (i.e. second-home owners, or cruise ship passengers docking at a port for a few hours)

Figure 1.2 The reasons why people travel

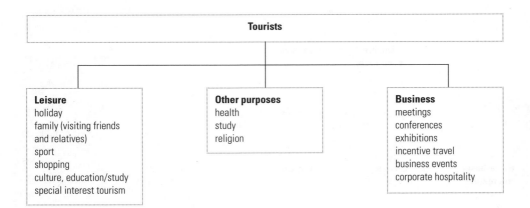

Leisure	**Other purposes**	**Business**
holiday	health	meetings
family (visiting friends	study	conferences
and relatives)	religion	exhibitions
sport		incentive travel
shopping		business events
culture, education/study		corporate hospitality
special interest tourism		

2. The second aspect is concerned with *time*: (i.e. for how long does a person need to be away from home to be deemed a tourist?)
3. The third element that should be taken into account is *distance* (how far away does a person need to be from their home area to be considered a tourist?)
4. Fourthly – and perhaps fundamentally – a definition of a tourist should take into account the *purpose of visit* (i.e. for what reason: leisure, business, education, or health).

Example Business tourism: leisure tourism's younger cousin

Business tourism is the fastest-growing segment of the worldwide tourism market and has enormous growth potential in South Africa. The meetings industry (encompassing conferences, exhibitions, incentive trips, business events, corporate hospitality and meetings) injects over R2,6 billion into the country's economy and supports 12 000 jobs. South African Tourism, South Africa's national tourism organisation, aims for South Africa to be ranked in the ICCA's (International Congress & Conventions Association) Top 10 meeting and conferencing destinations by 2010. South Africa's conference industry was rated 31st in the ICCA's top 40 list of leading destinations in the world in 2006.

SA Tourism launched its Business Tourism Growth Strategy (BTGS) in 2007. The BTGS aims to educate and equip the trade to better sell South Africa, and to align and integrate marketing efforts in respect of growth of the business tourism industry. SA Tourism unleashed its 'Business Unusual' proposition at Meetings Africa (a business tourism trade show) in 2006. South Africa's main competitors include established business tourism destinations such as Spain, Austria, USA and the UK.

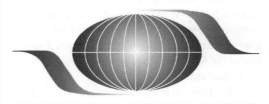

WORLD TOURISM ORGANIZATION
ORGANISATION MONDIALE DU TOURISME
ORGANIZACIÓN MUNDIAL DEL TURISMO
ВСЕМИРНАЯ ТУРИСТСКАЯ ОРГАНИЗАЦИЯ
منظمة السياحة العالمية

UN-WTO's logo

Discussion point

With reference to the UN-WTO definition of tourism, which of the following can be classified as tourists?

- a South African family staying in their second home in another town or province
- a group of American cruise-liner passengers docking at eThekwini for an afternoon
- a cross-border shopper from Mozambique visiting Johannesburg, but not staying overnight
- a German delegate attending a conference in Cape Town.

Example Cross-border shopper statistics

- Most cross-border shoppers come from Zimbabwe and Mozambique.
- Large numbers of shoppers also come from Swaziland, Botswana, and Lesotho.
- The majority of shoppers come to Johannesburg twice a month.
- The average length of stay is one to three nights.
- Accommodation used by cross-border shoppers varies from hotels, B&Bs, and dormitories, to staying at Park station. Many also stay with friends and family.
- High crime rates and a lack of suitable storage are the main concerns for cross-border shoppers.
- For most, cross-border shopping is the main source of income.

Source: COMMark Trust

Once there is an understanding of how tourism is defined, we can begin to analyse and appreciate the scale and global significance of tourism as an economic activity.

The significance of tourism

Tourism is of global significance. In 2006, there were 846-million people who travelled internationally, an increase of 5,4% over 2005 (UN-WTO, 2007). According to the WTTC, the global tourism industry is now worth US$6,500 billion a year, and is projected to achieve 4,6% annual growth over the next ten years. UN-WTO forecasts that international tourist arrivals are expected to exceed 1,6 billion by 2020 (see Chapter 17 – The future of tourism).

Page (2007: 3) explains the significant role of tourism globally:

- tourism is a discretionary activity
- tourism is of growing economic significance globally
- technology, such as the Internet, has made researching and booking holidays and travel-related products easy
- global travel is becoming more accessible for all classes of people in the developed world.

In South Africa, tourism is one of the key drivers of the economy, supporting around 947 500 jobs and generating over R100-billion every year. In 2006, tourism contributed (directly and indirectly) R141,86-billion, or 8,3% to South Africa's gross domestic product (GDP) (SA Tourism, 2007). It is well on course to overtake mining as the country's number one economic activity. According to South African Tourism (SA Tourism), the country's **national tourism organisation (NTO)**, over 9,07-million international (overseas and continental African) tourists visited South Africa in 2007 (see Figure 1.3); a 8,3% increase in visitor arrivals on the previous year (SA Tourism, 2008). Figure 1.4 shows that international tourist arrivals to South Africa have increased steadily year-on-year since the early 1990s. The release of Nelson Mandela on 11 February 1990, and the associated worldwide publicity, is one of the reasons for this increase, and even celebrity appeal. The transition to democracy with the first democratic elections held in 1994, has resulted in the country possessing a positive global image and high 'emotional pull' and celebrity appeal drawcards. Furthermore, there is good **value for money** (VFM) compared to other destinations, and foreign currency exchange rates are favourable.

After agreeing on a definition of what constitutes tourism, we can make use of the technical definitions used to measure tourism. Tourism statistics are important to assist tourism managers in decision-making.

Figure. 1.3 International tourist arrivals to South Africa, 1994–2006

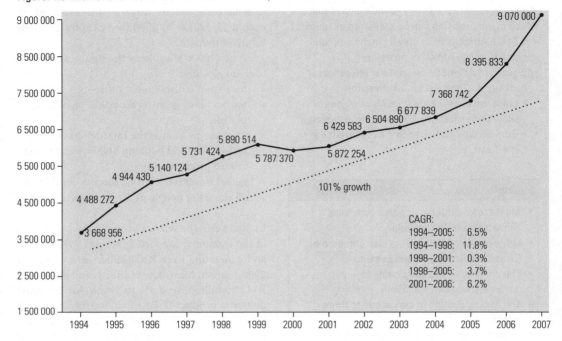

Discussion point

Examine Figure 1.3 above, and suggest reasons for the pattern of international tourists visiting South Africa over the last 12 years.

Measuring tourism flows

Tourism is essentially a series of flows or 'movements'. Monitoring these flows provides statistical data to help tourism managers understand current volumes of flows, and about where tourists travel to and from. The sources of data most widely used by academics are those collated and disseminated by the UN-WTO and the WTTC.

It is important to identify which countries are the major tourism generators and major tourism recipients. Table 1.1 shows the 'top ten' destinations, while Tables 1.2 and 1.3 list the 'top ten' spenders and earners to show international tourist arrivals by region in 2006. The UN-WTO rankings of top destinations put South Africa at 29th position in 2006 in terms of international tourist arrivals size.

In the next section, we examine the nature of tourism – what it is that makes it unique, and what implications it has for the tourism manager.

Figure 1.4 Tourist arrivals to South Africa (1965–2006)

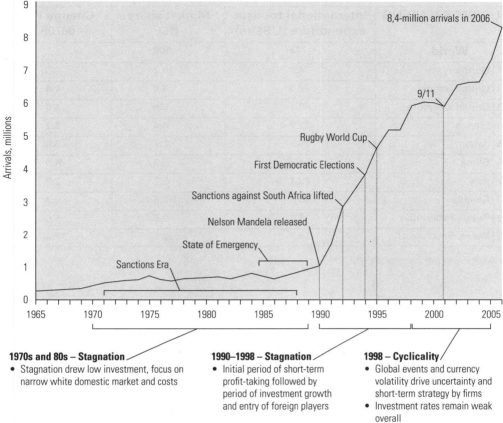

Source: SA Tourism, 2006. *2005 Annual domestic tourism report.* Tshwane: SA Tourism

Table 1.1 The world's top tourism destinations, 2006

Rank 2006	Country	Int'l Tourist Arrivals in 2006 (million)	Change % 06/05
1	France	79.1	4.2
2	Spain	58.5	4.5
3	United States	51.1	3.8
4	China	49.6	6.0
5	Italy	41.1	12.4
6	United Kingdom	30.7	9.3
7	Germany	23.6	9.6
8	Mexico	21.4	-2.6
9	Austria	20.3	1.5
10	Russian Federation	20.2	1.3

Source: UN-WTO (www.world-tourism.org)

Table 1.2 The world's top ten tourism spenders, 2006

TOURISM SPENDING		International tourism expenditure (US$bn)	Market share (%)	Change (%) 06/05
	World	733	100	
1	Germany	74.8	10.2	-0.3
2	United States	72.0	9.8	4.4
3	United Kingdom	63.1	8.6	4.6
4	France	32.2	4.4	2.2
5	Japan	26.9	3.7	3.8
6	China	24.3	3.3	11.8
7	Italy	23.1	3.2	2.2
8	Canada	20.5	2.8	5.7
9	Russia Federation	18.8	2.6	5.6
10	Korea, Republic of	18.2	2.5	18.4

Source: Based on information from the UN-WTO

Table 1.3 The world's top ten earners, 2006

TOURISM EARNING		International tourism receipts (US$bn)	Change (%) 06/05
	World	880	100
1	USA	85.7	4.8
2	Spain	51.1	6.6
3	France	42.9	1.5
4	Italy	38.1	7.7
5	China	33.9	15.9
6	United Kingdom	33.7	9.8
7	Germany	32.8	12.3
8	Australia	17.8	5.8
9	Turkey	16.9	-7.2
10	Austria	16.7	4.0

Source: Based on information from the UN-WTO

The nature of tourism

Tourism is not a simple business. It is a multi-sectoral, multi-faceted business, and encompasses many different sectors of the economy.

The following features of the tourism industry are important:

- *Complexity*. The tourism sector is variable and complex, comprising a number of directly and indirectly-related organisations, from B&B establishments to multi-national hotel groups; from curio sellers to casinos. Tourism businesses do not operate in isolation – from the consumer's perspective, the holiday experience consists of a number of elements (meals, accommodation, transport, sight-seeing, etc).
- *Fragmentation and diversity*. The supply of tourism is fragmented and diverse. In South Africa, as in most countries, the industry is highly concentrated and dominated financially by a small elite group of large, well-established, mostly locally-owned tourism enterprises, and by a considerable number of **small, medium, and micro enterprises (SMMEs)**. Large, mostly locally-owned tourism enterprises include major tourist agencies, transport operations, hotel-groups, and conference centres. Large players at the top end of the market include Tourvest (which comprises Seekers Travel Group, amongst others); Thompsons Travel Group (see Chapter 7); car rental companies such as Avis, Imperial, Budget, and Hertz; hotel groups such as Southern Sun, Sun International, Protea Hotels, and City Lodge, and air carriers such as South African Airways (SAA), Nationwide, and several others.
- *Volatility*. The demand for tourism **product-offerings** is extremely volatile and irrational and, for most destinations, tourism is a seasonal activity.
- *High fixed costs*. Most tourism businesses have high fixed costs. For example, the costs to a passenger-train operator do not change with the number of passengers; it will cost more or less the same to carry one passenger as it will to carry 150 passengers. This applies to other transport operators, such as airlines, as well as to the accommodation sector and, to a large extent, visitor attractions; most of the costs relate to the provision of facilities – land and buildings, for example – and the associated running costs are only moderately affected by the number of guests or visitors (see Chapter 12 – Managing finance for tourism).
- *Vulnerability*. The tourism industry is particularly susceptible to external events and adverse events, such as natural disasters, extreme weather patterns, climate change, terrorist attacks, economic downturns, and political crises. Recent examples include the outbreak of bird flu, rising oil prices and the war in the Middle East.
- *Resilient*. Nevertheless, the tourism industry has shown how resilient it is, recovering from setbacks such as 9/11 and Bali 2002 terrorist events, natural disasters such as the December 2004 tsunami in South East Asia, and the SARS (severe acute respiratory syndrome) and Hurricane Katrina (see Example box below).

Example Hurricane Katrina

Tourism products are making light of the storm that put 80% of New Orleans under water in September 2005, and dark humour is selling briskly. One of the best-selling post-Katrina tourist T-shirts makes fun of the looting that followed the storm: 'I stayed in New Orleans for Katrina, and all I got was this lousy T-shirt, a new Cadillac and a plasma TV'. T-shirts are not the only Katrina products on sale. One car bumper sticker around town reads 'New Orleans – Proud to Swim Home'.

Source: *Cape Times*. 12 June, 2006

Tourism is evidently a complex phenomenon. This leads us to ask: 'What is tourism management?' The Tourism Management Institute defines tourism management as:

> 'the activity of managing tourism in specific geographical locations for the economic, social and environmental benefit of the recipient business and residential communities'.

Clearly, the management of tourism involves taking into account the interests of a number of tourism organisations and role players.

According to Page (2007: 24–25), management of tourism occurs at three levels: at the individual business level, at the destination level, and at the country level.

- individual business level (the company)
- destination level (the destination management organisation)
- country level (the Ministry of Tourism).

In the next section, we ask why we should study tourism management, and examine how tourism can be studied from various perspectives.

Why study tourism management?

The academic subject of tourism has grown considerably internationally over the last few decades, in line with the international growth of tourism as an activity. According to the Centre International de Recherches et d'Etudes Touristiques (CIRET), in 2006 there were 641 academic institutions in 96 countries specialising in tourism.

Nevertheless, tourism is a relatively recent field of study. In South Africa, academic institutions began offering tourism education and training courses in the mid-1990s. Tourism has since increased in popularity at diploma and postgraduate levels, and is beginning to be recognised as a serious academic subject. Today, tourism education occurs at a variety of levels in South Africa, from school-based (Grades 10, 11, and 12) and further education training (FET),

to undergraduate and postgraduate courses at universities. Within the schools system itself, tourism was introduced in 2005 as part of the National Curriculum Statement (NCS), with the support of key tourism industry role players, in order to interest school leavers in a career in tourism.

Example The Institute of Travel Management Southern Africa (ITMSA)   www.itmsa.org

The Institute of Travel Management Southern Africa (ITMSA) is a non-profit company (Section 21) based on the ITM (UK) market.

What is evident is that tourism management involves more than the study of holidaymakers. Burns and Holden (1995: 1) note that studying tourism can be both enigmatic and bizarre: enigmatic inasmuch as there remain aspects of it difficult to define, and bizarre in that it sets out to make theoretical sense of people having fun. This in turn, has created an 'image problem' for the study of tourism in academia, as Leiper (1979: 392) asserts:

> 'The study of tourism as a focal subject has sometimes been treated with derision in academic circles, perhaps because of its novelty; perhaps because of its superficial fragmentation; perhaps because it cuts across established disciplines'.

Tourism is a multi-disciplinary field of study. It involves input from a variety of disciplines, including geography, sociology, business and management, and the social sciences.

Jafari and Ritchie (1981) presented a model of tourism studies as a field (see Figure 1.5). The model helps us to appreciate the multi-disciplinary nature of tourism studies, and that tourism can be studied from many perspectives. Throughout this book we shall be drawing on a number of disciplines in which to integrate the subjects of history, geography, sociology, economics, etc. in the context of tourism management. However, given a book of this nature, it is not possible to include the entire range of approaches to tourism.

Tourism courses are offered in various university departments and faculties – from 'Tourism Management' to 'Tourism Economics' (see Example box overleaf). Most courses are offered by schools of business and management. For the purposes of this book, tourism is examined from a business perspective.

Example The multidisciplinary nature of the subject of tourism
Tourism can be studied from a number of disciplines and subject areas including: • Sociology – social impacts of tourism • Agriculture – rural and farm tourism, ecotourism, environmental impacts of tourism • Business & Marketing – marketing of tourism offerings, management of tourism • Economics – economic impacts of tourism • Anthropology – cultural impacts of tourism, relationships between locals and visitors • Law – tourism laws, tourism legislation • History – evolution of tourism • Geography – spatial patterns of tourism • Psychology – tourism motivation, tourism consumer behaviour • Education – tourism education • Political science – tourism policy, influence of politics on tourism.

In the next section, we examine the tourism system, which incorporates an inter-disciplinary approach to the study of tourism. One of the key features of using the tourism system model is that it enables us to understand the different elements of tourism and how they are interrelated.

www

Browse this website: www.ciret-tourism.com

The tourism system

While it has been acknowledged that tourism is a business, several tourism researchers (such as Burns & Holden, 1995) suggest that tourism should not be viewed from this school of thought only, but from a **systems** approach. One of the most widely cited approaches is that of Leiper's (1979: 400) tourism system model. Leiper's tourism system provides a methodological framework for studying tourism (see Figure 1.6).

A system is defined as a group of interrelated, interdependent and interacting elements that together form a single functional structure, according to Mill and Morrison (1992: xv). The **tourism system** identifies tourism as being made up of five elements, namely generating, transit and destination regions, tourists, and the tourism

Figure 1.5 Jafari and Ritchie's tourism clock

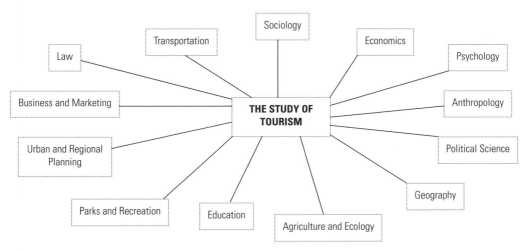

Figure 1.6 Leiper's basic tourism system

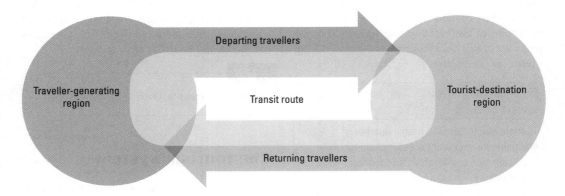

Source: Leiper, N. 1979 – The Framework of Tourism. *Annals of Tourism Research*, Vol. 6(4), 390–407

industry. These are embedded within a modifying external environment that includes political, social, physical, and other systems.

Tourists

Tourists are the travelling public: they are the human participants in the system. What a tourist is was defined in the previous section of this chapter. It is important for tourism managers to understand the way in which tourists make decisions to buy product-offerings. In Chapter 14 we will briefly explore the concept of consumer behaviour which lies at the core of tourism marketing theory.

Geographical elements

Leiper's (1979: 400) model outlines three main geographical components:

The tourist-generating region

The tourist-generating region is the area (e.g. country, province, city) from which the tourist originates, and is also referred to as the market or origin region. Factors at the generating region 'push' people to travel ('I need a holiday/to get away/a break'). It is in this region that the marketing activities are carried out. This region is where

consumers search and book their holidays, and where the demand for tourism occurs. Demand may be either:

1. *Effective* or *actual demand* – the number of people who are actually travelling (we referred to 'tourism flows' earlier in the chapter)
2. *Suppressed demand* – refers to the number of people at the generating region who do not travel (for reasons such as lack of time or income). Suppressed demand may be further divided into *potential* demand – those who will travel in the future if time and money allow them to do so, and *deferred* demand – demand that is postponed because of a lack of supply at the destination (for example, a lack of accessibility to the destination region, or perceptions of lack of safety at the destination)
3. *No demand* – those people who have no desire to travel or are unable to do so.

In reality, the majority of South Africa's population falls into the last two categories of demand – suppressed or no demand. In fact, only a small percentage of the total population actually engages in international tourism, due to a high percentage of people being economically inactive.

The transit region

The **transit region** comprises the places and areas that tourists pass through as they travel from the generating to the destination region. The transit region, however, may also be a destination of sorts – the places *en route*. For many people, travelling to the destination is as important as the destination itself. As the old adages go: 'getting there is half the fun!' (i.e. cruise holidays/boat trips) or 'the journey is the destination' (i.e. luxury train travel). The distinction between transit and destination regions is not always clear, given that a tourist's itinerary within a destination may include a variety of transit experiences. An inbound tourist staying in Johannesburg, for example, may choose to visit Kruger National Park, which requires a few hours' transit journey. A number of modes of transport are available to the tourist to travel between the generating and destination regions depending upon availability, frequency, price, speed, and comfort. The various modes of transport are discussed in Chapter 5.

The tourist destination region

The tourism **destination region** represents the places to which the tourist is travelling. It is the end point of a person's journey. According to Cooper *et al.* (2005: 9) this region is the 'sharp end' of tourism, which provides the 'pull' factors to energise the whole tourism system. Key 'pull' factors include climate, natural attractions, and value for money. Destinations are the focus of tourist activity, and where visitor attractions are located. They are the places that attract visitors for a temporary stay, and range from continents to countries, to provinces, to cities, to villages, to purpose-built resort areas (Pike, 2004: 11). The destination region is where the **impacts** of tourists and tourism are most felt. Attracting visitors to destination areas is a very competitive business, given the socio-economic benefits that tourism can bring to a wider range of national, provincial and local destinations (see Chapter 15).

The tourism industry

Leiper (1979: 401) defines the **tourism industry** as consisting of all those firms, organisations and facilities which are intended to serve the specific needs and wants of tourists. It therefore consists of all the businesses and organisations involved in the delivery of the tourism offering, from travel agents to car rental companies.

Lickorish and Jenkins (1997: 1) note that there is a lack of a common structure that is

Figure 1.7 Sectors and sub-sectors of the tourism industry

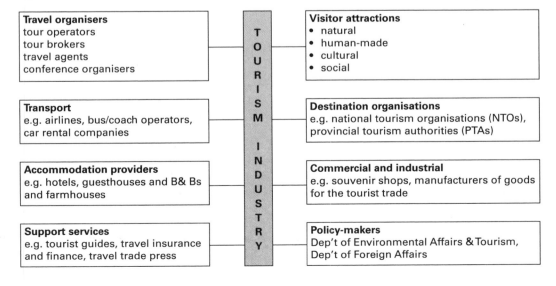

representative of the tourism industry in every country. In South Africa, for example, many tourists make use of guesthouses and bed-and-breakfast establishments, while in South East Asia such accommodation facilities are not available. Similarly, the main modes of transport used by holidaymakers travelling in South Africa are the motor car and bus, while in India most tourists travel by air.

The main sectors and sub-sectors which make up the South African tourism industry are shown in Figure 1.7.

The advantages of the tourism system model for studying tourism

The advantage of Leiper's (1979) tourism system model is that it provides a simple and orderly framework for the study of tourism. It allows for the various sub-sectors to be located, and highlights the process of tourism from the sides of both supply (the industry) and demand (consumer). This encourages multi-disciplinary thinking, which – given tourism's complexities – is essential to deepen our understanding of it (Burns & Holden, 1999: 29).

The model highlights the interaction between the five elements in terms of relationships and impacts. The model also emphasises that tourism is not seen in isolation from its human, sociocultural, economical, technological, physical, political, and legal environments.

It is also possible to apply the model to different scales – from a local destination to an international industry (see case study). Finally, the model assists in organising the structure and sets the context for this book.

Structure of the book

Managing Tourism in South Africa consists of 17 chapters, which are divided into four sections/main themes: tourism overview, the tourism industry, managing tourism businesses, and issues in tourism management.

Part I provides an overview of tourism. It seeks to explain what tourism is, and examines how tourism as an activity has evolved both histori-

cally and geographically. This chapter introduces the subject of tourism and provides the context for the book. Chapter 2 considers the historical evolution of tourism, and Chapter 3 discusses how tourism can be examined from a geographical perspective.

Part II of the book focuses on the tourism industry and covers the elements of the tourism system, including visitor attractions (Chapter 4), transportation (Chapter 5), accommodation (Chapter 6), intermediaries (Chapter 7), and the public sector (Chapter 8).

Part III covers the functional aspects of tourism management, including managing tourism businesses (Chapter 9), managing small tourism businesses and entrepreneurship (Chapter 10), human resource management (Chapter 11), accounting and finance in the tourism industry (Chapter 12), law and tourism (Chapter 13), and the marketing of tourism businesses (Chapter 14), which outlines the basic principles of marketing as applied to tourism businesses.

Part IV examines issues in tourism management, beginning with Chapter 15, which examines the economic, sociocultural, and environmental impacts of tourism which need to be managed. Chapter 16 considers how tourism is best managed in a responsible manner – tourism that does not disturb the environment or which is socially exploitative, and Chapter 17 concludes the book with a review of the future of tourism.

Conclusion

Tourism is a changing and dynamic phenomenon that requires sophisticated management to realise its full economic and sociocultural potential. This introductory chapter has considered the problems of tourism-related definitions. The significance and importance of tourism as an activity has also been discussed, as have the unique characteristics of tourism businesses. The major tourism flows were also identified. The chapter outlined the relative complexity of tourism, which has led to it being approached from various academic disciplines. However, a multi-disciplinary approach can lead to a better understanding of the management of tourism. For this reason, the interrelated elements of the tourism system were introduced before providing a framework for the book.

Review questions

1. Explain the definitional problems in relation to tourism.
2. Why is tourism described as a complex phenomenon?
3. Discuss whether tourism can be described as an industry.
4. Compare the top 10 international tourist destinations listed in table 1.1 on page 9 with the top 10 tourism revenue earners provided in table 1.3 on page 10. What factors might account for the discrepancies between the two tasks?
5. Why is the Leiper's (1979) tourism system model useful in studying tourism management?
6. Why is the business of tourism considered perilous and unpredictable?
7. Name five academic disciplines that can be applied to understanding facets of tourism.

Further reading

Leiper, N. 2004. *Tourism management*, 3rd edition. Malaysia: Pearson Education Australia

Mill, R. C. & Morrison, A. M. 1992. *The tourism system: an introductory text*, 2nd edition. London: Prentice Hall.

Tribe, J. 1997. The indiscipline of tourism. *Annals of Tourism Research*, Vol. 24, 638–57.

Journals

Annals of Tourism Research
Journal of Travel Research
Tourism Management

Websites

WTTC: www.wttc.org

UN-WTO: www.world-tourism.org

Centre International de Recherches et d'Etudes Touristiques (CIRET): www.ciret-tourism.com

South African Tourism: www.southafrica.net

Toursim Management Institute (TMI): www.tmi.org.uk

References

Boniface, B. & Cooper, C. 2001. *Worldwide destinations: the geography of travel and tourism*. London: Heinemann.

Burns, P. & Holden, A. 1995. *Tourism: a new perspective*. New Jersey: Prentice Hall.

Cooper, C., Fletcher, J., Fyall, A., Gilbert, D., & Wanhill, S. (Eds.). 2005. *Tourism: principles and practice*, 3rd edition. New York: Longman.

Gilbert, D. 1990. Conceptual issues in the meaning of tourism. In C. Cooper (Ed.), *Progress in tourism, recreation and hospitality management*. London: Belhaven.

Gunter, B. G. 1987. The leisure experience: selected properties. *Journal of Leisure Research*, Vol. 19(2), 115–130.

Jafari, J. & Ritchie, J. R. B. 1981. Towards a framework for tourism education. *Annals of Tourism Research*, Vol. 8(1), 13–34.

Leiper, N. 1979. The framework of tourism. *Annals of Tourism Research*, Vol. 6(4), 390–407.

Lickorish, L. J. & Jenkins, C.L. 1997. *An introduction to tourism*. Oxford: Butterworth-Heinemann.

Mill, R. C. & Morrison, A. M. 1992. *The tourism system: an introductory text*, 2nd edition. London: Prentice Hall.

Page, S. J. 2007. *Tourism management: managing for change*, 2nd edition. Oxford: Butterworth-Heinemann.

Pearsall, J. (Ed.). 1999. *The concise Oxford dictionary*, 10th edition. New York: Oxford University Press.

Pike, S. 2004. *Destination marketing organisations*. London: Elsevier.

South African Tourism. 2007. *Strategic Research Unit, 2006 Performance Report*. Johannesburg: South African Tourism.

Torkildsen, G. 2005. *Torkildsen's guide to leisure management*, 5th edition. Longman: Harlow.

United Nations World Tourism Organisation (UN-WTO). 2004. Tourism Satellite Accounts in Depth: Analysing Tourism as an Economic Activity. www.world-tourism.org (accessed May 2006).

United Nations World Tourism Organisation (UN-WTO). 2007. Another record year for world tourism. www.world-tourism.org (accessed February 2007).

World Travel and Tourism Council. 2006. *Blueprint for new tourism*. London: WTTC.

Case study

1

Domestic tourism in South Africa

Objectives

- to understand how the elements of the tourism system can be applied to domestic tourism
- to appreciate the importance of domestic tourism to the South African economy.

Domestic tourism is when people take day trips, short breaks and longer holidays in their own country. **Domestic tourism** (also known as 'internal tourism') is regarded as of great importance globally. On a world-wide basis, domestic tourism far exceeds international tourism. UN-WTO's research found that domestic tourism accounts for as many as 80% of all tourist trips.

Despite the major contributions to tourism made by domestic tourism, very few countries collect domestic tourism statistics. There are obvious difficulties in measuring data on domestic tourism flows, as domestic tourists do not cross frontiers/borders, or exchange money. Domestic tourists also often stay with friends and relatives (the VFR market), thus making it difficult to keep accurate statistics.

One of the characteristics of domestic tourism is that it is considered to be important during times of economic and political difficulty. For example, the terrorist attacks of 11 September 2001 in the

United States, which put many people off travelling internationally, prompted national governments to support tourism businesses by promoting their domestic tourism sector. Domestic tourism is robust. Even if there is war in another part of the world, or one of South Africa's main international source markets' economies is in trouble, South Africa is little affected by it, because of its citizens' travel patterns inside the country.

Domestic tourism is the hidden treasure of the South African tourism industry. It is the backbone of the tourism economy, and sustains a large tourist industry – for example, cultural and heritage attractions, national parks, coastal regions, special events and festivals, and built attractions such as holiday resorts and casinos. In 2006, South Africa's domestic tourism expenditure amounted to R16,5-billion (SA Tourism, 2007). During the year, 12,1-million adult South Africans took, on average, 3,1 trips within their own country, resulting in 37-million trips (see Table 1). These domestic tourists stayed on holiday for 7,6 nights' length-of-stay and, on average, spent R444 per trip.

Research on the domestic tourism market conducted by South African Tourism (SA Tourism) shows that the major factor motivating South Africans to travel within their own country is VFR (visiting friends and relatives), accounting

Table 1.4 Domestic versus international tourist trips and spending in SA, 2006

	Trips (millions)	Spending (R billion)
SA residents	37,1	R16,5
International visitors	8,4	R66,6
Total	45,5	R83,1

Source: SA Tourism, 2006

for approximately 78% of all travel. Domestic tourism for holiday purposes, although a small percentage (7%), accounts for an economic value of 18% of all expenditure. Domestic travel (both generating and destination) is dominated by KwaZulu-Natal, Gauteng, and the Western Cape, and these provinces account for 65% of all domestic tourist revenue.

Some of the advantages of domestic tourism are its ability to combat issues such as seasonality and to spread the benefits of tourism across the country. Domestic tourism in South Africa is an all-year-round industry. Special events, such as music and sporting events and festivals, which are held throughout the year, also boost domestic tourism. Another benefit is that, geographically, it is distributed more evenly compared to international tourism, largely because of the high rate of VFR travel.

The demand for domestic tourism in South Africa has the potential for high domestic travel volumes, given the large geographical size of the country and the difficulty of travel to other countries (distance, visa requirements, etc). The sheer size of South Africa and its diversity of high-quality resources assure a high volume of domestic tourism, compared to international outbound tourism. Yet, in reality, approximately only 12,1-million South Africans engage in domestic travel out of a total of 48 million people (28,7-million of whom are over 18 years of age (42,2%)).

The propensity for domestic travel in South Africa is determined by a number of factors. First, employment levels have a significant impact on demand for travel. The number of people employed and the types of jobs they have is an important consideration. Approximately 30–40%

of the adult population in South Africa is economically inactive, and cannot afford the luxury of holidays and travel. Secondly, economic determinants, such as high interest rates and inflation rates, affect domestic travel patterns and determine the amount of discretionary income enjoyed by the population. **Discretionary income** is the amount of money left over after taxes have been paid and the basics of life have been provided for. Similarly, exchange rates may influence whether individuals choose to travel internationally or domestically. Finally, domestic travel demand is a function of the values of the population. Over the years there has been a general lack of a culture of travel in South Africa. Many South Africans have not had the privilege of being tourists, and do not know what it is to be one.

The challenge now is to unlock segments of the domestic market who can afford to travel, yet who are not experienced travellers. The majority of tourism products and services that exist in the country do not cater for budget or group domestic travellers. Rather, many of the businesses cater for the 'top end' of the market, and few products cater to the 'mass' market. The Department of Environmental Affairs and Tourism (DEAT) and SA Tourism, through their promotional campaigns and marketing strategies, aims to ensure that all citizens have equal access to tourism services as both consumers and providers, and aims to create a culture of travel in the country.

Case study questions

1. Incorporate the major elements of Leiper's (1979) tourism system model to domestic tourism flows in South Africa.
2. With reference to Leiper's (1979) model, explain how the various external environments can affect domestic tourism flows.
3. Discuss some of the problems associated with the validity of domestic tourism statistics.
4. Identify the key barriers to tourism (domestic) demand that an individual might experience.
5. Visit SA Tourism's website at *www.southafrica.net*. What are DEAT and SA Tourism doing to promote and encourage domestic travel within the country?

2

The history of tourism

Chris Saunders and Tanya Barben

The Wilderness Hotel and Village in 1937

Purpose

The purpose of this chapter is to discuss the history and growth of tourism through the ages, to show how tourism in the past differs from modern tourism, and to suggest ways in which tourism may develop in the future.

Learning outcomes

After reading this chapter, you should be able to:
- understand why the history of tourism is important
- appreciate why tourism has taken different forms at different times
- explain how the South African tourism industry has evolved
- identify milestones of the 20th century which laid the foundation for the South African tourism industry today.

Chapter overview

In the first part of the chapter we examine some of the factors that have influenced the development of tourism. To begin with, we need to define what is meant by 'tourism'. People have always travelled from one place to another, for a variety of reasons. In very early times they moved to find

food or water or, perhaps, to escape drought and, as more sophisticated economies developed, they travelled to trade or to find work. Herodotus, a fifth century BCE Greek traveller, known as the 'father of history', travelled widely over the Greek and Persian territories of the Mediterranean world, and visited Babylon and Egypt. He recorded all he saw 'to prevent the traces of human events from being erased by time, and to preserve the fame of the important and remarkable achievement produced by both Greeks and non-Greeks' (Herodotus, 1998: 3). It is debatable, however, as to whether there was 'tourism' in its modern-day meaning in Ancient Egypt and Rome, although in the Roman Empire it was possible to travel safely over long distances. While some people did travel to visit others or to see interesting sights, they did not do so in an organised way. In the Middle Ages travel for religious reasons was common. Christian pilgrims visited holy sites such as at Santiago de Compostela in Spain, while Muslims went on the hajj to Mecca, and Christian crusaders waged war on the 'infidel' in the Holy Land. A few adventurous men traversed vast distances to learn how others lived, and recorded their experiences. For example, Marco Polo, a Venetian, travelled to China, Persia (now Iran), Tibet, and Burma (now Myanmar) in the late 13th century, while Ibn Battuta, a 14th century Arab from Tangiers, travelled extensively and crossed the Sahara to visit the great African empire of Mali.

Some argue that it was only in the 18th century, when privileged people began to enjoy leisure time, that tourism was born. Tourists began to visit the Lake District in England, for example, and, on what was called the European Grand Tour, young men from Britain travelled for educational purposes through mainland Europe, some going as far as Egypt. Although the Revolutionary and Napoleonic Wars, which began at the end of the 18th century and continued until 1815 ended the Grand Tour, in the early 19th century, as the industrial revolution gained momentum and new forms of transport developed, mass tourism began. Railways in particular, together with the availability of leisure time, made it possible for large numbers of people to visit spas and seaside resorts. Some even travelled to other countries for pleasure and enlightenment, either as individuals on a whim, or on some form of organised tour. Mountain ranges such as the Alps, previously regarded as hazards to be avoided, now came to be seen as places of beauty to be visited and enjoyed. Travel agents and tour operators began to take advantage of improvements in modes of transport, and were able to offer people the opportunity to participate in organised tours. As globalisation has increased in the 20th century, one of its by-products has been the considerable growth of modern mass tourism.

Before we consider this, let us pause and ask: Why study the history of tourism? One cannot understand the present without understanding the past. Without a knowledge of history, one might assume that tourism has always been a dynamic and important sector of many countries' economies. Furthermore, it is only by knowing how things have developed to the present that we may be able to think rationally about the future. Modern mass tourism, as we have just seen, is a recent phenomenon, and reflects changes in the global economy. Tourism is related to stability in the world system, and its future will depend on such stability continuing. Major changes in climate or the outbreak of war may have a considerable impact on tourism in the future.

Introduction

For most of human history, travel entailed very little pleasure. The Middle English (via Old French from Medieval Latin) origin of the word for travel is *travail*, meaning 'painful or laborious'. Our word 'holiday' comes from the Old English '*haligdæg*', or 'holy day' – a day with religious significance on which people could enjoy leisure and recreation. Longer paid vacation periods and early retirement have meant that holidays have become regular events for many people. Modern **mass tourism** has become a complex business, involving transport, accommodation, souvenirs, attractions, and tourist guides. In the past, some have suggested that 'travellers make their own choices; tourists have their decisions made for them' (Sharpley, 1999: 100), but tourists often want to make their own decisions about how and where to travel. Another unhelpful generalisation is that of the novelist Paul Bowles, who wrote that 'while the tourist accepts his own civilisation without question; not so the traveller, who compares it with others, and rejects those elements he finds not to his liking' (1990: 6).

Wars and tourism

Although the wars waged from the 1790s to 1815 brought an end to the **Grand Tour**, wars generally influenced tourism positively. World War I (1914–1918), for example, helped change tourism from something reserved for the elite to becoming an activity in which all could engage. After the war it became cheaper to travel, while the horror of war motivated people to get away from their familiar environments. Some visited battlefields to pay homage to deceased loved ones, or out of morbid curiosity (this is referred to today as 'dark tourism' – see Foley & Lennon, 2000). As class distinctions diminished, the masses wanted to enjoy the privileges hitherto available only to the upper classes. The experiences of combatants who had served in foreign countries during World War II (1939–1945) aroused a curiosity about overseas travel amongst the less affluent. In many countries the war effort resulted in an efficient transport system being developed. South Africa's railway infrastructure, for example, grew dramatically during and after World War II, making faster, safer, heavier, and longer trains possible. Similarly, the United States of America experienced a great increase in domestic travel after World War II due to the removal of petrol rationing, more automobile production, and the growth in air, rail, and coach travel.

The development of spas and seaside resorts

The development of **spas**, where one could bathe in mineral spring water, was yet another step in the evolution of tourism. Spas, first established during the time of the Roman Empire, became popular once more in the late 17th and 18th centuries in Britain and on the European Continent. They were visited by the wealthy for their therapeutic qualities, as well as for the entertainment facilities that opened up around them. The spas of Bath in England were first used by Romans, but enjoyed renewed popularity, especially among rich merchants and the landed gentry. Places like Tunbridge Wells, Droitwich Spa, and Sadler's Wells flourished, not only because of the excellence of their waters, but also because of the popularity of their theatres and music halls. In Germany, Italy, Czechoslovakia, and Hungary, spas were also popular. South Africa was to develop its own hot springs and spas at places such as Warmbaths, Badplaas, Montagu, Caledon, and Aliwal North, all of which were visited both for purposes of recuperation and health and general relaxation.

The swimming pool at Aliwal North hot springs in the 1920s

Seaside resorts became popular as sea bathing came to be considered more beneficial than 'taking the waters'. Doctors who suggested these places to their patients therefore played a role in the development of tourism. In the second half of the 19th century bathing in the sea and going to the coast grew in popularity for the healthy as well as the sick, and places like Brighton, Blackpool, Ramsgate, Margate, and Scarborough in England became favourite destinations. The affluent acquired properties there, and members of the middle and lower classes made day-trips to the coast. Several South African seaside resorts on the KwaZulu-Natal south coast have been named after their British counterparts.

Travel agents and tour operators

The development of tourism created a niche market for a new activity: that of travel agents and tour operators. The first steamship agent was Robert Smart of Bristol, England, who in 1822 booked passengers on steamers to ports in the Bristol Channel and to Dublin in Ireland. The excursion train was 'invented' by Rowland Hill in the 1830s, but Thomas Cook was the first rail excursion agent offering the first publicly advertised excursion train in 1841. Cook's company was to grow rapidly. It expanded its activities to provide tours to Europe, Egypt, the Holy Land and North America, and organised the first world tour in 1872. Cook later pioneered the '**packaged tour**'. His company dominated the market for such tours until World War II, organising entire itineraries including transportation, accommodation, and banking services, and introducing innovations such as Cook's travellers' cheques, which were cashable worldwide. Thomas Bennett (1814–1898) became the first operator to specialise in individual inclusive travel (today referred to as **fully independent travel** – FIT). Bennett, the secretary of the British consul general in Oslo, Norway, embarked on a secondary career as 'trip organiser' in 1850, providing tourists with itineraries and meeting all their travel requirements. The American Express Company, founded in 1850, began issuing travellers' cheques in 1891, and later operated as travel agents.

Vladimir Raitz, a Polish refugee living in London, introduced what was to become the modern air-charter package holiday. In 1951 he chartered a Dakota to take a group of tourists to Corsica. This was the forerunner of the modern air-charter package holiday. By 1971, over 50% of overseas holidays were packages. The growth of charter flights led to the establishment in 1960 of the International Air Transport Association (IATA), which regulates airfares.

The development of transportation

The Romans began building roads in Italy around 150 BCE. A roadbed was dug, and then lined with stones and lime mortar. Paving stones were placed on top of it, and the road edged with curbstones and cambered for drainage. The Romans created an excellent road infrastructure throughout their empire, which facilitated travel and tourism. Some of their roads are still in use today. In the late 1700s, a system of road construction based on scientific principles was introduced in Britain by two Scottish engineers, Thomas Telford and John McAdam. A network of well-constructed roads was built in France at much the same time.

Example Gateway to the eastern districts

The Hottentots-Holland Mountains east of Cape Town were the gateway to travel to the eastern districts of the Cape Colony but were a major impediment to vehicular traffic. In the nineteenth century the British authorities slowly improved travel between Cape Town and the interior. The construction of Sir Lowry's Pass, opened in 1830 and named for Sir Lowry Cole, the Cape Governor who authorised its construction, was the first substantial road-making project undertaken by a government in southern Africa. By 1845 a hard-surface road had been constructed across the sandy Cape Flats so day-trippers were able to flock to the summit of the pass to admire the panoramic view across to the Cape Peninsula.

The name 'stagecoach' derives from the practice of taking people from stage to stage in a coach; a large four-wheeled horse-drawn enclosed carriage. Invented in Hungary in the 15th century, the stagecoach provided regular transport on designated routes. Stagecoach trips between London and the larger towns in 17th-century England were introduced, and taverns provided lodging for passengers. However, the development of the railways in the 19th century heralded the end of the stagecoach era.

In southern Africa, transport riders travelled between Mozambique's Delagoa Bay and South Africa's Highveld in the late 19th century. Hotels sprang up to cater for horse riders, diggers, hunters and other travellers. When gold was discovered in 1884 in Barberton (in what is now the province of Mpumalanga), men of all nationalities flocked to the old South African Republic. Coach drivers had to cut their own roads in places, and encountered wild animals, local Africans whose land they were crossing, highwaymen, and floods (Klein 1972: 95). As travellers required accommodation en route, small hotels and inns were developed for this purpose. Marabastad, or Eerstegond, was a staging-post on the Pietersburg-Pretoria line of the Zeederberg Mail Coach Company (Erasmus 1995: 205)

The introduction of the steam locomotive brought the greatest advances in travel in the early 19th century. The first railway was built in England in the 1820s. This signalled the advent of rail transportation and 'the technological revolution which brought about the birth of mass tourism' (Sharpley, 1999: 46). Services for passengers developed rapidly, and soon railways were being built in many parts of the world. The development of London's sophisticated underground rail network began in the 1880s. The unprecedented mobility afforded by rail transport accelerated the development of tour operators, such as that of Thomas Cook, and saw the publication of travel guidebooks like John Murray's famous 'red handbooks'. These first appeared in 1836, and assisted tourists in their travels around Holland, Belgium, and the Rhineland.

Construction on the first railway line in South Africa between Cape Town and Wellington started in 1859. When minerals were discovered in the interior, railways were extended to the new centres of wealth. The Nederlandsche Zuid-Afrikaansche Spoorweg Maatschappij (NZASM) line linked Pretoria (now Tshwane) to Delagoa Bay/Lourenco Marques (now Maputo) by 1895. The South African Railways (SAR) added 8 800 kilometres to existing railway lines in the 14 years following the establishment of the Union in 1910. In recent years, luxurious trains in South Africa such as the Blue Train and Rovos Rail have become tourist attractions in their own right.

The 'Train de Luxe', built in 1901, was the antecedent of the well-known Blue Train. The colour of its deep blue dining-car, introduced in 1923, proved to be so popular that the whole train was later painted that colour. South Africa is one of the last bastions of the steam locomotive; steam trains such as the Apple Express (which runs on the line between Port Elizabeth and Avontuur in the Eastern Cape) and the Outeniqua Choo-Tjoe (which runs between George and Knysna in the Western Cape) are still in use today.

Travel by sea

It is believed that the Egyptians sailed out over the Mediterranean to Syria and Crete before 3000 BCE. The Phoenicians were some of the earliest traders and travellers in the Mediterranean region. They were motivated by a sense of curiosity and a desire to find new trading partners and new trade routes. They gradually won maritime superiority after the development of ship-building in Egypt declined, and by 800 BCE they had established a series of trading posts along the Mediterranean coastline. They built ships which were tub-shaped wooden craft with a single square sail. These were used primarily for trade in a range of goods including cloth, ivory, gold, olive oil, perfumes, and spices.

The peoples of Oceania undertook remarkable sea voyages in small dugout canoes from about 500 CE, some sailing over 3 200 kilometres to Hawaii. They navigated their way across vast expanses of the Pacific by interpreting celestial bodies, ocean swells, clouds, and bird flights. Indian and Indonesian traders used the trade winds to travel between the Indian mainland and the Indonesian archipelago, as well as to Madagascar and the east coast of Africa.

Sea travel, although for the most part the only option available, was not popular. It was associated with inherent dangers such as piracy and shipwrecks. Ships were small and uncomfortable, particularly for second- and third-class passengers, who generally had to provide their own bedding and meals.

Market boats were transporting passengers and goods on ship canals in England by 1772. Steamboats began cruising Britain's major rivers from 1815; cruises from London commenced in 1833. Excursions on the River Thames soon became permanent features – so much so that by 1841 a weekly 'Steamboat Excursion Guide' was issued. A trans-Atlantic steamship service between Britain and the United States began in 1840. The first sea 'cruise' was organised in 1844 by Arthur Anderson, co-founder of the Peninsular and Oriental Steam Navigation Company (later P&O), thereby initiating affordable sea travel in the form of organised pleasure-cruises. Passengers sailed from England around the Mediterranean and home again, stopping at ports along the way. The opening of the Suez Canal in 1869 further stimulated the demand for P&O services to India and other distant destinations. Famous ocean liners, such as those belonging to the Cunard Steamship Company and the White Star Line, plied the Atlantic between Europe and North America. Until 1945, when it was largely superseded by air travel, sailing in an ocean liner was the main form of transportation between Europe and the Americas.

Sea travel brought the majority of visitors to South Africa prior to air travel becoming a viable option. Two British steamship companies, the Union and Castle Lines, sailed between South Africa and England. Both companies initially offered a mail service, carrying passengers as a sideline. They later amalgamated to form the Union-Castle Mail Steamship Company, which enjoyed a long monopoly in passenger cruises between South African ports and Southampton, England. These cruises were very popular until air travel took precedence, as they catered extensively for the needs of pampered passengers out to have a good time during the voyage. Berths in different classes were offered, and crew members were employed to keep the passengers entertained and happy.

UNION-CASTLE: A British steamship company which sailed weekly between South Africa and England until 1977

Automobiles and motorcoaches

Travel by rail declined steadily after the introduction of the motor car. Developed in 1908, Henry Ford's affordable Model T, or 'Tin Lizzie', revolutionised travel in the USA and elsewhere. More and more people found a freedom and independence that enabled them to decide for themselves where they wanted to go, as they were no longer tied to the routes of public transport services. Road users demanded an improvement in road infrastructure, and by 1920 the USA had a system of roads in place. All this resulted in the dominance of road travel over other modes of transport, which is still the case today. Road transport in South Africa expanded rapidly between 1924 and 1929. South Africans started touring the country, picnicking and camping. Country hotels stocked tyres and petrol before service stations were opened. A bus service from the train station at Bot River to Hermanus in the Western Cape was offered from 1912. Hermanus, already well-known for its 'champagne' air, rapidly transformed into a popular seaside resort. As road conditions and cars improved and people became more prosperous, a new field of tourism was pioneered when luxury buses using regular and scheduled routes were introduced.

Air travel

The first aeroplane flight, by the Wright brothers at Kitty Hawk, North Carolina, took place in 1903. They flew 37 metres in 12 seconds. The German company, Deutsche Lufthansa, started the first scheduled air service in 1918. The airline operates very successfully today. The first flight to Cape Town from England was made in 1920 by Pierre van Ryneveld and C. J. Quinton Brand. 1927 was a significant year in aviation history. In that year Charles Lindbergh made his historic solo flight from New York to Paris, and Charles Levine became the first transatlantic air passenger when he flew non-stop from New York to Germany. South African Airways (SAA) began offering scheduled flights in 1934. Although SAA's aircraft were converted for military use during World War II, its commercial air services resumed in 1944. The very popular Springbok Air Service between Johannesburg and London first took to the skies in 1945.

developed reputations as health destinations (see Example box).

> **Example** Travelling by air
>
> South African Airways developed from Union Airways which began in 1929 with five open Gypsy Moths, each seating only one passenger who donned goggles and a flying helmet. In 1930 a six-seater Fokker began flying between Port Elizabeth and Cape Town. The first regular air service between London and Cape Town was offered by Imperial Airways from 1932. Until 1950 the most comfortable from of air travel was in flying boats. They took six days to travel between England and South Africa, landing en route on suitable stretches of water, such as the Vaal Dam.

> **Example** Matjiesfontein as a health resort
>
> Matjiesfontein near Touws River was established in 1883 as a health resort by James Douglas Logan, a Scottish entrepreneur. Logan, who suffered from a weak chest, realised that both the health of fellow-sufferers and his pocket would benefit from the clear, crisp air of the Karoo. He developed Matjiesfontein as an international health resort, easily accessible by train from Cape Town. It attracted visitors from far and wide, including celebrities such as Lord Randolph Churchill, the Sultan of Zanzibar, Olive Schreiner, Rudyard Kipling and Cecil Rhodes.

Developments in passenger aircraft, such as the Boeing, made affordable commercial flights possible and led to their acceptability as a form of long-distance transport that soon eclipsed sea and rail travel. SAA acquired its first Boeing 707 in 1960. The first jumbo jet flight took place in January 1970 from New York to London. These aircraft further reduced the cost of an air ticket and, consequently, increased still further the popularity of air travel. SAA flew its first wide-bodied jet in 1971, and in subsequent years has increased its flights to destinations throughout the world and improved its service considerably. Fast, comfortable, and reliable, air travel is the dominant mode of public transportation today.

The South African tourism industry, its history and development

Early days

Before the opening of the Suez Canal in 1869, the Cape was a popular stop-over for British civil servants and soldiers on leave from India. The Cape attracted visitors because of its agreeable climate. Various places, one such being Matjiesfontein,

Grahamstown in the Eastern Cape was advertised in 1887 as a health and holiday resort with game shooting, trout fishing and wooded 'kloofs' as major visitor attractions. At more or less the same time, Oudtshoorn, in the Little Karoo, started to attract visitors to the nearby Cango Caves, which were opened to visitors in 1891. The South African War of 1899–1902 drew worldwide public attention to the southern tip of Africa, and Thomas Cook & Sons, already considered pioneers in the industry, recognised the potential of marketing the country for 'war tourists' in 1900, while the war was still in progress. The South African Railways (SAR), already a major player in the local tourism industry at the time, established a publicity department in 1906. This department opened an office in London, which marketed South Africa as a health resort. Meanwhile, rudimentary domestic tourism had already begun during the second half of the 19th century, as people living in the interior travelled to the coast on holiday. False Bay's Muizenberg, on the suburban railway line from Cape Town, became a favourite destination during the summer, especially for wealthy holiday-makers from Johannesburg.

The Wilderness Hotel and village nestling at the foot of forest-clad hills, with the Wilderness lagoon in the background taken in 1937

Example Honeymooning in Wilderness

George Bennet, a well-travelled and adventurous Englishman, bought a property on the coast near George on the Garden Route in 1877 for a mere £500. This was to become Wilderness, one of South Africa's most popular holiday resorts since the 1920s. The origin of its name, perhaps, explains its particular popularity as a destination for honeymooners. When Bennet's fiancée, a Miss Melville, was shown the land on which he intended to settle, she is said to have exclaimed, 'Oh what a wilderness' – and so this beautiful spot, then a veritable wilderness, was named. The property was divided into plots in the early 1900s, and in the 1920s Bennet's original homestead was converted into what was to be the first Wilderness Hotel. Since then Wilderness has been one of South Africa's most sought-after holiday resorts.

The hospitality sector in South Africa

As South Africa increased in popularity as a tourist destination in the first half of the 20th century, more – and better – hotels were needed. With the use of motor cars becoming more widespread in the 1920s, as in the United States, motorists could travel further and seek accommodation away from the railway line. The hospitality industry, as a result, became more competitive. By the mid-1930s there were over a thousand hotels, of which 65% were country establishments, with the rest serving the needs of visitors to the cities and larger towns.

Example South Africa's oldest inn

The Houw Hoek Inn in the Overberg (Western Cape) was built in 1834. It is probably the oldest wayside inn still in use today. It was established at a spot where transport riders unhitched their oxen and set up camp, and an earlier inn had operated there since the late 18th century. The innkeeper profited by serving meals to passengers when the railway service from Cape Town to Caledon was introduced.

It was not until 1965 that a controlling body was established to coordinate standards in hotels. The Hotel Board licensed hotels and improved standards by the implementation of a grading system. The South African hotel sector grew dramatically in the 1970s, thanks in part to the activities of Southern Sun Hotels. The group's Sol Kerzner, who was later to contribute significantly to the development of an outstanding accommodation sector in South Africa, and who played a leading role in the establishment of the Sun City complex, said of tourists in 1970: 'You have to have somewhere to put them when you get them here. What we need are hotels as good as the tourists get anywhere else in the world, but at half the price'. Kerzner and other hotel developers carried out their ambitious plans, and a range of more than 40 quality hotels sprang up along popular tourist routes (*Financial Mail*, March 1970).

The promotion of tourism

The unification of South Africa in 1910 made it easier to market the country overseas. The South African Parliament voted £25 000 for this purpose in 1914, but the outbreak of World War I prevented the implementation of this strategy. An Overseas Advertising conference was held in Johannesburg in 1919, a year after the end of World War I. It was attended by representatives of various government departments, chambers of commerce, publicity associations, and participants in the tourism industry, such as Thomas Cook & Sons and the Union-Castle Steamship Company. The conference aimed at advertising all of South Africa's industries in order to – among other things – attract more tourists to the country. The South African Railways was a major role-player in the conference, and its Publicity Office in London was transformed into the Public and Travel Bureau when the conference ended. The Bureau conducted a vigorous marketing campaign, issuing travel guidebooks, pamphlets, and press releases. It publicised South Africa at exhibitions, in illustrated lectures and films, as well as in window displays at railway stations in the main cities and towns of the United Kingdom and Europe. The Railways' involvement in tourism was to grow exponentially over the years (Norval, 1936: 127–128).

As more and more cruise ships from the United States and Europe visited South Africa, bringing with them an increasing number of visitors, SAR was tasked with encouraging the tourists to visit destinations in the interior. The country was sharply segregated at the time, and the African population only featured in the tourist imagination as 'other'. Tourists enjoyed the comforts to which they were accustomed, while being exposed to 'wild Africa' under carefully controlled conditions. As few African communities were prepared to be put on display for Western tourists, encounters with the 'primitive' had to be stage-managed. By the mid-1920s, tourists on their way to the Victoria Falls could stop at a rural village in what was then Bechuanaland (now Botswana) to experience the 'real Africa', its traditional foods and tribal dancing.

Example Kruger National Park

As early as 1897, game reserves or 'prohibited hunting areas' were established in what was to become South Africa. Since 1884 President Paul Kruger had considered creating a wildlife sanctuary between the Crocodile and Sabie Rivers, an area unattractive for human habitation because of the presence of tsetse fly and the prevalence of tropical diseases. This became a reality in 1898 when a government game park was established – the embryo of what was to become the Kruger National Park in 1926.

The Park rapidly acquired a world-wide reputation. The first three cars entered the Park in 1927, followed by 180 cars in 1928. The popularity of the Park increased at an enormous rate, and stimulated the formation of other game parks in the 1930s. The Kruger National Park became an increasingly important tourism asset.

Bulpin, T.V., 2001: *Discovering South Africa*. Muizenberg: Discovering South Africa Publications

---

SAR remained the main destination marketing agency until 1938, promoting tourism within the Union of South Africa and overseas through its Publicity and Travel Department. Its work was assisted by the South African Publicity Association, which played a major co-ordinating role. The Tourism Development Corporation was founded in 1938 to promote South Africa as an international tourism destination, but could not fulfill its mandate because of World War II. The South African Tourism Corporation (SATOUR) was established in 1947 with the same aim. At that time the Smuts government was in power, and South Africa was well-regarded internationally because of its involvement in the war against Germany. The country was a member of the Commonwealth, and its racial policies of segregation were only just beginning to come under fire at the new United Nations. This changed, however, after 1948 when a new government came to power, following the National Party's victory at the polls.

Tourism under apartheid

The change in government in 1948 brought into office a party committed to the policy of apartheid, which meant that South Africa became increasingly isolated in the decades that followed. Tourism was a low priority for the new government, which did little to lure visitors. During the 1950s the tourist market remained predominantly regional, with visitors coming from neighbouring southern African countries such as Rhodesia (now Zimbabwe), and Mozambique. In 1952, only 17% of tourists were from overseas; half of them coming from the United Kingdom, most by a sea journey that took up to two weeks each way. In the 1960s, however, after the suppression of the liberation movements, the economy boomed and the country appeared to be stable. Improvements

to the country's infrastructure increased its tourist potential. By the early 1960s the use of jet aircraft had begun to revolutionise air travel, and the Jan Smuts International Airport in Johannesburg (now O.R. Tambo International Airport) took over from Cape Town as the country's main tourist gateway. Between 1958 and 1973 the number of tourists soared from 25 624 to 294 690. The importance of tourism was acknowledged by the establishment of a separate government department of tourism in 1963, and SATOUR (now known as South African Tourism) expanded, opening branch offices in Europe, America and Australia.

Because the government insisted on targeting high-income (as opposed to high-volume) tourists, the full potential of the international tourism market was not exploited. The government did not

Figure 2.1 Overseas tourists visiting South Africa from 1969 to 1989

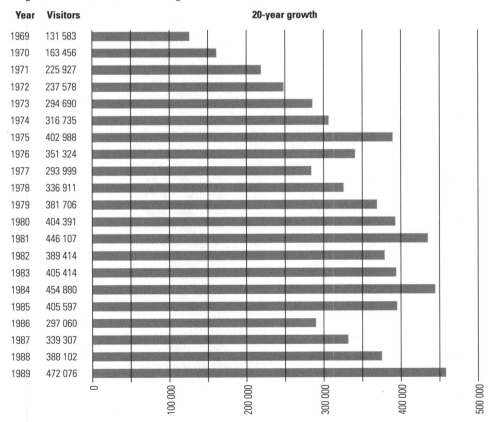

Year	Visitors
1969	131 583
1970	163 456
1971	225 927
1972	237 578
1973	294 690
1974	316 735
1975	402 988
1976	351 324
1977	293 999
1978	336 911
1979	381 706
1980	404 391
1981	446 107
1982	389 414
1983	405 414
1984	454 880
1985	405 597
1986	297 060
1987	339 307
1988	388 102
1989	472 076

Source: Annual report of South African Tourist Board, 1989: 17.

want South Africa inundated, as had happened in Spain and the Caribbean, by relatively low-budget 'mass' tourists with 'loose' morals (Ferrario 1991: 61). Nevertheless, by the early 1970s the tourism industry had become the fifth-largest earner of foreign revenue. The country's apartheid policies did not act as a consistent deterrent to the growth in overseas tourist arrivals. Until the mid-1970s, few overseas tourists had qualms about visiting the country, and South Africa's tourist arrivals for the period 1965 to 1970 outstripped the rate of tourist arrivals world-wide. Whereas world tourism figures showed a 7,2% growth rate, South Africa enjoyed a higher increase of 11,4% in tourist arrivals. From the time of the Soweto Uprising of 1976, however, international criticism of apartheid intensified and the country's isolation grew. In the 1980s the country seemed heading for a racial civil war. Many of SATOUR's promotional overseas offices had to be closed down. Despite all this, however, South Africa remained one of Africa's top destinations for overseas visitors, with most tourists ignoring the brutalities of the racial system and confining their visits to safe 'white' areas.

Figure 2.1 illustrates the enormous growth in foreign tourists visiting South Africa over the 20-year period 1969–1989.

Apartheid stifled the potential of domestic tourism. Restrictive laws meant that black people could not move about the country freely, and there was little scope for the emergence of a black middle class. Apartheid did, however, open up opportunities for gambling tourism, for casinos were permitted in the so-called 'homelands', whereas they were forbidden within the borders of South Africa. The most successful of these, Sun City, in what is now North West province, mushroomed into a major holiday resort, and was to survive the abolition of apartheid and the transition to a democratic society.

Tourism in post-apartheid South Africa

The tourism industry was helped by the 'miracle' of a relatively smooth political transition and by the fall in the value of the rand. Tourism has now emerged as the leading economic growth sector, and is one of the largest contributors to South Africa's **gross domestic product** (GDP). The number of overseas visitors increased more than tenfold, from the low of the mid-1980s to more than 8,4-million in 2006. Of the millions of visitors to South Africa, more than five million people come from African countries beyond our borders. Relatively few of them, however, make use of tourist facilities.

Established tourist sites have not lost their appeal. The breathtaking splendour of the Cape, the attraction of the Winelands, the spectacular coastline and beautiful beaches, and the call of the wild remain major drawcards for international visitors. Tourism, however, has become more diversified in a way that was not possible during the isolationist apartheid years. Seven United Nations Educational, Scientific & Cultural Organisation (UNESCO) World Heritage Sites have been proclaimed since 1999 (Robben Island, the Cape Floral Kingdom, the fossil hominid sites of Sterkfontein, Kromdraai and its environs, the Drakensberg Park, the Vredefort Dome, Mapungubwe, and the iSimangaliso Wetlands Park, formerly the Greater St. Lucia Wetlands). Township tours have emerged as popular tourist activities, as has 'struggle tourism', where tourists visit places associated with South Africa's struggle for democracy and liberation from apartheid. These visitor attractions include Robben Island, where Nelson Mandela and other political prisoners were incarcerated. Other such museums – some newly established – which tell the story of what happened during the apartheid years – are the District Six Museum in Cape Town, the Apartheid Museum in Johannesburg, the Hector Pieterson Museum in Soweto, and the Nelson Mandela Museum in the Eastern Cape. Among the new initiatives is the opening of a tourist route from Robben Island to Cuito Cuanavale in southern Angola, the site of a major battle in 1987–88 in which Cuban, Angolan, and Namibian troops got the better of the South African Defence Force for the first time. This led ultimately to the independence of Namibia, and helped to end apartheid in South Africa.

Conclusion

In this chapter we have looked at the evolution of the various aspects of the tourism industry. We have also examined earlier developments in tourism, such as the Grand Tour, the growth of spas, and the popularity of seaside resorts. We have discussed the impact of wars and the introduction of new modes of transport to tourism. The growth of tourism in South Africa is of specific interest, because we need to understand which events and developments have made our tourism industry what it is today. While reading this book, you need to remember what you have learned about the history of tourism, as an understanding of the past will better enable you to grapple with the concerns of the present and deal with the challenges of the future.

Review questions

1. When did modern mass tourism develop, and why?

2. Explain the development over time of different modes of transportation in South Africa, and how this contributed to the growth of the country's tourist industry.

3. How has the organisation of the tourist industry in South Africa developed since 1910?

4. What was the impact of apartheid on South African tourism?

5. What has the advent of democracy meant for South African tourism?

6. Analyse the history of any one tourist site in South Africa.

Further reading

Butler, R. W. & Wall, G. (Eds.). 1985. The evolution of tourism: historical and contemporary perspectives, *Annals of Tourism Research*. Vol. 12(3), 287–296.

Foley, M. & Lennon, J. 2000. *Dark tourism*. London: Continuum.

Inglis, F. 2000. *The delicious history of the holiday*. London: Routledge.

Rogerson, C. & Visser, G. (Eds. 2004. *Tourism and development in contemporary South Africa*. Tshwane: Africa Institute.

Swinglehurst, E. 1982. *Cook's tours: the story of popular travel*. Poole, Dorset: Blandford Press.

Towner, J. & Wall, G. 1991. History and tourism, *Annals of Tourism Research*. Vol. 18 (1), 71–84.

Websites

www.sa-venues.com/unesco_world_heritage_sites.htm

www.sahistory.org.za/pages/mainframe.htm

www.robbenisland.org.za

www.apartheidmuseum.org

References

Boekstein, M. 1998. *Hot spring holidays: visitors guide to hot springs and mineral spa resorts in Southern Africa*. Cape Town: Mark Boekstein.

Bowles, P. 1969. *The sheltering sky*. London: Penguin Books.

Bulpin, T. V. 1950. *Lost trails on the Lowveld*. Cape Town: Timmins.

Bulpin, T. V. 2001. *Discovering Southern Africa*. Muizenberg: Discovering South Africa Publications.

Erasmus, B. P. J. 1995. *On route in South Africa*. Johannesburg: Jonathan Ball.

Ferrario, F. F. 1991. *An evaluation of the tourist resources of South Africa*. Unpublished PhD University of California.

Financial Mail, 6 March 1970.

Goeldner, C. R., McIntosh, R. W., & Brent Ritchie, J. R. 2000. *Tourism: principles, practices and philosophies*, 8th edition. New York: John Wiley.

Herodotus. 1998. *The histories*. Oxford: University Press.

Johnston, R.H.1975. *Early motoring in South Africa*. Cape Town: Struik.

Klein, H. 1972. *Valley of the mists*. Cape Town: Timmins.

Norval, A. J. 1936. *The tourist industry: a national and international survey*. London: Pitman.

Sharpley, R. 1999. *Tourism, tourists and society*, 2nd edition. Huntingdon, Cambridge: ELM Publications.

Towner, J. 1985. The Grand Tour: a key phase in the history of tourism. *Annals of Tourism Research*, Vol. 12(3), 297–333.

Case study
2

Mineral spa resorts in South Africa

Mark Boekstein

Objective

- To understand the importance of thermal springs in the development of tourism in South Africa

Some of the earliest forms of tourism were based on the apparent curative powers of mineral-rich thermal springs. Travel to such springs for the sake of health and healing can be traced as far back as the ancient Greeks and Romans. The Romans laid great stress on both the therapeutic and social value of hot springs, which they called *thermae*. Many of the famous European baths, such as Aix-les-Bains and Vichy in France, Aachen and Baden-Baden in Germany and Bath in England were developed by the Romans. By the 18th century, 'taking the waters' had become popular among the upper classes of Europe, and European springs had developed into sophisticated spa resorts offering medical treatments in leisure environments. The Dutch soon discovered thermal springs in the vicinity of the settlement at the Cape. Some of the earliest holiday resorts in South Africa, including Caledon and Montagu in the Western Cape, Aliwal North in the Eastern Cape, Warmbaths (Bela-Bela) in Limpopo, and Badplaas in Mpumalanga were developed around these springs.

By 1710 the Caledon hot springs were being visited. They became known as *die bruin bronne*, 'the brown springs', because of the reddish-brown colour of the water, which has a high iron content. The water was found to be highly effective for treating skin diseases and rheumatism. At first, the baths were utilised only by those seeking some form of medical treatment, but when a new bathhouse with furnished rooms and excellent food was completed in 1821, they were visited by people from all walks of life for relaxation as well as for medicinal purposes. When the railway from Cape Town reached Caledon in 1902, the time required for travelling there was considerably reduced. A palatial three-storey 'Caledon Baths and Sanatorium' was built, and the town became the 'Baden-Baden' of South Africa. The building was destroyed by fire in 1946, and all that remains today is a single hot pool known as the 'Victorian Spa Bath', now part of the Caledon Casino Hotel and Spa.

Over the years other spa resorts were developed around natural thermal springs in the Western Cape. The Baths, near Citrusdal, began in 1739 as a military outpost when the Dutch East India Company erected a stone building and a few bathing huts. Today the resort is characterised by its well-preserved Victorian buildings.

Warmwaterberg Spa, between Barrydale and Ladismith, was drawing visitors as early as 1778. The guesthouse and 'sanatorium', built in 1908, remain part of the resort to this day. Avalon Springs, outside Montagu, and Goudini Spa, near Worcester, date back to the mid-19th century. A number of hot springs in the Western Cape, which at one time had facilities for bathing and accommodation establishments, are no longer open to the public. The springs at Brandvlei, near Rawsonville, are the hottest and strongest in South Africa, providing 126 litres of water per second, at 64°C. A bathhouse was built in the early 1800s, but it closed down in the 1940s. Brandvlei is now located on private land, and although the springs can be visited, there are no longer facilities for bathing there.

The largest mineral spa resorts in South Africa today are at Bela-Bela (Warmbaths) and Badplaas. Members of a Voortrekker party discovered the hot springs at Warmbaths in 1837. The springs had long been known to the indigenous people as 'Bela-Bela' (that which boils on its own). People with various ailments soon began to arrive, camping and digging their own baths in the mud, which they encircled with screening shelters of reeds and blankets. Badplaas was known by the Swazis as 'Emanzana' (where the waters heal). After being discovered by a local farmer in 1876, the springs attracted thousands of people, who would camp there during the icy Highveld winter.

In the years following the South African War, many people visited the saline springs at Florisbad, near Bloemfontein, to bathe and for the highly sought-after mud-pack treatments administered by owner Floris Venter, who had a reputation as a 'healer'. In 1912 an earthquake opened up a new spring eye, and fossil bones and stone artefacts were brought to the surface with the water. Further research led to the discovery in 1932 of the 'Florisbad Skull', which dates back more than 40 000 years. The site is now administered by the National Museum in Bloemfontein.

By the late 20th century, most thermal springs in Europe were being used almost exclusively for medicinal purposes, but in South Africa medicinal use of hot spring resorts had declined to the point where they all functioned primarily as family leisure resorts. Only three, Warmbaths, Badplaas, and Caledon have sophisticated health spa facilities. They offer a wide range of spa treatments including hydrotherapy, reflexology, mud treatments, and general beauty treatments. Recent years have seen a decline in demand for the medically-oriented services offered by traditional mineral spas, and an increase in demand for facilities and experiences focusing on a healthy lifestyle, fitness, and relaxation – a change in emphasis from 'health' to 'wellness'. There has also been a revival of the tradition of 'taking the waters' as an antidote to the stresses of urban living.

Case study questions

1. Show how, over time, different people have used South Africa's thermal springs for healing purposes.

2. Thermal springs in South Africa developed differently from those in Europe. What are the main differences?

3. Mineral spa resorts in South Africa cater mainly for the domestic market. How could South Africa's mineral spa tourism product be developed to attract more international tourists?

3

The geography of tourism

Gustav Visser

Purpose

The purpose of this chapter is to discuss the relationship between tourism and geography.

Learning outcomes

After reading this chapter, you should be able to:
- explain the relationship between tourism and geography
- understand the role of core tourism resources and attractors
- provide an overview of the geography of core tourism resources and attractions in South Africa
- understand current trends in tourist flows of international, regional and domestic tourism markets
- understand that there is a link between the geography of a destination region and different types of tourist.

Chapter overview

This chapter begins with a discussion of the relationship between geography and tourism. A definition of tourism geography (or 'geotourism') is provided, and the link between geography and tourism explained. The chapter further describes what core tourism resources and tourist attractors are. The discussion shows that the physical and human geography of a destination region presents tourism managers with a range of core tourism resources that can be used as tourist attractors. In the last part of the chapter our attention turns to South Africa, and key divisions are drawn between 'overseas', 'regional' and 'domestic' tourists. With these different tourism market segments in mind, we are able to see that different tourist attractors apply to each market segment and are reflected in different international, regional, and domestic tourist flows.

The case study illustrates the significance of cities as key tourist attractions in South Africa. It shows how different physical and human geographical attributes in cities affect the way that tourists make use of those cities. The case study will provide the tourism manager with a useful tool for the development of urban-centred tourism programmes that are relevant to the needs of tourists from different regions.

Introduction

Tourism is an activity which is dependent upon the social, cultural and natural environment within which it occurs and, consequently, its success is dependent upon the environment in which it operates. Geography as an academic discipline investigates where things are located on the surface of the earth, why they are located where they are, how places differ from one another, and how people interact with their natural and human-made environments. Consequently, geographers are intuitively interested in tourism, as it involves the understanding of different places and spaces, as well as why and how people interact with them. In addition, tourists modify, or create, new spaces and places which geographers also aim to understand.

This chapter will show that differences in the geographies of different places are at the heart of the tourism system. The physical and **human geography** of a destination is the context in which all tourism activity takes place. No matter what type of tourism management skills one might have, it is the different physical and human geographical attributes of a particular place or region that makes people want to travel. These geographic characteristics of a place that the tourism manager has at his or her disposal are referred to as *core tourism resources* which, in turn, can act as tourist attractors. It is for this reason that geographers since the 1920s have been interested in studying tourism. In fact, geographers were among the first to recognise the need for systematic academic reflection on the location of tourism resources, and how they might be managed in such a way as to become tourist attractions.

The relationship between tourism and geography

Historically, tourism geography developed from the chorology approach to geography. This mainly entailed the cataloguing of places and their characteristics. We might think of this as the mapping of the location of a number of places a tourist might find interesting, and the things they would like to see or explore. Several tourism geography textbooks have been written from this perspective in the past. These textbooks were primarily designed for the 'training' of tourism and leisure students – that is, to teach them where touristic things are in the world. Although this is of practical use it is not, in fact, the kind of geography that excites most people who conduct research into contemporary tourism geography (Lew, 2001: 105).

Geographers are interested in the processes that create and shape the places where people live. They aim to understand the intimate workings of people's lives that are fundamental to an understanding of those processes that create and shape places. Tourism infrastructure, traveller behaviour, and traveller experience are of interest to geographers particularly because of how they shape people, who in turn shape places.

Some commentators argue that the social and economic processes that transect space and drive tourism, recreation, and leisure, and the resulting impacts that these have on the creation of real places and spaces are just as important. Indeed, it is the understanding of the *why* and *how* of tourism's impacts that is the most common theme running through much of geographers' contributions to tourism studies.

One of the most useful ways of viewing tourism geography is by means of the recently introduced concept of 'geotourism'. This is concerned with preserving a destination's geographic character – the entire combination of natural and human attributes that make one place distinct from another. **Geotourism** encompasses both cultural and environmental concerns regarding travel, as well as the local impact tourism has upon communities and their individual economics and lifestyles. Seen in this context, tourism is essentially a geographical activity (Lew, 2002).

The tourism system and its geographical components

People travel because they want to experience geographical difference. These experiences can take place simply by being away from the normal workplace or place of living, or merely through new interpretations and experiences of familiar spaces. Chapter 1 discussed the fact that tourism generally has three main geographical components: the tourist-generating region, the transit region and the tourist-destination region (Leiper, 1979). Tourism geographers are interested in all three of these components. It is important for tourism managers to recognise that there are many geographical questions related to these three components of the tourism system. The information that tourism geographers create in terms of all three components is important to the tourism manager, because it can result in more responsible and more competitive tourism management.

Tourist-generating region

In terms of tourist-generating regions, geographical questions relate to who the tourists are, where they live and what they do. Geographers are also interested in how these facets link up with the different types of tourism offerings tourists want, and where. They aim to satisfy these needs spatially. Other questions relate to who the role players (for example, travel organisers, such as travel agents) and institutions (for example, **destination marketing organisations** – DMOs) are that enable these travel-decision choices.

More complex questions relate to how tourists' absence from the generating-region impacts upon that place. Other questions geographers focus on relate to what impact travelling has on the tourists themselves (physically and psychologically). Some geographers investigate the impact of tourists on the generating region once they have returned from their holiday (see Chapter 15 – Managing the impacts of tourism). Tourism geographers, in asking these questions, aim to understand the impact the tourist destination region has made upon the tourist's home environment. Here, questions such as lifestyle changes or changes in the types of recreation and leisure facilities which people seek out in their home environments come to mind. For example, the tourist might have developed an intense affinity for certain types of food (French country-style cooking); a way of approaching life (making more time for a long and relaxed lunch); or architectural (Tuscan-styled homes) and interior styles (minimalist modern furniture or ceremonial West African masks). These are all issues that relate to the experience of geographical difference elsewhere, but which also impact upon the tourist generating region.

The transit region

The transit region refers to those places, routes and areas tourists pass through, and the mode and means by which they travel to their destinations. Transport geographers investigate this aspect of tourism. Typical questions geographers ask relate to the nature of tourist flows (for example, how many tourists travel, and when do they travel?) and the modes of transport (for example, jet aircraft, private motor vehicle, bus, or train). Currently, tourism geographers are linking these questions to other issues because of their particular interest in the very complex relationship between tourism, transportation modes, and climate change. The key reason for this interest is because the air transportation system is one of the single largest contributors to global warming. In this respect tourists, as individuals, and the transportation system as a whole, have an impact on all destination areas – even on those where tourists have never set foot (Hall & Higham, 2005).

Other aspects concerning the transit region which have been of significant interest to tourism geographers relate to it as a destination area or region in its own right. Different approaches have been taken. Some geographers have investigated certain types of tourists, such as backpackers, who often do not have a particular destination in mind when travelling (Richards & Wilson, 2005). Similarly, there has been considerable interest in the development of 'route tourism', such as the Western Cape Wine Route and the Midlands Meander in KwaZulu-Natal. These investigations consider the different types of economic linkages into the communities around a particular tourism route and which benefits, or negative impacts, this might bring about. Other questions relate to which forms of transport in the transit region might be most beneficial to a range of activities and people along a route. The point is that there are different potential benefits derived from people traversing an area by motor vehicle, train, bicycle, on foot, or by airplane.

The tourist-destination region

The aspect of tourism that has been of most interest to tourism geography since the 1920s is the destination region. Much of what is contained in this book deals with a number of reasons why people are interested in visiting a particular region or destination area. Key generic characteristics that attract tourists are discussed head-on and at length later in this chapter, as well as in Chapter 15 – Managing the impacts of tourism. The aspects of tourism that geographers are interested in are vast in scope. It is enough to say that tourism geographers have been investigating which areas or regions have developed, and in what way, because of which aspect of tourism development. Typical questions include the tourist types, the types of accommodation they use, the magnitude of the economic linkages in the host community, the economic sectors that are involved, and the type and scope of employment creation that tourist numbers enables.

Earlier tourism geography researchers were interested in mapping the characteristics as well as highlighting the benefits of tourism development in a range of different geographical locations. Tourism geography investigations have become very critical of tourists and the tourism industry over the past three decades. The reason for this is the direct environmental impacts of **mass tourism**. For example, the construction of fast-developing hotels in resorts had devastating impacts on local environments in towns along the Mediterranean coast during the 1970s and 1980s. In addition, the impact of tourists' use of various amenities such as beaches, rivers, and historical sites has also been examined. Many of the investigations were linked to concerns over the **carrying capacity** of a destination region. Tourism's impact upon a destination's cultural and social systems has also become the subject of investigation for tourism geographers (see Chapter 15).

Core tourism resources and attractors

As discussed in the previous section, tourism geographers are interested in a vast array of issues associated with the tourist-generating, transit and tourist-destination regions. In this chapter, however, we focus on the tourist-destination region. No matter how important the first two components of Leiper's (1979) tourism system model are, it is the geographical differences in the destination region that attract tourists. These geographical differences can usefully be linked to countless combinations of the natural, human-made and socio-cultural characteristics of a destination region. The identification and description of these core resources represented the bulk of earlier tourism geography research, and remains of considerable interest to this sub-discipline.

One of the great challenges facing tourism managers is how they can best understand the factors that motivate individuals to choose one particular destination over countless others. When a tourist decides to travel to a specific destination, that destination meets the tourist's basic desire in respect of its core resources and attractors – that is, its geography. Core resources and attractors comprise natural, human-made and socio-cultural tourist attractions (see Example box below).

> **Example** Examples of core tourism resources and attractor types
>
> Ritchie and Crouch (2003) highlight a number of core resources and attractors which include a range of natural, human-made, and socio-cultural tourist attractions:
>
> The *physical geography* of the destination, most particularly the landscape, scenery, and climate. In effect, it is the visual and sensual pleasure derived from these elements that provides some of the most fundamental physical enjoyments of tourism.

Aspects of the *human geography* that are characteristic of the destination, such as elements related to the culture and history of a destination, provide much of the intellectual satisfaction that arises from visiting a particular place.

The scope of *special events* presented in a destination area creates much of the dynamics and the uniqueness that make a destination memorable.

Fundamental to a destination area's success is its *infrastructure*, such as hotels, restaurants, museums, and those services that tourists require when travelling to and around it.

The types of *entertainment* found at a destination are frequently designed to complement the different activities and events that a destination offers. Conversely, for other destinations the strength of the entertainment may itself be the primary appeal.

The strength of *market ties* frequently serves as a major catalyst for destination visitation that involves human relations.

The *blend of different activities* available at a destination provides the primary foundation of both the physical and emotional stimulation that excites and challenges the visitor.

TO DO

Draw up a list of core tourist attractors for the region in which you live.

Natural tourist attractions: Physical geography as critical tourist attractors

Natural tourist attractions are among the most important determinants of destination competitiveness. These attractions relate to the **physical geography** of a destination area. The central elements of the physical geography of a destination region include climate (absolute, relative, variability, consistency); the topography, size, water masses (lakes, rivers and oceans); forests, deserts, rural and urban areas, air quality, scenery, and the flora and fauna (Ritchie & Crouch, 2003: 112).

Climate

The extent to which the natural climate and terrain are hospitable to humans provides a set of natural parameters that either endow a destination with competitive appeal or create barriers that must constantly be adapted to, overcome, or circumvented. For example, a relatively comfortable climate with extremes that are not too significant immediately provides a baseline of attractiveness for the great majority of tourists. However, it has to be remembered that there are niche markets – such as adventure tourists – who seek unique and demanding climates, although they are generally the exception. Those destinations that are well endowed with a 'natural edge' have become increasingly attractive. Moreover, a high concentration of natural amenities often enables the development of adventure, natured-based, wildlife, and ecotourism attractions.

The majority of destinations that have a favourable climate tend to build their competitive position around this natural advantage. Italy, Greece, Spain, and other Mediterranean coastal regions, for example, as well as numerous island destinations in the Caribbean and South Pacific, all benefited from the 'rush to sun', offering tourists the 'three Ss' (sun, sand, and sea). Quite controversially, some destinations have, over time, added the fourth 's', for sex ('**sex tourism**').

Landscape

Closely linked to climate is the actual physical character of the destination. The extent to which the physical geography of a destination is hospitable to human activity again provides very important competitive advantages or disadvantages in terms of tourism marketing and management. A relatively even vegetation-covered terrain that has convenient access to water masses and high-quality recreation areas provides humans (and animals) with a physical environment that most easily accommodates their physiology. While variations in topography as well as in vegetation and wildlife add novelty, the human body prefers to avoid extremes (Ritchie & Crouch, 2003: 114).

It has to be pointed out, however, that some tourist destinations may not have favourable climates, but might have spectacular scenery. A whole range of destination regions with rugged mountain ranges or vast expanses of open, arid terrain provide some of the world's most attractive scenery. The Alpine regions of Europe, the Himalayas in Asia, the Andes in South America, and the Rockies of North America provide some examples of mountain ranges. In addition, the desert landscapes of Chile, Peru, and Namibia represent natural attractions which, because of their unique extremities of weather, are very desirable tourist attractions. These natural landscapes offer extraordinary views and mountain passes, as well as hiking, extreme sports, and mountaineering opportunities. As outlined in Table 3.1, a large part of the global tourist system has devised a range of different strategies to overcome a lack of physiographic and climatic attractors.

Although natural attractions in terms of unique or picturesque landscapes can motivate travel, the use of these natural resources can be highly problematic and lead to the degradation of parts, or all, of the attraction owing to overuse. Much of the tourism geography research in the 1960s, 1970s, and 1980s set out to uncover the negative impacts tourism can have on natural tourist attractors. In this respect, one might consider the extensive damage caused to the Costa del Sol in Spain and to other coastal resorts along the eastern seaboard of Spain, the islands of Majorca, Ibiza, and the Canaries because of tourist overuse. Spain, for example, was already attracting over six million tourists every year by 1960, and this was to grow to 30-million by 1975. Striking a balance between development and usage has become a critically important issue, debated at length across the world. Generally, it has become part of the so-called sustainable tourism debate.

Not all negative impacts on the natural resources base are directly linked to tourist use, but rather to increased population growth. However, tourism and climate change need to be understood as a 'two-way partnership', as tourism is itself an important contributor to climate

Table 3.1 Strategies to overcome a lack of physical geographical and climatic attractors

There are different strategies that might be deployed to overcome different physical barriers, including:
• Building artificial environments that negate the environmental inhospitality of a region. In this respect one might think of the use of air-conditioning and enclosed mall and entertainment complexes.
• Using a unique attraction that will make tourists bear the inconvenience of either an unattractive physical environment or inclement weather. Here one might think of attractions such as those of ancient Egypt.
• Development of events or attractions that capitalise on extreme weather or physical geography, such as skiing tournaments or ice landscapes.
• Enhancing the overall awareness of a destination through media attention resulting from particularly unpleasant aspects of a destination region. In this respect we can consider a number of 'justice tourism' sites such as Robben Island, or the Hector Pieterson Memorial in Soweto.
• Using mega-events to build the global reputation of a destination and to leave behind visible legacies that may, in time, become destination icons. In this respect one might think of the Eiffel Tower in Paris, which is just one remnant of a series of world exhibitions hosted by that city.
• Establishing niche attractions in an otherwise very unattractive or uninteresting destinations, such as the casino resorts of Las Vegas.

Adapted from Ritchie, J.R.B. & Crouch, G.I., 2003. *The Competitive Destination: a sustainable tourism perspective.* Wallingford: CABI Publishing

change as a result of the large amounts of fossil fuels needed for tourist transport, accommodation and activities. It is expected that climate change will increasingly affect travel behaviour, both as a result of altering conditions for holidaymaking at the destination level and because of climate variables being perceived as less or more comfortable for tourists. As a consequence, it is important for tourism managers to understand climate and landscape changes as they impact directly on the desirability of a destination. The Example box below highlights some of the issues surrounding tourism and climate change.

Example Tourism and climate change.

The effect of climate change on tourism has been the focus lately of several research studies. Thus some investigations have sought to access the consequence of climate change on the tourist industry for nations, destinations, or particular sectors of tourism such as ski tourism. Elsewhere the threat of rising sea-levels have led to banking institutions refusing to finance loans to beach resort developments in some island states.

Most researchers have warned that tourist destinations will lose attractiveness, as demonstrated by the loss of snow in ski resorts, the obliteration of glaciers, as well as the loss of sandy beaches owing to sea-level changes or frequent severe storm damage. Conversely, there might be benefits in terms of less rain or extended summer seasons at particular destinations.

There have been attempts to understand the effects of increasing temperatures and related parameters (such as rain) on tourists' choices of destination and time of departure. For example, an analysis of the travel patterns of British tourists aiming to identify optimal holiday temperatures found that the maximum preferred daytime temperature was 30.7°C, with even small increases above this level leading to decreasing numbers of visits. Other studies have found that tourists from Europe and North America preferred an average temperature (day and night temperatures aggregated) of 21°C at their destinations during the hottest month of the year.

The studies conclude that tourists may shift to other destinations or travel during other times of the year because of a scenario of climate change. Implications for the economies of nations and destinations of such changes might be severe. It has also been suggested that tourists probably do not care much about climate change, and they might merely substitute one destination for another, or one travel date for another.

Source: Gössling, S. & Hall, M., 2006

Socio-cultural attractors

It must be pointed out that the physical geography and climate of a destination region do not always play a central role in acting as a core tourism resource or tourist attractor. Socio-cultural attractors which include a very broad array of products besides the relative attractiveness of the physical geography of a destination are a very powerful and important dimension of destination attractiveness. In many ways, much of what qualifies as socio-cultural attractors can be interpreted as being human-made tourist attractions. However, as discussed below, there are some differences in the sense that human-made tourist attractions are developed with tourists in mind, whereas socio-cultural attractors have developed organically in a particular area, independently of the potential of tourist use or desirability.

It has been argued that the cultural and social characteristics of a region were, historically, the key reason why people 'become tourists' (McKercher & Du Cros, 2002). Indeed, as far back as ancient Rome, people travelled to numerous destinations to see and experience different cities' and regions' cultural and social practices and associated rituals, public buildings, and monuments. Currently, cultural and social characteristics have been shown to be critical to the desirability of a destination area, second only to its natural beauty and pleasant climate. The central elements of socio-cultural attractiveness in contemporary tourism are diverse. Scholars such as Ritchie and Crouch (2003: 115) argue that this would include some or all of the following elements:

- *Handicrafts of a region*, such as the leather products of Argentina and Spain; the unique masks of West African countries, or handicrafts made from a number of recycled materials in South Africa.
- Few experiences make one so acutely aware of being in a different country than *differences in the language* spoken by the residents of the destination area. Many people find that their experiences of countries are enhanced because they are in a different linguistic domain.
- *Regional traditions* also enhance the experience difference. Here one might consider the various traditions of Italy or Spain, celebrating particular local practices such as harvests.
- *Gastronomy or style of food preparation* particular to the region. Whether markets, foods and stalls in Mexico, night-markets in Thailand or China, or bistros and cafés in France, the different types and ways of food consumption and preparation can significantly enhance a tourist's experience of a destination.
- *Art and music* identified with the region, including paintings, sculpture and concerts. One might consider the enormous lure of the Louvre in Paris, the public sculptures of Florence, or the concerts held at Glastonbury in the United Kingdom.
- *History of the region*, including its visual reminders, can make a significant impact on a tourist's experience of a particular destination. Often the history of a destination is enhanced through a range of physical features, such as its architecture or the manner in which certain types of work are performed.
- *Methods of work or technology* particular to a region, such as unique ways of fishing and farming, make the experience of a destination very unique;
- *Architecture,* both exterior and interior, which lends a distinctive appearance to a region. No tourist can possibly confuse the stone houses of Tuscany with the whitewashed cottages

of Greek seaside villages or the grandeur of Parisian boulevards and public buildings.
- *Religion and religious practices* that are of particular significance to a region, including their visible manifestations. Think of the imposing mosques of the Middle East; the monks of Buddhist temples in Asia, or the Gothic cathedrals of Europe.
- The presence of expatriate communities across the globe has resulted in *visiting friends and relatives (VFR)* becoming a growing reason why people travel to a range of different regions. In this respect South Africa represents a prime example, with emigrant communities in Australia and the United Kingdom presenting new source markets for those travelling to visit relatives and friends in South Africa.
- The *education system* that is characteristic of the region. The collegiate university towns and cities such as Oxford, Cambridge, Grahamstown, and Stellenbosch are distinctive landmarks.
- *Leisure activities* reflecting the distinctive lifestyles of a region. Here we can think of surfing off the coast of Hawaii, or in Jeffrey's Bay.

Human-made tourist attractors

Numerous human-made (or built) attractions that might make a particular destination an attractive place to visit have been created to overcome the limitations of its physical geography, as well as its lack of either unique or attractive socio-cultural attractions. Human-made tourist attractions have been the focus of tourism geography research since the 1950s, largely because of the emergence of resort tourism and casino developments at the time.

Furthermore, the development of human-made attractors have, particularly over the past two decades, received considerable attention from a range of development agencies ranging from all levels of government to parastatal companies and private sector investors. Indeed, numerous city and regional governments have developed tourism strategies that focus on the creation and building of human-made tourist attractions (for example casinos and conference centres). These attractions typically act as vehicles for stimulating tourist flows as part of a local economic development strategy. One has to keep in mind, however, that often human-made attractors are not necessarily developed only with tourists in mind, as they might merely be part of the socio-cultural traits of a particular place.

Currently there is a range of human-made tourist attractions available. Two commonly deployed types of human-made tourist attractors relate to hallmark and mega-events, as well as landmark developments.

Hallmark and mega-events. It is often very difficult for places to compete with destinations that have extraordinary natural or unique cultural attributes, long and distinguished histories,

outstanding design, engineering, or architecture. However, if, as with many other destinations, it must rely on innovative insight and/or simply hard work to create for itself a unique characteristic that makes it stand out in the marketplace, then the development of special events has proved to be one way to achieve visibility and to build a reputation. Although large-scale events can elevate a destination from obscurity to international prominence, there are only so many ready-made events that can be staged and promoted (Ritchie & Crouch, 2003).

As a consequence, destinations strive to develop their own showpiece or hallmark events. The events include world fairs or expositions (such as Brisbane 1988, Lisbon 1998 & Hanover 2000); unique carnivals and festivals

Table 3.2 A typology of planned events

Cultural celebrations	Educational and scientific
Festivals	Congresses and conferences
Carnivals	Workshops
Religious events	**Recreational**
Parades	Games and sports for fun
Heritage commemorations	Amusement events
Art and entertainment	**Political and state**
Concerts	Inaugurations
Exhibits	Investitures
Award ceremonies	VIP visits
Business and trade	Rallies
Fairs, markets, sales	**Private events**
Consumer and trade shows	Anniversaries
Expositions	Family holidays
Meeting and conferences	Rites of passage
Publicity events	Parties, galas
Fund-raiser events	Reunions
Sport competitions	
Professional	
Amateur	

Source: Adapted from Ritchie & Crouch, 2003: 124

(for example, the Mardi Gras in New Orleans and Sydney); major sporting or mega-events (such as the Olympic Games or FIFA World Cup), and important historical milestones (the Australian Bicentenary in 1988, and the 500th anniversary of the European discovery of America in 1992). Classic commercial and religious events (e.g. wine expos in Bordeaux and London, and Papal visits), major political personage events (presidential inaugurations), and major political leadership events – such as the World Summit on Sustainable Development (WSSD) hosted in Johannesburg in 2002 – are also included in this category.

Few events however, are of great significance. Most events are smaller in size on the whole, and more frequent in their presentation. Table 3.2 provides a typology of planned events which many destinations present to greater or lesser degree.

Landmark developments: Often the hosting of events, irrespective of whether or not they are hallmark or mega-events, leads to the development of physical structures. In time these structures themselves become tourist attractions. In this regard one might think of the Eiffel Tower in Paris, which was only meant to have been a temporary structure linked to a world fair.

Recently, however, there have been very conscious tourist developments initiated, and landmarks created with their tourism potential in mind. In this respect we might think of the development of a range of art, cultural, and history museums, such as the Guggenheim Museum in Bilbao, Spain, the Constitution Hill development in Johannesburg, the Apartheid Museum and the Nelson Mandela Bridge in Johannesburg, and the Victoria & Alfred Waterfront in Cape Town. Other examples of such landmarks include theme parks such Disney World, Legoland, or cultural villages such as Shakaland in KwaZulu-Natal.

South Africa's core tourist attractions and their linkages to tourist flows

We have reviewed some of the generic core tourist attractors, and are now able to turn our attention

to how these relate to South Africa. South Africa is fortunate in having an abundance of natural and socio-cultural tourist attractors. Indeed, the strength of South Africa as a tourist destination lies in the variety of its many offerings, which range from its highly variable topography relative to its size, an excellent climate with temperature ranges generally not seen as excessive (including the fact that the country has some of the highest numbers of sunshine hours anywhere in the world), a differentiated economy, a tumultuous history, different cultural and social practices, and a range of unique political features (Cornelissen, 2005).

It is, however, very important to remember that, as far as the tourist attractors are concerned, different aspects of the South African tourism geography are utilised and experienced by different market segments in different ways. Of key importance, in the South African context, is the fact that the natural, socio-cultural or human-made attractors which draw tourists to a particular place have everything to do with where their home base is.

The following sections outline South Africa's core tourist attractors, whilst also demonstrating that there are clear links between the geography of the tourist-generating region, the geography of the transit region, and the geography of the tourism-destination area. For example, natural attractions are of critical importance to the overseas tourist market, but only of marginal importance to tourists from the African continent. As a consequence, it is extremely important to the South African tourism industry whether one is an international tourist from 'overseas', an international regional tourist from elsewhere in Africa, or a domestic tourist (for an extensive review of these linkages refer to Rogerson & Visser, 2006).

International tourists and South Africa's tourist attractors

Since the early 1990s there has been an explosion of international tourism arrivals to South Africa. In 2005, South Africa received the largest number of foreign visitors in its history of recording tourist statistics. The 7,4-million international tourist arrivals, of which more than two million came from other continents, ranked South Africa 32nd in terms of international tourist receipts. Figure 3.1 shows the sources of foreign visitor arrivals to South Africa for 2005. The African market generates the largest volume of international tourist arrivals for South Africa. Indeed, over 70% of South Africa's international tourists are intra-regional tourists from the African continent. Moreover, by far the largest category of arrivals from Africa originated from South Africa's neighbouring states.

Figure 3.2 highlights the leading 20 countries generating sources of foreign arrivals to South Africa. The four leading source markets, and six out of the leading eight source markets, are South Africa's neighbouring states. The largest tourist-generating markets are Lesotho, followed by Swaziland and Botswana. The key overseas source markets are the United Kingdom, Germany, and the USA.

South Africa's two groups of 'international' tourists visit the country for very different reasons (Table 3.3). In terms of overseas markets, North American and European tourists visit South Africa mainly for holiday or leisure purposes and different tourist attractors. In contrast, the majority of regional African tourists are visiting South Africa because of business-related attractors (SA Tourism, 2005).

Overseas international tourists and South Africa's core attractors

In terms of overseas tourist markets, the following distinctive tourist offerings might be identified as giving South Africa a competitive advantage over many other international tourist destinations:

Figure 3.1 The geography of international visitor arrivals in South Africa, 2005

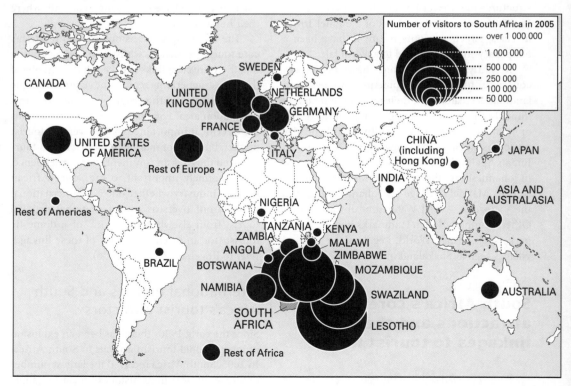

Source: Rogerson, C.M. & Visser, G. 2006. International tourist flows and urban tourism in South Africa, *Urban Forum*, Vol 17(2), 199–213

Figure 3.2 Leading country sources of foreign arrivals in South Africa

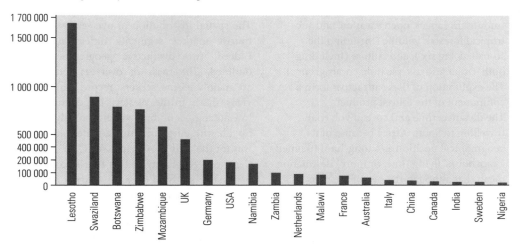

Source: Rogerson, C.M. & Visser, G. 2006. International tourist flows and urban tourism in South Africa, *Urban Forum*, Vol 17(2), 199–213

Table 3.3 Purpose of visit to South Africa, by geographical origin (by percentage)

	Holiday	**Business**	**VFR**	**Other**
Angola	38,5	31,4	16,1	14,1
Australia	50,0	18,7	25,6	5,6
Botswana	11,5	60,0	19,8	8,7
Canada	55,9	21,1	16,9	6,2
China	43,7	41,4	11,0	4,0
France	73,7	17,3	6,5	2,5
Germany	76,7	13,0	6,8	2,5
India	22,7	59,3	15,1	2,9
Italy	72,7	19,8	5,7	1,8
Lesotho	9,7	35,1	40,8	14,4
Malawi	27,8	47,2	16,5	8,4
Mozambique	17,7	71,5	7,6	3,1
Namibia	25,9	20,1	47,0	7,1
Netherlands	78,1	10,3	8,1	3,5
Swaziland	22,7	42,1	25,5	9,6
Sweden	63,1	25,4	7,4	4,1
UK	70,1	10,8	16,7	2,4
USA	61,0	21,9	10,3	6,9
Zambia	25,9	41,9	20,7	11,4
Zimbabwe	38,2	26,9	28,4	6,6

Source: South African Tourism, 2005. *2004 Annual tourism report*. South African Tourism Strategic Unit. Johannesburg: SA Tourism

- South Africa's attractors centre on unique natural and social features such as landscape (mountain ranges, open savanna, and sub-tropical forests), wildlife (including the so-called 'big six'), and culture (including both settler and diverse indigenous groups). The exploration of these attractors form a key component of the tourist product.
- The distance, time and costs involved in travelling to South Africa because of its geographical position as a **long-haul** (defined as six hours' flying time, or more) destination mean that although the size of the market is smaller, these visitors spend more and stay longer than those from short- or medium-haul destinations.
- Despite its natural appeal, South Africa is not regarded or marketed as a significant beach tourism or **resort destination**. This is in contrast to many other destinations in the developing world, not least of which is North Africa and most islands where the sort of infrastructure for so-called 'stay-put' vacationing has been well developed. Consequently, distinct from the 'sun, sand, sea, and hotel' visitors, overseas tourists to South Africa are characteristically not linked to one locale.
- Travel domestically in South Africa, particularly to destination regions such as KwaZulu-Natal, is a very important aspect of the country's tourist offering.

These features are not unique to South Africa, but, in terms of overseas visitors, South Africa's distinction lies in its status as an African country, and its tourist appeal is linked to this. The idiosyncrasies of South Africa's social and political history, moreover, make it a paradoxical destination. The fundamental attraction of the country resides in its geographical location on the African continent, and the opportunity it presents to tourists who are interested in viewing and experiencing uniquely African attributes (to sum up, the vastly different landscape, people and cultures, and wildlife) (Cornelissen, 2005).

Overseas tourists to South Africa

The spatial distribution of overseas and regional tourist market segments differs significantly. Indeed, two distinctive geographies can be outlined. The mass of overseas tourists, who are mainly leisure seekers, record a high level of visits, firstly to the Western Cape, and secondly to Gauteng – a finding which is mostly explained by Johannesburg's function as international gateway for the country. Cornelissen (2005) unpacked the travel geography of this tourist cohort in an exhaustive study of overseas tourists' travel itineraries, in which she showed that the typical tour for overseas tourists to South Africa ran from Johannesburg in the north of the country to Cape Town in the south. An example of such a tour is presented in the Example box below.

> **Example** A typical overseas tourist's travel itinerary
>
> Tourists typically arrive at the O.R. Tambo International Airport in Johannesburg, and then visit Gauteng's urban attractions – such as the Apartheid Museum, Gold Reef City, Sandton City, and the Union buildings in Tshwane. The tour then goes on to Mpumalanga (private game reserves), the Kruger National Park, Swaziland, Zululand, and then eThekwini. In the city of eThekwini beaches and a cultural village are visited. From there tourists go on to Port Elizabeth, the gateway to the Garden Route, and the resort towns of Knysna and Plettenberg Bay are the main focal points. From there the town of Oudtshoorn is visited, with the tour moving on to Cape Town. In Cape Town, key attractions include the V&A Waterfront and the Cape Town Central Business District, with visits to the Castle of Good Hope, the Company Gardens, St George's Mall and St George's Cathedral, the Cape Town Parliamentary Buildings, and, more generally, different examples of Cape Dutch architecture.
>
> Cornelissen, 2005: 687–688

Typically, South Africa's most important visitor attractions include those attractors which overseas tourists find it important to see (Figure 3.3

Figure 3.3 Location of key South African tourist/visitor attractions

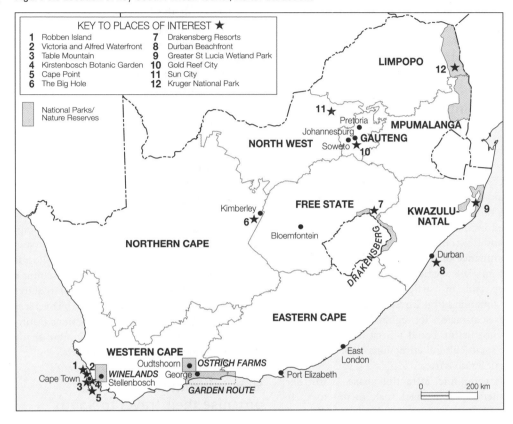

Source: Rogerson, C.M. & Visser, G. 2006. International tourist flows and urban tourism in South Africa. *Urban Forum*, Vol 17(2), 199–213

Table 3.4 South Africa's 10 premier visitor attractions

Rank	Tourist attraction	Location
1	Victoria and Alfred Waterfront	Cape Town, Western Cape
2	Table Mountain National Park	Cape Town, Western Cape
3	Cape Point	Cape Town, Western Cape
4	Wine Route	Winelands, Western Cape
5	Garden Route	Western Cape
6	Kirstenbosch Botanical Gardens	Cape Town, Western Cape
7	Ostrich Farms	Little Karoo, Western Cape
8	Robben Island Museum	Cape Town, Western Cape
9	Attractions in Tshwane, e.g. Union Buildings	Tshwane, Gauteng
10	Kruger National Park	Mpumalanga

Source: Cornelissen, S. 2005. *The global tourism system: governance, development and lessons from South Africa.* Aldershot: Ashgate

provides an outline of the main tourist attractions and their geographic distribution, and highlights the top 10 main overseas tourist attractions). As seen in Table 3.4, the main tourist attractors are mainly related to natural and human-made attractors.

Regional international tourists and South Africa's core attractors

As far as visitors from African regions are concerned, a very different picture emerges in which Gauteng, South Africa's economic heartland, and the cities of Johannesburg and Tshwane, are the most significant focus for regional tourism, followed by the provinces of the Western Cape and KwaZulu-Natal. This is the result of the dominance of business travel in the agenda of this market segment, the core focus being Gauteng and, in particular, Africa's economic hub – Johannesburg. These findings show that the tourist attractors for regional tourists are very clearly not nature-based tourist attractions, but mainly socio-cultural attractions – the economic system of South Africa.

The economic attraction base is further strengthened by the fact that, owing to their geographical proximity for land travellers, a specific province emerges as a significant focus for visitors from a specific source. Thus, Mpumalanga is important for visitors from Swaziland and Mozambique; Free State for visitors from Lesotho; Northern Cape for visitors from Namibia, and the North West province for visitors from Botswana. Again, the economic aspects of South Africa's socio-cultural landscape are the key attractors implicated in these tourist flows.

International tourists and their length of stay in South Africa

A significant difference between overseas and regional tourist markets is disclosed in terms of the length of stay of international tourists in South Africa. This, in conjunction with the key reasons for travelling to South Africa, provides insight into what the key tourist attractors are for different international tourist-generating regions. The most common length of stay in South Africa

by regional African tourists is between two and four days, with the highest figure recorded by travellers originating from Nigeria and Tanzania (six days), followed by Kenya, Namibia, and Zambia (four days), and Zimbabwe (three days). The short stays and more frequent visits to South Africa by regional tourists should be compared to the much longer length of stay of overseas visitors from Europe (14 days) or the USA (seven days) (South African Tourism, 2005).

One factor that underpins this pattern is the existence of differential entry conditions for nationals from different countries (Cassim & Jackson, 2003). However, more importantly, the nature of the visit is very different, with regional visitors conducting business (often shopping) visits, whilst the overseas visitor mainly pursues leisure activities. Thus, the regional visitor is engaging with specific aspects of the socio-cultural attractor base – the retail economy, which requires relatively limited time spans – whilst the overseas tourists engage with a range of attractions featuring natural, socio-cultural, and human-made attractors requiring larger time-budgets.

How international tourists organise their travel to South Africa

On the whole, travellers to South Africa prefer independent travel options. By far the majority of African tourists to South Africa fall into the category of **fully independent travellers** (FITs), rather than tourists visiting the country on some form of inclusive tourism (where airfare, accommodation, internal travel, and food are included) or package (airfare and accommodation) arrangement. Overall, the market segment that makes the greatest use of all-inclusive packages comprises tourists from France, China, and Japan; reflecting the fact that these markets are still not that highly familiar with South Africa. Moreover, the English-language barrier is a factor that prevents many of these tourists from engaging in independent travel, particularly when considering the far higher levels of independent travel among tourists from English-speaking countries such as Australia, the UK, and the USA.

International tourist spending in South Africa

During 2005, the total direct spend (TDS) in South Africa by foreign tourists was R47,8-billion. The total spend by African visitors was estimated at R25-billion, which represents roughly a 53% share. This figure should be compared to the nearly R13-billion contributed to the tourist economy by visitors sourced from Europe, and R2,5-billion from the Americas. Despite the higher average spend patterns of overseas visitors as opposed to African travellers, African countries still represent five of the most significant source markets, as measured by total direct spend. Of note is the fact that some of the highest average spend figures within South Africa are recorded by regional travellers from African destinations.

Profile of South Africa's domestic tourism market

Since the demise of apartheid South Africa has recorded a burst of growth in domestic tourism flows. The dismantling of apartheid (beginning in the 1980s), the end of restrictions on access to tourist attractions and amenities, and a growing prosperity among some sections of the black, coloured, and Indian communities precipitated an expansion of black domestic tourism from the 1980s (see Chapter 2 – History of tourism). Over the last 15 years, several domestic national tourism surveys have been undertaken in South Africa. The most recent data suggests that the size of the domestic tourism market is currently valued at R21,2-billion, which is comparable to the R53-billion (2005) earned from international tourism (South African Tourism, 2005). The total number of domestic trips, 36,2-million, far exceeded the number of international arrivals in South Africa, a total of 7,4-million for 2005 (Rogerson & Lisa, 2005).

Travel categories of domestic tourists in South Africa

Figure 3.4 provides a breakdown of the domestic market in terms of five major categories of travel.

It is important to note the reasons why domestic tourist travel does not fit neatly with the key attractors concerning either overseas visitors or regional tourists to South Africa. It is clear that **visiting friends and relatives** (VFR) is the main reason why South African tourists travel to particular destinations in South Africa (Rule *et al.*, 2001). Although nearly two-thirds of all trips are for VFR purposes, Figure 3.4 overleaf shows that holiday travel, which would be impacted by core nature, socio-cultural, or human-made tourist attractors, accounts for only 16% of trips. Moreover, business travel is the third most important segment of domestic tourism as indexed by share of value.

Surveys of the activities undertaken by domestic tourists reveal the significance of social activities (in terms of visits to friends and relatives), followed by shopping for personal use, nightlife (theatre, restaurants), and water-based activities. Together this segment engages a range of natural, human-made and socio-cultural tourist attractors. However, it is significant that these attractors are not the same as those which attract international overseas tourists (Rogerson & Visser, 2005).

Destination regions of South Africa's domestic tourists

Figure 3.4 shows that there is considerable spatial unevenness in domestic tourism flows within South Africa. It is recorded that 60% of all domestic travel overall occurs intra-provincially, and only 40% of domestic tourism involves inter-provincial travel (SA Tourism, 2004). The most significant inter-provincial flow occurs from Gauteng to the coastal areas of KwaZulu-Natal and to the game parks of Mpumulanga. For these domestic tourists, however, although natural attractors are important, they are evidently not necessarily seeking the same attractors as those visited by overseas tourists. Three key provinces, namely KwaZulu-Natal, Gauteng, and the Eastern Cape account for 64% of total trips in terms of source of travel, and correspondingly receive 60% of the domestic tourism trade. It is significant that the Western Cape province, which includes six

Figure 3.4 The geography of domestic tourism in South Africa: most important destinations for key segments

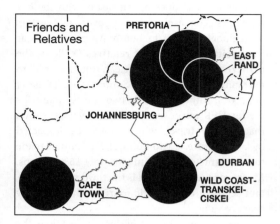

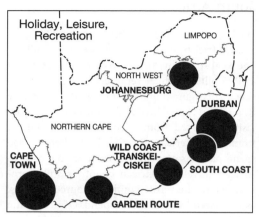

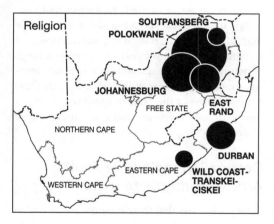

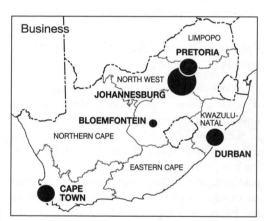

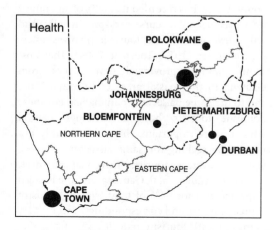

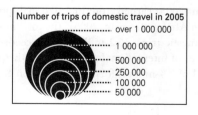

Source: Rogerson, C.M. & Lisa, Z., 2005. 'Sho't Left': changing domestic tourism in South Africa. *Urban Forum*, Vol 16(2/3), 88–111

of the top ten-ranked visitor attractions for over-seas tourists, is placed only fourth among South Africa's nine provinces in the league of domestic tourism destinations. In this respect, different natural attractors are important, as is the fact that socio-cultural elements induce travel to these regions (Rogerson & Lisa, 2005).

Volume and distribution of domestic tourists

Based upon the spatial information provided in the 2001 national domestic tourism survey (Rule *et al.*, 2001), a more detailed profile of the geography of domestic tourism can be constructed. Figure 3.4 illustrates the volume of estimated trips and leading destinations for different segments of domestic tourism – namely VFR tourism; leisure tourism; business tourism; religious tourism, and health tourism. Figure 3.4 shows that geographical variations clearly exist in the patterns of domestic tourism and local impacts on the different segments of domestic tourism. The VFR market is spread approximately in proportion to patterns of the national population, and is dominated by flows to the major inland urban centres of Johannesburg, Tshwane and Ekurhuleni, as well as to Cape Town and eThekwini. The Wild Coast, Transkei, and Ciskei areas, which are major focuses of out-migration, also emerge as leading destinations for VFR travel.

The coastal areas of KwaZulu-Natal, the Western Cape, and the Garden Route are dominant in terms of leisure travel. Of note, however, is that Johannesburg ranks as the third most important individual **node** for leisure travel. What is important here is that socio-cultural attractors motivate tourism flows, while natural attractors are of critical importance to overseas tourists. Business travel is heavily concentrated on South Africa's major commercial centres, with the dominance of Johannesburg strongly evident. Domestic health tourism also focuses mainly on the major urban centres where the quality and availability of health care is greatest. Once again, Johannesburg is the leading node. Finally, the spatial flows of religious tourism in South Africa are the most

distinctive of all the five segments of domestic tourism. Figure 3.4 illustrates the overwhelming dominance of the Polokwane region, where Moria is the national focus of the annual gathering of members of the Zionist Christian Church (Rogerson & Lisa, 2005).

Conclusion

Tourism is driven by human and physical geographical difference. Indeed, if it were not for these differences, there would be no reason to travel. In this chapter tourism geography, as an approach to understanding and investigating the tourism system, was introduced. It was argued that there are various issues which tourism geographers investigate in the tourist-generating, transit and destination regions. The focus then turned to the tourist-destination region, and generic core tourist attractors were discussed. It was the contention that geographical differences in terms of physical and human attributes drive tourism. These geographical attractors were divided into physical, socio-cultural and human-made tourist attractors. The impact of these attractors on tourist motivation and the impact of tourists on these tourist attractors were also outlined. The discussion then focused on South Africa's core tourist attractors. An important observation was that different tourist attractors are of relevance to tourists from different geographical regions.

Review questions

1. What is tourism geography?

2. Outline some examples of core tourism resources and attractors.

3. Describe some of the strategies to overcome a lack of physical geographical and climatic attractors of a destination region.

4. Describe South Africa's main tourist markets.

5. Describe the current trends in South Africa's international tourist flows, relative to core tourist attractors.

Further reading

Shaw, G. & Williams, A. M. 2002. *Critical issues in tourism: a geographical perspective*, Oxford: Blackwell.

Shaw, G. & Williams, A. M. 2004. *Tourism and tourism spaces*, London: Sage.

Rogerson, C. M. & Visser, G. 2004. *Tourism and development issues in contemporary South Africa*, Tshwane: Africa Institute of South Africa.

Rogerson, C. M. & Visser, G. 2007. *Urban tourism in the developing world: the South African experience*, New Brunswick: Transaction Publications.

Journals

Annals of Tourism Research

Tourism Geographies

Tourism Geography

Websites

South African Tourism: www.southafrica.net

Open Africa: www.africadream.org

Refeerences

Cassim, R. & Jackson, W. (Eds.). 2003. *International trade in services and sustainable development: the case of energy and tourism in South Africa*. Unpublished report, Trade Knowledge Network.

Cornelissen, S. 2005. *The global tourism system: governance, development and lessons from South Africa*. Aldershot: Ashgate.

Gössling, S., Bredberg, M., Randow, A., Svensson, P., & Swedlin, E. 2006. *Tourist perceptions of climate change: a study of international tourists in Zanzibar. Current Issues in Tourism*, 9(4&5), 419-435

Hall, C. M. & Higham, J. (Eds.). 2005. *Tourism, recreation and climate change*. Clevedon: Channelview Publications.

Judd, D. R. & Fainstein, S. (Eds.). 1999. *The tourist city*. London: Yale University Press.

Leiper, N. 1979. 'The framework of tourism', *Annals of Tourism Research*, Vol. 6(4), 390–407.

Lew, A. A. 2001. 'Defining a geography of tourism' in *Tourism Geographies*, Vol. 3(1), 105–114.

Lew, A. A. 2002. 'Internationalising tourism geographies' in *Tourism Geographies*, Vol. 4(3), 225–226.

McKercher, B. & Du Cros, H. 2002. *Cultural tourism: the partnership between tourism and cultural heritage management*. New York: Haworth Press.

Richards, G. & Wilson, J (Eds.). 2005. *The global nomad: backpacker travel in theory and practice*. Clevedon: Channel View.

Ritchie, J. R. B. & Crouch, G. I. 2003. *The competitive destination: a sustainable tourism perspective*. Wallingford: CABI Publishing.

Rogerson, C. M. & Lisa, Z. 2005. 'Sho't left': changing domestic tourism in South Africa', *Urban Forum*, Vol. 16(2/3), 88–111.

Rogerson, C. M. & Visser, G. 2006. International tourist flows and urban tourism in South Africa. *Urban Forum*, Vol. 17(2), 199–213.

Rule, S, Struwig, J., Langa, Z., Viljoen, J. & Boure, O. 2001. *South African domestic tourism survey: marketing the provinces*. Tshwane: Human Sciences Research Council.

South African Tourism. 2005. *2004 Annual tourism report*. South African Tourism Strategic Research Unit, Johannesburg: SA Tourism.

United Nations World Tourism Organisation (2005). *The congress and conventions market in the Americas: basic introductory report*. International seminar held in Santiago, Chile, 25-26 May.

Durban International Convention Centre

Cities as places of geographical distinction: urban tourism in SA

Scarlett Cornelissen

Scarlett Cornelissen

Objectives

- to illustrate the significance of cities as key tourist attractions in South Africa
- to indicate how different physical and human geographical attributes in cities affect the way tourists make use of those cities
- to demonstrate some of the management implications of urban-centred tourism in South Africa.

Natural attractions (such as landscape, wild animals, or beaches) and nature-based activities (such as hiking, kite-surfing, or river rafting) are key components of South Africa's overall tourism economy. Distinctive geographical features, which include an enticing topography, interesting fauna, and in some instances (such as is the case with fynbos) unique flora account for this, causing natural attributes to be one of the most important tourism assets that the country has.

Cities and towns in South Africa are also geographical features, but they are predominantly human-made. Indeed, as tourism destinations, cities encompass the complete range of attractors that usually draw tourists: they contain socio-cultural attributes; natural features (Table Mountain in Cape Town or the beaches in Port Elizabeth, for example), and man-made

attractions (such as the Big Hole in Kimberley, or the International Convention Centre in eThekwini). Cities, in other words, are key *places* or geographical sites for tourism consumption.

In world terms, cities occupy important positions in the wider international tourism system.

There are two reasons for this. Firstly, cities are the locations for major transportation hubs and, secondly, because of their appeal – particularly of the major cities – as historical, commercial, cultural, or entertainment sites. In this regard, think of the allure of Paris, New York, Singapore, or Sydney – and the strong tourism associations that these cities have.

Cities also are an important part of South Africa's spatial tourism economy: they constitute nodes for transportation (air, rail, and road) that help direct tourist flows; they provide a ready stock of tourist accommodation, and most major tourism organisations (such as tour operators or car rental companies) have their headquarters in urban areas, due to locational efficiency and the possibility to create economies of scale.

Despite this, urban tourism is a neglected element of study in South Africa. Urban tourism involves all aspects of tourism production and consumption that are located in cities or towns. Urban tourism is distinct from types of tourism

Table 3.5 Urban distribution of foreign tourism to South Africa, 2004

	Gauteng		KwaZulu-Natal		Western Cape*	
Quarterly percentage of foreign tourists to provincial cities	Johannesburg	85,5	eThekwini	86,8	Cape Town	78,9
	Tshwane	24,8	Pietermaritzburg	21,1	Stellenbosch	27,2
					George	21,3
					Knysna	23,2

* figures add up to more than 100%, since more than one city was visited

(Source: South African Tourism: Quarterly Provincial Reports)

such as rural, eco-, or nature tourism, in that what a city offers as a tourist destination stems from all of the infrastructural elements of a given urban area, the topography and natural context within urban development that has taken place, and the socio-cultural fabric of that city. People are thus attracted to cities to engage in leisure activities (particularly sightseeing), experience various modes of culture (such as a visit to a museum, a township shebeen, or to view distinctive architecture), or to make use of infrastructure that assures convenience, novelty, or inimitability (such as visiting Las Vegas or travelling on the *Shinkansen* or 'bullet train' in Tokyo). In all, the urban complex makes for distinctive tourist forms and experiences.

Judd and Fainstein (1999) have provided a typology of different tourism cities, identifying three – 'the resort city' (which includes seaside towns and other resorts), the 'tourist-historic city' (where the production and consumption of historical or heritage goods are important elements of tourism in that city), and the 'converted' city. The concept of the 'converted' city refers to the move to tourism development in post-industrial cities where often, as part of urban regeneration strategies, urban authorities develop derelict and under-utilised urban sites, such as harbours, into tourist attractions; or where other mega-projects, such as the building of convention facilities or major sporting stadia, are intended to boost tourism.

The typology referred to above is useful for locating South African cities in the country's wider tourism economy. Port Elizabeth, Langebaan or Knysna may be identified as resort cities *or towns*. Parts of Tshwane, as the seat of the executive branch of government, may be

regarded as displaying certain historical or heritage features; while Cape Town's V & A Waterfront is a clear example of a 'brownfield development' typical of post-industrial types of tourism development, where formerly under-utilised industrial sites are adopted for tourist use. It is the country's three prime cities, however – Johannesburg, eThekwini, and Cape Town – that constitute the central destinations for urban tourism. Table 3.5 indicates visitation by foreign tourists to South Africa's three major cities.

Johannesburg, eThekwini, and Cape Town not only dominate their respective regional economies, but are also the main driving forces of the national economy. Each occupies a different niche in the industrial make-up of the country. Transportation is a key function of both Cape Town and eThekwini, which have harbours, and for Johannesburg, which is a centre for rail and air transport. Johannesburg is a commercial centre, while eThekwini and Cape Town are nodes for the production of chemicals and of textiles respectively.

There are also distinctions in the tourism markets and types of tourism that each city draws. Johannesburg may be regarded as a hub within the Southern African regional subsystem. Thus, its proximity to other African centres and its overall commercial strength causes the city to draw a large component of the country's African visitors (mainly from neighbouring countries). Shopping tourism and business tourism are two key market segments in this city. Cape Town draws a comparatively larger proportion of overseas leisure tourists than any other city in the country (60% of the 1-million visitors to the city are overseas travellers). Another niche market that has developed in Cape Town over the past few years has been the gay/lesbian, or so-called 'pink' tourism market. Further, the Mother City has become distinguished as a convention destination. Indeed, Cape Town and eThekwini (which has also become a major location for the conducting of business tourism) are two of only three African cities (the other is Cairo) which are ranked in the United Nations World Tourism Organisation's list of international convention sites. In that organisation's 2005 report, Cape Town was ranked 38th, and eThekwini 65th in world terms (UN-WTO, 2005).

There are, therefore, significant differences among the cities with respect to the main functions that they fulfil as urban tourism destinations. Geographical distinctions, such as differing topography, variable infrastructural development, and socio-cultural differences that affect the tourist image of each city account for this. These differences also yield diverse factors to be considered by tourism managers in each city. These factors include decisions on how to diversify tourism markets, given the fixed character of geographical resources; how to reduce the metropolitan dominance within regional spatial tourism economies so that smaller towns and cities can draw benefits from tourism in the major metropoles; how to reduce the negative impacts of tourism on the provision of urban services (such as potage, sewage, and waste removal), and how to balance the demands of tourists with the needs of urban residents. Cape Town is an example of the way in which intermittent unrest in the city's poorest urban areas underscores the large disparities in development between such areas and the city's central tourism locales.

Case study questions

1. What are the main geographical distinctions between urban and rural or nature-based tourism?

2. Develop a listing of the main urban tourism destinations in South Africa. Identify the predominant market segments of each destination, along with the prime natural, socio-cultural and man-made features in each.

3. How does the management of tourism in cities differ from that in rural areas?

The tourism industry

4

Managing visitor attractions

Sabine Lehmann

Table Mountain Aerial Cableway Company – offering breathtaking trips to the top of one of the world's iconic mountains

Purpose

This chapter examines the key issues in managing visitor attractions.

Learning Outcomes

After reading this chapter, you should be able to:
- define visitor attractions
- understand the role of visitor attractions in the tourism industry
- apply the concept of the product life-cycle to the management of visitor attractions
- identify the main issues in managing visitor attractions
- identify future issues that may impact on visitor attraction management.

Chapter Overview

The chapter begins by establishing how visitor attractions are defined and categorised. It then discusses the role of visitor attractions in the South African tourism industry. Next, the product life-cycle model in relation to the visitor attractions sector is discussed. The chapter then discusses the marketing, financial, human resource, visitor, and operational issues that managers of visitor attractions need to consider. Finally, the future trends affecting the visitor attractions sub-sector are examined.

The case study focuses on the management of environmental issues at a prominent South African visitor attraction: Table Mountain Aerial Cableway Company Ltd. (TMACC).

Introduction

Visitor attractions form a key component of the tourism system. They are a drawcard for luring tourists, both domestic and international, to cities and regions in South Africa.

Visitor attractions, or tourist attractions, as they are sometimes called, play a key role in a country's tourism industry. Throughout this chapter, the term 'visitor attractions' rather than 'tourist attractions' is used to reflect tourism industry practice; also because many attractions are visited by as many of the local residents of an area as they are by tourists. Attractions probably play the most important role in creating a successful destination, and are usually what stimulates the tourist to travel in the first place. As Swarbrooke points out: 'Without attractions, there would be no need for other tourism services. Indeed, tourism, as such, would not exist if it were not for attractions' (2002: 3). Such strong sentiments as to the place and importance of visitor attractions means that tourism managers need to investigate the subject to understand their importance, as well as the management issues pertaining to attractions.

Defining and categorising visitor attractions

In many cases when people think of a destination they think of an attraction. This usually forms the foundation of a **destination marketing organisation's** (DMO) branding and marketing campaign. Indeed, in cases where no clear image of an attraction comes to mind, marketers may have difficulty defining a reason for tourists to travel there.

Visitor attractions provide the primary motivation for tourists to visit a destination. South Africa is fortunate in having many iconic and easily recognised attractions that are known world-wide (for example: Robben Island Museum, Table Mountain, and Kruger National Park). South Africa's **national tourism organisation** (NTO), South African Tourism (SAT), uses these and other images to draw visitors to South Africa.

Attractions are important both at the destination as well as *en route* to the destination, as they entice visitors to the region (see the tourism system in Chapter 1). Attractions need to have a number of characteristics if they are to be successful in growing the brand and popularity of the destination, creating employment, and becoming part of the tourism hub at each destination.

Swarbrooke (2002) identified the following features common to visitor attractions:

- that they are managed specifically with the aim of attracting visitors, and may or may not charge entrance fees
- that they provide the necessary facilities to ensure that the needs and interests of visitors are catered for
- that they provide an environment in which people can spend their leisure time, and aim to provide a pleasurable experience for the visitor
- that they are specifically designed to achieve the above goals.

However, these features do not necessarily cover all visitor attractions. For example, how would the West Coast flower season in South Africa fit into the above criteria? The flower season is not one site that is specifically managed, but it is marketed as an attraction in which people can spend their leisure time. Similarly, the famous waves at Jeffrey's Bay on the Garden Route are not managed in any way – and yet draw many surfers to the region. Some wilderness areas are also managed in a manner that does not specifically provide amenities and facilities suitable for visitors. In this instance, the attraction in itself is the fact that one is in an untouched wilderness area (the Richtersveld National Park on the Orange [Gariep] River, for example).

Middleton and Clarke (2001: 246) provide a succinct definition of an **attraction**: 'a designated resource which is controlled and managed for the enjoyment, amusement, entertainment, and education of the visiting public'. It is important to note again that the emphasis is on the fact that the attraction is *controlled* or *managed*. Middleton and Clarke (2001: 246) add a slight amendment to the definition when defining **managed attractions**: 'designated permanent resources that are controlled and managed for their own sake and for the enjoyment, amusement, entertainment, and education of the visiting public'. Note the expansion of the definition to include the terms 'permanent' and 'for their own sake'. This implies that managed attractions often have a dedicated reason for their existence; either as a profit-making entity, as an educational site, or as a site to preserve and manage a resource.

Tourism researchers admit that there is a lack of clear definition of what constitutes a visitor attraction.

Considering that this chapter is about *managing visitor attractions*, we will primarily consider sites that need control and managing. These may be many and varied. One should note that many attractions begin as unmanaged sites that interest people and, on becoming popular, perhaps then enter a management phase. Certainly, what will become clear throughout this chapter is that, for visitor attractions to be managed successfully, there are many and varied issues that need to be taken into consideration.

Not only is there lack of consensus on how to define a *visitor attraction*; researchers have also had difficulty agreeing on a method of categorising visitor attractions.

Swarbrooke (2002: 5) divides attractions into four main groups:
- *natural environment* (for example, Cape Point, Drakensberg, the Karoo)
- *built environment* that was designed for purposes other than attracting visitors (e.g.

Sydney Harbour Bridge – now an attraction, but at first a functional bridge)
- *purpose-built* buildings and structures which were specifically built to attract visitors (museums, theme parks, casinos, aquaria, golf courses)
- *special events* (for example, the Hermanus Whale Festival; concerts held in a city)

Many researchers divide attractions into two categories, namely natural and human-made. These can each be further divided into permanent and events-based attractions (see Table 4.1).

This discussion leads to the identification of four main categories of attractions, as discussed below. The sub-groupings are shown in Table 4.1.

Natural attractions

Natural attractions are all those features that make up the physical environment – for example the landscape, climate, wildlife, plants, and forests. Natural attractions may be further divided into those which are managed and those which are left in their natural state (Page, 2007: 278).

Built attractions

The second type of visitor attraction is **built attractions**. Built attractions (also referred to as human-made attractions) are not necessarily constructed only for tourists and visitors. For example, the Victoria & Alfred Waterfront in Cape Town attracts tourists, but also serves the needs of local shoppers and fishermen. Other build-

Table 4.1 Categories of tourist attractions

Visitor attraction			
Natural		Human-made	
Permanent	**Events**	**Permanent**	**Events**
• National parks and conservation areas • Beaches • Fauna and flora, e.g. floral kingdom in Cape Town	• Big Wave Competition in Cape Town • Flower Season on West Coast • Sardine Run	• Theme Parks • Casinos • Aquaria • Museums • Cultural traditions and patterns • Arts and crafts • Urban areas of interest, e.g. Soweto	• Concerts • Races e.g. Two Oceans Marathon • Reed Dance in Swaziland

ings, such as the Union Buildings in Tshwane, are not open to the public and tourists, but are included on tours so that tourists can see them and take photographs. There are also buildings that are built mainly for tourists – holiday resorts and theme parks, for example. A built or human-made attraction, therefore, can be defined as any building that attracts tourists or visitors.

Cultural attractions

Cultural attractions have become one of the most popular types of visitor attractions in recent years. Cultural attractions are places or things which are reflective of a particular community. Monuments, memorials, statues, traditional restaurants, shows, art, cultural villages, architecture, clothing, food, religion, rituals, and ceremonies are all examples of cultural attractions. On a township tour for example, visitors may taste *chibuku* at a spaza shop, learn about gumboot dancing, and have their future told at an African traditional healer-training school.

Social attractions

Social attractions are those where the visitor has an opportunity to see or be part of the way of

Table 4.2 Categories of visitor attractions

Attraction category	Attraction types	Constituent attractions
Natural	Scenic beauty	beaches, mountains, climate, rivers, waterfalls, fountains, lakes, forests, coastal areas, caves, flora, fauna
	Animal attractions	Game reserves, zoos, rare-breed farms, aquaria, wildlife
	Parks, gardens, and reserves Country parks Health	Botanical gardens, public parks, national parks, gardens, nature reserves, marine reserves country parks, reservoirs, marinas spas, hot mineral springs
Built	Leisure and theme parks	outdoor parks, beach resorts, ski resorts, casinos, shopping centres, dams
	Workplaces	mines, factories, docklands, farms, wineries
	Convention centres Transport	steam railways, cruise liners, luxury train safaris
Cultural	Historical sites	castles, historical houses, monuments, battlefields, memorials, statues
	Archaeological sites	cave rock art, ruins
	Religious sites	churches, temples, mosques and monasteries, ceremonies, rituals
	Museums and galleries	art galleries, museums
	Tourist routes	township tours, wine routes, whale routes, heritage routes, battlefield routes, slave routes, flower routes
	Rural life	cultural villages, food
	City/town life	architecture, cafés, restaurants, theatres, shows
	Arts and crafts	curios, handicrafts such as paintings, sculptures, and wood-carvings
	Events	markets, sports events, cultural festivals, hallmark events

life of the local population of specific communities. Tourists wish to socialise with local people, eat with them, drink in local bars and pubs, and experience life as they do. In some cases, visitors can live with a family and join them in their daily tasks and errands (for example, on farm stays).

Unusual tourist attractions are attractions, people, places, and accommodation establishments that are strange or off-beat. For example, farms that used to just breed ostriches have opened their doors to tourists who can now visit the farms and even ride the ostriches. Other examples include the following (as described in George, Slabbert & Wildman, 2006):

- a visit to the Big Pineapple in Bathurst, Eastern Cape
- go on a tractor-trailer ride at Protea Farm in the Breede River Valley
- a visit to the Owl House in Nieu-Bethesda, near Graaff-Reinet, Eastern Cape
- a Mystery Ghost Bus tour in Johannesburg
- an overnight stay in the old jail at Philippolis in the Free State.

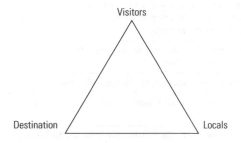

The role of visitor attractions in the tourism industry

Visitor attractions are a vital element of the visitor experience (Dewhurst & Dewhurst, 2006: 287; Page, 2007: 273). 'Visitor attractions and events play a key role in tourism destinations; as they entice visitors to the destination' (George, 2004: 335). What need, after all, would there be for accommodation establishments, transport providers and other amenities if there were no visitor attractions to draw people to the region in the first place? For most tourists, the attractions are the main reason for visiting a destination. This was certainly the case in the past when visitors

would simply 'tour or visit' specific sites that were of interest to them. Visitor attractions are important as destinations in and of themselves, and as attractions *en route* to a final destination (Page, 2007: 273).

There has been, in recent years, an increase in the amount of leisure time and disposable income available. Easier travel by air and road has created a larger base of potential visitors to local and international attractions. This has given rise to the 'day visitor'; often local people visiting attractions in their area. Many attractions could not remain in operation without the support of local visitors (see Example box).

> **Example** Gold Reef City
>
> 'We ignore the local market at our own peril. The diversity of our offer to visitors, who are looking for a secure environment where families are able to enjoy attractions – many of which are comparable to international theme parks at a fraction of the cost, and within an hour's reach of the majority of visitors – needs to be recognised, understood and constantly examined.'
>
> Steve Cook, MD, Gold Reef City Theme Park, Johannesburg

The role of visitor attractions may vary according to the **stakeholder's** mandate. This is the objective that the attraction's guiding body has highlighted. A private business may see its visitor attraction as a profit-making business, and have goals that are purely profit-driven. Theme parks often fall into this category, as do private attractions that provide an income to the business owner or shareholders.

Other visitor attractions may have a chief mandate to educate the public (for example, Walter Sisulu Gardens in Gauteng (part of the SA National Biodiversity Institute – SANBI), and the National Zoological Gardens (Tshwane Zoo) in Tshwane. Some visitor attractions may exist primarily as preservation sites, designed to preserve a rare item or to expand a conservation area (for example, national parks in South Africa). In such cases visitors may, in fact, be discouraged.

SOUTH AFRICAN
national
biodiversity
institute
S A N B I

One such example is the Maropeng Site in Magaliesberg. Visitors have been actively diverted from the Sterkfontein Caves, site of the famous archeological find 'Little Foot', and encouraged rather to visit Maropeng, which is 10 kilometres away. Both sites are within the World Heritage Site (WHS) the 'Cradle of Mankind', but each site has a very different role to play. The Sterkfontein Caves are still being excavated, and that site's role is to add knowledge and provide context for the area. Maropeng, on the other hand, is run as a business, and needs to create revenue to pay back the building costs. It is also seen as a major boost to economic activity and employment in Gauteng (see Example box below).

Visitor attractions thus play a strong role in a number of tourism sectors. We will now discuss the visitor attractions' role in destination growth, economic impact, and regional or urban regeneration.

Example Sterkfontein Caves

The world famous Sterkfontein Caves were declared a World Heritage Site in 1999 by the United Nations Educational, Scientific and Cultural Organisation (UNESCO). The declaration seeks to encourage the identification, protection, and preservation of cultural and natural heritage around the world considered to be of outstanding value to humanity. To maintain the status of a WHS, we have to adhere to a number of regulations, one of which is to make sure that no undue pressure is placed on the site due to too many people visiting the caves. As a result Maropeng, a visitor interpretation centre, was created to alleviate this pressure. A mere 10 kilometres away from the caves, the Maropeng visitor centre presents the scientific evidence found in Sterkfontein and other fossil sites in a manner that is highly interactive and fun for the whole family. 'This does not impact on the environment of the caves and visitors can see, touch, feel, and hear in an environment where they do not feel as though they are intruding', states Anton Post, General Manager of Maropeng a Afrika.

Destination growth

It has been argued that some attractions are the starting point from which a destination is established and grows (Swarbrooke, 2002). This is often true of natural phenomena (for example, Victoria Falls) or tourist icons, for example, the Pyramids of Giza, the Great Wall of China, Taj Mahal in India, and Kruger National Park (see Example box below). The increased number of visitors to an attraction may result in the need for support amenities and sub-sectors such as accommodation, transport, and restaurants. Over time, other attractions are added to diversify the mix. This is known as the **destination mix**. The aim, initially, may be to encourage people to stay an extra day, or to occupy people on a rainy day (for example, a museum near an outdoor attraction); but the result is that, as more visitors arrive, more support structures are required – and thus the destination grows.

Using an attraction to create a **node** on which a destination can start adding can be specifically designed – for example, the Guggenheim Museum in Bilbao, Spain. This small Spanish town created a visitor attraction powerful enough to draw visitors, and thus establish Bilbao as a destination requiring accommodation, transport, and restaurants. Table 4.3 lists a few examples of attractions as icons. Indeed, many icons form part of a destination marketing organisation's (DMO) marketing strategy (see Chapter 8).

Example Kruger National Park

Kruger National Park (KNP) is rated as one of South Africa's iconic tourist destinations, and is the most visited national park in the country. More than one million tourists visit KNP per year. The income earned by KNP represents 0,34% of the value of Mpumalanga's economy. Its contribution to the provincial economy is thus relatively small. But KNP is a major visitor drawcard, attracting people to the province. Thus, KNP draws visitors through the province, encouraging stopovers and extra spend there.

Table 4.3 Visitor attraction icons and their locations

Country	Attraction icons
South Africa	Table Mountain, Kruger National Park, Garden Route, Soweto
Zimbabwe and Zambia	Victoria Falls, Lake Kariba, Great Ruins, Victoria Falls
Namibia	Namib Desert, Etosha National Park
UK	Big Ben, Buckingham Palace, London Eye
France	Eiffel Tower, Champs Elysées, The Louvre
Italy	The Colosseum
Spain	Guggenheim Museum
Australia	Sydney Harbour Bridge, Sydney Opera House, Mt Uluru
USA	Statue of Liberty, Golden Gate Bridge, Empire State Building

TO DO

List five natural attractions that may have been the catalyst for destination growth. For example, Victoria Falls – Victoria Falls village; hotels, shops, bungee jumping, and river rafting.

Economic impact of visitor attractions

There is no doubt that visitor attractions create an economic impact on the destination area. The economic impact may be in the form of providing jobs (both direct and indirect jobs), taxes for local and regional governments, and income to local businesses as service providers (see Example box below and Chapter 15 – Managing the impacts of tourism). Visitor attractions are also a major source of foreign currency for the host country. Visitor attractions can thus be manipulated to achieve some or all of these aims. Dubai in the UAE (United Arab Emirates), for example, is building the world's largest theme park, Dubailand. This attraction is likely to lure tourists from all over the world, and thus create income for the UAE that is not based on its primary natural resource, oil.

Some attractions aim to do business in the quieter visitor season, so as to smooth the income and visitor arrival curve for the region. The Western Cape, for example, actively identifies and promotes attractions that happen outside its traditional visitor season. The Cape Town International Jazz Festival in March/April of every year is one such attraction. Furthermore, tourism during the Western Cape's winter – the 'green season' – is also actively promoted, with special rates being offered to visitors.

Attractions may also be established to act as a drawcard to encourage visitors to explore an area they perhaps would not otherwise reach. The Midlands Meander in KwaZulu-Natal, for example, encourages visitors to travel away from the metropolis and into relatively remote areas, where they can create an economic impact and support local farms and their produce. Local authorities have also set up traditional markets and trading stalls *en route* to attractions. For instance, outside Hluhluwe on the N2, there is a curio market that encourages visitors to stop and shop on the way to Hluhluwe, Sodwana, or St Lucia.

The government may gain from visitor attractions both in terms of taxes paid and in terms of a revenue stream, as, in many cases, the visitor attraction may be owned by the government. Revenue raised by Robben Island Museum in Cape Town, for example, is used to cover the costs of maintaining it as a World Heritage Site (WHS).

Example Johannesburg Zoo

Johannesburg Zoo was established in 1904, and is operated by the City of Johannesburg. In 2006 it was registered as a Section 21 (non-profit) company. The Johannesburg Zoo is an important recreational facility and visitor attraction. It receives about 150 000 visitors annually, most of whom are domestic tourists local to the area. The Zoo also acts as an important research, conservation, and educational facility.

Johannesburg Zoo employs 160 permanent staff and 200 outsourced staff. The Zoo also supports indirect employment, in that many suppliers support the zoo and thus create their own jobs.

Regional and urban regeneration

Governments, at both provincial and local levels, have recognised the potential of tourism as an economic development tool. Visitor attractions may be used as an urban (city-wide) or provincial tool to encourage regeneration (Swarbrooke, 2002). The aim is that major new visitor attractions can provide the hub for local spending patterns, and thus drive the regeneration process (Page, 2007: 273).

Examples in South Africa include the Victoria and Alfred Waterfront development in Cape Town; the proposed Urban Design Framework around the FNB Stadium in Johannesburg, and the planned Point Road development in eThekwini. Authorities may use government land and finance to develop areas as mixed-use attractions with varying degrees of success. This aspect of attraction development is often difficult, as various stakeholders may have different ideas of what is required in the area.

Visitor attractions and the product life-cycle

The **product life-cycle** (PLC) concept has long been accepted in marketing as a model of how product-offerings evolve through different stages during their lifetime. The model implies that offerings have a limited life; that profits increase and decrease as the product moves through different stages, and that each stage in the life-cycle offers different challenges and rewards for management to deal with. Ultimately, it implies that different management strategies are required at different stages of the product life-cycle (see Chapter 14 – Marketing tourism businesses).

The PLC has also been applied to tourist offerings (George, 2004: 195–197) and visitor attractions (Page, 2007: 288–290). The PLC is a planning tool that can help attraction managers understand the change in management strategies required as the attraction moves through its life-cycle.

The product life-cycle curve is 'S'-shaped. In the initial stages arrivals are high, as visitors and media become aware of a new product and flock to see it. Over time, visitor numbers level off or slow down, as competitors enter the marketplace

Figure 4.1 The product life-cycle

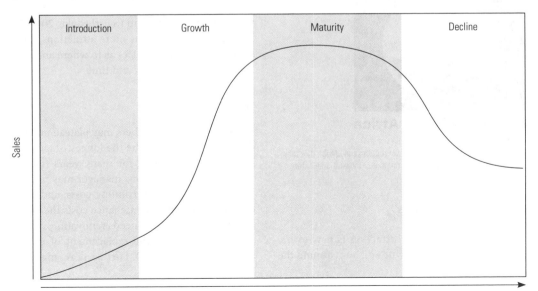

or the attraction fails to offer something new, and thus fails to draw repeat business.

However, Swarbrooke (2002: 55) argues that the PLC is of less relevance to visitor attractions, as it is problematic to identify when the introductory phase starts, with a natural attraction such as beaches. Was it when the first locals used the beach, or when the first visitors arrived because they had heard about a special beach? The aim of these attractions may not be to maximise profits. However, inevitably, as even natural attractions become part of a destination mix, these too may become formalised and start to become part of the product life-cycle. Thus, for example, many South African beaches now aim for 'Blue Flag Status', an international standard denoting a certain level of cleanliness, amenities, and safety (See Figure 4.2). With this, inevitably, comes some sort of record of visitor numbers and their increase, which is kept to justify the expense of new amenities, life guards, and marketing.

For most attraction managers, it is still useful to understand the PLC, as each stage offers different management challenges. The four stages that a visitor attraction passes through are described below. Each stage will have its own management implications, and require different strategies.

Blue Flag South Africa

Figure 4.2 The Blue Flag – gives visitors the knowledge that their beaches are clean and adhere to a number of international safety, environmental and facility standards

Introduction stage

At this stage, the visitor attraction is new to the market. There is often a hype and buzz around the new offering, as media and marketing initiatives create awareness. The introduction stage often enjoys a large buy-in from locals, who flock to see what the new attraction in their area has to offer. One caution at this stage is that some attractions may open before they are completed, as managers wish to gain entrance fees as soon as possible. This may result in negative feedback, as visitors do not get the full experience offered.

This early stage of the new attraction is important, as it often creates **word-of-mouth** (WOM) advertising among locals – the effects of which linger on long after the introduction stage is over. Few attractions fail at the introductory stage (Swarbrooke, 2002: 51), as in-depth feasibility studies have usually ensured that there is enough demand, at least at the introduction stage.

Growth stage

This is the stage that sees a steady increase in growth, and usually also profit (George, 2004: 196). The PLC indicates that it is at this stage that competitors may enter the market. This may be slightly different for the international iconic attractions, as it is difficult to identify the competition. For example, is the main competitor to the Eiffel Tower the Sydney Harbour Bridge, or Table Mountain? However, competition exists in the marketplace in terms of the visitor's time and their discretionary spend (Swarbrooke, 2002: 52). As the destination gains more attractions, so the visitor has to make choices as to where and when they spend their money and time.

Maturity stage

Profits and visitor numbers may plateau and slow down. This is likely to be the longest stage in the life-cycle, often lasting for many years (George, 200: 196). The attractions manager may find that there is an increase in running costs, and thus a decrease in profits. Maintenance costs increase as the attraction ages and needs renovating, or there may be a need for the replacement of exhibits and rides (for example). Furthermore, marketing costs increase as the attraction competes with others for attention and it becomes harder to get media coverage with no new product developments attracting media attention.

The quality of the attraction's offering becomes an issue (Page, 2007: 289). As fashions change, so attractions need to keep up with new trends and ensure that quality standards are always high. Amenities such as restaurants and shops may need to be upgraded, and the attraction needs to ensure that the experience offered remains relevant, up-to-date, and in line with consumer trends. Pricing also becomes an issue, as locals may already have visited the attraction and may need discounting to encourage return (see Example box below). Research into consumer perceptions and re-invention of the visitor attraction may be necessary in order to prevent the attraction from moving into the next stage – the decline (George, 2004: 196).

Visitor attractions may remain at the maturity stage for a very long time. The Eiffel Tower in Paris, for example, was built in 1889 and still attracts hundreds of thousands of visitors annually. It was initially seen as a white elephant and, in fact, was almost torn down in 1909 at the end of its 20-year lease; but it is now a French icon, and continues to enthral thousands of visitors to Paris every day. Some attractions re-invent themselves with re-launches and innovations. Table Mountain Aerial Cableway Company (see Case Study) for example, re-launched itself during the maturity stage by building a new and improved cableway with rotating floors. The media coverage coupled with the improved technology resulted in a vast increase in visitor numbers after the 1997 upgrade.

Example Two Oceans Aquarium, Cape Town

The Two Oceans Aquarium opened in November 1995, and within the first 18 months received over 1,5-million visitors. The novelty of being Africa's largest Aquarium, and the only Aquarium to open in the Western Cape, drew a large number of local and domestic visitors. Increasing competition both locally and nationally, however, has meant that the Aquarium has had to re-invent itself to keep abreast of the increasing demands of its visitors. This was achieved through the introduction of two new major temporary exhibit galleries: 'Fangs' in 1999, and the 'Living Dead' in 2001. Innovative pricing strategies targeted at bringing in more local visitors were introduced. These include the aquarium's annual membership programme and, more recently, the 'Kids for Free' winter campaign; both of which have assisted in maintaining visitation over the traditionally quieter months.

Decline stage

Although decline is not inevitable without intervention, many attractions may reach the stage of low sales and, consequently, low profits (Swarbrooke, 2002: 51). Visitor attractions can linger in this decline stage for a long time, until they are either closed, or upgraded and re-launched. A museum, for example, may have a steady decline in visitor numbers until, finally, the doors are simply closed as having staff on duty at the admissions kiosk is no longer justified. Some visitor attractions may not be expected to show a profit due to their historical or social value, and may remain in the decline stage for a long time.

Management of visitor attractions

Traditional marketing practice states that the product-offering must match the benefits sought by the consumer (Kotler, 2000: 17). This is also true of visitor attractions. One problem that attraction managers encounter is that the attraction may mean many things to different people, and thus that visitors do not all have the same expectation as to what they should experience on site (Ryan, 2005: 203) (see Example box 'Kgalagadi Transfrontier National Park' overleaf).

Example Kgalagadi Transfrontier National Park

This vast wilderness area needs to accommodate visitors with very different needs. There are 4x4 enthusiasts who wish to explore the area and test their 4x4 skills. There are international and local visitors who would like a comfortable experience with air conditioners, good food, and wine available even in the remotest camps. There are visitors who wish to have a simple, unspoilt experience camping in the rest-camps, while some visitors prefer to camp and provide everything themselves – and be alone in the vast wilderness.

Example De-marketing

In some cases, marketers may actively *dis*courage potential visitors from visiting their attraction. Marketing may opt to not create any awareness of the site; to forego publishing maps and brochures, and to actively steer visitors away from the site. Visitors may be encouraged not to visit the site at all, or not at certain times of the year. This is usually applied to very sensitive sites, where footfall above a certain level would be detrimental to the attraction. De-marketing has its own complications in that visitors may be disappointed with either not seeing the site, or seeing a substitute site, and this can have an unintended consequence with regard to raising awareness of the site (Boyd & Timothy, 2006: 59). Maropeng and the Sterkfontein Caves site are good examples of where this tool can be effectively used.

As with other business entities, the attractions manager will need to be successful at managing various business functions if the site is to be a well-known and popular visitor attraction. Commentators have listed a number of areas that managers should focus on, from ethical challenges (Swarbrooke, 2002: 299) to strategic partnerships (Dewhurst & Dewhurst, 2006: 297).

Management functions can be divided into five main areas: marketing, revenue and financial management, human resource, visitor management, and operations management. These will be explored further below.

Marketing

Successful marketing strategies are key to the success of all types of visitor attractions. Whether the aim is to raise awareness (for example, zoos, museums, game parks, or beaches) or to raise income, the intent is usually to ensure that the visitor always has a positive, memorable engagement with the attraction offering.

There are, however, some cases where a marketing success story may in fact impact negatively on the site (Boyd & Timothy, 2006: 56), as is the case when sensitive sites become overly popular (see Example box below). In this case, increased foot traffic may impact negatively on the site.

For larger visitor attractions, a dedicated **marketing** manager may be employed to oversee marketing activities. Smaller, often owner-run, attractions may fulfil this function themselves. The attractions manager may also consider outsourcing some of the marketing functions to a professional consultant, allowing the manager time to focus solely on managing the attraction itself.

Some of the challenges that an attraction manager faces when understanding the marketing aspect of a site are as follows:
- The definition of the attraction. Is the site a historical site, nature site, or cultural site? Robben Island Museum, for example, can be defined in a number of categories.
- The variety of visitors that the attraction may appeal to: each has different needs, and may need to be accessed through different marketing strategies (Boyd & Timothy, 2006: 57). As shown in the Kgalagadi Transfrontier National Park Example box above, one site may have many types of visitor, with differing recreational and educational needs.

- The intangible nature of the attraction.
- The benefits of visiting an attraction are often difficult to communicate. In most cases the customer cannot experience the attraction unless they are physically there on site (Swarbrooke, 2002: 199). Consider an outdoor concert: the marketer may list the names of bands playing, but the atmosphere and the whole 'vibe' of an outdoor concert can only be experienced by those who are there.
- Other stakeholders also market your site, and the attractions manager has little control over this (Swarbrooke, 2002: 201). SA Tourism uses local icons to market South Africa; tour operators include the attraction in their brochures, and word-of-mouth visitors encourage friends and family to visit. The attractions manager may have little control over how their attraction is positioned in such circumstances.

Middleton and Clark (2001: 252) have highlighted three major operating constraints at attractions that may affect the marketing of the site. These are:

- The relationship that exists between fixed costs and variable costs. **Fixed costs** are the costs of running the attraction that remain unchanged, regardless of whether one has few or many visitors. These are costs such as maintenance of buildings, staff costs, building costs, etc. Fixed costs at attractions are usually very high. To run a theme park or museum for 100 visitors or 2 000 visitors per day costs almost the same amount. In particular, this affects attractions that are weather-dependent. It costs the same, regardless of weather it rains or shines, for Ratanga Junction Theme Park (Cape Town) or Gold Reef City Theme Park (Johannesburg) to be open and ready for business on a weekend, yet their visitor attendance figures will look very different.
- Seasonality has a great influence on attractions. Most attractions have about 20 'peak' days per year. Most visitor attractions need to encourage visits for the remainder of

the year, and in particular during the quietest periods.

- Repeat visits are usually the minority of visits. Most attractions expect only one visit per visitor per year. Some have built-in programmes designed to encourage repeat visits (for example, Botanical Society membership that allows free entrance to all national botanical gardens for a year, and Johannesburg Zoo membership, also valid for one year). This indicates how important it is for attractions to continually focus on first-time visitors, as these form the major portion of their visitors.

These challenges imply that sophisticated marketing techniques need to be employed to influence the volume of visitors, to affect the seasonality of visitor patterns, create brand awareness, reach budgeted revenue, and stand out from the clutter of all the other options to buy and experience that the consumer/visitor encounters on a daily basis.

Promotional tools

There are many types of marketing tools and promotional materials that can be used (see Table 4.4). These range from traditional brochures that inform the potential visitor about the site to subtle press releases telling readers about the attraction, and ensuring that it remains in the forefront of their minds (ToM).

Example Cape Town's 'Big 6'

A good example of strategic partnership is Cape Town's 'Big Six' initiative. The marketing managers of Cape Town's top six attractions meet once a month to discuss joint initiatives with the aim of encouraging international and domestic visitors to visit all six attractions. Cape Town's 'Big Six' are: Table Mountain Aerial Cableway; Robben Island Museum, Victoria and Alfred Waterfront, the Constantia Wine Route, Cape Point, and Kirstenbosch Botanical Gardens.

Table 4.4 Promotional tools available to the visitor attractions manager

The visitor attractions manager would need to assess each tool in terms of their costs and their advertising reach, as well as their suitability for the market that he or she is trying to reach.	
Advertising	Various traditional advertising media may be used, from print media (magazines, newspapers) and radio adverts to posters, annual guide books, and TV adverts.
Marketing collateral	Brochures, newsletters, flyers, leaflets, maps, booklets, and information guides.
Public relations (PR) and press	Free editorial coverage in the media may be gained by providing relevant and interesting stories of suitable interest to the target audience. An engineering magazine, for example, may feature a story on the engineering issues of pumping fresh and sea water into large tanks in the uShaka Marine World, eThekwini. An environmental magazine may be interested in a story on how uShaka Marine World manages to keep its water usage to a minimum, and on what recycling plans are in place.
Sponsorship	Attractions may sponsor issues that are of interest to their own target market. The Two Oceans Aquarium in Cape Town, for example, sponsors a beach clean-up once a year. This raises awareness in the community, and is reported in the press.
Internet Marketing	Use of the Internet to generate interest in the attraction. This may be through competitions on the net, advising customers of specials, or video footage provided by webcams focused on water-holes.
Sales Promotions	Discounted offers, usually during the attraction's quieter times. See Chapter 14 – Marketing tourism businesses – for a further discussion on pricing issues.
Exhibitions and Trade Shows	Many attractions take stands at local and international exhibitions and trade shows, where they can reach many potential customers at the same time.
Signage	Signposting to the attraction is important so that visitors may find their way, but also so that an aspect of 'impulse buying' can be accommodated (Ryan, 2005: 210).
Educationals	Given that that best way to sell an attraction is to actually experience it, the industry invests much time and budget in educationals. Influential customers are encouraged to visit the site to experience it for themselves. These could be tour operators, press, tour guides, or teachers .
Strategic Partnerships	Marketing and promotional partnerships may be built so that information, resources, and promotional material can be shared. (see Example box for 'Big 6 of Cape Town')

Revenue and financial management

Clearly, for most visitor attractions, managing income and expenses is an integral part of managing the attraction. Even if the site is a not-for-profit organisation, the usual aim is at least to cover costs.

The main source of income is usually the entrance fee itself (Cochrane & Tapper, 2006: 104). For this reason the **lead adult price** (the main adult entrance fee, the full price an adult would pay with no discounts) at an attraction is the main income-driver.

Once discounting, free tickets, and reduced ticket prices for groups of children, etc., have been taken into account, the income per visitor usually rests at about 20% of the lead adult price.

Attractions seek to reduce their sole reliance on entrance fees by offering vistors opportunities to spend more on site. This may be at restaurants, cafes and vending machines, shops, and kiosks. South African National Parks (SANParks), for example, offers day walks and night drives, restaurants and curio shops to encourage extra spend from their visitors. Souvenirs may also be sold via the Internet, in an effort to create additional revenue.

A common issue, certainly in countries with much social and economic inequality, is the issue of a two-tier pricing system or 'differential fees' (Cochrane & Tapper, 2006: 104). At some attractions, local visitors pay a reduced rate, while international visitors pay a higher fee, often in dollars.

Differential fees may increase revenue, but the practice can create a negative image for the international visitor, who may question why they have to pay more for the same service. At the same time, many attractions, particularly those with a conservation or educational component to them, wish to ensure that domestic tourists make up a good percentage of the visitors, as this is an excellent way of ensuring their sensitivity to, and the longevity of, the site.

The Department of Environmental Affairs & Tourism (DEAT) as a rule has not encouraged the use of up-front differential pricing. However, many attractions have worked it in through their marketing plans. The WILD Card issued by SANParks is, in effect, such a system (see Example box). The domestic market pays less for such a card, and gets a reduced entrance fee, whilst international visitors pay more. Some attractions offer specials that are aimed at locals only – often primarily at a time of day or year when the domestic market travels.

Example SANPark's WILD Card

In 2003, South African National Parks (SANParks) revised its conservation fees, which had not risen for some years. As a parastatal, SANParks has the responsibility to ensure that South Africans – especially economically disadvantaged citizens – are not excluded from the country's national parks by rising conservation fees. The solution was the introduction of the WILD Card, essentially a season ticket allowing 365 days of access at a hugely discounted price.

The WILD Card has been enormously successful, with over of 400 000 sold, and Cape Nature, Msinsi Holdings, Big Game Parks of Swaziland, and KZN Wildlife have since joined the programme.

Source: Stephen Hulbert, WILD Card Coordinator, SANParks. www.sanparks.org.za

SANParks' logo

Some of the important financial management issues that an attraction manager needs to manage are as follows: (Swarbrooke, 2002: 269)

- *Budgeting*: this usually covers a financial year, and consists of budgeting for the number of annual visitors, translating this into an income stream, and forecasting any expenses that may be incurred. Managers from all departments will then be expected to manage their income and expenses within the planned and set budget. Budgets may be set per department as well as per revenue stream, so that how well each aspect of an attraction is doing can be monitored easily. Thus the budget for a shop or restaurant on site may be separate from that of the admissions desk.

- *Information management*: the finance department aims to provide information that is useful to managers, so that they can evaluate how they are doing and make decisions on managing the site. Thus, information such as breakdown of visitor numbers and ticket type, visitor spend, and staff costs are monitored on a daily and monthly basis.
- *Monitoring of the environment*: it is important that the financial manager is aware of any external issues that may affect revenue and expenditure at the site. He or she would have to ensure that the impact of such information is passed on to relevant managers at the attraction. Thus the impact of any changes in taxation, financial regulations, accounting practices, interest rates, inflation, and competitor spending would need to be assessed and analysed.
- *Control*: this is an important function and necessary to control costs (i.e. is the attraction getting the best price for services?) and control income (i.e. ensure that there is no theft or shrinkage).

The focus is constantly on finding innovative ways to generate income and contain costs. This can be achieved only by attending closely to financial matters on a daily basis. Each decision made within an attraction will create financial benefit or expense, and these constantly need to be weighed up so that the correct balance is achieved.

Human Resource Management (HRM)

Swarbrooke (2002: 244) believes that the **human resource management** (HRM) function of attractions management may be the most important aspect to get right. Visitor attractions are usually quite labour-intensive; therefore labour costs are likely to be high, and make up a significant portion of the costs budget. Moreover, attractions arguably fall in the services sector, and thus the service offered by staff is an important aspect of the attraction offering.

The seasonal nature of many visitor attractions means that a significant portion of staff are often employed on temporary or short-term contracts. In addition, the types of jobs offered at attractions are often monotonous, have long and unsociable hours, and offer low pay. For this reason, staff turnover can be high (Swarbrooke, 2002: 246). Effective HRM strategies are thus an important aspect of attractions management to support seasonal and full-time staff, as well as managers (Dewhurst & Dewhurst, 2006: 299).

Human resource tools that may be used to manage attraction staff professionally include:

- *Human Resource Planning*: whereby seasonal plans are made in advance to enable managers to recruit the right people for the right job, and have time to train them
- *Recruitment and Selection*: clear job descriptions describing the skills and competencies required to complete the job effectively are a precursor to a good recruitment and selection strategy
- *Induction*: whereby staff are introduced to the company and their new job, and standards and expectations are set
- *Training*: Training needs to take place to ensure that staff obtain the skills needed to perform their job to the expected standard.

The same high standards of recruitment induction, training, and performance management should be applied to both seasonal and full-time staff. In too many cases seasonal staff are treated differently, it should be remembered that the visitor is likely to be unaware who is permanent and who is seasonal, and therefore the same standards should be applied to both. Refer to Chapter 11 – 'Managing human resources in tourism' for a more detailed discussion on HRM in tourism.

Visitor management

Attraction managers have to balance two fundamentally opposing demands. They need to preserve and manage their site, and at the same time encourage as many visitors as they can to visit the attraction (Gale, 2006: 298; Shackley, 2006: 84). Ultimately, the attractions manager has to intimately understand the visitor's experience of his or her site in order to manage the site effectively (Page, 2007: 296) (See Example box below).

Visitors themselves are often an integral part of the experience (this is referred to as '**inseparability**' – see Chapter 14). If there are too few visitors, the attraction may feel empty and quiet; too many and the visitor may have to spend too much time in queues affecting the overall visitor experience.

Managing the visitor effectively and sensitively, therefore, is an essential component of attraction management. The start of effective visitor management is access control: knowing when, how, and where visitors access your site. Control at this point will enable the manager to control the visitor flow as well as ensure that ticket revenue is managed.

There are a number of tools that can be used to control visitors:

- Opening hours (e.g. gates at Kruger National Park are closed between sunset and sunrise)
- Pricing: reduced rates at certain times of the day or year may encourage visitors to visit out of peak season.
- Pathways and channeling the flow of visitors (e.g. one-way flows in and out) (Pender & Sharpley, 2005: 207)
- Signage: to direct visitors to specific sites of interest
- Brochures and information leaflets can act as direction pointers, and can be used to educate and inform visitors as to expected behavior on site
- Capacity management: only allowing a certain number of visitors on pre-booked tours or shows
- Restrictions on visitor numbers: some sites have a set maximum that they allow per day, and most events have a maximum number that is allowed (this may be as much for visitor safety as for managing the visitor experience)
- Providing an alternative product (Boyd & Timothy, 2006: 59): Maropeng was

specifically designed to draw visitors away from the sensitive Sterkfontein site.

Maropeng's logo

The manner in which the actual experience is delivered to the visitor also needs to be carefully managed and assessed. Are the different learning styles adapted to all visitors? Reading material, for example, could be presented for adults as well as younger visitors to read.

The balance between maintaining the quality of the experience offered and the sustainability of the site is an aspect of visitor management that needs to be assessed (Shackley, 2006: 84). Visitors wish to see attractions in their relevant context, and attractions managers need to continuously assess how their attraction meets the experience needs of its visitors. Thus, if the visitor groups are primarily families, the attraction needs to ensure that the entire experience is family-orientated. Are there enough prams and child seats for the restaurants? Are there taps and toilet facilities suitable for young children? Is there enough for the adults to do while they watch their children enjoying the site? Is there enough for parents to do while their children are participating in child-related activities?

> **Example** Visitor Management at World Heritage Sites
>
> World Heritage Sites, in particular, need to balance site conservation with visitor revenue generation. Shackley (2006: 84) highlights three main issues in visitor management at World Heritage Sites. These are: maintaining the spirit of the place (allowing the visitor to see the site in its proper context), crime and security (often an issue in isolated sites), and cultural sensitivity (respecting the local use and interpretation of the site, which may be in opposition to visitor needs).

Operations management

Operations management is the day-to-day running of the site. The attractions manager needs to use all the tools at hand to ensure that their clients have the best possible experience. This means using staff, on-site resources such as amenities, and any technology at hand to provide a memorable experience.

A good operations manager needs to understand that not everything on site is under their control. He/she needs to understand and control what *is* under their control, and identify and minimise that which is not. Weather – something that affects many attractions – is clearly not under the manager's control. Nevertheless, provisions need to be made so that customers are protected from the sun and rain. This may mean that extra shelter is added on such days, and extra water stations may be set up on very hot days. This may imply that extra staff are on standby for such days, which in turn means that plans for such eventualities must be in place.

Attractions managers have two tools available when managing their site: managing the resource at hand, and managing the number of visitors (Middleton & Clark, 2001: 245). This impacts on the quality of experience offered. Too many visitors using the attraction at the same time will impact on the how well the amenities such as restaurants, toilets, pathways, tourist guides and so on cope. In some cases, too few visitors at an attraction can also impact on the quality: a concert that is poorly attended lacks atmosphere.

This highlights the fact that an operations manager needs to work closely with the rest of the management team. He/she needs to let HR know when more staff are needed or what training is required; and at the same time work with marketing managers to ensure that promotions do not occur during peak or busy periods when the site cannot cope with more visitors.

One problem that most operations managers need to deal with is that of seasonal fluctuations in visitors. Peak season can be problematic, in that demand for the product cannot be met, and visitors may be turned away or the site will not cope adequately. During quieter months of the year, the manager may find that he/she has staff on hand, but that there is nothing for them to do. Managers therefore need to plan for seasonal fluctuations, and use them to their best advantage. Staff may be given annual leave or attend training during quieter months. Maintenance may be planned for the low season. In some cases an attraction may be closed altogether, and only reopened when sufficient visitors are on site again.

Swarbrooke (2002: 291) highlights some of the skills that an effective operations manager needs to possess:

- thorough knowledge of all aspects of the site, staff and machinery
- attention to detail, as well as an understanding of the overall picture
- planning skills – to be able to plan in advance and have contingency plans for emergencies
- communication skills to communicate to staff, management, and visitors
- crisis management skills and the ability to work under pressure, as they are often working in the public eye
- quality control and quality improvement.

Future issues for attractions managers

The successful attraction and attractions manager always has one eye on the future. As fashion changes, competitors enter the market, and visitors become more demanding, so the attraction will have to adapt to ensure that entrance figures do not drop.

Dewhurst and Dewhurst (2006: 293–294) identified the major factors that may affect attractions in the future. These are: changing visitor demand patterns, increase in competition, and stakeholder expectations.

Patterns in the way visitors manage their leisure time have changed over recent years. People are cash-rich and time-poor. This means that they have less time, or shorter amounts of time, to spend on leisure. In addition, visitors expect attractions to be open when it suits them. This means the attraction manager has to consider being open 365 days a year. Ease of access is a major issue in South Africa, where public transport is not readily available. Many visitor attractions are not readily accessible to visitors (both domestic and international) who do not have access to private transport. Even popular visitor attractions such as the Walter Sisulu Botanical Gardens in Gauteng and Kirstenbosch Gardens in Cape Town are not easily accessed, except by car.

Changes in population also need to be taken into account. Europe has an ageing population (Dewhurst & Dewhurst, 2006: 299), and attractions need to accommodate this visitor market suitably. In South Africa, attraction managers need to be able to accommodate the diverse cultures of both international and domestic tourists. Halaal foods, for example, need to be considered, as well as signage and other reading materials in a variety of South African languages.

Competition in the marketplace for leisure spend and leisure time is increasing. Whilst there are generally more leisure activities available, consumers also have higher expectations of what they wish to do in their leisure time.

Conclusion

Visitor attractions are an important part of the destination mix, often acting as the node for drawing visitors to a region. They may have significant economic impact, providing both direct and indirect job opportunities. In many cases, visitor attractions act as the basis for regional and urban regeneration schemes. Attractions, as with other products and services, move through a product life cycle (PLC), and profits increase and decrease as the offering moves through different stages. Each stage of the life-cycle presents various challenges and rewards for management to deal with. For example, attraction managers will be required

to change their management focus as their offering enters into the introductory, growth, maturity, and decline phases.

The management of visitor attractions is a complex interplay of visitor needs and expectations, and the management of the attraction itself. Small attractions may be run by one manager (sometimes the owner-manager), having to ensure that a wide variety of management issues are covered. Larger attractions may have specialist managers focusing on marketing, revenue and financial management, operations, and human resource management. Managing visitors on site, arguably the reason for an attraction to exist in the first place, is an important aspect of site management. Visitor management techniques use a number of methods to control, inform, guide, and manage visitors on site.

Future management issues include the need to create an authentic experience. Visitors want to experience sites, yet not feel that they are impacting on the site in any way. More research is required to understand how visitor attractions can meet the needs of their visitors in the future, and how to appropriately manage the increased number of visitors at sites.

Review questions

1. Discuss the various ways of classifying visitor attractions.

2. How would you define a successful visitor attraction?

3. Explain why visitor attractions are an important component of the tourism system.

4. List and discuss the main market segments that visit theme parks in South Africa.

5. Discuss the future trends in visitor attraction management, and how technology may play a part in solving some of the current problems.

Further Reading

Leask, A. & Fyall, A. (Eds.). 2006. *Managing World Heritage Sites.* Oxford: Butterworth-Heinemann.

Swarbrooke, J. 2002. *The development and management of visitor attractions*, 2nd edition. Oxford: Butterworth-Heinemann.

Websites

Visitor attraction consultants: www.visionxs.co.uk

Attractions Management magazine: www.attractions.co.uk

International Association of Amusement Parks and Attractions (IAAPA): www.iaapa.org

World Heritage Sites: www.whs.unesco.org

SANParks: www.sanparks.org.za

SANBI: www.sanbi.org

References

Boyd, S. W. & Timothy, D. J. 2006. *Marketing issues and World Heritage Sites*. In A. Leask & A. Fyall (Eds.), *Managing World Heritage Sites*. Oxford: Butterworth- Heinemann.

Cochrane, J. & Tapper, R. 2006. *Tourism's contribution to World Heritage Site management*. In A. Leask & A. Fyall (Eds.), *Managing World Heritage Sites*. Oxford: Butterworth-Heinemann.

Dewhurst, P. D. & Dewhurst, H. 2006. *Visitor attraction management*. In J. Beech & S. Chadwick (Eds.). *The business of tourism management*, Harlow: Prentice Hall, pp. 287–336.

Gale, T. 2006. *Mass tourism businesses: tour operators*. In J. Beech & S. Chadwick (Eds.), *The business of tourism management*, Harlow: Pearson Education. pp. 399–414.

George, R. 2004. *Marketing South African tourism*, 2nd edition. Cape Town: Oxford University Press.

George, R., Slabbert, D. & Wildman, K. 2006. *Offbeat South Africa*. Cape Town: Struik.

Kotler, P. 2000, *Marketing management: analysis, planning, implementation and control*, 8th edition. London: Prentice Hall.

Middleton, V. T. C. & Clarke, J. 2001. *Marketing in travel and tourism*, 3rd edition. Oxford: Butterworth-Heinemann.

Page, S. 2007. *Tourism management: managing for change*, 2nd edition. Oxford: Butterworth-Heinemann.

Pender, L. & Sharpley, R. (Eds.). 2005. *The management of tourism*. London: Sage.

Ryan, C. 2005. Site and visitor management at natural attractions. In L. Pender & R. Sharpley (Eds.), *The management of tourism*. London: Sage, pp. 202–215.

Shackley, M. 2006. *Visitor management at World Heritage Sites*. In A. Leask & A. Fyall (Eds.). Managing World Heritage Sites. Oxford: Butterworth-Heinemann, pp. 84–93.

Swarbrooke, J, 2002. *The development and management of visitor attractions*, 2nd edition. Oxford: Butterworth-Heinemann.

Case study

4

Table Mountain Aerial Cableway Company Ltd.

Objectives

- identify the main management issues prevalent in managing a visitor attraction
- understand how areas of business interact in managing an attraction.

Table Mountain is recognised as one of the world's most striking natural wonders. It is South Africa's most recognised icon and Cape Town's most famous landmark. It is also one of Cape Town's most visited attractions, as the Table Mountain Aerial Cableway Company (TMACC) transports approximately 750 000 visitors annually to the summit of Table Mountain. It is situated within a National Park, which is part of a World Heritage Site and one of the world's unique floral kingdoms.

TMACC is aware of the potential negative impact that such high-traffic tourism can have on the site, and have therefore committed themselves to environmentally sound and sustainable business practices. Management identified the need to formalise an environmental management system (EMS) in order to manager the site effectively. In order to report the progress of the EMS effectively to all stakeholders, the attraction manager identified the need to have the EMS formally benchmarked. This led to the managing director identifying the ISO 14001 standard as the standard to aim for. The ISO 14001 standard is independently audited by the South African Bureau of Standards (SABS).

The attractions manager needed to integrate several areas of business for the company to attain the ISO 14001. The initial phase thus consisted of obtaining co-operation from all managers, as their departments would be integral parts of the system. Areas that had to be integrated in order to attain this standard were: marketing, revenue management, human resource management, visitor management, and operations management.

After a five-year process of implementation, TMACC's EMS (Environmental Management System) was awarded ISO 14001 certification by the South African Bureau of Standards (SABS) in May 2003. This can be regarded as an environmental achievement of the highest international standard.

Human resource management

The company identified environmental performance as a high corporate priority, and established the Environment Policy as a driving force for the implementation, maintenance, and improvement of TMACC's EMS. For this reason, the environmental policy had to be endorsed from the very first. The HR department publicised to all staff that the Board and all managers had signed the environmental policy as part of their employment contract. The next step was for the HR department to find a way of communicating the EMS to all staff. A workshop was arranged for each department, to explain each staff member's role in the environmental system. For example, cleaners were made aware how important it is that stormwater drains were not used for anything but rainwater, and administration staff were made aware of how their paper use and recycling affects the EMS. Thereafter each employee was also asked to sign the environmental policy.

All new Cableway staff, whether permanent or on short-term contract, participate in an induction workshop on the environmental policy and its relevance to their specific job description.

Environmental awareness of staff is raised as part of an ongoing training process throughout the year, and on days when the Cableway is unable to operate due to adverse weather conditions, training sessions take place. This includes job-specific environmental training, and training workshops that focus specifically on the impact their jobs could have on the environment. Employees are also motivated to be role models for environmental performance on an ongoing basis.

The staff notice board and monthly newsletters are used to inform staff of environmental issues and environmental competitions, and include a 'plant/animal of the month' section. Ongoing internal communication is an important tool in educating staff and providing ongoing motivation to ensure that the highest environmental standards are met and kept.

Financial management

The EMS system had to be supported by the budgetary process. For example, a budget had to be allocated for extra staff (a full-time environmental officer was employed). Although management identified that it was was unlikely that this project would create income for the company, the financial manager still had to identify, budget for, and manage all costs associated with ensuring that this policy could be implemented. This included expenses such as training courses, waste

management, subscriptions, consultancy fees, the cost of using environmentally friendly products, etc. In addition, the manager had to be aware that some aspects of the policy may negatively affect profit. For example, popular items previously on sale may not be sold, due to the environmental policy. Cost savings were also assessed and noted, such as reduced waste removal costs due to recycling, and reduced water consumption.

Visitor management

Managing the 750 000 visitors a year who visit the Cableway, and ensuring that their footprint would be as small as possible, forms an important part of the company's EMS. A number of visitor management tools were assessed, and the most relevant of them were implemented.

On the summit of Table Mountain, a two-kilometre circular double-looped pathway system was designed for the efficient flow of visitors, to optimise their viewing experience and to mitigate adverse impacts on the natural environment. The footpaths are constructed of materials which blend in with the natural conditions, and boardwalks have been used to bridge sensitive drainage areas. The footpath was diverted from particularly sensitive areas, thereby channelling the majority of visitors to less sensitive areas. Despite this, some visitors still stepped off the pathway and trampled the vegetation. It was thus decided to fence the pathways with an environmentally and aesthetically acceptable, low visual impact fence.

Signage is used at the lower and top stations to direct visitors to specific sites of interest (and away from sensitive areas). Information leaflets are also given to each visitor, and are used to educate and inform them as to expected behavior on site. The cabin masters were trained to deliver a speech with environmental do's and don'ts as the cable car ascends the mountain. Maps and other information were made available at the curio shops at the top and bottom, and two free daily guided walks are provided in conjunction with volunteers from the Mountain Club of South Africa.

Marketing

The marketing manager was tasked with devising a strategy that not only communicated the

Table 4.5 Operational issues identified as part of the EMS programme

Operational issues identified	These concerns addressed by
Prevent degradation of the vegetation	Well-designed pathways with viewing decks and bridges over sensitive drainage areas.
Reduce damage caused by visitors	Fencing of pathways to stop the trampling of vegetation.
Minimise water consumption	Educate staff and visitors on water scarcity. Install toilet facilities that use less water and waterless urinals; devise cleaning policies that use minimum amount of water. Water consumption target set and actively managed.
Waste water removal from Upper Cable Station to Lower Cable Station	All waste water is removed from the top station.
Air pollution	Control the idling times of coaches parked at the Lower Cable Station.
Minimise litter generation and manage waste disposal	Minimise the use of polystyrene packaging. Use of paper bags in takeaway, souvenir shop, and kiosks. Minimise the use of glass products. Encourage the use of cans in preference to glass and plastic containers. No pamphlets or leaflets are allowed to be distributed within the area by third parties. Eliminate the use of straws with paper wrappers, as the wrappers were found to be a significant cause of litter. Recycle cans, glass, paper and cardboard, and used oil. Responsible hazardous waste disposal. Restrict smokers to a smoking area, with ashtrays to reduce cigarette butt litter along pathways, consequently reducing the associated fire hazard.

company's commitment to its EMS, but would also educate the public on environmental issues. The project 'Class in the Clouds' was born.

'Class in the Clouds' provides an opportunity each year for approximately 25 000 schoolchildren in the Western Cape to experience Cape Town's most famous landmark. It is aimed at school groups of all ages, and is a unique educational school outing, allowing students to explore Table Mountain and their natural heritage at a greatly reduced rate.

TMACC sourced a communications partner *(Coca-Cola)* and put together the 'Class in the Clouds' project in 2001 as an important part of **community development**, in the belief that the children of today are the guardians of the mountain in the future. It has now become a regular feature on the school calendar, encouraging more children to come to Table Mountain.

An inevitable consequence of such large numbers of children is the increased potential for litter. This was successfully curbed by providing teachers and teacher assistants with paper bags for litter, donated by Sappi's 'War on Waste' campaign.

The 'Class in the Clouds' project is a good example of an initiative that involved all management areas. Budgets needed to be set, HR needed to recruit and train teachers' assistants, and operations needed to ensure that queues were managed and that the impact of litter was minimised.

Operations management

The EMS significantly affects the operational management of the site. As a part of the formulation of the EMS, TMACC initially identified all the key environmental activities that may have potential positive or negative impacts that arise as a result of TMACC operations.

The identification of environmental issues is an important and ongoing part of TMACC's EMS. In order to address the environmental issues, objectives and targets are set and incorporated in the Environmental Management Programme of the EMS, specifying time frames and responsibilities. Operations managers worked closely with the environmental officer to plan ways to address environmental issues. Some of the issues addressed are outlined in Table 4.5.

TMACC is proud to be considered the premier visitor attraction in Cape Town, with international environmental standards in place that function in order to ensure the continuing conservation of Table Mountain for many generations to come.

Management identified the EMS as a project they wished to undertake and worked as a team, holding weekly and monthly meetings to ensure that the project was successfully completed. TMACC was audited by the SABS in May 2001, and received the ISO 14001 accreditation.

By minimising the environmental impacts of the business, the company is able to provide a visitor experience of high quality without compromising the integrity of the natural environment. This provides a good example of how all management areas need to integrate to ensure that the attraction meets the needs of its visitors.

Case Study Interview: Bonte Edwards, Environmental Control Officer, TMACC.

www

www.tablemountain.net
www.iso.org

Case study questions

1. Discuss the key elements that the attractions manager had to consider when implementing the Environmental Management System (EMS).

2. Consider other methods that the Cableway could use to manage visitors and the impact of their footfall. Draw up a table describing the advantages and disadvantages of each method.

3. List all stakeholders that are involved in this attraction. How would you communicate the EMS to each of these stakeholders?

4. How does the attraction benefit by the implementation of an ISO14001 EMS?

5. Describe how management commitment ensured the successful implementation of an EMS.

5

Transport for tourists

Anton Brits

1Time aircraft in flight

Purpose

The purpose of this chapter is to demonstrate the importance of transport as a key sector of the South African tourism industry.

Learning outcomes

After reading this chapter, you should be able to:
- explain the relationship between transport and the tourism system
- understand the governance of transport in South Africa
- understand the role of air transport in the tourism industry
- understand the role of land transport in the tourism industry
- understand the role of water-borne transport in the tourism industry
- identify the main aspects of the transport infrastructure.

Chapter overview

This chapter introduces the different modes of air, water and land-based transport and the governance thereof. It begins with the structure of the Department of Transport and the various agencies managing transport on a national basis. It then discusses air transportation with reference to the air transport system. Land transport modes and the distinction between road and rail transport are examined. Next, the third main transportation mode – water transport – is discussed. The last part of the chapter provides an overview of transport infrastructure, and discusses transport as the focus of tourist activities such as sightseeing and cruising.

The concluding case study examines 1Time, a low-cost domestic airline operating in South Africa.

Introduction

The most fundamental element of the concept of *tourism* is travelling. All definitions of tourism, whether they differ in some respects or not, are based on travelling, an activity which implies the utilisation of transport (see Chapter 1). Transport itself is defined in terms of the creation of a time and place utility. Transport is thus the backbone of tourism, since tourists travel from the generating-region to the tourist-destination region (place utility) on a specific date at a specific time (time utility). When they return at the end of their journey to their place of origin, place utility as well as time utility are created again, since they need to be at the place of origin at a certain time. The total process can be defined as the *tourism system* (Page, 2005: 15).

Transportation, while an important sector of the tourism industry, must also provide services which are not solely for tourists. Road, rail and air transport services all carry freight, whether separately or together with passengers. In addition, many transport carriers provide a social and commercial service – for example, buses and trains provide essential commuter services for workers travelling between their homes and workplaces.

Transportation in South Africa is provided by both the public and the private sectors. The public sector transport offering is focused on the supply of transport to serve the community as a whole, fulfilling its social and economic responsibilities – the focus being on break-even financial objectives. The public transport sector has the role of providing a transport infrastructure, which requires a huge capital investment as well as the responsibilities of supplying and maintaining whatever infrastructure is needed by the local population (commuters). Moreover, the public transport sector must take cognisance of the infrastructure's economic, environmental, and strategic influence. The private sector provision of transport is profit-orientated, and may therefore be more inclined to offer transport for tourists where the transport experience itself is integrated with the tourism experience.

An understanding of the operation of transport is extremely important for the tourism industry, since the effectiveness of transport will directly influence the income and profitability of the tourism industry. The safety of all modes of transport is crucial, and must be considered in transport strategies. The safe operation of modes of transport is subject to the safety regulations prescribed by the South African government.

Discussion point

Tourism is not possible without transport. Discuss this statement.

Characteristics of transport

The principal modes of transport are by air, land, and water. Air transport refers to all means of movement in the air, such as mechanical flying machines, air balloons, parachutes, and hang-gliders. Land-based transport includes mechanical motor vehicles, each defined according to the infrastructure used, such as roads and rail tracks. Vehicles driven by human energy, such as bicycles, also fall into this category. Water transport refers to mechanically-driven water vessels as well as human energy-driven boats. The **modes of transport** can either be offered in ways that are complementary to each other, which is also known as *inter-modal* transport, or in competition with each other.

All forms of transport in South Africa, whether offered by the public or the private sector, are subject to government safety regulations. Safety regulation is paramount and non-negotiable, because transport accidents may be fatal for both passengers (who may include tourists) and crew alike. In addition, the environment in which transport in general operates, be it economic, strategic, or international, necessitates governmental intervention.

Transport and infrastructure in South Africa is regulated and managed by the Department of Transport (DoT). This makes use of various agencies, as indicated in Figure 5.1 opposite. The offering of private transport is subject to the safety

Figure 5.1 Department of Transport and the establishment of agencies

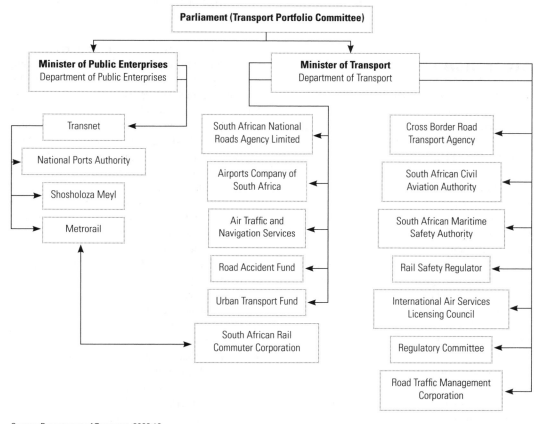

Source: Department of Transport, 2006:13

and economic (where applicable) regulations prescribed by legislation and promulgated by various governmental departments and agencies.

The demand for tourist transport

In general, the mode of transport that a tourist chooses is linked to his or her purpose for travelling. For example, a business traveller who is required to attend a meeting or conference is likely to choose the quickest mode of transport. The factors that influence a tourist's choice of transport include:
- cost of the service
- speed/travel time of the service
- distance

- comfort/luxury of the service
- status and prestige
- safety of the service
- frequency and reliability of the service
- perceptions of the quality of service delivery
- convenience accessibility of the service
- range of services offered (including the terminal).

Each form of transport has specific attributes that will influence the relative importance of the above demand factors for that specific mode of transport. For example, aircraft are known for their speed, and therefore transport passengers over long distances in a relatively short time span. Travel time and comfort will therefore be primary influences.

We will now discuss the various forms/means of transportation for tourists, and the competitive advantages of each.

Air transport

In South Africa, air transport is governed by the South African Civil Aviation Authority (SACAA), the International Air Services Licensing Council (IASLC), the Domestic Air Services Licensing Council (DASLC), the Airports Company of South Africa (ACSA), and the Air Traffic and Navigation Services (ATNS) (See Figure 5.1 on the previous page).

Air transport is generally associated with high speeds and long distances, and therefore ideally satisfies the demand for the rapid movement necessary for effective domestic and international tourism. The emergence and development of jet aircraft over the last 30 years has significantly increased the demand for global tourism as new markets and opportunities for travel have widened (Page & Connell, 2006: 4).

Air transport is, however, not necessarily the only economically viable mode of transport over long distances, but enjoys a competitive advantage for specific distances, depending on circumstances and the ability of other modes to compete with it in terms of cost and service quality. Where the terrain is favourable, various forms of land transport are also able to compete economically with air transport over longer distances. Where cost is a more important consideration than speed, the competitive position of the other modes vis-à-vis air transport improves considerably. However, where speed is a factor and tourists have to be moved across water or some other difficult terrain, other modes of transport are not really in a position to compete with air transport, even over short distances.

Because of the economic, technological, and operational characteristics of air transport, it is clearly unique because:
• it frequently takes place across national borders and through the airspace of sovereign states
• safety is of paramount importance

• it has great significance for a country's international relations, political prestige, and even defence.

As a result, air transport is an important factor in planning and in the development of tourism, notwithstanding its relatively small share in the overall national transport system. The importance of air travel for the South African tourism industry is, however, evident by the implementation of a South African Airlift Strategy (SAAS) for a period of five years (approved by the Cabinet in July 1996). This strategy is specifically aimed at the regulation of air transport in support of the Department of Environmental Affairs and Tourism's (DEAT) Tourism Growth Strategy (TGS). DoT supports this strategy, and is 'putting the final touches to a National Airlift Strategy' (*Travel News Now*, 23 June 2006). The objectives of the strategy are to:
• boost tourism
• promote business travel
• extend the role of aviation and low-cost airlines
• remove obstacles to growth through bilateral and multi-lateral negotiations, both regionally and internationally
• improve market access to support growth and competition in the air services industry.

These objectives will be achieved through the creation of an enabling regulatory framework that allows for capacity to be negotiated ahead of demand, and unlocks that capacity by introducing mechanisms such as the 'use-it-or-lose-it' principle. (The 'use-it-or-lose-it' clause was introduced to prevent an airline from keeping rivals out of a certain route by obtaining sole air traffic rights, but failing to provide a service within 12 months).

The Minister of Environmental Affairs and Tourism, Marthinus van Schalkwyk, confirmed the intentions of an international air-lift, while the President of South Africa, Thabo Mbeki, has asked several departments, including DEAT, DoT, and the Department of Public Enterprises (DPE) to examine the airlift issues (*Travel News Now*, 13 June 2006).

South Africa's mission for air transport is: *'To maintain a competitive civil aviation environment which ensures safety in accordance with international standards, and enables the provision of services in a reliable and efficient manner, improving levels of service and cost while contributing to the social and economic development of South Africa and the region' (White Paper on National Transport Policy, 1996).*

As far as the African continent is concerned, African countries decided to promote the air transportation industry in Africa and follow an 'Open-Skies for Africa' policy approach to liberalise air services across the continent. The *Yamoussoukro Decision,* which is intended to strengthen African airline carriers, to improve their capitalisation, and to minimise operating costs, was signed on 14 November 1999 by Ministers responsible for Civil Aviation in West and Central Africa. However, to date only Botswana, Kenya, Ethiopia, Uganda, Libya, Gabon, Egypt, and South Africa have agreed to implement the key elements of the Yamoussoukro Decision. These include improvement and the removal of physical and non-physical barriers.

According to the Secretary-General of the African Airlines Association (AAA), Christian Folly-Kossi, 'Intra-African liberalisation would create the appropriate environment for the most proactive carriers of the continent to quickly extend their networks and offer air services where they are now missing' (Airlift Strategy, 2006: 19). African tourism will be influenced positively if more access to the continent is made available through the Yamoussoukro Decision.

International airline alliances and competition

In terms of the global air transport environment South African Airways (SAA), owned by national government, is defined as the national airline carrier. The airline joined STAR Alliance, the largest organisation of its kind in the world, as its 18th member on 10 April 2006. SAA is, therefore, the first African airline to join the STAR Alliance. The international airline industry is dominated by three alliances: *One World*, led by British Airways (BA) and American Airlines; *Sky Team*, led by merged Air France and KLM Royal Dutch Airlines; and US-based Delta Airlines and the *STAR Alliance*, led by German airline Lufthansa, Singapore Airlines, US-based United Airlines, and US Air. The aim of each alliance is to be able to be able to provide world-wide coverage through connecting flights with a single ticket. They also achieve economies of scale through joint purchasing and shared facilities such as shared lounges and check-in facilities. SAA is, at the time of writing (January 2007), the only African airline to be a full member of an alliance, although Kenya Airlines, which is partly owned by KLM, is an associate member of Sky Team. BA/Comair is a franchise holder of BA, which owns 14% of Comair. Passengers travelling on SAA flights will benefit from all the advantages which the members of the alliance enjoy. These include, among others, a network of more than 15 500 daily flights serving 842 destinations in 152 countries, through check-in and access to more than 660 lounges (STAR Alliance Press Office, 10 April 2006).

However, some Middle Eastern airlines, which were started up by oil-rich governments for the express purpose of developing a tourism industry in their home countries, attracting service industries to them and building up their domestic airports into international hubs, are offering powerful competition to the alliances. They are developing extensive international route networks offering connecting flights to many regions of the world, often at lower rates than the alliance, with the added incentive of a free night in a hotel in their home cities. In recent years they have succeeded in attracting South African outbound travellers to travel by indirect routes, even to destinations such as Australia and Europe, because of their lower airfares.

Some **low-cost airlines** are beginning to compete with the full-service airlines in the international scheduled airline market; notably Scottish airline Globespan, which added flights between Cape Town and Manchester to its route network in October 2006.

As explained, the airline industry is complex and constantly exposed to innovations in the tourism, economic, technological, operational, and management spheres. Moreover, the environment in which it operates changes all the time. At both the national and international levels economic regulation is giving way to market competition. Vast sums of capital have to be invested in infrastructure, such as airports and aviation systems, which take a long time to develop and establish.

The air transport system

The South African Civil Aviation Authority (SACAA) (see Figure 5.1) is an important role-player in the South African air transport system. SACAA, which was established in October 1998, is the authority responsible for promoting, regulating and enforcing civil aviation safety and security.

The term 'air transport system' encompasses all the subsystems needed to meet the demand for air transport tourism, and includes the following:
* aircraft
* airports
* air traffic control
* route services.

These subsystems are interdependent, and deficiencies in one system automatically affect the ability of the system as a whole to provide a satisfactory service. It is evident that the air transport system can affect air transport demand either positively or negatively, depending on the extent to which it succeeds in providing safe and effective services that meet tourists' needs. It is imperative that the various subsystems interact, and that the equilibrium of the overall system should not be disturbed too often. Efficient aircraft, for example, cannot compensate for an inefficient traffic system.

Aircraft constitute the system's mobile units and, as such, they perform the basic transport function, which is to move tourists and other passengers through space between an origin and a destination. Aviation technology has advanced considerably in recent decades, and the rate at which new aircraft are being developed, produced,

and commissioned has effectively kept pace with the needs and requirements of operators and tourists in the market. However, it is far more difficult to adapt the capacities and characteristics of the airport subsystem to changing circumstances, of which the newly developed Airbus 380 is a good example (see Example box).

Example Airbus 380

In 2008, the Airbus 'superjumbo' A380 is due to enter service – a double-decker aircraft seating between 550 and 800 passengers.

The national and international routes on which airlines operate are basically determined by demand for such a service. National routes, however, are controlled by the government, which can restrict this right to national carriers, whereas international routes are assigned by bilateral agreements (see air transport infrastructure section) between the airline and the country whose airspace will be utilised. Bilateral agreements are negotiated between governments, which then allocate the air traffic rights between airlines applying for them. This helps to explain why Virgin Atlantic was unsuccessful for many years in obtaining rights to fly first to Johannesburg, and then to Cape Town. SAA was successful in persuading the South African government to limit the rights granted to British airlines, and British Airways was successful in persuading the British government to grant limited rights to Virgin Atlantic. The South African government's policy of protecting SAA's market share has been relaxed since 2006, in favour of encouraging more inbound tourists to the country.

The above discussion has dealt briefly with the functioning of the air transport system and its interaction with tourists' demand for air transport. Such functioning and interaction, however, cannot take place freely. While it is true that population growth and industrial expansion, more leisure time, and increased disposable income create new and larger tourist markets for air transport, factors such as conservation, safety regulations, and a lack of finance can hamper growth and effective operation. The authorities generally impose regulations to control the air transport system in the interest of tourists. Airlines are subject to the usual constraints that inhibit other forms of business enterprises, and are associated with the environment in which they operate.

Air transport service types

Worldwide tourist demand for air transport has grown more rapidly than the demand for more traditional modes of transport, for the following reasons:
- **economic growth** and increase in the wealth of individuals
- the growing importance of international tourism
- the greater availability and increasing importance of leisure time
- technological advancements in aviation, which have resulted in greater availability of air transport and declining operating costs, due to economies of scale.

It is this rising demand that places the air transport system and its subsystems under increasing pressure to provide a safe and effective service. Air transport services are categorised as scheduled and non-scheduled; charter, taxi and helicopter services.

Scheduled and non-scheduled air transport services

Scheduled air transport services are the most common. They play an important role in planning. Tour operators need to take these services into consideration when they plan the total tourism offering, because the offering is based on pre-determined routes and timetables. This service is focused on the demand of the general public, and is also used by business travellers, since it allows them the opportunity to work during the journey. Scheduled airline services may be expensive in terms of other services, since a scheduled service must be undertaken, irrespective of the demand for it. The demand for such a service may, however, be increased through specially reduced

fares offered for bookings made well in advance – the fare system known as the Advanced Purchase Excursion (APEX) being an example of this.

Non-scheduled airline services are offered whenever the demand for such a service is sufficient. By manipulating schedules, they may be able to offer lower tariffs than the scheduled airlines by maximising their average load factor, which is the ratio of occupied seats in relation to available seats. On the other hand, scheduled air services are required to operate in accordance with published and predetermined schedules, regardless of the number of passengers.

Leisure tourists are generally price-sensitive, since they usually have a limited holiday budget, have more time available, and do not necessarily require services of an exceptionally high quality. They therefore usually use Economy Class. Since they plan their holidays well in advance, such holidaymakers make use of scheduled airline services and therefore do not need a highly flexible service. Business travellers, on the other hand, prefer scheduled services, since they need maximum flexibility in order to change or cancel a flight if necessary. Since the company usually pays for the flight, the business traveller is generally less price-sensitive.

Various international carriers such as Emirates, Virgin Atlantic, British Airways (BA), Lufthansa, Air France, KLM, Cathay Pacific, Singapore Airlines, and Air India operate scheduled flights to southern Africa. Air India has announced that it intends to restore a service to South Africa that it withdrew several years ago, but had not yet started one by January 2007. Domestically, SAA – with the government as the sole shareholder – dominated the market before the 1990s. Very few airlines were able to enter the market, and smaller carriers such as BA/Comair and Nationwide competed for a share of the local market. The deregulation of the air transport industry took place after the promulgation of the Domestic Air Transport Policy in 1991, which had clear objectives, namely to ensure:
- the safety of passengers at all costs
- the equal treatment of all role-players
- that users' views and interests be taken into consideration

- that economic decisions are left to market forces to resolve.

The South African government relaxed certain aspects from July 2006, such as its protection of the national flag-carrier, but not at the cost of passenger safety. This resulted in a number of new airlines entering the market, which increased choices for passengers. At present, privately-owned South African airlines which provide scheduled low-cost airline services include Comair/Kulula.com; Nationwide, Inter-Air, 1Time, Airlink Regional, and Pelican Air Services. Although Nationwide's normal fares are pitched slightly below those of SAA and BA/Comair, it does not market itself as a low-cost airline. Similarly, Inter-Air and Airlink do not describe themselves as low-cost airlines. Mango, a low-cost airline which was launched in 2006, is state-owned (SAA) and run by a separate management.

Non-scheduled international services are based on the national laws of a country. In South Africa, such services are regulated by means of a Foreign Operator's Permit (FOP). During 2006, 11 scheduled and 68 unscheduled licensed air service providers were registered in South Africa (Airlift Strategy, 2006: 16)

Charter services

Charter airlines fly on routes where they can operate high load factors, typically 85 to 90%. They are not obliged to fly regardless of load factor as scheduled airline services are, and therefore their revenue per flight may be much higher than that of scheduled airlines. They also limit their marketing costs and offer less in the way of services in the air, compared with those of scheduled airlines. Tour operators are particularly content to make use of charter flights, since this allows them to reduce the price of a tour – depending, of course, on the category of tourist and visitor attraction. Tour operators tend to purchase or form their own charter airlines. They use these airlines for their own tours, but also take on other groups and sell empty seats to individual passengers (Mill & Morrison, 2002: 414).

Another form of charter air service for tourism is the *inclusive tour charter air service*. The inclusive tour package usually includes airfare, accommodation, transfer arrangements between the airport and accommodation, and other land arrangements for tourists (see Chapter 7 – Managing tourism distribution). In South Africa, this applies to people who will be visiting the country for at least seven days.

A *charter package for tourism and seat-only air service* is also offered. This is a combination of a package tourism service (an *inclusive* tour) and a seat-only service when spare capacity is available. This combination of services may compete with scheduled air services, especially during off-seasons, since the scheduled air service has to be provided irrespective of low demand.

Charter air services in South Africa from destinations not serviced by scheduled air services and intra-African services are allowed freely, but are subject to safety and security regulation.

Taxi services

The term 'air taxi' refers to a private charter plane that usually carries between 4 and 18 passengers, and is generally chartered by business executives and teams. They offer the advantages of convenience and flexibility. Flights can be arranged at very short notice to just about any destination. This service is primarily used by larger corporations, whose managers need to travel quickly and at the last minute to remote destinations not served by scheduled or non-scheduled airlines.

Helicopter services

The cost of operating helicopters is high in comparison with other modes of air transport, and therefore such services focus on business travellers. However, helicopters are ideal for sightseeing, and such services (helipads) are offered at specific visitor attractions such as the V&A Waterfront in Cape Town, the Champagne Sports Resort in the Drakensberg, and upmarket private game lodges and retreats.

National and international air transport services

National or domestic air transport services refer to air transport services within the geographical borders of a country. Tariffs for South African domestic air services are not regulated by the DoT, and are determined by market demand. The provision of general control over economic activities applicable to all industries specifically conducts regulation in terms of the Competition Act of 1998. As a result, two low-cost domestic airlines, Kulula.com and 1Time, emerged – attracting a huge proportion of the domestic passenger market.

SAA, however, launched a third low-cost airline service, Mango, in October 2006, with an initial fare of around R200 between Johannesburg and Cape Town. Kulula.com, Nationwide, and 1Time are keeping a watchful eye for signs that Mango is being subsidised by the taxpayer, and warn that they will complain to the Competition Commission if they find evidence of any practice they consider irregular.

Competition between the low-cost airlines is widespread and, with the entrance of SAA's Mango service, the existing low-cost airlines will need to employ innovative marketing approaches. Kulula.com has launched a credit card which can be used in shops like other credit cards, but which, in addition, earns the user points towards free flights. Similarly, 1Time has linked up with Galileo, a **global distribution system** (GDS) – the intention being that international travel agents book flights for their clients with 1Time, since most people use travel agents for overseas holidays. 1Time has a fleet of nine planes (see chapter case study).

Low-cost air transport services may influence the choice of mode of tourist transport. This could especially be the case with long-distance journeys, such as between Johannesburg and Cape Town, which are approximately 1 600 kilometres apart. This is because the cost of using the traditional mode of domestic tourist transport, the motor car, may well be far more than that of a return air ticket and hiring a vehicle at the destination.

'International air transport services' refers to global air transport services crossing the borders of various countries. Tariffs for international air services are generally deregulated and left to be determined by market demand, but are also subject to the control over economic activities applicable to all industries. Air service agreements usually make provision for a liberal 'double disapproval' tariff system, which allows for flexibility in filing of tariffs to address competition concerns.

International air transport is usually based on bilateral agreements, the first of which was the Paris Convention of 1919, where the sovereignty of states over the airspace above their territories was recognised. The traffic rights of airlines flying over a particular country were initially very restrictive, because of various political and technical problems. These issues were addressed at the Chicago Conference in 1944, of which the most important outcome was the signing of the Chicago Convention by various countries. South Africa adopted the Chicago Convention by signing into law the Aviation Act No 74 of 1962.

The Chicago Convention regulates all facets of the air transport industry. Non-scheduled flights were granted the right to fly over the territories of contracting states and the right to land in foreign states, while scheduled flights require prior approval. The Chicago Conference formulated two important documents – the International Air Services Transit Agreement, also known as the Two Freedoms Agreement, and the International Air Transport Agreement, known as the *Five Freedoms of the Air* agreement. The International Civil Aviation Organisation (ICAO) was also founded during the conference. (The objectives of ICAO are named after the five freedoms).

The following 'Freedoms of the Air' have been introduced for scheduled international air services:

- The *first freedom* is the right of an airline from country A – South Africa, for example – to overfly country B, Madagascar, without landing, to get to destination C, for example Singapore. This is the right of overflight.
- The *second freedom* is the right of an airline from country A (i.e. South Africa) to land in country B (i.e. Canary Islands, Spain) for purposes other than the carriage of passengers or freight; for example for the purpose of refuelling, maintenance, or repair work only, *en route* to country C (i.e. USA). Such landings are generally necessary because of the great distance between points

of origin and destination – for example South Africa and the United States of America.

- The *third freedom* is the right of an airline from country A (i.e. South Africa) to offload passengers, mail, or freight from which those passengers, mail, or freight originated (i.e. Singapore).
- The *fourth freedom* is the right of an airline from country A (i.e. South Africa) to carry passengers, mail, or freight to which those passengers, mail or freight are destined back from country B (i.e. Singapore).
- The *fifth freedom* is the right of an airline from country A (South Africa) to carry passengers, mail, or freight between country B (Singapore) and other countries such as C (Thailand) or country D (China). This freedom cannot be used unless countries C and D also agree.

However, the operation of international scheduled airline services sometimes necessitates supplementary rights for which the Two or Five Freedoms Agreements do not make provision. These rights are agreed upon by the contracting states and are referred to as the sixth, seventh, and eighth freedoms. They entail the following:

- *Sixth freedom*: The use of the third and fourth freedom rights by an airline of country A (South Africa) to carry traffic between two other countries, using its base in A (South Africa) as a transit point. This effectively means that the airline, without having been granted the fifth freedom, manages to carry traffic to and from two foreign states, say Singapore and Argentina, by interrupting the journey to land in its home state (South Africa). Although the sixth freedom is seldom formally acknowledged in aviation agreements, it is taken into account during capacity negotiations.
- *Seventh freedom*: The right of an airline of country A to carry traffic between country B and country C. As an example, for many years a US airline had such a right to operate a shuttle service between Tokyo and Seoul in Korea.

- *Eighth freedom*: The right of an airline of country A to carry traffic between two points within country B. This freedom is more commonly known as *cabotage*, and in commercial air transport applies to traffic on domestic routes, or on routes between the granting state and its overseas territories or former colonies (for example, the UK and Hong Kong, China). Cabotage rights are, however, usually reserved for the national carrier, and are very seldom granted to foreign airlines (Wells & Wensveen, 2004: 43–546).

The objectives of the ICAO are to develop the principles and techniques of international air navigation, and to foster the planning and development of international air transport so as to:

- ensure the safe and orderly growth of international civil aviation worldwide
- encourage the arts of aircraft design and operation for peaceful purposes
- encourage the development of air routes, airports and air navigation facilities for international civil aviation
- meet the needs of the peoples of the world for safe, regular, efficient, and economical air transport
- prevent the economic wastage caused by unreasonable competition
- ensure that the rights of contracting states are fully respected and that every contracting state has a fair opportunity to operate international air services
- avoid discrimination between contracting states
- promote the safety of international aviation
- generally promote the development of all aspects of international civil aeronautics.

The International Air Transport Association (IATA) is a voluntary international trade body representing the interests of more than 80% of the world's major airlines. IATA was founded in Havana, Cuba in 1945, as the successor to the International Air Traffic Association, which was established in 1919 and represented mainly European countries. In contrast to the ICAO, whose members consist of individual states,

IATA's members are individual airlines. IATA's objectives are:

- to provide a means for collaboration between airlines engaged directly or indirectly in the provision of international air transport services
- to promote safe, regular, and economical air transport for the benefit of the world's population
- to nurture air commerce and to study the problems connected with it; and to cooperate with the ICAO and other international organisations.

An airline qualifies for membership of IATA if it has been designated by a country qualifying for membership of the ICAO and licenced to undertake air services in terms of a bilateral air services agreement. IATA's involvement, which commences once the bilateral agreement has been signed and the relevant airlines have been licenced, covers virtually all spheres of air transport operations.

IATA's logo is widely recognised by the travelling public

The future of air transport

The future of air transport will be subject to technological innovations; such as the development of the Airbus A380, infrastructure development to facilitate aircraft developments, global integration, and corporate alliances.

An important future development in air transport is space tourism. Space travel emerged with the development of safe space travel. Space Tourism (ST) is, however, very expensive because of the intensive training the 'tourist' has to undergo and the operational costs of spacecraft. Only the super-rich have access to such a tourist adventure. Mark Shuttleworth was the first

South African to undertake such a journey (see Chapter 17 – Future of tourism).

Road transport

Road transport is governed by the South African National Roads Agency Limited (SANRAL), the Road Traffic Management Corporation (RTMC), and the Urban Transport Fund (UTF) (See Figure 5.1).

When tourists travel distances which are impractical for air transport, the alternative is either motor car, bus, or rail transport. The unique feature of the motor car is its accessibility and flexibility. It can be parked at the tourist's place of accommodation, and can be driven within walking distance of a destination. No schedules – as is the case with formal transport – are applicable, since the time of use depends on the preferences of the individual tourist.

Car transport

The car mostly dominates road transport in South Africa, and is used by tourists. Rental cars are available at international airports and major cities in South Africa, and are an important means of transport supply for travellers, especially international tourists and business travellers, as they enable travellers to travel at their own pace to attractions of their choice, such as private game reserves, which are often difficult to reach any other way. There are a number of **multi-national corporation** (MNC) car hire companies, such as Hertz, Avis (which also owns Budget Rent-a-car), and Imperial operating in South Africa, as well as hundreds of smaller local car hire companies. These companies charge similar prices, but offer a choice of cars, hiring locations and flexibility (for example, the ability to pick up a car at one location and drop it at another). Flexibility and convenience are important factors for business tourists, who tend to be less price-sensitive, but who also require fast service, reliability, and a more luxurious standard of car than leisure travellers. Most of the larger car rental companies also hire out camper vans, caravans, and recreational vehicles (large mobile holiday homes). There are literally dozens of small local car rental companies, who generally offer a limited choice of cars, but a low price, and the convenience of a local collection point – although perhaps from only one or two locations.

For domestic tourists the motor car is the preferred mode of transport, since public transport is usually expensive and limited at tourist destinations. Travelling on South African roads can be dangerous due to the following factors:

- the number of accidents on the road increases during the holiday seasons
- many cars on South African roads are not roadworthy, which means that they are not safe to be driven on the road
- drivers of vehicles tend not to obey the rules of the road, and therefore endanger both their own lives and those of other road users.

Bus transport

Public bus transport in South Africa is subsidised by the DoT by means of interim and tendered contracts. Municipal bus services are usually owned solely by the municipalities, and are a function within the municipal structure. Tourists very seldom use these bus services. The terms 'bus' and 'coach' are often used interchangeably. Buses are scheduled transport which tourists may use in the destination at which they are staying. Coaches are used for touring, and they are usually chartered. In South Africa, a bus trip is defined as a trip of 24 kilometres or less, whereas a coach trip is one longer than 24 kilometres.

Private bus transport – chartered coaches – is an important means of tourist transport, especially for international tourists travelling around the country. Various configurations of coach are offered, according to the number of passengers who need to be transported and the comfort required, which usually depends on the distance to be travelled. Most coach companies specialise in certain activities. Some operate and market their tours nationally, while others focus on incoming tourists and tour operators by offering half-day or full-day sightseeing excursions (see Example box), transfers between airports and accommo-

dation establishments, or coach tour holidays for inbound international tourists.

Example Open-top buses for sightseeing

As in cities such as Seoul, Amsterdam, and London, buses are used for sightseeing in Cape Town, Port Elizabeth, eThekwini, and Johannesburg. Open double-decker buses are used to provide tourists with an optimal view of the sights of the city. Such a bus operating in Cape Town is the Cape Town Explorer. The tour includes the V&A Waterfront, the city centre, Table Mountain and Kloof Nek, and a coastal drive through Camps Bay. Passengers can 'hop on, hop off', so that that they can access all the major visitor attractions in the Mother City. The tour includes the services of an experienced, qualified tourist guide, who points out all the major attractions and places of interest while narrating the history of the city.

Public bus transport in tourist destinations is usually predetermined by the position of bus stops and terminals, which may well not be near the place of origin or destination. The availability of bus transport is also determined by time schedules.

In the South African tourism industry scheduled long-distance coaches are used as an alternative to rail or car travel to the destination. Such transport is mainly offered on major routes, for example between Tshwane and Cape Town by coach companies such as *Intercape* and *Greyhound*. In some instances, these long-distance coach services are in direct competition with low-cost airlines such as Mango and Kulula. com. Coach transport is a very important mode of transport in the South African tourism industry, particularly for the VFR market.

The advantages of bus transport on major routes are as follows:

- It is convenient, because it offer a door-to-door service. Passengers can be picked up at a central point near their home and dropped off at the tourist destination

- The bus and coach network is more dense than the rail network, offering more destinations
- Schedules and the frequency of the service are set, and therefore planning can be done efficiently
- The total cost of travel is known beforehand, without any unforeseen additional costs, and is usually lower than other formal modes of travel
- The journey can offer scenic views from the coach
- Passengers can interact socially with one another
- Physiological effects, such as the stress of driving on roads, are avoided.

Coach transport as part of a tour package not only offers transport for the tourist, but can also be a tourism adventure itself (see Example box on previous page). Page & Connell (2006: 23) refer to this phenomenon as 'transport as tourism'.

In South Africa the transportation of passengers for remuneration is subject to the National Road Traffic Act (Act No. 93 of 1996) and the National Road Traffic Amendment Act (Act No. 21 of 1999). The Road Traffic Act of 1998 stipulates, *inter alia,* that drivers of passenger vehicles are required to hold a professional driving permit (PrDP).

Bus services can be categorised under the following headings:
- buses
- mini-buses of which the Gross Vehicle Mass (GVM) exceeds 3 500kg, or which have 12 or more seats including the one for the driver
- motor vehicles conveying persons for reward
- motor vehicles conveying 12 or more persons including the driver.

The authority to drive a vehicle conveying persons is categorised as 'P', and endorsed on the driving licence card where applicable. A transport permit is issued by the DoT. Safety regulations as prescribed by the National Road Traffic Act (Act No. 93 of 1996) are applicable, and are an important means of ensuring the safety of tourists.

Taxi transport

The taxi industry plays an important role transporting tourists within South African towns and cities. There are two types of taxis in South Africa, namely metered and un-metered taxis. Metered taxis charge passengers per kilometre travelled. Tourists tend to use metered taxis to get to and from accommodation establishments, restaurants, visitor attractions, and other transport terminals such as airports, bus, and train stations.

Un-metered taxis, or minibus taxis as they are known, charge a set rate for different destinations, and dominate the public transport mode on a national basis. Local people use minibus taxis mainly for getting around towns, as well as for longer distances between cities. Minibus taxis are perhaps the cheapest form of motor transport, and they are generally more frequent and accessible than local buses.

Unfortunately the minibus taxi's operational environment reveals that:
- it is dominated by severe harassment, intimidation, and violence
- the industry has been never been regulated, and any attempt to do so is viewed with great suspicion
- profit margins are limited, and 'break-evens' not acceptable
- reckless and negligent driving takes place, since a specific daily revenue is targeted
- training and working conditions are not given high priority by employers.

(National Household Travel Survey, 2003: 80-81*).*

Furthermore, minibus taxis are not always operated according to economic principles. Often, no provision is made for depreciation, and therefore no capital is available for the replacement of vehicles. This results in the continued use of old and unroadworthy vehicles, thereby endangering the lives of passengers and bystanders. These negative aspects of the minibus taxi industry motivated the DoT to plan a Taxi Recapitalisation Project (TRP), whereby old and/or unroadworthy minibus taxis will be replaced and the minibus taxi industry regulated.

The future of road transport

The future of road transport is based on the 2010 Transport Action Plan of the South African government. The need for long-distance travel services, which include taxi and bus services, tour packages, and private car hire, will peak when the FIFA World Cup is staged in South Africa during 2010. Challenges are enormous, among others:
• tourism travel plans and packages
• domestic distance travel
• localised travel demand planning and service provision.
(DoT, 2006, Section B:14).

Investment in vehicles and road infrastructure, which is urgently needed, is also planned. The sustainability of such investment is unquestionable when future growth patterns are scrutinised.

Rail transport

In South Africa, rail transport has not yet adapted to the needs of tourists. To some extent trains in South Africa are considered a second-rate means of passenger transportation. The long distances between South African cities make it difficult for trains to compete with private motor cars and low-cost airlines in terms of the time it takes to travel. There is also a need for improved marketing to raise awareness of the options available to tourists. In addition, the safety of passengers needs to be addressed, and the quality of service delivery needs to be improved. In general, the most important reasons for travelling by train are as follows:
• safety
• speed
• personal comfort
• the ability to view scenery en route
• the ability to move around the coach
• environmentally-friendly mode of transport
• arriving at the destination point rested and relaxed
• centrally located termini.

Rail transport in South Africa is governed by the Department of Public Enterprise (DPE),

the South African Rail Commuter Corporation (SARCC), Shosholoza Meyl (SM) and the Rail Safety Regulator (RSR) (See Figure 5.1).

The development of rail transport in the second half of the 19th century dominated the land passenger transport market, until the development of road and air transport technology took place. This, and the associated economic advantages over rail transport, resulted in a declining demand for rail passenger transport in certain markets. The introduction of high-speed trains, especially in countries such as France, Germany, and Japan, however, fuelled the demand for rail transport over distances of approximately 500 kilometres, because of travelling-time advantages. For example, Japan's *Shinkansen* (Bullet Train) travels at speeds up to 300 kilometres per hour, and is capable of travelling city-centre to city-centre between Tokyo and Osaka in less than three hours – compared with an hour's flying time between airports – covering a distance of 500 kilometres in less than two hours. Japan takes great pride in its bullet trains – where delays are counted in seconds, rather than minutes. Such long distance high-speed rail services are not yet available in South Africa.

The Gautrain, a high-speed intercity train service, has been planned to operate in Gauteng, and at the time of writing construction of the infrastructure had already commenced. 2010 is the projected date for completion of this rapid rail service between Hatfield, Tshwane, and Park Station in Johannesburg, with a link between Sandton and O.R. Tambo Airport. Although the Gautrain focuses on relieving traffic congestion between Johannesburg and Tshwane, the service between O.R. Tambo Airport and Sandton, which is an important business hub with a variety of accommodation options, will benefit international tourists especially.

Long-distance passenger rail transport

In South Africa, long-distance public passenger rail transport services on all the major routes are offered by Spoornet, a business unit of Transnet, which is the responsibility of the Minister of the

Department of Public Enterprises. Although the mainline passenger services offered are an important means of travel for residents in South Africa, they are also marketed to attract tourists, because train travel is an excellent means of sightseeing and viewing the scenic beauty of the country. Long distance passenger rail transport in South Africa can therefore be defined as 'transport as tourism' as opposed to 'transport for tourism'.

Spoornet operates the *Shosholoza Meyl*, the *Premier Class* and the *Blue Train* services.

- The *Shosholoza Meyl* has eight major routes linking South Africa's cities, with smaller towns along each route.
- The *Premier Class* offers luxury accommodation, fine dining, personal assistance and a scenic route between Cape Town and Tshwane (and vice-versa).
- The *Blue Train* combines the luxury of the world's leading hotels with the charm of train travel. The luxury of the Blue Train is partly due to suspension, braking, lighting, and under-floor heating systems that have been designed to give comfort to the passengers and allow them the experience of a smooth, pleasurable ride.

Private long-distance passenger rail transport

Private tourist trains in South Africa are offered by private companies, such as JB Train Tours. This private rail transport tourism sector generates more than R70-million for the South African economy, and transports some 19 000 passengers every year (*Travel News* 16-08-06). Rail transport in South Africa, however, depends on the infrastructure and rolling stock (coaches) being made available by Spoornet, and the risks associated with such an offering must be considered by the private rail transport tourism providers.

One of the advantages of rail transport as a means of 'transport as tourism' over competing modes of transport is the feature of integration of movement and accommodation (which is also applicable on sea and inland water cruises). Another advantage is that many people are opting

for rail transport as roads and air networks become more congested.

Urban passenger rail transport

Urban passenger train services in South Africa experience a number of problems because of ageing rolling stock (coaches) and infrastructure. Unfortunately, under-investment took place during the past 30 years. Urban passenger services are offered in the main metropolitan areas such as Cape Town, eThekwini and Tshwane.

International tourists visiting South Africa generally do not make use of urban rail transport. Research has shown that 71% of local users of train services are unhappy about the level of overcrowding on trains, while 63% consider that security on trains is not up to standard (DoT, 2006: 31–32).

The future of rail transport

The South African government is aware of the underinvestment in railway rolling stock and infrastructure, and has therefore developed a National Passenger Rail Plan, which entails an overall strategy for the passenger rail sector and, secondly, regional and route-specific business and operational plans with the aim of devolving commuter and rail functions to the local transport authorities.

The Gautrain, construction of which began in October 2006, may be regarded as the future of urban passenger rail transport in South Africa. Construction of the Gautrain itself, as well as its infrastructure, will utilise the latest rail transport technologies available. The train itself will, however, not be integrated with the existing rail systems because of technological differences, especially the width of tracks to be used.

It is likely that environmentalists will continue to lobby for rail as the preferred mode of transport over air transportation. Low-cost airlines in particular have been criticised for the air pollution they generate.

Water transport

Water transport is governed by the National Ports Authority (NPA) and the South African Maritime Safety Authority (SAMSA) (See Figure 5.1 on page 83).

In the South African context, inland or river transport is limited because of the non-existence of viable waterways and rivers. The development of air transport technology in terms of a safe, efficient and effective transport service has negatively affected sea transport; in particular ocean-going cruises between South Africa and other continents such as Europe and the Americas. If transport is used as a service for tourism, another reason is that people normally have holiday time constraints, and therefore the time to travel the vast distances between South African destinations is not available.

Water transport as 'transport as tourism'

Water transport is important; not as a means of transportation, but rather as a visitor attraction. Examples are the cruises around the coast of South Africa, and trips to destinations such as the Portuguese Island and Mozambique. International cruise liners also dock at harbours such as those of Cape Town and eThekwini, allowing passengers to go on excursions to inland visitor attractions such as the wine farms, township tours, and museums.

International cruise ships have been developed as 'floating holiday resorts', which are self-contained in terms of the various visitor attractions on board (See Example box opposite). This approach is specifically followed to attract tourists and to supplement the demand for the cruising market. Therefore, holistically, the cruising experience can be defined as 'transport as tourism'.

The advantage of cruise liners is that they integrate accommodation and transportation with excursions at different ports. Other advantages relate to the characteristics of sea transport, including:
- The supporting infrastructure is free, since ships are supported by the sea, and the sea

lanes in which they travel are usually outside the territorial waters of the country being sailed past, which is normally 19 kilometres from the low-water mark.
- Entry into a country's territorial waters is based on what is known as the 'right of innocent passage'. A country may, however, prohibit ships from entering its territorial waters – particularly if hostile activities are expected.
- On the open sea, deviations from the course within certain parameters are possible.
- The docking costs at terminal facilities for cruise liners are relatively low, when compared with air transport.
- Propulsion through water requires less power, and therefore less energy than on land.

The disadvantages related to cruising are, mainly, the original costs of constructing the ship and the necessary terminal facilities. However, over the long term, the average costs decline continually, since the original costs are divided by constantly increasing passenger numbers.

Example Freedom of the Seas

The *Freedom of the Seas* is the world's biggest cruise liner – four times heavier than the Titanic, and with decks that would accommodate 25 football pitches. Built for the US-Norwegian company Royal Caribbean Cruises, *Freedom of the Seas* can accommodate 4 375 passengers and 1 365 crew, and weighs 158 000 tons. The ship is 339m long, 56m wide, and 72m high, and has a kitchen staff of 240. It hosts a pool with artificial waves big enough to surf on, a 135sq. m shopping centre, a rock-climbing wall, an ice rink, a mini golf course, and a casino. *Freedom of the Seas* also has three F-16 fighter jet replicas and a real Morgan sports car just for decoration!

The ship, however, will lose its top slot as the world's biggest liner when the *Genesis*, which is expected to carry 5 400 passengers, makes her inaugural voyage in 2009!

Other forms of water transport as tourism

In South Africa, coastal leisure cruising is offered between or in harbours, along the coast to bays, such as from Table Bay to Clifton or Hout Bay, while ferries are used for short-haul water transport and within docking areas, such as within eThekwini and Cape Town harbours. A distinction between 'transport for tourism' and 'transport as tourism' can, however, be vague – since this mode of transport may be used for both purposes.

A 'ferry' is defined as a form of short-distance water-borne transport (Holloway, 2006: 369). This includes ferries such as the Robben Island ferry service, which links the city of Cape Town with Robben Island, and which has become a primary 'must-see' visitor attraction for international and domestic tourists.

Another local sea cruise that operates in South African waters is the *RMS St. Helena* (also see Chapter 15 case study). This is an unusual form of transport, because it transports cargo as well as passengers to and from the island of St Helena in the Atlantic Ocean. The *RMS St Helena* is the only operating mail ship in the world, and carries up to 128 passengers. The ship features many of the luxuries that a cruise liner provides, including a cinema, a sundeck, sports facilities such as table-tennis, a swimming pool, and volleyball. These activities keep passengers entertained during their seven-day voyage to St Helena Island, which is only accessible by sea.

Inland waterways, such as canals, provide exceptional opportunities for recreation as well as a form of urban transport. In Cape Town, for example, visitor attractions such as the Cape Town International Convention Centre (CTICC) and the Victoria and Alfred Waterfront can be reached by water from the city centre. Sailing boats are used between ports and for cruising, and – specifically for the adventurous tourist – river boats are used as floating restaurants and sightseeing platforms on dams such as the Hartebeespoort Dam in the North West province and the Vaal Dam in the Free State.

Holiday resorts with water features often make canoes and other pleasure craft, such as pedal boats, available to guests and visitors. These are used either for sightseeing or adventure tourism

Watersite development

The closure of some of South Africa's docklands provided an opportunity for redevelopment of the sites for leisure and tourism. The restoration of waterfront property in sites such as Cape Town's V&A Waterfront and eThekwini's Victoria Embankment Waterfront has, in turn, generated tourism income for these sites following the construction of their marinas and the introduction of visitor attractions such as ferry services, boat tours, cruises, and floating restaurants.

The future of water transport

The future of water transport will depend on the shipping industry and the effect of marketing cruise-liner operations. Cruise liners are likely to continue becoming ever larger, resembling 'floating hotels' that offer a full range of leisure facilities. Marketing research will play an important role in designing vessels and craft which are more fuel-efficient, larger, faster, and more comfortable.

Transport infrastructure

The success of transport itself depends on the infrastructure available. The importance of a successful tourism system with all its value-added benefits depends on the approach which says that the development of transport infrastructure should be integrated with tourism demands. It is a view which should be considered when new transport infrastructure is developed, or existing infrastructure upgraded.

Research carried out in the USA emphasises the importance of transport infrastructure integration with tourism by concluding that, providing tourism over time is a multi-faceted and mutable product, it affects various factors within the broader tourism system such as the:

- access flow from the dispersion of attractions
- extent of trip-chaining
- markets from which the tourists are drawn

- specific needs of different categories of visitors
- adequacy of available modes for connecting visitors to destinations (NCHRP Synthesis 329, 2004: 31).

We will now discuss the infrastructure for different modes of transport.

Air transport infrastructure

Airports

Airports facilitate the deviations of air transport's infrastructure. An airport primarily consists of runways, terminal buildings, facilities, and access systems. Various important activities in the air transport chain take place at airports. The functions involve the concentration and dispersion of passengers. Its effectiveness depends on the airport's transport access system and parking facilities. The processing of arriving and departing tourists is accomplished inside the terminal buildings by means of appropriate facilities, the transfer of tourists between land and air modes, and between different aircraft. Runways, terminals, and access systems are fixed assets with a long service life that require the investment of vast sums of capital. Since the capacity and location of these facilities are largely fixed, it is extremely difficult to adapt them to changing circumstances. Since only minor changes are possible, and in most cases these are extremely costly, it is imperative that these facilities be planned in such a way that they can readily be adapted as circumstances change. The Airports Company of South Africa (ACSA) operates the main public airports in South Africa.

Air traffic control

Air traffic control and navigation services are the most important route services. Air traffic control is basically concerned with the safe and effective flow of aircraft at airports and in the air, particularly when air traffic is dense and visibility is poor. The key requirements for effective air traffic control include equipment for observing traffic, navigational aids, weather data, and the existence

of rules and procedures. Air Traffic control can be classified as either:

- the control of aircraft movements on the ground, which is generally accomplished from the control tower
- the approach and *en route* control, which is usually accomplished from specialised control centres.

The **Air Traffic and Navigation Service** (ATNS) company is the primary provider of navigational services in South Africa, provides services at 21 airports, and covers approximately 22-million square kilometres of airspace. An annual increase of 5,4% is expected between 2006 and 2018 (Airlift Strategy, 2006: 22).

Road and rail infrastructure

In South Africa, road and rail infrastructure developments are taking place, of which the Gautrain is an example. The upgrading of the O.R. Tambo International Airport is also necessary, to make provision for a terminal for the Gautrain.

Intelligent transport systems, transport planning, the construction of roads, and the allocation of R180-million to improve the rail system will be included in the Public Transport Infrastructure Fund (PTIF). This fund forms part of the transport budget related to the 2010 FIFA World Cup, which has recently been increased to R3,74-billion. According to the DoT, at least 70% of infrastructure has to be up-and-running by mid-2009.

Water infrastructure

Water infrastructure in South Africa refers to the different ports, such as Cape Town and eThekwini, with their docks, handling facilities, and navigational support systems. Ports are fixed long-term assets requiring huge initial capital investment, and cannot easily be adapted to changing circumstances. In terms of tourism, handling facilities at docks refer to the transfer facilities of passengers between the ship and the dock.

The navigational support systems are navigation itself, communication, and weather forecasts. The purpose of this system is to support and assure the effective movement and operation of shipping in and outside ports

Other modes of transport

Other modes of transport for tourism will depend on the specific demand for movement. Such modes include walking, cycling, canal boats, rickshaws, motorbikes, scooters, balloon flights (see Example box), and overhead cableways.

Example Air ballooning
AIR Ventures Hot Air Ballooning offers flights taking off from the Rhino and Lion Nature Reserve on the outskirts of Johannesburg. The four-hour 'special' includes a short game drive through the reserve to the balloon launch site; tea, coffee, and biscuits; a one-hour flight, champagne and orange juice, a full English breakfast, and a visit to the big cat breeding area and animal creche, where lion and tiger cubs can be viewed.

Conclusion

Air transport plays an important role in tourism in South Africa, since it is the major mode of transport for international tourists, because of the country's geographical location in relation to continents such as Europe, Asia, and the Americas. Foreign capital is generated when it is brought into the country by international tourists.

The operation of international airlines is complex, because nations control the air space above their area. This implies that airlines need to negotiate for the space through which they fly. The 'Freedoms of the Air' were established in order to make provision for the routing and scheduling of various flight operations.

Land-based modes of transport are particularly important, not only for domestic tourists, but also for international tourists upon entering the country. Various modes of land transport are used, such as the motor car, buses, hire cars, and rail. Each of these modes has specific advantages, and the specific tourist priorities will determine the demand for a specific mode.

Review questions

1. Which factors will influence tourists' demand for transport? Discuss briefly.

2. The operation of airlines internationally is complicated by utilising the air space of foreign countries. Explain ways of overcoming this operational burden.

3. List the functions of the ICAO and IATA, and indicate the difference between the two organisations.

4. Discuss the attributes of road transport in the tourism experience.

5. Explain why, under certain circumstances, rail transport and sea cruising can be regarded as 'transport as tourism'.

Further reading

Department of Transport. 2005/06. *Strategic Plan,* Tshwane: DoT.

Doganis, R. 2002. *Flying off course,* 3rd edition. London: Routledge.

Page, S. J. 2005. *Transport and tourism,* 2nd edition. Pearson: Prentice Hall.

Journals

Transport Management

Journal of Transport Economics and Policy

Websites

ACSA: www.airports.co.za

SA Department of Transport: www.transport.gov.za

Gautrain: www.gautrain.co.za

Spoornet: www.spoornet.co.za

IATA: www.iata.org

References

Department of Transport. 1996. *White Paper on National Transport Policy.* Tshwane, DoT.

Department of Transport. 2003. *Technical Report. The first South African National Household Travel Survey.* Tshwane, DoT.

Department of Transport. 2006. *Strategic plan 2005/6.* Tshwane, DoT.

Department of Transport. 2006. *Transport Indaba.* Tshwane, DoT.

Holloway, J. C. 2006. *The business of tourism,* 7th edition. Harlow: Longman.

Mill, R. C. & Morrison, A. M. 2002. *The tourism system: an introductory text,* 4th edition. London: Prentice Hall.

NCHRP Synthesis 329. 2004. *Integrating tourism and recreation travel with transport planning and project delivery.* Washington: Transportation Research Board.

Page, S. J. 2005. *Transport and tourism,* 2nd edition. Pearson: Prentice Hall.

Page, S. J. & Connell, J. 2006. *Tourism: a modern synthesis,* 2nd edition. London: Thomson Learning.

South African Tourism. 2006. *South Africa: Domestic Tourism Growth Strategy,* SA Tourism.

United Nations World Tourism Organisation. 1991. *Resolution of International Conference on Travel and Tourism,* Ottawa, Canada. Madrid: UN-WTO.

Wells, A. T. & Wensveen, J. G. 2004. *Air transportation: a management perspective,* 5th edition. Belmont: Thomson Learning.

Objective

- to understand the role played by air transport in the South African tourism industry

In 2003, Glenn Orsmond, ex-financial director of British Airways/Comair, began a partnership with Rodney James, Gavin Harrison, and Sven Petersen to start 1Time, a low-cost airline to compete with kulula.com in the South African domestic airline market.

1Time Airlines' first scheduled flight took place on 25 February 2004, with three return flights on the Johannesburg/Cape Town route. Since then, the airline has expanded to eight routes in South Africa. 1Time is now planning to fly to African destinations, but has encountered resistance from various countries' governments, which allocate air traffic rights to specific airlines (priority being their state-owned airlines); and which have thus closed off the African market to 1Time for the time being. 1Time is also not without its battles in South Africa, where the government allocates air traffic rights to SAA or state-owned SA Express in preference to the likes of 1Time, kulula.com and Comair.

1Time flies on the major domestic routes in South Africa with its five MD-80 aircraft and two DC-9s. The MD-80s are twin-jet passenger aircraft carrying 157 passengers in a 3-2 seating configuration. On-board standards are impressive, with leather seats and greater leg-room than most other airlines.

Orsmond realised that 1Time could be a profitable low-cost airline, because its own real costs would be lower than those of kulula, since it would not be tied to a full-service airline (kulula's costs are subsidised to some extent by the shared use of Comair's facilities). Hence, 1Time is advertised as a 'true low-cost airline'.

The words 'more nice, less price' appear on all the company's advertising. The name '1Time' is a reflection of the company, and the phrase 'one time!' is derived from the South African colloquialism meaning 'for real!'. The airline's slogan is *Azuikho lo nonsense* which means 'no nonsense' or 'no bull', and which further reflects the airline's determination to cater for consumers' desire for a company that is 'for real', with no small print or pricing conditions.

1Time operates in the same way as other low-cost airlines, where the first seats to be sold on every flight are at the lowest advertised price and, as the flight fills up, the prices increase until they near the advertised maximum price. Indeed, the advertised maximum is rarely in fact charged, but the latest seat to be sold on any one flight always cost more than the first seats sold.

1Time's business model is based on price and service. Quite simply, price attracts customers to 1Time, and they are retained through service. To ensure quality service, Orsmond flies regularly on his own planes to identify possible problem areas and rectify them. In order to keep costs low, the airline has opted for ticketless air travel. Most of 1Time's reservations are made through its call centre; others are made via its Internet booking site or its ticket sales counters at O.R. Tambo International Airport and Cape Town International Airport. It also manages to keep costs down by running a tight business without 'frills'. Food and beverages are available on board, but at a cost to those passengers who want them. 1Time does not offer 'loyalty' or 'frequent flyer' programmes (FFPs), as these contribute to the high cost of airfares; nor do they take part in code-sharing (the industry term for 'link-ups') with any international carriers, as do most local airlines. Other than partnerships with Avis and City Lodge Hotels, they do not extend their brand significantly. Indeed, 1Time attracts an increasing number of business tourists, who make use of car hire and accommodation options. It is also attracting an increasing number of first-time fliers, who are flying for the purpose of holidays and visiting friends and relatives (VFR).

The South African domestic airline market is made up of over 7-million passengers each year, and is growing at a rate of between 15% and 20%, largely due to the vibrant economy, but also because of the influx of low-cost airlines operating in South African skies which has created access to air travel for less affluent people. The growth of 1Time illustrates that the owners did indeed get it right – no bull!

Case study questions

1. Explain how 1Time contributes to the tourism industry in South Africa.

2. Are you able to identify the business and managerial skills that Glenn Orsmond exhibits, as described in this case study? Discuss.

3. What marketing strategy would you recommend traditional full-cost carriers adopt to compete with low-cost airlines? Do they need to compete with them, or can they coexist in harmony?

6

Managing accommodation for tourists

Delano Caras

Purpose

The purpose of this chapter is to explore the role of tourist accommodation establishments and how they currently operate in South Africa.

Learning outcomes

After reading this chapter, you should be able to:
- understand and describe the nature, range, and diversity of tourist accommodation in South Africa
- discuss the history and recent development of the tourist accommodation sector in South Africa
- explain the nature of the 'no-frills' hotel product-offering, why it evolved in South Africa, and its profound impact on the hotel industry
- demonstrate understanding of the nature of demand for tourist accommodation, and how it is manifested in South Africa
- explain how tourist accommodation is priced
- discuss the importance of quality, standards and grading to the tourist accommodation product
- explain the challenge of operating tourist accommodation.

Chapter overview

This chapter begins with a description and classification of the various types and forms of tourist accommodation. It then looks at the modern history of hotel and other tourist accommodation in South Africa from the pre-1960 period to the present.

Attention is paid, in particular, to the reasons for and the fact of the emergence of the so-called 'no-frills' hotel.

Occupancy (volume) and rate (price) are the two drivers of accommodation revenue; their interrelationship is examined.

The question of quality and its management is then considered, together with the related issue of accommodation grading. The chapter then discusses what attracts people to enter the business of providing tourism accommodation, as well as some of the reasons for the many hotel failures that occur. It then proceeds to examine various performance measurements and their implications. Finally, the chapter looks at the various regimes that occur in the sector, from owner-operated entities to leases and management contracts.

The concluding case study illustrates how the theory contained in this chapter can be applied to a practical situation within the accommodation sector in the South African tourism industry.

Introduction

Tourist **accommodation** is by a long way the largest sub-sector of the tourism industry (Sharpley, 2005: 15). Although it has experienced astounding expansion and diversification in modern times, in its simplest forms it has very old historical roots. The evolution of tourist accommodation has also been witnessed in South Africa, where inns and the rather simple and modest establishments of earlier times have given way to a plethora of accommodation types that will be discussed below. The development of the sector in South Africa in recent years reflects the country's transformation from its apartheid past into a young democracy, riding the wave of sustained tourism growth since the early 1990s.

The rapid and substantial growth of international tourism to South Africa over the last decade-and-a-half has stimulated the accommodation sector, as has the emerging interest in travel by a large, previously excluded segment of South Africa's population of **historically disadvantaged individuals** (HDIs). These dynamics are bringing about not only an expansion in the overall supply of tourist accommodation, but also a rich diversification in the kinds and styles of accommodation, to suit the ever-growing demand for different experiences, tastes, and pockets of travellers.

The nature of tourist accommodation

Hotels, perhaps because they are amongst the oldest and most conventional and visible forms of tourist accommodation, spring readily to mind when one thinks about places, other than the homes of friends or family, that may accommodate tourists. Of course, hotels take many different forms: large, high-rise city hotels; suburban 'boutique' hotels; family-orientated establishments in coastal resorts; no-frills business hotels, etc.

Indeed, the word 'hotel' is a somewhat restrictive term. It is probably more useful to talk of 'tourist accommodation', given the range of establishments that might and do accommodate travellers today (see Example box opposite). An incomplete list would include: guesthouses, bed-and-breakfast establishments ('B&Bs'), holiday flats, holiday homes and holiday farms, game lodges, bush lodges and tented camps, backpacker establishments, youth hostels, caravan parks and campsites, resorts, golf estates, casino hotels, conference hotels, **timeshare**/sectional-title developments, long-stay and all-suite hotels, and self-catering establishments. Even trains and cruise-liners, in specific circumstances, may be defined as tourist accommodation. It is clearly beyond the scope of this chapter to describe and discuss every kind of hospitality accommodation product. We can do no more than deal in a general way with tourist accommodation. In doing so, this chapter will often use the example of a hotel, although nearly all the principles covered can be applied equally to the many other forms of tourist accommodation.

Figure 6.1 Four examples of the many forms of tourist accommodation

Example Preamble in an international travel guide's listing of accommodation in SA

The whole range of accommodation available is a reflection of the diversity of the country itself. A fantasy resort hotel like the Palace of the Lost City at Sun City, and Cape Town's elegant Mount Nelson, offer every conceivable luxury and bear comparison with the best in the world. Charming alternatives are the guest cottages found in most *dorps* (country villages), where tranquillity and hearty, home-cooked fare is valued far more than modern convenience. Farmsteads and safari lodges provide a lavish and expensive Africa experience, while campsites and backpacker hostels offer basic amenities and cater for the younger visitor on limited budgets.

bed and breakfast	a family (private) home, where the manager/owner lives in the house or on the property, that provides accommodation (with or without an en-suite bathroom) and breakfast
self-catering	a house, cottage, chalet, bungalow, flat, studio, apartment, villa, houseboat, tent, or any accommodation where facilities and equipment are provided for guests to cater for themselves
backpacker and hostelling	an accommodation establishment that provides communal facilities, including dormitories, for transient guests
caravan and camping park	a facility that provides ablution and toilet amenities and space for guests to provide their own accommodation such as a tent, motor home, or caravan.

In its monthly publication of tourist accommodation statistics, Statistics South Africa (Stats SA, 2006), categorises accommodation types as:

- hotels
- caravan parks and camping sites
- guesthouses and guest-farms
- other accommodation.

On the other hand, the Tourism Grading Council of South Africa (TGCSA) (2006) categorises tourist accommodation according to the following types, and provides a definition of each:

hotel	provides accommodation to the travelling public, has a reception area, and offers at least a breakfast room or communal eating area
lodge	an accommodation facility located in natural surroundings, and usually charging rates inclusive of all meals and the experience offered at the lodge
guesthouse	an existing home or purpose-designed building, which is a commercial enterprise, providing overnight accommodation with public areas for the exclusive use of guests

Although neither of these two classification systems is rigorous or comprehensive, they provide some assistance in delineating the most common forms of tourist accommodation in South Africa today. Despite its considerable diversity, the common thread and defining characteristic of all tourist accommodation is that it is accommodation provided to transient guests – that is, to tourists. Chapter 1 (Introduction to tourism) referred to the United Nations World Tourism Organisation's (UN-WTO) definition of a tourist as 'a person travelling to and staying in places outside their usual environment for not more than one consecutive year for leisure, business or other purposes' (UN-WTO, 2004). This definition rules out the many so-called 'residential hotels' in South Africa, which seems appropriate, at least insofar as any study of *tourist* accommodation is concerned. A large resort may feature more than one type of accommodation. *Sun City*, for example, includes the downscale *Cabanas*, with small, rather cramped but modestly-priced rooms, as well as the ultra-luxurious *Palace of the Lost City*, with deluxe, spacious, and expensive accommodation.

Tourist accommodation in South Africa – a brief modern history

Pre-1960s

South Africa has boasted inns, taverns, and public houses since the early history of European settlement (see Chapter 2 – History of tourism). According to Norval (1936: 104), however, it was not until 1913 that the country consciously began to seek to attract foreign visitors as an economic activity for the purpose of national gain. This first effort took the form of an advertising campaign run by the (then) South African Railways and Harbours (SAR&H). More than two decades later, the same writer observed that 'South African hotels…are [not] all that can reasonably be expected of them. There is much room for improvement, particularly amongst the small country hotels, which have almost entirely neglected the accommodation side of their business and concentrated unduly on the bar side' (Norval, 1936: 227).

This preoccupation with liquor was a consequence of government policy which, until the 1960s, although nominally supportive of economic development through tourism growth, was in practice driven by a desire to control the sorts of premises in which alcohol could be consumed. An establishment with 10 bedrooms that provided meals was deemed eligible for a liquor licence, and many public houses ('pubs') merely added 10 basic rooms with minimum facilities in order to qualify for one.

There were 1 144 licensed hotels in South Africa by 1935. More than half of them had 24 or fewer rooms, and many of these were owned and operated by individuals seeking 'their fortune in the liquor trade' from establishments that were 'nothing but subterfuges for bars' (Norval, 1936: 234–247). This lamentable state of affairs persisted until the early 1960s.

Mid-1960s to late 1970s

Matters were precipitated by the shock announcement in 1962 that Johannesburg's old Carlton

Hotel, without doubt South Africa's most important hotel at the time, was to close, with poor profits and low returns cited as the reason (*Financial Mail*, 1962). The government's response was to appoint a commission of enquiry into the hotel trade. At that time there were 1 650 licensed hotels in South Africa (*Financial Mail*, 1963). A Hotels Act was promulgated in 1965, in pursuance of the recommendations of the Hotel Commission. A Hotel Board was established and a grading system introduced for the first time in South Africa in 1966, followed by the roll-out in 1967 of a set of income-tax allowances designed to encourage the development of new, better hotels. These tax allowances were linked to the grading system in such way as to grant tax concessions on a sliding scale related to the hotel's grading. For example, a 5-star hotel could write off its cost of development against income over 13 years, and a one-star hotel over 23 years. In future, a hotel's tax status was to be driven by its grading, which would be policed by the Hotel Board.

A flurry of hotel development across South Africa followed the implementation of these policy initiatives, some milestones of which were:

- 1965: Sol Kerzner (later to be labelled the 'Sun King' by the media for his role in bringing the famous *Sun City* resort to fruition) opens his first – and, at the time, South Africa's most luxurious – new hotel, the *Beverly Hills* at Umhlanga Rocks, and Cape Town's city council approves tenders for a new 5-star hotel (the *Heerengracht)* in the CBD.
- 1967: the 5-star *President Hotel* opens in Johannesburg, and Cape Town's *Mount Nelson Hotel* is substantially upgraded.
- 1968: the Holiday Inn group is launched in South Africa, with plans to develop a country-wide chain of middle-market hotels.
- 1969: South African Breweries, in partnership with Kerzner, forms a new subsidiary – Southern Sun Hotels.
- 1970: the *Elangeni* hotel is launched on eThekwini's beachfront, and the *Tollman Towers* hotel opens in Johannesburg.
- 1971: the *Malibu Hotel* opens in eThekwini, a new *Holiday Inn* commences operations

adjacent to Johannesburg's O.R. Tambo airport, and the 5-star *Elizabeth Hotel* is completed in Port Elizabeth.

- 1972: the new 600-room *Carlton Hotel* – hailed as the largest in the southern hemisphere – opens in downtown Johannesburg, and the *Beacon Island Hotel* at Plettenberg Bay is completed.
- 1973: the 5-star *Landdrost Hotel* opens in Johannesburg.
- 1977: the 21st Holiday Inn in southern Africa opens in Vanderbijlpark.
- 1978: eThekwini's 5-star *Maharani Hotel* opens.
- 1979: Southern Sun, with 25 hotels (4 300 rooms) is listed on the Johannesburg Stock Exchange (JSE), and *Sun City* opens.

The hotel industry in South Africa flourished during the 1970s, with average annual occupancies seldom falling below 65% (Bureau of Financial Analysis, January 1975 to December 1979). Kessel Feinstein Consulting correctly observed that the hotel industry in South Africa came of age during the 1970s: 'before the 1970s, South Africa had only a very few first-class hotels; by the end of that decade, the country could boast hotels of international standard in all its major cities' (1992: 49).

The 1980s

Towards the end of the 1970s and in the early 1980s, the award of casino licences in South Africa's supposedly independent *Bantustan* 'states' – especially the Transkei and Bophuthatswana – spurred the development of major hotel resorts in these jurisdictions against the background of a general prohibition on gambling (other than horse-racing) elsewhere in South Africa at that time. The huge profits from casino operations provided returns that could justify significant capital investment in, amongst others, *Sun City* (1979) in Bophuthatswana (the North West province), and the *Wild Coast Holiday Inn and Casino* (1981) in the Transkei (the Eastern Cape's Wild Coast). It is almost certain that without casino rights the building of these and other large and lavish resorts would never have been contemplated.

Other, non-casino, hotel development was initiated in the major cities during the 1980s, following a further improvement in the income-tax incentives in 1980. These afforded an even more generous writing-off of hotel development costs for 3-, 4- and 5-star hotels. Amongst the new properties to be built at this time were:

- 1982: the Sandton *Holiday Inn*
- 1983: the 5-star *Cape Sun*
- 1984: the *Sandton Sun* and Tshwane *Holiday Inn*
- 1985: the eThekwini *Holiday Inn*
- 1986: the 800-room *Johannesburg Sun*.

Apartheid largely excluded black South Africans from the mainstream hotel industry. Protests against apartheid led to unstable social conditions, which impacted on the hotel industry. South Africa's hotel occupancies averaged only 56% during the five years between 1983 and 1987, and in 1986 dropped to an unprecedented low of 49% (Bureau of Financial Analysis and Central Statistical Service).

The grading-linked income-tax incentives for new hotel development were withdrawn in 1988. Since then, all new hotel developments have been entitled to only a 5% per annum building-cost write-off, regardless of grading.

Current conditions

The sustained growth in international tourism, which began in the latter part of the 1980s, gathered momentum with the country's transition to democracy in 1994, and continued through the course of the 1990s. Overseas tourist arrivals increased more than threefold between 1990 (0,5-million) and 2000 (1,6-million), while total foreign tourist numbers grew over eightfold; from one million in 1990 to almost 8,4-million in 2006.

As may be expected, this considerable growth in foreign tourism, accompanied by a steady expansion of domestic tourism (mostly white South Africans) on the back of a growing economy, represented a considerable boom for the tourist accommodation sector. It inspired a burgeoning in the supply of all forms of tourist accommodation, including a proliferation of guesthouses, B&Bs, game and other lodges. Other major new ventures which stimulated and supported the growth of tourist accommodation in recent years include:

- Cape Town's Victoria and Alfred Waterfront (inaugurated in 1988), visited by 22-million people a year (*Cape Times*, 2006: 23; *Business Day*, 2006: 15). The first of its many hotels, the *Victoria and Alfred Hotel*, opened in 1990
- The construction of international-calibre convention centres in Midrand (1993), eThekwini (1997), Sandton (2000), and Cape Town (2003)
- Significant upgrading and extension of all South Africa's international airports.

According to *Stats SA*, there is now a total of about 5 500 tax-registered public and private enterprises in South Africa that are mainly engaged in providing tourist accommodation (*StatsSA*, 2006: 7). The general trading conditions of modern-day tourist accommodation operations in South Africa are examined below.

Example New Soweto hotel

Soweto's first 4-star hotel – the 46-room *Freedom Square Hotel* – recently commenced operations in the Walter Sisulu Square of Dedication in Kliptown, in what *Finweek* (2006: 92) predicts will contribute towards 'the rapid transformation of Soweto from a once dusty and derelict township into a fully-fledged commercial hub'.

Emergence of the modern 'no-frills' product

Following the lead set in North America and Europe, a new type of hotel emerged in South Africa in the late 1980s. This was the so-called 'limited-service hotel'. Possibly ahead of its time, the first such establishment to be built here was the 123-room *City Lodge,* which opened in Randburg (adjacent to Johannesburg) in 1985.

It was also the first hotel venture of the new City Lodge Group. This was the early prototype of a novel kind of establishment, variously referred to as a budget hotel, economy hotel, no-frills hotel, restricted-service hotel, or limited-service hotel.

A **limited-service hotel** is one that offers guests no or very few facilities other than sleeping accommodation. Such non-accommodation facilities or services as may be offered are usually simple ones that are generally undemanding in terms of equipment, labour, and management.

From the outset, limited-service hotels were promoted as being something different from lower-graded hotels – that is, from hotels that were merely cheap. The focus of this new product would be on providing simple, minimalist establishments with clean, small, but comfortable guest bedrooms, and to severely curtail, if not altogether eradicate, all other facilities, amenities, and services commonly associated with hotels: not only restaurants, bars, and room service, but also valet and laundry services, shops, meeting/conference rooms, banqueting facilities, gymnasiums, hairdressing salons, etc.

In fact, there were a number of important motivations underpinning the emergence of this new product-offering concept:

- *Market pressures*: various factors, including the declining rand exchange rate, were increasingly putting conventional hotels beyond the pockets or reach of South African holidaymakers, and many business travellers too. Limited-service hotels offered the prospect of an affordable alternative.
- *Rising labour costs and union pressures*: these were having the effect of driving up wages in the catering and hotel sectors. Limited-service hotels, because of their radically lower staffing requirements, provided management with the means of largely obviating these productivity-related issues in an otherwise highly labour-intensive sector.
- *Operational pressures*: limited-service hotels, with their virtual absence of food and beverage operations, banqueting and other complex functions, are far simpler to run, have fewer departments, and a much smaller staff complement to manage. Indeed, Cooper

et al. (2005) see this disaggregation of accommodation from other hotel services as an important general trend in the hotel sector (2005: 399). This is very much in evidence in the USA too, through the contracting-out of restaurants in particular: a trend that is also in evidence to some extent in South Africa (for example, Café Maude in the Garden Court Sandton City, and Villamoura in the Sandton Sun).

- *Lower risk*: international research (such as *Deloitte's Hotel Benchmark Survey*, 2003, quoted in Global Hotel Network, 2003) demonstrates that in times of economic contraction or in oversupply situations, the market trades down; i.e. higher-graded hotels have to discount their prices, or lose business to hotels offering cheaper rates. Limited-service hotels generally trade at a far higher margin than full-service hotels, and they therefore have more capacity to withstand price competition.
- *Financial pressures*: the absence of extensive public areas – restaurants, bars, meeting rooms, and the like – as well as the back-of-house facilities they imply (kitchens, stores, goods-receiving bays, cold-rooms, staff change-rooms, canteens, etc) greatly reduce the capital cost of a limited-service hotel compared with a full-service hotel of equivalent capacity.

As Payne (2005) points out, '…the capital required to build one medium-size, mid-price, full-service hotel could build three or four economy/limited-service hotels'. A profitable operation requiring a relatively small capital outlay translates into a high **return on investment** (ROI). All other things being equal, a new full-service hotel is unlikely to generate as high an ROI as a new limited-service hotel in its early years. This should not be taken to imply that a limited-service hotel will necessarily produce a higher amount, that is rand value, of profit than its full-service equivalent, but it will very likely generate a significantly higher *ratio* of profit relative to its capital cost.

When first unveiled in South Africa, this concept was greeted with some scepticism in industry circles, even though the first examples were not quite as 'pure' or austere as their counterparts overseas: amongst other things, the South African version provided guests with the option of a cooked breakfast in contrast to the typical overseas model at that time, which usually provided only a Continental-style breakfast (breads with coffee or tea) on a self-service or buffet basis.

It took some time for the limited-service hotel product to catch on in South Africa. It was not until 1992 that Southern Sun made a serious foray into this segment. It firstly converted a number of its conventional hotels into limited-service *Holiday Inn Garden Courts* (recently re-branded *Garden Court*), which were followed later by purpose-designed hotels of this type and brand, and, secondly, entered into a joint venture with the French group Accor to roll out the latter's *Formule 1* (its name later modified to *Formula 1*) limited-service brand in South Africa. Amongst other brands soon to emerge were *Days Inn* (from the USA) and *Landmark Lodge* (a locally-developed product, later adopted by Protea Hotels).

This new type of hotel is quite well developed in South Africa today, and has expanded and diversified into many different brands. There is, in fact, a hierarchy of brands nowadays within the limited-service segment which is partially illustrated in Figure 6.2 overleaf.

There is some blurring at the edges of the limited-service segment, so that in some cases it is not always obvious what the fundamental difference is between this type of tourist accommodation and, say, a holiday flat. Also, as Payne (2005) has noted, the product is always in transition. New amenities and services are added (sometimes referred to as 'service creep') in an effort to make a particular property more appealing than its competitor. For example, following trends elsewhere in the world, both *City Lodge* and *Garden Court* have added well-equipped exercise rooms to some of their hotels. There is presumably the danger that if service creep continues, and as additional staff and costs accrue, the product will start to undermine the fundamentals that enable it to operate more cost-effectively than its full-service counterpart. For the time being, this danger seems somewhat

Figure 6.2 Differences within the limited-service segment

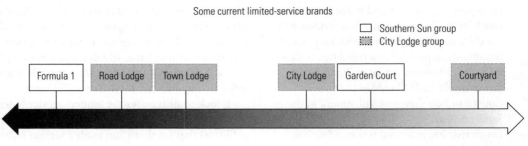

Some current limited-service brands

☐ Southern Sun group
▦ City Lodge group

| Formula 1 | Road Lodge | Town Lodge | City Lodge | Garden Court | Courtyard |

Lower price – smaller room – fewer facilities   Higher price – larger room – more facilities

theoretical; at least based on the evidence of the City Lodge group, which has been able to post increasing rather than declining ratios of EBITDA (earnings before interest, tax, depreciation and amortisation, expressed as a ratio of total revenue): in 1999 the ratio was 49,3%; in 2003 it was 51,8%; and in 2005 it was 52,5% (City Lodge, 2005: 17).

Accommodation demand

The nature of accommodation demand

According to Cook, Yale, and Marqua: 'even before a new property opens for business, sales and marketing efforts begin and should never end… no matter how simple or complex the marketing effort, the ultimate goal is to attract future bookings…' (2006: 199). Indeed, business in significant quantities will not 'automatically' or inevitably materialise merely because the establishment has been built and exists.

As Holloway points out: 'the demand for hotel bedrooms stems from a widely-distributed market, nationally or internationally; whereas the market for other facilities which the hotel offers – such as restaurant meals, meeting facilities, and banqueting – will often be localised' (2006: 285). It is normally useful for managers and marketers to segment demand into different categories based on such criteria as geographic origin (for example, domestic and overseas), purpose of

travel (for example, leisure and business), travel method (independent and group), etc., since each category is likely to have different needs and requirements, pricing sensitivity, seasonal preferences, and so on, and also because there may be varying expectations about the future growth of particular segments.

Roubi and Litteljohn (2006: 380–381) point out that demand for accommodation is, to a great measure, *derived demand*, in the sense that it follows from and is secondary to the more primary decision to travel: typically, travellers first make a decision about *where* they want to travel to, and then make a decision about where they will *stay* when they get there. Roubi and Litteljohn note, however, that there are exceptions to this in the case of what are called 'destination hotels', which is where the accommodation itself is the primary motivation for the holidaymaker (2006: 380–381). South African examples, amongst others, include resorts such as *Umgazi River Bungalows* at Port St John, *Club Mykonos* on the Cape west coast, and *Sun City*.

Demand for accommodation is, to a greater or lesser extent, seasonal. Resort properties tend to experience a fairly high degree of **seasonality**, with demand peaking in the summer months and/or during holiday periods. The Western Cape, as a winter rainfall area, experiences a fairly severe drop in occupancies between May and August; often as much as 40 percent. City hotels on the other hand, generally experience far less volatility, although business demand may drop quite low over the December and early-January period.

An intriguing feature of accommodation demand is that the person who actually stays in the accommodation may not be what Roubi and Litteljohn refer to as the 'travel decision-taker'; namely the person placing the booking (2006: 381). This might be the case, for example, when package tours are sold or when business-travel arrangements are made by the traveller's host (or an intermediary such as a **professional conference organiser** (PCO).

Assessing demand when contemplating new development

It is logical that a new hotel should not be built unless and until the developer has undertaken a proper feasibility study, starting with a careful analysis and assessment of the likely demand for the project contemplated. Indeed, many financiers and institutional investors today correctly insist that such an exercise be undertaken as a first and fundamental prerequisite to serious consideration of an application for financing. Some financiers, to encourage objectivity, will require the feasibility study to be undertaken by independent, professional experts.

This process may be a repetitive one, in which the original concept is modified, firstly until it properly correlates with the target markets that have been identified, and secondly until the project can be shown to be likely to generate an acceptable financial return on the estimated investment outlay. This process is illustrated schematically in Figure 6.3 below.

The potential for additional accommodation at any particular location will reflect the current success of the area, in tourism terms, and investors' views on how this might be affected by future social, economic, and travel trends (Roubi & Litteljohn, 2006: 379). These considerations will normally be manifested in the market study, particularly in its assumptions about future demand for and supply of accommodation.

The purpose of the market study is to assess:
* the expected level of demand for the project and its facilities, primarily in relation to accommodation, but also in terms of food, beverage, entertainment, meetings, banqueting, sport, and other facilities

Figure 6.3 The feasibility-assessment process

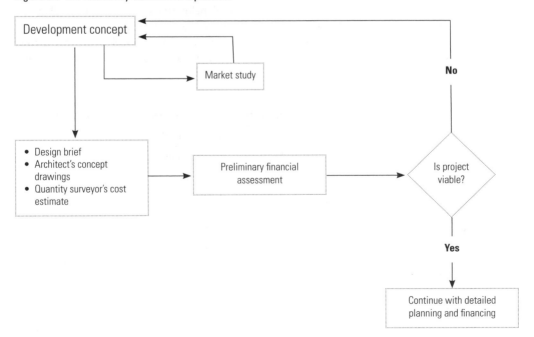

- the expected seasonality of that demand
- the likely mix of demand (as between leisure and business, domestic and international, etc.)
- a suitable standard and style of facilities
- an appropriate tariff structure that will be competitive in the light of what is to be offered and what competitive providers of tourist accommodation are offering.

Location is, without a doubt, of cardinal importance in the establishment of a new property, both in terms of the general area and also the particular siting of the project within that area: its visibility, access, orientation, views, neighbouring buildings, zoning stipulations, etc. As Holloway notes: 'location is... fixed for all time; if the resort itself loses its attraction for its visitors, the hotel will suffer an equivalent decline in its fortunes' (2006: 284). In fact, the question of location is very closely tied to the type of facility that is to be established – a business hotel will rate certain locative factors more important than, for instance, a resort hotel or a bush lodge, as illustrated in Table 6.1.

Because it is often difficult to convincingly demonstrate the viability of proposed new tourist accommodation projects, and because of general investor and financier wariness when it comes to funding them (hotels and other tourist accommodation are long-term in nature, and are often regarded as problematic and highly risky

investments), more project concepts fail than succeed in actually coming to fruition.

Trends in tourist accommodation marketing

International hotel chains have tended to diversify their brands in an effort to tap into different market segments and, in aggregate, to achieve as large a market penetration as possible. This has also happened to a degree in South Africa in chains such as Southern Sun and City Lodge and, to a lesser extent, Protea Hotels.

The Internet has had, and continues to have, a profound impact on the sale and distribution of accommodation (see Chapter 7 – Managing tourism distribution). As Holloway points out: 'it is making the large hotel groups far more independent [from airlines' global distribution systems] in their interface with customers' (2006: 299).

Internet websites such as *Orbitz* (www.orbitz.com), *Expedia* (www.expedia.com), lastminute.com, and *Travelocity* (www.travelocity.com) feature hotels, airlines, and car-hire; and have drawn a significant volume of business from travel agents. Holloway attributes the growth in website marketing to the fact that prices offered to consumers are often well below those available through more traditional outlets (2006: 273).

With more and more travellers content to book their own cheap airline seats and accommodation,

Table 6.1 Relative importance of selected locative criteria

Criterion	Business hotel	Resort	Bush lodge
proximity to major roads	High	High	Low
good visibility	High	Low	Low
close to restaurants	High	Low	Low
close to shopping	High	Low	Low
close to entertainment	High	Low	Low
good scenery	Low	High	High
hi-quality environment	Low	High	High
recreational amenities nearby	Low	High	Low
close to a business centre	High	Low	Low

together with the fact that most airlines no longer pay commissions to travel agents, '...few agents, apart from those dealing regularly with business travellers, are keen to handle hotel bookings as distinct from comprehensive travel services' (Holloway, 2006: 299).

However, according to eTurboNews (2006), online travel is no longer a novelty, and competition is intensifying as airlines and hotels redouble their efforts to get travellers to buy on their own site. Shares in online travel companies were reported to be flagging somewhat in the US in 2006. The large hotel groups, notes Holloway: 'are relying increasingly on their own websites to reach customers, in an effort to cut costs by avoiding payment of commission to intermediaries, airline – hotel and rental-car companies also vow that consumers can get the best deals on their

sites' (2006: 299). Future prospects for the online travel companies are said to be more favourable for international than for domestic bookings.

Levels of accommodation demand in South Africa

As indicated earlier, the strong growth in tourism through the 1990s was a bonanza for the tourist accommodation sector. Figure 6.4 illustrates that overall demand, expressed as average occupancy, has remained above 50% for the decade to 2005, rising to above 65% by the end of that period (a level last experienced in 1982); this despite a significant expansion in the accommodation stock and strong growth in average rate. Revpar – the combination of occupancy and average rate – has, as a consequence, also grown strongly in

Figure 6.4 A decade of key South African hotel trading statistics (1996–2005)

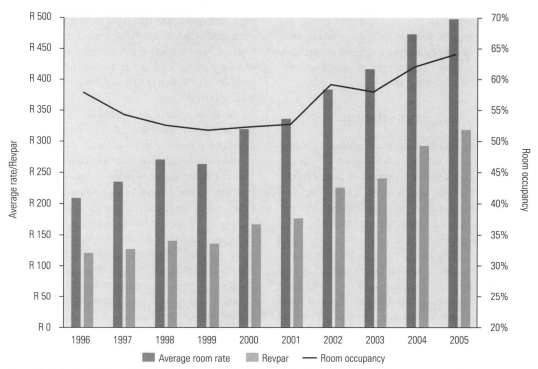

Source: Statistics South Africa: 1996 to February 2004 – Hotels: trading statistics (report P6441); September 2004 to 2005 – Tourism accommodation (report P6410); data for intervening period interpolated by author.

Table 6.2 Tourist accommodation statistics, 2005

	Hotels	Caravan parks and campsites	Guest-houses and guest farms	Other	All tourist accom-modation
Rooms or sites available	44 000	11 000	11 000	33 000	99 000
Average occupancy	64,0%	19,8%	46,6%	38,0%	48,5%
Average rate	R497	R185	R332	R292	R412
Revpar	R318	R37	R155	R111	R200
Accommodation revenue as a ratio of total gross revenue	64,4%	64,1%	70,2%	67,7%	65,5%

Adapted from Statistics South Africa, 2006

the last 10 years ahead of the rate of inflation in South Africa.

Hotels tend to attain significantly higher average rates of occupancy than other accommodation types. In contrast, caravan parks and campsites usually average rather low **occupancy** rates. Hotels also, on average, achieve appreciably higher rates than other forms of tourist accommodation (see Table 6.2 above).

Prices for accommodation

The actual accommodation facilities ('rooms operations') of tourist establishments generate substantially the greatest portion of both revenue and profits of the business. As Cook, Yale, and Marqua observed: 'a great deal of management effort is therefore logically directed towards devising strategies for maximising occupancy levels and room rates' (2006: 204). Pricing is, therefore, a key management preoccupation, especially given the product's high degree of **perishability** (see Chapter 14 – Marketing tourism businesses). Indeed, as Sharpley notes: 'the core product – selling bedrooms – is perishable; that is, an unsold room is business lost forever. Thus, a principal management task is to optimise profitability by balancing occupancy levels with room rates' (2005: 19).

This quest to maximise revenue is a relentless imperative which is all the more acute in

the case of tourist accommodation, because it is a high fixed-cost business; that is because hotels, lodges, and the like are highly capital- and labour-intensive; they usually have fixed interest costs and high staff overheads that have to be paid, whether occupancy rises or drops, and whether revenue is high or low. A hotel must generate revenue that at least exceeds its **fixed costs** (called the 'break-even' level of activity) to avoid incurring losses or 'falling into the red'.

In their efforts to maximise occupancy at the best price, accommodation establishments commonly have several different rates, so that revenue can be derived from a variety of markets. For example, whereas walk-in guests typically pay the standard tariff (also known as the '**rack rate**'), other categories of guests may be given a variety of discounts. For example, airlines which can guarantee the take-up of a negotiated minimum quantity of rooms a year will be offered a discount of perhaps 30% or 40%. Certain high-volume corporate customers would usually be charged discounted rates, as would conference organisers in relation to group bookings for specified conventions or other large events. Other groups who may receive preferential rates include senior citizens, frequent guests, and government employees. Special discounted rates may also be offered during off-season periods (or commissions offered to travel agents and tour operators for bookings made for these times), and special offers may be extended for accompanying children, or rates quoted which include breakfast and/or other meals, game drives, and the like. According to Holloway, a business hotel may offer packages with substantial discounts over weekends when its occupancy levels drop, and discounts of up to 50% are extended to guests who book late in the day, 'the hotel management recognising that any sale is better than none'(2006: 285).

In short, '…hotel operators are willing to forego higher rates in exchange for guaranteed consistency and revenues' (Cook, Yale, & Marqua, 2006: 204). And, as a consequence of this, 'rack rates… are rarely achieved, [and] yield, measured against potential, rarely runs at much more than 60% in the mid- to upper-market levels of the hotel industry…' (Cooper *et al.*, 2005: 387). The adoption of flexible pricing as a management tool for maximising revenue is commonly referred to as **yield management**, a term borrowed from the airline industry. Sophisticated software packages have been developed to implement and monitor yield management in hotels.

The practice of discounting also has a downside, though. As Roubi and Litteljohn caution: 'offering low prices which only make a contribution to fixed costs is not a strategy that can be maintained for all customers. Discounting may also become a problem when there is an overall downturn in demand, and many hotels at the same location engage in price competition' (2006: 387). Just such a situation developed that had dire consequences for many operators in South Africa. The volatile social conditions in South Africa during the 1980s, and their deleterious effect on the hotel industry (referred to in *Tourist accommodation in South Africa – a brief modern history* above) led to a price war, which saw the *real* (i.e. adjusted for inflation) nationwide average rate decline by 26,5% between 1984 and 1989, accompanied by a 5% drop in occupancy during the same period (Caras, 1990). Not only did rate-discounting during this period fail to stave off an overall drop in occupancy; it left many hotels deeply in the red.

Yield management is the process by which management deliberately and systematically applies strategies for maximising revenues that optimally price its accommodation capacity. This usually involves the setting and adjustment of rates that cater for fluctuations in demand caused by seasonal factors and other market dynamics.

Quality and grading

Service and the tourism-accommodation sector

According to Wright (1990: 194), hotels initially concentrated in the main on providing better physical facilities to differentiate themselves from their competitors. This type of distinction, however, is no longer sufficient to sustain superiority: 'the battle for the hearts and minds of guests [is being] fought out in the service areas of the hotel' (Wright, 1990: 194). This evolution has also occurred in South Africa over the last 30 years. In the mid-1960s, an en-suite bathroom, wall-to-wall carpeting and in-room air-conditioning would have been regarded as sumptuous; the height of luxury. These amenities are routinely available today, even in limited-service hotels!

Customer expectations have advanced in tandem with a general improvement in the physical facilities provided by establishments. A hotel may still be able to generate a higher occupancy and tariff by virtue of its superior location, or larger and more luxurious guest bedrooms; but these physical distinctions become increasingly difficult to sustain when newer, more luxurious competition is built in a similarly good location. Hotel operators have come to realise that, important though the physical features of their product are, the standard and quality of service they provide may be what ultimately distinguishes their product from others. 'Human' issues, such as guest recognition, friendliness, courtesy, skill, helpfulness, and efficiency, applied consistently by well-trained staff, may garner more customers and a greater frequency of repeat business that ultimately translates into higher occupancy at better tariffs. As Dallas and Buoy point out in their discussion of the 'customer-for-life' concept, 'servicing repeat guests is more profitable than prospecting for new ones' (1999: 16–17). Indeed, research conducted by Knowles (1998: 293) suggests that the cost of acquiring a new customer is five times higher than retaining an existing one.

The service challenge

Managing quality is a difficult challenge in most industries. Three challenges in tourism make it especially problematic for the hospitality industry:

- it is difficult to know if the client is satisfied – a mere absence of reported complaints is no assurance that customers are not dissatisfied
- since the service is consumed at the same time that it is created, it is impossible to control its quality in advance – the customer tests it
- consumers nowadays are better-travelled, more experienced, probably have higher expectations than before, and have become more critical in their perception of quality.

In an industry where the 'product' is, mainly, services provided by fallible human beings, there is no guarantee that today's perfection will be carried forward to tomorrow. Managing service quality is a relentless process. Sharpley contends that this is the main challenge facing the accommodation sector (2005: 16).

Yet striving for service quality may often be the most realistic way of improving profitability. Clearly, profits can only be increased by either reducing costs or increasing revenue. In the case of tourist accommodation, though, the scope for reducing costs and overheads is limited. Of course, it is management's task to constantly apply its vigilance, energy, and ingenuity to minimising and containing input costs and overheads. However, there are practical thresholds below which costs cannot be reduced without fundamentally changing the nature of the business and its product-offering in the segment of the market in which it operates. Management's only other avenue for greater profit is to increase revenues. There are, essentially, only two ways in which this

can be done: by increasing volume (occupancy) or by raising prices (rates). Tourist accommodation providers try to do both, of course – that is, to maximise occupancy at the best possible rate. In many cases though, it may be more difficult for a single business to achieve increased profitability through higher volume than through a higher price, since there are many factors beyond management's control that might affect volume. Price of accommodation is more directly related to quality, and quality is something that is mostly under management's control.

Customers are prepared to pay a premium for quality, because tourism services are extremely personal to the user or purchaser. In some cases quality may, to a large degree, stem from the physical standard of the facilities, equipment and product-offering. However, in most cases, quality is also significantly a function of the *standard* of service delivery. Although it is by no means easy to attain and maintain high service standards, they are at least something entirely within management's domain. For example, a hotelier may not be able to do much about the inconvenient location of his or her establishment, the smallness of its rooms, the new competition which has opened nearby, etc. Management, however, can certainly influence the friendliness of its reception staff, the efficiency of room-service, and so on, and management can be instrumental in introducing the personal touches which make ordinary guests feel special. In addition, various aspects of service can often be improved without necessarily incurring additional costs: a good attitude costs no more than a surly one. Diligent management should cost no more than sloppy management, and so on.

While it would be simplistic to suggest that volume is driven by external factors alone, or that price is entirely a function of service (currency exchange rates are an example of an external factor that does impact on price), it is certainly true that it becomes easier, within reason, to justify higher prices when better standards of service are offered. People will pay more for better service. Put another way: 'a customer will forgive a hotel with a poor, outdated product if he or she receives memorable service' (Wright, 1990: 195).

Managing and measuring service

A requirement for effective quality management is that it should be a holistic, continuous process embedded in the ordinary operations of the business. It should be an integral part of the business' corporate culture. According to Knowles, the concept of total quality management comprises six interrelated elements (1998: 297–299):

- the institution of recognition-and-reward systems whereby employees are recognised and rewarded (financially and otherwise) for providing consistently good service (e.g. an 'employee of the month' award)
- the provision of appropriate, skills-based education and training
- effective communication with both guests and staff . The latter should be from management to staff and *vice versa*, as well as horizontally across departments in order to ensure commonality of understanding and purpose with respect to guest requirements and service delivery
- the inculcation of an attitude and commitment in which every manager and staff member feels they are 'on the same side', and with management showing that it 'practises what it preaches'
- systems and methods in which processes are well documented, so that improvements are recognised and defects systematically identified, analysed, and eliminated
- the setting of targets and goals that are well defined and communicated, and regularly reviewed and adjusted.

The above principles reinforce the idea that in a service-oriented business, such as the provision of tourist accommodation, the quality of service delivered is inextricably related to the quality of the establishment's staff – their attitude, training, competence, skills, and level of job satisfaction. A study by Iacobucci (2000) shows the statistical association between employee satisfaction and customer satisfaction, and argues that the reverse is also true: happy customers provide a better working environment.

There are several ways of monitoring service quality; among them:

- guest/customer satisfaction questionnaires (CSQs) – these often take the form of 'tent' cards in guest bedrooms, inviting the guest to answer set service-related questions
- *ad hoc* surveys of customers' perceptions – preferably designed and executed with the assistance of independent specialists to ensure objectivity
- the use of 'mystery guests' (again, preferably according to a programme administered by independent specialists/researchers) who, at randomly-timed visits under the guise of regular guests, assess and record particular aspects of service.

These and other research methods, if executed in a consistent and objective way and administered correctly, can serve both as a meaningful indicator of service quality and as effective management tools when converted into the proper corrective action.

Standard grading systems

From the consumer's perspective, the likely or probable standard of the tourist accommodation he or she has booked remains unknown and unverified until it is actually experienced. By then, of course, there is little practical redress for a disappointed customer. In most cases it would probably be too late to secure alternative accommodation, and it might be difficult or even impossible to extract a refund or any other compensation from the establishment which has provided the below-expectation experience. The disappointed guest's only remedy is not to patronise that establishment again. But this is cold comfort, for example, to someone on a once-in-a-lifetime visit to a particular destination.

Faced as it is with this sort of 'gamble', the travelling public (directly or through their agents) have looked to independent gradings or ratings to provide some basic **benchmark** when selecting an accommodation establishment. Various accreditation systems have emerged to grade or rate hotel accommodation and other tourist and hospitality services; their object being to signal to the potential user the standard and also, explicitly or implicitly, the relative cost of the relevant service. Perhaps one of the most famous of these is *The Michelin Guide*, the European restaurant-rating publication. Similar official or unofficial classification systems have been developed for hotels and other tourist accommodation. They often take the form of a 5-star grading system, with one star being the lowest (and cheapest) grading, and five stars the highest (and most expensive). This approach enjoys widespread use throughout the world, although there are vast differences in how these gradings are applied from one country to another. Even so, they provide some guidance to a traveller in determining the relative standard of establishments within a particular geographic jurisdiction. Of course, any grading system is very much a blunt instrument; one that does not cater for the nuances and subtle differences between establishments that are so important to guest enjoyment.

TOURISM GRADING COUNCIL
OF SOUTH AFRICA
TGCSA's distinctive and easily recognisable logo

Grading accommodation in South Africa

When the hotel tax incentives in South Africa were withdrawn in 1988 (see *Tourist accommodation in South Africa – a brief Modern History*), the grading system lost its impetus and effectiveness. It defaulted to a voluntary system, and ultimately lost considerable credibility when many operators and some major groups opted out of it altogether. This void was filled by other accommodation-grading schemes, including one run by another government entity, the South African Bureau of Standards (SABS) with its so-called Crystal Grading Scheme. There was for a while, a bizarre situation where two competing government

agencies vied for recognition as *the* official grading agency (*Cape Times*, 2002; *Business Report*).

Eventually, the Tourism Grading Council of South Africa (TGCSA) (established in 2000) was resuscitated. It set about the business of re-grading tourist accommodation establishments in 2001 with a new star-grading system and fee structure. SABS announced in 2004 that it would abandon its system in deference to that of the TGCSA (*Travel News Now*, 2004).

TGCSA claims that, currently, more than three-quarters of tourist accommodation rooms have been graded under its system (TGCSA, 2006). Importantly, this national grading system extends beyond hotels to other forms of tourist accommodation. It is being further broadened to encompass other tourist facilities and services such as meetings, exhibitions, special events, and restaurants. While the system remains a voluntary one, government is using moral persuasion (some might say bullying) to induce compliance by all operators.

The grading criteria of the TGCSA relate to the functional and physical characteristics of the establishment seeking grading, and to the range and level of services the establishment provides to its guests. Its serviced accommodation grading criteria (SAGC) cautions that taste and fashion have no influence on its grading. There are, however, minimum requirements pertaining to the maintenance of the buildings, structures, grounds, fittings, fixtures, and furnishings, including specifications as to bedroom size, quality of beds, furniture, bathrooms, lighting, curtains, and a plethora of other physical characteristics and features, as well as a raft of requirements concerning the range of services and amenities to be made available to guests, depending on the applicable category of accommodation (referred to in *The nature of tourist accommodation* above).

The grading process involves a TGCSA assessor carrying out an on-site assessment benchmarked against its documented Minimum Requirements and Grading Criteria for the category of grading sought by the establishment. The assessor's recommendation is referred to the TGCSA Awards Committee, which confers the grading. This is carried out according to a 5-star scale for each of the accommodation categories. TCGSA has confirmed (*Business Report*, 2003) that there is no such thing as a 6-star hotel grading, and that claims about particular establishments being of 6-star quality are a 'marketing myth'. A grading is only valid for 12 months, and each property is re-assessed once a year. TGCSA also employs a mystery-guest system to monitor adherence to grading standards.

www

Browse this website: www.tourismgrading.co.za

Discussion point

Discuss the benefits that accrue to an accommodation provider from accreditation by the TGCSA.

Other quality-assurance resources

The Internet provides a simple but most effective alternative means to enable a traveller to predetermine the likely quality and suitability of tourist accommodation. One website that can assist a traveller in this way, for example, is *TripAdvisor* (www.tripadvisor.com). Aside from serving as a search engine to link to sites with booking facilities for hotels worldwide (which many other websites nowadays do), it also provides frank and objective reports on a large database of hotels, both positive and negative, by guests who have stayed at them recently.

This sort of authentic, informal feedback by actual guests is likely to be far more persuasive to a potential visitor than either the establishment's own promotional blurb or gradings conferred by impersonal agencies against perhaps unknown criteria. It is likely that the practice of seeking quality endorsements of this sort through the Internet will become more widespread in the future.

Hotel operations, and hotel failures

There have been many hotel failures in South Africa. This no doubt contributes to the general perception amongst financiers that the sector is a high-risk one. Some fine old hotels with

proud histories have disappeared, such as the *Grand Hotel* in Cape Town's CBD; Johannesburg's *Carlton Hotel* (both the original property and its successor), and many others. Some newer and flashier properties have gone the same way (the *President* and *Johannesburg Sun* hotels, for example). In some cases, entire chains have failed, been wound-up or taken over, including *Aventura*, *Karos Hotels*, *Stocks Leisure* and *Cullinan Hotels*.

The reasons why businesses in the tourist accommodation sector fail are diverse and not necessarily always easy to pinpoint. There are, no doubt, instances when a combination of factors can contribute to their demise. These reasons can be conveniently grouped into several categories:

- *Faulty product concept*: the wrong or inappropriate product for the intended market; a poor location; an oversupply situation in the relevant market at that location; development costs that are too high and cannot be sustained; or a project that is not financially viable for other reasons.
- *Inappropriate financing*: the business's gearing is too high (meaning that there is too much borrowing relative to owners' equity); the loan terms are too onerous and cannot be serviced from available cash flow; the practice of 'borrowing short to invest long', that is trying to finance fixed assets such as land and buildings with short-term borrowings, like a bank overdraft, that can be called at any time; or sourcing loans in a strong foreign currency which must be repaid later out of depreciated rands.
- *Inept management*: a poorly-run operation which gets a bad reputation, causing occupancy to drop and the achieved average rate to wilt; poor/ineffective cost and revenue controls resulting in low or declining profitability; badly-targeted or insufficient marketing; poor information, accounting and/or operating systems; poor staff-management practices leading to low employee morale and a drop in standards; etc.
- *Exogenous events*: deterioration or environmental degradation of the area in which the establishment is located; political

or social instability that results in a decline in tourism; crime and violence; severe economic contraction; intractable industrial disputes; etc.

- *Other reasons*: over-ambitious group expansion; ill-considered diversification, and other strategic blunders.

Although beyond the scope of this chapter, it would be instructive to carefully analyse the various South African hotel failures in recent history, if for no other reason than to learn how to avoid similar pitfalls in the future.

Conclusion

The rather simple idea of 'a bed away from home' has developed into an almost bewildering array of types, styles, and brands of tourist accommodation serving the needs of all manner of travellers and their diverse preferences and requirements. This complexity places new and more intricate demands on all those who work in and serve the industry.

Notwithstanding technology's pervasive intrusion into peoples' lives, the hotel and its equivalent is still more dependent on actual human interaction than on call centres and automated responses: a warm welcome is more important than a high-speed modem. Even so, tourist accommodation is currently one of the most extensively-traded commodities on the Internet, and the growing use of this medium has already revolutionised the role of intermediaries in the hospitality chain.

Despite the many challenges of developing and then successfully running tourist accommodation in today's world, tourism destinations 'could not exist without accommodation' (Roubi and Litteljohn, 2006: 378). Ron Stringfellow, CEO of *Tsogo Sun Hotels*, says hotels are part of Africa's core infrastructure, and that their development should be high on every African leader's agenda (*Business Report*, 2004). Tourist accommodation certainly is, and will remain, an integral part of South Africa's economy.

1. What are the main management challenges facing accommodation establishment owners in South Africa?

2. How has the 'no frills' accommodation product-offering developed in South Africa since the late 1980s?

3. Outline the key characteristics of demand for accommodation.

4. Is the TGCSA grading scheme a good method of grading hotels and other forms of accommodation in S.A.? Suggest some ways in which the scheme may be improved.

5. What are some of the unique characteristics of the accommodation sector compared to other services businesses? To what extent does this represent a constraint to the implementation of quality service delivery?

Further reading

Journals

Journal of Hospitality and Tourism Research

International Journal of Hospitality and Tourism

Websites

FEDHASA: www.fedhasa.co.za

Global Hotel Network: www.GlobalHotelNetwork.com

HospitalityNET: www.hospitalitynet.org

Statistics South Africa: www.statssa.gov.za

TGCSA: www.tourismgrading.co.za

References

Bureau of Financial Analysis. *Hotel ratios* (various issues up to and including 1979), University of Tshwane, Tshwane.

Business Day 2006. 21 September *'V&A Waterfront sale 'will attract more foreigners'*

Business Report 2002, 2 May *'Hotel grading systems fight it out'*

Business Report 2003. 23 November, *'Six-star hotel ratings are a myth'*

Business Report 2004. 1 December , *'Hotels are part of Africa's core infrastructure'.*

Cape Times 2002, 1 May. *'Reach for the stars – or maybe crystals – in choosing accommodation'*

Caras, D. 1990. *'Beware of cutting rates to fill rooms'* in Hotelier & Caterer, July 1990.

Central Statistical Service (now Stats SA), Statistics of registered hotels, various issues from 1987 to February 2004.

City Lodge Hotels Limited, 2005. Annual report. '20 Years of the fundamentals', Sandton, p.16

Cook, R. A., Yale, L. J. & Marqua, J. J. 2006. *Tourism: the business of travel*, 3rd edition. New Jersey: Prentice Hall.

Cooper, C., Fletcher, J., Fyall, A., Gilbert, D., & Wanhill, S. (Eds.). 2005. Tourism: principles and practice, 3rd edition. New York: Longman.

Dallas, J. & Buoy, T. 1999. *'Industry trends: a glimpse into the new millennium'.* In 1999 National Lodging Forecast, New York: E and Y Kenneth Leventhal. 1999.

Financial Mail 1962. 14 December. *'Good-bye Carlton Hotel.'*

Finweek, 2006. 18 May. *'Hoteliers eye Soweto'*, p.92, Muller, J.

Holloway, J. C. 2006. *The business of tourism*, 7th edition. Harlow: Pearson.

Iacobucci, D. 2000: *'Golden rules for customer service'* 'Mastering Marketing', *Business Day*, 15 May 2000.

Global Hotel Network, 2003. [online]. Available from: www.ghr@globalhotelnetwork.com [8 January 2003]

Kessel Feinstein Consulting, 1992, Proposed income-tax allowances and incentives for tourist accommodation,

South African Tourist Board and The Federated Hospitality Association of South Africa, unpublished report.

Knowles, T. 1998. *Hospitality management*, 2nd edition. New York: Longman.

Norval, A. J. 1936. *The tourist industry: a national and international survey.* London: Pitman.

Payne, K. 2005. *'Economy lodging: always in transition'*, hospitality NET, [online]. Available from: www.info@hospitalitynet.org [28 January 2005].

Roubi ,S. & Litteljohn, D. 2006 'The accommodation subsector'. In Beech J & Chadwick S (Eds.). The business of tourism management, Harlow, England: Prentice-Hall, pp.377–399.

Sharpley, R. 2005. *'The accommodation sector: managing for quality'* In Pender, L. & Sharpley, R. *The management of tourism*. London: Sage Publications Ltd, pp.14–27.

Statistics South Africa (formerly: Central Statistical Service), 2006, Tourist accommodation, Statistical Release P6410, March, Tshwane.

TGCSA. 2006, Tourism Grading Council of South Africa [online]. Available from: www.tourismgrading.co.za [14 September 2006].

Travel News Now, 2004, *'Crystal Grading Scheme abandoned'*, Travel News Now [online]. Available from www.traveleditorial@nowmedia.co.za [5 July 2004]

eTurboNews, 2006, *'Online travel stocks stranded* [online]. Available from www.eturbonews.com [28 March 2006]

Wright, J. 1990. *'The service challenge'*, Quest 1990, pp.194–200.

Case study

6

Camps Bay Retreat

Objectives

- to provide an example of a boutique hotel
- to illustrate the diversity of factors that may affect strategy around the development of tourist accommodation

Camps Bay Retreat is an up-market boutique hotel situated on a secluded estate in the Glen area of Camps Bay, Cape Town. It has superlative sea and mountain views, and is within walking distance of both Camps Bay and Clifton beaches, and of the historic Round House and Glen Forest, which are part of the Cape Peninsula National Park.

Boutique hotels are a relatively new segment of the accommodation sector, and also one of the 'sexiest'. However, in general there is a lack of an accurate definition for the term 'boutique hotels'. It can encompass small single hotels, large luxury resorts, or hotels where modern design is the main attraction. Various names are embodied such as concept, townhouse or design-led.

The focal point of Camps Bay Retreat is a grand, two-storey manor-house (c.1929) – known as Earl's Dyke Manor – which is set in four secluded acres of attractive fynbos forest between two rugged ravines with flowing streams and pools.

This residential property was purchased in 2002 by Village and Life, a Cape Town-based group that operates hotels and self-catering tourist accommodation in the form of villas and apartments. It is perhaps best known for its novel street hotel – De Waterkant Village – in Cape Town's famous and picturesque Bo-Kaap precinct.

Two further adjoining residential properties have since been added to Camps Bay Retreat, bringing its total accommodation to 15 spacious rooms. Though the establishment has a 5-star guesthouse grading, it styles itself as a 'boutique hotel' located in a private nature reserve. Its facilities and services include:

- fully equipped guest rooms (with tea- and coffee-making facilities, satellite television, DVD player, mini-bar, air-conditioning, ADSL Internet access, etc)
- a fully-functional restaurant serving top-quality cuisine (breakfast, lunch, and dinner)
- room service until 10:00 p.m.
- a dining room, lounge and library
- a wellness centre, offering massages and treatments
- a gym, sauna, and spa bath
- guided walks in the grounds and forest
- pre-packed picnic baskets
- several swimming pools

- floodlit tennis courts
- business services.

Village and Life's CEO, Maree Brink, regards the defining feature of Camps Bay Retreat to be its secluded natural beauty, and the unique tranquility this bestows on the property, despite being within a stone's throw of the hustle and bustle of Camps Bay beachfront. 'Even when the hotel's full', says Brink, 'a guest can enjoy a quiet and peaceful ambience, feel at one with nature, and experience virtual solitude if he or she wants to'. Indeed, his vision for Camps Bay Retreat has been 'to create a unique nature reserve that transforms and unites the space between a suburban landscape and an alien forest, creating an inspiring, yet sustainable environment'. To this end, Camps Bay Retreat has engaged the full-time services of a qualified horticulturist, whose job it is to maintain the property's natural landscapes and gardens, and to restore them to their original indigenous state.

Brink stresses that the emphasis on the environment in the case of Camps Bay Retreat is fundamental, and even overrides return on investment. While the construction of a further two or three unobtrusive chalets within the wooded sections of the property is being considered, the company has rejected any notion of redeveloping it into a much larger accommodation complex, or even of substantially extending the existing facilities, which the site's large size could easily accommodate. The new chalets will be eco-friendly and designed with a 'very light footprint', so as not to detract from the natural environment.

The occupancy of Camps Bay Retreat is largely dependent on international demand, and is therefore quite seasonal. Village and Life's financial objective is to aggressively increase its average room rate over time, principally by enhancing and improving the property's natural environment. Based on experience to date, the company believes that this strategy can be successful in the niche market of discerning, high-spend tourists who seek comfort and privacy and who value nature, but who wish to be close to Cape Town, with all its attractions. By this means, and through the modest and judicious increase in accommodation capacity, Brink believes Camps Bay Retreat will be able to generate sufficient revenue to adequately cover its relatively high overheads (about R80 000 monthly), and therefore generate a positive cash-flow. This, he says, will be sufficient payback, even though it may not amount to a market-related return on investment in the conventional sense. 'Not everything can, or should, be measured purely in terms of financial returns', he says.

Case interview: Maree Brink, CEO of Village and Life, 14 November 2006.

www

www.campsbayretreat.com

Case study questions

1. It is sometimes argued that full-service accommodation establishments have to be relatively large, because economy of scale is needed to generate revenue sufficient to ensure viability. Is the case of Camps Bay Retreat likely to support or defy this argument?

2. Is the idea of restricting the extent of accommodation at Camps Bay Retreat, in favour of preserving the property's natural beauty, naïve sentimentality or a shrewd business strategy? Explain your answer.

3. Discuss some of the reasons behind the growth of the boutique hotel concept.

4. Based on the factors which describe Camps Bay Retreat as a boutique hotel, produce a definition of a 'boutique hotel', and develop a set of criteria which a genuine boutique hotel should meet to be classified as such.

7

Managing tourism distribution

Richard George

Purpose

This chapter explores the role of distribution in the South African tourism industry.

Learning outcomes

After reading this chapter, you should be able to:
- explain the importance of intermediaries in the distribution of tourism offerings
- define the nature and structure of intermediation in tourism
- identify the different types of distribution channels that are used for tourism offerings
- explain the role of travel agents as a component of the tourism industry
- identify the functions performed by a travel agent
- define the role of tour operators
- explain the functions of a tour operator as a component of the tourism industry
- illustrate the impact of information and communication technology (ICT) on tourism distribution.

Chapter overview

This chapter explores the issues facing tourism managers in relation to the distribution of tourism offerings. It begins with a discussion of the role of distribution channels in the tourism industry. The functions of intermediaries (the middlemen) who sell offerings within the tourism industry are outlined, and the impact of integration on tourism – one of the greatest influences that has shaped the industry in recent years – is examined. The chapter then focuses on the activities of two key intermediaries; the tour operator and the travel agent. Finally, the developments in information and communication technologies (ICT) which influence the manner in which tour operators and travel agencies operate are discussed.

The concluding case study applies the theory contained in this chapter to Mo Happy People Travel & Tours, a tour operating company based in Mpumalanga.

Introduction

Tourists require a wide range of tourism services, ranging from airline tickets, accommodation, admissions to visitor attractions, and information about interesting activities and special events. The success of tourism businesses depends on their ability to access and meet targeted consumers' needs effectively and efficiently. Linking the supply of tourism offerings to consumer demand is the task of intermediaries. The primary means through which tourism offerings are sold to consumers is through channels of distribution using intermediaries such as travel agents and tour operators (see Figure 7.1). Recent technological developments in the tourism industry, however, have revolutionised the way consumers deal directly with tourism businesses. These affect all tourism enterprises, from small, medium and micro enterprises (SMMEs) to multi-national corporations (MNCs). Information and communication technologies (ICT), in particular the Internet and online booking (WWW and e-mail), have created a virtual form of distribution for SMMEs bound by limited resources for reaching customers, thereby opening up new markets and enabling them to work in the global marketplace. This same technology, however, can pose a threat to both travel agents and tour operators, since consumers can book flights and hotel rooms directly at a lower cost than through an intermediary.

Distribution, or 'place', is often regarded as the least 'sexy' of all the marketing management functions, but it should not be underestimated, as it is where tourism businesses can gain a competitive advantage. It is the battleground of strategic tourism management.

As we saw in Chapter 1, distribution plays a vital link in the tourism system, linking tourism supply and demand. It also plays an important role in providing both information and services to tourism consumer markets.

TO DO

Draw up a list of intermediaries operating in the services sector.

Figure 7.1 Distribution channels: manufacturing vs. the tourism industry

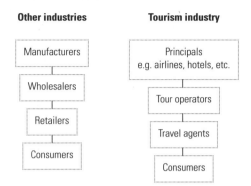

Distribution channels in tourism

Distribution channels (also known as *the chain of distribution*) describes the system by which an offering is distributed from a tourism provider to consumers. Offerings are traditionally distributed through a number of **intermediaries**, who link tourism suppliers with consumers. These intermediaries are either wholesalers (such as tour operators) who buy in bulk, or retailers, such as travel agents, who form the link in the **chain of distribution** and sell individual offerings or bundled packages to consumers. The role of intermediaries is to bring consumers (buyers) and providers (sellers) together. Intermediaries improve the flow of information and offerings (termed distribution channels) between principals and consumers. Tourism providers are not obliged to sell their offerings through the chain of distribution. Indeed, many choose to sell directly to the consumer or retailer, thereby cutting out some or all of the middlemen. Similarly, tour operators may sell offerings direct to the consumer, avoiding the retailer. The latter method is referred to as *dis-intermediation*.

The number and types of links in the chain of distribution varies, depending on the nature of the tourism offering to be distributed, the type of tourism organisation, and the type of customer. Smaller tourism businesses, for example, may sell directly and/or through one type of intermediary to one type of customer. Most of the larger tourism organisations and MNCs have more complex distribution strategies, using a variety of distribution methods which reflect the different market segments that the organisation aims to target.

Levels of distribution channels

Tourism offerings can be sold to the consumer in a number of ways. In other words, there are several types of distribution channels that can be used to access tourism product-offerings and information about services. These channels range from one-level direct access to more complex three-level arrangements involving several intermediaries. In general, the longer the distribution channel, the higher the cost of the tourism offering to consumers. Figure 7.2 shows one-, two- and three-level distribution channels for tourism organisations.

Figure 7.2 The principles of distribution and the important role of travel agents and tour operators

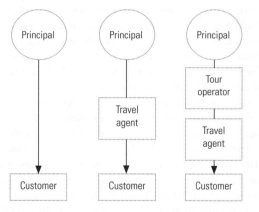

Intermediaries in tourism

As we have seen earlier, an 'intermediary' refers to any dealer – a business or person – in the chain of distribution who acts as a link, or 'go-between', or 'middleman', between the tourism **principal** and its consumers (see Figure 7.3). An intermediary, therefore, is a person or an organisation who liaises between the tourist and the tourism provider. The best-known intermediaries in the tourism industry are travel agents, who mainly transact with tourism principals such as airlines, hotel groups, car hire companies, coach operators, and tour operators.

Nowadays, both tourism principals and consumers have a great deal of choice of distribution methods, including travel agencies, call centres, tourist information centres/offices, electronic point of sales (EPOS) systems, supermarkets, **destination management companies** (DMCs), sales representatives, travel clubs, and the Internet. Distribution channels both influence consumer behaviour and determine the ability of the industry to respond efficiently to consumers' requests (Cooper *et al.*, 2005: 422).

In tourism the concept of intermediation is complex, as principals and intermediaries are able to switch roles in the chain of distribution. An intermediary such as a tour operator may act as a principal and, vice-versa, a principal may act as an intermediary. An example of the former is when a travel agency sells elements of a holiday package on behalf of a tour operator. An example of the latter is a hotel that becomes a 'tour operator' by packaging its surplus capacity to offer mid-week

Figure 7.3 How tour operators package the elements of a holiday together

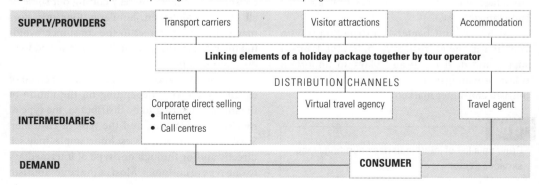

Source: Page, S.J., 2007. *Tourism management: managing for change*, 2nd edition. Oxford: Butterworth-Heinemann

breaks aimed at the domestic leisure tourism market, and sells coach operator or airline tickets and admissions to visitor attractions in an all-inclusive package.

The benefits of intermediaries

Intermediaries in distribution channels are useful to both the consumer and the organisation. They provide various convenient services to the consumer, and function almost like external reservations and sales staff for the organisation. In addition, distribution channels offer management of the whole travel package or travel arrangements and itineraries. Some of the reasons why tourism businesses decide to use intermediaries are as follows:

For tourism businesses:

Save costs
Tourism principals save the cost of dealing directly with customers; specifically the cost of employing sales staff and the renting or buying of premises. These economies allow them to invest more in their core business activities. Intermediaries also collect individual payments to **suppliers**, thus again saving costs.

Retailing
Tourism businesses cannot afford to have hundreds of retail outlets throughout the country. SAA, for example, have several *SA Travel Centre* (franchised travel agencies) branches in towns across South Africa. Sales representatives, multiple and independent travel agents, the Internet, **call centres**, and tour operators do the rest of their selling for them in other places.

Reduce risk
Intermediaries have a function of reducing risk in terms of inventory for principals. By using middlemen, a car-rental company, for example, can reduce the risk of being left with unused rental cars, thereby leading to lost revenue. Intermediaries therefore increase a principal's number of distribution channel options.

For consumers:

For consumers, the advantages of using an intermediary include:

Convenience
For consumers there is the convenience of having a third party (intermediary) deal with arrangements which necessitate a level of expertise beyond that of the consumer (for example, industry contacts, offering knowledge, language skills, etc.).

Provide specialist knowledge
Intermediaries provide expert product knowledge and advice to consumers. For example, an inbound tour-operating business specialising in adventure travel will be expected to have better knowledge of the offerings available in the region in which it operates.

Cost savings
Bulk purchasing provides a guaranteed level of occupancy to principals. As such, tour operators are able to keep prices down by buying in bulk. Consumers making use of an intermediary are also able to minimise holiday search costs, and thereby save time and money. This is the reason why certain travel agents are often able to sell airline tickets at a cheaper price than they would cost if bought directly from the respective airlines.

Greater choice
Consumers also have greater choice through aggregation of products and services. A prospect, for example, may have booked a room at a guesthouse searched via the Internet.

Consumer protection
The use of an intermediary grants certain rights not afforded to the independent traveller – for example, when service standards do not match those advertised in a tour operator's brochure.

Reduced risk
Consumers reduce their risk of purchasing a less desirable offering by receiving knowledgeable advice and recommendations from travel agents, tour operators, and **tourism information centres** (TICs).

The disadvantages of using an intermediary

There are, however, problems with respect to the use of intermediaries. Pender (2005: 70), for example, cites that control is a major issue for tourism principals. The more frequently an organisation in the tourism industry uses intermediaries, and the more distant these intermediaries are from the organisation, the more difficult it is to control them. Relations with customers can be built up if the tourism business has direct contact with them. Similarly, the cost of distribution has also become an emerging issue in recent years, thereby influencing principals to cut out the middleman and sell directly to the consumer (any sale made without the use of an intermediary can be said to be a direct sale). As George points out, holidays sold directly to consumers are not always cheaper: tour operators and travel agents purchase elements of the tourism experience from principals and suppliers by buying in bulk at significant discounts which they, in turn, pass on to the consumer (2004: 232).

Many tourism businesses, however, distribute both directly and via intermediaries. This is both a balancing act and a management challenge for these businesses, as intermediaries may not recommend with enthusiasm those suppliers who blatantly deal directly with customers. Were the suppliers to have a strong pull on their customers, it is likely that the power of the intermediaries to influence choice would be reduced.

Integration in the tourism industry

Most of the tourism businesses which dominate the market place do so because of their size and market share. Many of these have acquired such power due to **integration** (the formal linking arrangement between organisations), mergers, acquisitions, and takeovers (see Example box). This integration then allows one organisation to offer various elements of the holiday product to consumers – because it owns the travel agency,

the tour operator, the transport providers, and sometimes the accommodation provider too. The extent of integration in the global tourism industry has been such that there are large tour operators now linked with travel agency chains, yet these linkages are not always recognised by consumers.

Example Founders to buy out Flight Centre

Flight Centre, Australia's biggest travel agent, yesterday agreed to a buyout by its founders that valued the company at A$1,6-billion (R9,4-billion) as customers switched to direct Internet bookings with airlines and hotels.

The buyout will increase the value of takeovers in the global tourism industry to $10, 4-billion this year [2006] as the Internet spurs competition. Flight Centre has outlets in nine countries, including South Africa.

Source: Vesna Plojak, *Cape Times Business Times*, 1 November, 2006, p.3

Integration entails the linking (through changes of ownership such as mergers, acquisitions, and takeovers) of different stages of the chain of distribution to form larger, more powerful organisations. It is a way of expanding a tourism business – by bringing in a wider range of offerings (vertical integration), or by gaining a wider market share of the business's current market (horizontal integration). SAA is a good example of this, for it is part of Star Alliance, which has a global alliance with several major airlines such as Lufthansa, Singapore Airlines, United Airlines, and Thai Airways International – thereby giving it a worldwide network of routes and destinations. Globalisation is an inevitable consequence of the growth of the international airline business. A strategic alliance offers opportunities for rapid global growth, along with marketing benefits that cannot be achieved as an individual airline. For example, alliances enable airlines to reduce costs by using larger aircraft, as well as sharing operational costs, such as counter space at airports.

Integration can occur both horizontally and vertically:

Horizontal integration

Horizontal integration occurs when connections are made along the distribution chain; for example when two similar organisations – such as small tour operators – merge or are amalgamated, or where one is taken over and absorbed by the other (horizontal axis in Figure 7.4). An objective of horizontal integration is to gain greater control within an organisation's own sector (such as two travel agencies or two tour operators). Horizontal integration also reduces operating costs, especially if merged companies can use one administration centre. Integration of this type is always subject to the monopoly and merger laws of the country in which the companies are based (see Chapter 13 – Tourism businesses and the law). The company formed must not be so big that it totally dominates the market, leaving no room for competition.

Vertical integration

Vertical integration describes the process whereby an organisation at one level of the distribution chain links with one at another level (vertical axis in Figure 7.4). An example of this is when an airline acquires or forms its own tour operations company.

This integration can be forward (or downward in the direction of the chain), as in the case of a tour operator which buys its own chain of travel agents (sometimes referred to as *multiples)*, or it can be backwards (or upwards against the direction of the chain), such as where the tour operator buys its own airline. If integration moves further away from the actual consumer (when a tour operator gains control over a company that manufactures small tour buses, for example) then *backward integration* occurs. If the integration moves closer to the consumer (for example, where a tour operator acquires a chain of travel agencies), the process is known as *forward integration.*

Vertical integration implies that an organisation is gaining control over more elements of the tourism supply chain as a way of ultimately maximising its profits (such as when the middleman is eliminated, and therefore there is a saving on commission fees).

Figure 7.4 Integration in the tourism industry

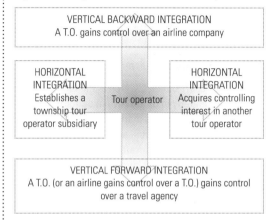

An example of vertical integration in the South African tourism industry is that of Imperial Car Rentals, a company in the broader Imperial Holdings Group. There are a multitude of integrated companies in the South African market. There have been several mergers and take-overs between tour operators in the South African tourism industry which have brought both advantages and disadvantages to role players. Issues in recent years such as **black economic empowerment** (BEE) and transformation have influenced the integration of tourism organisations in the South African tourism industry.

The largest travel groups in South Africa are BIDTRAV (mainly comprising travel agents and foreign exchange bureaux such as Rennies Travel, and part of the Bidvest Group); Tourvest, and Cullinan Holdings (which includes the Thompsons Travel Group).

Cullinan Holdings' two major businesses are in- and outbound wholesaling. These businesses are widely supported by third party supply operators and retail distributors. The Outbound Wholesale division (Thompsons Tours) distributes through the widest range of agencies compared to other tour operators in South Africa (see Table 7.1 and Example box overleaf).

Tourvest operates four divisions: Inbound Tourism Services, Outbound Travel Services, Financial Services, and Retail Merchandising. In recent years, Tourvest has acquired numerous companies to add to its portfolio which include travel agencies, hotels, tour operators, game lodges, souvenir shops, restaurants, and foreign exchange bureaux (see Figure 7.5).

Example Bidvest acquires 20% of Comair

In January 2007, Bidvest, which is the largest holdings company in South Africa, acquired 20% of Comair. Bidvest owns many travel and tourism companies in South Africa, such as ground handling companies, aircraft cleaning services, tour operators, and travel agents.

www

Browse this website: www.tourvest.co.za

Example Thompsons Travel Group

The Thompsons Travel Group is a division of Cullinan Holdings. It was founded in 1978, and today employs almost 800 qualified and experienced travel professionals. The company, which has offices in Johannesburg, eThekwini, and Cape Town, has been voted *Best Africa Tour Operator* and *Best International Tour Operator* for the past five consecutive years.

Thompsons has, through its partners in the South African tourism industry, access to booking a variety of principals – from airlines and hotels to luxury trains and car-hire worldwide. Thompsons has perfected the fine art of tours in a worldwide environment – inbound and outbound – with a global network of travel and tourism industry partners.

www

Browse this website: www.thompsons.co.za

The advantages of integration

Integration offers the advantage of greater control over the quality of the tourism product-offering. A tour operator which, for example, owns and operates its own hotel, is able to ensure the availability and price of rooms. According to Gale (2006: 407), integration offers a number of benefits for tourism organisations, including that:

- it deters new entrants to the mass market
- it consolidates purchasing power over principals (especially in respect of accommodation, where large numbers of mostly small independent operators mean that supply conditions resemble those of perfect competition, whereas the concentration of ownership among tour

Table 7.1 Thompsons Travel Group of companies

Company	Tour operator brands	Offerings
Thompsons Travel Group	Thompsons Tours	Cruising, ski holidays, group tours
	Thompsons Africa	Transfers, specialised tours in Africa for groups and individuals
	Thompsons Africa Touring & Safaris	Escorted tours, private day tours, safaris, adventure activities and transfers
	Thompsons Gateway Africa	Tours for groups and individuals from SE Asia
	Thompsons Corporate Travel	Tailor-made corporate travel packages
	Thompsons Leisure Travel	Global holiday packages

Figure 7.5 An example of integration in the South African tourism industry – Tourism Investment Corporation Ltd (Tourvest Ltd).

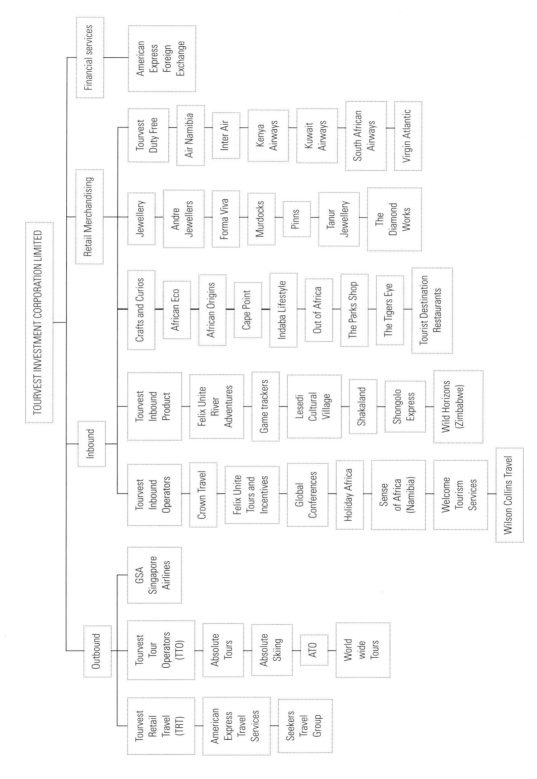

operators mean that demand is delivered under **oligopolistic** conditions)
- it provides a greater influence in the sale of package holiday products
- it allows for the possibility of 'instantly' diversifying into emerging and profitable niche markets.

TO DO

Find an example of integration in the tourism industry. Prepare a mini-presentation to show the key features of collaboration, alliances, and partnerships.

The role and functions of tour operators

In Chapter 2, the manner in which the pioneer Thomas Cook organised and conducted the first tour in 1841 was discussed. Cook used a variety of management, marketing, and financial skills to assemble, package, sell, and escort that organised tour.

A **tour operator** is an individual or organisation that arranges domestic, inbound, and/or outbound **inclusive tours** (or 'package tours'). Tour operators have played a significant role in the growth of international tourism over the last 25 years. For many tourism principals, especially those with limited resources, tour operators have been the only means of reaching international markets (although the Internet is changing this).

The business of tour operating is an important and dynamic sub-sector of the tourism industry. It is highly competitive, and is characterised by expansion, mergers, and acquisitions.

The primary function of a tour operator is to assemble the main elements of a holiday (transport, accommodation, ancillary etc.) into a single product (or 'package'), and sell this to consumers through a travel agent, airline sales office, or other intermediary. In the chain of distribution, tour operators are the 'wholesalers' (or 'middlemen') of the tourism industry, buying bulk from principals (for example, airlines, hotels, car rental companies) and reselling through retail travel agencies. In the tourism industry, tour operators take on the role of a **wholesaler**, since they buy their different tourism offerings, such as airline seats or hotel bed spaces, in bulk for subsequent sale to travel agents or directly to the tourist. The terms 'tour operator' and 'wholesaler' are often used interchangeably. Tour operators also carry out a number of functions including conducting research, contracting suppliers, costing the package, and marketing and selling the holiday package.

An inclusive tour (or 'holiday package') can be divided according to:
- type of accommodation, (e.g. a city hotel becomes a tour operator by packaging its surplus capacity to offer as weekend or short breaks)
- mode of transport, such as a coach holiday (e.g. Springbok Atlas)
- international or domestic packages

Table 7.2 Components of an inclusive tour (package holiday)

Core elements	Add-ons
Aircraft seat	Car hire
Transfer from airport to accommodation establishment and back to airport (transfer companies)	Excursions/tours (excursion providers)
Accommodation at destination	Activities, e.g. paragliding
Restaurant meals	
Insurance	
Services of a tour operator representative	

- distance – short haul (less than six hours' flying time) or long haul (more than six hours' flying time)
- length of holiday, such as a short break (typically less than four nights), or a longer holiday (typically more than four nights)
- destination type (e.g. special interest tourism (SIT) holidays or city breaks).

The components of a typical holiday package might include: transport (for example, a return flight from Johannesburg to London with SAA); a transfer from airport to hotel, accommodation (seven nights' full board at a City Lodge hotel), and optional travel services such as car hire (see Table 7.2).

The specialised roles of tour operators

When we think of tour operators, we almost always tend to think of them as outbound tour operators (transporting tourists out of the country). However, tour operators fulfil a number of different roles. They may organise holidays domestically (within the country); handle incoming foreign tourists (inbound tour operators), or specialise in a particular aspect of operating. We will now examine each of these:

Domestic operators

Operators that organise package holidays and tours in South Africa form a much smaller component of the tourism industry. The reason for this is that it is relatively easy nowadays for tourists to organise their travel arrangements within their own home country. An example of one of the leading domestic tour operators in South African is Thompsons Tours. The longest-established programmes are coach tours, operated by well-known companies such as Springbok Atlas.

Incoming operators

Organisations specialising in handling incoming foreign (African and overseas) tourists have a different role to that of outbound operators. Some are groundhandling agents, ranging from those

that organise hotel accommodation on behalf of an overseas tour operator, to those offering a comprehensive range of services such as coach tours, booking theatre tickets, arranging tours of townships and other visitor attractions, study tours, or **special interest tourism** (SIT) holidays. Various tour operating companies also specialise according to the markets they service, catering for inbound North Americans (e.g. Abercrombie & Kent), Asians (e.g. Wendy Wu), or Scandinavians (e.g. My Travel), for example. Most incoming operators are relatively small companies, and are marketed as part of a **consortium** through the travel trade and sectoral organisations (one such being Southern African Tourism Services Association – SATSA). They also work closely with destination marketing organisations (DMOs) such as regional tourism organisations (RTOs) (see Chapter 8).

Specialist operators

Specialist (or independent) tour operators cater for niche tourism markets. Some outbound operators choose to specialise according to the *mode of transport* by which their customers travel; such as coach travel (especially the **visiting friends and relatives** (VFR) market in South Africa), cruise liners, or railway companies.

Tour operators may specialise in the selection of products they offer, or the markets they serve. At one extreme, for instance, there are the mass market operators – the larger integrated operators, such as Infinity (the tour operator belonging to Flight Centre); Thompsons Tours (Cullinan Holdings), and Absolute Tours (Tourvest), which offer a range of holiday brands to appeal to very broad market segments. Then there are the *specialist tour operators* that may target particular niche markets and special interest tourism (SIT) activities; for example, sports enthusiasts (golf, angling, skiing, etc.), single travellers, female travellers, 'pink' tourists (gay and lesbian travellers), hobbies (bird watching, antique collecting, painting, photography, naturism, cycling, wine tasting, gastronomy), adventure (hiking, rock climbing, white-water rafting, motorcycle tours, safaris, balloon safaris, shark cage-diving), or even marine tourists (see Example box). Activity and adventure holidays are one of the fastest-growing sectors in the tourism industry.

Specialisation by market is also common. Some tour operators appeal to a particular *age group*, such as the student or youth markets (i.e. Contiki Holidays 18-35), or the over-50s (Saga Holidays, for example). Tour operators such as Le Voyageur offer luxury tailor-made tours to exotic destinations (for example: 'Star of the Indian Ocean' to Mauritius and 'River of the Pharaohs' to Egypt), which are aimed at up-market travellers.

There are also the operators that specialise in *geographic destinations,* such as Thai Tours (to Thailand), Mozaic Travel (to Mozambique), or African Routes (to Namibia). Most of these specialist operators carry small numbers of tourists, and make use of guesthouses. They are also reasonably flexible, and have the ability to switch destinations and adjust itineraries at the last minute. Staff employed by specialist tour operators are expected to be knowledgeable about the holidays and destinations they offer.

---

www

Browse the *Tourism Update* (a journal for tour organisers) website: www.tourismupdate.co.za

---

Example Specialist marine tourism operator

Specialist marine tourism company, Strandloper Safaris, offers coastal expeditions led by specialist marine biologists to discerning clients interested in learning more about the marine environment. One of the business partners, Professor George Branch, author of the bestselling *The Living Shores* and *Two Oceans: a Guide to Marine Life of Southern Africa*, has assembled a team of enthusiastic guides who will share their knowledge and enthusiasm for the marine world as they lead marine tourists through some of the Cape's premier tourist attractions. These include Cape Point, the penguins at Boulders Beach, the West Coast, encounters with white sharks, whale-watching in Hermanus, and the Two Oceans Aquarium.

Types of tour offered by tour operators

Tour operators offer three main types of tours, including:

- *Escorted tours*: An escorted tour includes the services of a designated tour escort or tourist guide, who accompanies the group throughout their tour.
- *Hosted tours*: Hosted tours include the services of a tour manager, who oversees all of the arrangements for the group, but does not usually escort them on excursions. These types of tours allow more flexibility than escorted tours, enabling participants to choose their own activities at the destination.
- *Independent tours*: An independent tour enables members of the tour group to choose from a range of elements of a tour, such as accommodation options, transport, and sightseeing activities.

There are over 50 inbound tour operators in South Africa, represented by their own trade organisation – the South African Tour Operators Association (SATOA). SATOA is the representative body for the Wholesale Tour Operators in South Africa (see Example box below). Many South African tour operators are also members of the Association of South African Travel Agents (ASATA).

SATOA is the tour operators' division of ASATA; currently there are 26 members. The organisation is shortly due to undergo a re-branding process.

Example South African Tour Operators Association (SATOA)

The South African Tour Operators Association (SATOA) was established to represent the interests of tour operators.

SATOA's objectives are:
- to further and secure the interest of SATOA and its members;
- to reflect the consensus of its members and present their views to all sectors of the public, the Government, and the business community
- to act on behalf of its members in deliberations and negotiations with other sectors of the travel industry

- to continually assess and evaluate the needs of its members, with a view to providing them with meaningful services and benefits
- to consider and promote the highest standards of professionalism and ethics among its members in their dealings with the public and each other
- to promote systematic training within those sectors of the travel industry falling within the scope of SATOA
- to consider all legislation and/or proposed legislation brought to its notice affecting, or likely to affect, the travel industry, and to take such action as considered to be in the interest of its members
- to play an active role in the international community of the travel industry.

www

Browse this website:
www.asata.co.za/pages_public/join_satoa.asp

The economics of tour operating

Tour operators rely on the **economies of scale** generated by bulk buying of the elements of the holiday package. In turn, this allows packages to be sold to potential holidaymakers at attractive prices. Tour operators therefore enable different tourism principals, such as holiday resorts and transport providers, to sell their offerings (stock) well in advance. For example, a tour operator will purchase airline seats from an airline, airport shuttle services from coach operators, and taxi rides to be pre-sold to consumers at the booking stage or at the destination. As a result, tourism principals are able to fix their costs in advance, and tour operators achieve economies of scale by heavily discounted rates on their purchases. Essentially, the mass tour operator assembles the various elements of a holiday, promotes and sells them, and uses third-party agents to deliver them on the ground. Tour operators calculate all the input costs and overheads, and mark them up at a

price attractive to consumers, ultimately making a profit for themselves. There is a growing trend among consumers to book holidays much later, very often within a week of departure.

The tour operator's brochure

An essential part of a tour operator's marketing armoury is the brochure which communicates the holiday package to the consumer. The primary aim of the tour operator's brochure is to attract attention. In addition, it should reinforce an image of quality and reliability. The text and images in the brochure should be attractive as well as honest, accurate, and easily understood. The brochure should have a well-structured layout, feature high-quality photographs, and be printed on quality paper. The terms and conditions of the holiday package should be included in the brochure.

The information required in a tour operator's holiday brochure should include:

- the name of the company responsible for the holiday
- modes of transport used (in the case of air transport, the name of the carrier, type, and class of aircraft used should be included)
- full details of destination, **itinerary**, and times of travel
- duration of each tour (number of days/nights' stay)
- full description of the location and type of accommodation used
- details of prices for each tour, including taxes (sometimes as an insert in the brochure, or on request, due to changes in prices, taxes and surcharges)
- full conditions of booking, including cancellation conditions and non-refundable deposits and several other clauses must be included
- details of any insurance coverage
- details of travel documentation required, such as visas and health certificates (this varies depending on the traveller's nationality). Notification should be given that there are visa requirements and health precautions which need to be checked.

Tour operators must establish a policy for the distribution of their brochure to selected travel agencies.

TO DO

Carry out research into one of South Africa's major outgoing tour operators. Describe the scale and structure of the organisation and the offerings it provides.

Tour operator sales representatives

Many tour operators employ sales representatives to maintain and develop their business through travel agents. The main functions of sales representatives are to call on existing and potential contacts, advise and update travel agents of the services they offer, and support them with merchandising material. (This is a similar arrangement to representatives of pharmaceutical companies who service medical doctors).

Sales representatives act as the main point of contact between travel agents and tour operators. They also receive useful feedback from consumers about client and agency attitudes towards the company and its offerings. Tour operating companies, increasingly in recent years, have made use of telephone sales calls with agents. Sales representatives need to be well-trained and knowledgeable about their operator's offerings.

Tour brokers

Tour brokers that bulk buy tourism offerings and sell them in smaller quantities are most frequently found in the **distribution system** within the air transport sector (Holloway, 2006: 169).

Tour brokers assemble tour packages for groups/clubs such as religious groups, a group of pensioners, or a sports club. These are usually organised by a tour leader or manager, who may charter a coach, and who arranges details of the travel itinerary including booking tickets to visitor attractions, booking restaurants, and contracting the services of a tourist guide.

Groundhandlers

Groundhandlers are agents that work on behalf of international and South African tour operators, travel agents, and principals (see Example box). They facilitate all the ground arrangements for tourists at destinations, such as the booking of accommodation, transfers to and from their accommodation and airport, car hire, excursions, and the reservation of any activities ranging from shark diving to restaurant bookings and golf tee-times.

> **Example** African Experience Golf Tours & Safaris
>
> African Experience Golf Tours & Safaris, which was formed in 1999, has evolved from a small golf tour operator based in KwaZulu-Natal to offering golf and generic travel packages throughout South Africa. Over the years, the company has created partnerships with more than 10 international tour operators and travel agents. African Experience Golf Tours & Safaris essentially act as a local **groundhandler**, assisting with the arrangement of all ground activities, such as accommodation reservations, transport requirements, golf, and day tours. The company also offers various travel packages throughout South Africa, which include sports tours, generic sightseeing holidays, themed holidays, and safari tours.
>
> African Experience Golf Tours & Safaris' competitive advantage over mass-market operators is the ability to offer specialised service and knowledge in relation to the specific themed package holiday, such as Battlefield Holidays. They are able to offer and provide the personalised services of experienced tourist guides who offer a service to the clients by passing on valuable information while re-enacting the events of the themed holiday. The company subcontracts the tourist-guiding services and hosting for each themed holiday.

Examples of South African tour operators

The role of travel agents

Travel agents are perhaps the best-known inter-mediaries. They act as the retailing arm of the tourism industry, and are an important source of distribution in it. Essentially, they function as convenient sales outlets at which holidays and other travel-related offerings can be purchased. Travel agents generally act on behalf of princi-pals (such as hotels, airline companies, and car rental companies), as well as other intermediaries (including tour operators and groundhandlers). As such, they do not purchase tourism offerings or hold 'stock' of any travel product-offerings. (This is sometimes referred to as 'consignment sales', where there is no actual transfer of owner-ship). Only when a consumer has decided on a purchase do travel agents approach the principal on the consumer's behalf to make a purchase. This has an important implication for the business of tourism distribution, as travel agents do not carry any financial risk in terms of unsold stock (unused bed spaces, empty seats on aircraft, or places on tours), because they do not purchase offerings in advance. This means that any financial risk lies with the principal. Nonetheless, when there is high demand for a particular offering and supply is short, the travel agent can make the sale only if the tour operator provides sufficient availability: thus, travel agents cannot adjust supply for popu-lar destinations. They do, however, have to have

guarantees for the value of their air ticket stock, this often being a substantial amount.

The main task of a travel agency is to supply the public with travel services. The range of offer-ings that a travel agency chooses to provide will vary depending on the **commission** rates, as well as the demand from the consumer market-place. Services range from accommodation bookings, transportation (air, rail, coach, cruise tickets, and car hire) to hotel and package tours. Different commission rates are paid by different sub-sectors. Car-hire commission, for example, is usually higher than rail or cruise commission. Most of the travel agent's revenue comes from selling package holidays. In recent years, there has been a trend towards airline companies refusing to pay commissions to travel agents.

Besides their main role of selling holidays and travel, travel agents also act as a source of information and advice on travel services: for example, they arrange travel documentation such as visa applications, make reservations for visitor attractions and entertainment venues, and plan travel itineraries. Ancillary services, including the sale of travellers' cheques, travel insurance, and foreign currency exchange may also be offered. Customers pay an additional fee for some of these value-added services. Many full-service travel agents have evolved into more specialised 'holiday shops' – one-stop travel shops where consumers can purchase a range of travel-related

Examples of well-known South African travel agencies

products (ranging from luggage to photograph processing) (See Example box below).

Example Seekers Travel Group – a one-stop travel shop

Seekers Travel Group is the retail travel arm of Tourvest. The Group has several Seekers Travel Centres located in South Africa's main centres. Each centre offers travel information and bookings for a wide variety of tours and destinations around southern Africa. Most of their stores have everything under one roof. Besides an information and booking centre, there is a film developer, gift shop, jewellers, wine shop, and a foreign exchange bureau. Seekers aim at both international and domestic tourism markets.

---

www

Browse this website: www.seekers.co.za

ASATA's logo is widely recognised by the travel trade

Example Association for South African Travel Agents (ASATA)

The Association for South African Travel Agents (ASATA) was founded in 1956, as the leading trade body representing both travel agents and tour operators in South Africa. It is a voluntary organisation (members do not have to belong to ASATA). In mid-2006 there were approximately 640 members (retail travel agents, tour operators, and tourism associations) affiliated to ASATA. ASATA acts as a facilitator between its members and the travelling public using such members.

ASATA liaises with various industry stakeholders, and relays legislation and information of national importance to its members, particularly issues which affect the tourism industry.

ASATA members comply with the ASATA constitution, and the specific terms and conditions which govern its different divisions. A broad overview would be that ASATA stands for professionalism, advice, value, and integrity.

---

www

Browse this website: www.asata.co.za

Characteristics of travel agents

In South Africa, there were, at the time of going to press, approximately 581 travel agents affiliated to the Association of South African Travel Agents (ASATA). These members are bound by ASATA's constitution and code of conduct, which promotes integrity in dealing with an ASATA travel agent or tour operator. ASATA has over 200 travel partners, including airlines, hotels, and car rental companies as members (see Example box above).

Travel agents perform a number of functions. These include:

- stocking a wide range of brochures
- planning travel itineraries
- making reservations
- promoting merchandise in attractive displays
- calculating tickets and fares
- advising consumers on a wide range of offerings
- providing travel advice (on safety issues, resorts, travel companies, carriers, world-wide travel facilities, etc.)
- complaints handling (e.g. dealing with dissatisfied customers)
- communicating both verbally and in writing with consumers (e.g. forwarding flight changes to customers)
- transmitting tickets to consumers.

Travel agencies earn their income mainly from the commission they receive from each sale involving principals, tour operators, and other intermediaries, as well as other ancillary and support services for consumers' bookings, using **computer reservation systems** (CRSs). Many travel agents make additional income selling 'extras' such as foreign currency and car hire. Notably, travel agents provide significant after-sales services when dealing with flight changes, for example. The only tangible elements that they stock are information in the form of brochures, leaflets and data, and the professional expertise of travel consultants; which, of course, is intangible.

Travel agency staff (usually referred to as travel consultants) require extensive product-offering knowledge. In particular, they should possess the skills to source travel information, such as 'best buy' airfares, and should be familiar with the latest technology, including accessing travel websites and computer reservation systems (CRSs). A number of internationally recognised courses – to provide skills in airline fares and the issuing of tickets – are available. These include those offered by SAA in South Africa, which meet International Air Transport Association (IATA) requirements/ Fares and Ticketing Part II.

Quality customer service (QCS) is paramount if the agency is to succeed in the competitive retail travel business. QCS will ensure that the needs and wants of an agency's customers' are satisfied, help gain repeat business, and give the agency a competitive advantage. Travel agency managers need good interpersonal skills to be able to manage a team of people, as well as the necessary technical skills in financial management of accounts and cash flows, the invoicing of customers, and in the control and running of a business (see Chapter 12 – Managing finance for tourism).

Types of travel agencies

There are several ways of categorising travel agencies:

1. Travel agencies can either be *generalist* travel agencies, selling a wide range of travel offerings, or *specialist* agencies, selling particular types of offerings. Shopping mall/High-street generalist agencies such as Sure Travel or Harvey World Travel deal with high volumes of clients, and are equipped to sell all types of leisure and business travel to individuals or groups. Specialist agencies, such as Birdfinders SA, only sell specialist products to specialist markets, and are therefore niche travel agencies.

2. *Multiples, miniples,* or *independents*. Multiple travel agencies are private companies, usually with a main street presence in most major South African cities. Many of these are household names in the tourism industry, such as Sure Travel, Pentravel, Club Travel, Seekers Travel, and Flight Centre. These travel agencies are sometimes part of large (or parent) organisations. Seekers Travel Group, for example, is owned by Tourvest, while Pentravel and a chain of 16 retail agents is owned by Cullinan Holdings. Similarly, the Flight Centre, Student Flights, and FCM Travel Solutions are within the Flight Centre Group. Miniples travel agencies have a number of branches located in a particular part of the country, meeting a regional demand, e.g. Woodstock Travel, with branches mainly in the southern suburbs of Cape Town. Miniples do not benefit from 'economies of scale' to the same extent as multiple travel agents, but they are able to build close relationships with business and leisure tourists. Their success, however, often makes them prime targets for takeovers, mergers, or acquisitions. Independent travel agents are private companies that are not part of a travel agency chain. They offer as wide a range of holiday and travel products as the multiple travel agents. Most independent travel agencies are small, family-run businesses, in which the owner acts as manager and employs two or three members of staff. The independent travel agency market in South Africa is very competitive, and thus is making increasing use of marketing tools and modes of distribution to maintain its presence.

3. Travel agencies can be *leisure* or *business travel agents*. Leisure travel agents are located

in South Africa's major cities and large towns. Sure Travel, Pentravel and Harvey World Travel would be examples of this. Student travel agencies such as STA Travel and Student Flights would be examples of this. They tend to be sited at street level or in shopping centres, and make travel arrangements for individual leisure travellers. Business travel agents, for example Rennies Travel and FCM Travel Solutions, exist solely to offer travel services for business clients. This is an extremely specialised and competitive market. Business travellers tend to be very demanding of time and customer service; their prime requirement is the saving of time, and they usually make bookings at very short notice. They are, however, less price-sensitive than leisure travellers (as costs are usually met by their employer). Agents earn either commission or management fees for all the business they handle for a corporate company or association. A corporate travel agency (or a **destination management company** – DMC) manages the travel arrangements for a company's employees, from proposing accommodation venues to booking tours and entertainment. In some cases DMCs are housed within the premises of the company concerned.

4. *E-travel agents* (or e-retailers) are electronic retailers. Traditional travel agencies are competing with 'virtual' on-line travel agencies (VTAs) such as *lastminute.com, Expedia, eTravel, Travelocity,* and *Travelstart* – which allow consumers to have access to information and make online bookings (see Example box below).

Example Travelstart

Launched in South Africa in August 2006 by Stephan Ekbergh, Travelstart is one of the most popular South African online travel agencies. Travelstart is a new breed of e-travel retailer that believes in offering customers VFM (in part, by charging low service fees) through maximising the potential of technological platforms.

'You can compare the prices of all carriers and filter the list of results. You can also search on specifics like departure time or arrival time, and you can combine searches', Ekbergh claims. 'Nevertheless, if users experience any problems in transacting online, or if they merely prefer to liaise with a human being instead of a computer, they are welcome to contact the company's call centre for assistance'.

Travelstart aims to be a one-stop shop for meeting the travel requirements of its customer base. However, as the service is still in its growth phase, only airfares and hotel accommodation are offered at this stage. Nonetheless, the array of airline tickets is considerable. Tickets for low-cost airlines (e.g. kulula.com, 1Time, Mango, etc.) are available for the budget-conscious market, and the more sophisticated traveller can choose from SAA, BA, etc. Even the low-cost carriers in foreign markets (e.g. Ryanair or easyJet), often not known to South Africans, are included in the offering to enable international travellers to obtain the best deals possible.

---

www

Browse this website: www.travelstart.co.za

The impact of ICT on tourism distribution

The distribution of tourism offerings is the component of the tourism industry that is most susceptible to change in the future, as new technology enters the marketplace enabling consumers direct access to tourism products. It is likely that the role of tour operators and travel agents will decrease, as full package holidays are increasingly being purchased directly via the Internet. This reinforces the volatile nature of the tourism industry, especially tourism distribution and intermediaries (see Chapter 1 – Introduction to tourism).

Travel distribution has been affected most by information and communication technologies (ICT). Internet-based (on-line) booking systems, with their facilities to search, compare, and buy tourism offerings, have revolutionised the tourism industry and are being increasingly used to eliminate the traditional travel agents from the chain of distribution. It is becoming ever easier for leisure tourists to make their own bookings, buying individual elements of the holiday package from different providers.

Travel agencies have to compete by developing specialised knowledge and advice to maintain their competitive edge. In essence, they must compete by providing extra and more superior service than their competitors. Developments in ICT have been a 'double-edged sword', bringing both opportunities and threats to travel agencies. It has helped them on the one hand, by providing fast global communication and **global distribution systems** (GDSs) (for example, Galileo); databases of customers, and efficient billing and ticketing systems, as well as developing an on-line presence of their own. ICT has also enabled travel consultants to prepare complicated travel itineraries rapidly, and to provide up-to-date schedules, prices, and availability data. On the other hand, traditional travel agents are threatened by the competition which has arisen because Internet access has given the consumer direct contact with travel industry principals and tour operators.

The tourism industry is well suited to ICT. Tourism offerings differ from many other types of products and services (see Chapter 14 – Marketing tourism businesses). They are **intangible**, which makes it impossible for consumers to try them out before purchase. Likewise, tourism offerings are **perishable**, and cannot be stored for later sale. As a result, holidays and other tourism offerings may be 'inspected' via the Internet (for example, 'blog sites' which enable consumers to read about the experiences and tales of previous travellers), or through the use of e-brochures. ICT also offers a number of functions to travel intermediaries (see Table 7.3). It enables users to make immediate bookings, determine the availability of transportation and accommodation providers, process

tickets, invoices and travel itineraries, and process accounting and management information rapidly.

Table 7.3 ICT used in tourism

- Internet/Intranet/Extranets
- Office automation, reservation, accounting, payroll, and procurement management applications
- Internal management tools such as management support systems, decision support systems, and management information systems
- Tailor-made internal management applications
- Databases and knowledge management systems
- Networks with partners for regular transactions (EDI or extranets)
- Networking and open distribution of offerings through the Internet
- Computer reservation systems (CRSs)
- Global distribution systems (GDSs)
- Switch applications for hospitality organisations (e.g. THISCO and WIZCOM)
- Destination management systems (DMSs)
- Internet-based travel intermediaries (e.g. eTravel, Travelstart, lastminute.com)
- Wireless/mobile/WAP-based reservation systems
- Interactive digital television (IDTV)
- Kiosks and touch-screen terminals (see Example box).

Source: Adapted from Buhalis, D. 2003. *eTourism: information technology for strategic tourism management.* Harlow: Pearson Education, p. 234.

Example Self-service check-in

In 2007, the Airports Company of South Africa (ACSA) introduced self-service check-in kiosks at four international airports around the country. Over 100 'Flightcheck' kiosks have been installed, which are used by major airlines such as KLM, SAA, South African Express, and Airlink. Self-service check-in enables passengers to complete the check-in procedure – including reserving a seat, obtaining boarding passes, and proceeding to the relevant boarding gate.

Travel agents currently make use of GDSs (such as Galileo and Amadeus), which provide an effective reservation system which, in turn, supports travel agencies in obtaining information, making reservations, and issuing travel documents in minutes (see Example box below). Similarly, tour operators' reservations are accessed via CRSs connected to agents. Travel agencies, therefore, use ICT to access tourism suppliers' databases, to verify availability and rates, and to confirm reservations (Inkpen, 1998: 185). This allows for a comprehensive journey to be planned, booked, and paid for in advance. For example, travelling from Frankfurt to London using various modes of transport (i.e. coach, train and ferry) can be processed by dealing with one travel consultant.

Example Galileo

With 30 years of experience, Galileo has the expertise that airlines, other travel suppliers, and travel agencies around the world depend on. Maybe that is why they are one of the world's leading providers of electronic global distribution services – connecting approximately 44 000 travel agency locations to 470 airlines, 24 car rental companies, 56 000 hotel properties, 430 tour operators, and all major cruise lines throughout the world.

Galileo is backed by a strong staff of approximately 2 000 professionals, who take a truly unique approach to its business. Its employees understand and utilise technology as a means to an end, and unfailingly make customer service the highest priority.

Travelwire, part of Galileo's EMEA region, maintains a commitment to technology and automation of the travel booking process, and tackles the rigorous demands of software production and IT solutions by utilising state-of-the-art TCP/IP technology (Intra/Internet), including the virtual travel agency (VTA), which provides a complete software package for web-based or traditional travel agencies wishing to distribute, administer, and sell a full range of inventory via the Internet.

Headquartered in Parsippany, New Jersey, USA, Galileo International has offices worldwide, with a presence in 116 countries.

Increasingly, tour operators and travel agencies will have to compete with new forms of business-to-consumer (B2C) technology such as electronic tickets (or 'e-tickets') and ticketless travel (where the passenger is provided only with a reference number, rather than being issued with a coupon for travel), both of which are bypassing the travel agent and airlines 'GDSs' and selling directly to consumers. These technologies are rapidly being introduced by major airlines to reduce costs, while at the same time speeding up check-in processes. Tourism principals such as airlines, for example, are creating their own websites. Similarly, technologies such as cellular telephones (interacting with the Internet and TV channels) and interactive digital television (IDTV) enable travellers to call up information anywhere and at any time, check availability, and book travel arrangements. Besides the Internet, travel agencies also face additional competitors that distribute travel offerings, such as food and clothing retailers (see Example box below), banks, even petrol stations – and enable consumers to make purchases via electronic point-of-sale (EPOS) systems and cellphones.

Example Soon you'll be able to buy Mango with your mango

Groceries and air tickets will soon be available in the same shopping cart. South African travellers will be able to buy air tickets at food and clothing retailers. And passengers will also be able to buy air tickets via their cellphones.

Low-cost air carrier Mango said it would officially announce its plans to allow consumers to pay for their travel at retailers within the next month.

This was in an effort to target the country's huge 'unflown' market – people who, until now, have not used air travel – and make travel more accessible, said Mango CEO Nico Bezuidenhout.

Source: Thembisile Makgalemele *Weekend Argus*, November 4, 2006, page 1.

Conclusion

In this chapter we have examined the role of tour operators and travel agencies – two of the main intermediaries in the tourism chain of distribution. The process of disintermediation is, undoubtedly, a threat to these intermediaries, but also presents an opportunity for tour operators to sell directly to consumers. Travel agencies, too, have responded to technological advances such as the Internet and direct selling, as well as to adjustments to earning levels (caused by a reduction in commission rates), by offering value-added services (or 'add-ons'); charging fees for such professional services (itinerary planning, for example), and providing quality customer service (QCS). In essence, travel agents are becoming an agent for the traveller, instead of the tour operator or principal.

For many tourism businesses, distribution is an important facet of strategic management. As we saw in Chapter 1 (Introduction to tourism), distribution is also a vital link between tourism supply and demand in the tourism system. Tourism managers need to be familiar with the diversity of distribution channels now available, as well as how best to manage them.

Review questions

1. Explain the role of intermediaries in tourism distribution channels

2. Discuss integration in the context of tour operators and the implications for consumers.

3. What role do travel agents play in the structure of the tourism industry? Why does their role continue to be an important one as a source of distribution?

4. What are the differences between one-level and two-level tourism distribution channels?

5. Compare two channels of distribution for the following tourism principals:
    - a low-cost airline
    - a large hotel group

- a mass-market tour operator.

(Use different examples for each one).

6. Should travel agents expand on the range of services they currently retail? If so, what should they offer?

Further reading

Buhalis, D. & Laws, E. 2001. *Tourism distribution channels: practices, issues and transformations*. London: Continuum.

Websites

Association of Independent Tour Operators: www.aito.co.uk

Association of South African Travel Agents (ASATA): www.asata.co.za

Business travel agent website: www.biztravel.com

STA Travel: www.statravel.co.za

Thompsons Tours: www.thompsons.co.za

Tourism update (online tour operator trade magazine): www.tourismupdate.co.za

Travel information website: www.travelmole.com

References

Buhalis, D. 2003. *eTourism: information technology for strategic tourism management*. Harlow: Pearson Education.

Cooper, C., Fletcher, J., Fyall, A., Gilbert, D., & Wanhill, S. (Eds.). 2005. *Tourism: principles and practice*, 3rd edition. New York: Longman.

Gale, T. 2006. Mass tourism businesses: tour operators. In J. Beech & S. Chadwick (Eds.). *The business of tourism management*. Harlow, England: Pearson Education pp.407.

George, R. 2004. *Marketing South African tourism*, 2nd edition. Cape Town: Oxford University Press.

Holloway, J. C. 2006. *The business of tourism*, 7th edition. Harlow: Pearson.

Inkpen, G. 1998. *Information technology for travel and tourism*, 2nd edition. London: Addison-Wesley.

Page, S. J. 2007. *Tourism management: managing for change*, 2nd edition. Oxford: Butterworth-Heinemann.

Pender, L. 2005. Managing tourism distribution. In L. Pender & R. Sharpley (Eds.). *The management of tourism*. London: Sage Publications, pp.67–83.

Case study 7

Mo Happy People Travel & Tours

Objective

- to understand the operations of small-sized tour company

Businessman Kealeboga Gift Mogapi and Cindy Florence Shongwe, a former educator, set up their first company, called Sub-Saharan Travel and Tours, in 2004. The name of the tour operating business soon changed to Mo Happy People Travel & Tours, following the experience of their first ever tour, a five-day festive package between Gaborone in Botswana and eThekwini. During the journey Gift and Cindy played the song 'Happy People', and started singing along with it. Their passengers joined in, and the driver of the coach soon had to put the CD on repeat mode. 'Happy People' was sung and danced to during both the outbound and return trips. Every passenger in the coach was labelled a 'Happy Person', and Gift and Cindy decided to honour their very first clients by renaming their company 'Mo Happy People Travel & Tours'.

The company remains small by tour operating standards with a staff of just six, based in an office at the Kruger Mpumalanga International (KMI) airport outside Nelspruit in Mpumalanga. Five members of staff occupy the following permanent positions:

- Managing Director – responsible for the overall management of the company
- Office Manager – responsible for the daily running of the KMI airport office
- Marketing Manager – responsible for the advertising and communications efforts of the company
- Transport Manager – responsible for all the chauffeuring services of the company
- Customer Services Manager – responsible for all customer needs and requirements before and after using MHPTT products and services

The company also outsources services to various sectors of the industry such as hostesses, bodyguards, and tourist guides, as and when the need arises.

Mo Happy People Travel & Tours is busy expanding its products and service base, with the aim of becoming a one-stop travel and tourism company. It specialises in travel agency services, airport/hotel road transfers, point-to-point shuttle services, VIP bodyguard and chauffeur drive services, tailor-made tour packages, and open vehicle safaris. It has enjoyed an enormous growth in business as a result of word-of-mouth referrals. The company operates in South Africa,

Swaziland, Mozambique, Zimbabwe, Zambia, and Namibia. According to Gift, it aims to have offices in all these countries by 2010. The company has a website, www.mhptt.co.za, which markets it clearly to people all over the world and produces brochures for distribution throughout southern Africa as well as overseas.

MO Happy People Travel & Tours identifies the following challenges:

- the need to meet the expectations of often demanding customers
- the fragmented tourism structure in Limpopo
- the need to gain a competitive advantage
- finding ways of communicating successfully in the marketplace

The biggest challenge that Gift and Cindy have had to face in the industry is the racial divide caused by South Africa's fractured past. They were evidently not made to feel welcome on their arrival in Mpumalanga. While operating in Cape Town, they had been members of a fully-fledged and properly functional tourism structure, Cape Town Tourism. In Mpumalanga they found many different tourism bodies fighting each other over the same turf. This is still the case today, and is made worse by the fact that the private tourism sector and government are pulling in different directions. This has resulted in a great deal of confusion, and delays in the growth of the structures of tourism in Limpopo. Mo Happy Travel & Tours has decided to follow its own style, taking things one step at a time; doing its 'thing' slowly but surely, and thereby creating credibility for the company.

Gift and Cindy are convinced that once the structures of the tourism industry are established and functional, Limpopo will be a major player in South Africa's tourism industry. Their enthusiasm and their desire to work in conjunction with all structures is infectious. The tour company has, consequently, been approached for guidance by organisations and individuals in the industry to assist them in resolving some of their problems.

Today, the company largely targets wealthy foreign visitors seeking a southern African experience, and offers them destinations whose tailor-made itineraries are mainly cultural or safari-based.

Mo Happy People Travel and Tours has come a long way from its humble beginnings and, today, is considered among the leading young and up-and-coming travel companies in South Africa, because it offers a personalised professional service, efficiency and effectiveness in providing travel, tour and hospitality services, and advice to people from all over the world.

Case interviews:
Kealeboga Gift Mogapi, Managing Director; Cindy Florence Shongwe, General Manager, Mo Happy People Travel & Tours.

Case study questions

1. What competitive advantages do small specialist tour operating companies have over the larger tour operators?

2. Discuss the pros and cons of dropping the brochure entirely, and relying on a website to market Mo Happy People Travel & Tours.

3. Would you recommend that Mo Happy People Travel & Tours remains small, focusing on customer service delivery, or should Gift grow the company to compete with larger tour operating businesses?

8

environment & tourism

Department:
Environmental Affairs and Tourism
REPUBLIC OF SOUTH AFRICA

The government and tourism

Richard George

Purpose

This chapter examines the role of government in the management of tourism.

Learning outcomes

After reading this chapter, you should be able to:
- explain the role played by government in the planning and promotion of tourism
- explain what is meant by tourism public policy
- illustrate the importance of government involvement in all aspects of tourism
- assess the roles of public sector tourism bodies at an international level
- detail the structure of public sector tourism in South Africa
- identify and describe the functions of DMOs in South Africa.

Chapter overview

This chapter discusses the role played by national, provincial and local governments and their agencies in the planning and promotion of tourism in a country. The chapter begins with a discussion on the importance of public sector involvement in tourism. It then explores the key functions of government organisations' intervention in tourism from an international scale (i.e. the UN World Tourism Organisation) through to national (the Ministry of Tourism) and local levels (tourist information centres). The last part of the chapter explores several quasi-government organisations and sectoral (trade) tourism organisations, and the important role that they play in representing the public and private sectors of the South African tourism industry.

The concluding case study examines the government's Global Competitiveness Programme (GCP) for the South African Tourism Industry 2005–2010.

Introduction

Chapter one introduced the concept of Leiper's (1979) tourism system model as a way of better understanding the management of tourism. The system's model shows that tourism is affected by socio-cultural, economic, political, and legal macroenvironments beyond the control of the company, and that these environments are indirectly and directly managed and influenced by government. As Hall points out, governments shape the economic climate for the tourism industry, help provide infrastructure and educational requirements for tourism, establish the regulatory environment in which business operates, and take an active role in promotion and marketing (2005: 219). Government plays an important role in tourism, as it provides the overall regulatory framework within which the tourism industry operates, as well as directly intervening in many components of the tourism system.

The unique nature of the tourism industry

Before looking at government involvement in tourism, we first need to look at what it is that is unique in the nature of the tourism industry that highlights the importance of government intervention in it.

- traditionally the tourism industry is dominated by small, medium, and micro enterprises (SMMEs) and relatively few large multi-national corporations (MNCs) that have market presence
- the fragmented nature of the tourism industry
- seasonality (variations in the demand for tourism offerings makes it difficult to sustain business all year round)
- the geographical spread of tourism
- tourism is seen as a development tool (to rejuvenate economically depressed regions).

Tourism public policy framework

Chapter one discussed the fact that there exist a myriad of tourism definitions, and that there is no universally accepted definition of 'tourism'. Similarly, 'public policy' is equally problematic to define. According to Hall and Jenkins, tourism **public policy** is whatever governments choose to do or not to do with respect to tourism. This definition covers government action, inaction, decisions, and non-decisions regarding the tourism industry (1995: 7).

Public policy-making is the focal point of government activity (Hall & Jenkins, 1995: 1). Tourism public policy-making has become an important part of the system of many governments. According to Turner (1997), public policy in tourism is a function of three interrelated issues:

- the intentions of political and other key sectors
- the way in which decisions and non-decisions are made
- the implications of these decisions.

The World Travel & Tourism Council's (WTTC) *Blueprint for New Tourism 2006* (a document setting out the vision for a partnership between the private sector and public sectors geared to deliver tourism that benefits everyone in the twenty-first century) states that governments should:

- show leadership by defining coherent and streamlined management structures that can efficiently drive New Tourism.
- elevate tourism to strategic national level with senior policy-making
- factor tourism into all its policies and decision-making, to promote growth that respects both business needs and the well-being of citizens (WTTC, 2006: 11).

Policies exist at national, provincial and local government levels in South Africa. The Department of Environmental Affairs and Tourism's (DEAT) 1996 *White Paper on the Development and Promotion of Tourism in South Africa* provides the policy framework for tourism in the country. The paper contains a number of programmes that contribute to the growth of tourism in South Africa (see Example box).

Example The White Paper on the Development and Promotion of Tourism in SA

Tourism growth:
- facilitating increased tourist volumes, tourism spend and the geographical spread of tourism
- facilitating investment in infrastructure and product development in tourism priority areas
- creating awareness of the economical potential and impacts of tourism
- promoting domestic tourism
- monitoring tourism trends and providing timely information to the public and private sectors.

Government involvement in tourism management

In the study of tourism management it is important to include the sometimes unfashionable public sector to enable us to gain an understanding of the role and structure of tourism organisations at all levels.

Tourism is a major industry, and the government plays an important role in influencing and supporting the industry. The term 'government' is the name usually given to the public agencies that interact and implement the decisions of politicians and parliament. It is used interchangeably along with public service, public administration, the state, and the public sector (Hall, 2005: 218).

Although tourism as a 'business' should essentially be driven and operated by the private sector, there are several reasons why the government should be involved in planning and promoting tourism, including the facts that:
- thousands of businesses in South Africa depend in whole or in part on tourism – government can help diverse businesses to recognise their common interest in working together
- many core visitor attractions are public goods (national assets): these include natural features such as beaches, national parks, and heritage sites – particularly UNESCO World Heritage Sites (WHSs). Governments have a duty to protect a country's heritage

- many activities such as planning, research, transformation, and regulation can only be carried out effectively by government organisations who have the funds and power
- the lack of marketing (see Chapter 14) and human resources management (HRM) expertise (see Chapter 11). SMMEs in particular have inadequate funds to promote themselves
- social and political reasons need to be taken into account. For example, in South Africa the national airline (SAA) is state-owned and controlled. While the income accruing from the operation of the airline is important to the government, there is also the political prestige of operating an airline, even if the national flag-carrier is economically non-viable
- the private sector cannot do it alone – tourism requires partnerships with the public sector (ideally it should be public sector-led and private sector-driven).

Hall (1994) outlined six main functions of government in relation to tourism. These include: coordination, planning, legislation and regulation, stimulation, promotion, and a social tourism role.

Coordination

The first and perhaps most important role of government is that of coordination, which refers to the formal institutionalised relations between existing networks of organisations. This is a key issue, as the success of all the other roles is dependent on the ability of government to co-ordinate its various roles in the tourism development process. Indeed, Hall points out that the need for a coordinated tourism strategy has become one of the great truisms of tourism marketing, **policy**, and planning (2005: 223). Due to the fragmented nature of tourism within the economy, coordination for tourism usually occurs both vertically – for example, between different levels of government (e.g. national, provincial, local) within an administrative framework, and horizontally – for example, between different government agencies which may have responsibilities for tourism-related activities at the same level of governance (for example, transport, national parks, NGOs). The government plays a dominant role in tourism in South Africa, and is fully conscious of the need, on one hand, to provide the basic infrastructure for tourism development, while on the other to allow the private sector to drive tourism. The government's accelerated and shared growth initiative for South Africa (ASGISA) has identified tourism as an 'immediate high priority sector' (see Example box).

Example SA Deputy President backs tourism

South African Deputy President, Phumzile Mlambo-Ngcuka, officially opened Tourism Indaba 2006, highlighting the need for government to create 'an enabling environment' for tourism to grow. Among their priorities, she said, were air access, security, and reliable modern infrastructure. 'Furthermore, we need an efficient and reliable visa regime. In our case, we are working towards a Southern African Development Community (SADC) 'uni-visa' that will facilitate travel in all SADC countries', she said. Another challenge posed by the Deputy President was skills development. South Africa needs a skills revolution in which tourism benefits. The people to be trained are needed by employers, who must take greater responsibility than has been the case thus far to invest in human capital', she said. These and other obstacles will have to be addressed if the South African tourism industry is to reach the ambitious target set by government: growing arrivals to South Africa to 10-million a year by 2010; creating 400 000 new jobs in the industry by 2014; and raising the industry's GDP contribution from 8% to 12% by 2014.

In March 2006 Mlambo-Ngcuka also launched the joint initiative on priority skills acquisition (JIPSA), which will identify and advise on scarce skills in a bid to help the country achieve the accelerated and shared growth initiative for South Africa's (ASGISA) goal, namely a growth of 6% by 2010 and a 50% reduction in unemployment by 2014. Tourism-related skills are one of JIPSA's priorities.

Source: www.deat.gov.za

Planning

Government planning for tourism takes place in several forms (for example, development, infrastructure, land and resource use, promotion, and marketing), institutions (different government agencies, for example), and scales (for example national, regional, provincial, and local).

Legislation and regulation

Government possesses a variety of legislative and regulative powers which directly affect tourism, such as legislation and parliamentary discussion papers, which may specifically refer to tourism. The South African national government, for example, introduced the Tourism Act in 1993 and devised the *White Paper on the Development and Promotion of Tourism in South Africa* (DEAT, 1996) and *Guidelines for Responsible Tourism* (DEAT, 2002).

The South African tourism industry is governed by a wide range of laws and regulations spanning environmental protection, coastal management, health and consumer protection, trade, development, employment, education and training, competition, agriculture, transport, liquor sales, foreign currency, building and planning permissions, visa requirements, and much more. The industry is subject to the authority of various government departments at the national, provincial, and municipal level. The regulatory regimes imposed by these different authorities are not always as coherent and coordinated as might be desired.

DEAT has primary responsibility for tourism development, and is also responsible for developing policy and regulations specific to the sector, as well as for environmental and conservation issues. DEAT shares responsibility for the tourism sector with a number of other government departments and statutory authorities. The Department of Trade and Industry (dti) offers incentive schemes for businesses in the sector, including support for small business, and develops strategies to improve investment, competitiveness, and growth. It also governs the distribution of liquor. The Department of Home Affairs is responsible for visa regulations. The Department of Transport (DOT) develops and implements policy regarding aviation, taxi and tour operations, and transport for tourists in general (see Chapter 5). The Department of Arts and Culture is responsible for regulations pertaining to heritage issues. Zoning legislation is developed at local government level. Land management policy is the responsibility of the Department of Land Affairs (DLA). Health and safety regulations are developed at local government level, while the National Department of Health sets standards for the handling of food.

The need for tourism businesses to be aware of and compliant with the wide range of regulations applicable to them, together with their need to interact with a number of government departments and statutory bodies on specific issues, creates a considerable burden of 'red tape' for firms in this sector. A number of studies of the tourism industry in South Africa have identified regulation as an area requiring government attention. The dti has identified 'excessive' or 'unnecessary' regulations imposed by national, provincial, and local authorities as a constraint to the growth of firms in the tourism industry.[1] A 2006 Small Business Project (SBP) study looked in detail at the costs incurred by the tourism industry in complying with regulations – finding that tourism firms incur compliance costs up to 30% higher than firms in the broader economy.[2]

www

Browse this website: Visit the SBP's website: www.sbp.org.za

Stimulation

One of the main activities of government is to stimulate tourism development in ways, for example, such as providing financial incentives to tourism principals, sponsoring research on tourism, and marketing and promotion. In South Africa, DEAT works closely with local communities, small, medium and micro enterprises (SMMEs), and emerging entrepreneurs. An initiative such as the Tourism Enterprise Programme (TEP) –

a joint DEAT and Business Trust (BT) initiative – was launched to promote economic growth in the tourism industry. TEP's objective is to develop skills capacity and the participation of historically disadvantaged individuals (HDIs) within the tourism economy. TEP also aims to encourage and facilitate the growth and expansion of SMMEs within the tourism economy, resulting in job creation and economic growth (see Example box below).

Example Tourism entrepreneurs get a head start

The Tourism Enterprise Programme (TEP) is a job creation project for black entrepreneurs wishing to venture into the tourism industry. TEP aims to help small, medium and micro enterprises (SMMEs) to grow.

The programme helps SMMEs to identify viable business opportunities, and helps with International Organisation for Standardisation and South African Bureau of Standards (SABS) quality certification; debt and equity finance; business planning; packaging; legal advice; technology needs, and marketing.

The programme targets cultural groups, bed-and-breakfasts, lodges, tour guides and transport services, and arts and crafts.

TEP was launched in 2000 with an investment of R60-million from the Business Trust, ending in June 2004. In July 2004 the Business Trust and DEAT renewed the contract, investing another R80-million for three years.

Promotion

One of the actions of government in tourism is the promotion of tourism through marketing and promotional campaigns, which may be targeted at generating international or domestic tourism demand, as well as attracting investment. The task of promotion lies with government agencies called 'destination marketing organisations' (DMOs), as well as with public-private sector partnerships. We will examine the roles and responsibilities of DMOs later in the chapter.

> **Example** Government involvement in tourism
>
> The reasons for involvement of government in tourism development include:
> - to increase foreign exchange earnings
> - to create employment
> - to maximise the net benefits to the host region
> - to build the image of the country as a tourist destination
> - to market regulation to protect consumers and prevent unfair competition
> - to provide public goods and infrastructure as part of the tourism offering
> - to protect resources and the environment
> - to regulate aspects of social behaviour – for example, gambling
> - to monitor the level of tourism activity through surveys
> - social aspects, for example, improved well-being of citizens
> - a long-term growth and development strategy.
>
> Source: Adapted from Cooper *et al.*, 2006: 509. Reprinted by permission of Pearson Education Inc.

Discussion point

With reference to the example box above, why are governments interested in attracting more tourists to a country?

Social tourism

According to Hall (2005: 228), **social tourism** involves the extension of the benefits of holidays to economically marginal groups such as low-income groups, single-parent families, the elderly, the handicapped, and other deprived members of a population. Assistance may be offered in the form of finance (i.e. grants, low-interest loans), or as direct support through the provision of free coach trips, holiday accommodation, or reduced-priced holiday packages

The South African government has embarked on a series of campaigns to create a culture of travel within South Africa in recent years. In particular, it aims to encourage the participation of historically disadvantaged individuals (HDIs), many of whom have never been exposed to the tourism industry. An example is the Sho't Left

campaign, which has been the main driver behind promoting domestic tourism to South Africans. SA Tourism's slogan 'It's possible' was devised with domestic tourism in mind, and to encourage all South Africans that it is both affordable and possible to travel in and around South Africa (see Example box below).

The Sho't Left logo

> **Example** The Sho't Left campaign
>
> The phrase 'Sho't Left', which is a minibus taxi term for 'jump off just around there, or around the corner', was adopted by DEAT and SA Tourism as part of a marketing campaign during the last few years to target the domestic tourism market. The slogan attempts to encourage South Africans to travel; to 'get off around the corner', where the whole world meets them! There are over six million people in South Africa who are able to travel and want to, but, because of historical disadvantages, do not know where to start. Many South Africans are not familiar with the concept of travelling for leisure purposes. The campaign also addresses the issue of seasonality by encouraging domestic tour operators to package special offers for the local market during the off-peak seasons.

Government tourism organisations

Governments are involved with tourism organisations at international, regional, national, provincial, and local levels.

International government agencies

At an international level, governments, along with other member countries, are partners in such operative bodies or 'multinational agencies' as the United Nations World Tourism Organisation (UN-WTO), the World Travel and Tourism Council (WTTC), the Organisation for Economic Cooperation and Development (OECD), and the International Air Transport Association (IATA).

United Nations World Tourism Organisation (UN-WTO)

The United Nations World Tourism Organisation (UN-WTO) has its headquarters in Madrid, Spain, and assists approximately 150 member countries to provide a means for governments and industry members to work together to discuss issues and set global standards (see Example box). The re-designated UN-WTO[3] is a specialised UN agency, which has status within the UN system and a voting role in inter-agency mechanisms, such as the chief executives' board.

UN-WTO provides international tourism statistics, and advises on polices and best practices to improve **tourism planning**, education, and training. The UN-WTO was founded in 1946, with a mission to develop tourism as a significant means of fostering international peace and understanding, economic development, and international trade. Vellas and Becherel (1995) describe the UN-WTO as the principal source of statistics on international tourism. The organisation has released a series of studies and reports such as the Tourism Satellite Accounts (TSAs), which have set the benchmark for measuring the economic contribution of tourism for national accounts (ranging from GDP to job creation). Over 75 countries are currently using TSAs (see Chapter 15 – Impacts of tourism).

UN-WTO plays a dominant role in collecting and collating statistical information on international tourism. This world governing body on tourism represents public-sector tourism bodies from most countries in the world, and the publication of its data enables comparisons to be made of the flow and growth of tourism on a global scale.

UN-WTO also works with the World Trade Organisation (WTO) to support broad-scale liberalisation of the tourism sector through the WTO's General Agreement on Trade Services (GATS).

> **Example** The World Tourism Organisation (UN-WTO)
>
> The World Tourism Organisation (UN-WTO), a specialised agency of the United Nations, is the leading international organisation in the field of tourism. It serves as a global forum for tourism policy issues and as a practical source of tourism know-how.
>
> UN-WTO's functions include:
> - assisting member countries, tourist destinations, and businesses to maximise the positive economic, social, and cultural effects of tourism
> - assisting in tourism planning as an executing agency of the United Nations Development Programme (UNDP)
> - advising on the harmonisation of policies and practices
> - sponsoring education and training, and identifying funding sources
> - promoting the broader relationships of visitors to the physical and social environment, by defining 'sustainability' as development which meets the needs of present tourists and host regions, while protecting and enhancing opportunities for the future
> - encouraging the implementation of a Global Code of Ethics for Tourism for the observance of human rights and fundamental freedoms.
>
> Source: www.world-tourism.org

> **www**
>
> Browse this website: www.world-tourism.org

WORLD TOURISM ORGANIZATION
ORGANISATION MONDIALE DU TOURISME
ORGANIZACIÓN MUNDIAL DEL TURISMO
ВСЕМИРНАЯ ТУРИСТСКАЯ ОРГАНИЗАЦИЯ
منظمة السياحة العالمية

The UN-WTO's logo

Organisation for Economic Cooperation and Development (OECD)

The Organisation for Economic Cooperation and Development (OECD) groups together 30 member countries which share a commitment to democratic government and the market economy. With active relationships with some 70 other countries, NGOs, and civil society, it has a global reach. Best known for its publications and statistics, its work covers economic and social issues from macroeconomics to trade, education, development and science, and innovation.

OECD also has a Tourism Committee, consisting of tourism officials drawn from its member countries, which provides regular reports comprising comparative data on tourism development to and within these countries. The Tourism Committee aims to enhance the capacity of OECD governments to adjust their policies and actions to support sustainable tourism growth, and to better integrate **tourism policy** issues. In addition, it attempts to raise awareness of international issues and to foster international co-operation. The OECD has produced several reports, including *Measuring the role of tourism OECD economies* (2000), a manual detailing the application of Tourism Satellite Accounts (TSAs) in 16 OECD countries.

www

Browse this website: www.oecd.org

World Travel & Tourism Council (WTTC)

The World Travel and Tourism Council (WTTC) is a privately-sponsored pressure ('lobby') group representing the interests of the world's leading tourism companies. Formed in 1988, the WTTC works with governments to maximise the benefits that tourism can bring to the world economy. It is the only body representing the private sector in the global travel and tourism industry. Its members are drawn from more than 30 leading airlines and tourist organisations. This body also regularly commissions and publishes research data highlighting the significance of tourism as a generator of income and jobs. For example, more recently, its *Blueprint for New Tourism* (2006) encouraged governments to unlock tourism potential by adopting its policy framework for sustainable tourism development.

www

Browse this website: www.wttc.org

International Air Transport Association (IATA)

The International Air Transport Association (IATA) is a voluntary international trade organisation representing over 270 of the world's leading passenger and cargo airlines operating on international routes (approximately 95% of all airline traffic). IATA has been operating for more than 60 years. Its main aims are to:

- ensure that its members' aircraft can fly around the globe safely, securely, and efficiently under agreed rules and regulations
- ensure that people, mail, and freight can also move around the globe efficiently
- control ticket costs and ensure that tickets (including e-tickets) are universally usable
- work with governments to set global standards of safety and efficiency.

www

Browse this website: www.iata.org

Pan-regional government agencies

There are, in addition to the international tourism agencies, a variety of pan-regional agencies/bodies that have a specific region of the world as their focus. These agencies, which are also referred to as 'regional tourism organisations', are non-profit-making organisations. They have the task of promoting tourism to their specific regions on behalf of their member NTOs. Pan-regional government agencies primarily undertake activities such as marketing, development, and market research. For example, the Regional Tourism Organisation of Southern Africa (RETOSA) has a mandate to promote southern Africa (the SADC region) as an attractive destination through public relations, market research, and travel trade promotions. The other major regional government agencies are the Pacific Asia Travel Association (PATA) (see Example box), European Travel Commission (ETC), Indian Ocean Tourism Organisation (IOTO), and the Organisation of American States (OAS).

Example Pacific Asia Travel Association (PATA)

Founded in 1951, the Pacific Asia Travel Association (PATA) is the recognised authority on Asia Pacific travel and tourism. PATA provides leadership and advocacy to the collective efforts of over 100 government, state and city tourism bodies, more than 55 airlines and cruise liners, and hundreds of travel industry companies. In addition, thousands of travel professionals belong to dozens of PATA chapters worldwide. PATA's mission is to enhance the growth, value and quality of Asia Pacific travel and tourism for the benefits of its membership. PATA is a non-profit organisation.

---

www

Browse this website: www.pata.org

We will now look closely at two of these regional tourism agencies: the ETC and RETOSA

European Travel Commission (ETC)

The European Travel Commission (ETC) is responsible for the promotion and marketing of Europe as a tourist destination. ETC, which was established in 1948, comprises NTOs of 37 European countries (from Austria to the Ukraine). It is a non-profit organisation, which provides a forum for the directors of all the European NTOs to meet regularly and exchange ideas.

---

www

Browse this website: www.etc-corporate.org

Regional Tourism Organisation of Southern Africa (RETOSA)

The Regional Tourism Organisation of Southern Africa (RETOSA)'s main objective is to spread the benefits of tourism across the **Southern African Development Community** (SADC) region (14 countries), and to market and promote the region as a world-class destination using a cooperative approach involving the regions' national tourism organisations (NTOs), the private sector, and local communities (see Example box).

Example RETOSA

Tourism is seen as one of the greatest assets of Southern Africa. The Southern African Development Community (SADC) established the regional tourism agency known as the Regional Tourism Organisation of Southern Africa (RETOSA) in 1995. RETOSA is a private and public sector organisation which aims to promote the region as a world-class tourism destination.

RETOSA promotes the rich wildlife in game reserves and national parks, as well as natural attractions such as the Okavango Delta, Mount Kilimanjaro, Table Mountain National Park, and Victoria Falls. RETOSA also promotes the region's historical and cultural heritage to major markets in Europe, North America, and Asia.

RETOSA carries out its objective to spread the benefits of tourism across the region through sustainable tourism. It also aims to increase the number of tourists who visit the region, and it encourages cross-border (intra-regional) travel. RETOSA works closely with the region's NTOs, such as South African Tourism and Namibia Tourism.

RETOSA's logo

www

Browse this website: www.retosa.co.za

Government tourism agencies in South Africa

South Africa's **national tourism organisation** (NTO) is South African Tourism (SA Tourism), which reports directly to the Ministry of Tourism

– the Department of Environmental Affairs and Tourism (DEAT). The country's nine provinces all have their own tourism authorities (provincial tourism organisations), which work fairly closely with SA Tourism and DEAT in promoting and developing tourism to international tourism markets.

There are five types of government sector tourism agencies with interests in destination tourism development and promotion in South Africa:

1. The Ministry of Tourism, Department of Environmental Affairs and Tourism (DEAT), which is responsible for government policy on tourism developments.
2. A national tourism organisation (NTO), South African Tourism, which aims to increase the total number of international tourists to South Africa.
3. Nine provincial tourism authorities (PTA) – (e.g. the Gauteng Tourism Authority), which aims to promote individual provinces to international and domestic tourists.
4. Regional tourism organisations (RTOs) in each province (approximately four to seven; this varies per province), to promote regions within their respective provinces.
5. Local tourism organisations (LTOs) – managing services for visitors (the number of these varies for each province). In the Western Cape, for example, there are approximately 70 LTOs.

Figure 8.1 The structure of tourism administration in South Africa

The role of local, provincial and national government tourism agencies is to maximise tourism growth and the development opportunities of their respective regions. Figure 8.1 (on the previous page) shows the structure of tourism administration in South Africa.

www

Browse this website: www.environment.gov.za

We will now take a look at each of the government tourism agencies.

Department of Environmental Affairs & Tourism (DEAT)

In the structure of tourism administration in South Africa, the Department of Environmental Affairs and Tourism (DEAT) sits at the top (see Figure 8.2). DEAT, which is the Ministry of Tourism for South Africa, is an influential agency that is responsible for tourism policy, regulation, and development (see Example box). DEAT plays a dual role, in that it is responsible for environmental affairs as well as tourism.

DEAT consists of five branches:
1. Environmental quality
2. Marine and coastal management
3. Tourism
4. Conservation
5. Biodiversity and conservation.

Example The Department of Environmental Affairs and Tourism

Vision and mission
DEAT's vision is to create a prosperous and equitable society, living in harmony with the country's resources.

DEAT's mission is to lead sustainable development of our environment and tourism for a better life for all, by:
• creating conditions for sustainable tourism growth and development
• promoting the sustainable development and conservation of our natural resources
• protecting and improving the quality and safety of the environment
• promoting a global sustainable development agenda
• transformation of the department, statutory bodies, and economic sector.

www

Browse this website: www.deat.gov.za

Figure 8.2 Structure of DEAT's support system.

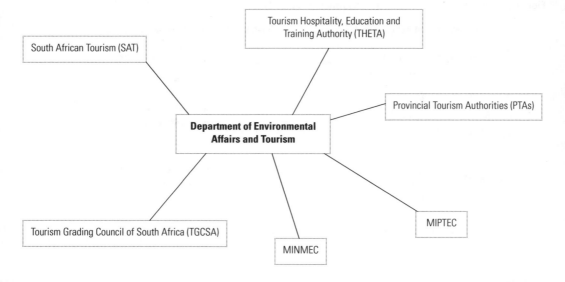

Discussion point

Is there a case for a separate tourism minister in South Africa?

Department of Trade and Industry (dti)

As tourism is a priority sector of the economy, in addition to being supported by a ministry, it is also supported by a small unit in the Department of Trade and Industry (dti). The responsibility of the tourism unit in the dti is to:

- devise and implement (in partnership with DEAT and other bodies) a tourism sector development strategy
- recruit local and foreign investment into the sector
- increase exports in tourism (literally foreign tourist arrivals).

The first objective includes resolving barriers to competitiveness such as restrained airlift, inadequate skills development, lack of transformation, and the absence of **Tourism Satellite Accounts** (TSAs). Many of these projects are necessarily championed elsewhere (by DEAT, or the Department of Transport, or Statistics South Africa). Increasing investment levels involve co-ordinating activities across the various investment promotion players, establishing investment promotion platforms, developing a database of scoped investment projects, etc.

The last objective (export promotion) is supported through the financing of mini-pavilions at international trade shows for high-growth niche industry associations, as well as the financing of hosted buyers' missions to the country. In this regard, the dti supported Backpacking South Africa (BSA) to represent the youth, student, backpacking, and volunteer tourism segments at three global trade shows in 2006. It also funded Fair Trade in Tourism South Africa (FTTSA), which represented accredited responsible tourism businesses at the Reisepavilion Trade Show in Germany. The dti sponsor about 50 business

tourism buyers (buyers on behalf of corporate, government, association, and incentive travel) to attend Meetings Africa, the major annual business tourism event in South Africa.

www

Browse this website: www.thedti.gov.za

A range of other ministries and government departments, however, influence and impact on tourism. Tourism relies, for example, on adequate skills development, and this is associated with the ministries of education and labour. It also requires a safe and secure environment for tourists – hence the Ministry of Safety and Security plays a role, as does the South African Police Services (SAPS). Transportation is also key to facilitating tourism and creating the enabling environment described earlier, so the Department of Transport also has to become involved.

MINMEC and MIPTEC are two co-ordinating structures to ensure that policies and strategies are aligned. MINMEC and MIPTEC also facilitate communication and collaboration between DEAT and provincial governments.

MINMEC

MINMEC is a forum comprising the Minister of Environmental Affairs & Tourism, national ministers, and the Members of Executive Councils (MECs) responsible for tourism in the nine provinces. This is where the policy matters and issues between national and provincial governments are decided.

MIPTEC

MIPTEC is an inter-provincial technical committee (ITC), which brings together national and provincial officials, heads, and the CEOs of provincial tourism authorities (PTAs) to coordinate provincial and national tourism offices in support of MINMEC.

Destination Marketing Organisations (DMOs)

The promotion of tourism is carried out at national tourism organisation (NTO), provincial tourism authority (PTA), regional tourism organisation (RTO), and local tourism organisation (LTO) levels. The most commonly used term which encompasses all of these organisations is a destination marketing organisation (DMO)[4].

Destination marketing organisations (DMOs) are non-profit entities aimed at generating tourist visitations for a given area (Gretzel, *et al.*, 2006). According to Pike (2004: 14), a DMO is any organisation, at any level, which is responsible for the marketing of an identifiable destination. DMOs have the role of marketing cities, areas, regions, provinces, and countries to tourism intermediaries (the travel trade) and individual travellers (George, 2004: 337). DMOs also co-ordinate most private and public tourism role players and provide information to tourists.

Due to the complex nature of the tourism industry and its role players, DMOs face numerous challenges in formulating and implementing effective marketing strategies. Table 8.1 outlines six challenges for DMOs. DMOs have the primary role of selling places.

Pike defines a destination marketing organisation as:

> 'any organisation, at any level, which is responsible for the marketing of an identifiable destination. This therefore excludes separate government departments which are responsible for planning and policy' (2004: 14).

DMO names

There currently exists a plethora of DMO names, including:

- agencies (Gauteng Tourism Agency)
- authority (Zimbabwe Tourism Authority)
- associations (Tshwane Tourism Association)

Table 8.1 Challenges for DMOs

Challenge	Factors
Adapting to technological change	Lack of human and financial resources Internet technology is not just a substitute for old ways of marketing Websites not catering to customers' unique needs
Managing expectations	Leadership role of DMOs in local communities Communicating more effectively by recognising changes in consumer behaviour Need for community relations plan
From destination marketing to destination management	More complex DMO responsibilities Increasing involvement in planning and development projects Need to change LTA structures
Confronting new levels of competition	Fight for market share with other destinations emergence of non-profit destination management companies Compete with other sectors for increasingly limited funding
Recognising creative partnering as the new way of life	Partnerships beyond geographical boundaries Lack of incentives for partnering Need for creative partnering ideas
Finding new measures of success	Increased need to demonstrate accountability Finding the benchmarks and benchmarking partners Responsibilities and marketing tools have changed, but evaluations still based on traditional methods

Adapted from Gretzel, U., Fesenmaier, D.R., Formica, S. & O'Leary, J.T. 2006. 'Searching for the future: challenges faced by destination marketing organisations'. *Journal of Travel Research*, Vol. 45(2), 116–126

- boards (Eastern Cape Tourism Board)
- bureaux (Darling Tourist Bureau; convention and visitor bureaux)
- councils (International Marketing Council)
- corporations (Lesotho Tourism Development Corporation)
- departments (Department of Economic Development & Tourism)
- directorates (Mpumalanga Tourism Directorate)
- ministries (Namibia Ministry of Environment & Tourism)
- tourist offices (South African Tourism London Office)
- organisations (Khayalethu Community Tourism Organisation)
- regions (Regional Tourism Organisation of Southern Africa)
- commissions (Swaziland National Trust Commission)
- centres (Cape Town Tourism Centre).

Several DMOs have incorporated 'tourism' and 'destination' into their names – such as 'Tourism KwaZulu-Natal', and the 'visit' in 'VisitBritain' and 'VisitScotland' – also 'Destination Australia' and 'Destination Pakistan'.

The main DMO goals can be summarised as relating to the following four themes (Pike, 2004: 45):
- enhancing destination image
- increasing industry profitability
- reducing seasonality
- maximising the economic contribution of tourism.

The roles of DMOs, which are similar around the world, include the following:

Marketing

The primary responsibility of DMOs at all levels is destination marketing. Advertising and promotional activities are the most visible actions of a

DMO and, as such, are likely to receive mixed reviews by the local community. Key DMO marketing activities include: identifying target markets (research), advertising, PR and publicity, direct marketing, sales promotions, and personal selling. DMOs are increasingly making use of a relatively new approach to marketing; namely integrated marketing communications. The main aspects of integrated marketing communications are the development of profitable consumer relationships, effective relationships with stakeholders, and synergy of messages. According to Pike, integrated marketing communications represent the way forward for DMOs confronted by significant changes in the destination marketing paradigm (2004: 154).

A typical table of contents for a DMO marketing plan generally includes the sections as shown in Table 8.2 below. It is important that a clear and succinct mission (in the form of a mission statement) is articulated to stakeholders, because of the political dynamics of destination marketing. Some examples of DMO mission statements are listed in Table 8.3 overleaf.

www

Browse this website: www.destinationmarketing.org

Table 8.2 Table of contents for a DMO marketing plan

1. Executive summary
2. Mission and vision
3. Environmental analysis
   - macro-environmental analysis
   - resource auditing
   - competitive positioning analysis
   - product analysis
4. Goals and objectives
5. Target market selection
6. Marketing mix
7. Action plan timelines
8. Budget
9. Performance measures

Table 8.3 DMOs' mission statements

Organisation	Mission statement
Swaziland Ministry of Tourism	To ensure sustainable and equitable development through the promotion of sound environmental principles, conservation of our national heritage, and efficient communication infrastructure, which is conducive to Swazis and attractive to international visitors, and to ensure efficient and effective custody of all recorded information.
Zimbabwe Tourism Authority (ZTA)	To work with various stakeholders to sustainably develop and promote Zimbabwe as a leading tourist destination through setting and monitoring high standards, market research, and product development.

Monitoring service and quality standards

One of the main roles of a DMO is to ensure the provision of good-quality accommodation, welcoming hosts, attractive prices, and high standards at visitor attractions, as well as good accessibility. An accommodation classification system – the Tourism Grading Council of South Africa (TGCSA) – was launched in 2000 by DEAT. The current mandate of the TGCSA is to provide a framework and process for grading across all relevant sectors of the tourism industry in South Africa. TGCSA performs the important role of ensuring that a standard of quality is achieved across all the services and facilities offered by the South African tourism role-players.

Coordination of the tourism industry

One of the major functions of DMOs is to develop a cohesive approach among stakeholders – for example, government, private sector industry 'trade' associations, tourism businesses, host communities (citizens), and other NGOs. DMOs

also provide a vision/mission for all stakeholders to increase destination competitiveness. This entails sharing resources, in an effort to create a greater impact in the market.

Enhancing community relations

An important function of DMOs is to inform the local community, which ultimately delivers DMO's promises, of the organisation's purpose and role. It is important that the host community's values are respected and included. One of the ways that this can be achieved is through delivering consistent messages that repeat key terms (such as 'economic development' and 'job creation').

National tourism organisations (NTOs)

A nation's government is usually responsible for the establishment of a national tourism organisation (NTO). According to Pike (2004: 14), the term NTO is used to represent the entity with overall responsibility for marketing a country as a tourism destination. NTOs are therefore responsible for promoting the destination to international and domestic tourist markets.

The functions of NTOs

NTOs, which are part of the destination organiser sector, play an important role in influencing tourists and potential tourists to a country. However, there is a dearth of academic literature on the structure and role of NTOs. Indeed, no universally accepted model for NTO structure currently exists (Pike, 2004: 39).

The marketing department devises the NTO's marketing strategy, which would include several promotional and advertising campaigns. Besides the traditional promotional tools, NTOs target the travel trade through **familiarisation trips** and attendance at travel trade shows (see Example). NTOs also operate and administer offices in key markets, which act as 'shop windows' to potential tourists, enabling them to obtain information and brochures about the host destination.

environment & tourism

Department:
Environmental Affairs and Tourism
REPUBLIC OF SOUTH AFRICA

SOUTH AFRICAN TOURISM

www.southafrica.net

SOUTH AFRICA
It's possible

South African Tourism's imposing head office and SAT's branding logo

Example SA Tourism targets the Japanese travel trade

During 2006, South African Tourism hosted some 2 000 foreign travel agents and other tourism stakeholders. The first trip saw 50 Japanese delegates embark on a week-long journey throughout South Africa. Their visit culminated in a gala event hosted at the Maropeng Interpretation Centre at the Cradle of Humankind in Gauteng.

The familiarisation trip is one component of SA Tourism's relationship with the Japanese trade in its quest to grow arrivals from Japan (over 27 000 Japanese tourists travelled to South Africa during 2005).

Source: Natalia Thomson, *Southern Africa Tourism Update*, August 2006: 4.

Cradle of Humankind©
Ⓡ World Heritage Site

Discussion point

Discuss why government should or should not fund tourism promotion in South Africa.

South African Tourism (SA Tourism)

South African Tourism (SA Tourism), which is the NTO of South Africa, has as its main function the marketing of South Africa as an attractive destination to foreign tourists. It aims not only to increase the total number of tourists to the country, but also to spread visitors evenly throughout the provinces all year round. SA Tourism is a statutory body of DEAT, by virtue of its having its own chief executive officer (CEO) and board of directors. The organisation works on a total annual budget of about R500-million to spend on marketing initiatives. SA Tourism has 12 business units at its headquarters, each with its own business plans and budget, and each reporting to a Business Unit Manager. The units are: Americas, Asia, Europe, Africa, Central Marketing, Research, E-business, Communications & PR, Finance and Administration, HR, office of the CEO, Strategic Relations, and Business Tourism.

In the past, SA Tourism's primary role was to market South Africa as an international tourism destination. SA Tourism, however, is currently playing a more pro-active role in boosting domestic tourism and encouraging travel by South Africans within their own country. This follows the decision by DEAT to include domestic tourism as part of SA Tourism's mandate.

Business tourism now has its own unit within SA Tourism, because of its importance in terms of tourist expenditure and the unique servicing requirements of the meetings industry (corporates, associations, and inter-governmental) travel markets, compared to leisure tourism.

SA Tourism employs more than 140 people and has a total of 10 overseas offices, based in a number of strategically located long-haul markets.

1. Europe – Amsterdam, Frankfurt, London, Milan, and Paris
2. North America – New York
3. Asia Pacific – Beijing, Sydney, Mumbai, and Tokyo

SA Tourism offices are each responsible for raising awareness of the offerings, activities, and destinations which South Africa offers. SA Tourism offices also promote the business tourism sector to their respective markets.

Over the last few years SA Tourism, in conjunction with DEAT, devised an in-depth marketing strategy, the Tourism Growth Strategy (TGS). This was first announced in 2002, and has subsequently been updated to the TGS 2005–2008. The aim of the TGS is to market the country and to put into practice an action plan to reposition the brand and to encourage domestic and international tourism in South Africa. Also announced was the Tourism Transformation Strategy (TTS), which aims to develop black-owned businesses within the tourism industry and the Business Tourism Growth Strategy (launched in 2007). Following research on the domestic market, DEAT and SA Tourism produced a Domestic Tourism Growth Strategy 2004–2007.

DEAT and SA Tourism have partnerships with sectoral organisations such as the Tourism Business Council of South Africa (TBCSA) and the Business Trust (BT) (to be discussed in the next section).

National government plays a key role in South Africa in funding SA Tourism's government-led marketing activities. In addition, SA Tourism's international marketing activities are part-funded by the levies raised through Tourism Marketing South Africa or TOMSA (see Example box). The funds are collected through a consumer levy on tourism products in South Africa, such as a bed

tax and an international airport departure tax. NTO partnership between private and public sector partnerships is extremely powerful in marketing destinations.

> **Example** Tourism Marketing South Africa (TOMSA)
>
> TOMSA (Tourism Marketing South Africa) is the name of a trust account originally set up by the TBCSA, to raise funds for the generic marketing of South Africa internationally. TOMSA was founded in 1996 after the establishment of TBCSA. The funds are collected through a consumer levy on tourism products in South Africa. In consultation with the hospitality sector, a 1% addition to all accounts was agreed. Car hire companies agreed to a 1% addition to their daily/weekly rates, and coach operators agreed on a set amount per passenger. The levy is voluntary, from both a consumer and a tourism establishment perspective. TOMSA contributed more than R50-million to SA Tourism's total marketing budget during 2005 (approximately R500-million per year).

> **www**
>
> Browse these websites: www.tomsa.co.za
> www.tourismlevy.co.za

SA Tourism's marketing activities

SA Tourism carries out a number of marketing activities targeting consumers as well as the trade, including:

- producing promotional material – printed media brochures, promotional videos, CDs and DVDs, and newsletters to the travel trade

- participating in travel trade shows including the Tourism Indaba (in South Africa), the Internationale Tourismus-Börse (ITB) in Berlin, the World Travel Market (WTM) in London, and business tourism trade shows, such as the IMEX in Frankfurt, Germany
- organising PR events
- educating the trade seminars, workshops, and events in co-operation with tour operators and partners such as the South African Tour Operators Association (SATOA)
- educating the trade, such as the FUNDI programme (see Example box)
- sponsoring events such as the Scandinavian Masters Golf Tournament (held in South Africa).

Example Fundi e-training programmes

The Fundi (meaning 'expert') e-training, a specialist destination programme, is delivered via the SA Tourism web site. Two courses, an international and a domestic programme, which are both divided into eight modules, are offered. SA Fundi programmes are used by the international and domestic travel trade to ensure that travel agents and wholesalers understand the local consumer, and at the same time know which product offerings and experiences to sell to international and local travellers. SA Fundi graduates receive additional support from SA Tourism, and become eligible for a range of incentives.

SA Tourism's marketing research activities

SA Tourism has invested significant funds in market research over the last few years to gain market intelligence, to help it identify core market segments clearly, and to examine SA Tourism's image as an international tourist destination in key markets. SA Tourism currently has a number of 'growth' markets (those markets which offer opportunity for growth) and 'defend' segments (those which should just be defended). Research into market segments is commissioned to a UK-based research company, Monitor Group. Monitor Group is a global market research company, which conducts qualitative and quantitative research amongst tourism stakeholders and tourists.

Provincial tourism authorities (PTAs)

Provincial tourism authorities (PTAs) are responsible for marketing and promoting the **unique selling points** (USPs) of an area as a tourism destination. PTAs (also referred to as provincial tourism organisations) manage and align themselves with policies and strategies devised at national level by DEAT and SA Tourism (such as the National & Provincial White Papers on Tourism and the National TGS).

In South Africa, each of the nine provinces has its own PTA. Each PTA receives an annual marketing budget from their respective provincial governments to develop marketing strategies. To date, the success of tourism marketing, promotion and development has varied across the provinces.

At provincial level there are four provinces where tourism development, marketing and regulation are outsourced to public entities/bodies. These provinces are ECTB, GTA, KZNTA and MTA. Four other provinces all conduct these functions 'in-house': Free State Department of Tourism, Environmental and Economic Affairs; Limpopo Department of Economic Development, Environment and Tourism (DEDET), North West DEDET and Northern Cape Department of Economic Affairs and Tourism. The Western Cape's Department of Economic Development and Tourism outsources the tourism marketing function to CTRU.

Regional tourism organisations (RTOs)

Below the level of PTAs, regional tourism organisations (RTOs) are tasked with promoting tourism to their respective regions. For example, in Limpopo province there are five RTOs, each responsible for promoting the attributes of their tourist region: Waterberg, Capricorn, Vhembe, Mopane, and Sekhukhune.

RTOs are government agencies, which also rely on funding from membership fees. These fees are derived from a variety of sources, including local authorities, private businesses, and the PTAs – all with an interest in the region.

RTOs are largely membership organisations. Businesses have to pay a fee to join and, in return, receive RTO services which include marketing and promotion of their offerings, information dissemination (via brochures, website, information officers), and support. RTOs receive an annual operating budget from national government, although they are also dependent for funding on membership fees paid by private sector tourism businesses and on contributions from local municipal departments.

> **Example** Regional Tourism Organisations (RTOs)
>
> The term 'region' has a number of different meanings, ranging in geographical scope from a trans-national area, such as southern Africa, to a local area. In South Africa, RTOs refer to regions within a province, which are responsible to PTAs.

> **Example** Durban Tourism
>
> Durban Tourism's role as a CUB is to market Durban as the ideal business, event, incentive, and leisure tourism destination. It aims to:
> - Promote and position Durban as a unique tourism destination, providing a true African experience
> - Use conventions and events as tactical marketing tools for positioning and branding.
> - Use the diversity of Durban's unique 'world-in-one' product offerings and cultural and heritage background as a tool to attract both domestic and international markets.

Local tourism organisations (LTOs) and tourist information centres (TICs)

Local tourism organisations (LTOs,[5] also called local tourism bureaux or boards), have the role of managing services for visitors, via tourist information centres (TICs), which provide a contact point for domestic and international visitors. TICs (sometimes referred to as visitor information centres) play a particularly important role in disseminating information about tourism in their local areas. They provide up-to-date information on a range of accommodation options, events, attractions, activities, and transport providers to visitors. TICs have the following functions:
- to promote the local tourism authority
- to distribute brochures
- to make bookings
- to provide information.

TICS are becoming increasingly commercial in their operations, by charging for their services and selling a range of products such as curios, books, and maps. Ultimately, they provide a service to visitors and satisfy the craving of today's tourists for travel destination information.

Sectoral tourism organisations and trade associations

There are a number of organisations that represent the private and public sector bodies of the South

African tourism industry. These sectoral organisations work in partnership with the government and the private sector and are usually non-profit making. The overall aims of these organisations, in general, are to ensure that national and provincial tourism policy and strategic directions will be a joint undertaking. For example, the Tourism Business Council of South Africa (TBCSA), a statutory body, acts as a conduit between the private and public sectors of the tourism industry and, in so doing, strives to be a voice for the South African tourism industry on issues that affect tourism, and to mediate the best and most sustainable position across the industry.

Trade associations (sometimes called membership organisations), such as the Federated Hospitality Association of South Africa (FEDHASA), represent their own interest groups and functions. THETA (Tourism, Hospitality & Sport, Education and Training) is accountable to the Department of Labour, although DEAT serves on THETA's board and signs off their sector skills plan.

Indeed, many trade associations are themselves members of sectoral tourism organisations, such as TBCSA (see Example box). Trade associations make a huge contribution to the South African tourism industry, as their members are often strongly associated with tourism at a grassroots level. The aims of these sector organisations are outlined in Table 8.4 overleaf.

Various tourism trade associations' logos

> **Example** Tourism Business Council of South Africa (TBCSA)
>
> Formed in 1996, the Tourism Business Council of South Africa (TBCSA) is the umbrella tourism industry body, whose main function is to grow the tourism economy for the benefit of all South Africans. TBCSA engages with all stakeholders, including SA Tourism, THETA, TGCSA, DEAT, and SANParks in developing overall strategies that create an environment conducive to the development of tourism.
>
> Over the last 10 years, TBCSA has been at the forefront of transformation in the industry; instrumental in improving airline access to the country, improving standards and quality in accommodation establishments, and providing access to statistical information related to tourism. It has also been successful in attracting funding for projects and acting as an incubator for ideas that have resulted in sustainable tourism developments.

Conclusion

The role of government in influencing the direction of the development and marketing of tourism is crucial in the shaping of the tourism system. In this chapter we have examined the main role and functions of government intervention in tourism, and defined tourism public policy.

Governments are involved in supporting powerful inter-governmental agencies such as the UN-WTO at an international level. At a national level, government and the private sector need to work more closely to manage, plan, control, and develop tourism. The South African government plays an important role in relation to tourism. The Ministry of Tourism, DEAT, is responsible for tourism policy, regulation, and development in South Africa. SA Tourism's main role is marketing and creating a brand image of the country. Tourism is important to the South African economy, and is seen as a saviour regarding issues such

Table 8.4 Various sectoral tourism organisations and trade associations in South Africa

Acronym & website	Name of organisation	Aims
ASATA www.asata.co.za	Association for South African Travel Agents	To represent travel agents, inbound and outbound tour operators as well as protect the rights of consumers.
BABASA www.babsa.co.za	Bed & Breakfast Association of South Africa	To ensure customers receive quality, service and excellence in the hospitality industry.
BARSA www.barsa.co.za	Board of Airline Representatives of South Africa	To facilitate, promote, represent, and protect the commercial and professional interests of its members in South Africa.
BSA www.btsa.co.za	Backpacking South Africa	To ensure that people, who visit the country as backpackers or independent travellers, can be assured that there is an organisation that is interested in making their stay the most enjoyable in the world.
FEDHASA www.fedhasa.co.za	Federated Hospitality Association of South Africa	To protect and serve the needs of the hospitality sector.
FTTSA www.fairtourismsa.org.za	Fair Trade in Tourism South Africa	To facilitate improved access to tourism markets for disadvantaged tourism enterprises.
SAACI www.saaci.co.za	Southern African Association for the Conference Industry	To maintain and improve standards of efficiency and professionalism in the conference industry in southern Africa.
SAATP www.tourismprofessionals.org	Southern African Association of Tourism Professionals	To represent the collective interests of individuals operating at a professional level in southern Africa.
SATSA www.satsa.co.za	Southern Africa Tourism Services Association	To represent the private sector of the tourism industry. It established, promotes and represents the views of the tourist industry.
TBCSA www.tbcsa.org.za	Tourism Business Council of South Africa	To ensure that the business sector of the tourism industry is effectively represented at provincial and national government levels.
TGCSA www.tourismgrading.co.za	Tourism Grading Council of South Africa	To provide a framework and process for grading across all relevant sector of the tourism industry in South Africa.
THETA www.theta.org.za	Tourism , Hospitality & Sport Education and Training Authority	To help tourism fulfil its potential by promoting and facilitating training and skills development.

as employment creation and poverty alleviation. As such, tourism is high on the government's policy agenda. Notwithstanding, administrative and policy co-ordination between different government agencies, as well as entering into partnerships with the private sector, remain key issues and challenges in the management of tourism in South Africa.

Notes

1. DTI, 2003, Annual Review of Small Business in South Africa – 2003, 77–78.

2. For further detail, see 'Counting the cost of red tape in the tourism sector, SBP, November 2006', and 'Counting the costs of red tape for business in South Africa, SBP, June 2005'. These reports can be accessed on the SBP website, www.sbp.org.za

3. In December 2005, the Madrid-based World Tourism Organisation (WTO) – added the letters UN (UN-WTO), to differentiate it from the other WTO, the Geneva-based World Trade Organisation.

4. This level of DMO is also referred to as other names in different parts of the world, such as regional tourism board (RTBs) in the UK, and **convention and visitor bureaux** (CVBs) in the USA.

5. A term used to represent both a local tourism administration and a local tourism association; the former may be a local government authority, while the latter is a form of cooperative association of tourism businesses.

Review questions

1. Why do governments get involved in tourism management?

2. Why is coordination such a crucial issue regarding tourism development?

3. Explain the role of various global inter-governmental organisations in tourism. (i.e. the UN-WTO RETOS etc.).

4. Discuss the role of DEAT and SA Tourism in respect to the management, development and marketing of tourism in South Africa.

5. Identify a southern African country and define the roles and functions of its NTO.

Further reading

Lennon, J. J. 2006. *Benchmarking national tourism organisations and agencies: understanding best practices*. London: Elsevier.

Pike, S. 2004. *Destination marketing organisations*. London: Elsevier.

Websites

Global

United Nations World Tourism Organisation (UN-WTO): www.world-tourism.org

Tourism Office Worldwide Directory (TOWD): www.towd.com

World Travel & Tourism Council (WTTC): www.wttc.org

Regional Tourism Organisation of Southern (RETOSA): www.retosa.co.za

Pacific Asia Tourism Association (PATA): www.pata.org

European Travel Council (ETC): www.etc-corporate.org

Organisation of American States (OAS): www.oas.org

Indian Ocean Tourism Organisation (IOTO): www.ioto.org

South Africa

DEAT: www.environment.gov.za

South African Tourism: www.southafrica.net

References

Cooper, C., Fletcher, J., Fyall, A., Gilbert, D., & Wanhill, S. 2006 (Eds.). *Tourism: principles and practice*, 3rd edition. New York: Longman.

Department of Environmental Affairs and Tourism. 1996. *White paper: development & promotion of tourism in South Africa*. Tshwane: DEAT.

Department of Environmental Affairs and Tourism. 2002. *Guidelines for responsible tourism*. Tshwane: DEAT.

Gretzel, U., Fesenmaier, D. R., Formica, S. & O'Leary, J. T. 2006. 'Searching for the future: challenges faced by destination marketing organisations.' *Journal of Travel Research*, Vol. 45(2), 116–126.

Hall, C. M. 1994. *Tourism and politics: policy, power and place*. Chichester: John Wiley.

Hall, C. M. 1999. *Tourism planning: policies, processes and relationships*. Harlow: Prentice Hall.

Hall, C. M. 2005. 'The role of government in the management of tourism' in L. Pender & R. Sharpley (Eds.). *The management of tourism*, London: Sage Publications, pp. 217–231.

Hall, C. M. & Jenkins, J. M. 1995. *Tourism and public policy*. London: Routledge.

Leiper, N. 1979. 'The framework of tourism.' in *Annals of Tourism Research*, 6(4), 390–407.

Lennon, J. J. 2006. *Benchmarking national tourism organisations and agencies: understanding best practices*. London: Elsevier.

Pike, S. 2004. *Destination marketing organisations*. London: Elsevier.

Turner, J. 1997. 'The policy process'. In B. Axford, et al. (Eds.). *Politics: an introduction*. London: Routledge, pp. 409–439.

Vella, F. & Becherel, L. 1995. *International tourism*. London: Macmillan.

World Travel and Tourism Council. 2006. *Blueprint for new tourism*, London: WTTC.

Case study
8

Global Competitiveness Programme (GCP) for the South African Tourism Industry, 2005–2010

Objectives

- to identify the key strategic challenges facing South Africa as a tourism destination
- to understand the government actions required to address these challenges

The Global Competitiveness Programme (GCP) 2005–2010 was published by the Department of Environmental Affairs & Tourism (DEAT), the Department of Trade & Industry (dti), and South African Tourism (SAT) in November 2005. It focuses on upgrading South Africa's tourism business environment by developing product-offerings that meet visitors' demands and expectations. The aim of the programme is to sustain a differentiated and competitive position for South Africa's tourism industry. The GCP identifies the following key competitiveness challenges and actions to address these challenges:

Black Economic Empowerment (BEE) transformation

Strong growth in the tourism industry provides an opportunity to drive BEE through growth, and not through the redistribution of an existing 'cake'. Tourists are looking for experiences centred around arts, history, entertainment, and African authenticity and uniqueness – black South Africans are ideally placed to move into these gaps. An emerging domestic market is seeking experiences closely aligned to many of the experiences demanded by tourists, and will be the driver for improved demand and new product development by black entrepreneurs.

Actions:

- increasing transformation partnerships between government and the private sector
- measuring transformation with information management systems
- supporting BEE at enterprise level, e.g. through the establishment of a tourism-specific institutional capacity dealing solely with BEE issues
- government interventions: incentives, black investment support, skills development, enterprise development, and social responsibility programmes.

Market access

Limited capabilities in terms of market knowledge and marketing (financial and human) were identified as key constraints for individual companies to enter the tourism market. In addition, the

South African leisure tourism economy generally favours large companies that are able to realise competitive prices. Many of South Africa's tourism offerings depend on bookings through large outbound tour operators and travel agents, while these depend on competitively priced products.

Actions:

- supporting the emergence of collaborative marketing initiatives such as destination marketing organisation (DMO) structures
- promoting information-sharing within the industry around product development and business partnerships
- marketing support programmes for emerging enterprises through industry associations
- creating market access opportunities for new offerings through collaboration between government and travel agents/tour operators.

Air access

Major constraints on the ability of South Africa to generate tourism growth are airlift challenges regarding capacity and pricing/competition on routes. The choice by airlines to invest in additional capacity is generally constrained by seasonality, availability of equipment, and bilateral air services' regulatory regimes, regulating frequencies, and competition on routes between nations. Airfares from the major source markets (Europe and USA) are a big part of the cost of the holiday package and an important barrier to travel to South Africa.

Actions:

- a tourism-focused international aviation policy/strategy realising a flexible bilateral framework for capacity adjustments in response to demand
- promoting competition on domestic and international flights
- aviation information systems to monitor and track aviation capacity and pricing
- a review of the regulatory and pricing regime at airports (e.g. taxes & fees).

Public transport

Public transport in South Africa is generally configured to serve a commuter market, not tourist needs. Licensing for charter and tourism transport services (e.g. tour buses) was also found to be difficult and time consuming, constraining flexibility.

Actions:

- integrating tourism into government's transport planning
- promoting investments in tourism-related transport services
- reviewing regulations around charter tourism transport services (e.g. licensing).

Safety and security

Issues around safety and security in South Africa remain key constraints for future tourism growth. South Africa is often perceived as an unsafe destination by potential tourists and therefore not considered.

Actions:

- addressing tourists' perceptions by reviewing the government's communications and public relations strategy
- revising tourist information services (e.g. websites, catalogues, brochures, etc.)
- facilitating accurate information to tourists and focused police crime prevention in high tourism-density areas
- public-private partnerships to provide permanent safety monitoring at visitor attractions and transport services
- marketing the SA Tourism call centre as the one-stop service for tourists who have questions and concerns regarding safety.

Information

The availability and accessibility of tourism-related information represents one of the most significant barriers to the development and competitive upgrading of tourism in South Africa. Information-sharing and linkages between businesses are rare, while potential tourists are lost due to problems with the availability, quality, and suitability of relevant consumer information.

Actions:

- developing physical and electronic information platforms for tourists and intermediaries as a collaboration of the tourism industry and SA Tourism/PTAs
- increasing collaboration between industry and tourism information publishers
- further development of physical TICs, infrastructure, and systems at key visitor attractions to upgrade the tourism experience
- the implementation of a Tourist Satellite Account (TSA) for the creation of robust industry information sets

Innovation, product development, investment & SMME development

The GCP identified gaps in the current tourism offering, especially around cultural experiences, quality accommodation at affordable prices, diverse activities for repeat tourists, tours, holiday resorts, and theme parks. The lack of investment in these product areas is caused by a deficiency of available and accessible information around such market opportunities, particularly for SMMEs. Other factors are inadequate skills to develop innovative products and enter the tourism market, insufficient resources for funding investments, or the inability to access such funds.

Actions:

- developing new and upgrading existing offerings, especially around cultural tourism
- establishing platforms in support of investment, skills/enterprise development, and innovation management.

Skills development and quality assurance:

Despite current industry beliefs, tourists' quality expectations of South Africa's universal tourism offerings (i.e. hotels, airports, hospitality services) are, on the whole, higher than their expectations of unique South African products (e.g. game lodges, wildlife, natural beauty). For delivering the expected quality, the industry is experiencing major difficulties accessing a workforce with adequate skills in their local areas.

Actions:

- renewed investment to build legitimacy and support for the TGCSA
- ensuring consistency to restore trust levels in TGCSA grading, particularly with outbound tour operators in the major source markets.

Building local clusters and the role of government

The emergence of strong local tourism clusters made up of companies that can collaborate, integrate, and play as a team when entering tourism markets will be of great benefit for the South African tourism economy. The industry also holds a strong view that government should focus on issues of international marketing, infrastructure and information provision, as well as barriers to investment and skills development.

Actions:

- tourism-focused planning and development in appropriate areas
- facilitating the development of leadership in local clusters by creating effective partnerships and forums, ensuring a clear tourism vision and strategy
- establishing local tourism organisations to manage joint programmes and monitor their impact

Source: DEAT/dti/SAT Global Competitiveness Programme for the Tourism Industry in South Africa 2005–2010, November 2005.

Case study questions

1. Explain which of the strategic challenges will be particularly relevant against the background of the 2010 FIFA World Cup.

2. What integrated system could be imposed to manage/monitor the action plans? Where do you see issues of (de-)regulation?

3. How could collaboration and alignment between government and the private sector be facilitated, short, medium, and long-term?

PART III Managing tourism businesses

9

Managing tourism businesses

Jennifer Nel

Purpose

The purpose of this chapter is to give you clear guidelines on how to manage a tourism business successfully in order to achieve its goals and make it a success.

Learning outcomes

After reading this chapter, you should be able to:
- identify the four main tasks of management in tourism
- explain the different levels of management
- describe the importance of each of the management tasks
- discuss the different types of plans
- describe the planning process
- explain the meaning of organisational structure
- discuss the characteristics of effective leaders
- discuss motivation and communication in terms of leadership
- explain management challenges facing South African tourism.

Chapter overview

This chapter focuses on the important function of management within a tourism business. It begins by discussing the role of management and identifying the different levels of management. The chapter then examines each management task: planning, organising, leading, and control in detail, and highlights the significance of each. Finally, the chapter examines some of the management challenges facing the South African tourism industry, and concludes by considering how innovation can be used to manage change effectively.

The concluding case study illustrates how the theory contained in this chapter can be applied to the preparation of a South African Airways (SAA) aircraft for flight.

Introduction

As can be seen in previous chapters, this book focuses on tourism in South Africa. As the title of this book, *Managing Tourism in South Africa*, suggests, however, it is important to look at what is actually meant by the term *management*. This term is often used ambiguously, and its application is frequently neglected. The different functions of management, including marketing, finance, and human resources, among others, are often examined. A detailed study of the function that integrates all these tasks, however, is very often omitted.

Tourism managers in today's dynamic and growing tourism industry need to be skilled in order to ensure that they are proactive, goal-orientated, and can gain the greatest competitive advantage possible in the business. No matter what role you play, whether it be the CEO (chief executive officer) of a leading hotel group, the marketing manager of a tour operator, or the reservation clerk in a small tourist guiding business, it is important to know and understand the basic tasks of management and to be able to apply these tasks in practice.

As discussed in chapter one, management for tourism takes place at three levels: the individual business level, destination level, and country level. For the purpose of this chapter, we will focus on management at the individual business level. Let us start by defining the term *management*.

What is management?

Management can be defined as the process of co-ordinating an organisation's human and physical resources so as to achieve its goals. A manager, whether of a large hotel, airline, tour operator, small guesthouse, car rental company, or tourist guiding business, must effectively allocate and direct the business's resources, including its people, finance, technology, and materials, in such a way that the objectives of the organisation are realised.

Managers in any typical tourism organisation are constantly making decisions, co-ordinating, delegating, communicating, motivating, and interacting with people. In performing these activities they are, in fact, continually carrying out four basic tasks. These are planning, organising, leading, and controlling – the basic tasks of management, which must be performed in the sequence depicted in Figure 9.1.

It is also important to note that management is an integrated and continual process. These management tasks, as well as the tourism organisation's objectives and resources, must not be seen as a separate, but rather as a combined approach. Planning activities lay the foundation for these objectives, while organising, leading, and control activities are aimed at implementing the plans. This is an ongoing process, conducted to accomplish the objectives of the tourism organisation; namely, to provide a memorable experience for

Figure 9.1 Basic tasks of management

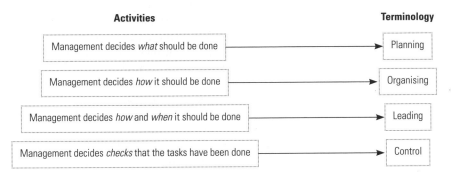

Activities	Terminology
Management decides *what* should be done	Planning
Management decides *how* it should be done	Organising
Management decides *how* and *when* it should be done	Leading
Management decides *checks* that the tasks have been done	Control

Source: Cronjé, D.J. de J., Du Toit, G.S. & Motlatla, M.D.C. (Eds.), 2003. *Introduction to business management*, 6th edition. Cape Town: Oxford University Press.

the tourist, and ultimately to make a profit for the business. The four elements that comprise the management tasks are described below:

1. **Planning** determines *what* the tourism organisation wants to achieve in respect of its vision, mission, and goals, and how it is going to accomplish these with what resources. Planning includes processes used to anticipate the future position of the organisation within the changing environment in which it operates, and the strategies employed to achieve this desired state. It takes place on all management levels, and all management activities are focused around it.

2. **Organising** is the next step in the management process, and it determines *how* things should be done. Organising requires tourism managers to co-ordinate tasks into a formal framework. Resources are allocated to specific departments or sections, where they will be used appropriately to complete the tasks required to achieve the organisation's goals. Every tourism establishment will have its own organisational structure due to the differing nature, size, and objectives of each business.

3. **Leading** involves giving *orders* to people; determining *who* should do which task, and by *when*. Tourism managers at all levels can motivate and guide their staff to perform the necessary tasks successfully, and realise the organisation's goals and plans through strong leadership and good communication.

4. **Control** *checks* that the orders and tasks have been carried out correctly. This management task is essential in evaluating the tourism organisation's performance and determining whether its objectives have been fulfilled. It continually requires management to review its plans to establish whether deviations have occurred, as well as to reconsider the organisation's future direction.

Levels of management

Organisations traditionally consist of three levels of management – top, middle, and lower management. These levels of management form a management hierarchy, and are described as follows:

Top management consists of a small group of managers, referred to as the executives, including the CEO, managing director, board of directors, and partners, who are accountable for the organisation as a whole. Top management determines the tourism organisation's vision and mission, and is responsible for the long-term planning that will ensure the success of the business. Managers at this level establish the way forward for the organisation, and encourage everyone involved in the tourism business to strive towards achieving its vision.

Middle management is responsible for specific departments or functions, and includes branch managers, division managers, and functional heads – such as a financial manager, marketing manager or front office manager. This level of management develops medium- to long-term plans and implements the plans, policies, and strategies determined by top management.

Lower management, also referred to as supervisory management, includes a larger group of managers, in positions such as supervisors, team leaders, and section chiefs. This level of management is responsible for short-term planning and carrying out the plans introduced by middle management. They work closely with their subordinates and inspire them to complete their tasks correctly, by managing the performance of day-to-day activities within their department.

It is important to keep in mind that levels of management may vary between different types of tourism organisations, depending not only primarily on the size and nature of the business, but also on the competitive and market environments within which the business operates. Table 9.1 shows the levels of management and different types of managers within a large hotel, tour operator, small tourist guiding business, and a guesthouse.

Table 9.1 Levels of management and types of managers

Business	Hotel	Tour operator	Tourist guide	Guesthouse
Level of Management				
Top Management	Board of directors Managing director	Board of directors	Owner	Owner-manager
Middle Management	Front office manager Executive housekeeper Food & beverage manager Financial manager Security manager Marketing manager	Marketing manager Financial manager Product manager Operations manager Human resources manager	Tourist guide	
Lower Management	Head reservationist Head of housekeeping Head chef	Sales executive Reservation clerk	Receptionist	Receptionist
Subordinates	Receptionists Housekeeping staff Kitchen staff	Bookkeeper Secretary	Drivers	Cleaning staff Kitchen staff

TO DO

With reference to Table 9.1, draw a similar table, and complete it by filling in the different levels of management for a large car rental company or for a local travel agency.

Chapter 1 noted that while the tourism industry in South Africa is dominated by a small group of large, well-established tourism enterprises, the vast majority of South African tourism enterprises are small, medium, and micro enterprises (SMMEs), with a wide range of tourism offerings of one kind or another. Bennett, Jooste, and Strydom (2005: 167) pointed out that small businesses are often run by owner-operators, who maintain close control and supervision over them. Guesthouses, private game lodges, small hotels, B&Bs, self-catering accommodation, local travel agencies, small transport companies, touring companies, and tourist guiding businesses are examples of SMMEs (see Chapter 10 – Managing small tourism businesses and entrepreneurship).

Small tourism enterprises often overlook the importance of implementing a formal management structure and operate their businesses in an *ad hoc* (as and when needed) manner. The owner-manager usually takes on all the management responsibilities. This frequently results in a lack of communication, exclusion of employees in decision-making, and misused finances. All of these have negative consequences, including wasted resources, high staff turnover, and liquidation. These are critical weaknesses in the management of a tourism business. Larger tourism organisations, however, also have weaknesses. Many large tourism organisations employ a formal management structure, but fail to include middle and lower-level management in the planning stage of the management process. This, too, can result in despondent employees, poor decision-making, and a variety of financial problems.

It is vital, therefore, regardless of how big or small your tourism business may be, to establish a formal and systematic management approach. This, together with effective planning, organising, leading, and control will facilitate effective decision-making, empower everyone involved, and create a corporate culture based on teamwork.

The above representation of the principles of management will enable us to consider each of the basic management tasks in more detail.

Planning

Boone and Kurtz (2006: 269) define **planning** as the process of anticipating future events and conditions, and determining courses of action for achieving organisational objectives. Planning can further be described as a process of forecasting potential opportunities and threats, and then determining what is to be performed and how it is to be completed. It plays a very important role in the tourism industry, and is central to the success of any tourism business. Doswell (1997: 183) suggests that, to be successful, the plan is best implemented by the people who have participated in its preparation. The preparation and implementation of plans is part of management. It is therefore essential that tourism businesses encourage the involvement of as many staff members as possible in the planning process, as this gives them a sense of ownership and facilitates implementation and achievement of the organisation's plans and objectives. According to Rogers and Slinn there is substantial evidence indicating that successful organisations are good at planning and use it as a vehicle for challenging management, motivating staff, and controlling activity (1993: 36).

In today's busy lifestyle and dynamic business environment, tourism managers often become trapped in their day-to-day routines and challenges, only to discover, once it is too late, that they have not planned correctly. The consequences of this are a form of crisis management. Tourism managers are therefore encouraged to undertake a proactive management role. This will enable them to anticipate future conditions and maintain a competitive advantage, rather than following a passive approach, where they are forced to react and adapt to unforeseen situations.

It is important to emphasise that planning needs to be an ongoing process, and not just part of a once-off plan. It can be performed in either a formal or informal manner, but it must always take the organisation's available resources and current operations into account.

In the next section we examine the important role that planning plays, and look at the different types of planning.

The importance of planning

Planning is essential for the following reasons:
- it presents management with guidelines for the decision-making process
- it provides direction and promotes a future-orientated approach
- it encourages co-operation and team-building, as well as shared responsibilities amongst staff
- it enables management to generate performance standards and measurement controls
- it allows management to take advantage of new industry and technology developments
- it fundamentally facilitates the attainment of the organisation's goals
- it presents a proactive approach to management and minimises the possibility of crisis management, thereby encouraging stability.

Types of planning

The four approaches to planning, as used in tourism management, are described below:

Strategic Planning. Top management within an organisation is responsible for formulating **strategic plans**. These are long-term plans (generally three to five years or more) that focus on the entire organisation. The purpose of strategic plans is to ensure that the tourism organisation achieves its goals. Top management, in consultation with middle and lower-level management, creates a vision and mission for the organisation, and then translate these into long-term goals and objectives. These are performed to attain the organisation's vision. For example, the vision of an airline could be 'to become the leading domestic airline company in South Africa'. To achieve this goal, the airline's top management may, as one of their strategic plans, aim to expand market share from 10% to 25% over the next five years.

Tactical Planning. Tactical plans are the primary responsibility of middle level management. They are medium-term plans (one to three years), and are more specific. Tactical planning is directed at the different departments of the organisation, including marketing, human resources, finance, front office, food and beverage, and other departments, depending on the type of tourism organisation. The aim of each of these functions is to implement the strategic plans formulated specifically for them by top management. These plans may also be referred to as functional plans. To reduce staff turnover by 5% over the next two years, for instance, may be a human resource objective, and a medium-term plan for a hotel.

Operational Planning. Middle to lower-level management is accountable for operational plans. These short-term plans (one year or less) prescribe specific methods and procedures to ensure the correct execution of day-to-day, weekly, and monthly activities. Operational plans are detailed and quantitative, to ensure that everyone in the particular department knows exactly what is required of them, and how it is to be achieved. For example, the head reservations clerk of a car rental company may have a meeting with all the reservation staff every Monday morning, to delegate

specific tasks and motivate them to achieve their monthly targets.

TO DO

Levels of management and types of planning: Complete the table below by filling in the appropriate level of management and type of planning that is responsible for each of the scenarios.

While it has been acknowledged that planning is generally divided into strategic, tactical, and operational planning, several tourism researchers suggest a fourth type of planning.

Contingency Planning. Even when the above-mentioned types of planning have been conducted, it is impossible for management to anticipate every situation in the future. According to Jasenko (2004: 83), unexpected events occur in every system, which happen more or less coincidentally, and we have no direct influence on them. These events can significantly influence the

Scenario	Level of management	Type of planning
A holiday resort intends to employ 25 extra lifeguards during the Easter weekend.	Lower management	Operational planning
A local tourist guiding business aims to increase the number of tours conducted annually by 12% over the next two years.		
A hotel aims to attract, develop, and retain the best employees.		
A travel agency aims to increase domestic accommodation bookings to Cape Town by 4% in the next month.		
A theme park aims to extend its business hours during the Christmas season.		
A tour operator wants to expand market share from 12% to 20% over the next five years.		
An airline aims to increase its number of international flights by 18% over the next two years.		
A tourist attraction wants to launch a three-month promotional campaign aimed at attracting December holidaymakers.		
A car-rental company aspires to become South Africa's preferred car-rental company.		
A guesthouse aims to increase room occupancy by 15% during the next three years.		

planned events in the operation and behaviour of the business systems, as they fundamentally prevent the achievement of goals. Boone and Kurtz (2006: 271) explain that major accidents, natural disasters, and rapid economic downturn can throw even the best-laid plans into chaos. To handle the possibility of business disruption from events of this nature, many firms use contingency planning, which allows a firm to resume operations as quickly as possible after a crisis while openly communicating with the public about what happened. Recent international events include the September 11 ('9/11') 2001 terrorist attacks; the tsunami in South East Asia in 2004, the war in the Middle East, and the constant threat of terrorist attacks in many regions of the world, as well as local events. Events such as the floods in the Western Cape, electricity blackouts, and various countrywide strikes are testament to the importance of these types of plans. Even though many contingency plans may never be implemented, it is vital that some form of emergency plan is formulated at every planning level.

While the type of plan and amount of time spent developing each will differ at every management level, top, middle, and lower management all share responsibility for formulating plans. It is vital that a 'team involvement' philosophy be established in the planning process, and implemented throughout the entire organisation to further strengthen the organisation and ensure that not only are its goals achieved , but also those of each department, and every individual working in the organisation.

In the following section we will examine the process that is required to ensure successful planning.

The planning process

The planning process is a logical list of steps that need to be followed to realise the organisation's vision, mission, and goals. These steps are shown in Figure 9.2.

Step 1. Situation analysis. Due to the volatile external environment that a tourism business operates in, the dynamic nature of the tourism industry, and the characteristics of its internal operations, tourism organisations need to continually identify any opportunities or problems that require planning.

Step 2. Establishing goals. An organisation first formulates a vision that it aims to achieve. This

Figure 9.2 The planning process

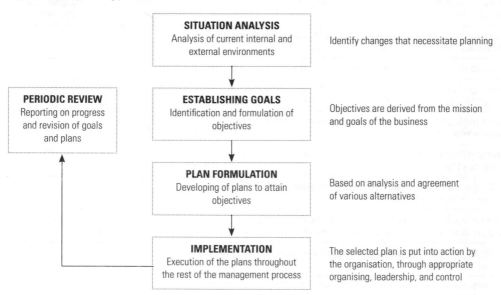

Source: adapted from Cronjé, Du Toit, & Motlatla (2003: 120); Page & Connell (2006: 479–480); Smit & Cronjé (2002: 98– 99)

vision is translated into a mission statement, and further broken down into long-term goals and objectives, providing the business with direction for all its operations.

Step 3. Plan formulation. Once a situation analysis has been conducted and goals have been identified, different options are examined and the most appropriate alternative chosen. Specific plans are formulated to achieve the tourism organisation's objectives.

Step 4. Implementation. The selected plan is put into operation by the tourism organisation. Through appropriate organising and supportive leadership, it is applied to the remainder of the management process.

Step 5. Periodic Review. Management at all levels needs to continually report on the progress that is being made towards the achievement of the tourism organisation's goals. Control must be exercised, and revision of the original plans must be made, should any changes be necessary.

Now that you are familiar with the planning process and different types of plans, it is important that you understand how these plans are organised within a business of any size.

Organising

Planning is the first task in the management process, but a formal framework is required to put these plans into operation. According to Cronjé, Du Toit and Motlatla (2003: 131), **organising** means that management has to develop mechanisms to put the strategy or plan into effect. Arrangements have to be made to determine what activities will be carried out, what resources will be employed, and who will perform the various activities. This task involves dividing work and resources into a logical system and assigning them to specific people. Detailed tasks and procedures are specified, along with the required levels of responsibility, to enable the tourism business to attain its objectives. Organising is the process that establishes a structure to guide people towards achieving the business's goals. To begin with, let us examine the importance of organising.

The importance of organising

An organisational structure is important for a number of reasons (adapted from Rogers & Slinn, 1993: 44; Smit & Cronjé, 2002: 192):
- it facilitates the co-ordination of activities and tasks within the organisation
- it establishes visible channels of communication throughout the organisation
- it defines the levels of responsibility and authority in the organisation, so that every person knows what they are accountable for
- it facilitates the allocation and distribution of resources to the relevant staff and departments
- it develops relationships between staff members and departments, as well as between the organisation, its suppliers, and its customers.

Organisational structure

As mentioned earlier, the tourism industry is made up of organisations of different sizes, each requiring their own framework to structure their business. The owner of a small guesthouse is usually also the manager. The owner-manager handles all bookings, purchasing, financing, and marketing for the guesthouse, and may hire several employees to be responsible for cooking and cleaning, resulting in a very basic organisational structure. In comparison, a much more complex structure is used by the owner of a large hotel, which is operated by a board of directors and a managing director who, in turn, may employ a front office manager, an executive housekeeper, a food and beverage manager, a financial manager, a security and control manager, and perhaps even a marketing manager, as well as all the relevant staff within each department.

This requires a well-defined structure, so that all employees know what is required of them, who to report to, and how they contribute to meeting the tourism organisation's goals. This is often represented by an organisational chart, which Boone and Kurtz (2006: 284) define as a visual representation of a firm's structure that illustrates job positions and functions. It depicts the levels of authority and responsibility, as well as the channels of communication within the organisation. There are many different types of organisational structures, and all tourism organisations, whether big or small, need to formulate one. Figures 9.3 and 9.4 illustrate examples of organisational charts formulated by a guesthouse and a hotel respectively.

From this, it is evident that although everyone involved in the tourism organisation contributes various resources and carries out certain tasks to achieve the business's objectives, each of them works at a different level within the organisation. Furthermore, the type of organisational structure can vary from a very flat structure, such that of a guesthouse, to a more comprehensive one, as in the case of a large hotel.

Organisational charts are often included in company's annual reports. Visit the websites of South African Airways (SAA), South Africa National Parks (SANParks) and Avis Rent-a-Car to compare the framework of their organisational

structures. These annual reports also provide valuable and interesting information about each tourism organisation's vision, mission, objectives and strategies, as well as the achievement and results of these goals. To view each of these organisation's annual reports, explore 'About Us' at:

www

Browse these websites: www.flysaa.co.za, www.sanparks.co.za, www.avis.co.za

Logos: Avis, SAA, SANParks

Figure 9.3 Organisational chart of a guesthouse

Figure 9.4 Organisational chart of a hotel

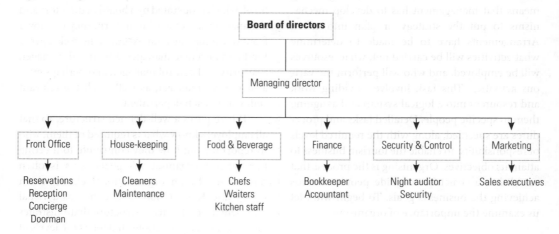

Determining the type of organisational structure

The following factors help to determine the type of organisational structure that a tourism organisation should implement (adapted from Boone & Kurtz, 2006: 284; Cronjé, Du Toit and Motlatla, 2003: 144; Rogers & Slinn, 1993: 50):

- the vision, mission, goals, and objectives of the organisation
- the type of industry in which the organisation functions
- the size of the business
- the level of technology it employs
- the environmental circumstances in which it operates
- the corporate culture of the organisation
- the number and type of staff employed
- the activities that shaped its past
- the organisation's strategy for future growth.

By taking responsibility for his or her actions, exercising authority, and delegating tasks, a tourism manager can effectively co-ordinate various functions and ultimately organise the business to achieve its goals.

In the next section we examine why managers need to motivate their staff, and consider what characteristics are essential to lead the tourism organisation to success.

Leading

Smit & Cronjé (2002: 279) define leadership as the process of directing the behaviour of others towards the accomplishment of the organisation's goals. It is frequently regarded as the most important task of management, as it is the driving force which ensures that the tasks which were developed during planning are organised and implemented correctly. Furthermore, since tourism is a service industry and people are involved in both the production and consumption of the tourism offering termed **inseparability**[1]. It is imperative that the skills of an effective leader are employed not only to achieve the goals of the

organisation, but also to ensure that the tourist or visitor has a memorable tourism experience.

The quality of *leadership* plays such an essential role in management that it frequently determines the success or failure of a business. Smit and Cronjé (2002: 276) suggest whenever an organisation finds itself in trouble, it should investigate its leadership as a possible cause of the problem. A leader may be unable to adapt to change, or find it hard to take others' ideas into account. This can result in unproductive personnel and unorganised tasks. A leader must be flexible, and able to inspire others to pursue the vision of the organisation. Furthermore, leadership is not only necessary at top management level, but can be carried out at any management level by anyone who is accountable for the performance of others.

There is a difference between a manager and a leader. It is important to keep in mind that a good manager is not always a good leader, and *vice versa*. Tourism organisations are, therefore, encouraged to employ someone who is both; or, failing that, at least to employ a manager who, through training and experience, has the potential to become a good leader.

Leaders derive power and authority from a variety of sources, including the management position they hold, their knowledge and experience, or their personality. They use this authority to guide subordinates to complete their tasks willingly.

Characterisics of effective leaders

Effective tourism leaders need to possess a number of essential characteristics. They should be able to (Adapted from Cronjé, Du Toit and Motlatla, 2003: 149; Boone & Kurtz, 2006: 279; Page & Connell, 2006: 232; Smit & Cronjé, 2002: 279):

- motivate and encourage others to move in the same direction
- empower others
- communicate expectations, tasks, and consequences effectively
- delegate tasks and give orders in an understandable manner

- acknowledge and reward successful accomplishment of tasks and objectives
- show honesty, integrity, and commitment in everything
- take calculated risks and be willing to experiment
- manage conflict
- show initiative and possess passion for their work
- be responsible and accountable for their actions
- be flexible and able to adapt to changing environments
- be objective when dealing with others.

Great leaders, however, do not share all these traits or have all the same qualities, but two characteristics are fundamental: effective tourism leaders must be able to motivate others and communicate well.

Discussion point

With reference to the 'characteristics of effective leaders', who would you classify as an example of a leader in the South African tourism industry?

Motivation

Motivation, in the context of management, is defined as the ability to encourage others to do something willingly. It stimulates interest in something or the achievement of something. For example, travel consultants working at travel agencies are motivated to achieve specific sales targets by a variety of incentives, including cash, travel, or career advancement rewards.

Tourism is a service industry and a people business. Different people have different needs and, this being said, different things motivate different people. According to Rogers and Slinn (1993: 95), motivational theories are particularly significant for managers in the tourism industry, which traditionally employs a large number of relatively unskilled and low-paid workers, and yet whose interaction with the customer is of prime importance. Furthermore, there are only a limited number of management positions available in many establishments within this labour-intensive industry, and this often results in a lack of career development and a lack of self-motivation. It is essential, therefore, that a leader identifies what motivates each employee and then tries to satisfy him or her in the best way possible. This will ensure that they are continually inspired to strive towards achieving the tourism organisation's goals.

Communication

Effective communication is essential in all relationships and in all tourism businesses. Boone and Kurtz (2006: 339) define *communication* as a meaningful exchange of information through messages. Tourism managers spend a significant amount of time communicating with people. Due to the nature of the tourism industry, they are not only communicating on a daily basis with their staff, but they also frequently communicate with their customers (tourists and visitors).

For effective communication to take place, it is vital that the information or message conveyed is correctly interpreted. This is particularly important in South Africa, as people come from many diverse cultures and backgrounds, and speak different languages. These circumstances may result in information being misunderstood, with serious consequences. Furthermore, constant feedback must be encouraged, as this is a valuable method of monitoring whether problems exist, as well as identifying any potential opportunities.

Bennett, Jooste & Strydom (2005: 182) state that the largest part of a tourism manager's workday is spent on communication, and it may be downward (to explain exactly what is expected of a subordinate), upward (through progress reports) or horizontal (to coordinate tasks at the same level within or between departments).

It is important, however, that open two-way communication must be encouraged in all tasks, no matter in what direction it occurs, as this will ensure that everyone within the tourism business works in the same direction to achieve the organisation's goals (see Example box opposite).

Example Effective Communication

A guest staying at a game lodge goes to reception to report that the air-conditioning in his room is not working. The receptionist informs the guest that housekeeping will be there *'just now'* to see to the problem. The guest returns to his room, and expects that the person will come in the next five minutes. However, the person from housekeeping only arrives half-an-hour later. This is a very unhappy guest – and all because of the way the information was communicated.

TO DO

Read the Example box above, and then answer these two questions:
1. If you were the receptionist at this game lodge, what could you have said to the guest to ensure that this situation did not occur and that the guest did not have to wait so long?
2. List three recommendations to ensure effective communication in the game lodge.

Control

Godfrey and Clarke (2003: 156) define *control* as the tactical activity carried out to close the gaps between actual performance and daily, weekly, or monthly targets identified by monitoring. **Control** evaluates whether the tasks that were planned, organised, and directed have been successfully completed. It also determines whether deviations from these plans have occurred, and whether, as a result, the plans need to be revised. Although often referred to as the 'final' step in the management process, it is important to remember that control should be conducted on an ongoing and systematic basis. By implementing this approach, your tourism business will operate in a proactive manner, thereby allowing you not only to take corrective action where necessary, but also to take advantage of any potential opportunities. To ensure that continuous monitoring occurs,

four basic steps need to be carried out during the control process:

The control process

Step 1. Determine performance standards. During planning, a set of performance standards must be developed against which success can be monitored. The plans are formulated into objectives, and then transformed into evaluation criteria that are used to measure performance and to determine whether any deviations from the plans have occurred.

Step 2. Monitor actual performance. The actual performance and completion of tasks within a business must be measured on a continual basis. To evaluate whether deviations have occurred, it is essential that the pre-set standards are quantifiable and reliable.

Step 3. Compare actual performance with established standards. Once actual performance has been observed, any variations from the set criteria must be evaluated. It is important to establish the level at which deviations are allowed to differ from the original set of standards; to understand why the standards have not been met or exceeded, as well as to decide what corrective action will be required.

Step 4. Take corrective action if required. It is imperative that all the necessary actions are taken not only to correct, but also to improve the business's current situation. This may include adjusting the actual operation of tasks, or amending performance standards, based on the current conditions in the businesses environment.

It is essential that the control process be systematically implemented throughout all departments and functions of the tourism business. Budgets, statistical data, reports, internal audits, focus groups, questionnaires, personal observation, and interviews are methods that can be used to exercise control.

The executive housekeeper in a hotel may write weekly reports to monitor the cleanliness of the hotel and the satisfaction of guests. Monthly budgets may be monitored to ensure that a community tourism project stays within its allocated funds. Visitor attractions, such as theme parks and museums, may analyse daily visitor numbers to control overcrowding. These examples all highlight the significance of control.

Discussion point

With reference to the abovementioned control methods, briefly discuss which method you would employ in each of the following scenarios:

- To ensure effective control of visitor numbers in the Kruger National Park
- To determine on a weekly basis the number of South African Airways' flights that depart on time
- To ensure that customers experience excellent service at the Palace of the Lost City.

The importance of control

Control plays an important role in tourism organisations for the following reasons:

- it helps to determine whether all the functions and activities of the tourism organisation are working together towards achieving its goals
- it is able to make adjustments to adapt to the changing business environment by evaluating the organisation's current situation
- with proper control processes and systems in place, tourism managers are able to delegate tasks more easily, as they know that the tasks will be continually monitored
- through regular observation and feedback, problems can be identified early and the necessary action taken
- frequent and systematic monitoring helps minimise both the expenses and time involved, since the possibility for human error is reduced
- it helps ensure that the visitor or guest enjoys a memorable tourism experience.

TOURISM GRADING COUNCIL
OF SOUTH AFRICA

Example Tourism Grading Council of South Africa (TGCSA)

In September 2000 the (then) Minister of the Department of Environmental Affairs and Tourism (DEAT) founded the Tourism Grading Council of South Africa (TGCSA). The primary role of the TGCSA is to provide the South African tourism industry with a grading structure which ensures that a uniform standard of quality is realised by all tourism organisations. By means of consumer feedback, visitor expectations are monitored to certify that the grading system is reliable and objective. Tourism organisations are informed about amendments that need to be made, and are encouraged to continually improve their quality rating.

TGCSA recognises and rewards tourism organisations for their quality standards with a star grading. Furthermore, TGCSA promotes an attitude of shared accountability among all stakeholders, and ultimately ensures a memorable tourism experience for the visitor.

www

Browse this website: www.tourismgrading.co.za

It is important to remember to keep control systems and procedures simple and flexible. Complex systems become too difficult and complicated to handle. It is recommended to focus rather on accuracy and relevance, and to use basic processes and procedures. This allows management to objectively evaluate the situation and make adjustments where necessary.

Throughout this chapter, we have focused on the four tasks of management (planning, organising, leading, and control) and what management is responsible for, to ensure the tourism organisation achieves its goals. However, even when all these management tasks are performed correctly, there will always be a number of external challenges that have to be managed. A detailed discussion of the future of tourism will be found in Chapter 17, where various trends and other issues confronting the tourism industry will be analysed. However, we will now look briefly at some of the challenges currently facing tourism businesses.

Management challenges facing tourism businesses in South Africa

Due to South Africa's vibrant history and the fast-evolving nature of the tourism industry, tourism managers are faced with a number of challenges that they have to manage correctly to ensure the success of their business.

South African tourism managers are faced with a diverse and multi-cultural workforce, and they therefore need to be sensitive to cultural differences and to look for ways to empower their staff (see Chapter 11 – Managing HR in tourism). To ensure that future South African generations will benefit from the tourism experiences we are currently enjoying, managers need to operate their tourism business responsibly and sustainably (see Chapter 16 – Managing tourism responsibly). Together with these challenges, tourism managers have to manage various economic issues, political events, competitive forces, and technological and international developments, as well as deal with one of the biggest challenges – the ability to effectively manage change.

Change management

Change is a significant, and inevitable, characteristic of any tourism business. Changing customer needs; the desire to experience something different, technological advancements, and growing worldwide competition are some of the main forces that cause change within the tourism industry. The reaction and management of these challenges will determine the success of a tourism organisation. One way to respond to such changes is through **innovation**.

Innovation involves introducing new offerings, methods, or ideas, and, as described by Page (2007: 326), it is often seen as one way in which businesses may seek to gain a competitive advantage, especially where innovation in the face of competition leads to growth, survival, or enhanced profitability. Page (2007: 327) stresses that managers need to understand the role of innovation and its potential to improve business processes and the client-organisation interface, and to add value to the business (for example, it may lead to cost savings). A tourism manager may enter a new market, or launch a new or improved offering, such as the 'no-frills' flights offered by low-cost airlines such as kulula.com and 1Time. A manager can use creativity and initiative to find a new supply source. This is particularly important in South Africa, where locally produced products are being promoted, as is evident by the 'Proudly South African' (PSA) initiative.

PSA's distinctive logo

The challenge for tourism managers is to find suitable ways to employ innovation, and then to effectively implement the change. Furthermore, there may be some resistance to change. It is therefore important that tourism managers, firstly, establish an environment that is favourable to change, and then involve staff in the change process. It is also vital that management provides a clear vision, conveys it to everyone from the very beginning, and also presents clear guidelines on how to achieve the change. Tourism managers, consequently, need to be flexible, encouraging, and supportive. However, tourism managers can only accomplish this and manage change successfully if they make use of excellent management skills.

Conclusion

Tourism managers need to make successful use of the basic tasks of management to effectively co-ordinate the organisation's resources and ensure the achievement of its goals in today's vibrant and developing tourism industry. This chapter examined the important role of management in a tourism business, and outlined the four tasks of management: planning, organising, leading, and control. The different types of planning and the planning process were discussed, and guidelines for determining which type of organisational structure to implement were presented. Characteristics of effective leadership were identified, and motivation and communication were highlighted as the two most important of these. The process to ensure effective control was outlined, and the significance of each task was also highlighted. The chapter concluded with a brief look at the management challenges facing the South African tourism industry, and how the ability to use innovation is able to manage change effectively.

Notes

1. Inseparability is a characteristic of tourism offering: they are produced and consumed at the same time, and cannot be separated from their providers.

Review questions

1. Illustrate, by means of a diagram, the four tasks of management.

2. Explain the role of contingency plans in relation to tourism.

3. Discuss the importance of an organisational structure within a tourism establishment.

4. Why are motivation and communication considered the two most important characteristics of effective leadership?

5. Discuss the four basic steps carried out during the control process.

Further reading

Boone, L. E. & Kurtz, D. L. 2006. *Contemporary business 2006*. Florence, KY: Thomson/South-Western.

Websites

AVIS: www.avis.co.za

South African Airways: www.flysaa.co.za

SANParks: www.sanparks.co.za

Tourvest: www.tourvest.co.za

References

Allison, S. 2006. A flight is born. *Sawubona: South African Airways in-flight magazine*. Randburg: Mafube Publishing.

Bennett, A., Jooste, C. & Strydom, L. (Eds.). 2005. *Managing tourism Services: a southern African perspective*, 3rd edition. Tshwane: Van Schaik.

Boone, L. E. & Kurtz, D. L. 2006. *Contemporary business*. Florence, KY: Thomson/South-Western.

Cronjé, G. J. de J., Du Toit, G. S. & Motlatla, M. D. C. (Eds.). 2003. *Introduction to business management*, 6th edition. Cape Town: Oxford University Press Southern Africa.

Doswell, R. 1997. *Tourism: how effective management makes the difference*. Oxford: Butterworth-Heinemann.

Godfrey, K. & Clarke, J. 2003. *The tourism development handbook: a practical approach to planning and marketing*. London: Thomson.

Page, S. J. 2007. *Tourism management: managing for change*, 2nd edition. Oxford: Butterworth-Heinemann.

Page, S. J. & Connell, J. 2006. *Tourism: a modern synthesis*, 2nd edition. London: Thomson.

Rogers, H. A. & Slinn J. A. 1993. *Tourism: management of facilities*. London: Pitman.

Smit, P. J. & Cronjé, G. J. (Eds.). 2002. *Management principles: a contemporary edition for Africa*, 3rd edition. Cape Town: Juta.

South Africa.Department of Trade and Industry (dti). 2006. *The Tourism Sector*. http://www.thedti.gov.za/publications/tourism.htm (accessed September 2006).

Tourism Grading Council of South Africa. 2006. *What do we do?* TGCSA: www.tourismgrading.co.za. (accessed September 2006).

A flight is born

- to appreciate the importance of planning in the preparation of an aircraft to take you to your destination
- to understand how the control process influences the successful flight of an aircraft

So you've booked your flight. Whether for business or leisure, air travel is exciting. You think about a number of things on the way to the airport. For some people it is just the stress of getting there on time. Have you ever considered, though, the preparation that goes on behind the scenes in order for the aircraft to be waiting for you? It's all too easy to take for granted, without realising what is involved in preparing the aircraft to take you to your destination.

The process actually began up to a year before the flight's departure. An annual timetable is worked out. First of all, SAA decides which routes it would like to service. The next step is to determine that the right number and type of aircraft will be available to fulfil the timetable obligations. Finally, the airline has to bid for slots. Airports around the world allocate departure slots, so that they can move all the traffic without delay. The busier the airport, the more difficult it is to get slots, and airlines have to bid for them.

Now that it has been decided when and where flights will be going throughout the year, there is another important element that needs to be planned. Aircraft have to be maintained to very stringent regulations. Some maintenance is carried out at a time interval, while other maintenance tasks are carried out according to the number of hours the aircraft has flown. The maintenance schedule has to be worked out in conjunction with the timetable of scheduled flights.

Now that we have an aircraft for the flight, we'll need a crew to operate it. Both cockpit and cabin crew have to be qualified to fly the particular aircraft type. A Boeing 747 crew does not fly an Airbus A340. A crew roster is worked out each month. There are rules governing the number of hours a day a crew can work; both in terms of flying time and duty time. All of these factors have to be taken into account when the roster is created.

SAA uses a software program called Pegasys to assist with drawing up the timetable, scheduling of crew, and aircraft maintenance. It is important for an airline to make optimum use of its people and equipment. A crew that flies from Johannesburg to eThekwini and back, for example, will not have done a full day's work. Pegasys is used to pair the eThekwini flight with another local flight, so that the crew and aircraft are well utilised.

During the flight, you'll want something to eat and drink, and if you don't sleep during the flight, you'll need to be entertained; so a choice of meals and a variety of movies and music have to be provided.

All this behind-the-scenes planning ensures that an aircraft and crew is available for the flight, but there is still a lot to be done. The aircraft has to be in position on the apron. Check-in staff have to be ready at the check-in desk. Buses have to be arranged if the aircraft is parked away from the terminal building. A flight plan has to be filed with air traffic control services for every flight. Clearances have to be obtained in order to overfly foreign countries.

Obviously, we won't be able to go anywhere without fuel. It's not a simple case of filling the tanks, though. Fuel is heavy – a flight from Johannesburg to London will carry in the region of 130 tons of fuel. If the aircraft is too heavy, it won't be able to take off. Transporting extra weight also costs money, so it makes no sense to carry fuel unnecessarily. The exact quantity of fuel loaded is determined by weather conditions and expected delays at the destination.

On the day of the flight, the number of meals required is determined according to the number of passengers. As with fuel, any unnecessary food will also add to the weight of the aircraft.

SAA operates to a precision time schedule, which determines, to the minute, when an activity should take place. The ramp co-ordinator uses this schedule to oversee the preparation of the aircraft once it is on the apron. Should something not happen – for example, the cleaners don't arrive on time, the ramp co-ordinator will contact the relevant contractor. It is essential to notify the operations control centre if the problem might cause a delayed departure.

Forty minutes before departure, the international flight is closed, meaning no more passengers can be checked in. The reason for closing the flight is to allow passengers time to get through immigration, in the case of an international flight, and to the boarding gate. It also allows time to get the baggage on board. Once the flight has been closed and all the baggage has been weighed, the weight of the aircraft can be calculated more accurately. The pilots can then do their final performance calculations. The pilots call air traffic control for a departure clearance. Air traffic control problems could cause a delay, but air traffic control services are not run by SAA. For that reason, if they do delay the flight, it's out of the airline's hands.

The final stage of the process is to get you, the passenger, on board and to your seat. After placing your hand luggage in the overhead locker, you can sit back and relax. So, next time you fasten your seat belt, remember everything that has happened behind the scenes so that you can fly to your destination.

Source: Adapted from Allison, S. 2006. A flight is born. *Sawubona: South African Airways in-flight magazine*. Randburg: Mafube Publishing.

www

www.flysaa.co.za.

Case study questions

1. With reference to drawing up a timetable, scheduling the crew, and maintaining the aircraft, explain the importance of planning in the preparation of an SAA aircraft.

2. Various operational plans are made during the preparation of an aircraft. Give three examples of such plans.

3. Discuss the four steps of the control process as they apply to the amount of fuel, the number of meals, and the weight of baggage – which ensure that the aircraft has a successful flight.

4. In the light of current tourism trends and the change towards low-cost ('no-frills') airlines, where airlines are offering fewer in-flight services, what can SAA do to manage this change in customer requirements, and how can they use innovation to remain competitive?

10

Managing small tourism businesses and entrepreneurship

Cecile Nieuwenhuizen

Purpose

The purpose of this chapter is to explain the importance and the contribution of entrepreneurial businesses, their different types in the tourism industry, as well as the variety of approaches and skills required to manage these businesses successfully.

Learning outcomes

After reading this chapter you should be able to:
- explain the meaning and value of entrepreneurship to the economy
- differentiate between entrepreneurial and small businesses
- identify the contribution of small, medium, and micro enterprises (SMMEs) to the economy
- describe the role of tourism entrepreneurs in the economy.
- distinguish between entrepreneurship, management, and entrepreneurial leadership for the successful management of SMMEs and growth of entrepreneurial businesses
- determine the important management and entrepreneurial skills of successful SMMEs
- identify entrepreneurship in the medium and large business sectors.

Chapter overview

This chapter introduces the concepts of small, medium, and micro enterprises (SMMEs) and entrepreneurship; their role in the tourism industry, and their contribution to the economy of a country. It compares the total entrepreneurial activity of South Africa to that in other countries, and discusses some of the unique features of the South African situation with regard to SMMEs and the tourism industry. The entrepreneur, or SMME owner, and differences in respect of their entrepreneurial, management, and leadership styles, are also discussed. Essential management and entrepreneurial skills of successful entrepreneurs – as identified by various researchers – are highlighted. Finally, entrepreneurship in medium and large businesses is discussed, in the light of the fact that entrepreneurs are not limited to SMMEs, and usually grow their businesses to become medium and large undertakings. The concluding case study illustrates the difference between entrepreneurial businesses and small businesses, and the importance of both to a nation's economy.

Due to the nature of entrepreneurship and SMMEs, their attributes and principles apply to all fields of business, not only to tourism; therefore the focus will not be on tourism businesses alone.

Introduction

In most countries, the tourism industry consists of **multi-national corporations** (MNCs) and large businesses such as travel operators, hotel groups, and transport providers (for example airlines, rail companies, and bus and coach operators). These MNCs, in turn, are supported by a multitude of small, independent tourism businesses, including specialist tour operators and tourist guiding companies, boutique hotels, lodges, guest houses and B & Bs, cultural experiences, craft and curio shops and stalls, restaurants, and **agri-tourism** (agricultural tourism) businesses. Despite the prominence of large companies, the tourism industry, in reality, is numerically dominated by small businesses (Szivas, 2001: 163), and thus entrepreneurship is a critical factor in tourism development both globally and regionally (Russel & Faulkner, 2004: 556).

It has been established that the motivation for entrepreneurial entry into the tourism business is often non-economic – or, if economic, it is matched on the one end of the scale by non-economic factors such as lifestyle preferences. On the other end of the scale are entrepreneurial small, medium, and micro enterprises (SMMEs), driven by the growth motives of the 'Schumpeterian type' of entrepreneur. Innovative behaviour, which is characteristic of an entrepreneurial enterprise, involves one or a combination of the following: the introduction of new goods, the introduction of new manufacturing methods, the opening of new markets, the opening of new supply sources, and industrial reorganisation (Schumpeter, 1934: 66). High-potential, or Schumpeterian-type entrepreneurs intend to grow their businesses. Such entrepreneurs are responsible for growth and job creation in the economy, and can be found in their own enterprises, as part of a team owning an enterprise, or as corporate entrepreneurs and 'intrapreneurs' in large companies and in the public sector. Their own business is, however, the most natural place for entrepreneurs to be, and that place is found mostly in SMMEs, and often in larger businesses which they have grown from SMMEs.

Growth and profit-orientated entrepreneurs are valuable as far as a country's economic development is concerned, since they grow and create jobs. It is important, therefore, to keep in mind that not everyone who starts a new business is, in reality, an **entrepreneur**. Some might be enterprising, but true entrepreneurs habitually create and innovate to build and grow something of recognised value. Some SMMEs do not achieve anything new or different; do not grow, and do not find new customers. They merely survive, or cannot obtain finance. Although small businesses contribute to, and add value to, a nation's wealth creation, not all SMMEs are necessarily entrepreneurial and, unfortunately, the majority of tourism-related businesses remain small (Getz & Peterson, 2005: 220).

There is a distinct difference between growth and profit-orientated entrepreneurs and autonomy and lifestyle-orientated entrepreneurs; to such an extent that autonomy and lifestyle-orientated entrepreneurs are usually regarded as SMME owners rather than entrepreneurs. The primary aim of entrepreneurs with an autonomy orientation is to be in control of their own lives and careers, and not necessarily to establish and grow a business. Lifestyle-orientated entrepreneurs have a distinct inclination to align their careers with their preferred – and usually more comfortable – lifestyles; a more leisurely or family-focused lifestyle, for instance. Growth and profit-orientated entrepreneurs display different business characteristics, such as the type of business they operate in. Their primary intention is to establish and grow high-potential businesses, and the profit motive is very strong in these entrepreneurs. Businesses established by these entrepreneurs ensure growth in the economy, since they do something new or different to create wealth for the entrepreneur and to add value to society. The entrepreneur is 'a person who undertakes a wealth-creating and value-adding process, through developing ideas, assembling resources and making things happen' (Kao, Kao & Kao, 2002: 42).

Economic growth is largely dependent on growth and profit-orientated entrepreneurs, but the majority of SMME owners in the tourism industry are lifestyle-orientated. Lifestyle motivations are typical of travel and tourism business owners such as guesthouses, game lodges, restaurants, shops, and other businesses in tourism areas such as the Midlands of KwaZulu-Natal, the Western Cape, and Clarens in the Free State (Rogerson, 2005: 630).

Entrepreneurs in the tourism industry are attracted to tourism because it is often seen as an excellent opportunity to combine a passion for a type of tourism activity or location with a business opportunity. For example, a person who is passionate about exciting and adventurous activities, and who has a need to achieve by establishing a business, will establish a business specialising in adventure tours. Another entrepreneur might have a need to live in a specific area, for example in a coastal village. To be able to afford this lifestyle, it may be necessary to start a business, such as a guest lodge, or a specialist tour operator, such as one offering dolphin-watching sea cruises. It is often found that tourism entrepreneurs have a strong lifestyle orientation, and combine their lifestyle needs with the type of business they establish.

Economic impetus of SMMEs and entrepreneurial businesses

SMMEs and the level of entrepreneurial activity contribute directly to the economic development of a country (Schumpeter, 1934; Bird, 1989). The ability to grow businesses, create wealth, and sustain a competitive advantage has become imperative in high-growth, global, competitive economies. Entrepreneurship is associated with the adaptation and change of economic systems, and often contributes to national and economic growth. Job creation is highly correlated with the level of start-up activity: there is a positive, statistically significant association between national economic growth and entrepreneurship (Bygrave, Reynolds & Autio, 2004: 5).

Employment is closely linked to the state of the economy. Fewer employment opportunities are available when there is no growth in the economy. Access to employment in South Africa is low, with an approximate unemployment rate of 25,6% (Statistics South Africa, 2006). SMMEs in general, not necessarily only entrepreneurial businesses, form 97, 5% of all businesses in South Africa. In the United Kingdom it is estimated that 99% of businesses in the travel and tourism industry are SMMEs, while the figure in Australia is 95%. However, it is important to note that the few large tourism organisations control between 60% and 70% of the industry in South Africa, and that the high proportion of SMMEs is responsible for the rest of the economic activity in the industry. A recent (2005) Department of Trade and Industry (dti) calculation determined that there are in excess of 50 000 tourism SMMEs in South Africa (Rogerson, 2005: 628).

The South African tourism industry is a three-tiered hierarchy, with the top tier consisting of a small group of large businesses responsible for the major travel and tour agencies, transportation, hotels, casinos, and conference centres. The middle tier consists of SMMEs operating as travel and touring businesses, small hotels, self-catering accommodation, bed-and-breakfasts, backpacking hostels, and game farms. The lowest tier is made up of registered micro-enterprises and informal businesses. Due to the lack of available statistics, it is not clear what the contribution and size of each tier are (Rogerson, 2005: 629).

Tourism SMMEs in South Africa are of two very different types, largely stratified along racial lines. At the one end of the scale are well-established, mainly white-owned, small businesses. These include travel and touring companies, restaurants, small hotels, self-catering accommodation and resorts, game reserves, bed-and-breakfasts, and backpacker hostels. The owners of many of these establishments have used their personal savings as start-up capital. Many have moved into tourism from other sectors, often motivated by lifestyle choices.

At the other end of the scale is the emerging black-owned tourism economy, consisting mainly of formally-registered micro-enterprises, as well as informal enterprises. Many, though not all, of these enterprises are survivalist in nature. Survivalist enterprises are often driven by a lack of alternative job opportunities and, in many cases, barely make a profit (Strategic Business Partnership, 2006: 11).

SMMEs generate 35% of South Africa's **gross domestic product** (GDP); contribute 43% of the total value of salaries and wages paid in South Africa, and employ 55% of all formal private sector employees (Ntsika Annual Review 2002).

High-potential entrepreneurs intend to grow their businesses. They are responsible for growth and employment creation in the economy. The results of *the Global Entrepreneurship Monitor: South African Report for 2004* indicate that the small and medium enterprise sector employs 1 210 838 people in 575 246 start-up businesses. It employs 1 195 033 in 292 930 new firms, and 1 669 374 in 290 161 established firms. This gives a total of 4 075 245 people employed by small and medium enterprises (SMEs) in South Africa (Orford, Herrington & Wood, 2004: 25). Start-up enterprises are defined as businesses which have not yet paid any salaries or wages, or have done so for less than three months. New firms are businesses that have paid salaries and wages for more than three months, but less than three-and-a-half years. Established firms have paid salaries and wages for more than three-and-a-half years (Orford, Herrington & Wood, 2004: 28).

The above figures indicate the importance of established firms for economic growth, employment creation, and sustainability. The survival rates of start-up and new enterprises are very low, even though only a very limited number of the population ventures into their own enterprises. According to Statistics SA (2006), 16% of economically active South Africans work for themselves, with 25,5% of white males, 19,6% of African women, and 18,6% of Asian men being involved in their own businesses.

The total entrepreneurial activity (TEA) in South Africa, as measured by the Global Entrepreneurship Monitor, was 5,4% (Orford, Herrington & Wood, 2004: 3). This percentage relates to the entire population of South Africa, and is not a percentage of the economically active population. This is very low if compared with the average of 9,4% in all 34 countries, and 21% in the developing countries, included in the 2004

survey. The South African TEA rate is in line with those of Poland, Hungary, and Croatia; countries that were also suppressed by legal and political systems which made it illegal for citizens in socialist countries to start their own businesses, as was the situation here for black people under the apartheid system. The implication is that these systems have a long-term effect on the attitudes, skills, and economic structures of these countries, and this explains the lower-than-expected TEA rates. The expectation is that South Africa should have a TEA rate of at least 15% (Orford, Herrington & Wood, 2004: 11).

An additional reason for the low total entrepreneurial activity in South Africa is that there is a low survival rate among start-ups. This is a matter of concern, as start-ups do not actually contribute to economic development, employing less than one person on average, as opposed to new business that employ – on average – 2,5 people per business (Orford, Herrington & Wood, 2004: 13). These facts highlight the importance of developing and helping individuals with entrepreneurial potential to ensure increased survival of start-up and new enterprises, as well as promoting the establishment of higher levels of successful businesses. According to Schussler (De Lange, 2006: 1), the average number of employees has decreased from 42 employees per business in 1982 to 12,7 employees per business in 2006 , thereby indicating the increasing importance of small businesses to job creation in South Africa.

The success of developed countries such as the United States of America, Japan, and the UK has proved that the only growth sector in the economy is the entrepreneur-driven small, micro and medium enterprise (SMME) sector. This means that SMMEs need to become established and to grow, as established and growth-orientated businesses contribute significantly to the economy through employment creation. In contrast, employees of large businesses are often laid off, or become self-employed. They also become employed by new SMMEs that are formed as some of the activities of large businesses are increasingly contracted out. In addition, some of the sections of these large businesses are closed down, or sold off to function as SMMEs. Once again, entrepreneurs play an important rôle. They are responsible for the formation of new businesses, to which non-core functions are outsourced, and often take over or buy the sections that would have been closed down.

Given the importance of entrepreneurs to the South African economy, their determination, resilience and contribution is even more admirable in view of the restrictions and regulations that they have to comply with. For instance, the number of regulatory instruments increased from 521 in 2002 to 1 309 in 2004. These include labour regulations, such as those for registration, together with other regulations for employment equity, tax, and value-added tax, with some sectors such as those for tourism, textiles, clothing, vehicles, and pharmaceuticals being particularly heavily regulated. Regulations cost the business sector 6,5% of GDP or, in rand terms, R79-billion in 2004 alone. The cost implications of this for businesses with a turnover of less than R1-million per year is 8,3% of their turnover. This decreases to 0,2% if the turnover of a business is more than R1-billion per year. Other implications are that the regulatory cost per worker is ten times higher for a business with five employees than for one with 200 employees (Paton, 2004).

Limited statistics with regard to SMMEs in the tourism industry specifically are available, and few if any studies focus on the contribution of these businesses to the economy of the country.

The role of tourism entrepreneurs and small businesses in the economy

The difference between SMMEs in the tourism industry and the tourism economy is that the tourism industry consists of the following three sub-sectors:
- accommodation providers (guest houses, small hotels, B&Bs, self-catering, backpacker hostels)
- hospitality and related services (restaurants, visitor attractions, arts and crafts)

- the travel distribution system (tour operators, travel agencies, and tourist guides) (Rogerson, 2005: 628).

The tourism economy is a broader concept, and includes businesses involved in providing services to the tourism industry – for example, laundry services or products such as toiletries specifically and only made for the tourism industry. SMMEs in the broader tourism economy are not usually regarded as tourism SMMEs.

It is significant that limited attention is paid and information available about the role of SMMEs in tourism. There is a lack of theoretical and empirical data on travel and tourism SMMEs, with much of the knowledge still at the information-generation stage and generated by small business researchers, rather than tourism researchers or specialists. A more developed knowledge base is essential for the development of tourism businesses and the contribution that research can make to policy-making, planning, and the future prosperity of tourism, as well as to addressing the needs of the tourism SMME sector (Page, Forer & Lawton, 1999: 436).

Sustainable tourism development is seen as the management of resources to ensure the fulfilment of economic, social, and aesthetic needs while maintaining cultural heritage, essential ecological processes, biological diversity, and life-support systems (see Chapter 16 – Managing tourism responsibility). It is important to ensure an environment that enables responsible entrepreneurial development, taking the demands of sustainable development as points of departure (cited in Lordkipanidze, Brezet & Bakman, 2005: 787).

Tourism provides benefits such as revenue generation, employment, regional development, and economic prosperity to destination communities. However, concerns have been raised about the extent to which the indigenous communities benefit from tourism development in their areas; the way in which they are exploited by foreign MNCs, and the indifferent attitude of the tourism industry towards the local or indigenous communities in which new tourism opportunities are identified.

Lordkipanidze, Brezet & Bakman (2005: 796) highlight the importance of innovative entrepreneurs in the development of local economies. Small tourism businesses and entrepreneurship play an important role in the tourism industry, as they contribute to the development of tourism businesses in rural areas – nature-based, hospitality, crafts, and adventure tourism. They transform local resources into tourist products and services. The potential economic, socio-cultural, and environmental advantages of tourism entrepreneurship are manifold, as indicated in Table 10.1.

Tourism has been recognised as having the potential to help communities resolve some of their socio-economic development challenges, as it represents a sector of international growth. This is because of all the new destinations, and the tendency among tourists world-wide to move away from traditional tourism destinations towards tourism with a more socially responsible approach to vacationing (Kokkranikal & Morrison, 2002: 8).

There seems to be a shift from the traditional '4 Ss' ('sun, sea, sand, and sex') and the generally passive nature of tourism, to the '4 Is' (information, insight, involvement, and inspiration), and a more active approach (Middleton, cited in Buhalis & Paraskevas, 2002: 427).

Tourism is an emerging sector in modern economies, and is a dynamic, ever-changing industry. Entrepreneurs play a central role in the evolution of destinations, but their rôle has either been underestimated or incompletely understood in the unstable tourism industry (Russel & Faulkner, 2004: 556–557). Schumpeter identified the image of entrepreneurial activity as a chaotic process. He has suggested that 'the entrepreneur destroys the equilibrium with a perennial gale of creative destruction' (cited in Russel & Faulkner, 2004: 56). Due to the nature of the entrepreneur, it is expected that entrepreneurs adapt well to the continually evolving and changing tourism industry, with its many opportunities.

Table 10.1 Potential economic, socio-cultural and environmental advantages to a region by stimulating entrepreneurship

Economic advantages	Socio-cultural advantages	Environmental advantages
• An increase in overall employment • An increase in employment outside agriculture • A diversification of local economic activity • Strengthening and expansion of existing enterprises • An increase in the number of investors • An increase in the number of local tourism enterprises (by turning locals into entrepreneurs).	• Strengthening the local culture and identity through promoting local products/services • Keeping local population stable; as a result there will be decreased migration, good occupational opportunities, and an educational background for succeeding generations • Improvement in the quality of life • Increased awareness of the value of heritage and the need for its protection • Improved educational level (knowledge about managing business).	• Protection and preservation of the rural/natural heritage • Reduction of resource use, minimising waste, and safeguarding environmental qualities, thus preserving biodiversity • Promotion of sustainable development of tourism products and related business areas • Sustainable land management • Less environmental impact due to the small-scale character of rural tourism entrepreneurs.

Source: Lordkipanidze, M., Brezet, H. & Backman, M. 2005. The Entrepreneurship Factor in Sustainable Tourism Development. *Journal of Cleaner Production*, Vol.13, 787–798

Entrepreneurship, management and entrepreneurial leadership

The vast majority of businesses initiated by entrepreneurs originate as micro or small businesses. These businesses are usually started and entrepreneurially managed by one person. They can grow and become larger small businesses, or even medium and large businesses, if the entrepreneur does not become a manager. The entrepreneur has a distinctly different mindset from that of the manager or bureaucrat, but the entrepreneur often becomes complacent with a specific level of achievement in his or her business. The entrepreneur then becomes the contented manager of a small business, who is averse to risk, change, and **innovation**. The entrepreneurial business is then replaced by a managerially-focused small business.

The people behind good ideas might be competent, but they often do not know how to manage a business, and have no underlying appreciation of business fundamentals. The business then fails, due to a lack of management skills, behaviour, and the necessary knowledge of the different functions of a business. Businesses that have been successfully established often fail at a later stage in the business life-cycle, due to the entrepreneur's inability to adapt to the changing needs of the business, which often includes the need for a more managerial and functional approach.

The true entrepreneur is a leader, and is adaptive, innovative, and willing to take risks. The need for a more managerial style however, becomes particularly important when the business has grown and become medium-sized (see Chapter 9 – Managing tourism businesses).

The success of entrepreneurs is determined by their ability to not only establish businesses, but also to adapt their managerial and leadership styles to changes required in the growth phases of the business. However, entrepreneurial differences occur, in that some entrepreneurs are satisfied to establish a business and then continue to manage it, while others are interested in the growth and extension of their businesses to become medium or large businesses, and continually seek new areas for development and growth. The growth-orientated entrepreneurs are vital to wealth and job creation, and contribute to the economic growth of a country. It would certainly be advantageous to South Africa if the entrepreneurs with growth intentions and the ability to adapt to change and develop with their businesses were to be identified.

Entrepreneurship can be seen as both the intention to grow and the managerial capability to manage actual growth, as well as the actual activity of establishing a business. The propensity to introduce changes is strongly related to growth intentions, this being one of the main defining features of the entrepreneur (Gray, 2002: 69). Thus, although SMMEs contribute to wealth creation and adding of value, not all are necessarily entrepreneurial.

Management and leadership skills are equally important in determining the growth rate of SMMEs. Fernald, Solomon & Tarabishy (2005: 7) identified eight common characteristics between leaders and entrepreneurs, namely:

- visionary, which indicates an explicit identification of a domain for competitive behaviour, a set of sources of competitive strength, and a profile for resource capability. A good vision is realistic and feasible, and implies a capability construct.
- risk-taking, which implies weighing the multitudinous factors involved, while understanding that no-one can predict the future with certainty.
- achievement-orientated, which refers to a person's need to do things better, faster, and more efficiently; set challenging yet achievable goals, and show persistence and determination in pursuing goals
- able to motivate others, showing a talent to inspire others to voluntarily do their best to achieve the objectives of the business
- creative, meaning that they are able to involve the adjustment or refinement of existing procedures or products, the identification of opportunities, and the identification of solutions to problems.

- flexible, indicating that they can adapt to changing circumstances
- patience, namely the ability to exercise patience until a task has been completed and a goal has been reached.
- persistent, to have confidence in themselves and their businesses, and to continue in spite of setbacks, difficult situations, and problems.

Gray confirmed strong positive links between growth-orientation, setting of financial objectives (as opposed to lifestyle goals), propensity to introduce changes, and actual growth (2002: 61). SMME owners generally set non-financial objectives for their businesses, and those entrepreneurial businesses that do set more classical financial strategic objectives are in the minority. Entrepreneurial businesses facing the growth challenge play an important role as change agents for economic change and innovation. Unfortunately, most small business owners are reluctant to accept this challenging role, resist change, and become non-entrepreneurial once they have established a business. Few small companies are seriously interested in growth; their primary motives are autonomy and independence. Organisational complexities associated with growth and innovation, as well as the non-economic personal motivations of many SMME owner-managers, present real external and internal psychological barriers to sustained entrepreneurial behaviour in most SMMEs. In line with Schumpeter's (1934: 69) observation that most firms settle for non-entrepreneurial stability, Gray confirms low intention to grow in most small businesses (2002: 67). Growth-orientated business owners are also more inclined to introduce constant or major changes within their businesses.

Although there are some general beliefs that the entrepreneur, or entrepreneurial leader, should be replaced by a professional manager after the successful establishment of a business, studies have found no evidence that professional managers performed better in high-growth firms than the original entrepreneur did. In their study, Willard, Krueger & Feeser (1992) found that many entrepreneurs learn how to manage growth effectively. Swiercz & Lydon (2002: 380) are in

agreement, and in their study reveal the process by which successful entrepreneurs transform themselves into successful professional managers. They build on the business life-cycle approach in creating a two-phase entrepreneurial leadership model, consisting of the formative growth phase and the institutional growth phase.

In the first phase, the leader establishes the business on free-form energy and, as the business grows and matures, it becomes more formalised. The second phase requires focus on long-term stability without neglecting the innovative, entrepreneurial spirit that ensured success in the first phase. At the transition point where the business moves from phase I to phase II, a strategic inflection point occurs. It is here that the entrepreneur must acquire new leadership competencies. The entrepreneurial leadership model defines the characteristics of the business in the formative growth or first phase as spontaneous and free spirited, with informal communication and centralised decision-making. The second phase of institutional growth is characterised by the efficient operation of tasks, formal communication during scheduled meetings, and policies and procedures (Swiercz & Lydon, 2002: 383).

Bolton & Thompson (2003) identified talents, and ranked them according to how difficult it is to get and exploit a specific talent. For example, the 'follower' talent is the least buried and easiest talent to exploit, whereas the 'inventor' talent is the most difficult to exploit. Five other talents fall in between these two categories, ranging from the easiest to exploit to the most difficult:

Followers
Operational managers
Enterprising managers
Project champions
Leaders
Entrepreneurs
Inventors

The research of Bolton & Thompson (2003) clearly indicates how difficult it is to exploit entrepreneurial talent, second only to the inventor talent, which has been found to be the most difficult to exploit.

Management and entrepreneurial skills of successful entrepreneurs

Lerner & Haber (2000: 77–78) found that in small tourism businesses, managerial skills provided the strongest association with success, while their absence was one of the main barriers to that success. The tourism business owner has to be involved in all areas of activity, and therefore has to be provided with tailored regional business and management training tools to ensure business development and success. Small tourism business profitability is contingent on human capital, especially the skills of the entrepreneurs in the business. Managerial skills are so crucial for the success of the business that the main objective of advisors should be to promote managerial competencies.

Essential management skills for successful entrepreneurs identified through research (Nieuwenhuizen & Kroon, 2002) are as follows:
- planning an enterprise before it is established
- general management skills (planning, organising, leading, and control)
- customer service
- knowledge of competitors
- market orientation
- the importance of quality products/services
- expertise in financial management
- the use of advisers when necessary
- knowledge and skills needed for a specific industry
- sound human relations, indicating interpersonal relations in the broader sense, including internal and external stakeholders in the business.

A study by Szivas (2001: 170) identified useful skills for running a tourism business are as follows:
- the ability to handle people
- a knowledge of finance and accounting
- a knowledge of marketing
- the ability to make contacts
- a knowledge of the tourism industry
- the ability to use computers
- a knowledge of economics and

- the ability to speak foreign language/s.

The management skills identified as important by both these as well as other studies agree on the importance of the ability to 'handle' people, or good interpersonal relations; expertise in financial management, knowledge of marketing (which includes knowledge of competitors), and knowledge of the specific – or tourism – industry.

The important managerial skills identified are varied and comprehensive and, due to the importance of these skills in the management of small tourism businesses, are expanded upon briefly:

1. *Planning* a business before it is established and general management skills (planning, organising, leading, and control) are essential skills for success in any business. A well-considered business plan ensures that the entrepreneur launches the enterprise with confidence, because it means that the necessary research and planning has been done. It also implies that the entrepreneur is, and will be, personally involved in the management of the business (see Chapter 9 – Managing tourism businesses).

2. *Sound human relations*. Entrepreneurs have a close involvement with people. They realise they cannot be successful in isolation. They apply human processes that are important for the successful management of people: motivation, team-building, communication skills, and conflict management. They also know how to build contacts and networks to the benefit of the business. They find it important to ensure long-term relationships and to stay on good terms with suppliers, clients, and others involved in the enterprise. Closely related to sound human relations is good customer service.

3. *Good customer service*. Entrepreneurs who maintain good human relations are sensitive to clients' needs, and so provide very good customer service. Personal service is important. Examples are after-sales service – attention to details such as serving refreshments tastefully when a client visits the business enterprise. Personally, they are

presentable individuals, have attractive premises, and their premises are user-friendly, as with a neatly-ordered shop. Administrative and technical factors are also crucial to sound customer service. Keeping records and filing systems for reference and stock control; a diary to ensure proper planning and keeping of appointments; contract planning and target dates for completing projects; contracts, and job files for information on clients are a few examples of a methodical approach that can help to ensure effective customer service.

4. *Market-orientated*, including knowledge of competitors. Successful entrepreneurs are market-orientated. They know who their target market is; what the needs and demands of the target market are, and how to meet them profitably. A market-conscious entrepreneur has developed products and services to satisfy the requirements of the client. A market-conscious entrepreneur is positioned realistically in relation to competitors. This means that the entrepreneur's products and/or services are distinct from those of competitors, to ensure profitability and a competitive edge. The utilisation of the Internet to market small tourism businesses has been found by Elliot & Boshoff (2005: 91) to be essential. To ensure successful Internet marketing of small tourism businesses, Elliot and Boshoff's research found the following criteria to be important:

- there should be a product champion in the business, meaning that someone – ideally the owner manager – should recognise the potential of Internet marketing and be involved in its implementation
- a network of effective alliances, including personal contact networks, social, business, industry, marketing, and other tourism businesses networks
- a high level of owner-manager involvement in the Internet marketing strategy
- clear owner-manager vision.

5. *Knowledge of competitors*. Successful entrepreneurs know who their competitors are; how many competitors they have; the size of their competitors' businesses; the segment of the market their competitors control; the quality of their competitors' products/services (offerings); how to distinguish themselves from their competitors and so ensure an increase their share of the market; how to discover their competitors' strengths and weaknesses, and how to convert a competitor's weakness into a profit opportunity for their own business.

6. *Recognise the importance of quality products/ services*. This activity is part of the marketing function as well as the purchasing function. The client is the focus of the business, and products and/or services are developed and adapted to meet the client's wants and needs. Quality offerings are not necessarily expensive offerings. But the client expects the quality of the offering to be in keeping with the price charged, and, for that reason, value for money is important. A successful entrepreneur aims to offer clients a quality offering, while still remaining profitable. Costs must be kept in check without affecting the quality of goods. Quality products and services contribute to marketing, as they generate new clients through personal recommendation by existing, satisfied clients.

7. *Expertise in financial management*. Successful entrepreneurs realise that they must be able to understand their own accounting systems (see Chapter 12 – Managing Finance for Tourism. Simplicity and usefulness are the most important features of such systems. A simple system that suits the business is essential. The entrepreneur must understand what has to be done and why it must be done, so that the information it provides can be properly utilised. If the size and complexity of a business are such that the accounting cannot be done internally, a qualified person must be appointed to perform this function. The usefulness of the information provided by the accounting system is of cardinal importance. The information obtained from the accounting system allows the entrepreneur to make decisions on how to improve the management of the business. For the entrepreneur, the main purpose of accounting is to provide insight into the use of financial information. The accounting must be simple enough not to demand too much time. However, it must be comprehensive enough to ensure effective

decision-making and management. The successful entrepreneur exercises financial discipline, understands what to spend money on, and how it must be done in order to ensure success.

8. *Knowledge and skills needed for a specific industry*. Successful entrepreneurs usually have enough knowledge and skills regarding their business to ensure success. Knowledge of and experience in the tourism industry are essential for the success of a tourism business. Successful entrepreneurs are also thoroughly aware of their own limitations, and make use of experts to provide them with advice and to help them, in this way ensuring improved performance. Successful entrepreneurship does not involve a person becoming an expert in management, but rather that they become an expert in the product or service for which there is a need in the market or, even better, a specified target market.

9. *The use of advisers when necessary*. Entrepreneurs know what is needed for success in a specific business, and are intent on developing their skills in these critical areas of performance. If marketing the enterprise's offerings is the critical area of performance, and significantly determines the success of the business, the entrepreneurs know how to do marketing. If they don't have the necessary expertise themselves, they appoint trained staff or outsource the function to specialists. They understand the environment in which they are competing, and are well-organised.

Entrepreneurs must also be fully aware of management skills they do not have (weaknesses). These can be corrected by using other people, such as employees, consultants, contractors, or professional experts; self-development and conscious efforts to make up for deficiencies by learning new skills and gaining new knowledge.

Entrepreneurial/personal skills

In addition to managerial skills, entrepreneurial skills are important for success of a SMME. Creativity and innovation, a willingness to take risks, leadership, and networking – the distinguishing personal skills of entrepreneurs – were identified as having a strong relation to the success of entrepreneurial businesses. Involvement in the business and giving priority to a high quality of work also indicates that successful entrepreneurs realise that their presence in the business is as critically important as the quality of their products or services.

Creativity and innovation: Creativity is the generation of new and usable ideas to solve any problem or use any opportunity. In the long term, an enterprise's success is determined by the degree to which good ideas are generated, developed, and implemented. Creativity consists of people being open to new ideas and new approaches to the business, and focusing on what can be done differently to ensure success in the enterprise. In other words, effective entrepreneurs take the initiative to solve problems in a unique manner. Although they understand the importance of innovation, they often view the risk and the high investment that the development of innovative products or services requires as out of proportion to its profit potential. This explains why the owners of small businesses often creatively adopt the innovations of competitors by, for example, product adjustments, marketing, and client service. Entrepreneurs tend to be creative, but are not necessarily innovators. They are not necessarily focused on the research and development of new or unique products, services or methods. Innovators challenge existing systems and change them. They take an opportunity, and use it to develop innovative solutions. This explains why innovators lead, and others often follow. Innovators ensure flexibility, competition, and improved reactivity in their enterprises by constant innovation.

Risk orientation: Successful entrepreneurs do not take chances, but sometimes feel it necessary to take calculated risks. Unsuccessful entrepreneurs, on the other hand, do not take any risks, or take expensive, impulsive decisions that they don't think through. Entrepreneurs investigate the situation and calculate the probable results before they take decisions. Successful entrepreneurs avoid opportunities where there is a high probability that they will be unsuccessful, regardless of the reward. Entrepreneurs manage the risk of their enterprise by accepting control, and by being involved in the basic aspects of the enterprise. They control their enterprise by getting access to information. They reduce their exposure to financial loss by involving investors, often at the risk of losing control. They shorten the period between the conceptualisation of an idea and making the product or service available in the market. In this way, they often limit the risk of competition. Hasty actions also often involve risk, and can be harmful because the incubation period of the idea is insufficient and the time calculation poor (Bird, 1989: 88).

Leadership in a SMME is unique, and different to leadership in a large organisation, because it focuses on different forms of interpersonal behaviour. The character, vision, and contributions have a direct impact, because the owner is involved in all of them. Team effort and cross-functional approaches are required, because the SMME owner is often responsible for all or most of the organisational functions. They are multi-dimensional, with a broad foundation of interests in various disciplines. The influence of decisions is larger in small businesses, and they spend less time giving direction, and more time bringing out the best in people. To be comfortable with people and have good personal interactions; to confront problems; to be amenable to differences in opinion; to trust people and to give recognition where it is deserved, are behaviours that are linked to leadership. The successful entrepreneur is a team-builder, and allows people to feel worthy by giving them responsibility and credit for what they have achieved. They know how to work with people and motivate them; how to build a comprehensive network of contacts which they know will possibly be useful in the future.

Conditions for success in entrepreneurial tourism businesses are as follows:
- a task-related motivation that includes a vision for the business
- skills and expertise that include present knowledge and acumen, as well as the ability to develop and acquire skills that will be needed in the future for the type of business

- an expectation of personal gain, whether financial or other (for example, autonomy or lifestyle)
- new technologies, such as information and communication technologies (ICT)
- a supportive environment with conditions and policies that support the performance of the entrepreneur.

A study by Copp & Ivy (2001: 346) found that a small business venture (enterprise) benefits from networking through interaction with and the support of other entities. A *network* is defined as a group of two or more businesses that have come together to carry out some new business activity that they would not do independently. Examples in the tourism industry are a group of guest houses, lodges, and small hotels that form a *consortium* to purchase guest toiletries and other supplies. By grouping together, they are able to negotiate better prices than they would as individuals. Another example is when a few businesses group together to advertise their services and products. An example of this would be five wine estates in the Winelands region in the Western Cape co-operating to market their estates and offering a multiple wine tasting experience. Visitors buy a pass that provides for wine tasting and accompanying snacks at these estates. This cooperation between the estates enables them to market themselves better, since the cost is shared and they can create a combined awareness of the area in a larger region.

Networks can be broadly grouped into informal and formal categories. The informal or social network consists of individuals such as family, friends, former colleagues, and employees who are contacted to listen, give advice and support, and who are used extensively by entrepreneurs, particularly in rural or developing areas. Formal networks involve links between the entrepreneur and other organisation/s, rather than individuals, and include advisory agencies, chambers of commerce, small business associations, banks, accountants, and lawyers (Copp & Ivy, 2001: 347). These networks contribute in various ways, including the marketing of small tourism businesses.

Management and entrepreneurial skills of small tourism businesses and entrepreneurs, as well as a thorough knowledge and application of various business functions, such as human resources management (HRM) (see Chapter 11), finance (see Chapter 12), marketing (see Chapter 14), and technology (see Chapter 7) further contribute to their success.

Entrepreneurship in the medium and large business sectors

Entrepreneurial skills at the medium and large business level are distinctly different from those at the small business level. A fine balance between entrepreneurial and managerial skills is essential at a medium and large business level. Specialisation in areas of the medium-sized business is necessary due to size and manageability, with different departments for functions such as management, finance, marketing, and HRM. Entrepreneurial businesses are inclined to remain flat in structure, even when they become medium or large – but those with a more administrative method of adaptation sometimes become hierarchical. The entrepreneur at this level has to be, or to become, more adept at managing different functional areas and levels from a managerial and strategic level. Managing growth by way of expansion, diversification, and vertical integration becomes more critical in medium and large businesses.

Entrepreneurs in the large business sector are often excluded from the definition of an entrepreneur, but, in actual fact, those who have grown their businesses into large and often diversified enterprises are the ultimate entrepreneurs. Their contribution to the economy and employment creation is also not included in the statistics of small and SMMEs, and is therefore not usually seen as the involvement of entrepreneurs. In this sector we find our more prominent entrepreneurs in the tourism industry, often in public companies – for example, Sol Kerzner of *Southern Sun* and *Sun International*; Glenn Orsmond of *1Time* and Luke Bailes of *Singita Game Lodges* (see Chapter case study).

Conclusion

Small tourism businesses as well as growth-orientated entrepreneurs in the tourism industry make an important contribution to the country in their own unique ways. Competent management of these businesses is essential to ensure their continued success and growth, in order to provide much-needed tourism visitor attractions, offerings, amenities, and value towards a sustainable tourism industry in South Africa. Important entrepreneurial, managerial, and other functional business skills should be developed and applied, as these skills are essential to ensure continued success of tourism SMMEs in South Africa.

Review questions

1. Distinguish between small business and entrepreneurship.

2. Identify and describe three small tourism businesses, as well as three entrepreneurial businesses in the tourism industry.

3. What is the contribution of small tourism businesses and entrepreneurship to the economy of South Africa?

4. List management and business management functions that are important for success in tourism SMMEs.

5. Name the economic, socio-cultural and environmental advantages of a region in stimulating entrepreneurship.

Further reading

Getz, D. & Peterson, T. 2005. Growth and profit-orientated entrepreneurship among family business owners in the tourism and hospitality industry. *Hospitality Management.* Vol. 24, 219–242.

Lerner, M. & Haber, S. 2000. Performance factors of small tourism ventures: the interface of tourism, entrepreneurship and the environment. *Journal of Business Venturin.* Vol.16, 77–100.

Lordkipanidze, M., Brezet, H. & Backman, M. 2005. The entrepreneurship factor in sustainable tourism development. *Journal of Cleaner Production*, Vol.13, 787–798.

Websites

www.seda.org.za

www.tradepage.co.za

www.tourismcapetown.co.za/xxl/_lang/en/_site/
entrepreneur/index.html

References

Bird, B. J. 1989. *Entrepreneurial behaviour.* Glenview, Illinois: Scott, Foresman and company.

Bolton, B. & Thompson, J. 2003. *The entrepreneur in focus.* London: Thomson.

Buhalis, D. & Paraskevas, A. 2002. Entrepreneurship in tourism and the context of experience economy. *Tourism Management*, Vol. 23, 427–431.

Bygrave, W. D., Reynolds, P. D. & Autio, E. 2004. *Global Entrepreneurship Monitor:* 2003 Executive Report. London: Babson College.

Copp, C. B. & Ivy, R. L. 2001. Networking trends of small tourism businesses in Post-Socialist Slovakia. *Journal of Small Business Management*, Vol.39(4), 345–353.

De Lange, J. 2006. SA maak werk van werkloosheid. *Beeld, Sake Beeld.* 27 September. p.1.

Elliot, R. & Boshoff, C. 2005. The uitilisation of the Internet to market small tourism businesses. *South African Journal of Business Management*, Vol.36(4), 91–103.

Fernald, L. W. Solomon, G. T. & Tarabishy, A. 2005. A new paradigm: entrepreneurial leadership. *Southern Business Review*, Spring 2005, Vol. 30(2), 1–10.

Getz, D. & Peterson, T. 2005. 'Growth and profit-orientated entrepreneurship among family business owners in the tourism and hospitality industry' in *Hospitality Management.*Vol. 24, 219–242.

Gray, C. 2002. Entrepreneurship, resistance to change and growth in small firm. *Journal of Small Business and Enterprise Development*, Vol. 9(1): 61–72.

Kao, R. W. Y., Kao, K. R. & Kao, R. R. 2002. *Entrepreneurism: a philosophy and a sensible alternative for the market economy.* London: Imperial College Press.

Kokkranikal, J. & Morrison, A. 2002. Entrepreneurship and sustainable tourism: the houseboats of Kerala. *Tourism and Hospitality Research*, Vol. 4(1), 7–20.

Lerner, M. & Haber, S. 2000. Performance factors of small tourism ventures: the interface of tourism, entrepreneurship and the environment. *Journal of Business Venturing.* Vol.16, 77–100.

Lordkipanidze, M., Brezet, H. & Backman, M. 2005. The entrepreneurship factor in sustainable tourism development. *Journal of Cleaner Production*, Vol.13, 787–798

Nieuwenhuizen, C. & Kroon, J. 2002. Identification of entrepreneurial success factors to determine the content of entrepreneurship subjects. SA *Journal for Higher Education*, Vol.16(3), 157–166.

Orford, J., Herrington, M. & Wood, E. 2004. *Global Entrepreneurship Monitor: South Executive African Report 2004.* Cape Town: University of Cape Town, Graduate School of Business, Centre for Innovation and Entrepreneurship.

Page, S. J., Forer, P. & Lawton, G. R.1999. Small business development and tourism: *Terra incognita? Tourism Management*, Vol. 20, 435–459.

Paton C. 2004. Myriad laws burden economy. *Financial Mail.* 19/11/2004.

Rogerson, C. M. 2005. Unpacking tourism SMMEs in South Africa: structure, support needs and policy response. *Development Southern Africa*, Vol 22(5), 623–642.

Russel, R. & Faulkner, B. 2004. Entrepreneurship, chaos and the Tourism Area Lifecycle. *Annals of Tourism Research*, Vol. 31(3), 556–579.

Schumpeter, J. 1934. *The theory of economic development.* Cambridge, Mass.: Harvard University Press.

South African Tourism Strategic Research Unit, 2006. *2005 Annual Tourism Report*, August. Tshwane: South African Tourism.

Statistics South Africa. 2006. Labour force survey. *Statistics South Africa.* September.

Strategic Business Partnership (SBP). 2006. *Counting the cost of red tape for tourism in South Africa.* Johannesburg: Acumen.

Swiercz, P. M. & Lydon, S. R. 2002. Entrepreneurial leadership in high-tech firms: a field study. *Leaderhip & Organisation Development* Journal, Vol. 23(7), 380–388.

Szivas, E. 2001. Entrance into tourism entrepreneurship: a UK case study. *Tourism and Hospitality Research*, Vol.3(2), 163–172.

Willard, G. E., Krueger, D. A. & Feeser, H. R. 1992. In order to grow, must the founder go: a comparison of performance between founder and non-founder managed high-growth manufacturing firms. *Journal of Business Venturing*, Vol. 7, 181–194.

World Travel and Tourism Council. 2003. *South Africa: travel and tourism – a world of opportunity.* London: WTTC.

Singita Game Reserves

Objectives

- to understand what it means to be an entrepreneur
- to determine what entrepreneurial businesses contribute to a country
- to identify some important managerial skills of successful entrepreneurs

Singita Game Reserves is a world-class eco-tourism and leisure operation, offering award-winning safari adventures coupled with specialised and sophisticated hotel experiences. Singita Game Reserves has lodges in South Africa, Zimbabwe, and Tanzania. Singita currently operates nine distinctive lodges of varying sizes. Singita Ebony & Boulders Lodges are in the Sabi Sand Reserve; Singita Lebombo & Sweni Lodges are in the Lebombo Concession, Kruger National Park; Singita Pamushana is in Zimbabwe and Singita Grumeti Reserves in Tanzania consists of Sasakwa Lodge, Faru Faru Lodge and Sabora Tented Camp on the border of the Serengeti National Park in Tanzania.

Originally a game farm belonging to James Bailes, the decision was made in 1994 to open Singita, adjacent to the Kruger National Park in Mpumalanga, to discerning visitors. Singita Ebony Lodge and Singita Boulders Lodge were conceived

later that year, the brainchild of Luke Bailes, James Bailes' grandson. Bailes saw that there was a need in the market for a superior luxury product.

'Singita', which means "the place of miracles" in Shangaan, is regarded as an international enterprise, as the majority of guests are international visitors. Few South Africans get to visit these luxurious resorts, as at R7 500 per person a night it is simply too expensive. Singita Ebony and Boulders, with a total of 24 luxurious suites, are two exquisite lodges in the Sabi Sand Game Reserve overlooking the Sand River, and attract some of the world's wealthiest visitors. Suites comprise of a lounge, bedroom, bathroom, wooden deck, private pool, and both an indoor and outdoor shower. In addition, the secluded Castleton Camp has six bedrooms.

Singita's mission is to create and operate exceptional products that are economically sustainable and environmentally responsible. Through an encompassing dedication to service excellence, the group aims to be the most successful ecotourism and leisure operation in Africa.

Most of Singita's staff are locals. They receive expert training, as service is a vital component in the success of this enterprise. When a tracker, the person who to is responsible for finding and following the animals for observation by the guests, for example, is ready for promotion to game ranger position, he or she is flown to a 5-star hotel in Cape Town for the experience. For some of them it will be their first time on an aeroplane and/or staying at a hotel. Trackers attend a six-month course involving training in customer service, based at the lodges. Singita Game Reserves also has an in-house guide training and development program run from the lodges. The staff contribute to the ambience by exuding warmth, informality and the spirit of *ubuntu*. They love their jobs, their guests, and each other.

Singita has earned some of the highest international accolades for exceptional standards in accommodation, service, and cuisine. It has been rated Number One by several of the world's leading travel magazines as the ultimate game lodge experience. Readers of America's biggest-selling travel magazine, Condé Nast Traveller, rated it the top hotel in the world in 2004. It also achieved the seemingly impossible and unprecedented score of 100% for its two lodges on all accounts – rooms, service, food, and location. No other hotel has achieved this score in the 13 years of the award's existence. American magazine *Travel & Leisure* voted it the second best hotel in the world and the best in Africa and and the Middle East 2007. In the connoisseur's travel guide *Harper's Hideaway*

Report rated Singita Private Game Reserve the 'best international resort hideaway' in 2003. It also received the *Tatler Travel Guide Magazine's* (UK) 'Word's best five house-style destination' in 2004.

Recently, Singita received yet more prestigious awards, and has expanded the lodge with additional exquisite accommodation. Family suites have been added to Singita Ebony & Boulders, taking suite numbers to 24 at Singita Sabi Sand Reserve. Undoubtedly, from humble beginnings, Singita has evolved into the world's premier safari destination.

www

www.singita.com

Discussion questions

1. Would you describe Luke Bailes as a small tourism business owner or an entrepreneur? Motivate your answer.
2. Explain how Singita contributes to the tourism industry in South Africa.
3. Discuss the entrepreneurial and managerial skills Luke Bailes exhibits that you can identify through the case study?

11

Managing human resources in tourism

Pieter Grobler

Purpose

The purpose of this chapter is to introduce you to the management of human resources in the tourism industry.

Learning outcomes

After reading this chapter, you should be able to:
- explain the importance of human resource management in the tourism industry
- describe what human resource planning entails
- explain the objectives and uses of job analysis
- describe the processes of recruitment, selection, placement, and orientation
- discuss the purposes and techniques of employee training, development, and performance appraisal
- describe the primary elements of employee compensation
- describe the nature of the health and safety field and its role in companies
- define a human resource information system
- discuss some of the major legislation affecting human resource management.

Chapter overview

This chapter introduces the issue of human resource (HR) management in the tourism industry. It begins with a debate on why HR management is important in the industry. It considers the role of the human resource manager in a company. Thereafter, a classification framework for individual HR functions is proposed. The chapter also contains a discussion of these functions.

The concluding case study illustrates how the theory contained in this chapter can be applied to a practical situation in the tourism industry.

Introduction

As indicated in Chapter 1, there is no doubt that the world tourism industry is profitable, and expanding. The South African government, has recognised the importance of this industry to the economy in its accelerated and shared growth initiative for South Africa (ASGISA) (Department of Foreign Affairs, 2006). Tourism as a service industry is highly people-intensive, and in this context the management of employees working in this industry is a critical function (Baum & Kokkranikal, 2005: 86). It is acknowledged within all the sub-sectors of this industry, be they visitor attractions, transport operators, accommodation providers, or travel organisers, that the people employed in these organisations are one of their most crucial assets. The success of an individual tourism organisation or destination is dependent on its employees' contribution and commitment (see Example box). The human resource is one therefore, that needs to be nurtured properly.

Example Vision of City Lodge Group

People caring for people
- We will be recognised as the preferred Southern African hotel group.
- Through dedicated leadership and teamwork, we will demonstrate our consistent commitment to delivering caring service with style and grace.
- We will constantly enhance our guest experience through our passionate people, ongoing innovation, and leading-edge technology.
- Our integrity, values, and ongoing investment in our people and hotels will provide exceptional returns to stakeholders and continued sustainable growth'

Source: Website: www.citylodge.co.za. Used with permission, accessed 26/6/2006.

The question that immediately comes to mind is: 'How can the goals listed above be achieved?' The answer lies in having sound **human resource management** practices. This chapter focuses on what these practices entail, and how you as a tourism manager can ensure that they are implemented correctly.

Why are HR practices necessary for tourism businesses?

According to De Waal (2007: 3–11), people are the most difficult asset to manage. They are unpredictable (at least to some extent); they have their own will and plans (which do not necessarily fit in with those of the organisation), and they are affected by the external and internal environments. Despite these issues, people are the source of the competitive advantage of any company (Burud & Tumolo, 2004: 12). Thus, getting the best out of people to improve organisational performance makes sense; especially in the tourism industry, where employees are constantly working with customers.

There is no doubt that some tourism companies are more successful than others at attracting and retaining talented people. In order to establish why this is so, Dychtwald, Erickson & Morison (2006: 125) compared the HR practices of highly successful companies with those that were not so successful. The results show that the following HR practices allowed talent-winning companies to perform better than their competitors:
- they make work challenging
- they demand personal responsibility in completing the work
- they include subordinates in decision making
- they provide quick and immediate feedback and recognition.

According to Armstrong (2006: 54), these findings place enormous pressures on organisations to improve the ways in which they manage their human resources. In consequence, the full range of HR practices is indispensable. The challenge here is to create policies and practices that enhance the company's ability to attract and keep the talented employees who are vital for successful service delivery in the different tourism businesses.

Although these findings do not necessarily prove the connection between HR practices and the ability to attract and retain talented people, they are consistent with the view that there is a link between organisational capability and the way companies manage their human resources (Jackson & Schuler, 2000: 3–7).

While the tourism industry offers well-qualified individuals, such as graduates, exciting and rewarding career opportunities, the industry also needs a vast number of operational staff (Haven-Tang & Jones, 2006: 91). Low entry barriers and high turnover pose particular HR challenges to tourism management in this area. There is no doubt, however, that the application of HR practices in the tourism industry can only lead to better staff utilisation and service delivery. What these HR practices entail, and who is responsible for them within a company, will be discussed in the next section.

The HR professional

Who is responsible for an organisation's HR practices? In a small business, a characteristic of the tourism industry, these aspects are normally handled by one of the functional managers – namely, the marketing or financial manager, or even, sometimes, the owner. As the business grows, this task requires more and more time and attention, until a person is eventually appointed to perform these specific activities. Such a person is usually called a human resource (HR) officer or a personnel officer (Armstrong, 2006: 71). As the

business develops further and the HR officer can no longer cope, additional people are appointed, and eventually a human resource department is established, with a human resource manager. This person is normally a member of the HR professional body, known as The South African Board for Personnel Practice (SABPP).

www

Browse this website: www.sabpp.co.za

HR practices and their classification

The most important task of the HR manager in any organisation today is to help other managers in the business to fully utilise the employees allocated to them, so that the company can improve its competitive advantage. HR management can therefore be regarded as an aid or staff function; as it advises other line functions such as marketing, finance, etc. This activity normally takes place by means of HR policies. To ensure optimum effectiveness, the HR policies should be in writing, and should be communicated to all employees. This is traditionally done by the publication of an HR policy manual.

Figure 11.1 Effective HRM

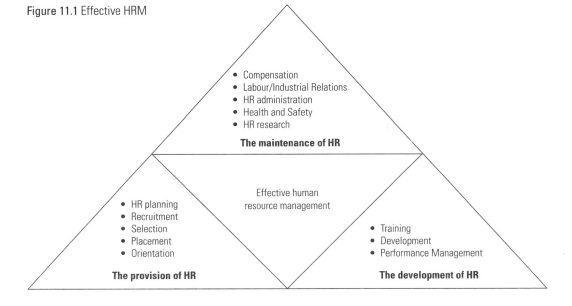

According to the literature (Byars & Rue, 2000: ix; Bernardin, 2003: ix; Mathis & Jackson, 2003: iv), the HR practices found within organisations can normally be classified into three main groups; namely, the provision of human resources; the development of human resources, and the maintenance of human resources. The three main groups, with their sub-components, are illustrated in Figure 11.1 (on the previous page).

It is important to realise that, to be effective, these three main groups of activities, with their sub-components, cannot operate in isolation, but must be integrated with one another as well as with the overall company strategy. This is known as the strategic HR management approach.

It should also be noted that, irrespective of the size of the company within the tourism industry, be it a guest house, tour operator, travel agency, major car rental operator, airline company, or MNC hotel group, the full range of HR practices are essential to improving the organisation's capability, and thus its particular competitive advantage.

In the next section, we will discuss the individual components within each of the three main HR areas.

The provision of human resources

From the foregoing, it is clear that one of the main activities of the HR function is to ensure a continuous flow of human resources (employees) to the company. The HR manager must thus ensure that the company has the right number and the right quality of employees to perform its activities at all times. The sub-activities of human resource planning, recruitment, selection, placement, and orientation, as well as the smaller activities of which they consist, are engaged in by the HR manager in order to ensure the efficient performance of her/his role; namely the effective provision of human resources.

Human resource planning

Human resource planning involves estimating the quantity and quality of employees who will be required for the business in the future, and determining whether this can be met by the current workforce. This is an issue which has become more and more difficult, as a result of the HIV/AIDS epidemic in South Africa. According to Mello (2006: 211), there are five major objectives in HR planning, namely:

- preventing over- or under-staffing. For example – if a new hotel opens with too few staff, proper customer service delivery will be hampered. On the other hand, if too many staff are appointed, they will get in one another's way, which will also lead to poor customer service delivery.
- ensuring that the company has the right employees, with the right skills, in the right places, at the right times. This will enable the hotel to provide an excellent service to its customers.
- ensuring that the company is responsive to changes in its environment. Doing this will help the hotel group to determine what the customers would like to have and, as such, enable them to provide this service
- providing direction and coherence of all HR activities and systems. By determining the quantity and quality of staff needed in a hotel, the HR manager can focus his or her energy in the right direction
- uniting the perspectives of line and staff managers. This will enable the staff managers, for example HR, to provide sufficient staff members to the line managers to enable them to do their jobs well.

Job analyses and job descriptions are used to identify the work being done in a company now, while a job specification identifies the type of employee needed to do the work, and human resource forecasting assists in determining the number of employees that will be needed in the future.

Job analysis and job description

Job analysis is the process by which all relevant information regarding a specific post is gathered. Various methods exist to gather this information. These include observation, interviews, and questionnaires. In the case of observation, the job analyst observes precisely how the task is performed by the job incumbent. This method is used specifically where physical labour is performed by the incumbent, and it is easy to observe how the job is performed. An example would be that of a housekeeper making a bed in a hotel room. During the interview, the job analyst conducts an interview with the incumbent, during which the employee explains precisely how she/he goes about performing her/his job. A good subject for this research method might be the reservation clerk at the front desk of a hotel or accommodation establishment.

The third approach involves surveys. In this instance, questionnaires are compiled, consisting of specific questions relating to how the incumbents perform their job, as well as what is required from them in its execution. This approach is very popular, as job incumbents can complete the questionnaire in their own time. This method would be suitable for the crew and cabin staff of an airline, or for staff working on a luxury cruise liner.

A job description is a written account of the information obtained through one of these research methods. It will normally start with a summary of the total job; i.e. the title of the job and where it fits into the company structure. This will be followed by a brief description of the main tasks, duties, and responsibilities associated with the job. The finer details and practical examples serve as sub-sections. It is important to remember that the contents of each job should be written up, so that the incumbent knows exactly what the job entails and what the expectations in respect of its performance are.

Discussion point

What information is necessary to develop job descriptions? What are some of the qualities of a well-constructed job description?

Job specification

Having established the job content, the second step in the HR planning process needs to be undertaken. This is the drawing up of a job specification (sometimes called a person specification), which outlines the requirements to be fulfilled by an incumbent in respect of qualifications, experience, skills, behaviour, etc. It is noteworthy that the qualifications of the current job incumbent should not be taken as a criterion when the job specification is compiled, as, in practice, the incumbent may or not meet the requirements of the post, or may even exceed them. The job specification should therefore be seen as separate from the job incumbent.

Human resource forecasting

Human resource forecasting is the process through which forecasts are made on a continuing basis about the type and number of employees needed by the company. A number of factors need to be considered when doing this – these include the labour market, the economy, and the future expansion plans of the company. Available forecasting methods vary from simple projections to sophisticated computer models. Two types of forecasts are made; namely those relating to the external and internal supply of labour, and the internal and external demand for labour. Internal supply forecasts relate to conditions inside the organisation, such as age distribution, terminations, and retirements. External supply relates to the possible supply of labour from outside the organisation. Both internal and external demand forecasts, on the other hand, depend primarily on the behaviour of some business factors, such as projected sales or product volume, to which human resource needs can be related (Casio, 2006: 179). After reliable estimates have been made for both the supply and demand of employees, an anticipated shortage or surplus of employees will be realised. Mello (2006: 215) identifies a number of strategies at the grass-roots, which may be followed in both cases. Strategies for managing shortages can include—recruiting new employees, offering incentives to postpone retirement, or attempting to reduce turnover or redesign job processes so that fewer employees are needed. In the case of surpluses, interventions such as the freezing of posts and leave substitution; the offer of early retirement, or the expansion of operations can be instituted. It is important to remember that these are only forecasts, and that external as well as internal factors can impact on these forecasts – such as the prevalence of HIV/AIDS in the labour market.

Recruitment

The primary purpose of *recruitment* is to attract applications from candidates who possess the required skills and attitude to fill vacancies. The HR manager has two options in this regard – firstly to recruit from within the company (thus providing opportunities for promotion for existing staff), or to recruit from external sources. Both strategies have advantages as well as disadvantages. In practice, however, companies seldom follow a policy of recruiting only externally. Most companies combine internal as well as external recruiting, by first looking internally and then recruiting externally if no suitable internal candidate can be found. The most effective recruiting method is advertising. The key to effective advertising is knowing when and where to run a job advertisement so that it will be viewed by the greatest number of qualified readers (Tanke, 2001: 96).

Besides the traditional methods of advertising for candidates (for example, newspapers, journals, and radio), electronic recruiting (E-recruiting) systems are being increasingly utilised. E-recruiting methods make use of company Internet web sites and online resumè databases. The cost of recruitment is a significant factor and everything, including the time needed to fill vacancies, that may contribute to cost-effective recruitment must be taken into consideration. With the implementation of the Labour Relations Act No 66 of 1995 (as amended by Act 12 of 2002); the Basic Conditions of Employment Act No 75 of 1997 (as amended by Act 11 of 2002), and the Employment Equity Act No 55 of 1998, a number of important issues relating to where to recruit, as well as who to target, have arisen. Employers will have to carefully scrutinise their recruitment policies and procedures and, where necessary, compile new recruitment and selection procedures (as discussed in the next section), to be applied consistently and fairly to all job applicants. Failure to do so could have major implications for companies, such as costly litigations.

Discussion point

From an inexperienced job applicant's point of view, which recruitment method is more attractive?

Selection

Selection entails choosing from a number of candidates a person who, in the judgment of the selector/s, is best qualified to meet the required performance standards. A decision to appoint a particular candidate in a job depends, therefore, on the assumption that the person concerned will be successful in the job. The appointment is made after individual differences between the applicants and the specific job requirements have been considered. Selection principles apply equally to the appointment of new employees in entry-level jobs; to transfers, and to the promotion of candidates to higher positions. The selection process normally consists of a number of steps – such as initial screening, completion of the application form, testing, interviews, reference checks, medical examination and, finally, the selection decision. The selection process itself has become of critical importance to companies in South Africa since the implementation of the Employment Equity Act No 55 of 1998. All forms of discrimination, whether direct or indirect, are forbidden. Employers should not disqualify applicants because they are unable to complete an application form unassisted, unless personal completion of the form is a valid test of the standard of English required for the safe and effective performance of their job. This issue is especially applicable in the tourism industry. In addition, any test administered for the job must be valid and reliable; be applied fairly to employees, and not be biased against any group of applicants. In the area of medical testing, numerous legal aspects must first be clarified before this can be undertaken. For example, employers are prohibited from requesting a candidate to undergo an HIV/AIDS test for appointment purposes. Finally, in view of the present labour legislation, companies are now obliged to keep a complete set of records pertaining to the recruitment and selection of staff.

Placement

Placement is the process whereby individuals are placed in jobs in the company. This process also governs the movement of individuals within the company where promotions, transfers, and terminations of service are concerned. However, placement is primarily the follow-up of the selection process. Approved applicants are appointed at this stage (mostly in entry-level jobs). The main difference between the placement and the selection process is that the former is concerned with the internal labour market, while selection concentrates mainly on the external labour market. Placement for other than new appointments is normally based on additional information, such as the employee's performance since his or her appointment; her/his own preferences pertaining to career development; her/his perception of the status of the position; opportunities for promotion within the organisation, and opportunities for changing jobs. Successful placement therefore entails striking a careful balance between the employer's need to fill a job, and the employee's career expectations.

Orientation

It is essential that the new employee fits into his or her job environment as soon as possible, so that he or she can become productive immediately. This can be realised through the availability of an *orientation* programme. The purpose of the orientation programme is twofold. It offers a general orientation with respect to the activities of the company, and it orientates new employees (at all organisational levels) in respect to their responsibilities within the company. A typical checklist for the orientation of a new employee is shown in Table 11.1. In its broadest sense, the orientation process can be thought of as an extension of the recruitment and selection processes.

Orientation programmes vary in both length and content, and should take place every time an employee begins a new position and/or or takes on new responsibilities; when the organisation undergoes changes in its structure or policies, or following a merger or an acquisition (Tanke, 2001: 158–160). It is essential that the programme

is structured, as an unstructured process can, in the long term, be very destructive.

Table 11.1 A typical checklist for the orientation of a new employee

- Words of welcome
- History of the company
- Company culture
- Service philosophy of the company
- Company structure
- Sexual harassment policy
- Review of job descriptions, hours and days of work, job duties, and responsibilities
- Rate of pay, pay policies, and periods
- Gratuities and tip reporting
- Employee benefits
- Special uniform requirements
- Break periods and meal hours
- Review of rules of conduct and employee handbook
- Unforeseen absences and tardiness
- Tour of operation and work unit
- Introduction to co-workers
- To whom to report, when, and where
- List of frequently-called phone numbers
- Safety procedures
- Performance evaluations and salary increases
- Career development and opportunities for promotion
- Progressive discipline
- Grounds for termination
- Emergency situations

Adapted from Tanke, M. L. 2001. *Human Resources Management for the hospitality industry*, 2nd edition. Albany, NI, Delmar. Delmar is a division of Thomson Learning. Used with permission.

According to Stone (2005: 351–353), specific benefits can be derived from a proper orientation programme:

- Higher job satisfaction
- Lower labour turnover
- Greater commitment to values and goals
- Higher performance as a result of faster learning times
- Fewer costly and time-consuming mistakes
- Reduction in absenteeism
- Better customer service through heightened productivity
- Improved manager/subordinate relationships
- Better understanding of company policies, goals, and procedures.

Thus, tourism companies that make a genuine effort to welcome new employees, teach them about the company and its mission statement, and encourage them to be part of a team, will reap the benefits of a staff that is highly motivated to make a long-term commitment to their employer (Hicks, Peters & Smith, 2006: 45). The role-players in the orientation process are numerous, but ideally all levels of management must be involved in the programme in one way or another. It cannot be the responsibility of the HR manager only.

A final component of the process is its evaluation. The benefits arising from evaluating the process include:

- that the company is spending its money wisely and achieving positive results
- that the methods used to assist new employees to integrate and become effective workers in the company are the most suitable.

Discussion point

Do you agree that only new employees should undergo orientation?

Depending on the type of programme used, evaluation may cover many aspects, and can be carried out at different levels. This could include interviews with new employees after a few weeks of employment in the company; monitoring turnover statistics; conducting exit interviews, and looking regularly at sickness and absenteeism rates.

Once the appointment of suitable staff has been successfully completed, the HR manager has the first task; namely that of the provision of human resources. This brings us to the HR manager's further task: the development of these human resources.

The development of human resources

The growth of a tourism company is closely linked to the development of its human resources. When employees fail to grow and develop in their work, a stagnant company will most likely result. Although a strong employee development programme does not necessarily guarantee a company success, such a programme is generally found in successful, expanding companies. To enable the HR manager to perform the development activities within the company successfully, she/he has to perform sub-activities such as training, development, and performance management. In the next section, we will look briefly at each of these activities.

Training

Once employees have completed their orientation, they must focus only on the job for which they were employed. Able and motivated employees are a company's greatest asset, but these qualities do not come naturally, and effective *training* is necessary to achieve the required level of competence. In the tourism industry, for example, employees need to be competent, courteous, credible, responsible, and responsive (Rao & Das, 2002: 101). Training is the responsibility of the tourism company, if it wants to ensure that employees are competent and motivated. In South Africa in particular, HR managers are faced with enormous challenges. This is because the country's employment situation is unique. There is a serious shortage of skilled employees on the one hand, and a high rate of unemployment among unskilled employees on the other. South Africa urgently needs to bridge the gap between the lack of productivity among lower-level workers and the need to be highly productive, particularly at the lower levels of employment (Grobler et al., 2006: 20–21). This is a serious problem facing most tourism businesses in South Africa today. Training is the means by which this can be corrected. To assist in this regard, the South African government has, over a number of years, promulgated the following Acts: the Skills Development Act 97 of 1998; the Skills Development Levies Act 9 of 1999, and the South African Qualifications Authority Act 58 of 1995.

As indicated in Table 11.2, a number of training methods are available to the HR manager. These methods are divided into two groups: on-the-job training and off-the-job training. Any training methods employed will have to depend on the needs of the employees in a particular situation, as there is no 'correct' combination of these that can be used. It is important to note that, before training can begin, a needs assessment must be undertaken. This should be conducted at the organisational, operational, and personal levels.

Table 11.2 Training methods

On-the-job training
- job rotation – here, hotel employees are moved between different jobs to gain experience
- apprenticeship/learnership training – numerous jobs within the hotel industry require learnership training; e.g. chefs

Off-the-job training
- role-playing – here managers are normally exposed to situations such as dealing with difficult staff, and shown the correct way
- in-basket training – here managers at all levels in the hotels are exposed to numerous tasks, to see whether they can cope under pressure
- management games – here managers at senior management level in hotels are exposed to different scenarios, and have to solve problems
- brainstorming – here groups of workers at different levels in hotels get together to solve problems
- university non-degree courses – here hotels can enrol their staff, e.g. the front desk staff, to undergo a short course in communication skills
- lectures – hotels can nominate a number of managerial staff to attend a lecture on leadership

---

According to Desimone, Werner & Harris (2002: 128), a needs assessment can identify:
- an organisation's goals, and its effectiveness in reaching the goals
- discrepancies or gaps between employees' skills and the skills required for effective current job performance
- discrepancies (gaps) between skills and the skills needed to perform the job successfully in the future
- the conditions under which the training activity will occur.

Besides the traditional methods of training as indicated in Table 11.2, new developments that have taken place in the training field over the last few years also need to be mentioned, as they impact directly on the training effort in the tourism industry. These innovations include computer-based training (CBT) programmes, as well as web-based training (WBT) Yorks (2005: 180–181). CBT provides instruction via the medium of computers, and allows the employee to proceed at his own pace. A further development of CBT is the use of WBT, where instruction is delivered over the World Wide Web (WWW). In this case, individual tourism businesses, such as large hotel chains, can economically institute training courses at any time and anywhere in the world, and are able to constantly upgrade or modify the training material (Tanke, 2001: 183).

Discussion point

How have technological advances changed the training and development methods available to tourism employers?

Once the training programme has been developed and delivered, it is necessary to establish whether it works. The evaluation is, perhaps, therefore, the most critical element in the training programme. Unfortunately, not many tourism companies make any effort to determine whether their training programmes are working or not. Evaluation can only be effective if it is based on clear and specified objectives which have been determined beforehand. Evaluation must be continuous, and not a once-off exercise. It must be based on uniform, objective methods and standards. A number of measurement techniques can be used. These include a survey conducted among individuals across the organisation; a critical internal review, and a review of a range of delegate feedbacks or benchmarking performance against acknowledged excellence (Thorne & Mackey, 2003: 102).

Development

The *development* of employees – especially managers – is aimed at equipping them with the knowledge, skills and attitudes needed to enable them to manage their subordinates, develop strategies, and successfully achieve organisational goals. In other words, improved performance and productivity and the achievement of goals are all essential aspects of running a tourism business successfully. Various development methods are available, as indicated in Table 11.3. Each one provides a slightly different focus on the intended outcome of the development programme. Many tourism companies use a combination of these methods to achieve their goals.

Table 11.3 Development methods

On-the-job methods
Coaching – here, for example, restaurant staff are shown how to serve customers
Mentoring – here, junior managers are assisted by senior staff in how to perform better in their jobs in their future
Job rotation – here, junior managers in the hotel industry are moved between jobs to gain experience

Off-the-job methods
Sensitivity training – with the workforce diversity in hotels, groups are brought together to better understand each other
Team building – here, different groups are brought together to build a team – for example, the front desk staff
Assessment centres – senior managers in the hotel industry are brought here to identify their managerial abilities

---

Two of the methods which are fairly prevalent in the tourism industry are coaching and mentoring. We shall take a brief look at each of these methods.

One way of helping individuals to fulfil their potential is to develop a *coaching* environment. In this environment, a coach plays an important role. He or she guides, rather than manages. The reinforcement of a person's learning is one of the prime roles of a coach, who is often the new manager's or exceptional employee's supervisor. The coach answers questions, lets the employee participate in making decisions, stimulates the employee's thinking, and helps when problems occur. Trust, cooperation and mutual respect are imperative for coaching to be helpful (Thorne

& Mackey, 2003: 121–136). *Mentors* are usually nominated within a company to provide guidance and insight to others. They are usually experienced people with a high level of knowledge of the company, and how things are done in it. The role of a mentor tends to be far less proactive than that of a coach. A mentor usually only provides the knowledge, guidance, and insight on request. A mentor may be appointed to a new employee in the company, and remain as the learner's mentor throughout that person's career (Thorne & Mackey, 2003: 136–137).

Performance management

The assessment of an employee's *performance* or task accomplishment is a sensitive matter that must be approached with great circumspection by managers and supervisors. The result of such an assessment correlates directly with the employee's self image, and her/his status among fellow-workers. In practice, this process of assessment is known as performance review, annual appraisal, performance evaluation, employee evaluation, or merit evaluation. The appraisal is normally done by those superiors who are best acquainted with the employee's performance, and who are therefore in a position to observe the employee's work behaviour on a daily basis. The results of the process provide important information regarding any training deficiencies of the employee, and can also serve as a basis for wage adjustments. Various factors may contribute towards inefficient task performance. Generally, these factors can be linked to the system of appraisal itself, as well as the person carrying out the appraisal. To be successful, the process requires performance standards against which the employee's performance can be measured. These standards must be determined accurately, and must relate directly to the work outputs required for a particular job. The standards may certainly not be determined arbitrarily. Job analysis (discussed earlier) provides the information required to set appropriate performance standards. These standards must be defined as performance criteria which constitute the criteria for appraisal. A performance appraisal form is used to do the assessment.

After completion, the results must be discussed with the employee concerned. Feedback in the performance appraisal process means that employees are told how their performance can be improved upon in the light of an objective appraisal of the existing situation. A performance appraisal interview provides an excellent opportunity for summing up performance over the past few months by pointing to occasions where success was achieved, or where something went wrong. It is important to note that feedback is most effective when it happens as soon as possible after appraisal. The feedback can either be negative or positive. In Table 11.4, a number of appraisal methods are indicated.

Table 11.4 Performance Appraisal Methods

Category rating methods
• Graphic rating scale/non-graphic rating scale
• Checklist of critical incidents

Behavioural/objective methods
• Behavioural rating approaches
• Management by Objectives (MBO)

Comparative methods
• Ranking
• Forced distribution
• Paired comparison

Narrative methods
• Critical incident
• Essay

Other methods
• Multirater, or 360-degree appraisal.

Some benefits can be derived from the appraisal: improved performance, improved job satisfaction, increased productivity, and a stronger commitment to the company. However, not all appraisals are done in this positive atmosphere, and errors do occur. According to Redman and Wilkinson (2006: 165–168), the most common errors include rater (appraiser) bias (here the appraiser may give a high rating to the captain of the football team); the halo effect (when one particular aspect of an employee's performance may influence the evaluation of the other aspects of performance); central tendency (when appraisers evaluate everyone as

average); leniency (the appraiser gives everyone a high rating); strictness (appraisers give consistently low ratings), and recency effect (the appraiser only remembers events close to the rating time). Tanke (2001: 240–241) suggests that performance expectations need to be identified and communicated to all employees; performance appraisals need to be conducted on a regular basis, and the appraisers need to be properly trained to ensure that an effective performance appraisal is instituted within a company.

An appraisal method which has become very popular in the tourism industry is that of the 360-degree appraisal. In this appraisal feedback is obtained from a number of sources; these being the employee's supervisor; peers; subordinates; the employee him/herself, as well as the customer. This method is popular, as the feedback comes from a variety of people, rather than from one supervisor. It is important to remember that the appraisal process is also tied to the existing labour legislation mentioned earlier, and that care must be taken in how it is executed within a company, especially when dismissing an employee on grounds of poor work performance.

Discussion point

Discuss the most common rater errors which can occur during performance appraisals.

This completes our discussion on the human resource development function, the second primary HR function. Attention can, therefore, now be directed to the third HRM activity – namely, the maintenance of human resources.

The maintenance of human resources

According to research undertaken by Weiss (1997: 3), the two main issues affecting retention in the tourism industry can be identified as pay and general working conditions (e.g. long hours). Having obtained and developed its human resources, the company must ensure that these resources do not leave. In order to improve retention, increase morale, enhance customer service, and boost productivity, the HR manager has to perform sub-activities such as compensation, health and safety, labour relations, HR research, and HR administration. We will now look at each of these sub-activities.

Compensation

The issue of *compensation* has long posed problems for the HR manager. How should jobs be evaluated to determine their worth? Are wage and salary levels competitive? Are they fair? Is it possible to create an incentive compensation system tied to performance? The management of the compensation process is a complex and sensitive issue. Compensation in its simplest form means the payment received by workers for services rendered. 'Payment', in this sense, denotes all forms of monetary reward received by the worker; whether it be a wage, salary, financial benefits, non-financial benefits, or deferred benefits. The object is to attract, retain, and motivate employees to realise the goals of the company. The foundation on which many of the above decisions are based is called the job evaluation.

Job evaluation is a method used to determine the relative worth of a job in relation to other jobs in a company. Job evaluation implies that the value of a job (job worth) can be measured, and that employees in posts with greater responsibilities should receive compensation at a higher level. Many techniques for evaluating the financial worth of jobs are available, and include– amongst others – the Patterson Method; the Hay method; TASK (Tuned Assessment of Skills and Knowledge); Peromnes; the Job Appreciation System (JAS); the ranking method, factor comparison method; classification method, and the point method (Pilbeam & Corbridge, 2006:242). It is incumbent on the HR manager to ensure that the compensation paid by the company to its employees corresponds as closely as possible to what similar companies allocate to jobs in the same business sector. Such correspondence is called *external equity*. The purpose of compensation surveys is to enable the HR manager to ensure that the compensation system of the company conforms to an acceptable degree of equity.

Compensation surveys can therefore serve as a diagnostic instrument. A compensation system should attract, retain, and motivate employees. A high labour turnover or rejection of employment offered is probably due to inadequate compensation levels. When an HR manager decides to make use of compensation surveys, one of two possible approaches may be adopted: the organisation can undertake its own in-house survey, or a survey can be undertaken by a consultancy company.

An increasingly important part of compensation is employee benefits. Core benefits often include sick leave, maternity or paternity leave, vacation leave, life assurance, private medical insurance, critical illness or long-term disability insurance, personal accident insurance, and pensions. Examples of additional benefits include company car schemes, childcare, financial planning, a home or mobile telephone package, parking facilities, relocation expenses, wellness programmes, and employee assistance programmes.

Discussion point

Outline at least four reasons why an organisation needs a compensation system.

Because the cost of benefits for many companies now averages as much as 40% of total payroll costs, employers are attempting to control benefit costs without seriously affecting the overall compensation programme.

The tourism industry in South Africa is now turning towards some new ideas in the area of compensation; such as 'pay-for-performance'. This concept includes a variety of individual and group incentive plans such as gain-sharing, commissions, bonuses, profit sharing, and employee stock ownership plans (Sutherland & Canwell, 2004: 45). Important legislation which impacts on the compensation and benefits employees receive is the Basic Conditions of Employment Act 75 of 1997 (as amended – Act 11 of 2002).

Health and safety

A more contemporary area of concern to the employee today is *health and safety*. Each year, accidents, injuries, and occupational diseases cost billions of rands in medical expenses, medical insurance, equipment damage, and production problems. These can all have a major impact on the tourism industry in South Africa. Although much is being done to improve the workplace environment, there is still considerable room for improvement. Legislation which the HR manager needs to take cognisance of in this area includes the Occupational Health and Safety Act 85 of 1993, and the Compensation for Occupational Injuries and Diseases Act 130 of 1993. At present, health issues prevalent in the South African workplace which directly affect employees in the tourism industry include stress, burnout, and HIV/AIDS. As far as HIV/AIDS is concerned, employer groups in South Africa are finding their health budgets under siege by rising medical costs in this regard (Van Jaarsveld, 2004: 33). However, a number of options are available to companies. To assist employees, the HR manager should implement an Employee Assistance Programme (EAP) within the company. According to Tanke, such a programme can be defined as 'a management tool to assist employees in dealing with personal problems before they seriously impair job performance' (2001: 366). The problems covered by a typical EAP are indicated in Table 11.5.

Table 11.5 Problems covered by an EAP

- Alcohol abuse
- Alcohol dependency
- Career development difficulties
- Children/adolescent
- Depression/burnout
- Domestic violence
- Drug abuse
- Elder-care issues
- Emotional difficulties
- English as a second language
- Family issues
- Gambling, compulsive
- HIV/AIDS
- Legal problems

- Life transition
- Literacy
- Marital difficulties
- Mental health
- Personal financial problems
- Psychological
- Single parenting
- Stress-related problems.

Source: Tanke, M. L. 2001. *Human Resources Management for the hospitality industry*, 2nd edition. Albany, New York: Delmar is a division of Thomson Learning, p.365. Used with permission.

Even the smallest tourism business can implement an EAP. The most popular method for companies that cannot afford to operate their own programme is to appoint a contractor. An aspect closely related to this is the establishment of a wellness programme. This programme normally has three components:

- It helps employees identify potential health risks through screening and testing
- It educates employees about such health risks as high blood pressure, smoking, poor diet, and stress
- It encourages employees to change their lifestyles through exercise, good nutrition, and health monitoring.

The most common wellness activities offered by employers include:

- Smoking cessation
- Health-risk appraisals
- Back care
- Stress management
- Exercise/physical fitness
- Off-the-job accident prevention
- Nutrition education
- Blood pressure checks
- Weight control. (Grobler *et al.*, 2006: 399–400.)

As far as safety is concerned, two issues of importance are unsafe working conditions and unsafe acts. Unsafe working conditions include defective equipment, inadequate mechanical protection, the danger of explosions or fires, unsafe designs, unsafe machines, and the unsafe location of machinery and equipment. Unsafe acts, on the other hand, refer to the incorrect use of tools and equipment and the failure to adhere to safety regulations. In the area of unsafe acts, accidents are directly related to human error. Proper training to sensitise employees in this regard must, therefore, be implemented to reduce the risk (see Example box).

Discussion point

Should an employer have an employee assistance programme (EAP)?

> **Example** Health, safety and environmental issues at SAA
>
> The Health and safety of the company's employees, passengers, contractors, and others affected by its operations and activities is a top priority for management. The company views itself as being environmentally responsible, and is committed to ensuring that it operates its business in compliance with worldwide environmental standards.
>
> Enhanced security measures have had, and will continue to have, a significant impact on SAA's flying experience for passengers. While these security requirements have not impacted aircraft utilisation, they have impacted on our business. The company has invested significantly in facilities, equipment, and technology to make travelling with SAA a memorable flying experience.
>
> Source: South African Airways Annual Report 2005. Year ended 31 March 2005, p.64. Used with permission.

Labour Relations

There is no doubt that *labour relations*, or employment relations, are of special importance to HR managers in South Africa. Especially in the tourism industry, industrial disharmony can be cataclysmic and can have an immediate effect on customer satisfaction. Hence, ensuring a healthy and peaceful labour relations climate is essential for the survival of the tourism industry. HR managers have, however, particularly in large

organisations, handed this new facet of human resource management over to labour relations managers. Not all companies (particularly smaller companies) are fortunate enough to have the services of a labour relations manager or officer, and many do not have separate labour relations sections or departments. In these cases, labour relations are the human resource manager's responsibility. The HR manager's neglect of this responsibility will be detrimental to the progress of the company. The Labour Relations Act No 66 of 1995 (as amended by Act 12 of 2002) greatly influences the South African environment in this regard.

What does the Act mean for workers and employers?

The Act benefits workers by giving them the right to:
- Join trade unions and participate in union activities (the Food and Allied Workers Union – FAWU)
- Strike
- Picket in support of a protected strike, or against a lockout
- Be consulted by employers on various proposals if there is a workplace forum, e.g. job grading, plant closures, and new technology
- Joint decision-making in various proposals, if there is a workplace forum (such as disciplinary codes)
- Information on matters affecting workers at work
- Fair dismissals
- Protection against victimisation for exercising any rights in terms of the Act (Grobler *et al.*, 2006: 428).

Employers benefit by having:
- The right to join employers' organisations and to participate in their activities
- The right to lock out workers
- Less production time lost (through a decrease in labour unrest)

- The possibility of successful restructuring of the workplace through information sharing and consultation
- The joint solution of problems, training, and development
- Quick, inexpensive and non-legalistic procedures for the adjudication of dismissal cases
- The accommodation of the needs of small business (Grobler *et al.*, 2006: 428).

For more information on this Act and the other Acts discussed in this chapter, see www.labour.gov.za

Discussion point

Compile a list of the major labour laws that have been discussed in this chapter.

HR research

The ability to conduct research and solve HR problems, such as absenteeism and staff turnover, is critically important for HR managers. Through *HR research*, managers are able to substitute facts about human behaviour for armchair theorising, hunches, guesswork, and gut reactions. This aspect is vital, because of the labour-intensity of the tourism industry. Specific uses of HR research include the evaluation of current policies, programmes, and activities, and the prediction of conditions, events, and behavioural patterns. Numerous research techniques exist, including surveys (e.g. job satisfaction surveys), and exit interviews. Research can be undertaken in any of the three main areas of HR discussed in this chapter. Besides the information gathered through research conducted within the company, information can also be obtained from research undertaken externally by consultants on a regional or national basis.

Human resource administration

From the overview provided in this chapter on the different HR practices to be used by the tourism industry in South Africa, it is clear that, for them to be successful, they need to be properly managed.

Not only must the activities be integrated with each other as mentioned earlier, but they must also be tied in to the strategic direction of the company. To achieve this goal, the HR manager needs the assistance of a computerised Human Resource Information System (HRIS). This system should form an integral part of the Management Information System (MIS) of the company. The HRIS will be the primary transaction processor, editor, record-keeper and functional application system at the heart of all computerised HR work. According to Grobler *et al.* (2006: 40), this system will maintain employee, organisational, and HR planning data sufficient to support most, if not all, of the HR functions. A number of methods exist to access the HRIS, such as:

- via the intranet, using web-type methods by operating purely within one company or location
- via Extranets, encompassing two or more companies
- via Portals, offering links to internal information and services, but also accessing the World Wide Web through the Internet.

The benefits of having an HRIS system are that it reduces errors, increases efficiency, and reduces costs for the company. Paperwork is reduced, forms are standardised, and reports for decision-makers are generated faster. The HRIS consists of a number of identifiable components such as hardware; a central processing unit (CPU), personal computers (PC's), and software. In larger companies this system is normally supported by a computer programmer, while in the case of smaller companies use is made of outside vendors. It is essential for company efficiency for the HR professional working with the HRIS to possess computer skills and an understanding of the interface between computer technology and HR functions.

PeopleSoft is a typical HRIS programme available in the marketplace at present.

Discussion point

What is the purpose of a human resource information system (HRIS)?

Besides the management of the HR activities through the HRIS, it is also possible to deliver some HR services on-line through web-based HR home pages. This has become known as e-HR. According to Karakanian (2000: 3–6), e-HR can be described as 'the overall HR strategy that lifts HR, shifts it from the HR department and isolated HR activities, and redistributes it to the company and its trusted business partners, old and new. e-HR ties and integrates HR activities to other corporate processes such as finance, supply chain, and customer service'. The HRIS will thus form the backbone of the e-HR system.

This system will interface with the company's Intranet, connect to HR service suppliers and business partners via an Extranet, as well as have links to the Internet via HR portals. This entire process will allow cost-effective universal access to HR data by all authorised parties including employees, managers, executives, HR service providers, relevant communities, and the public at large. It will also reduce the distance between the HR department and its internal customers, and thus provide a quick and efficient administrative service.

The maintenance of human resources requires that the HR manager create a working environment in which employees will want to work and, very importantly, continue to work. However, this task can become very frustrating for the HR manager, as she/he has only limited control over factors that make it pleasant for employees to do their job.

Conclusion

The HR manager is responsible for the management of employees – the company's greatest asset. Not only is the HR manager expected to utilise the employees more effectively, but it can be anticipated that the employees will also make greater demands regarding their job satisfaction, compensation, training and development, and labour relations. To address these issues, HR managers, specifically in the South African tourism industry, will have to employ the latest techniques available in the HR field to ensure that they achieve their goals successfully.

Review questions

1. What are the most critical challenges facing HR managers in the South African tourism industry today?

2. Has advertising become more of a recruitment technique in recent years? Why?

3. List the major methods used in performance appraisals

4. What is the difference between employee evaluation and job evaluation?

5. Should a tourism company have an employee assistance programme (EAP)?

Further reading

Baum, T. & Kokkranikal, J. 2005. Human resource management in tourism. In L. Pender, & R. Sharpley (Eds.). *The management of tourism*. London: Sage Publications.

Brewster, C. Carey, L. Dowling, P. Grobler, P. Holland, P. & Wärnich, S. 2003. *Contemporary issues in human resource management: gaining a competitive advantage*, 2nd edition, Cape Town: Oxford University Press South Africa.

Grobler, P. A., Wärnich, S., Carrell, M. R., Elbert, N. F. & Hatfield, R. D. 2006. *Human resource management in South Africa*, 3rd edition. London: Thomson Learning.

Websites

www.labour.gov.za – Department of Labour

www.ccma.org.za – Commission for Conciliation, Mediation & Arbitration

www.sabpp.co.za – SA Board for Personnel Practice

www.ipm.co.za – Institute of People Management

www.irasa.org.za – Industrial Relations Association of SA

References

Armstrong, M. 2006. *A handbook of human resource management practice*, 10th edition, London, Kogan Page.

Baum, T. & Kokkranikal, J. 2005. Human resource management in tourism. In L. Pender, & R. Sharpley (Eds.). *The management of tourism*. London: Sage Publications.

Bernardin, H. J. 2003. *Human resource management: an experiential approach*, 3rd edition. New York: McGraw Hill Higher Education.

Burud, S. & Tumolo, M. 2004. *Leveraging the new human capital*. Palo Alto, Davies-Black Publishing.

Byars, L. L. & Rue, L. W. 2000. *Human resource management*, 6th edition. New York: McGraw-Hill Higher Education.

Casio, W. F. 2006. *Managing human resources: productivity, quality of work life, profits*, 7th edition. New York: McGraw-Hill.

De Waal, A. 2007. *Strategic performance management: a managerial and behavioural approach*. Houndmills, Hampshire: Dalgrave Macmillan, pp 3–11.

Desimone, R. L., Werner, J. M. & Harris, D. M. 2002. *Human resource development*, 3rd edition. Sea Harbor Drive, Orlando: Harcourt.

Dychtwald,K.,Erickson,T J&Morison,R.2006.*Workforce crisis:how to beat the coming shortage of skills and talen*t. Boston, Massachusetts, Harvard Business School Publishing.

Grobler, P. A., Wärnich, S., Carrell, M. R., Elbert, N. F. & Hatfield, R. D. 2006. *Human resource management in South Africa*, 3rd edition. London: Thomson Learning.

Haven-Tang, C. & Jones, E. 2006. Human resource management in tourism business. In J. Beech, & S. Chadwick (Eds.). *The Business of Tourism Management*. Harlow: Prentice Hall.

Hicks, S., Peters, M. & Smith, M. 2006. Orientation redesign. *Training & Development*, Vol. 60(7), 43–45.

Jackson, S. E. & Schuler, R. S. 2000. *Managing human resources: a partnership perspective*, 7th edition. Cincinnati: South Western College Publishing.

Karakanian, M. 2000. Are human resources departments ready for E-HR? *Information Systems Management*, Vol. 17(4), 36.

Mathis, R. L. & Jackson, J. H. 2003. *Human resource management*, 10th edition. Mason: Ohio, South Western a division of Thomson Learning.

Mello, J. A. 2006. *Strategic human resource management*, 2nd edition. Mason: Ohio South-Western, part of the Thomson Corporation.

Pilbeam, S. & Corbridge, M. 2006. *People resourcing: Contemporary HRM in practice*, 3rd edition. Essex: Pearson, Education.

Rao, N. & Das, R. P. 2002. Reorienting HRD: Strategies for tourists' satisfaction. *Journal of Services Research*, Vol. 2(1), 95–105.

Redman, T. & Wilkinson, A. 2006.*Contemporary human resource management*, 2nd edition. Harlow, Essex: Pearson Education.

South Africa. Basic Conditions of Employment Act No 75 of 1997 (as amended by Act 11 of 2002) Tshwane: Government Printer.

South Africa Compensation for Occupational Injuries and Diseases Act No 130 of 1993. Tshwane: Government Printer.

South Africa. Department of Foreign Affairs. 2006. Information document compiled by the Communication Resource Centre of UK/20060606/Financial Times – South Africa, pp.1–17.

South Africa Employment Equity Act No 55 of 1998. Tshwane: Government Printer.

South Africa. Labour Relations Act No 66 of 1995 (as amended by Act 12 of 2002) Tshwane: Government Printer.

South Africa Occupational Health and Safety Act No 85 of 1993. Tshwane: Government Printer.

South Africa Qualifications Authority Act No 58 of 1995. Tshwane: Government Printer.

South Africa. Skills Development Act No 97 of 1998, Tshwane: Government Printer.

South Africa. Skills Development Levies Act No 9 of 1999. Tshwane: Government Printer.

Stone, R. J. 2005.*Human resource management*, 5th edition. Milton, Australia: John Wiley.

Sutherland, J. & Canwell, D. 2004. *Key concepts in human resource management*. Houndmills, Hampshire: Palgrave MacMillan.

Tanke, M. L. 2001. *Human resources management for the hospitality industry*, 2nd edition. Albany, NY: Delmar, a division of Thomson Learning.

Thorne, K. & Mackey, D. 2003. *Everything you ever needed to know about training*. 3rd edition, London: Kogan Page.

Van Jaarsveld, A. 2004. Running a healthy company. *HR Future*, September, p 33.

Weiss, T. B. 1997. Show me more than the money, (Employee retention strategies). *HR Focus*, Vol.74(11), 3.

Yorks, L. 2005. *Strategic human resource development*. Mason; Ohio: South-Western part of the Thomson Corporation.

Case study
11

Springbok Hotels

Cape Photo Library

Objectives:

- to understand the process of determining training needs within the hotel industry
- to appreciate the importance of evaluating training effectiveness.

When Bruce Smith, the owner and founder of Springbok Hotels, retired because of ill-health in 2005, he appointed John Motlana as CEO of Springbok Hotels.

With a MBA degree from University of Cape Town and five years' experience with the company, John was eager to take over. He believed that his university training had prepared him well. One of the first things John wanted to do was to get the managers in the organisation to move closer to the frontline staff of the company. After all, it was these people who had frequent contact with the guests and, as a result, would either leave a positive or negative perception of the hotel they visited. Springbok Hotels has, since its establishment in 1975, expanded rapidly, and today has 35 hotels throughout South Africa, employing 4 000 staff, with a total of 1 500 rooms. The occupancy rate for the hotels over the past five years was over 80%. However, the market in which Springbok Hotels operate has become highly competitive, and new initiatives are required.

Surely managers who occasionally spend time performing the day-to-day activities of employees would have a better appreciation of the problems these employees face? Yes, they do; but reality tells us that only a few companies do anything about it. However, Springbok Hotels is an exception to the rule.

Springbok's CEO, John Motlana, recognised the importance of sound corporate training programmes. For the company to succeed in its highly competitive market, he knows that all employees, from the company CEO to the hotel cleaning staff, must have a complete understanding of the hotel's daily operations. Consequently, through his actions, Springbok's so-called 'In-Touch Day' programme was born.

The purpose of this training day was to enable management to better understand the day-to-day activities involved in running the hotel. Not having spent time at the grass-roots level prior to this programme, many of these executives were far removed from the problems employees faced in dealing with guests. The object was to bring managers closer, through direct hands-on experience. For example, one purchasing manager was assigned to spend the day working as a cleaning staff employee at the Springbok Hotel in Gauteng. During the course of her day, the purchasing manager encountered a major obstacle – there wasn't enough clean linen to make the beds. What had caused this problem? Apparently, corporate managers had not acted on a request to purchase additional linen.

As fate would have it, this same purchasing manager had been the one delaying the approval of the acquisition of sheets and towels for the hotel. Her seemingly innocent action at corporate headquarters meant that she had to strip the beds, launder the sheets and towels, and then return them to the rooms. What a waste of time, and what a learning experience! John Motlana's 'In-Touch Day' has become a special 'treat' for Springbok employees. Giving company executives insight into how their actions affect employees, and ultimately customers, promotes better employee relations and customer service.

Case study questions

1. Using the process of determining training needs, describe how John Motlana decided to develop the 'In-Touch' Day for Springbok Hotels.

2. How would you evaluate the training effectiveness of Springbok's 'In-Touch' Day? What would you evaluate? Given the information about the programme, how effective would you estimate 'In-Touch' Day to be?

12

Managing finance for tourism

Richard Chivaka

Purpose

The purpose of this chapter is to discuss the management of finance within the tourism industry.

Learning outcomes

After reading this chapter, you should be able to:
- identify and provide examples of the basic cost elements involved in the running of tourism businesses
- classify the basic cost elements according to management information needs
- classify the basic cost elements according to how they behave, and explain the significance of cost behaviour in financial planning
- apply cost-volume-profit analysis principles for planning purposes
- define the break-even point, calculate it, and explain its importance
- define a budget and discuss the budgetary control, using variances
- discuss the cash budget process and explain how it ties into the wider process of budgeting and budgetary control
- discuss how management helps makes decisions such as outsourcing, specials, discontinuing a service line or segment of the organisation, and the use of scarce resources.

Chapter overview

This chapter discusses some of the key principles in the management of finance within the tourism industry. The first section looks at financial planning 'building blocks'. It discusses the basic cost elements, and then moves on to examine cost behaviour and the importance of understanding how costs respond to changes in activity level in running a tourism business. The second section focuses on cost-volume-profit analyses, including contribution margin, the break-even point, methods of calculating the break-even point, and the importance of margins of safety in tourism businesses. This section also discusses budgeting and budgetary control, and we address the principles underpinning the preparation of budgets and how budgets are used for control purposes via variance analysis. Attention is then focused on cash budgets. In the last section we discuss how management makes decisions such as outsourcing, special promotions for tourism consumers, and the use of scarce resources in service delivery.

The concluding case study illustrates how some of the key financial planning principles can be applied in the context of the tourism industry.

Introduction

The global economic environment is changing rapidly, due to the interplay of several factors. Over recent years, competition has intensified as a result of the opening up of hitherto 'closed' economies due to global economic reforms, coupled with the introduction of new and revolutionary technologies (Magretta, 1998: 74). Such technologies have also precipitated information exchange and **e-commerce** beyond national and regional boundaries. These changes have resulted in the increased availability of a wide range of products and services at affordable prices. Furthermore, due to the availability of products and services from anywhere in the world, consumers are not compelled to buy from the same supplier; hence customer loyalty has decreased. Customers are also ever-changing in terms of quality, functionality, and service requirements. Consequently, the global market is now characterised by shorter product and service life-cycles (Mirra, 1999: 5; Drury, 2005: 13).

In order to survive, tourism organisations have to 'mass customise' most of their offerings to satisfy the diverse needs of changing market and consumer needs (Lee, 2000: 31; Vollman & Cordon, 1998: 687). In addition, tourism organisations have to create new product offerings speedily in order to meet the ever-changing needs of customers (Johnston & Lawrence, 1988: 96). This requires flexibility in terms of response to market changes, supported by higher levels of employee productivity, as well as cost management. Therefore, attaining a sustainable competitive advantage requires monitoring of the marketplace for changes in customer requirements; rapidly designing offerings to satisfy consumers' needs; customising offerings depending on the needs of the market segment being served, and making sure that offering costs are contained, so as to compete favourably with other players in the same market. In order to do this, tourism managers require relevant information to make strategic, operational, and tactical decisions.

The need for financial information

Information in any business is a weapon that is used to gain a competitive advantage over other role-players in the same industry. As such, financial information is used by management to plan and, consequently, to execute the plan; to review the results of the plan, and to make adjustments in order to respond to market changes. The following section defines what financial information is, as well as the nature of the financial information that management requires to run a tourism business and understand the impact of their decisions on the profitability of the organisation.

Financial information

Financial information shows the impact of management decisions on the revenues and costs of an organisation. Financial information is, therefore, required to support decision-making as well as to highlight the result of decisions that have already been taken. The types of financial information used by a tourism organisation include:

Financial accounting

This is the part of financial information that shows what has been accomplished during a financial year: it is, therefore, historical. Financial accounting aims to report the results of a tourism organisation at the end of the **accounting period**. This part of financial information is largely meant for external stakeholders such as shareholders, government, prospective investors, and general employees, who would be considered 'external'. This information is produced according to accounting principles known as Generally Accepted Accounting Principles (GAAP).

Management accounting

Management **accounting** is produced for internal use only; it is produced for the management of the tourism organisation, and hence it is called 'management accounting'. It is meant to support strategic and operational plans as well as the day-to-day running of an organisation. This information is produced as projections into the future, such as budgets, and contains sensitive information (the margins of a business, for example) that management uses to make useful decisions on how to compete in the market. This chapter will focus on management accounting, as opposed to financial accounting. It is important to point out that in order to make decisions, management needs to define costs properly, understand how they are classified, and how they behave. These are the focal points of the following sections.

Financial planning 'building blocks'

Tourism organisations develop internal financial reports and schedules. These are referred to as management accounts for the purposes of running and managing their operations. Management accounts provide far more detail regarding the organisation's financial activities than financial accounting statements, and thus comprise the organisation's financial information. Organisations require management accounts, which are part of an organisation's financial information, in order to carry out three main activities of management, namely: planning, decision-making, and control. As such, management accounts are used by tourism managers for decision-making at strategic, operational, and tactical levels. Financial information is defined as the information that shows the impacts of management decisions on an organisation's *costs* and *revenues*. Since management decisions impact on costs and revenues of the organisation, effective decision-making requires that tourism managers:

1. clearly define cost
2. understand the categories into which costs are classified (cost classification)
3. understand how costs respond to changes in activity level (cost behaviour).

Therefore, in order to effectively utilise financial information to prepare budgets as well as to make effective decisions, it is necessary for tourism managers to answer some of the following questions:

- What is cost?
- How can costs be classified in a way that enhances decision-making?
- How do costs respond to changes in activity level?
- How and why do costs change over time?
- Are costs fixed or variable?

However, before addressing these questions, we first need to consider the following basic cost terms:

Cost

The term **cost** refers to the value of resources sacrificed or foregone in the process of achieving a specific objective. In the tourism industry, the term 'cost' refers to all the resources, quantifiable and non-quantifiable, that are sacrificed in all the processes that result in the provision of an offering to tourists. This definition shows that tourism management should look at costs from a broader perspective, rather than a narrow definition that simply takes into account the cash costs incurred in achieving a specific objective. This means that, for the purposes of tourism management decision-making, both quantifiable costs (cash paid) and non-quantifiable costs (time and effort expended) arising from a service provided to consumers should be taken into account.

Cost object

'Cost object' refers to anything for which cost information is required – for example, a meal, a product-offering line, customers, and organisational departments. The way in which cost information is produced is dependent on the nature of the cost object that management is considering. For example, management may be interested in knowing the cost of a specific menu in a hotel restaurant. The menu becomes the cost object, and cost information should be produced in such a way that the menu costs are apparent to management. However, in some instances management may be interested in knowing the cost of running the hotel restaurant. In this case, the hotel restaurant is the cost object, and hence cost information should be produced to reflect the resources that are sacrificed in running the hotel restaurant. The understanding of cost information in relation to the running of a tourism business means more than defining costs properly. It requires an understanding of how costs can be put into specific categories rapidly; called *cost classification*, in order to facilitate decision-making. The following section deals with the main cost categories into which costs are classified in order to support management decision-making.

Cost classification

Cost information is used by management for various purposes. Thus, in order to provide relevant cost information to support the various management purposes, it is necessary to put costs into specific categories – *cost classifications* – to facilitate the generation of the information required by management. Table 12.1 summarises the main cost classifications, depending on the purpose for which cost information is required.

(i) General cost classification

The general approach applied in classifying costs depends on the type of tourism organisation involved, and the needs of management. This is because cost information is used by the management of a tourism business to make decisions based on the circumstances that the organisation is facing. The general categories into which costs are classified for a service organisation include:

Direct materials

These are materials that can be directly traced to the final service offering. They are materials that are an integral part of the finished offering and, as such, are easily traceable to the final offering. All costs of ingredients used to make meals are regarded as direct materials.

Direct labour

Direct labour is the cost of labour that can be physically and conveniently traced to individual offerings. This refers to the cost of labour of employees who are physically involved in the provision of a service. For example, the cost of a tour bus driver is a direct cost with regards to tour services.

Overheads

These are all costs of resources that are used in the provision of a service other than direct material

Table 12.1 Cost classifications

Basis of classification	Cost category	Purpose
(i) General	Material costs Labour costs Overhead costs	Preparation of financial statements
(ii) Predicting cost behaviour	Fixed costs Variable costs Mixed costs	Break-even analysis Profit planning/profit targeting
(iii) Assigning costs to cost objects	Direct costs Indirect costs	Product/service costing Product/service pricing Budgeting & budgetary control
(iv) Making decisions	Differential costs Opportunity costs Sunk costs	Outsourcing Capital budgeting Evaluation of the viability of specials Study of product/service alternatives

and direct labour. Organisations require other resources to support the service provision, for example, electricity, indirect labour (managers), and indirect materials (materials that cannot easily and conveniently be traced to the product, e.g. salt). The costs in the tourism industry arising from infrastructure such as a hotel, the maintenance of a fleet of tour buses, management of the business, and property taxes, are all examples of overheads. Other costs classified as overheads would be administrative as well as selling costs. Examples of administrative overheads would be salaries of CEOs/Managing Directors, clerks, finance personnel, secretarial, and public relations (PR) staff.

(ii) Cost classification for predicting cost behaviour

Costs are also classified in a way that facilitates the understanding of the manner in which they will respond to changes in activity level. This is important for budgeting purposes, as it enables tourism managers to understand the impact of their future plans on costs. The manner in which costs respond to changes in activity level is called **cost behaviour**. The following are categories into which costs are assigned, in order to understand their predictable behaviour when activity levels change (see the section on cost behaviour for a detailed discussion).

Fixed costs

Fixed costs are costs that remain the same, in a relevant range, when activity levels change. Fixed costs behave in such a way that when the activity level changes (rises and falls), they remain unchanged. An example of such costs would be property taxes, salaries of managers, rent, and the depreciation of assets.

Variable costs

Variable costs are costs that change, in total, in direct proportion to changes in activity levels. Examples of these costs are materials (consumables) and wages paid to casual workers on the basis of time worked. As activity level changes, i.e. more or fewer customers are served, the amount

of these resources consumed also changes in a similar fashion.

Mixed costs

A *mixed cost* consists of both the fixed and the variable components. Such costs are exemplified by the cost of metered electricity and of telephone services. These costs have a minimum amount that is always present, regardless of whether the activity takes place or not – for example, telephone line rental. The other component of a mixed cost (the variable part) is directly influenced by changes in activity levels, for example, charges for telephone calls made.

(iii) Cost classification for assigning costs to cost objects

Costs are classified to facilitate the calculation of the costs associated with a cost object, such as a hotel guest or a meal. Classifying costs this way enables management to: (i) establish the cost associated with a guest's stay at the hotel; (ii) establish the profitability of different tourism services provided to the public; and (iii) control the amount of resources spent in the process of service delivery. These costs are classified into the following categories:

Direct costs

Direct costs are costs that can easily and conveniently be traced to a specific service. A hotel would classify food and beverage as direct costs, because they can be easily and conveniently traced to each guest staying at the hotel.

Indirect cost/Overhead costs

Indirect costs, which are also known as overheads, are common costs incurred in the provision of service to clients, e.g. the salaries of all managers, office rentals (where the organisation does not own the property), electricity, water, and property rates (where the organisation owns the property). In addition, all head-office costs are classified as overheads. These costs are incurred to create the capacity for the organisation to provide services to its clients. As such, these costs cannot be associated with one specific line of service, or one particular customer.

(iv) Cost classification for decision-making

In order to facilitate management decision-making, costs are classified according to whether or not they have an impact on a particular decision. Costs, therefore, are classified into the following three categories:

Differential costs

Given the fact that decision-making involves choosing between at least two alternatives, differential costs are costs that are unique to an alternative chosen by management. For tourism businesses, for example, a differential cost will be the difference in cost between two alternative projects in which management can select to invest. Such a difference influences management to choose one of the two alternative projects.

Opportunity costs

These refer to the potential value of the next best alternative, sacrificed when a specific course of action has been selected. For example, if management chooses to develop and sell product 'A' instead of 'B', the opportunity cost of such an action will be the financial benefit that could have been realised from the sale of product 'B' (after subtracting all costs associated with the development and sale of product 'B'). What this means is that the real cost of selecting product 'A' is not only the cost associated with this product, but the opportunity cost arising from not choosing product 'B'. Failure to take into account the opportunity cost of the next best alternative, which has not been selected, has the effect of inflating the benefits arising from the alternative that has been chosen. This is because the real costs of the alternative selected are understated whenever the opportunity cost arising from the next best alternative foregone is not taken into account.

Sunk costs

Sunk costs are costs that have already been incurred: they are 'water under the bridge' or 'spilt milk'. These are costs arising from past decisions which cannot be changed by any current or future decision. For example, if management invested in computer hardware of a particular type several years ago, and the computer hardware is now obsolete due to fast-changing software development methods, nothing that management can do now can change the situation.

The importance of cost classification for tourism businesses

It is important for planning, decision-making, and control to classify costs correctly, depending on the decision to be made. It is the context of the intended cost information use that determines the manner in which costs are classified in order to facilitate the understanding of the impact of management decisions on future costs. However, in order to effectively use cost classification in three main activities of management, namely: planning, decision-making, and control, it is necessary first of all to discuss how costs respond to changes in activity level – cost behaviour, for example. This is the focus of the next section.

Cost behaviour

The manner in which costs respond to changes in activity level will be explored by looking at three main cost categories already discussed: fixed costs, variable costs, and mixed costs.

Fixed costs

Fixed costs are costs that do not change within a relevant range, or during the accounting period (for example, a month, quarter, or year). Within the relevant range, an organisation's present capacity is adequate to support increased volume, hence the costs associated with such capacity remain the same. Such costs do not depend on the level of business activity during the accounting period. For example, the cost of salaries of managers does not change from month to month, due to changes arising from an increase or decrease in customers in the same period. Other costs that would remain the same are property taxes and depreciation of assets (Drury, 2005: 34). Such costs are incurred regardless of activity level, i.e. they would stay 'fixed'.

Discussion point

Do you think total fixed costs are always fixed? Explain your answer with supporting reasons that draw from your understanding of the tourism industry.

In order to answer the above discussion question, think about what happens to the salary cost of running a tour operating company when the number of tourists increases in a sustainable way. If the tour operator currently employs five salaried tourist guides who can handle a maximum of 15 000 tourists per year, what happens when the number of tourists increases to 18 000 per year? Certainly, the current employees would be overwhelmed, as they would be stretched beyond their limits. One approach would be to hire someone on a contract basis. However, if the increase in tourists is a sustainable one, it makes sense for the tour operator to hire someone on a permanent basis to guarantee reliable service. Therefore, in practice, total fixed costs do not remain the

same regardless of the level of activity. Figure 12.1 shows what happens to total fixed costs as activity level changes.

Figure 12.1 shows that, in practice, total fixed costs respond to significant changes in activity level. The manner in which they respond is such that total fixed costs increase in chunks. What we end up having is what is known as *step-fixed costs* (Drury, 2005: 36). In other words, total fixed costs remain the same within the relevant range as activity level changes. However, beyond the relevant range, total fixed costs increase by a lump sum. The point at which the current capacity is exhausted and additional capacity is thus required is known as a *critical point*. This is the point, in the example given above, at which the tour operating company's current five employees can no longer handle the additional work available, resulting the in the owner employing an additional tourist guide.

An understanding how total fixed costs behave is very important in management planning, particularly in budgeting. For example, if the owner of the tour operating company anticipates that the number of customers requiring the services of the company will be more than the number that the current number of employees can handle, (for example, beyond the first critical

Figure 12.1 Total fixed costs graph

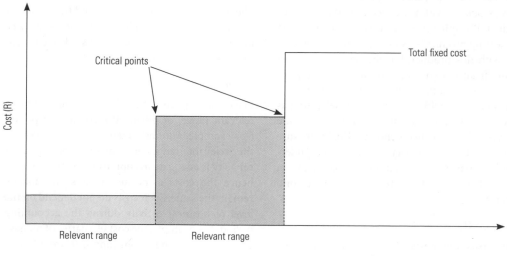

Activity level

point), then proper advance arrangements can be made to employ another tourist guide.

Fixed cost per unit

It is also important to understand how fixed costs per unit of activity behave. Do they change, or remain the same? What we are interested in here is the relation between the salary of managers, for example, to the level of activity in a given period. In other words, if we were to divide the salary of a manager by the output in a given month, what would be the cost of his/her salary per unit of that output measure? This is shown as a fixed cost per unit of activity, i.e. a fixed cost per every unit of the output measure. Figure 12.2 below shows the way fixed costs per unit behave as activity level changes.

Discussion point

Discuss the significance of the fixed cost per unit graph in running organisations within the tourism industry.

In order to address the above question, consider this scenario: if a tourist attraction such as the Robben Island Museum in Cape Town received 50 000 tourists in 2007, and the salaries of the managers on the heritage site amounted to R1 500 000 in the same year, what would be the salary cost per tourist? As can be seen from Figure 12.2, fixed costs per

unit decrease as activity level increases. This means that the more output in a given period, the lower the fixed cost per unit of the output measure. This is what is known as **economies of scale**, i.e. the higher the volume of output, given a fixed total cost, the lower the fixed cost per unit of the output measure.

Total variable costs

Variable costs, on the other hand, do change in total as the level of activity changes.

Discussion point

Discuss the practical significance of the total variable cost line in running a tourism business.

Variable costs per unit

While total variable costs increase as activity level increases, we are also interested in understanding how variable costs per unit behave. Variable costs per unit stay the same as activity level changes; for example, the cost per food item.

> **TO DO**
>
> Discuss whether variable costs per unit are always fixed. Illustrate your answer with practical examples of variable costs relevant in the tourism industry.

Figure 12.2 Fixed cost per unit

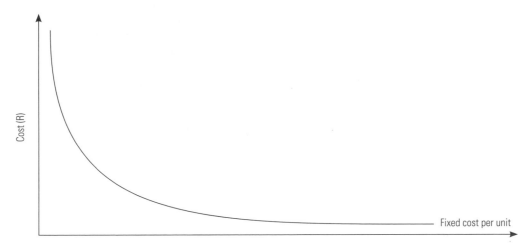

In order to answer the **TO DO** question on the previous page, try to think about the cost of ingredients for a hotel meal, such as beef. If the supplier charges a restaurant R12.00 per kg (this is the variable cost per unit), is it possible to reduce the cost per kg? Under what circumstances would this be possible? What is the significance of your understanding of variable costs per unit in the planning process?

The importance of understanding cost behaviour patterns in tourism businesses

Knowledge of cost behaviour assists management in understanding the impact of changes in the tourism business level on the cost per unit of activity (refer to your cost behaviour, especially the economies of scale). Knowledge of cost behaviour also assists management in budgeting, by helping to predict the impact of changes in activity level on costs (variable, fixed, and mixed costs). Once management understands cost behaviour, they can undertake scenario planning or sensitivity analysis, which enables tourism managers to predict the likely impact of different business scenarios on costs and profitability.

The next section discusses how cost behaviour principles are applied in two financial planning areas: cost-volume-profit analysis and budgeting.

Financial planning

This section is concerned with the application of the financial planning 'building blocks' in the process of financial planning. Cost behaviour concepts are applied in understanding the impact of changes in activity levels (tourist patronage levels) on total costs, as well as profit levels. Cost behaviour concepts are also applied in the process of budgeting.

Cost-volume-profit (CVP) analysis

Cost-volume-profit (CVP) analysis is a decision-making tool used by tourism managers to understand the interrelationship between cost,

volume of activity, and profit. This is achieved by exploring the relationship between four variables:

- Cost of a product/service
- Revenue from a product/service
- Volume of output a product/service
- Profit from a product/service.

CVP emphasises the analysis of cost behaviour patterns through different volumes of output. This enables tourism managers to undertake profit planning/profit targeting; to adopt appropriate pricing policies; evaluate the viability of specials for tourists, and evaluate the adequacy of the available service capacity. The starting point in the analysis of the relationship between **cost**, **revenue**, **volume of output**, and **profit** is the contribution margin.

Contribution margin (CM)

Contribution margin (CM) is the amount remaining from sales revenue after variable costs have been deducted. CM per unit of a product/service is given by:

Selling price per unit – variable cost per unit

CM goes to cover fixed costs, and any remaining CM after covering fixed costs contributes to the organisation's income. Given the fact that fixed costs constitute a significant proportion of the total costs for most tourism organisations, the ability of management to provide offerings with a high contribution margin is very important. This can be achieved in two ways: either the organisation provides offerings with a high unit contribution, or offerings that have a low contribution per unit, but which can achieve significant volumes (see Example box). Whichever strategy results in the highest total contribution would ensure that the high fixed costs are covered, and that there remains enough contribution to go towards profit.

Example Vuyokazi African Jewellery

Vuyokazi African Jewellery (VAJ) is an eThekwini-based medium-scale company formed in 1994, with the sole purpose of selling its products to foreign tourists. Employing women only, VAJ makes women's accessories (necklaces and bangles) from beads and dried seeds from the forest. The seeds are collected, washed, polished, and then dyed into several colours. All the products are marketed to the foreign tourists who throng the eThekwini coastline most of the year, and particularly during the festive season. The company uses a rented factory, in which tables and chairs are arranged 'classroom style'. Currently, VAJ produces and sells a total of 22 000 units (both necklaces and bangles) per annum. However, the company's production managers believes that with the company's current capacity, the number of units produced and sold could be increased to 31 000 per year. VAJ sells all its products, regardless of type (necklace or bangle), size, or style for R40 each. The company's variable costs are R12 per unit of product, and fixed costs (rent, salaries, and depreciation) amount to R310 000 per year.

TO DO

Assess the impact of the projected increase in output on Vuyokazi African Jewellery's profit.

The starting point here is to calculate the contribution margin per unit. This is done as follows:

Contribution margin per unit = selling price per unit – variable costs per unit

R40 – R12 = **R28**

It has been shown that a contribution is required to cover fixed costs and ultimately supply a portion of any profit. Therefore, we can use the contribution margin that we have calculated to generate total contribution at the different levels of output, and then assess the impact of the projected increase in output on profit, as shown in Table 12.2 below.

The calculations in Table 12.2 demonstrate that VAJ makes more profit when its output level increases while other costs remain the same. While contribution unit per unit has remained the same, the company is able to achieve more total contribution due to the higher output levels. What is more significant is the fact that the total fixed costs remain unchanged between the two output levels. This means that the company is still operating in the same relevant range (refer to the section on cost behaviour). Thus VAJ is leveraging its current cost structure (by taking advantage of total fixed costs that remain unchanged) to generate more profit from increased production and sales.

However, the above analysis is limited in scope, because it does not help management determine where the company break-even is; the break-even being the minimum quantity that VAJ should produce and sell in order to cover its total costs (both fixed and variable). The section below is concerned with break-even analysis.

Table 12.2 Impact of the projected increase in output on VAJ profit

Output level					
22 000 units			31 000 units		
		R			R
Total contribution	28 × 22 000	616 000	Total contribution	28 × 31 000	868 000
Less: Total fixed costs		310 000	Less: Total fixed costs		310 000
Net profit		306 000	Net profit		558 000

Break-even point (BEP)

A break-even point (BEP) is the activity level at which a tourism organisation is neither making a loss nor a profit, and above which it makes a profit, while below that point it makes a loss. The BEP is expressed either as units of product, or in terms of sales value. In terms of planning, the BEP is very important, because it tells an organisation the minimum units of offerings that it should *produce and* sell in order to sustain the business. The BEP therefore helps a tourism organisation to assess whether:

1. the organisation has enough capacity to produce the required minimum quantity before the organisation invests in that particular project
2. there is sufficient demand for the offering, so that the minimum sales volume that can be realised can enable the organisation to cover all its costs (both fixed and variable)
3. the organisation can sustain losses in the short-term if it is expected that sales volume will increase beyond the break-even point.

The BEP is expressed in either of the following ways:

BEP is a point where:

a) **Total sales revenue equals total cost (variable & fixed)**

or

b) **Total contribution margin equals total fixed costs**

It is necessary for planning purposes to calculate the BEP at the planning stage, in order to generate useful insights for management decision-making. It is therefore important to measure the break-even point of an organisation on the basis of its current cost structure, production methods, and market opportunities. The measuring of the break-even point is what is known as the break-even analysis.

Break-even analysis (BEA)

Break-even analysis is concerned with measuring the BEP in order to generate useful insights for management. For the purposes of this chapter, we will only discuss the *equation* and the *contribution* methods.

The equation method

In the *equation method,* the relationship between sales, variable and fixed costs, and profit is expressed as an equation in the following way:

**Sales/Total revenue =
variable costs + fixed costs + net profit**

In other words, the sales that an organisation realises are equal to total costs (variable and fixed), and profit. However, since we are interested in calculating the value of sales that only covers the organisation's total costs, i.e. break-even, it means that net profit at this level is zero. Thus this method can also be restated as:

Sales/Total revenue = variable costs + fixed costs

When using this method, it is important to remember that the sales or total revenue figure may not be given. However, you are always given the information that enables you to calculate it. The Example box below illustrates how the equation method is used to calculate the BEP.

Example Kruger Lodge

Kruger Lodge (KL) is a very beautiful lodge built to provide accommodation to tourists visiting the Kruger National Park (KNP). Located near one of the major watering holes in the KNP, KL provides tourists with accommodation located at vantage points to see the Big Five. In addition to accommodation, KL also provides breakfast and dinner to guests staying at the lodge.

All guests staying at the lodge at any given time eat breakfast and dinner. The cost to KL of providing the two meals, plus other variable costs, amounts to R500 per guest night. The charge for the service is R1 800 per guest night. The lodge's total annual fixed costs are R3 250 000.

TO DO

1. Calculate the number of guest nights that KL should have in order to break even.
2. Using the same information, calculate KL's break-even revenue.

Using the equation method, we know that sales/total revenue = variable costs + fixed costs. In the scenario in the Example box above, we are given the revenue per guest night (and not total revenue), variable costs per guest day (not total variable costs), and total fixed costs. We can use this information to formulate an equation. However, in order to do that, we first need to get total revenue and total variable costs. These are calculated as follows:

**Total revenue =
revenue per guest night $\times$ number of guest nights**

**Total variable costs =
variable costs per guest $\times$ number of guest nights**

What is apparent from the above is that we do not know the total number of guests. We can use a place-holder 'x' to represent the missing variable, i.e. the number of guest nights. We are now ready to formulate the equation as follows:

$$1\,800x = 500x + 3\,250\,000$$
$$1\,800\,x - 500x = 3\,250\,000$$
$$1\,300x = 3\,250\,000$$
$$x = 3\,250\,000 \div 1\,300$$
$$x = 2\,500$$

Therefore KL needs 2 500 guest nights in order to break even. The second part requires us to convert the guest nights into revenue. This can easily be done by multiplying the guest nights by the guest night revenue. Thus KL's break-even revenue is (2 500 $\times$ 1 800), or R4 500 000. The next section looks at how the contribution method is used to calculate the break-even point.

The contribution method

This method employs the contribution margin per unit of output that is required to cover total fixed costs. The following formulas are applied

to establish the break-even point using the contribution method. We have already discussed what a contribution margin is, and its importance in running businesses.

Break-even units are given by:

$$\frac{\text{Fixed cost}}{\text{Contribution margin per unit}}$$

What this formula establishes is the number of units that collectively generate a total contribution that covers total fixed costs, with each unit generating a given contribution. The Example box below illustrates how the contribution margin method is used to calculate the break-even point and profit.

Example Chopper Services

Chopper Services (CS) is a small charter tour company that operates a shuttle service from the V & A Waterfront in Cape Town to Robben Island and back. The company operates two helicopters, and each provides four return journeys per day. The following information refers to the company's daily operating costs:
*   Maximum number of passengers per flight = 8
*   Return tickets cost R600 per passenger

Costs of operating the above service are as follows:

Daily fixed costs:

Staff costs	R3 000
Insurance	R2 000
Helicopter rental	R4 000
Maintenance	R1 000
Other	R1 000

Variable costs amount to R200 per passenger, per return flight.

1. Calculate the number of passengers to be carried each day for CS to break even.
2. What would the daily profit (net income) be, given an average load factor of 75%?
3. Calculate the company's expected profit in a 365-day year, if the helicopters are each grounded for 12 days per year for maintenance, plus 60 days per year when weather conditions do not allow any flying. Furthermore, when the helicopters are flying, their average load factor is 75%.

By using the contribution method, we need to calculate the contribution margin per return trip and use it to calculate the number of passengers that should be carried in order for CS to break even. This is done as follows:

Contribution margin per passenger per trip is:
(R600 – R200) = R400

We can now use the contribution margin formula to calculate the break-even number of passengers. This is done as follows:

$$\frac{\text{Total fixed costs}}{\text{Contribution margin per passenger per return trip}}$$

$$\frac{(3\,000 + 2\,000 + 4\,000 + 1\,000 + 1000)}{400}$$

= 27,5

Therefore, CS should carry a minimum of 28 passengers in order to break even. Note that we do not use a fraction, but *always* round up the number we get to the nearest whole number. This is because CS cannot carry 27½ people.

The next question takes into account the realities of running any business; i.e. the fact that it is not always possible to operate at full capacity (to be precise, this is known as practical capacity). What we want to do here is to calculate the total contribution that CS gets when the company can only get (.75 x 8) six passengers per return trip. Once we have calculated the total contribution, we can then use it to calculate the company's profit by subtracting total fixed costs (see Table 12.3).

Table 12.3 Chopper Services daily profit

		R
Total contribution at lead factor 75%	[(6 × 400) × 4 trips × 2 helicopters]	19 200
Less: Total fixed costs	(3 000 + 2 000 + 4 000 + 1 000 + 1 000)	11 000
Net profit per day		8 200

The last question brings to the fore some of the challenges that tourism businesses may encounter – the impact of natural events such as extreme weather conditions, for example. In this case, we need to take into account the downtime caused by the weather, as well as the maintenance of helicopters. This means that the helicopters can only fly for a total of (365 – 12 – 60), or 293 days. What is also important to remember here is that even though the helicopters are grounded, CS continues to incur fixed costs. This is the point that was discussed earlier in the chapter – that many organisations in the tourism industry incur fixed costs which do not change with activity level. The solution to the last question is shown in Table 12.4.

Table 12.4 Chopper Services annual profit

		R
Total annual contribution at lead factor 75%	[(6 × 400) × 4 trips × 2 helicopters] × 293	5 625 600
Less: Total fixed costs	(3000 + 2 000 + 4 000 + 1 000 + 1000) × 365	4 015 000
Net profit per year		1 610 600

From the calculations shown in Table 12.4, it is clear that the company's average daily profit has gone down, due to weather conditions and the maintenance of helicopters. This can easily be established by dividing the annual profit by the number of days that CS was operating (R1 610 600 ÷ 293), giving us about R5 497 average profit per day. The company's daily profit has gone down from R8 200 per day to R5 497. This also illustrates the impact of fixed costs (which are largely unaffected by changes in activity levels, in this case lower activity levels) on the company's profit.

A better way of measuring the impact of fixed costs, and thus the risk inherent in a company's cost structure, is to use what is known as *margin of safety*. This is defined as the difference between normal sales level (actual or expected) and sales/revenue at the break-even point (Weetman, 2006: 212). In the case of CS above, if we take the break-even passengers (28) and multiply this number by the return ticket fare of R600, we get a break-even revenue per day of (28 x 600) R16 800. We can calculate the anticipated revenue from two helicopters that provide four return trips per day, and get [(2 x 4 x 8) x R600], or R38 400. When we compare the break-even revenue per day of R16 800 and the anticipated revenue per day of R19 200, we get the company's daily margin of safety revenue of (38 400 – 16 800), or R21 600. This means that the company's revenue will fall by R21 600 per day (or equivalent to the revenue from 36 passenger trips) before profit becomes zero.

In order to assess the real risk inherent in the cost structure of CS, we can consider the additional information given. We are told that the company's average load factor is 75%. This means that its expected revenue would be [(2 x 4 x 6) x R600], or R28 800. When compared to the break-even revenue of R16 800, we get a margin of safety revenue of R12 000 per day (or equivalent to the revenue from 20 passenger trips). Thus, there is a massive reduction in the company's margin of safety from R21 600 per day to only R12 000 per day. This means that a reduction of 25% in the company's revenue (i.e. its average load factor of 75%) causes its margin of safety (its cushion) to fall by 44.4%!!

The margin of safety revenue can also be expressed as a percentage, as follows:

$$\frac{\text{Normal sales/Expected sales} - \text{break-even sales}}{\text{Normal sales/Expected sales}}$$

In the case of CS, its margin of safety percentage before the 75% load factor is:

$$\frac{\text{R21 600}}{\text{38 400}} = 56{,}3\%$$

This means that for every rand in revenue that the company gets from passengers, about 56.3 cents goes towards covering fixed costs, and then contributes to profit. In other words, the company's revenue will have to go down by 56.3% before reaching the break-even point. This would be considered a very healthy margin of safety. When we consider the load factor, the company's margin of safety percentage is calculated as:

$$\frac{\text{R12 000}}{\text{R28 800}} = 41{,}7\%$$

As can be seen from the two margins of safety percentages, only about 42 cents is going towards covering fixed costs, and ultimately profit from every rand in gross revenue. Given the fact that the company's fixed costs remain unchanged, this means that less total contribution is available to cover fixed costs and generate profit. This demonstrates the risk inherent in costs structures that have a high fixed-cost component. When activity level falls, such companies find themselves rapidly moving down to the break-even point. The company will not be able to cover its fixed costs, resulting in loss if this situation persists.

The discussion above focused on the application of cost-volume-profit analysis in financial planning. The main objectives were to show the potential usefulness of this tool in planning and risk management. As discussed earlier, the planning section also deals with budgeting and budgetary control, as discussed below.

Budgeting

In order to survive in the global economic environment, all tourism organisations need to carefully decide and specify exactly how they will organise themselves, and how resources will be deployed to support the relevant activities and processes that result in the attainment of their objectives. The specific course of action that is decided upon in order to achieve corporate objectives is known as **strategy**. Thus, an organisation's strategy is the path that it chooses (among several others) to attain its long-term goals (Blocher, Chen & Lin, 2005: 277). In order to implement this chosen course of action, tourism organisations develop clear business plans that require the deployment of resources (people, material, equipment, and infrastructure) in a specific manner, in order to realise goals stated in the business plans. The goals specified in the business plans and the resources required to attain them are summarised in a budget. A **budget** is defined as an organisation's operation plan for a specified period (Blocher, Chen & Lin, 2005: 276). It can also be seen as a detailed plan for the acquisition and use of financial and other resources over a specified time period (Garrison, Noreen & Brewer, 2006: 378). Thus, a budget may be defined as 'a detailed plan based on clearly-stated and agreed business objectives and strategy, which specifies, in financial terms, the income and expenditure expected in a future period of time' (Weetman, 2006: 311).

What is apparent from the above definition of a budget is that it is a *plan*, and therefore refers to what a tourism organisation anticipates in terms of goals to be achieved and the resources required to achieve them. The above definitions of a budget contain key aspects that are important to remember. The first aspect is that a budget is based on clearly-stated and agreed business objectives. This means that all the activities budgeted for should be such that, when they are performed properly, they will result in the attainment of an organisation's business objectives. In other words, a budget is based initially on the principle of effectiveness. Effectiveness means doing the right things. As such, it is important that when a budget is prepared, management satisfies itself that the items budgeted for are in line with its stated business objectives.

The second aspect in the definition of a budget (given above) is that it specifies all the income and expenditure items in financial terms. Since the activities that are necessary to

support an organisation's business objectives are not identical (e.g. activities that fall within the administration function are different from those that form the selling and marketing function), it is necessary to use a commonly-understood language, i.e. monetary language. Also, budgets require funding; i.e. the resources required to perform activities. As such, quantifying such resources makes it easier to understand the value of the resources required. Finally, when budgets are implemented, it is necessary to monitor the results (this is discussed later under budgetary control), and therefore quantifying the resources required facilitates monitoring.

The purpose of budgets

Budgets serve a number of important management functions (Drury, 2005: 593; Garrison, Noreen & Brewer, 2006: 379; Weetman, 2006: 318). These include the following functions:

Communication

As a planning tool, a budget facilitates the communication of key goals that are to be achieved by a tourism business in a specified period. For example, for a private game reserve operator, such communication might take the form of management clearly stating the plans in place to increase the market share of the overseas tourism market during the next three years.

Target

In addition to stating the plans aimed at increasing market share, a budget can also be used to specify exactly what percentage the intended increase is going to be. The management of the private game reserve might say 'we want to increase our market share of overseas tourists by 7% in the next three years'. In numerical terms, the 7% increase might mean increasing the patronage of the private game reserve by 720 overseas tourists during the next three years. The 7% (or 720 tourists) becomes a target for the next three years, towards which the resources of the organisation are deployed. This *target* is then broken down into yearly targets. For example, year one's target might be 20% (.2 × 720), or 144 tourists; year two might be 35%

(.35 × 720), or 252 tourists; and, finally, year three 45% (.45 × 720), or 324 tourists.

Allocation of resources

Once the objectives to be attained are specified, a budget plays the role of a mechanism by which resources are allocated to the specific areas within the organisation where they can be effectively used to realise the objectives. For example, in order to achieve a 7% increase in the market share of overseas tourists, the management of the private game reserve may decide to embark upon an aggressive marketing campaign aimed at creating awareness of the key attributes of the game reserve that overseas tourists would enjoy. This would certainly require the right quantity of resources to be allocated to the relevant organisational sections, such as marketing, to drive the marketing campaign.

Coordination

Budgets are also an important way of coordinating the disparate organisational segments by integrating plans from various parts of the organisation. The private game reserve might be organised into three main sections; namely operations (all activities to do with game viewing), marketing, and administration (including finance). It is important that, while each of these sections has its own specific objectives, they all pull in the same direction. Budgets are used to ensure that resources are allocated in areas of these sections that, when they perform their functions properly, collectively realise the main goal of achieving a 7% market share in the foreign tourist market.

Control

Control through budgets involves monitoring to ensure that each of the organisational segments performs according to plan, and that resources are being used to achieve the goals set in the budget. The process of monitoring the use of resources and the performance of activities is known as budgetary control.

Budgetary control

Budgetary control is defined as the use of a budget to control the activities of an organisation in order to ensure that activities are not only effectively performed, but also efficiently executed.

Budgetary control is based on the two principles of effectiveness and efficiency. As discussed earlier, effectiveness refers to doing the right things. Thus, budgetary control involves making sure that people are actually performing activities relevant to the attainment of the stated business objectives (an aspect of effectiveness). Efficiency, on the other hand, means doing things right. This means that budgetary control entails making sure that the resources required to support the performance of activities are used without waste, i.e. in the most efficient manner.

In the example of the private game reserve, budgetary control involves a combination of the two principles – effectiveness (deploying the right quantity and quality of resources in the marketing campaign), and efficiency (using the resources allocated to all sections of the organisation with the minimum wastage possible). This increases the likelihood that the stated objective of increasing market share in the foreign tourist market by 7% over the next three years will be achieved.

Budgetary control requires that the results of the implementation of a branch budget be monitored on a regular basis. This requires that, on a monthly basis, the planned activities and the resources they are expected to consume in a particular month are compared against the actual activities performed and the actual resources they consume in that particular month. The difference between *planned* actual activity and resource usage and *actual* activity and resource usage gives rise to what is known as a **variance**. A variance is defined as 'a deviation of actual outcome from the planned outcome. This is the difference between the actual cost/revenue and the budgeted cost/revenue' (Weetman, 2006: 349).

These comparisons of actual versus planned activity and resource usage are contained in a document known as a Monthly Report, or Monthly Variance Report. In this report, variances arising from the expenditure and revenue aspects of the business are analysed to provide management with useful information for control purposes. On the expenditure side, the variances are analysed as follows:

- If actual cost is greater than budgeted cost, the variance is known as adverse variance, and is denoted by an 'A'.
- If the actual cost is less than the budgeted cost, the variance is called a favourable variance, and is denoted by an 'F'.

On the income side of the business, the variances are analysed as follows:

- If actual income is greater than budgeted income, the variance is known as a favourable variance, and is denoted by an 'F'.
- If actual income is less than the budgeted income, the variance is called an adverse variance, and is denoted by an 'A'.

The purpose of variance reports is to give management timely information with which to assess whether the planned and implemented course of action is yielding the desired results. This is because each variance should be justified in the context of the organisation's corporate objectives. Using the example of the private game reserve, variance analysis would involve monitoring the attainment of yearly targets on a monthly basis. This could involve the monitoring of the overseas tourist inflow on a monthly basis, to evaluate the effectiveness of the marketing campaign. Thus, budgetary control through variance analysis is an important control device at the disposal of management.

The importance of variance analysis

Variances are an important control device, in that a well-prepared budget does not, in itself, guarantee the realisation of the desired performance. It is therefore imperative that the outcome of the planned activities (as detailed in the budget) is monitored on a regular basis (usually on a monthly basis) to detect undesirable trends, either in the planned revenue or planned expenditure. By analysing the variances at the end of each

month, management is able to detect whether there is a trend in the adverse expenditure variances. Management is able to deal proactively with the adverse trend before the situation gets out of hand. As such, every significant adverse variance should be justified. Therefore a plausible explanation, which should reflect the business objectives, should be provided. An adverse variance could be due to lack of discipline in spending company resources on the planned activities. This kind of variance should be a cause for concern for management if it is an outcome of management behaviour that goes against the principle of efficiency.

However, not all adverse variances arise from a trend that should be a cause for management concern. For example, an adverse expenditure variance can arise due to the volume of the actual activity exceeding the volume of the planned activity. For example, the private game reserve may receive more than the anticipated additional 144 overseas tourists in the first year. The game reserve's costs associated with food and consumables would therefore have to be more than the amount budgeted for the additional 144 tourists. This type of adverse variance should be seen in good light by management, because it results from more business than was anticipated, and hence more revenue will have been generated than was budgeted for. In this situation, every component of the game reserve's operations cost budget (fuel for game-viewing vehicles, repairs, and maintenance) will be higher than budgeted. Again, such a variance (which is adverse) should be interpreted by management as the result of improved volume of business.

On the other hand, a favourable expenditure variance is not always a good development. In respect of the game reserve's strategy to embark on an aggressive marketing campaign, the marketing manager might not plan or execute the campaign properly, resulting in less money being spent on advertising. This certainly produces a favourable expenditure variance. However, in this case, the favourable advertising expenditure variance is at the expense of the creation of awareness of the game reserve among international and domestic tourists, and thus results in less than the desired future patronage. Such a favourable variance should not be seen by management as a good development.

Therefore, from the above discussion, it is important to note that whether an adverse variance is seen as bad or good is subject to the reason(s) why it arose in the first place. Obviously, adverse variances arising from inefficiencies should be tackled immediately by management; i.e. the sources of such inefficiencies should be dealt with decisively.

Having discussed budgeting, budgetary control, and the principles that govern the use of these planning and control tools, we focus now on one of the forms of budget – the cash budget – which provides useful information to management.

Cash budget

Cash management is an important management responsibility, because a profitable tourism organisation may go out of business due to poor cash management. This could be due to carrying too much stock, and/or the extension of generous credit terms to its customers. Thus, making profit and generating cash from sales is not necessarily one and the same thing. Profit is a result of deducting expenses from sales. However, cash is the result of actually realising the physical cash from sales, most of which may be done on credit. Consequently, a profitable organisation may find itself without adequate cash to meet its daily and periodic commitments, such as the payment of wages, salaries, and creditors. An organisation cannot expand its markets, train its staff, or implement capital expansion programmes without sufficient cash resources. Good cash management is vital to any organisation's survival.

Cash management in the tourism industry is even more important, because of a number of factors. First (as discussed in Chapter 1), tourism involves huge capital outlays in order to create the capacity to provide services to tourists. This locks up much of an organisation's cash resources, such as in the case of a hotel infrastructure. In addition to the huge infrastructure costs, a hotel has to buy food and beverages in advance, as well as

maintain salaried staff in anticipation of guests. Second, the service that is created by the assets is highly perishable; i.e. it cannot be stored for later use (see Chapter 14 – Marketing tourism businesses). This means that a hotel or a tour operator is not guaranteed patronage simply because of the capacity created to provide services. Therefore, cash streams from unutilised services cannot be recouped in the future (contrast this with a trader, who has physical stock that can be sold in the future).

Given the above factors, cash budgeting is very important for tourism businesses operating in the tourism industry. The following sections discuss the cash budgeting process, as well as the way in which a cash budget is constructed.

What does a cash budget show?

A cash budget shows the planned opening cash balance, cash inflows, cash outflows, and a closing cash balance for a specific period (usually a week or month) within the budget period (usually a year). A cash budget should be well-prepared, to generate useful insights to tourism managers and, as such, should be prepared to show the following key information:

1. planned cash balance at the end of the budgeted period (a week, month, etc.)
2. expected cash surpluses (for investment) and shortages (for which loans need to be arranged).

These two key pieces of information help tourism managers establish a reliable planning base for all aspects of cash management within the organisation. In addition, a cash budget enables management to co-ordinate cash management with other aspects of the business, such as working capital (a balance between inventories, debtors and creditors), general expenses, revenue/sales, and investment in fixed assets. As indicated in the last section, running a tourism business involves huge capital outlays as well as running costs requiring cash resources. This means that there are periods of rapid cash outflows that are not matched by cash inflows. A cash budget indicates when, for example, a hotel's cash outflows outstrip its cash inflows.

TO DO

Explain how a cash budget should be developed, taking into consideration what has been discussed so far.

How a cash budget is developed

A cash budget is prepared by taking into account two main aspects, namely cash flows and cash management targets. There are no standard measures of these variables and, as such, tourism managers should take into account the nature of the business they are running, the competitive environment, the level of risk, as well as other cash sources at their disposal.

Cash inflows and outflows

The preparation of the cash budget focuses on establishing the cash inflows and cash outflows arising from the activities planned in each period of the budget. Therefore, its construction usually involves a detailed analysis of other budgets (for example, sales/revenue, operations, and capital expenditure budgets) to assess their impact on cash inflows and outflows. This means that in order to properly project the cash inflows and outflows expected from a given level of tourist activities, it is necessary to prepare the budgets that capture the underlying transactions which give rise to cash inflows and outflows.

Cash management targets

As discussed earlier, a cash budget is part of the budgeting process that any organisation undertakes. It is, therefore, necessary that specific cash management targets are set during the process of cash budgeting. These targets take the form of the maximum allowable time for any debts to be outstanding. This is particularly important for hotels that may provide services on account. In order to improve cash inflows, the debt collection period should be as short as possible. Another target would be the maximum time that lapses before creditors have to be paid. The idea here is

to delay paying creditors for as long as possible, in order to minimise cash outflows.

The setting of these cash management targets requires past management experience. For example, if a hotel gives certain patrons a 30-day period within which to settle their accounts, it is reasonable to assume that this trend will continue unless changes are made. What is crucial in any cash management targets is that they ought to be as demanding as possible, to ensure that there is cash management discipline. As such, if the hotel's debt collection period is 30 days, then it should be strictly observed. Also, if the hotel has negotiated favourable payment terms with its suppliers, for example 60 days, paying suppliers before the 60 days had expired would be lack of cash management discipline.

TO DO

Discuss ways of improving the cash flow position of a hotel, a tour operator, or a heritage site.

Ways to improve cash flow

In order to improve the cash position of the organisation, management should deploy some of the following strategies. In order to speed up payment, it is necessary that invoicing of customers is done timeously and correctly, to avoid delays while amendments are being made. Where possible, management should take advantage of the Internet by using Internet banking. The idea here is that, using forms of payment other than hard cash, there is normally a time-lag between receiving payment – such as by cheque – and the availability of cash in the organisation's bank account. It is also important to do a thorough check of the calibre of customers to whom management offers services on credit. We have already discussed the fact that sales are not necessarily the same as cash, in that a sale happens when a service has been provided. However, if it is provided on credit terms, then the cash is not received immediately. The risk in offering credit is that, without a thorough credit check, the chances of some customers defaulting are high, resulting in less cash being received from the sales realised.

Decision-making using financial information

Management decision-making involves making choices about the future. As such, tourism managers are concerned about the impact of their decisions on future costs and revenues. Costs and revenues that influence management decisions about the future are known as *relevant costs* and *relevant revenues*, respectively. While what has happened in the past may offer useful lessons, we can never change what has already happened. Costs relating to past decisions are thus not relevant; therefore they are called sunk costs. Thus, what is relevant to management are the future cash flows (both costs and revenues) that impact on and are also impacted upon by a specific decision. These cash flows would be different (either more, or less) compared to the current position; hence they are also called incremental costs and revenues (Garrison, Noreen & Brewer, 2006: 603). It is also important to remember that making a decision often involves choosing between at least two alternative courses of action. This means that when management makes a final decision to invest in a particular project, there is often a second-best alternative project that will have to be sacrificed. Therefore, making decisions involves foregoing the benefit that could have been realised from the next-best alternative. The benefit sacrificed is known as an opportunity cost.

In order to apply the relevant costing concept in business, we need to use our knowledge of how costs respond to future decisions. Thus, a knowledge of costs behaviour is very important in relevant costing. The section on cost behaviour demonstrated that, in the short term, fixed costs remain unchanged, while variable costs always change in response to changes in activity level. It follows, therefore, that one of the key aspects of relevant costs is to understand the impact of the decision period (i.e. short- versus long-term) when considering costs. Generally, in the short term, fixed costs are unchanged by activity level changes. They are regarded, therefore, as

irrelevant in that particular decision. In other words, costs that remain the same, regardless of the decision taken, are irrelevant. However, it is important that we do not conclude that all fixed costs are irrelevant to a decision in the short term. Remember that we defined a relevant cost as one which belongs to the future, and which changes when a particular decision has been made. There are certain fixed costs that may be relevant in the short term. These are fixed costs that are unique to a product or service; hence they are called *product-specific fixed costs*. What this means is that if management makes a decision to drop that product/service, these costs will also disappear. Therefore, when making a decision in a business situation, management should ask the following questions (Weetman, 2006: 238):

- *Is this a future cost or benefit?*
- *Will the future cash flow change because of this decision?*

Costs and benefits are regarded as relevant if the answer to both questions is 'yes'. However, when making business decisions using the relevant costing concept, it is also important to consider what are known as qualitative factors; i.e. non-financial considerations that can either support what the numbers have indicated, or influence decision-makers to decide differently. Before looking at these non-financial measures, we should consider a number of decision contexts within which relevant costing is applied.

Decision contexts

Adding or dropping a product/service line

This decision is about considering the effect on the overall profits of the tourism company of dropping a product line. What is important in this decision is the impact on the cash flow position of the company arising from dropping a product/service. Compare the contribution lost by dropping the product/service line (this is the relevant cash flow cost of the decision) against the product-specific, service-specific fixed costs that are avoidable (relevant cash flow benefit of the decision). An organisation benefits from dropping a product/service if the relevant cash flow benefit is more than the relevant cash flow cost. However, the final decision requires more than this calculation. It requires that the organisation considers the strategic importance of the product/service offering line. Customers may be attracted to the organisation because they get a 'package' of offerings. Thus, dropping an offering entirely on the basis of the numbers may actually hurt the business. For example, a tour operator may offer other services, such as meals, which would be convenient for tourists. A decision to drop the provision of meals may force the tourists to go elsewhere. In addition, dropping a product/service line invariably results in retrenchment; thus damaging employee morale. This arises from the fact that employees remaining after others have been retrenched may feel insecure, which in turn may harm their productivity.

Special offers

An example of a special offer

Normally, companies offer 'specials' to customers, and organisations in the tourism industry are no exception. Specials are one-time offers that are meant to attract tourists' patronage to a particular place of interest within the specified period of time (see Chapter 14). In making a decision to offer a service such as this, the company consid-

ered incremental revenue arising from the extra tourists taking advantage of the 'once in a lifetime' offer, and the extra costs arising from taking care of the tourists. In making this decision, the extra revenue from the additional tourists taking advantage of this offer (the relevant cash flow benefits) was compared with the extra costs arising from the additional tourists. Please note that we are not talking about the costs and revenues derived from the company's normal business. We are focusing on the special offer, i.e. the one-time offer.

Apart from the financial considerations as discussed above, management should consider whether the company has excess capacity, enabling it to make the special offer without sacrificing capacity for its current (or normal) business. If, in the example given above, the company was already operating at full capacity, offering such a special would involve opportunity cost from lost revenue, as a result of sacrificing its normal business in order to accommodate the extra tourists taking advantage of the special. This would not be a wise decision, as it would result in poor relations with a company's regular customers.

Conclusion

This chapter has provided an overview of the challenges in the current global economic situation, and the importance of financial information in helping tourism managers to make useful decisions. The chapter presented the 'building blocks' used to manage finance in tourism businesses, and discussed how they support financial planning and management decision-making. It is important that tourism managers are well versed in the use of the financial planning tools discussed in this chapter. In order to effectively compete against other global players in the tourism industry and add value to shareholders, managers must be able to select and apply the most appropriate financial planning tools in a given situation. However, this chapter is in no way exhaustive in discussing the management of finance in the tourism industry. You are therefore encouraged to read the references below to further your knowledge of finance.

Review questions

1. What makes costs and revenues relevant to a management decision? Your answer should include practical examples within the tourism industry.

2. Why is it important for cost classification to be matched to the decision that management wants to make? Your answer should include practical examples within the tourism industry.

3. What is the impact of an increase in fixed costs on the break-even point, other variables remaining the same? Explain why this is important, given the high fixed costs and the perishability of services in the tourism businesses.

4. Discuss the importance of a cash budget within the budgetary process of tourism businesses.

Further reading

Blocher, E. J., Chen. K.H. & Lin, T. W. 2005. *Cost management: a strategic emphasis*, 2nd edition. New York: McGraw-Hill.

Garrison, R. H., Noreen, E. W. & Brewer, P. C. 2006. *Managerial accounting*, 11th edition. New York: McGraw-Hill.

Weetman, P. 2006. *Management accounting*. London: Prentice Hall.

Websites

www.tourism.govt.nz/tourism-toolkit/index.html

References

Blocher, E. J., Chen. K. H. & Lin, T. W. 2005. *Cost management: a strategic emphasis*, 2nd edition. New York: McGraw-Hill.

Drury, C. 2005. *Management accounting*, 6th edition, London: Thomson.

Garrison, R. H., Noreen, E. W. & Brewer, P. C. 2006. *Managerial accounting*, 11th edition. New York: McGraw-Hill.

Johnston, R. & Lawrence, P. R. 1988. *Beyond vertical integration: the rise of the value-adding partnership*. *Harvard Business Review*, Vol. 66(4), 94–101.

Lee, H. L. 2000. Creating value through supply chain integration. *Supply Chain Management Review*, Vol. 4(4), 30–37.

Mirra, P. 1999. New opportunities for management accounting in supporting value creation in *The role of Management Accounting in Creating Value, 1999 Theme Book*, International Federation of Accountants.

Vollman, E. & Cordon, C. 1998. Building successful customer–supplier alliances. *Long Range Planning*, Vol. 31(5), 684–694.

Weetman, P. 2006. *Management accounting*. London: Prentice Hall.

Case study
12

Sipho Zulu's 'African Hospitality'

Objectives

- to apply cost-volume-profit analysis principles to analyse the profitability of a planned business venture in the hospitality industry
- to use cost-volume-profit analysis principles to assess the potential risks and rewards inherent in different courses of action of a planned business venture in the hospitality industry.

Sipho Zulu, having come into a rather large sum of money, decides to go into the hotel business. Already involved in the tourism industry (via *Sipho Zulu's African Tours*), Sipho believes that owning a hotel, to be named *Sipho Zulu's African Hospitality*, is a natural extension of his tour business. Before leaping into the business, however, he decides that a little bit of financial analysis might be wise. Sipho obtains the following financial information with regard to the small hotel he is thinking of purchasing:

Capacity   20 Double rooms and 10 Single rooms
Potential annual guest-nights
$$[(20 \times 2) + (10 \times 1)] \times 365 = 18\ 250$$
Expected annual occupancy rate   80%
Variable costs per guest-night   R100
Bed & Breakfast rate per guest-night R300
Annual Fixed Costs   R2 420 000

Case Study questions

1. Assuming that the above information is accurate, what would Sipho's expected profit be from the first year of trading?

2. What would annual break-even occupancy be? (Expressed as a number of guest nights, and as a percentage)

3. What would his occupancy have to be to make R800 000 profit for the year? (guest nights and percentage)

   Sipho's annual occupancy rate is based on 100% occupancy for six months of the year (October to March, 182 days); a 70% occupancy for four months (April, May, June and September, 121 days), and a 40.8% occupancy for two months (July and August – 1 265 guest nights over a 62-day period)

4. Sipho is considering two different 'Come to the Cape in the Green Season' packages, both of which are intended to boost his occupancy levels and profits during the traditionally quiet months:

   - He could reduce his rate per guest night to R275 for April, May, June, and September, which he believes will raise his occupancy rate during this time to 84%. He also intends to reduce his rate per guest night to R250 for July and August, which should raise his occupancy rate to 60% during these months.

- Sipho's second option is to maintain his guest night rate at R300 for the full six quiet months, but include in this rate free daily tours to the Winelands and other places of interest. This will cost him an extra R50 per guest night in additional variable costs, but should boost his occupancy rates to 90% for the four quiet months, and to 75% for July and August.

First, evaluate Sipho's two proposals on the basis of total annual net income, to establish which of the two would be the most profitable. Second, which of the two proposals might be best for Sipho, and why?

13

Tourism businesses and the law

Patrick Vrancken

Photo: Harrow Services

Purpose

The purpose of this chapter is to introduce you to the diversity of the legal environment within which tourism businesses operate in South Africa.

Learning outcomes

After reading this chapter, you should be able to:
- explain the advantages of running a tourism business as a juristic person
- describe the legal regulation of passenger transportation
- explain the legal constraints on the provision of tourist accommodation and catering
- discuss the legal regime of tourism intermediaries
- describe the legal environment of visitor attractions
- list the legal implications of international tourism.

Chapter overview

This chapter introduces you to the diversity of the legal environment within which tourism businesses operate in South Africa. It begins by explaining the advantages of running a tourism business as a juristic person. It outlines the legal regulation of passenger transportation, and discusses the legal constraints on the provision of tourist accommodation. The chapter considers the legal regime of tourism intermediaries, and continues with an overview of the legal environment of visitor attractions. Finally, it introduces the legal implications of tourism across international borders.

The case study at the end of the chapter illustrates the legal complexities of tourism, and highlights the need to obtain expert legal advice.

Introduction

Although tourism is reportedly the world's largest industry, there has been very little attention to the subject in law, whether internationally or in South African law. Indeed, the only national legislation dealing with tourism is the Tourism Act 72 of 1993, and that legislation deals only with the national tourism organisation (SA Tourism) and tourist guides (Vrancken, 2000). Although each province has its own legislation, that legislation deals only with that province's government tourism agency and the registration of tourism businesses active in that province (Vrancken, 2006). For that reason, the legal rules impacting on tourism are scattered throughout a great variety of sources, a situation that is further complicated by the many different forms of tourism activities. As a result, tourism law is usually approached from the perspective of a specific sub-sector of the tourism industry, such as air transportation law, hospitality law, and gambling law.

It is beyond the scope of this chapter to discuss all the legal rules impacting on tourism and to provide answers to every legal problem that may arise. It is, in fact, highly recommended that expert legal advice be obtained in all but the most obvious situations. In uncomplicated or routine matters it may be possible to avoid relying on the services of an attorney by approaching the professional (or trade) organisation to which the business belongs (for instance, Federated Hospitality Association of South Africa, FEDHASA) or the public agency concerned (for instance, the South African Revenue Services, or SARS).

This does not mean that this chapter is of little use. On the contrary, one cannot manage a business successfully without being aware of the legal environment within which that business operates. More specifically, when taking a management decision, it is wise to take into account the main legal implications of that decision. Those would include the new legal duties that the business will have to fulfil. Those duties are likely to increase the running costs of the business, sometimes to the point of causing the business to go bankrupt.

For instance, when budgeting for the addition of a bedroom to a B&B, it is essential to include the cost of adequate insurance cover and/or appropriate burglar-proofing. This is because the owner may be liable for the theft of a guest's property, even if the owner did not steal that property, or was not negligent. To guard against such a possibility, it is necessary to be aware of and to make use of the legal tools that protect the business and the individuals who have an interest in it. A concept created by the law for that purpose is that of the *juristic person*.

Juristic persons

The legal duties of an individual are fulfilled by using that individual's legal rights. In order for individuals to avoid having to give away their *personal* rights in order to fulfil their *business* duties, those individuals may create a fictitious entity called a 'juristic person'. The individuals then run their business through that juristic person. The juristic person is separate from the individuals, and has its own rights and duties. This means that the duties of the juristic person may only be fulfilled by using that person's rights, and that the individuals running the business may not be compelled to give away their own personal rights. For instance, when a travel agency that is a juristic person sells a holiday package and that package is not delivered, the tourist may not obtain contractual damages from the individual to whom the tourist actually spoke, even if that individual has a lot of assets and the juristic person has hardly any.

Individuals may create a company with limited liability in order to obtain the required protection. The choice of the actual type of company depends on a number of factors, such as the size of the business, the amount and source of funding required, and the extent to which the individuals concerned are prepared to subject themselves to the complex rules imposed by the Companies Act 61 of 1973 (Le Roux, 2002: 114–131).

As Le Roux (2002: 131) explains, the purpose of the Close Corporation Act 69 of 1984 was:

'to provide a simple, less expensive and more flexible new legal form for a business venture that consists of a single entrepreneur or a small number of participants. Membership of a close corporation is limited, but there is no restriction on the size of the business or undertaking, or on the number of employees or creditors'.

This type of juristic person is particularly attractive in the tourism industry, where the proportion of small, medium, and micro enterprises (SMMEs) is particularly high (see Chapter 10). Entrepreneurs are better able to protect their personal assets if they run their tourism business as a CC. This is particularly important when one takes into account the fact that the law creates additional burdens, which vary depending on the services offered by the business. One example of such services is the transportation of passengers.

Passenger transportation

Tourists may be transported in a variety of ways. One of the most popular modes of transportation in South Africa is road transportation.

One mode of road transport offering consists of making cars available for hire. These cars must comply with the technical requirements of the Road Traffic Act 29 of 1989. It was confirmed in *Fourie v Hansen and Another* [2000] 1 All SA 510(W), that '[a] party letting out vehicles ... has a duty to apply expertise in ascertaining and checking the conditions of such vehicles when it rents them out'. There is, on the other hand, no specific legislation regulating the contractual relationship between tourists and car-rental companies. As a result, that relationship is governed by the common law relating to the contract of letting and hiring of a thing, unless the parties agree on specific terms and conditions. In practice, car-rental companies do not normally release a vehicle before a written document, sometimes called a 'Rental Agreement', has been completed and signed by both parties. It was decided in the *Fourie* case that one may not assume in such a case that the tourists have agreed to the terms and

conditions usually printed on the reverse side of the document. In fact, if a dispute arises in this regard, the company has to prove that the tourist knew those terms and conditions (Vrancken, 2002: 319).

In contrast to car rental, the National Land Transport Transition Act 22 of 2000 requires businesses operating charter services to hold an operating licence or a temporary permit. A **charter service** is a service involving 'the hire of a vehicle and a driver for a journey at a charge arranged beforehand with the operator, where (a) neither the operator nor the driver charges the passengers individual fares; (b) the person hiring the service has the right to decide the route, date and time of travel; and (c) the passengers are conveyed to a common destination'.

The legal relationship between the business that makes the vehicle and the driver available, on the one hand, and the person who hires the vehicle, on the other hand, is a complex one. This is because it presents features of a contract of letting and hiring of a thing (the hiring of the vehicle) as well as a contract of letting and hiring of services (the hiring of the driver). The exact nature of the contract will depend on the intention of the parties in each specific case (Vrancken, 2002: 319–320).

As in the case of charter services, the National Land Transport Transition Act requires a person to hold a licence, permit, or authorisation if that person operates a service for the carriage of passengers against payment. It is worth noting that courtesy services do not have to comply with this requirement. A **courtesy service** is a 'transport service for customers or clients provided by an organisation which is not a public transport operator, where the organisation provides its own vehicle or a vehicle provided by an operator in terms of a contract with that organisation'.

The Act is complemented by provincial legislation enacted in all nine provinces of South Africa, and in force within the territory of the provinces concerned.

In order for a contract of carriage of persons to be complete, the general requirements for a valid contract must be met. This means that the carrier and the passenger must agree on the terms of the contract. In this case, the parties must agree (i) on the person(s) to be carried, (ii) on the fact that the carriage will take place by road, and (iii) on the two points between which the carriage is to take place. Moreover, as in the case of any contract, the passenger must be capable of concluding a contract. The conclusion of the contract, the performance in terms of the contract, and the purpose for which the contract is concluded, must also be legal. Finally, the contract must be clear, and its enforcement must be possible (Mukheibir, 2002: 57–66). In practice, the contract is usually concluded when the carrier issues the passenger with a ticket that records the relevant particulars.

The main obligation of the carriers is to convey the passengers in accordance with the terms of the contract and within the times agreed upon. It was also confirmed in *Durham v Cape Town and Wellington Railway Company* 1869 Buch 306 that carriers must 'take every reasonable precaution to secure the safe transit of the passengers'. Should they fail to do so, the carriers will be liable for the injuries sustained by the passengers. Whether carriers are liable for the acts or omissions of their drivers depends on whether the drivers are free to do what they please and how they please in carrying out their occupation, or whether they are acting in accordance with prescriptions issued by the carriers. Carriers are only liable in the second case. Carriers frequently limit their liability by printing on the tickets issued to the passengers a notice stressing that the carriage is subject to terms spelled out in some document. In those cases, called 'ticket cases', the rule is that the passengers are bound by the terms of the document, whether they have read it or not, if the carriers have done what is reasonably sufficient or reasonable to draw the passengers' attention to that document (Vrancken, 2002: 322–324).

Tourist accommodation and catering

The legal relationship between the tourist and the business providing accommodation may take various forms (see Chapter 6 – Managing accommodation for tourists). Indeed, a distinction must be made between the cases where the relationship is based on a contract of *lease*, those where the relationship is based on a contract of *board and lodging*, or where the relationship flows from a *timesharing* scheme, as well as the cases where the relationship is governed by the rules of *innkeeping*. It must be stressed that the nature and features of the relationship do not depend on the name or appearance of the establishment concerned (Vrancken, 2002: 347).

The legal relationship between tourists making use of accommodation supplied to them, and the provider of that accommodation, may flow from a timesharing scheme. The timesharing industry is regulated by a code of conduct prepared by the Business Practices Committee, in conjunction with the Timeshare Institute of South Africa (TISA). The Property Time-sharing Control Act 75 of 1983 regulates the sale or lease of timesharing interests in immovable property. Timeshare products and practices are also regulated by the Share Blocks Control Act 59 of 1980, the Sectional Titles Act 95 of 1986, the Companies Act 61 of 1973, and the Estate Agents Affairs Act 112 of 1976 (Vrancken, 2002: 355–356).

If the relationship between the tourist and the provider is based on a contract of lease, which is likely to be the position in the case of self-catering accommodation, the supplier is referred to as the 'landlord/landlady' or 'lessor', and the tourist as the 'tenant' or 'lessee'. In terms of such a contract, the lessor agrees to give the use and enjoyment of the whole or part of the building concerned to the lessee on a temporary basis in return for the payment of rent. The relationship may be subject to the Rental Housing Act 50 of 1999. That legislation, for instance, expressly forbids lessors to unfairly discriminate against lessees on the basis of race, sexual orientation, religion, or language (unfair discrimination is actually forbidden in all spheres of tourism activities in terms of section 9(4) of the Constitution and the Promotion of Equality and Prevention of Unfair Discrimination Act 4 of 2000). It is also worth noting that the lessees are entitled to sub-let the property unless it has been agreed otherwise (Vrancken, 2002: 347–349).

If accommodation is supplied with meals, the relationship between the tourist and the supplier may be based on a contract of board and lodging. In that case, the supplier is referred to as the 'boarding-house keeper' and the tourist as the 'lodger' or 'boarder'. It was held in *McLaughlin v Koenig* 1928 CPD 102 that boarding-house keepers are only liable for injuries suffered by lodgers if they failed to observe the standard of care that the average diligent person would observe under the circumstances. It was also held in *Connel v Kluge* 1921 CPD 601 that the same standard applies to the lodgers' property.

The position is different if the relationship between the tourist and the supplier of the accommodation is based on a contract of innkeeping, which is likely to be the position in the case of B&Bs (see *Gabriel v Enchanted Bed and Breakfast CC* [2002] 6 SA 597 C). In that case, the supplier is referred to as the 'innkeeper', and the tourist as the 'traveller'. It remains unclear in South African law whether innkeepers have a duty to supply travellers with accommodation in all cases where there is no legitimate ground for refusal. However, once innkeepers have accepted travellers, certain rights and related duties arise with regard to the personal safety of the travellers and their property. On the one hand, innkeepers must not be negligent about the personal safety of the travellers. On the other hand, the liability of innkeepers towards property brought onto their premises by the travellers is much higher than that of the boarding-house keeper. Indeed, the principle is that innkeepers are liable for loss or damage to that property, even in the absence of fault or negligence on their part. Innkeepers will, however, not be liable if the loss or damage is caused by an event that could not be expected or avoided. Innkeepers will also not be liable if there would not have been any loss or damage if the travellers had taken the ordinary steps that a careful person would be expected to take under the circumstances. It is also possible for innkeepers to limit their liability, or exclude it completely, by agreement with the travellers. It must be stressed that it was decided in *Davis v Lockstone* 1921 AD 153, that the mere posting up of a notice for the purpose of limiting an innkeeper's liability will not affect the travellers'

rights, unless it can be proven that their attention was drawn to the notice and that they agreed to be bound by it (Vrancken, 2002: 352–355).

Businesses offering tourist accommodation often also offer food and beverages. Some tourism businesses focus exclusively on catering.

In terms of the Businesses Act 71 of 1991, a licence is normally required for the sale or supply of any foodstuff in the form of meals. One of the exceptions is where meals are prepared and sold in a private dwelling. When a licence is required, that licence is either an ordinary licence or a hawker's licence usually issued by the local authority where the business is located. Before issuing a licence, the licensing authority must check that the business premises comply with the applicable legal requirements relating to town planning as well as the safety and health of the public, and that all apparatuses, equipment, storage spaces, working surfaces, structures, and vehicles used comply with the applicable legal requirements relating to public health. The sale of any article or substance ordinarily eaten by humans is also controlled by the Foodstuffs, Cosmetics and Disinfectants Act 54 of 1972. The Act provides for criminal offences and for the inspection of premises and substances, as well as for the analysis of foodstuffs. The local authorities are responsible for making the necessary specific regulations (Vrancken, 2002: 356–357).

The retail sale of liquor is regulated by relevant provincial legislation. That legislation deals with the licensing or registration of retailers. It also provides for the terms and conditions applicable to the sale of liquor, such as trading hours, and persons to whom liquor may be sold.

Tourism intermediaries

Tourists often rely upon **intermediaries** to identify and secure offerings (see Chapter 7 – Managing tourism distribution). The legal regime of tourism intermediaries is particularly complex, and research in this field has received scant attention in South Africa.

One of the reasons for this is that the legal regime of travel agencies is difficult to describe, because travel agents perform various kinds of activities, with varying legal implications. The only legislative provision dealing specifically with travel agency is section 22 of the Tourism Act 1993, which states that:

> 'any person who, in the course of his business, sells facilities for a journey to any destination in a foreign country shall, when selling such facilities, offer ... to the buyer thereof his assistance in order to enable such buyer to obtain alternative travelling facilities for his return journey to the Republic in any case where the person who, in terms of the agreement in question, is obliged to provide such facilities should fail or should for any reason be unable to do so'.

Travel agents comply with this duty by merely showing on their premises a notice stating:

NOTICE TO CLIENTS

Assistance to obtain travel insurance in terms of section 22 of the Tourism Act, 1993, is available on request.

This very limited statutory protection is complemented by the Consumer Code for Travel Agencies, issued by the Consumer Affairs Committee and supported by the Association for South African Travel Agents (ASATA). It must be stressed that the Code is merely a statement of policy by the Committee about the desired conduct of travel agents. In other words, the Code is applied by the Committee when it is asked to assess whether a conduct complained of constitutes a harmful business practice. In terms of the Code, all travel agents are expected to comply with various accounting and financial requirements. They are also expected to:

- maintain an ethical and professional approach towards meeting customers' needs
- provide accurate and detailed information to customers regarding travel products
- give immediate attention to customers' requests
- provide written confirmation of, and information on, the status of a booking, when requested, as well as maintain a complete record of each booking

- bill relevant and reasonable services charges, when applicable
- act on the basis of absolute integrity in the handling and remittance of customers' funds
- make a recommendation to each customer to take out comprehensive insurance
- meet and comply with the promises and offers made in any advertising, the latter having to comply with the Committee's Advertising Code as well as the Code of the Advertising Standards Authority
- make available a brochure, leaflet or other publication containing minimum information for each inclusive tour or package product (Vrancken, 2002: 327–330).

When it comes to determining the nature of the contractual relationship between tourists and travel agents, a number of situations must be distinguished. If the travel agency acts on behalf of the business providing the offering (for instance, sells an airline ticket on behalf of the airline carrier concerned, or reserves a room on behalf of the hotel concerned), the agency indeed acts as an agent in law. In such a case the agency must act in accordance with the supplier's instructions, if any, as well as with the necessary care and diligence. If the agency does so, and the tourist is aware that the agency acted on behalf of the supplier, a legal relationship is established between the tourist and the supplier. Their legal position is then the same as if they had dealt directly with one another.

The travel agency can also act on behalf of the tourist (for instance, when the agency contacts a B&B overseas and makes a booking for the tourist). In such a case, the agency also acts as an agent in law, and must act in accordance with the tourist's instructions, if any, as well as with the necessary care and diligence. If the agency does so, and the supplier is aware that the agency acted on behalf of the tourist, a legal relationship is established between the tourist and the supplier. Their legal position is then the same as if they had dealt directly with one another.

The travel agency can also act as a tour operator, selling offerings that it bought from suppliers, and adding an amount for packaging them together. From a legal point of view, the difficulty in this case is that, when the tourists purchase the package from the tour operator, the legal relationship established as a result is only between the tourist and the tour operator. This means that there is no contractual relationship between the suppliers of the offerings included in the package, and the tourists. As a result, there are also no contractual remedies available to the tourists against the suppliers. In the case where the suppliers do not fulfil their duties towards the tourists, the tourists must sue the tour operators and, if the tourists are successful, the tour operators must then sue the suppliers.

Example The Boks at Twickenham

- The tourists were rugby supporters wanting to see the Boks playing against England at Twickenham.
- They bought a package including air travel from Johannesburg to London, accommodation in London, and tickets to the venue.
- They were told that the tickets would be given to them in London.
- Their flight was delayed, but they arrived the day before the match.
- They were given accommodation as agreed.
- They ultimately were not given tickets, and they had to watch the match on TV in London.
- They sued the travel agency for the price of the whole package.
- The travel agency was only prepared to refund the price of the tickets.

Source: *Tweedie & Another v Park Travel Agency (Pty) Ltd t/a Park Tours [1998] 4 SA 802 W*

Discussion point

Examine the facts in the Example box above. Assess the claim of the tourists. How would you justify the position of the travel agency? The court ordered the travel agency to refund the price of the whole package. Was the loss incurred by the travel agency actually limited to that amount?

Tourism businesses increasingly enter into contacts with tourists through the Internet without the services of intermediaries. Use of the Internet in South Africa is regulated by the

Electronic Communications and Transactions Act 25 of 2002, which applies over and above other consumer protection instruments such as the Consumer Affairs (Unfair Business Practices) Act 71 of 1988 and the Code of Advertising Practice. Section 43(1) of the Electronic Communications and Transactions Act requires a tourism business offering tourism services by way of an electronic transaction to indicate to the tourists on its website:

- its full name and legal status
- its physical address and telephone number
- its website and e-mail address
- the contact details of any self-regulatory or accreditation body to which it belongs
- the electronic address of any code of conduct to which it subscribes
- its registration number, the names of its office-bearers, and its place of registration
- the physical address where it will receive service of legal documents
- a sufficient description of the main characteristics of the services offered to enable the tourist to make an informed decision on the proposed electronic transaction;
- the full price of the services, including transport costs, taxes, and any other fees or costs
- the manner of payment that it will accept
- the terms of the agreement and the details of how those terms may be accessed, stored, and reproduced electronically by the tourists
- the time during which the services will be rendered
- the manner and period within which tourists can access and maintain a full record of the transaction
- the details of the alternative dispute resolution code to which it subscribes
- its security procedures and privacy policy in respect of payment, payment information, and personal information.

It must also be stressed that electronic data messages have, in principle, the same legal effects as messages conveyed by word of mouth, by post, or by fax. This means that a binding contract may come into being as a result of one e-mail containing an offer, and a second e-mail containing acceptance. In this regard the Act compels tourism businesses to provide tourists with an opportunity to review the entire electronic transaction, correct any mistakes, or withdraw from the transaction before finally entering into it. If the tourists go ahead, they have the right to a payment system that is sufficiently secure, with reference to accepted technological standards and the type of transaction concerned. Moreover, the Act allows tourists to cancel an electronic transaction without reason and without penalty within seven days of the conclusion of the agreement provided, obviously, that the services offered have not already been used. In such a case, the tourism business must refund fully any payment already made within 30 days from the date of cancellation (Buys, 2004: 152–156).

Visitor attractions

Visitor attractions are varied, and a study of the legal rules that govern all of them would lead to an almost complete overview of the South African legal system. Tourist guides play a central role at this level.

In terms of the Tourism Act, 1993, tourist guiding businesses employing tourist guides must be registered with the relevant provincial registrar of tourist guides. All registered tourist guides must have the required competence to be registered, and must have passed the prescribed quality assurance process. Tourist guides are bound by a code of conduct and ethics prepared by the National Registrar of Tourist Guides (NRTG). The code provides that a tourist guide must take all reasonable steps to ensure the safety of all the tourists whom the guide is accompanying. The code also requires tourist guides to render services of an acceptable standard. Any tourist unhappy with the conduct of a guide may lodge a complaint with the relevant provincial registrar. There is a right to appeal to the National Registrar of Tourist Guides (Carnelley, 2002: 365–366).

Natural attractions

South Africa's natural attractions are one of its main drawcards, and many tourism businesses capitalise on that market strength. In order to protect those assets, the National Environmental Management Act 107 of 1998 sets out the national environmental management principles with which all organs of State must comply. In conjunction with that Act, the Environment Conservation Act 73 of 1989 provides mechanisms for the inclusion of privately-owned land into protected areas, in order to safeguard and manage the specific ecological processes, natural beauty, indigenous wildlife and, more generally, the biotic diversity of those areas. The Act also prohibits littering on any land or water surface, street, road, or site to which the public has access. In this regard the Act compels any business in charge of a place to which the public has access to ensure at all times that containers or places are provided that will normally be adequate and suitable for the discarding of litter by the public. That litter must also be removed within a reasonable time. Furthermore the Act makes it possible for the Minister of Environmental Affairs and Tourism (DEAT) to prohibit activities that may have a substantial detrimental effect on the environment in general or in specific areas. Such activities may then only be undertaken with written authorisation (Carnelley, 2002: 368–369).

Other legislation regulates specific kinds of natural attractions. For instance, the National Forests Act 84 of 1998 states that everyone has the right to reasonable access to State forests for purposes of recreation, education, culture, or spiritual fulfilment. Tourists may, however, enter only designated areas and, when doing so, must comply with a number of rules and restrictions relating, for instance, to the number of tourists allowed at any one time and to the mode of transport utilised. Access to, and activities on, the seashore are regulated by the Seashore Act 21 of 1935. The detailed rules applicable in a specific section of the coast are set by the municipality concerned. Those rules usually deal with issues such as the use of vehicles and boats, trading conditions, bathing areas, the presence of animals, and the lighting of fires. Further out to sea, the Marine Living Resources Act 18 of 1998 protects South Africa's marine ecosystems and regulates their use. In terms of the Act, marine protected areas have been declared within which nobody may, without permission, engage in certain activities such as fishing, taking or destroying any fauna or flora, and erecting any building. The Act also regulates tourist activities such as whale-watching, for which a permit is required. Mention must also be made of the Sea Bird and Seals Protection Act 46 of 1973, which forbids anybody to set foot and remain on islands such as Bird Island in Algoa Bay, Seal Island near Mossel Bay, Seal Island in False Bay, Jutten Island, Marcus Island, Malagas Island and Meeuwen Island in Saldanha Bay, as well as Marion and Prince Edward Islands in the Southern Ocean, without a permit. The Act also forbids the killing, capturing, or disturbing of any sea bird or seal on those islands, the seashore of the mainland, or South African waters.

As far as hunting is concerned, the Firearms Control Act 60 of 2000 requires a licence for the possession of a firearm. Foreign tourists bringing their weapons into South Africa must have an import permit, which serves as a temporary licence. Unlawful hunting is an offence in terms of the Game Theft Act 105 of 1991, and the South African Police Service (SAPS) Act 68 of 1995. There are also several restrictions on hunting, as well as the transportation of animals and animal products in terms of the Animal Diseases Act 35 of 1984. As Carnelley explains, at provincial level:

'various other pieces of legislation deal with hunting. In the Eastern Cape, for example, the Cape Ordinance 19 of 1974 applies. That legislation creates a classification system of species of game. Some species, such as the rhinoceros, are protected and are prohibited from being hunted. Other animals may only be hunted with a permit. Special provisions exist regarding the season of hunting, the types of weapons that may and may not be used, and professional hunters' (2002: 381).

Cultural attractions

Cultural attractions are also one of South Africa's major drawcards (see Chapter 4). The main legislation in this regard is the National Heritage Resources (NHA) Act 25 of 1999, which makes any place or object of cultural significance a heritage resource. This includes places, buildings, structures, and equipment of cultural significance; places to which oral traditions are attached or that are associated with living heritage, historical settlements, landscapes and natural features of cultural significance, geological sites of scientific or cultural significance, archaeological and palaeontological sites, graves and burial grounds, as well as a whole range of movable objects. Heritage resources of national significance are managed by the South African Heritage Resources Agency (SAHRA), resources of provincial significance are managed by the relevant provincial heritage resources authority (for example, the Amafa aKwaZulu-Natal), and the other resources by the local authorities concerned. Once a place has been declared a National Heritage Site, it is forbidden to destroy, damage, deface, excavate, alter, subdivide, or change the planning status of that site without a permit. Regulations are also often made to safeguard heritage sites. The Act also prohibits the alteration or demolition of any structure that is more than 60 years old without a permit. Sites of outstanding universal value are protected by the World Heritage Convention Act 49 of 1999.[1] Those sites are managed by special bodies. Other relevant national legislation includes the National Arts Council Act 56 of 1997, the National Film and Video Foundation Act 73 of 1997, the Pan-South African Language Board Act 59 of 1995, the Culture Promotion Act 35 of 1983, and the Cultural Institutions Act 119 of 1998.

Built attractions

Tourists also require entertainment. In this regard, the Businesses Act 71 of 1991 requires certain types of health facilities and forms of entertainment businesses to be licensed. Those include businesses providing Turkish baths, saunas, or other health baths; businesses making the services of an escort, whether male or female, available to another person; businesses keeping devices designed for the playing of a recreational or amusement game upon payment; businesses keeping snooker or billiard tables; and businesses running a nightclub, discotheque, cinema, or theatre.

Gambling is regulated at national level by the National Gambling Act 7 of 2004. In terms of the Act, and as a matter of principle, all gambling activities, machines, premises, and industry employees must be licensed or registered, and must comply with a wide range of very specific requirements. The Act also excludes certain persons such as minors from gambling, and places restrictions on the advertising and promotion of gambling activities. Provincial legislation complements the Act in each province.

Social attractions

In view of the fact that an increasing number of tourists appear to engage in sexual activities with children, tourism businesses need to be aware that a number of wide-ranging measures to combat this scourge have already been taken, or are in the process of being adopted. For instance, the Sexual Offences Bill makes it an offence to make or organise any travel arrangements for or on behalf of any other person, whether that other person is resident within or outside South Africa, with the intention of facilitating the commission of any sexual offence against a child, irrespective of whether or not that offence is committed. Upon conviction, the offender is liable to a fine or imprisonment for a period not exceeding 20 years. The same applies to the printing or publishing, in any manner, of any information that is intended to promote or facilitate child sex tours. The Bill makes its provisions applicable outside the territory of South Africa. This means that a South African court has jurisdiction – even when the above offences have been committed abroad – if the perpetrators of those offences are South Africans or permanent residents in South Africa; if they have been arrested in South Africa, or if they are South African companies. On the other hand, the Child Care Act 74 of 1983 provides for the prosecution of any person directly involved in the commercial sexual exploi-

tation of children and makes it an offence for an owner, lessor, or manager of a property where the exploitation occurs to fail to report the occurrence within a reasonable period of time after becoming aware of it. Moreover, the conduct of the various role-players in child sex tourism falls within the definition of child sexual abuse in the Children's Act 38 of 2005.

Visitor attraction businesses, like all other tourism businesses, must comply with labour legislation, such as the Labour Relations Act 66 of 1995; the Basic Conditions of Employment Act 75 of 1997, and the Occupational Health and Safety Act 85 of 1993 (Vercuil & Fourie, 2002). They also need to select their employees carefully. One of the reasons for this is that the business will often be held vicariously liable towards tourists for the delicts of its employees. A **delict** may be described as the unreasonable behaviour of a person who acts either intentionally or negligently, and thus causes someone to suffer loss or damage' (Mukheibir, 2002: 76).

In order for this to happen, the following requirements must be met:
- there must be an employer/employee relationship between the business and the person with whom the tourist was in contact
- the employee must have committed a delict
- the delict must have been committed by the employee in the course and scope of performance of his or her duties.

As Vercuil and Fourie explain:
'when vicarious liability is established, the [business] and employee are both liable for the whole debt. In practice, the [tourist] concentrates his or her efforts on claiming damages from the [business] on the basis that it is usually in a stronger financial position than the employee. Once the [business] has paid, however, it has a right of recourse against the employee, which means that the [business] is entitled to claim back from the employee the amount that the [business] has paid to the [tourist]' (2002: 176).

Example The unruly barman

The claimant and his girlfriend visited the Umdloti Bush Tavern. The barman on duty served everyone except the claimant and his girlfriend. When he was approached by another barman, the claimant remarked that the first barman could take a few lessons regarding service from the second barman. The first barman heard this remark, became agitated and glared at the claimant, to whom he made a sign to come closer. The claimant reacted by saying words to the effect that he 'did not come for people like that': This further agitated the first barman, who occasionally stared at the claimant and appeared to be aggressive. When the claimant and his girlfriend were about to leave, he generously tipped the barman who had served them. The first barman saw this and quickly left the bar. When the claimant reached the corridor in the immediate vicinity of the bar, the first barman assaulted him, causing injuries which were reasonably serious. Immediately after the incident, the manager of the Tavern summarily dismissed the first barman, because he had broken the rules that regulated how he should perform his basic duties. The claimant sued the company that owned the bar and employed the barman.

Source: *Costa Da Oura Restaurant (Pty) Ltd T/A Umdloti Bush Tavern v Reddy 2003 (4) SA 34 SCA*

Discussion point

Examine the facts in the above example box, and assess the claim of the customer. On which basis did the customer claim damages? On which basis did the company argue that it was not vicariously liable? The court decided that the company was not vicariously liable. Do you agree with that decision?

Tourism businesses must also ensure that they are adequately insured against the legal costs that they may have to incur for breach of contract – for example, in the case of false description or disruption of a tourism offering. Legal costs can also be extremely high, for instance, in the case of personal injury claims as a result of a car accident, a bite by a lion at a game reserve, food poisoning or a contaminated swimming pool. This is because victims may not only claim compensation for hospital and medical costs already incurred, but also for future medical costs that will be required as a result of the injury. Moreover, victims may claim compensation for the income that they have already lost because they were unable to work while they were recovering, as well as for the income that they will not be able to continue earning if they cannot recover sufficiently to return to their professional activities. Finally, victims may also claim compensation for **non-patrimonial damages** such as pain, suffering, and disfigurement (Mukheibir, 2002: 89–90).

Liability insurance can be obtained from an insurer registered in terms of the Short-term Insurance Act 53 of 1998. As Woker explains, tourism businesses must:

> *'ensure that their policies cover the risks that they wish to insure against. In this regard exclusion and excess clauses are vitally important, as insurers always limit their liability, and an insurer will only accept liability for a loss that falls within the limits of the policy' (2002: 202).*

Tourism businesses must also check regularly that they are not under-insured because, if the insurance contract contains an average clause (which is very often the case), insurers will not compensate the insured for the whole loss suffered. It is also very important for tourism businesses to disclose all material facts to the insurer when insurance is being applied for, and whenever circumstances change afterwards. A **material fact** is a fact that the insurer takes into account when deciding whether to cover the risk and, if it decides to do so, what the premium and other conditions will be.

As Woker notes,

> *'should adequate information not be provided by the insured, the insurer is entitled to repudiate the contract, notwithstanding the fact that the insured did not deliberately withhold that information. The policy may be declared of no legal effect because the risk that the insurer agreed to run is actually different from the risk undertaken' (2002: 208).*

International tourism

The legal environment of tourism activities becomes even more complicated once international borders are crossed.

First of all, it is important to stress that tourists have no right in international law to enter the territory of a State of which they are not nationals. This means that each State is entitled to decide which tourists it wishes to allow to enter its territory, and under which conditions. In South Africa, these issues are regulated by the Immigration Act 13 of 2002.

International tourists are likely to have made arrangements with South African tourism businesses by the time they enter the country. The question then arises as to which legal system governs those contractual relationships. It is likely that the South African tourism businesses will want South African law to apply, while the foreign tourists will want their own legal system to apply. South African law does not provide that contracts entered into by South African tourism businesses with foreign tourists are automatically governed by South African law. The rule is that a South African court will apply to the contract either the legal system expressly or tacitly chosen by the parties to the contract or, if the parties have not chosen a legal system, the legal system 'with which the contract has its closest and most real connection' (Forsyth, 2003: 308). That legal system is the legal system of the State where the contract was concluded – unless the contract was, or is to be, performed in another State. In that case the legal system that is applied is the legal system of the State where the contract was, or is, to be performed. Those rules, however, are not rigid, because their application may lead to inappropriate results, as in the case where there is no meaningful link between the parties and the State where the contract was concluded. For example, a travel package may have been bought at a tourism trade fair that took place in a State with which neither the tourists nor the tourism businesses have a connection. It may also be difficult to determine in which State the contract is performed when a package involves travel and attractions in several countries. It must be noted that different rules apply in exceptional cases. South African courts deal with the issue of whether a contract is valid with regard to its form by determining whether the contract complies with the requirements of either the legal system of the State where the contract was concluded, or the legal system that governs the substantive aspects of the contract (Forsyth, 2003: 294–325).

The South African courts have not yet decided which legal system governs a dispute revolving around a delict. It seems that, as a matter of principle, the court will apply the legal system of the State where the delict was committed. For instance, a dispute revolving around a car collision in Lesotho will be resolved by applying the relevant legal norms of Lesotho. This may also lead to an inappropriate result, as when all the parties involved are South Africans. Because none of the parties has any meaningful connection with Lesotho, it would make little sense to apply Lesotho's legal system to the dispute. In such a case, it is clearly more appropriate to apply the legal system with which the delict has the closest connection – South African law, in this example (Forsyth, 2003: 325–338).

Another matter that requires attention in the case of international tourism is to determine which courts will have the authority to decide a legal dispute that may arise. It can be expected that foreign tourists would want to be able to approach the courts in their own country, while South African tourism businesses would want to be able to approach the South African courts. The best way to address this issue is to insert a clause in the contract stating which courts will have jurisdiction in the case of a dispute. It must be kept in mind, however, that the binding effect of orders of South African courts is limited to the South African territory. Proceedings will have to be instituted in the State of the foreign tourists to have the decision of a South African court recognised in that State and enforced by its authorities (Forsyth, 2003: 389–445).

Because the great majority of overseas tourists to South Africa reside in Europe, it is important for South African tourism businesses to understand the implications of the European Union's Directive 90/314/EEC on package travel, package holidays, and package tours. This instrument is relevant when businesses contract with European intermediaries which, in turn, contract with the European tourists. In other words, the Directive applies when European tourists purchase holiday packages to South Africa from European tour operators or travel agents. An inclusive, or 'package' holiday is defined as the pre-arranged combination of not fewer than two of the following when sold or offered for sale at an inclusive price, and when the service covers a period of more than 24 hours or includes overnight accommodation:

a) transport
b) accommodation
c) other tourist services not ancillary to transport or accommodation, and accounting for a significant proportion of the package. (article 2(1) of the Directive).

Probably the most important effect of the Directive, as far as South African tourism businesses are concerned, is that it compelled EU member States to adopt legislation making European tour operators and travel agents liable to the tourists for the proper performance of the obligations undertaken in terms of the packages that they are selling. This is irrespective of whether those obligations are to be performed by the tour operators and travel agents themselves, or by other suppliers of services included in the packages. Consequently, when South African tourism businesses fail to perform their obligations in terms of packages sold in the EU, the European tourists are able to sue in their own country the European tour operators or travel agents that sold the packages, despite the fact that those operators or agents have not done anything wrong. Obviously, the European tour operators and travel agents may then turn against the South African businesses. As explained above, this may prove quite difficult and, in practice, this seldom happens. The South African businesses will therefore escape having to compensate the European tourists, tour operators, or travel agents. They will, however, most probably be blacklisted by European intermediaries, and will certainly have tarnished the reputation of South Africa as a quality tourism destination (Vrancken, 2001).

Conclusion

This chapter has introduced some of the facets of the wide diversity of the legal environment within which tourism businesses operate in South Africa. In the process of dealing with juristic persons and illustrating the legal regulation of passenger transportation, tourism accommodation, tourism intermediaries, visitor attractions, and international tourism, it has been made very clear that the issues are often complex, and that it is necessary in most cases to obtain expert legal advice.

Review questions

1. Why is it better for tourism businesses to be juristic persons?

2. Describe the legal relationship between transport carriers and passengers.

3. What are the different legal relationships that may exist between tourists and accommodation owners?

4. Discuss the nature of the contractual relationship between tourists and travel agents.

5. Give examples of legislation impacting on visitor attractions.

6. Explain legal issues raised by international tourism.

Further reading

Grant, D. & Mason, S. 2003. *Holiday Law,* 3rd edition. London: Sweet & Maxwell.

Vrancken, P. (Ed.). 2002. *Tourism and the law in South Africa.* Port Elizabeth: Butterworths.

Websites

ASATA: www.asata.co.za

DEAT: www.environment.gov.za

dti: www.thedti.gov.za

FEDHASA: www.fedhasa.co.za

South African legislation: www.polity.org.za/pol/acts

References

Buys, R. 2004. *Cyberlaw@SA II,* 2nd edition. Tshwane: Van Schaik Publishers.

Carnelley, M. 2002. Attractions law. In P. Vrancken (Ed.). *Tourism and the law in South Africa.* Port Elizabeth: Butterworths.

Forsyth, C. F. 2003. *Private international law,* 4th edition. Cape Town: Juta.

Le Roux, L. 2002. Business entities. In P. Vrancken (Ed.). *Tourism and the law in South Africa.* Port Elizabeth: Butterworths.

Mukheibir, A. 2002. Law of contract and delict. In P. Vrancken (Ed.). *Tourism and the law in South Africa.* Port Elizabeth: Butterworths.

Vercuil, M. & Fourie, R. 2002. Labour law. In P. Vrancken (Ed.). *Tourism and the law in South Africa.* Port Elizabeth: Butterworths.

Vrancken, P. 2000. The national legal framework of tourism: past, present and future. *Stellenbosch Law Review,* Vol. 11(1), 85–98.

Vrancken, P. 2001. Package travel, holidays and tours in the European Union. *Obiter,* Vol. 22(2), 300–311.

Vrancken, P. (Ed.). 2002. *Tourism and the law in South Africa.* Port Elizabeth: Butterworths.

Vrancken, P. 2006. New Mpumalanga tourism legislation. *Obiter,* Vol. 27(2), 351–357.

Woker, T. 2002. Insurance Law. In P. Vrancken (Ed.). *Tourism and the law in South Africa.* Port Elizabeth: Butterworths.

Case study

13

Masters v Thain t/a Inhaca Safaris (2000 1 SA 467 W)

Objectives

- to apply the legal principles regulating tourism activities
- to apprecite the complexity of legal issues and the need to obtain expert legal advice

In this case, the travel agent specialised in arranging tours to, and holidays on, the Mozambican island of Inhaca. The tourist, who lived in Johannesburg, paid the travel agent for a 10-day holiday, commencing on 29 March 1996, on Inhaca. The only reason why the tourist took his family to Inhaca was that he and his daughter would be able to do some scuba-diving. His wife accompanied them, but did not intend doing any scuba diving. The tourist made this clear when he made his travel and hotel reservations with the travel agent. This was, in other words, a family holiday – which the tourist would not have contemplated, let alone undertaken, if he had known that he would not be able to partake in his favourite hobby, and the travel agent knew this.

The cost of the holiday amounted to R15 245, and included business-class airfares, transfers to and from the island of Inhaca, as well as hotel accommodation. The tourist and his family flew business class because it was cheaper than flying economy class and having to pay extra for their scuba-diving gear. The amount did not include the cost of scuba-diving. The tourist was informed that, once on the island, he would have to pay around R140 for each dive, and he was happy with that. Once the tourist arrived on Inhaca, he attempted to find a boat to take him and his daughter out to sea for them to do some scuba-diving. He then discovered that there were no boats available and that, for the whole duration of his stay at Inhaca, there would not be any boats available at the price quoted by the travel agent. Other, more expensive, boats were available for around R800 per dive, but the tourist refused to pay such a high price compared to the R140 he had been quoted by the travel agent.

The tourist did not adopt a complacent attitude and accept less that he had contracted for. The very first evening that he and his family arrived on the island, he immediately telephoned the travel agent to complain about the absence of scuba-diving facilities. He also instructed the travel agent to get him and his family back to Johannesburg as soon as possible. The travel agent agreed to do so. The first SAA flight back to South Africa was, however, fully booked. For that reason, the travel agent suggested that the tourist and his family should return anyway to the airport in Maputo so that, if they were indeed unable to get on the SAA flight, they could try to get on the LAM flight later in the evening. This did not work out. In fact, the tourist and his family had to spend four more nights on the island before they were able to return to Johannesburg.

The tourist asked the court to order the travel agent to reimburse the R15 245 that he had paid for the holiday. The travel agent pointed out that there were boats available, and that the tourist and his family had actually spent four nights on the island. The court granted the order requested by the tourist, and also ordered the travel agent to pay the legal costs.

Case study questions

1. Discuss to which extent the court's decision could or should have been different if the travel agent had not known the tourist's purpose when he bought the holiday.

2. Explain why the court's decision would have been different if the tourist had not immediately complained to the travel agent.

3. Assess how different the legal position of the tourist would have been if he had made all the necessary arrangements for his airfares, transfers, and accommodation on the Internet directly with the relevant tourism businesses.

14

Marketing for tourism

Richard George

Purpose

This chapter examines the main aspects of marketing as a management function for tourism businesses.

Learning outcomes

After reading this chapter, you should be able to:
- explain what is meant by marketing
- appreciate the characteristics of services and the implication of these for tourism marketers
- understand consumer buying behaviour in tourism
- explain the concept of tourism market segmentation
- identify the components of the tourism marketing mix
- appreciate the importance of customer relationship management and marketing research in tourism marketing
- understand the stages of the tourism marketing planning process.

Chapter overview

In this chapter we explore the role of marketing as a management function for tourism businesses.

Marketing is regarded as a core business function, concerned with matching offerings with the needs and interests of its potential and existing customers.

The chapter begins with an explanation of how tourism is part of the services sector, and requires different marketing approaches to those carried out in other industries, such as manufacturing. It then discusses consumer behaviour – why people choose to travel and select certain tourism offerings – which lies at the core of tourism marketing. One of the main principles of marketing, the concept of market segmentation, is also considered. We address the elements of the marketing mix that involve the key decisions in relation to the 'four Ps': product development, pricing decisions, appropriate distribution, and promotional methods. We also examine several tourism marketing approaches, such as customer relationship management (CRM) and tourism marketing research. Finally, we briefly outline the key stages involved in planning marketing in tourism and identify the content of a marketing plan.

The concluding case study illustrates how the theory contained in this chapter can be applied to a practical situation relating to the marketing of tourism in South Africa.

Introduction

A single chapter in a book such as this can provide only a flavour of the marketing discipline as it is applied to tourism. Marketing offers the tourism business manager a way of communicating the offering to the marketplace. All tourism businesses – from small guesthouses to multi-national tour operators with their own marketing departments – market themselves in one way or another. That said, the structures and style of managing marketing differ. For example, a small, medium and micro enterprise (SMME) may have no written marketing plan (unless a loan from the bank is required), while a multi-national corporation (MNC) may have written **strategic marketing** plans by brand, product-offering, or target market.

Marketing represents a business function which utilises a set of principles. It is not a discipline in its own right, but rather uses disciplines such as economics, sociology, and psychology. Marketing is a field of enquiry of business studies. While many of the principles were developed originally in North America and Europe for selling manufactured goods, they are now being practised all around the world in other service industries as well.

> **TO DO**
>
> How would you define marketing? You can do a Google search on the Internet for the words 'marketing', 'academic', and 'definition', or consult a dictionary and look up the word 'marketing'. Write down the key aspects of marketing and what you think it entails.

What is marketing?

What, then, do we mean by **marketing**? Usually one thinks of advertising or brochures. While these are the visible aspects of marketing, there is more to marketing than advertising and brochures (referred to as marketing collateral). Marketing is a whole range of activities designed to identify and satisfy customers. According to Kotler, Bowen, & Makens: 'marketing is a process whereby individuals and groups obtain the type of products or services they value' (2003: 13). These goods are created and exchanged through a process that requires a detailed understanding of consumers and their wants and desires, so that the product or service (offering) is effectively and efficiently delivered to the client or buyer.

Marketing is not a one-off activity to be used to solve business problems. It is a systematic process, and should be part of a tourism organisation's everyday business activities. The most important thing about marketing is that it needs to be practised correctly. It forces an organisation to identify and respond to customers' needs in a way which builds loyalty and, hence, profitability.

Tourism marketing managers face challenges in marketing a business that is essentially based on the provision of services, rather than physical goods. In the next section, we will examine the service nature of tourism businesses and the implications this has for the tourism manager.

Tourism marketing has been carried out for many years in South Africa

The service nature of tourism businesses

Before we look at some of the core principles of tourism marketing, we first need to understand the service nature of tourism businesses. Tourism is, after all, very much part of the **services sector** industry. Managers need to understand the unique service nature of tourism businesses. It is this unique quality which influences the management of tourism. The important characteristics that distinguish goods from services include **intangibility**, **inseparability**, variability, and **perishability**. The four characteristics have resulted in tourism marketers incorporating the additional three Ps of physical evidence, people, and processes into their marketing mix.

The four service characteristics are discussed in more detail below.

Intangibility

The essential difference between goods and services is that goods are produced, whereas services are performed (Rathmell, 1966: 32). A motor car can be taken for a test drive, clothes can be fitted, and a CD may be played in the store. Tourism offerings, however, cannot be assessed or touched prior to purchase. Someone considering purchasing a holiday can only imagine what the holiday on offer will be like, helped by holiday brochures and/or media images. The customer is likely to assess the different holiday destinations in brochures, websites, postcards, photographs, or in the media – comparing the descriptions of resorts, hotels, activities and tours. Money is paid weeks in advance, and the customer will not be able to find out if it is satisfactory until he/she arrives at the destination. Buying a tourism offering inevitably presents risk and uncertainty in the purchase decision-making process for the customer (discussed in the next section). One of the key functions of tourism marketing is to attempt to create a perception of tangibility for the offering in the mind of the consumer by communicating its benefits through promotion, branding, and quality customer service delivery.

Inseparability

Tourism offerings are sold first, and are then produced and consumed at the same time. This is referred to as 'simultaneous production and consumption'. Until the consumer uses the offering, the offering does not actually exist. In the case of a flight, for example, the passenger 'consumes' the service provided at the time of provision.

The consumer also has to interact with the service provider, or destination, in order to experience the offering. As a result, the customer participates in the service production process. Furthermore, as most tourism services involve more than one customer, other customers are involved in the service process. For example, tourists interact with each other while on a township tour. These encounters could enhance or detract from the overall quality of the tour experience. The challenge in this case is for the tour operator to live up to the promises made in the tour brochure, or from word-of-mouth recommendations.

Variability

Tourism is a people industry. Each experience relies on human interaction between customers and employees, so that each encounter is unique. Because a tourism offering is not an object, but rather an experience, each and every customer is likely to perceive it differently. For example, what one customer may perceive as fast, excellent, and professional service, another may interpret as rather mediocre. The **heterogeneous** nature of tourism offerings means that they cannot be standardised. Customers are actively involved in the delivery of an offering. The challenge for tourism managers is to manage the service encounter between staff and customers, to ensure that satisfied customers will use a tourism business again, or recommend it to friends, relatives, and colleagues. Thus, all staff involved in the service encounter (from boardroom executives to receptionists) work as 'marketers' for the tourism business. To reduce the problems that can be associated with **variability**, there is a need for tourism businesses to invest in quality customer service (QCS) training programmes for all staff. This includes staff of the tourism organisation as well as staff at the main points of traveller interaction; i.e. tourism information centres, petrol stations, grocery stores, chemists, on so on.

Perishability

Tourism offerings cannot be stored for sale at a later date. Unused bed spaces, empty seats on aircraft, or places on tours cannot be stored for sale later, and result in lost revenues. This presents challenges in forecasting and the impacts of seasonality, special events, and external events for tourism managers. They therefore have to devise complex pricing structures and promotional polices in an attempt to synchronise supply and demand. During the high season hotels, airlines, visitor attractions, etc. cope with peak demand by charging higher premium prices, or use queueing as a control mechanism. During quiet periods, however, there is a need for greater promotional activities. The impact on the quality of customer experience and operations as a result of uneven demand is an additional challenge. Visiting a museum on a busy day, for example, may mean waiting in long queues, whereas on a quiet day there may be no queues, but equally not much of an atmosphere.

TO DO

Relate the four characteristics of services marketing to the purchase of a holiday.

Now that we have we examined the service characteristics of tourism offerings, our attention turns to the issue of consumer behaviour.

Understanding consumer buying behaviour in tourism

At the core of tourism marketing is an understanding of individual consumer behaviour; that is, understanding the way in which consumers make decisions and behave in relation to the consumption of offerings.

The main aspects of consumer behaviour involve an understanding of *why* people buy holidays (motivation), *how* people go about selecting their holidays (the decision-making process), and *who* the consumers are (tourism market segments). By understanding its buyers and their decision-making processes, a tourism business can develop an offering which is appropriate, accessible, and attractive to customers, and at a price they are willing to pay. In essence, an organisation is better equipped to communicate through relevant channels to reach its desired market segments.

Tourist motivation

Firstly, a tourism manager needs to understand why consumers buy the holidays they take; in other words, what motivates people to choose particular tourism offerings and destinations. **Motivation** and purpose of trip and are closely linked, and in Chapter 1 we classified tourists into three broad categories: business, leisure, and other purposes (i.e. health, education, or religion). However, simply categorising tourists in this way only helps us understand their general motivation for travelling; it tells us very little about their specific motivation.

'Motivation' is derived from the word 'motivate', which is concerned with what causes a person to act in a certain way, or the stimulation of an interest (Pearsall, 1999: 928). There have been numerous studies on how motivation influences tourists' consumer behaviour. Many of these have utilised general motivational theories, such as that of Maslow (1958). Maslow proposed a hierarchy of individual needs, expressed as a pyramid. At the base of Maslow's (1978) pyramid are the basic physical needs for food, water, rest, and shelter that are necessary for survival. Maslow argued that these fundamental needs, along with the next layer of security and safety needs, must be satisfied on a reasonably regular basis before people will focus on higher-level needs such as the need for self-esteem and status. The implication of this for the tourism manager would be the need for him/her to appeal to consumers with higher-level needs, such as status. The most sophisticated level of needs is the need for self-development ('self-actualisation' in Maslow's terms). Self-development means an individual's striving for personal fulfilment (or growth) of his or her potential.

According to Middleton and Clarke (2001: 78), those most likely to travel are also most likely to be in the position to focus on their own self-development, something which many people associate with quality of life. The need for self-actualisation can be achieved in a number of ways, ranging from a desire to 'commune with nature' (achieved, for example, by going on scenic trips or on holidays) to the 'quest for knowledge' (i.e. cultural tours) and 'do-it-yourself' (i.e. farming getaway-weekends) holidays. Holloway asserts that, as people travel more and become more sophisticated or better educated, their higher-level needs predominate in their motivation for a particular holiday (2006: 71). Tourism managers need to recognise this, and to take it into account when developing new offerings for tourists.

Purchase decision-making processes

As well as understanding why tourists make decisions, it is also important to examine how tourists decide to buy specific offerings. Page (2003: 63) identified the following factors as key influencers on the decision to purchase tourism offerings:

- Personality of the buyer
- The point of purchase
- The role of the sales person
- Whether the individual is a frequent or infrequent buyer of holiday offerings
- Prior (buying) experience.

There are two types of factors that influence buying behaviour in tourism: personal and social. Each type involves its own complex series of factors affecting individual consumer buying decisions as to tourism offerings. For example, buyers are also heavily influenced by *peer groups* as well as *reference groups*. In the former, consumers may make choices based on those of whom they wish to emulate, such as those of immediate friends, work colleagues, fellow students, or others they come into regular contact with (even on television). In the case of the latter, the influence of 'celebrities' is becoming increasingly paramount, as the holiday choices and behaviour of TV and movie personalities increasingly influence buying patterns.

Market segmentation, targeting & positioning

Identifying market segments

After understanding why and how tourism customers make decisions, tourism businesses need to identify them. This involves dividing the overall **market** into segments or groups of customers who are sufficiently alike, so that they can be targeted. The main benefits of **market segmentation** are that it allows a company, regardless of size, to maximise its available budgets by specialising in and targeting small markets, and it enables the company to tailor its offerings to the specific needs of their market segment.

Before embarking on a segmentation exercise, it is important to make sure that the potential market segment is:

- substantial enough to warrant a separate marketing effort
- measurable in terms or purchasing power and size
- accessible – the company should be able to market to it and serve it effectively.

One of the most widely used and basic ways in which markets are segmented is by *socio-economic* or *demographic segmentation* – for example, by age, gender, educational background, income, occupation, and location. For example, the type of holiday chosen is likely to differ greatly between 20- and 30-year-olds, and 60- and 70-year-olds. These factors are important to tourism business managers, so that they can provide specific offerings that appeal to each market segment. This socio-economic and **demographic** information can be obtained from market research surveys and census statistics (i.e. Mintel reports, StatsSA).

Segmenting markets using socio-economic or demographic data, however, is considered too simplistic, as individual tastes and previous experiences within segments are likely to be very different. Furthermore, consumers' motives for undertaking travel to tourist destinations within segments will differ.

A more sophisticated way of segmenting the market is *psychographic* (or *lifestyle*) segmentation, which is often used to complement socio-economic and demographic data. With this approach, variables related to consumers' lifestyles (e.g. their interests, hobbies, and spending patterns), as well as their attitudes, opinions, and feelings towards travel are used to predict consumer buying behaviour. This more complex information can be gathered from field (or primary) marketing research sources such as **focus groups** and customer surveys, and from desk research, such as customer records, commercially-produced market research surveys, and other companies' mailing lists. This data helps marketers understand consumers' motivations to make decisions to buy certain types of tourism offerings. An example of psychographic segmentation is a specialised offering (or niche tourism) such as cruise holidays, using segmentation variables such as age profile of cruise tourists, how they book their holidays, and their motivations for taking a cruise.

Another way of segmenting the marketing is based on *transaction history and buying behaviour*. This technique tracks and analyses the purchase behaviour of customers. This information may be derived from in-house, such as payment records, customer/guest registration cards, and customer service surveys. For example, guest registration cards contain important information such as date and length of stay, rate paid, number of guests in the party, and contact information (such as email address, post code, etc.). This data, combined with periodic customer surveys, can be transformed into crucial marketing information. Table 14.1 displays the most common variables for consumer segmentation.

www

Browse this website: dmasa.org

DIRECT MARKETING ASSOCIATION OF SA

The Direct Marketing Association's (DMASA) logo

Table 14.1 Common variables for consumer segmentation

Variable	Typical classification
Geographic	Groups customers based on geographical area such as country, urban, suburban, city, postal code, climate.
Socio-demographic	Based on age, gender, income, family size, family life-cycle (single, married, etc.), occupation, education level, social class.
Psychographic	Based on people's special-interest and common lifestyle traits, as well as personality type.
Transactional history/buying behaviour	Based on the purchase behaviour of customers, including where and when they buy, how often, how much they spend, how purchases are made (travel agent, Internet, telephone, etc.), who makes the buying decision, and who makes the purchase.

Targeting markets

Having recognised different segments of the market, the next stage is for the manager to decide how many and which segments to target. Marketing targeting involves evaluating each segment's attractiveness (i.e. their size, growth rate, etc.) and selecting one or more of the market segments. There are three widely-used targeting approaches: **niche marketing**, differentiated, and undifferentiated.

- *Niche marketing* entails targeting small sections of a market, each with clearly defined characteristics, rather than trying to cover it all. In tourism, niche marketing can be a very effective strategy, since consumers are often willing to pay a premium for a more exclusive offering, for example, a cruise to Namibia (see Example box overleaf).
- *Differentiated marketing* involves selecting market segments to target, and designing different strategies to reach each segment selected.

- *Undifferentiated marketing* involves communicating to the mass market with one product-offering.

Markets are then targeted by selecting communication channels that will reach the identified segments, for example, the media – such as in special-interest magazine advertising. In turn, the appropriate magazine needs to be identified to make sure that it is read by the correct market segments (this data can be obtained from sources such as the South African Advertising Research Foundation's (SAARF) All Media Product Survey (AMPS). AMPS contains audience data on all types of electronic and printed media, and consumption figures for selected products and services.

Example Niche tourism markets

- Adventure/Agricultural/Alternative/Ancestry/Architectural/Artic & Antarctic tourism
- Backpacker/Beach/Benefit/Birding/Budget tourism
- Cycle tourism
- City/Charity/Clubbing/Cosmetic/Cruise/Culinary/Cultural/Cycling tourism
- Dark/Defence/Desert/Disabled/Disaster tourism
- Eco/Education/Elephant-back/Ethical/Ethnic/Extreme tourism
- Family/Farm/Film/Food tourism
- Gastronomy/Gay/Genealogy/Geotourism/Green/Grey tourism
- Health/Hedonistic/Heritage tourism
- Indigenous/Industrial tourism
- Jazz tourism/Jungle tourism
- Lake/Life-seeing/Lighthouse/Literary tourism
- Marine/Medical/Military/Moral tourism
- Nature-based tourism
- Off-beat tourism
- Party/Pink/Photographic/Poverty/Property tourism
- Railway/Rehab/Religious/Research/Road/Rural tourism
- Senior/Sex/Shock/Shopping/Social/Spa/Space/Spiritual/Sports/Struggle/Surfing/Sustainable
- Township/Transplant/Transport/Tribal tourism
- Urban/Underwater tourism
- Veteran/VFR/Volunteer/Virtual tourism
- Wellness/Wedding/Wildlife/Wine tourism

Market positioning

After the market has been divided and targeted, the tourism offering needs to be positioned for the target audience. Market **positioning** involves identifying the offering's **unique selling points** (USPs) upon which to gain a position in the marketplace. These USPs form part of the messages which are communicated to the organisation's targeted segments.

Blending the marketing mix

The **marketing mix** is one of the fundamental tools in marketing. Otherwise known as the 'four Ps', the marketing mix refers to the different elements that a tourism business can use to communicate with its target market. In other words, the '4 Ps' are the factors that need to be 'mixed' to enable a tourism business to achieve its marketing objectives.

These four P's – product, price, place, and promotion (McCarthy, 1960) – make up the traditional marketing mix. These elements form the core decision variables in any marketing text, and are located at the heart of a marketing plan. The theory of the marketing mix is that all the elements can be controlled by the marketer to some extent, and that they are related to one another. Regarding the latter point, it is important that the marketing mix elements are not conducted in isolation without cross-checking other elements on which they might impact. For example, a tour-operating business might launch an advertising campaign without distribution (place) having been finalised. The result is that consumers telephone a travel agency to book a holiday they have seen advertised, only to find it is not yet in the system.

Tourism marketing involves finding out what tourists want (marketing research), developing suitable offerings (product-offering development), telling them what is available (promotions), and providing instructions as to where they can buy the offerings (place), so they in turn receive value (pricing), and the tourism organisation makes money. Much of an organisation's marketing effort is made up of the design, implementation, and evaluation of these four Ps (see Figure 14.1).

Figure 14.1 The traditional marketing mix

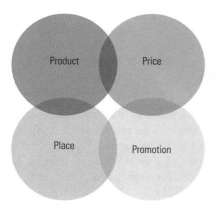

Product (offering)

In marketing, product refers to both goods and services. Throughout this book the term 'offering' has been used to denote both service and product aspects. Tourism experiences are often described as a mix or an amalgam of offerings.

There are two concepts or 'tools' in relation to the product-offering element of the marketing mix: the PLC and Branding.

The Product life-cycle (PLC) model

Product-offerings move through the **product life-cycle** (PLC) model, a framework which is useful to managers to assess their development. The PLC concept suggests that offerings have a limited life, during which they pass through four stages:

- Introduction – new to the market, will be purchased by 'innovators'
- Growth – sales increase
- Maturity – profits and sales growth slow down
- Decline – a decline in sales and profits.

At an individual product-offering level, the PLC is a useful tool in product-offering planning, since it can show peaks and troughs in sales performance, thereby giving pointers to possible new product-offering development and promotional opportunities. The concept does, however, have limitations for tourism marketing over and above those for consumer goods marketing. First, it cannot be used to forecast future developments;

for example, to predict when an offering will move from stage to stage. The PLC should, therefore, be seen as a diagnostic tool that can assist in making marketing mix decisions for different stages of an offering's life-cycle. Second, it is difficult to obtain accurate sales data, and this makes it unclear as to which life-cycle stage the offering is in.

Tourism managers need to think about replacing those offerings which have reached the end of their life-cycle with new ones. When developing and providing new offerings, managers need to be aware of the specific offering characteristics which might encourage customers to buy a specific offering. Offering characteristics are the specific features of an offering that customers see as being important – the features that attract them to buy or use it. Offerings need to be constantly adapted and devised to ensure that they continue to meet customers' needs. Marketing managers must identify gaps in the market where new offerings might be developed.

Branding

One of the main aspects of product-offering management is branding. **Branding** was first used as a marketing tool by tourism organisations such as Thomas Cook, who, back in the 1930s, launched one of the first international package tours to the south of France (see Chapter 2 – History of tourism). Branding is the practice of giving a product-offering a distinctive name, in the hope that it will be become more identifiable than its competitors, and take on an identity of its own. It involves the use of words (names and slogans) and symbols (logos and design) to represent the **image** of an offering and the benefits it offers to customers. Moreover, a brand is defined as 'a product or service made distinctive by its positioning relative to the competition, and by its personality in the context of the target market' (Hankinson & Cowking, 1993: 33). Branding is, therefore, closely linked to the concept of market segmentation discussed in the last section, with brands being developed to meet the needs of different segments of the market, but branding for tourism businesses offers several advantages, including:

- countering the effects of intangibility and variability
- establishing customer awareness and loyalty
- differentiating product-offerings
- targeting specific market segments in order to achieve a higher brand share.

For example, tour operators have well-established lifestyle brands for particular niche tourism markets (see Example box). Contiki Tours (for students), Saga (for mature travellers), or Sandals (aimed at couples) communicate to distinct and identifiable stages of the consumer life-cycle.

The concept of branding offerings has become a powerful marketing tool in tourism. One of the most noticeable differences between multinational corporations (MNCs) and SMMEs, however, is their ability to develop a strong brand image.Indeed, some of the most successful brands in tourism are corporate brands, whereby the value of the brand focuses on the organisation's corporate image, rather than on individual offerings. In this way both tour operators and hotel groups are usually differentiated on the basis of their corporate name and reputation, rather than on the specific services which they offer.

The concept of branding can also be applied to tourist destinations. There are however, problems with treating destinations as brands. Firstly, a destination is a multi-faceted composite, featuring many brands. For example, South Africa has many brands: Nelson Mandela, Table Mountain, the Big Five, and so on. Second, branding involves marketing different offerings to particular market segments (adventure tourists, business travellers, etc.), whereas destination marketers must market a destination to many different types of consumers, often through a single promotional campaign. Furthermore, as Pritchard and Morgan (1998: 217) note, destination marketers face unique challenges in branding initiatives: a lack of control over the total marketing mix, relatively limited budgets, and political considerations. See Chapter 8 – The government and tourism – for a more detailed discussion on destination marketing and branding.

Discussion point

Discuss why the branding of destinations is problematic.

Pricing

Once a tourism business has identified an offering, it must decide on the price at which it is going to be offered to its customers. Price is what a consumer must give up to obtain an offering. In reality, however, the term 'price' is seldom used in the tourism industry. More often terms such as rent (car hire), fare (rail journey), rate (tourist guide), or tariff (hotel) are used. Furthermore, not all tourism offerings carry a monetary price to the consumer. Museums; natural attractions, such as beaches and parks; shopping malls, or religious buildings may not charge a user fee. For most tourism businesses, getting pricing right is crucial.

Given the intangible nature of tourism offerings, customers often have few bases for evaluating one offering from another. Potential customers, therefore, often use price as an indicator of quality. It is also important to remember that customers not only give up money for using tourism offerings, but also non-monetary costs, such as time and search costs. In the case of the former, most offerings require participation of the consumer (inseparability), which may also involve waiting time. In the case of the latter, search costs include the effort invested in selecting the offering; for example, gathering information about holiday destinations. Tourism offering prices must therefore be set very carefully.

The art of successful pricing is to establish a price level which is sufficiently low so that an exchange represents good value to customers, yet is high enough to allow a tourism business to achieve its financial objectives. If an offering is priced too high, it will be seen as poor **value for money** (VFM) by customers, who will not buy it. On the other hand, if the price is too low, the offering may be perceived as inferior in quality. When using price to create demand, care must be taken to ensure that one does not create the wrong consumer perceptions about the offering's quality (see Example box). Over-pricing can lead to certain expectations not being met, and result in disappointed customers. Marketing managers need to attempt to create delight by offering the customer more than they expected.

Example Creating the wrong perceptions

A business person who has been under a lot of pressure decides to take a three-day holiday. She wants to stay in luxury accommodation, enjoy a spa, and receive exceptional food service. She is prepared to pay R700 a night for a room. She calls a hotel to hear that there is currently a special rate of R400. The hotel may be able to satisfy her needs, and has simply dropped its rate to encourage business. In this case, the hotel has dropped its rate too low to attract this customer. Because she has never visited the hotel before, she will perceive the hotel as being inferior in quality.

As we mentioned earlier, getting the price right is crucial for tourism businesses. It may well determine the financial success of a particular offering and, in part, the long-term success of tourism businesses. It is important that the tourism organisation conducts market research (for example, pricing surveys), to assess competitor prices and offerings in order to ensure desired positioning and choice of pricing strategy. There are several different pricing policies which can be implemented by tourism organisations:

Market-penetration pricing

This is usually used by tourism businesses wanting to get into a new market, in order to establish an offering. It might involve setting a lower price to attract new business or to undercut competition.

Competitive pricing

Often the prices charged by competitors will dictate what price an organisation can set for a particular offering (known as the 'going rate'). For example, B&Bs in a coastal resort will frequently charge very similar prices, since they know that to charge more would result in a loss of business.

Discount pricing

This pricing policy involves setting a reduced price for certain offerings. This type of pricing is widely used in the tourism industry, and includes numerous sales promotions and special offers such as 'two for the price of one', 10% off, and free child places.

Discretionary pricing

Tourism businesses can alter prices by market segment (customer type), time, or place of purchase. For example, visitor attractions may charge lower prices for early bookings, or lower entrance fees according to student, local resident, or pensioner status.

Market-skimming pricing

For certain tourism offerings, customers may be prepared to pay high prices for the quality offered and the status associated with using them. Tourism businesses such as upmarket game lodges (e.g. Singita) and luxury trains (e.g. The Blue Train) often adopt high price strategies to retain their exclusivity, status, and quality image.

For many larger tourism businesses, the combination of pricing policies can result in very complex pricing structures. A typical airline company, for example, will have literally hundreds of different prices, and each person on a given flight may have paid a different seat price to everyone else!

Place (distribution)

The perishable nature of tourism offerings makes distribution decisions critical to the success of tourism businesses. In recent years, technological advancements have changed the distribution options available to tourism businesses. Tourism businesses can choose to sell directly to customers (using the Internet and other forms of information and communication technologies – ICT) or indirectly, using intermediaries such as tour operators, travel agencies, TICs, sales representatives, and so on.

Tourism managers must choose the intermediary that most effectively reaches their target markets. Care must be taken when selecting intermediaries, as their direct contact with the consumer means they can influence levels of quality and satisfaction. The choice of intermediary also depends on the size and type of the organisation. A large organisation such as Sun International Hotels uses several distribution channels to reach different target markets. A small guest house, on the other hand, deals directly with consumers; many of whom will purchase at the location of the business or make enquiries, payment, and booking via the company website. The three factors which may influence a tourism organisation's intermediary selection are cost, control, and level of service (Holloway, 2004: 130–132). Chapter 7 – Managing tourism distribution – examines the role of tourism marketing distribution in more detail.

Promotion

'Promotion' means to advance or encourage something. Promotion is one of the main marketing functions for a tourism business. The intangibility of tourism offerings, which often means high-risk purchases for consumers, implies that promotion, however, due to its intangibility, means that it is also easy and tempting for tourism businesses to over-promise in tourism advertisements (they promote what cannot be delivered). Through the Promotional (or Communications) Strategy, the tourism marketer will identify channels in which to communicate to the identified target market segments.

The AIDA (Attention, Interest, Desire, Action) principle should be followed when carrying out any promotional activity – whether it be designing an advertisement, writing a direct mail letter, designing a brochure, or selecting promotional sales tools. If we take the example of designing a newspaper advertisement for a newly-opened visitor attraction, AIDA could be used as follows:

- **Attention** is achieved by getting the attention of potential customers
- **Interest** is generated by using colour and bold headlines
- **Desire** to visit the attraction is created by offering a discount voucher with the advertisement
- **Action** is triggered by clearly stating the opening times, including directions to get there, address, telephone number, e-mail address, and/or the website address for enquiries.

There are a number of different tools (referred to as the 'promotional mix elements') that can be used to promote tourism offerings, including advertising, public relations (including sponsorship, publicity and crisis management), marketing collateral (including brochures, business cards), sales promotions (including merchandising, point-of-sale), personal selling (face-to-face), direct marketing (including direct mail, telemarketing, and door-to-door distribution), networking, and exhibitions and trade shows. We will now examine some of these promotional mix tools in more detail.

Advertising (Above-the-line advertising)

People dream about visiting foreign countries. The job of your advertising is to convert their dreams into action.
– David Ogilvy

Advertising is the space or time in a medium such as a publication or on television which usually aims to persuade consumers to buy an offering. The role of advertising is to develop awareness, understanding, interest, and motivation amongst a targeted audience (Middleton & Clarke, 2001: 235). Remember that you will need a substantial budget to implement a successful advertising campaign.

Strategic media placement is the way to target certain identified segments. All Media Product Survey (AMPS) statistics are available on all media vehicles. For example, if you have a sports tourism offering that you would like to promote, first you will have to decide between domestic, international, or both; then you select the provinces and/or countries, then the media (i.e. the sports section of national newspapers, sports magazines, TV sports programme time slots, etc).

Advertising can be carried out by means of a variety of media, including:

Newspapers and magazines

Sunday travel supplement advertising is one of the most effective media for promoting both tour operators' and travel agents' offerings. National press advertisements are less expensive than other forms of mass media, such as TV advertising, and large national audiences can be reached. Furthermore, readers tend to have a travel-shopping mindset, and are looking for special offers.

Travel magazine advertising is an excellent medium for most tourism brands. It provides very good reproduction quality in full colour, and is an exceptional medium to 'tangibilise' the offering. Advertising in travel trade magazines should generally feature plenty of factual information to educate travel agents and other intermediaries about the organisation's offerings. Advertisements in local newspapers are very flexible – advertisements can be changed at relatively short notice, while the advertising message can be read at leisure, re-read, or even cut out and kept for future use.

Radio

This is a powerful tool to promote offerings to the local population. It is less expensive than TV advertising, and has the advantage that dialogue and sound effects can be used. Radio advertising is an effective way of promoting specific offerings and local events, particularly when it can be linked to PR activities such as live radio coverage of an event. Radio is also reasonably inexpensive, and costs can often be negotiated.

Outdoor

The use of posters is the oldest form of advertising. Posters can be displayed on bus shelters, on transport such as taxis, at sport stadia or on the walls of the tourism business's premises. One of the advantages of this type of advertising is that readers generally have time to read the advertising copy. Billboards are an excellent medium for tourism offerings. They can be used to dramatise offerings and, due to their size, allow for spectacular visuals. Another example of an effective outdoor advertising vehicle used in tourism marketing is sandwich boards.

TV

The main advantage of television is that is 'tangibilises' the tourism offering – it shows it in operation. In addition, the use of music, dialogue, personalities, colour, special effects, and animation can help make an effective visual impact on a mass audience. For most tourism businesses, the biggest disadvantage of TV advertising is the expense.

Public relations (PR)

Public relations (PR) is defined as all the activities designed to build and maintain mutual understanding between a tourism company and its publics (French, 1994: 1). The last word in this definition is used in the plural sense, since a company has to deal with a wide range of people while carrying out its business, including customers, suppliers, government organisations, communities, stakeholders, employees, and the press.

PR can be the most powerful, valuable, and cost-effective tool in the tourism marketer's armoury. This is largely due to the fact that tourism is perhaps more newsworthy than many other sectors. PR is generally used for generating awareness, building recognition, and creating a favourable image. For many new organisations and their offerings, it is publicity that creates the launch, not advertising. One of the main advantages of PR is that other people speak about your organisation and brand, thus giving it more credibility than advertising. Furthermore, unlike advertising, PR is usually expensive. Not all tourism organisations can afford an advertising budget, but most can afford some degree of PR. If tourism managers can devise some unique, different, or newsworthy information about their offering, organisation, or brand, media coverage will be easy to find.

Media relations is one of the main PR tools used by tourism businesses, and includes the writing of press releases and the preparation of press packs. The press release (or news release) is a written document that is used to communicate newsworthy information to the media. Press releases are sent to the media via e-mail, fax, or commercial newswire distribution. Press packs (or press kits) contain all the information that a writer needs to cover a story, such as releases, company fact sheets, brochures, a CD, biographies, etc.

Chapter 1 noted tourism's susceptibility to external events (ranging from product defects such as outdated lifts in older hotels, to on-location accidents, safety and security issues, and natural disasters). As a result, the PR activity of crisis management (also referred to as 'crisis communications') is especially important in tourism businesses. The potential for damage to corporate image and reputation by crisis situations requires skills training and professional management to be in place to deal with events that inevitably occur from time to time (see Example box).

Example 10 key points for handling crisis situations

There are 10 key points for handling a crisis situation:
1. Have a crisis plan in place before disaster strikes.
2. React immediately. Don't let rumours gain momentum.
3. Don't avoid the media in a crisis situation. If they don't get the information from you, they will get it from somewhere else.
4. Gather the facts. Try to respond with as many facts as are possible.

5. Be honest. Admitting responsibility will not make you appear weak. Trying to shift the blame will make you appear as if you're trying to avoid responsibility.
6. Turn negative into positive. If your company made a mistake, admit it, and then immediately focus on how it will remedy the situation.
7. Guide your responses by long-term perception objectives.
8. Demonstrate genuine care and compassion.
9. If you don't have an answer, say so, and then look for it. Never say 'no comment.'
10. In a time of crisis, you are the organisation. Stick with the facts, and don't offer personal opinions.

Besides the PR activities mentioned above, the following PR tactics can help tourism businesses generate publicity and awareness:

Networking

Networking (or 'Notworking', as it is sometimes called!) is the art of mingling with potential customers and other tourism providers at an event. You should be sure to be active in your community by attending all tourism offering-related launches, local business clubs, tourism industry forums, tourism industry association meetings, talks, and conferences. You should also consider attending local tourism organisation (LTO) and regional tourism organisation (RTO) meetings, and your business should be listed on a provincial tourism authority (PTA) and/or a RTO's database to ensure invitations. Networking with other tourism professionals is an excellent way of obtaining information that can result in new marketing strategies.

Attending travel trade shows

Travel **trade shows** are usually targeted at the trade, while some also aim at consumers. Some travel trade shows are general leisure trade shows, others specialise in adventure, backpacking, business tourism, luxury travel, etc. The biggest travel trade show in Africa is the Tourism Indaba, which is held annually in May. The International

Travel Exchange (ITB) in Berlin and the World Travel Market (WTM) in London are examples of premier annual international travel trade shows. For smaller tourism businesses, there is a trend towards shared or 'umbrella' stands, where they may achieve their objectives under a collective banner provided, for example, by a destination marketing organisation (DMO) (see Example box). Make sure that you only participate in the trade shows that are appropriate for your offering and which attract a targeted audience, as they can be quite costly if you hand out brochures to the wrong audience. To benefit more effectively from tourism trade shows, small businesses can attend them under the banner of the destination in which they are located, or as representatives of an association to which they belong. In this way they still get some exposure, but at a greatly reduced cost.

Memberships

Taking out memberships should also be part of a tourism business's networking strategy. Tourism managers need to make an effort to speak to people, tell them about what they do, and stay in touch with them. In particular, it is important for you to get to know tourism stakeholders in your local area. You can do this by taking out memberships of the various relevant tourism and business associations in your area.

Taking out memberships of appropriate tourism associations will also entitle a tourism business to certain benefits. Some of the associations provide discounted advertising for members, or put together annual membership books that will help to market the business, while others secure discounted insurance cover.

Other associations include local tourism authorities and sectoral organisations (or trade associations), such as Southern African Tourism Services Association (SATSA) and Backpacking South Africa (BSA). See Chapter 8 – The government and tourism – for a comprehensive list of South African tourism sectoral organisations.

Sending out newsletters

This is an excellent format to keep interested industry media and travel agents updated about news, as well as information about your organisation. The newsletter should be professionally designed and written, contain real news and updates, and be sent only to those who are interested. Newsletters can be delivered inexpensively via e-mail. However, e-mail newsletters should not be sent out too frequently, otherwise they will be perceived as junk mail.

Familiarisation trips

Familiarisation trips (or 'fam trips'; educational trips) are an excellent marketing tool for reaching travel agents and other publics such as journalists, TV crews, and trade delegates. Fam trips enable agents to actually sample the facility, offering, and destination. Innovative and effective fam trips include an activity programme, ranging from a welcome greeting through to sending out follow-up mail.

P   R   I   S   A
**PUBLIC RELATIONS &
COMMUNICATION MANAGEMENT**

The Public Relations Institute of South Africa's (PRISA) logo

www

Browse this website: www.prisa.co.za

Printed literature/ Collateral materials

All tourism organisations, regardless of their type or size, need some type of collateral material to promote them. **Collateral materials** come in many forms, such as a simple black-and-white flier, a leaflet, a rack brochure, a multi-page colour brochure, a map, and a DVD. Brochures and leaflets can provide detailed information about an organisation, and can act as a booking mechanism. For example, for a visitor attraction, a brochure can be designed to enhance visitors' experience by providing information such as a map, a description of the local area, opening times, directions to get there, location of toilets, and so on. Brochures and literature can also double as purchasing mechanisms through tear-off booking forms. Chapter 7 – Managing tourism distribution – looks at the importance of the tour operator's brochure. A DVD is highly effective marketing collateral: it is unique, ensures an experience of a destination, entertainment value, and portrays reality. Other basic collateral pieces include fact sheets, postcards (effective as reminders or follow-up or introductory mail items), and videos.

Collateral materials usually provide the first point of contact with prospective consumers, so it is crucial that they convey the right image of your organisation and offerings. Remember – for collateral to work for your business, it needs to be strategically distributed.

Sales promotions and merchandising (Below-the-line advertising)

Sales promotions are a popular promotional tool, aimed at generating last-minute purchases or improving public perceptions. Most tourism offerings, including hotels, car rental companies, and destinations have an opportunity to organise promotions at the point of sale or on the premises. Indeed, the term *merchandising* is often used to specifically mean sales promotion at the point of sale (Middleton & Clarke, 2001: 257). The main types of sales promotions include price promotions, contests, sampling, product placements, and celebrity endorsements. Sales promotions should not happen on an *ad hoc* basis (i.e. let's run a competition), or as a substitute for advertising. They should be integrated into the overall marketing campaign, and assessed as to their likely impact on the brand and on sales.

The main targets for sales promotions include individual customers, distribution networks (such as travel agents), and sales forces. Typical sales promotion techniques used by tourism businesses are outlined in Table 14.2.

Direct Marketing

The main aspect of a direct marketing strategy is creating a database. There are several ways of creating a database, such as running a competition, website newsletter subscriptions, collecting business cards and contact information at trade shows, seminars and familiarisation trips, and keeping sales records of visitors. You should aim to build a profile of each customer or supplier, which includes contact details such as the consumer's e-mail and physical addresses, history of the transaction, the type of offering most booked, the destination, etc. The database can then be used for mailing anything from special offers to 'thank you' cards or other marketing collateral.

Personal Selling

As we discussed earlier in the chapter, one of the characteristics of tourism offerings is that they are inseparable; both the service provider and the consumer have to be present. **Personal selling** involves persuading consumers to buy offerings in a 'face-to-face' encounter, and must therefore

Table 14.2 Typical sales promotion techniques used by tourism businesses

Individual customers	Distribution networks	Sales force
• limited time price offers (i.e. book before this date/Winter Special) • vouchers/discount coupons • free gifts and incentives • special offers • extra products (i.e. a free bottle of wine) • competitions/contests • prize draws	• extra commission • prize draws • competitions • parties/receptions • free gifts	• bonuses and other incentives • gift incentives • travel incentives • prize draws

be seen as an important promotional tool for the tourism manager. Although the clear objective of any selling activity is to achieve a sale, it should be seen as one to be used at all times that can help cement customer relationships, build loyalty, and improve customer service delivery. Personal selling is the direct contact between buyer and seller, face-to-face, by telephone or through video conferencing. This tool differs from other promotional tools in that there is a personal interaction between two or more people. It is likely that all staff in your tourism organisation are involved in some form of 'selling' in the course of their work.

Internet marketing

The rapid increase in the use of the Internet has meant that many tourism businesses, regardless of their size or marketing budget, have realised the benefits of having an Internet presence. The Internet has significant advantages over traditional communication tools, and is an excellent sales and marketing tool. The main benefits of the Internet are as follows:

- it is flexible. Information on your website can be kept up-to-date
- it is interactive. It allows tourism businesses to communicate with their consumers, and online bookings can be made in 'real time'
- it is on-going. Your website is available '24/7'
- it is measurable. You can measure the number of consumers, click-throughs, responses to specials and promotions, etc.

The design of your website should be a part of an overall E-marketing (or Internet) strategy, and its content will depend on your objectives. Objectives might be to provide information, educate, process reservations, communicate with consumers, handle requests, or all of these. The website should be designed with the user in mind, and care should be taken not to have too many sections (menu items) on the website; if there are too many, it will appear cluttered. If you do a lot of business with travel agents, it is worth having a referral section on your site. Providing local weather information can be a good strategy for those companies dealing with overseas consumers and intermediaries.

Make sure that you do not overload website visitors with unnecessary information.

Your website needs to be managed and updated to keep it interesting, and to invite repeat visitors. A website can be kept up-to-date by making use of the latest software, which allows simple text and graphic changes to be made without the need for a webmaster.

E-mail marketing is an extremely convenient, fast, effective, and inexpensive marketing tool. It should be noted that e-mail should not be unsolicited (you should send e-mail only to those who have agreed to receive it). Solicited e-mail can be used to send out a variety of communication tools such as special offers and last-minute discounts, company updates, newsletters, and digital brochures.

Integrated marketing communications

When you develop a promotional/communications strategy for your tourism business, all activities must be integrated. It is also important to ensure that clear messages are communicated to the target market. For example, if you run a sales promotion, such as a Winter Special, the Winter Special must be communicated through all other communication channels that the tourism business is using. Similarly, if your business launches a new product-offering or website, this information must be added to all other communication tools and messages.

Extending the marketing mix

The marketing mix of the four Ps has been adapted in the services marketing literature to become the seven Ps, with the addition of people, processes, and physical evidence. Booms & Bitner (1981) suggested an extended marketing mix, which recognises that the people who deliver offerings are important, and that the physical layout and atmosphere of the organisation are equally important.

As with the components of the original mix, the components of the extended mix are interrelated, and can also be controlled by the tourism manager. Any or all of them can influence consumer buying decisions, as well as levels of consumer satisfaction.

All three of these extended marketing mix components are very important in managing the quality of the service encounter and creating consumer satisfaction. For instance, the first encounter that a tourist has when checking in at the airport is with the airline's ground staff. The quality of that encounter will be judged by the process of checking in (the length of the queue and the wait), the attitudes and actions of the people (the knowledge and courtesy of the airline staff), and the physical evidence (the cleanliness and comfort of the airline gate area and the interior of the aircraft, as well as evidence of other tangibles such as tickets, food, and staff uniforms).

The extended mix is particularly useful for tourism, which is a high-contact service (people), a complex service (process), and an offering that can only be evaluated by consumers at the place of consumption (physical evidence).

Tourism marketing research

Marketing research is the process of gathering and analysing information and data about customers and markets. Tourism managers need to understand which markets they wish to serve – which prices to charge, which product-offerings to sell, which distribution channels will be effective, and which communication tools to use. The marketing research process is therefore closely linked to the development of an effective marketing mix, and is applicable at every stage of the marketing planning process.

Figure 14.2 shows the interdependent nature of the marketing mix and marketing research – how information is gathered from consumers and analysed; then how the mix is adjusted accordingly for future marketing decisions. Research also helps managers understand the marketplace in which they work and its tourism suppliers, tour operators, travel agencies, competitors, and consumers.

Two of the most commonly-used marketing research methods in tourism are primary research and secondary research.

Primary research (sometimes referred to as 'field research') is original data generated by new research, and includes techniques such as surveys, interviews, or observations. Primary research, which covers both quantitative and qualitative data, is research that is specifically commissioned by an organisation to contribute to its marketing decisions. It requires the gathering of data not available from any other desk or secondary source. For example, a survey commissioned by one hotel group to study the current attitudes of business guests towards its own and other hotels competing in the same market, would be primary research.

Secondary research (sometimes referred to as 'desk research') is information collected for purposes other than solving the problem at hand – in this sense, the researcher becomes the secondary user of the data (Aaker, Kumar & Day, 2001: 106). All published sources, including government sources, trade association statistics, and commercial companies' market surveys are classified as secondary data.

Most research will include secondary data collection to find out what work on the subject area has already been conducted. Secondary sources of information should always be consulted before collecting primary data, as the information needed may already exist.

Figure 14.2 Marketing research and the tourism marketing mix

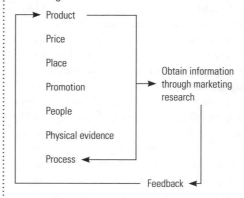

Customer Relationship Management (CRM)

Customer relationship management (CRM) is a very important but simple tool. CRM involves building customer loyalty and on-going business-customer relations. CRM also helps overcome some of the intangibility characteristic of services marketing. For instance, customers who feel a sense of loyalty to a tourism provider will have a reduced sense of risk when buying from that tourism provider. Furthermore, the problem of variability is also reduced, as loyal customers tend to be more forgiving and may overlook a one-off error in service delivery. Most of all, loyal customers usually pass on recommendations to generate repeat purchases.

Many tourism businesses implement loyalty schemes, such as frequent-flyer or frequent-guest programmes (FFP/Gs). Tourism organisations such as airlines, car rental companies, tour operators, cruise liner companies, and hotel groups have developed databases which combine loyalty schemes, customer histories, and other information, enabling them to interact with their existing and prospective customers through sophisticated CRM systems.

CRM can be inexpensive, which is good news for start-up tourism businesses. In its simplest form, CRM is the ability to identify and recognise repeat customers and to address them individually by name. For managers of tourism SMMEs, what it means is that each time they meet someone (through networking), or have a customer, they enter his or her details on to a spreadsheet or customer database. Whenever they run a special offer, have some news to announce, or want to jog their customers' memories, they can send out an e-mail to all the people on the customer database spreadsheet. Customer relations managers could also send a printed newsletter, but this costs more. These actions will help reinforce the concept of ToMA, 'Top of the Mind Awareness'. This simply means that a manager of a tourism business ensures that the customer does not forget about what the business offers.

Managers and all staff must work at building relations with valuable consumers, as well as with all of the other markets (for example, tourism intermediaries: travel trade and conference/event organisers, suppliers, and stakeholders) that affect the tourism organisation's success. A marketing manager should build relationships with suppliers, such as visitor attractions, accommodation providers, transportation carriers (airlines, car rental companies, cruise liners), the travel trade (tour operators, travel agents), and destination marketing organisations (regional tourist originations and tourist information centres). The objective of CRM with these markets is to develop co-operation between all the parties that can impact on the ultimate satisfaction of the consumer. These supplier members play an important role in delivering vital customer service quality.

DMOs face major difficulties in seeking to implement CRM practices. Among the reasons that inhibit the development of CRM is, firstly, that tourists are not contractual customers of the DMO. Secondly, for many visitors, particularly international tourists, the likelihood of a repeat visit to a given destination is comparatively low. This is especially true in the case of long-haul destinations from the generating country (for example, from either the UK or USA to South Africa).

Tourism marketing planning

Tourism managers can draw on theory from the academic fields of marketing and planning when devising a marketing plan. **Marketing planning** consists of a systematic process that includes stages of analysis, planning, implementation, and monitoring. These stages might be expressed as:

- What is our business?
- Where are we now? *Situation analysis*
- What do we want to achieve? *Planning*
- How do we get there? *Implementation*
- How effective have the plan and its activities been? *Monitoring*

Figure 14.3 The marketing planning process

These five questions are represented in Figure 14.3, and help to explain three concepts in marketing planning:

- Vision, goals and objectives
- Strategies (chosen routes for achieving goals)
- Plans (action programmes for moving along the route, and evaluating achievement against targets).

Marketing planning is as relevant to a small tour-operating business as it is to an international hotel group. Its sophistication and scale of planning will obviously vary according to the size of the tourism business and the diversity of its operations, but the essential approach is always the same.

It is also important to understand that the marketing planning process is not always a series of procedural steps. Quite often the process requires an interplay between the various stages, with the flexibility to move forwards as well as backwards. Marketing planning, therefore, requires constant refinement – it is an ongoing process – and a plan may well not be perfected until a number of drafts have been completed. In addition, as we mentioned in the last section, it is imperative that marketing research be conducted at every stage of the marketing planning process.

What is our business? (analysis stage 1.)

Before any planning takes place, it is important that the tourism organisation has a clear understanding and insight of what business it is actually in. The tourism organisation must agree on its overall mission statement, through conducting research. This mission statement (or 'vision', as some organisations call it) must reflect the aims of the organisation, and is usually expressed in terms of benefits offered to consumers (see Example box). It is also a guide that helps employees know the purpose of the organisation for which they work. The structure of mission statements varies, and may describe what the business wants to achieve, and also identify the user groups. More specifically, a mission statement should:

- be broad
- focus on markets
- provide inspiration.

The marketing plan should be designed to fulfill this mission.

> **Example** TMACC's mission statement
>
> Table Mountain Aerial Cableway Company's (TMACC's) mission statement is as follows:
> 'We strive to provide our customers with service levels of exceptional standards, and to serve the industry to the best of our ability'.

Where are we now? (analysis stage 2.)

The next stage in marketing planning is strategic analysis. This involves an analysis of the current and future *internal* strengths and weaknesses and *external* opportunities and threats (SWOT) facing the tourism business (also known as a 'situational analysis').

A **SWOT analysis** is a useful tool for identifying the microenvironmental (internal) and macroenvironmental (external) factors affecting the whole organisation. An example of an analysis of the microenvironment is when an organisation critically appraises itself in terms of how it compares with competitors, how it is seen by its consumers, and what resources and capabilities it has to enable it to deal with a changing market. The analysis of the macroenvironment entails identifying the social and global factors that affect a tourism organisation; for example, the economic environmental factors, such as interest rates. The macroenvironmental analysis enables tourism managers to identify trends that may present opportunities or threats to their organisations.

It is important that marketing planners not merely list every factor they can think of, but use only what is relevant and significant to a particular organisation. In addition, the SWOT is not an end in itself, but a means of deciding priorities for action. Its completion should be followed by recommendations on how to exploit the strengths, repair weaknesses, capitalise on opportunities, and avoid threats.

What do we want to achieve? (planning stage)

In this stage of the marketing planning process, tourism businesses need to articulate their objectives. An organisation's mission is often accompanied by a series of objectives. Objectives spell out the organisation's goals that it needs to achieve in order to realise its mission. Objectives need to be clearly defined, and should be 'SMART':

- **S**pecific – be clearly linked to a particular area of operation
- **M**easurable – have a method of measurement to gauge success and effectiveness
- **A**greed – be feasible and realistic, so that staff can work towards set objectives
- **R**ealistic – be compatible with the organisation's mission statement
- **T**ime frame – have deadlines for review – weekly, monthly, or annually.

Once objectives and target markets have been set, marketing planners must decide on appropriate

strategies to meet these objectives. Each objective should be examined very closely, and strategic options drawn up. For example, if one of the objectives for a guest house is to increase bookings, then this can be achieved in several ways: perhaps by charging a lower price, offering something different, or focusing on a new market.

Strategies are then developed to achieve objectives. Two strategic tools are used extensively in tourism marketing: *Porter's generic strategies* and the *Ansoff matrix*. The two aspects of strategic formulation include competition strategy and strategic direction. Porter's (1980) generic strategies framework is used for competitive strategy, and the Ansoff (1965) matrix for strategic development (or growth).

It is at this stage that the organisation should also plan which market segments it intends to target. It is also here that the marketing mix is used, to plan in order to achieve strategies. Each marketing mix component has its own strategy (product strategies, pricing strategies, distribution strategies, and promotional strategies). It is the application of the tactical plans, based on each component of the marketing mix. At the heart of marketing planning, therefore, is the design and management of the marketing mix (the seven Ps), which we examined in closer detail earlier in the chapter. These marketing mix elements should flow logically, with decisions on product-offering, price, distribution, promotion, people, physical evidence, and processes linked with each other and the tourism organisation's objectives.

How do we get there? (implementation)

Once strategies have been selected, the next stage of the planning process asks the question 'How do we get there?' It involves putting the plan into action. This means actually doing things based on the strategy for the whole time period that the marketing plan covers. Action plans are communicated – implementation is the action of the action plan! During implementation, performance is constantly monitored.

How effective have the plan and its activities been? (monitoring and evaluation)

The last stage in the marketing planning process is the issue of evaluation to interpret results. Evaluation answers the question: 'How effective has the plan and its activities been?' The marketing plan needs to be evaluated *during and after* implementation, so that any problems can be identified and remedied. Usually this involves a systematic review of all aspects of the marketing plan against targets set. The evaluation should be carried out on a regular basis, usually monthly or quarterly, so as to ensure prompt attention and action in areas where the results fall behind targets set. One of the easiest and most widely-used methods to evaluate marketing performance is to analyse the organisation's sales figures.

Sales data is easily accessible to the marketing planner, and is the most accurate method of analysing how consumers respond to adjustments made to the marketing mix. For instance, results are clear when there is an increase in the number of consumers coming to a hotel after a recent advertising campaign. Analysis of sales or bookings on a regular basis allows a marketer to adjust the plan accordingly in the short term, and to reallocate resources where necessary. However, managers must also take coincidental factors into account. If a holiday weekend occurs at the same time as a promotion, it could simply have been the holiday, and not the promotion, which caused higher sales.

At this stage of the marketing process, it is important that the organisation conducts on-going marketing research. For example, a tour operator who purchases advertising space in various tourism trade magazines would monitor any new business that may have resulted.

This would be achieved by compiling a marketing information system (MIS)/database, which would record the details of any enquiries, where the potential client heard about the organisation, etc.

The marketing plan

Marketing planning documents appear in many forms and sizes in the tourism industry. For most hotel groups, airlines, visitor attractions, and destinations, the planning format might well take a formal approach, and is often embodied in a document known as the marketing plan. The marketing plan is a structured guide to action, usually in written format. It is a document consisting of objectives, goals, and every aspect of future marketing activity.

The marketing planning process, discussed in the previous section, is on-going, but the marketing plan covers different time scales. A tactical marketing plan is usually carried out annually (a year plan), and strategic plans usually span between three and five years (see Table 14.3). A corporate marketing plan, on the other hand, covers five years or more.

As mentioned earlier, large tourism organisations may devise marketing plans for specific brands, key market segments, or product-offerings – for example, Thompsons Tours' *Cruising, Ski Holidays*, or *Africa City Stopovers*. Furthermore, some tactical plans may take the form of an integrated communications campaign on a shared message; for example, eThekwini Africa's 'Beyond the Beach', or Cybele's 'Inspiration for the mind, body, and soul'.

Table 14.3 A comparison of strategic and yearly marketing plans

Strategic marketing plan (3–5 years)	Tactical marketing plan (1 year)
Situation analysis *macro micro external internal*	Summary of *situation analysis SWOT*
Forecasts	Target segments and positioning
	Annual marketing objectives *in SMART format*
SWOT analysis	Product *[objectives] strategies tactics*
Target segments	Price *[objectives] strategies tactics*
Positioning statement	Place *[objectives] strategies tactics*
Marketing objectives	Promotion *[objectives] strategies tactics*
Marketing strategies *product price place promotion*	Monitoring, evaluation and control *including budget*
Evaluation and control *including budget*	

Adapted from Godfrey, K., & Clarke, J. 2000. *The tourism development handbook: a practical approach to planning and marketing.* London: Cassell.

Conclusion

This chapter has provided an overview of some of the marketing challenges faced by managers of tourism businesses, and links these challenges back to the services characteristics of the tourism offering.

As a manager of a tourism business, it is important to become familiar with marketing. Marketing is about satisfying customers' needs. However, managers cannot satisfy all customers; they have to choose their customers carefully. They must select their target markets; those that will enable the business to meet its objectives. To compete effectively for their selected customers, organisations need to design a marketing mix that provides their target markets with more value than their competitor's marketing mix.

Marketing should not be seen in isolation from other business functions and customer services. It influences the entire business, from management to front-line employees. Similarly, marketing plans require the entire organisation's commitment if they are to be successful.

It is not possible in a single chapter to explore marketing as a tourism business function in great detail. However, you are encouraged to read the references below to further your knowledge of marketing.

Review questions

1. Describe the differences between services and goods and the implications for tourism marketers.
2. Why is it important for tourism managers to understand tourism consumer behaviour?
3. What is meant by market segmentation?
4. What are the advantages of branding for tourism businesses?
5. Why is it important for tourism managers to carry out marketing research?
6. Explain why the topic of customer service is important to tourism businesses.
7. List and discuss the key elements of the marketing planning process.

Further reading

Evans, N., Campbell, D. & Stonehouse, G. 2003. *Strategic management for travel and tourism*. Oxford: Butterworth-Heinemann.

Finn, M., Elliot-White, M. & Walton, M. 2000. *Tourism and leisure research methods*. Essex: Longman.

George, R. 2004. *Marketing South African tourism*, 2nd edition. Cape Town: Oxford University Press.

Swarbrooke, J. & Horner, S. 2006. *Consumer behaviour in tourism*, 2nd edition. Oxford: Butterworth-Heinemann.

Websites

Direct Marketing Association of South Africa (DMASA) www.dmasa.org

International Marketing Council (IMC): www.imc.org.za

Public Relations Institute of South Africa (PRISA): www.prisa.co.za

References

Aaker, D. A., Kumar, V. & Day, G. S. 2001. *Marketing research*, 7th edition. New York: John Wiley.

Ansoff, H. I. 1965. *Corporate strategy: business policy for growth and expansion*. New York: McGraw-Hill.

Booms, B. H. & Bitner, M. J. 1981. Marketing strategies and organisational structures for service firms. In J. H. Donnelly & W. R. George (Eds.), *Marketing of services*. Chicago: American Marketing Association, pp. 47–51.

French, Y. 1994. *Public relations for leisure and tourism*, Exeter: Longman.

George, R. 2004. *Marketing South African tourism*, 2nd edition. Cape Town: Oxford University Press Southern Africa.

Godfrey, K. & Clarke, J. 2000. *The tourism development handbook: a practical approach to planning and marketing*. London: Cassell.

Hankinson, G. & Cowking, P. 1993. *Branding in action*. Maidenhead: McGraw-Hill.

Holloway, J. C. 2004. *Marketing for tourism*, 4th edition. Upper Saddle River, New Jersey: Prentice Hall.

Holloway, J. C. 2006. *The business of tourism*, 7th edition. Harlow: Pearson.

Kotler, P., Bowen, J. & Makens, J. 2003. *Marketing for hospitality and tourism*, 3rd edition. Upper Saddle River, New Jersey: Prentice Hall.

Maslow, A. H. 1954. *Motivation and personality*. New York: Harper and Row.

McCarthy, E. J. 1960. *Basic marketing*. Homewood, Illinois: Irwin.

Middleton, V. T. C. & Clarke, J. 2001. *Marketing in travel and tourism*, 3rd edition. Oxford: Butterworth-Heinemann.

Page, S. 2003. *Tourism management: managing for change*. Oxford: Butterworth-Heinemann.

Pearsall, J. (Ed.). 1999. *The concise Oxford dictionary*, 10th edition. New York: Oxford University Press.

Porter, M. E. 1980. *Competitive strategy: techniques for analysing industries and competitors*. New York: Free Press.

Pritchard, A. & Morgan, N. 1998. Mood marketing – the new destination marketing strategy: a case study of 'Wales the Brand', *Journal of Vacation Marketing*, Vol. 4(3), 215–229.

Rathmell, J. 1966. What is meant by services? *Journal of Marketing*, Vol. 1. October, 32–36.

Case study

14

Promoting the re-opening of the Big Hole, Kimberley

Objectives

- to understand the importance of promotions
- to understand and apply the tools of the promotional mix to a visitor attraction

Kimberley's Big Hole, which first opened on 19 November 1969, has recently undergone a major re-vamp. The Big Hole is the biggest hand-dug hole in the world. It was mined to a depth of 215 metres with a surface area of 17 hectares, a mean diameter of 457 metres, and a perimeter of 1,6 kilometres. This diamond-bearing volcanic rock has drawn thousands of domestic and international tourists over the years, due to its historical association with De Beers, a name synonymous with diamonds through its 60% share of the international diamond market. Nevertheless, the Big Hole has been under-utilised as a visitor attraction and, as a result, has undergone a comprehensive makeover.

In 2007, a Section 21 (non-profit) company was established between provincial government, the Sol Plaatje and Frances Baard municipalities in Kimberley, the Northern Cape Tourism Authority (NCTA), De Beers, and the private sector to manage the R52-million upgrade and re-vamp of the Big Hole. The project entailed the transformation of the old Big Hole museum into a new, dynamic, and functioning 'Old Town' (including

the open mine museum, Old Time Bar, a guesthouse, fast-food outlets, skittle alley, and diamond dig), and the installation of a new exhibition centre called 'Diamond World'. A new cantilever platform that stretches over the edge of the hole has also been constructed. In addition, a 90-metre viewing ramp provides visitors with an expansive view over the Big Hole, and an audio-visual (AV) theatre has been developed. In the theatre, visitors watch a 20-minute film giving insight into the formation of diamonds, the history of the discovery of diamonds, the subsequent mining operations in the Kimberley area, as well as the characters in the evolution of mines. A vault, which can hold 15 visitors, displays a collection of some of the biggest and rarest gems, including a 616-carat uncut diamond, different coloured diamonds, fluorescent diamonds, as well as the Eureka diamond – the first diamond discovered in the area. Finally, a world-class visitor centre, a first for Kimberley and the Northern Cape, was built after a decision made by De Beers in 2002 to invest R50-million into a three-year project.

Planning the promotions of the re-opening event

The Big Hole's marketing activities are handled by two marketers, employed by the Big Hole &

ESS (Compass Group). The Big Hole's main target markets are international (overseas tourists) and domestic markets (LSM groups 6-10). The re-opening launch took place on 23 November 2006: opened by the Deputy President, Phumzile Mlambo-Ngcuka, Northern Cape Premier Dipuo Peters, and De Beers chairperson Nicky Oppenheimer. The Big Hole project committee members were dressed in 19th-century period clothing, and fireworks at the end of the evening celebrated and marked the beginning of a new era for the attraction. The following marketing activities are on-going.

PR

Promotional activities include features in *Getaway*, national and local newspapers, the distribution of press/media kits (including fact sheets containing information on the Big Hole), and active involvement with key tourism bodies within the Northern Cape, including NCTA, Kimberley Tourism, and involvement with the media. Interviews were conducted on various local radio stations, which included phone-ins from listeners. All VIPs attending the re-opening event received a leather holdall, which included a site map as well as an event programme. Staff handed out Big Hole balloons to children at the Diamond Pavilion Mall, talked to community members, and ran a 'Diamond Draw' competition (see Direct Marketing below).

Advertising

Slots of one-minute advertisements were placed in various broadcast media to announce the re-opening of the Big Hole, including SABC radio stations (5FM and MetroFM), and local radio stations OFM and Radio Teemaneng.

Advertisements were placed in print media – South African magazines, such as *Good Taste*, *Getaway*, *TOGOTO*, SA Tourism's *Factfiler*, and in-flight magazines including British Airways' *Upfront* and SAA's *Indwe*. Two large billboards were strategically positioned on the N12 – the route from Johannesburg and Cape Town to Kimberley. The Big Hole's re-opening advertising theme was 'Opening Soon', with the objective of informing the marketplace that the old attraction still exists, but has a new look.

Website

A holding page was constructed for about three months, to coincide with the re-opening. The home page content included an overview of the rejuvenation project. The website is now up and running (www.thebighole.co.za).

Marketing collateral

Brochures were distributed at the Information Centre. A huge velvet-covered board with the new logo on it was on display, to notify oncoming visitors at the Shell Ultra City on the N12 from Johannesburg to Kimberley.

Marketing research

Customer surveys – personal interviews – are yet to be carried out with the local community to establish usage data (i.e. if, and how often, they had been to the Big Hole, with whom, etc.).

Direct marketing

Visitors to the site during the re-opening phase received a 'Diamond Draw' ticket, making them eligible to win a diamond on completion of a short application form (name, address, e-mail address, cellular phone number). This customer information was added to a database.

Branding

The Big Hole's marketing campaign included the launch of a new logo – a black-on-white and white-on-black picture of the 'Colesberg kopje' above a v-shape depicting the hole and landscape, which together form the outline of a diamond. Beneath the logo lies the slogan 'Diamonds & Destiny' (which refers to the fact that people over the years have found both diamonds and their destinies in Kimberley).

Case study questions

1. The Big Hole's re-opening campaign combines advertising, PR, and other tools. Analyse the promotional mix, and discuss its effectiveness.

2. Identify the target audiences for the Big Hole's re-opening campaign.

3. How did the re-opening launch target relevant audiences?

PART IV

Issues in tourism management

15

Managing the impacts of tourism

Richard George

The RMS St Helena arriving at St. Helena island

Purpose

This chapter examines the range of economic, socio-cultural and environmental pressures that tourism exerts on a destination, as well as the management implications of these impacts.

Learning outcomes

After reading this chapter you should be able to:
- explain the economic impacts of tourism
- demonstrate how to measure the economic impacts of tourism
- explain what is meant by the multiplier effect
- outline the concepts of linkages and leakages
- explain a range of socio-cultural impacts of tourism
- discuss the management implication of socio-cultural impacts of tourism
- illustrate the various ways in which tourism can impact on the environment.

Chapter overview

This chapter discusses the association between tourism and the destination region. The tourism industry is a mix of goods and services and, as such, is characterised by the close proximity between consumers and producers. For tourism to occur, tourists have to visit the destination to consume the tourism offering. There are inevitable consequences for the destination as tourists interact with the host community, and as a local tourism industry develops. These impacts of tourism can be defined as effects which may be positive or negative. There are three major impacts associated with tourism activity and development: economic, socio-cultural, and environmental. This chapter also considers the various management and planning tools for assessing and managing each of these impacts.

The concluding case study examines these different impacts in the context of the South Atlantic Ocean island of St Helena.

Introduction

Preceding chapters have focused on the role-players in the tourism industry, and how they manage their businesses. This chapter focuses on tourists and their impact on the destination region. One of the aims of tourism management at a destination level is to maximise the industry's economic, socio-cultural, and environmental benefits, while minimising its costs. The socio-cultural, environmental, and economic impacts are interlinked. For example, negative social reactions to tourism could result from its perceived economic and environmental costs. Tourism managers need to understand the potential positive and negative **impacts** generated by tourism – the economic, social, cultural, and environmental pressures, and the ways in which they can be managed.

Firstly, we look at the economic consequences for regions affected by tourism.

Discussion point

'Tourism is good, it's tourists that are bad'. Discuss this statement.

The economic impact of tourism

In South Africa, inbound and domestic tourism contributed over R100 billion in 2006. Tourism accounts for over 8.3% of South Africa's gross domestic product (SA Tourism, 2006). **Gross domestic product** (GDP) is the measure of the size and value of all the goods and services produced during a specified time period, usually one year. GDP can be divided into the *primary sector* (which includes mining and agriculture, for example); the *manufacturing sector* and also the *services sector*, which includes tourism services. It is made up of a number of items, found in the manufacturing and service sectors (including tourism) of an economy. The money earned from international tourists coming into South Africa (inbound tourists) is considered to be an invisible

export because it earns foreign exchange, bringing in revenue to the economy (in the same way that a South African textile business does when it earns money from exporting its garments), whereas the money that South African nationals (outgoing/outbound tourists) spend on holidays overseas is considered an *import*, because the products and services are paid for in foreign currency using money earned in South Africa, thereby taking money out of the South African economy.

Exact figures that illustrate to what extent tourism impacts on the economy are difficult to calculate, due to the nature of the tourism industry. Unlike other industries, such as the automotive or the textile industries, tourism includes not only the accommodation and catering sector, but also sectors such as transport or insurance services. Tourists contribute to the economy in many ways. They pay for flights, hire motor cars, book accommodation, go on safaris, use laundrettes, eat in restaurants, buy curios and other products, visit attractions an participate in recreational and adventure activities. Tourism, in fact, impacts on nearly all sectors of the economy in a direct or indirect way, as we shall see later.

Measuring the economic impacts of tourism

Impact multiplier

When measuring the positive or negative economic impacts that tourism has on the host region, economists often make use of an *impact multiplier*, also called an *income multiplier*, or quite simply, a *tourism multiplier*. Economists use models of the economy and calculate multipliers that reflect to what degree a change in the demand for a tourism offering impacts on other sectors. The particularly important feature of the impact is that sectors that are affected by an increase in demand impact in turn on further sectors, or maybe even link back to the original one, causing a whole chain of reactions throughout the economic system. In the end, the original impact on one sector – say, accommodation – has caused a certain amount of change in the economy as a whole. This amount, expressed as a number, is usually termed an impact **multiplier**.

Linkages and Leakages

Linkages

The strength of linkages between sectors in an economy is what determines the size of the impact multiplier. Inter-industrial linkages refer to the cooperation of different segments of the economy. There will be linkages between the wood industry and the furniture industry, for example. In the tourism industry, inter-industrial linkages might include contracts for the textile industry to deliver bed-linen to hotels, or for electronics firms to supply bus and coach companies with air-conditioning units for new tour buses. If the textile industry cannot make enough bed-linen, or if the bed-linen manufactured in the country is not of an acceptable quality, there is no inter-industrial linkage to increase the positive effect of tourism on the economy. In such a case, the bed-linen will need to be imported, and the local economy will not feel the benefit of tourism's growth in the form of increased demand for textile goods.

Leakages

Due to **leakages** and other phenomena the effects of tourism diminish as they travel through the economy. A certain proportion of the added value will be lost from the circular flow through leakages due to imports, such as the bed-linen in the example above. A study carried out by the non-government organisation (NGO) Sustainable Living, found that leakage in Thailand was estimated to be about 70% of all money spent by tourists (via foreign-owned tour airlines, tour operators, hotels, or payments for imported food, drink, and supplies). Estimates of leakage for other developing countries range from 75% in the Caribbean to 40% in India (York, 2005). Leakages will be far lower in economies where businesses supply each other, rather than import a high proportion of their inputs. Consequently, smaller economies will often have low linkages and high leakages, because the variety of goods produced is smaller than in larger, more diversified economies (see Figure 15.1 opposite).

Some main sources of leakages include:
- imported manufactured goods

- imported inputs, such as materials for the development of tourist facilities
- currency conversion, banking fees, etc., needed in connection with paying for imports
- remittance of wages by expatriates
- management fees or royalties for international franchises
- payments to overseas companies, such as airline carriers and tour operators
- international marketing costs, for example for promotion overseas.

Remember that here, also, the effects happen at different levels: those employed in the tourism industry also consume imported goods, so there are also leakage effects in the second round of impacts from tourism!

One of the major sources of leakage from the South African economy in the tourism industry is airline transportation. Tourists who use foreign airline carriers to come to South Africa spend nearly all their airfare outside the country. Some of the benefits reach South Africa in the form of landing and handling fees, taxes, fuel costs incurred while in the country, etc., but most of the revenue stays in the tourist-generating country of the airline (Raguraman, 1997).

Together, the number and strength of linkages within the economy, as well as the scope of leakages, determine the size of the impact multiplier. While linkages maximise the impact, leakages lower the multiplier by drawing money out of the economy. This, of course, implies that if a government wants to increase the economic impact of tourism, it must:

a. protect established inter-industrial linkages and support the creation of new ones; and

b. minimise leakages and consider possible leakage increases as a result of new policies.

Responsible tourism management (RTM) is all about creating local linkages – through employing locals, procuring local goods and services, investing in social services in the local area, and respecting the natural environment (see last section in this chapter).

There are a number of private-public sector initiatives aimed at maximising linkages and

Figure 15.1 Leakage of foreign exchange earnings: 12 countries

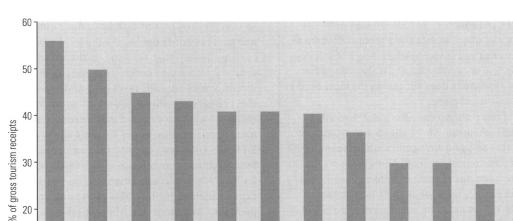

minimising leakages in South Africa. One of the ways to help reduce leakage is to encourage tourism spending in the local area. For example, South African Tourism's (SA Tourism) 'Sho't Left' domestic tourism marketing campaign has helped encourage people to 'buy local', and thus retain as much tourism expenditure in the local area as possible. The concept of '**Pro-poor tourism**' is another initiative which investigates how linkages can be maximised and reduced. The concept describes tourism that deliberately creates local linkages and economic benefits. This can involve a major tourism company deliberately employing local people, sourcing goods and services (such as food, crafts, linen and security services) from the local economy, assisting in setting up local enterprises, etc. Pro-poor tourism can be seen as an enactment of responsible tourism principles (see Chapter 16 – Managing tourism responsibly). Responsible tourism management aims to increase linkage and reduce economic leakages. The Example box opposite on **enclave tourism** illustrates where leakages are high, and where money leaks out of the local economy.

Example Enclave tourism

Enclave tourism refers to tourism development where most of the economic benefits of tourism are captured by the tourism business (which is often foreign-owned), and few felt in the host community, which is largely excluded from the tourism activities. An 'all-inclusive' tour package is an example of this. If tourists remain for their entire stay at the same resort, or on the same cruise liner – where everything they need is provided, and where they will make all their purchases – not much opportunity is given to local people to share in the benefits of tourism.

The Organisation of American States (OAS) carried out a survey of Jamaica's tourism industry that looked at the role of 'all-inclusives' compared to other types of accommodation. It found that 'all-inclusive' hotels generate the largest amount of revenue, but that their impact on the economy is smaller per US$ of revenue than other accommodation sub-sectors.

Certain resorts in the Caribbean actually limit the local community's access to hotel sites and beaches. Tourists are kept within the resorts, where all meals are eaten and where all activities and shopping take place. Not only does this limit economic benefits, it also means that the experience does not convey the local culture or a sense of place.

Cruise tourism can also be tantamount to enclave tourism, where guests are encouraged to stay on board and spend all their money on the ship. Fortunately in South Africa there are few, if any, examples of enclave tourism. Government and industry together promote local linkages, with opportunities for suppliers of tourism and other goods and services prioritised for support.

Discussion point

Discuss how SA Tourism's domestic tourism campaign *Sho't Left* can minimise linkages within the South African economy.

Direct and Indirect Impact

Put simply, the multiplier effect of tourist spending works in the following way: initial tourist spending has direct revenue effects for the hotel owner, the taxi-driver, or other services used by tourists (see Figure 15.2). Some of the services

used by the tourists, however, might be owned by people or companies from outside the economy, so that the direct revenue leaks to these outsiders, and generally does not benefit the local economy.

The money that remains in the destination area will be used to cover costs such as material inputs, wages to staff, taxes etc., and represents the primary, or direct, effect of tourism. The increase in labour demand will increase employment levels and/or wages to the benefit of the local labour force. The increase in demand for manufactured goods leads to increased revenue for local wholesalers and manufacturers, who will expand their capacities, also increasing employment and income levels. These local businesses, which form the secondary recipients of tourist spending, therefore also re-spend their money, and so on. This is referred to as the indirect effect of tourism on the economy – the second round, if you like. Goeldner, McIntosh and Ritchie (2003) termed this the *ripple effect of tourism expenditure*, but, more generally, it is termed the *multiplier effect*.

TO DO

Take one other part of the tourism product-offering that the tourist spends money on directly, and follow the chain for two links as in the diagram below. Try and include four items at each level for which the revenue is used. This way, you will end up having eight indirect beneficiaries of the original direct spend.

The size of the multiplier depends on a number of factors, namely:

Figure 15.2 Simple diagram of the multiplier effect of tourism

Tourist	Accommodation Transport Souvenirs Shopping Tourist guide Entry fees	rent wages to staff purchase of goods income for owner ('profit') interest payments to bank marketing costs etc.	purchase of raw materials wages for workman costs of machinery transport costs marketing costs income for owner ('profit')
	EXPENDITURE	**DIRECT IMPACT**	**INDIRECT IMPACT**

- the model or method used to calculate the multiplier: economists usually divide tourism multiplier models into four groups:
  i)   basic multipliers
  ii) economic models using the input-output tables and social accounting matrices
  iii) the newly developed general equilibrium models
  iv) the system of the satellite account
- the size of the economy: larger and more diversified economies tend to have lower leakages, and so higher multipliers
- the degree to which backward and forward linkages exist between different sectors of the economy. For example, do taxi drivers get spare parts for their locally-produced cars here in South Africa (*backward linkage*), and are many products they buy out of their incomes locally produced (*forward linkage*)?
- population size, as larger populations can better adapt to maximise benefits from tourist incomes
- the relation between the number of tourists and the local population: Studies have shown that regions with high numbers of tourists and small population numbers have lower multipliers
- the share of tourists coming from the major country of origin
- the political system and per capita income: studies also show that open, globalised democracies tend to have higher multipliers, as do more developed nations.

Calculating the economic impacts

The economic impact of tourism is calculated using economic models. The most commonly used model is based on the economy's *input-output table*. This table, a comprehensive and detailed list of all industries in the economy, shows the value of inputs used in each industry and the value of the output. It is a little like a system of accounts applied to products and industries. Economists can use input-output tables to see what would happen if, say, tourism increased by 5%. The numbers in the table would change to reflect the additional consumption, and the 'bottom line' of the table shows how each industry's output increases due to this boost in tourism. It is possible also to see other economic impacts, such as the increase in tax revenue or employment.

Applying methods such as input-output analysis for tourism-related research is problematic because, unfortunately, tourism is not an industry that can be immediately identified, as it is not separately classified in national accounts or input-output tables. Instead, it must be constructed by aggregating a number of different economic sectors which serve it directly.

In general, it is quite difficult to measure the extent to which tourist consumption of local goods and services supports domestic activities. Each activity must be measured as the tourists' share of total consumption of each good and service (United Nations, 1999). Other problems associated with economic modelling to calculate impacts include:

- unrealistic assumptions made about the economy, such as the availability of resources, free and fair markets, etc.
- the rigidity of a model that means that price changes cannot be taken into account
- results from such models cannot be compared to impact multipliers calculated for other countries, as the input-output table compilation is never the same in any two countries.

Using other models besides input-output tables can overcome some, but never all, of these issues. Another attempt to overcome the problems associated with comparing multipliers across regions has been the development of tourism satellite accounts (TSAs). A **satellite account** is a system to help measure the size and impact of sectors that cannot be defined as industries in national accounts. Other examples besides TSAs include ICT (information and communication technologies) satellite accounts, and environmental satellite accounts.

The United Nations World Tourism Organisation (UN-WTO), the Organisation for Economic Cooperation and Development

(OECD), and the European Commission (EC) have introduced a *tourism accounting system* that is consistent with the national accounts of every country. Because this system runs parallel to the national accounts format, it is called the tourism satellite account. The TSA can measure all goods and services consumed by tourists according to international standards of concepts, classifications, and definitions, making TSAs of different economies comparable to each other.

Because of the fact that they are comparable, TSAs are especially useful for policy and business strategies policy-makers and industry professionals. A TSA for South Africa has been planned for some years, but will only be completed in 2008 (SA Tourism, 2006). It will enable the measurement of:

- tourism's contribution to GDP
- tourism's ranking compared to other industries
- employment figures in tourism
- the volume of investment in tourism
- consumption by tourism
- tax revenues generated by tourism
- the impact of tourism on the national **balance of payments** (Stats SA, 2003).

Discussion point

1. Discuss why tourism is not classified as one industry in economic models. Name ten industries that are included, wholly or partially, in the tourism industry
2. What can TSAs help measure?

Employment

Growth in tourism has positive impacts, not only on the tourism industry, but also on many sectors of the economy. Similarly, job creation through tourism is also spread across many sectors. Tourism creates employment opportunities; not only in the accommodation and transport sectors, but also in the agriculture, manufacturing, and retail sectors.

The employment effects of tourism are often cited as the major benefit of tourism to local communities. Tourism is thought to be labour-intensive and low-skilled work, meaning that jobs

are created in particular for vulnerable and under-employed sectors of the community: women, those with little or no formal education, and those with little work experience.

Challenges that the South African tourism industry needs to deal with to maximise the creation of jobs include:

- the general change of capital-labour ratios around the world, but also in South Africa, meaning that labour productivity has increased at the expense of jobs. On the other hand, this means that each job is more challenging and fulfilling for the worker.
- hierarchies have tended to become flatter, meaning that fewer management staff are employed than previously. Middle management positions have taken over more menial work, replacing some less-skilled workers.
- trends in the concentration of market power: tour operators or hotel and restaurant industries, for example, have become more concentrated as small, privately-owned and -run businesses have been bought up and large companies, and chains have increased their market power. These large companies tend to use economies of scale that need less labour than small individual companies.
- including the informal sector in the formal industry; for example, by helping those involved to benefit from government support programmes for SMMEs (see Chapter 10 – Managing small tourism businesses and entrepreneurship).
- labour laws in South Africa are stricter than in competitor destinations such as Mexico or Kenya. This means that short-term employment is discouraged and that employers try to use their employees to the maximum, rather than employ more people.

South African labour laws are stricter, too, than in most other comparable middle-income countries, and can be compared with those of the wealthiest European states. This means that workers in this country are much better protected from insufficient pay, unfair treatment or abuse, unsafe working conditions, etc. This protection comes at a price, which is borne to a great extent by the employer, who is less able to retrench in times of low demand, for example. Better protection of workers raises the price of the tourism offerings (and other offerings, too), but it is felt that this is necessary and acceptable in order to protect the people.

A great deal of employment in the South African tourism industry is based in the informal sector. Examples of the informal sector operations which parallel the mainstream tourism industry are evident in sub-sectors such as guesthouses, crafts-related activities, souvenir vending, prostitution, tourist guiding, mini-bus shuttle services, tour operating, and food stalls. The informal sector is unregulated and external to the formal institutions of South African society. One of the disadvantages of informal sector employment is that businesses and workers generally do not pay any regular wages or taxes. As a result, informal earnings are not included in official calculations, and tourism's economic contribution may be even greater than supposed. The major drawback for those working in the informal sector is that they are not protected by labour laws such as minimum wages, or by access to other benefits. The government loses the tax revenues that formal employment of these people would create, so it should be in everybody's interest that these workers are included in the formal sector.

Skills levels and employee training

Employment needs to be seen not only as the number of jobs in total, but also to be divided into different types of jobs. Normally, labour economists talk about skills levels. It is often said that the employment created by tourism favours low-skilled workers. This would mean that tourism creates particularly high numbers of jobs for poor people who tend to have few or no skills. In reality, the jobs that are created by tourism are not any lower-skilled than those in the South African economy in general. Some sectors, such as accommodation and catering, require many low-skilled workers, such as cleaning staff and waitrons. However, it should be noted that tourism creates employment throughout the economy. Studies (i.e. Thiede 2005) show that, overall, the employment created also requires many skilled and highly skilled workers.

Table 15.1 shows that in the catering and accommodation sector the ratio of skilled to unskilled workers has improved for the unskilled – the decrease in highly skilled jobs is greater (37%) than the losses for skilled and unskilled jobs (26% and 28%, respectively). This is positive for government policy-makers, and shows that the 'pro-poor' policy may be working in tourism!

There may also be a need for training and development of the local population, so that they can take advantage of employment opportunities in the tourism industry. For example, a new visitor attraction may need tourist guides, receptionists, cashiers, catering assistants, and cleaning and maintenance staff. Whilst members of the local community may have the general skills and personal qualities required, it is likely that they will need additional training to meet the responsibilities of their new job. Training and development can take many forms. It may

Table 15.1 Number of employees in catering and accommodation services sector 1994–2005 by skill level

Year	1994	2000	2005	Decrease 1994–2005
Total employment	289 037,5	218 328,7	207 358,5	28%
Semi- and unskilled	71 954,98	54 117,62	51 851,03	28%
Skilled	177 387,3	135 757,8	130 695,5	26%
Highly skilled	39 695,17	28 453,28	24 811,96	37%

(Source: TIPS, 2006)

be provided by educational institutions such as universities and FET colleges, by individual tourism providers, by local government departments, by sectoral organisations (such as the Southern African Tourism Services Association), or by trade organisations (such as the Tourism, Hospitality & Sport Education and Training Authority – see Chapter 8 – The government and tourism). The overall effect of maximising the level and quantity of training is to develop the general skills base of the local community. This can result in very positive economic and social benefits for the whole community, by creating a more employable workforce. Where training is combined with the opportunity to gain recognisable qualifications, the benefits to the individual are even greater.

Government revenue through tourism

How does revenue generated through tourism serve governments? Tourism impacts on many different sectors of the economy. These positive effects on many parts of the economy are used by many national, provincial, and local government agencies as a rationale for tourism development and investment in recreation facilities for the local economy. These government agencies are keen to use the tourism industry as a catalyst for job creation, income and revenue. Tourism can be particularly attractive to governments of developing countries and regions, as it brings badly needed foreign currency into the country (which is needed to pay for imports).

Visitor attractions such as pristine beaches, national parks, cultural and historic landmarks, etc. are often located in economically backward regions, making tourism a good alternative to other industries (such as agriculture, fishing, forestry, etc.) as a means to increase local employment and income.

Marketing South Africa as a tourist destination

Government can influence the size of the economic impact of tourism in a number of ways, for example by:

- improving transport infrastructure, such as airports and roads
- facilitating access to the country by limiting formalities at border crossings
- offering flexible and attractive loans to encourage entrepreneurial activities in tourism and to help include the informal sectors often involved in tourism-related activities
- facilitating inter-industry cooperation and supporting local industry to maximise linkages
- marketing the region or country as a whole through a destination marketing organisation (DMO) or board
- ensuring stable and continuous growth rates in the economy, low inflation rates, and internal political stability to keep the region or country attractive for visitors.

The South African government is also involved in the marketing of the nation as a whole to international and domestic tourists. The country's **national tourism organisation** (NTO), South African Tourism (SA Tourism), is the official marketing arm of the Department of Environmental Affairs and Tourism (DEAT), which aims to promote the country as an international tourist destination (see Chapter 8 – The government and tourism). SA Tourism uses marketing activities to:

- maximise tourist volumes and expenditure
- increase the dispersal of all visitors across South Africa to spread the economic benefits and encourage development
- promote a unique African experience
- to co-ordinate, where appropriate, data, research, and product information for the industry nationally through regional co-operation
- to promote southern Africa as a tourism hub for the benefit of the whole region
- to offer visitors a quality-assurance instrument.

WWW

Browse this website: www.southafrica.net

Tourism activities are also an important source of taxation revenue (see Table 15.2). Levies such as the SA departure tax, a fee paid by all inbound and outbound travellers, are an attractive form of revenue generation for government, and are often hidden as part of a package arrangement or within the overall cost of a tourism offering, so that the consumer is often unaware of their existence. Consumer levies on tourism offerings – 1% on accommodation, car hire companies and coach operators in South Africa – also make up part of the final price for the consumer, but don't directly benefit the supplier. Other tourism providers collect a levy by other agreed methods.

Tourists also generate taxation revenue through the purchase of tourism offerings which are subject to sales tax and other levies. Hospitality tax is an example of *ad valorem* taxes (i.e. taxes which are set as a percentage of the price), while airport departure taxes and visas are *specific* (i.e. they are set at a given price).

Table 15.2 Total tourist expenditure by category of spend, 2005

Category of Spend	% of total
Accommodation	25
Transport	12
Food and beverages	11
Leisure and entertainment	10
Medical	18
Shopping	25
Total	100

South African Tourism, 2006. *2005 Annual tourism report*. Illovo: South African Tourism Strategic Research unit.

Stimulating regional development and regeneration

Besides income generation and job creation, tourism also promotes the development of regions where economic options are otherwise limited. For example, in South African coastal areas, such as the West Coast in the Western Cape, tourism is developed as a vehicle for regional economic development. In addition, national parks, farm stays (known as 'agritourism'), wineries ('wine tourism'), and gambling casinos contribute to the economic development of regions in SA (see Chapter 4 – Managing visitor attractions).

Tourism may also be used in regeneration schemes. According to Tribe, regeneration is generally about replacing the gap left by declining industries by implanting new centres of economic activity (2005: 297). Tourism provides a way of attracting expenditure and creating jobs. There is a threefold impact on regeneration. Firstly, local jobs are provided at the construction stage of new projects. Secondly, local jobs are created when the new projects are commissioned. Thirdly, tourism projects often attract spending from outside the local area.

Since the mid-1990s, South Africa's major cities such as eThekwini, Johannesburg and Cape Town have all enhanced their external image, attracting both tourism and investment. Hosting mega-events is also an effective way of kick-starting economies. The 2010 FIFA World Cup showpiece is projected to attract over 3-million visitors, increase the international profile of SA, and act as a catalyst for a range of residential, retail, and business developments.

With these issues in mind, our attention now turns to the negative impacts associated with tourism.

Negative economic impacts of tourism

According to Mason (2003: 35) some of the negative economic consequences of tourism to a local destination include the following:

- inflation/increased living costs – increases in the prices of local property, land, and food
- opportunity costs – the cost of engaging in tourism rather than another form of economic activity (for example, in a coastal region, with a predominantly rural hinterland, this could be the costs of investing in tourism instead of in arable farming or fishing)
- over-dependence on tourism – for example, small countries become dependent on tourism revenue to the extent that any change in demand is likely to lead to a major economic crisis.

There are also risks associated with excessive dependence on tourism in an economy. These include exposure to the effects of impacts such as natural disasters (for example, the South-East Asia tsunami in 2004), or criminal activities, such as those by terrorist groups. Tourists react quickly to such events, and can leave a tourist region without any income if there are perceived reasons to avoid the area.

The socio-cultural impact of tourism

As we have seen in the last section, tourism can be a strong force for economic benefit, creating employment and income. In this section we examine the positive and negative socio-cultural impacts of tourism – the somewhat more discreet and hidden effects. In general, it is difficult to distinguish between social and cultural impacts, as they are interlinked. However, the social impacts of tourism are more easily identifiable, and tend to have a more immediate effect on both tourists and host communities (for example, increased crime rates), whereas the cultural impacts (for example, changes in language) are those which lead to longer term, gradual change in a society's values, beliefs, and cultural practices.

Before examining these impacts, we will first consider the factors which determine the degree of socio-cultural impact of tourism and tourists on a destination area

The factors influencing socio-cultural change

It is inevitable that the presence of large numbers of tourists – many from different cultures from that of their hosts – will have an effect on the societies they visit (Brown, 1998: 66). A host community can act as an important attraction for tourists – including craft and art works, music, dance and religious festivals. The degree to which these impacts influence visitors and host communities depends on a number of factors.

In general, the greater the contrast between the tourist-generating country and the receiving (destination) country in terms of culture and economic development, the more significant the impacts are likely to be. For example, differences in the wealth of visitors and the host community have been shown to have a negative effect on a destination. This is particularly evident in certain developing countries, where the host community constantly witnesses the relative wealth of visitors and become dissatisfied with their own lifestyles. Another important factor is the type of tourist which the destination attracts. Mass tourists, such as holidaymakers on a package tour, are less likely to adapt to local norms, and will look for Western amenities, while explorer-type tourists, such as those visiting the destination because they want to experience local culture, usually adjust better to the local environment (see Table 15.3). Clearly, the second type of tourist is going to have less negative impact on the socio-cultural values and behaviour of the host community.

The other more specific factors influencing these impacts include:
- who the tourists are (what is their origin, are they domestic or international visitors, are they from developed or developing countries, how well travelled/travel experience?)
- what is the scale of tourism (how many tourists are involved?)
- the ratio of visitors to residents
- how developed is the tourism industry? (the speed and intensity of tourism development)
- what infrastructure (roads, telecommunications, and electricity supply) exists for tourism?

Table 15.3 Smith's typology of tourists (1992)

Type of tourist	Numbers of tourists	Adaptation to local norms
Explorers	Very limited	Adapts fully
Elite tourists	Few, rarely seen	Adapts fully
Off-beat tourists	Uncommon, but seen	Adapts well
Unusual tourists	Occasional	Adapts somewhat
Incipient mass tourists	Steady flow	Seeks Western amenities
Mass tourists	Continuous influx	Expects Western amenities
Charter tourists	Massive arrivals	Demands Western amenities

Source: Smith, V.L., 1992. (Ed). *Hosts and Guests: an anthropology of tourism.* Philadelphia: University of Pennsylvania Press

- the seasonality of tourism (time of year)
- the extent of foreign ownership.

Key socio-cultural impacts resulting from tourism

There are a range of negative effects resulting from tourism, including:

Crime

Despite the fact that crime against tourists is not a new phenomenon, the link between tourist victimisation and tourism demand is difficult to establish. This is because there are many exogenous factors involved in the tourist's decision-making process (see Chapter 14 – Marketing for tourism). Some of these factors include economic considerations, accessibility, climate, the extent and effect of a destination marketing organisation's (DMO) marketing activities, changes in consumer behaviour, and so on.

Tourists have been found to be susceptible to crime for various reasons, sometimes by chance (being in the wrong place at the wrong time), or because they are purposely targeted by local criminals. Tourists are considered 'easy targets', as they are clearly identifiable by appearance, language, dress codes, and mannerisms (they also tend to 'let their guard down' whilst on holiday). In addition, it is assumed that tourists carry with them significant sums of cash and other 'portable wealth', such as digital cameras, i-pods, and jewellery (see Figure 15.3).

Studies on the relationship between tourism and crime have been hampered by a lack of available data on tourist victims of crime. This can be attributed to systems which do not distinguish between crimes committed against tourists and

Figure 15.3 Factors that make tourists targets of criminal activity

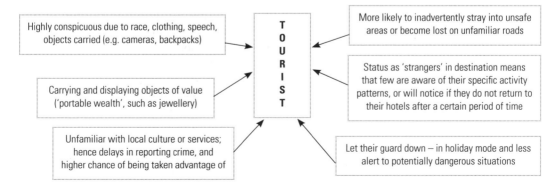

those against local residents (George, 2003: 2). Certain destinations have started to make this distinction, but are reluctant to release such data for fear of adverse publicity.

It is not only locals that take advantage of tourists, but also the tourism industry that participates in illegal activities. A number of local tourism businesses and individuals eager to 'chase the tourist dollar' and make money rapidly (referred to as 'fly-by-nighters') may contribute to giving a destination a 'rip-off' image.

Prostitution and sex

Tourism creates conditions under which prostitution can thrive. Tourists have left the restrictions of their own society, and may be willing to indulge in activities which they would not usually consider in their home environment. In addition, sex tourists in general are assured of anonymity.

European destinations such as Amsterdam, Hamburg, Soho in London, Asian cities such as Bangkok and Manila, and areas within South Africa such as Green Point in Cape Town and the Point in eThekwini, have become notorious sex-destinations. 'Sex Tours' to such destinations are openly promoted and advertised in some tourist-generating countries such as Japan and the USA. It should be noted that prostitution is legal in these all destinations, but not in South Africa. It is difficult, as with crime, to assess the extent to which tourism has led to an increase in prostitution as opposed to other factors (for example, increased population in the destination community). Most authors agree that the problem with **sex tourism** is not prostitution in general, but the illegal forms of it such as child prostitution and associated activities such as narcotics. Of particular concern is an increase in the popularity of child sex tourism, defined by the United Nations as 'tourism organised with the primary purpose of facilitating the effect of a commercial sexual relationship with a child'.

Gambling

Certain destinations that offer casino gambling – to meet the needs of visitors – are often associated with criminal activities such as organised crime, begging, and prostitution.

Rural-urban migration

In developing countries in particular, tourism can entice younger people to leave traditional activities in order to seek employment (and perceived higher wages) in the tourism industry.

Tourism, therefore, can have an adverse effect on other industries such as agriculture, fishing, and forestry by drawing people away from the land into employment in hotels, etc.

Health issues

Tourists travelling to destinations may introduce disease to resident communities, for example, HIV/AIDS and other sexually-transmitted diseases, avian flu, and the Ebola virus.

The demonstration effect

One of the most notable socio-cultural impacts of tourism is referred to as the 'demonstration effect', where local residents begin to adapt and change their values and modes of behaviour to imitate those of the visitors. The extent of the demonstration effect depends on the visible differences between the hosts and visitors. The **demonstration effect** is most likely to occur where the contacts between residents and visitors are relatively superficial and short-lived (Williams, 1998). To a certain extent the demonstration effect is inevitable: as Sharpley points out: 'whilst on holiday, tourists demonstrate levels of affluence that are usually beyond the reach of local people' (1999: 204).

The demonstration effect may be advantageous or disadvantageous to the host community. On the one hand, observing tourists may encourage locals, particularly in developing countries, to strive for possessions they lack. In other words, it may assist development. On the other hand, the demonstration effect may cause discontentment and resentment amongst locals because the degree of wealth and freedom of behaviour displayed by visitors imposes an impossible goal. As a result of the latter, increased consumption expectations among local populations aspiring to material standards of tourists may lead to the copying of consumption patterns (Wall & Mathieson, 2006: 239).

Language

One of the most widely cited socio-cultural impacts resulting from tourism is that of a decline in the use of the vernacular language, because the universal mode of conversation in tourism is in European languages, chiefly English and French. (Pearce, 1989: 219.)

Commodification

Another negative socio-cultural impact of tourism is the commoditisation of a destination's culture, or its conversion into a commodity in response to the perceived or actual demands of the tourist market (Greenwood, 1989). Crafts, ceremonies, and cultural performances may be modified in accordance with the demands of tourism. Problems occur when the reproduction and sale of cultural artefacts become more important than the meaning and qualities of the products.

Staged authenticity

Staged authenticity takes place when the locals provide tourists with 'staged' cultural experiences which appear 'authentic', and by so doing offer those tourists what they think is a genuine experience of another culture (MacCannell, 1989: 91). Examples of this are when Zulu tribal dancing is arranged for mass tourists as a form of cabaret, or gumboot dancing is staged as a set performance for groups of tourists at shopping centres and other tourist sites (see Figure 15.4). Tourists seek 'authentic African' arts and curios as souvenirs,

Figure 15.4 Authenticity and tourism

'Could you look a bit more…authentic?'
The ethics of travel photography

but are often content to buy what they believe to be an authentic example of artwork. This, in turn, has encouraged businesses to mass-produce poorly crafted works (also known as *airport art*) or local artists to change their traditional styles by reducing the size of their works to make them more transportable for tourists (Holloway, 2006: 129).

Tourism can often result in positive effects for the social and cultural characteristics of a destination area, including the following:

Preservation of culture and heritage

Experiencing culture and local heritage is often a major attraction for visitors. Many destination marketing organisations (DMOs) are keen to promote this aspect. Revenue accrued from tourism can be used to help restore or preserve heritage and historical buildings and sites (for example, landmarks pertaining to South Africa's struggle, such as the Robben Island Museum near Cape Town, the Hector Pieterson Museum & Memorial, and the Mandela Museum in Soweto). This can be achieved through revenue collected by the sale of souvenirs, entrance fees, and donations (for example, the percentage of receipts donated to local communities and schools by township tour operators and tourists).

Renewal of cultural pride

A sense of pride felt by residents in their culture can be reinforced or renewed when they observe tourists appreciating it (Inskeep, 1991: 370). Tourism can inject new life into ceremonies and rituals, skills, and crafts. Without tourism, such activities may cease to exist.

Promotion of peace and cross-cultural understanding between tourists and locals

Tourism can promote a culture of peace and understanding, due to direct contacts between visitors and host communities. Contacts between tourists and host communities can help to dispel stereotyping. In South Africa, direct contacts with American, British, and Asian tourists have contributed to the erosion of stereotypes held by some South Africans. However, this effect may also be reversed, and may reinforce stereotypes.

Improved infrastructure for the local community

Tourism, in most instances, results in improvements to the existing infrastructure in destination areas. Large-scale tourism development usually leads to improvements in the existing infrastructure which are required to meet the needs of tourists, such as roads, telecommunications, public transport, airports, water and sewage systems, etc. While these improvements are needed because of the increase of visitor numbers, they also may be of benefit to local communities.

Provision of community facilities and public services

Tourism development can result in socio-cultural benefits such as the development of additional facilities and services that can be enjoyed by the local destination community as well as tourists. For example, public services such as a tourist information centre (TIC) in a town centre may be provided primarily for visitors to the area. However, local residents will also benefit from being able to use the TIC to book tickets to festivals, events, and visitor attractions. Similarly, tourist destinations tend to have a wide range of restaurants and entertainment venues to cater for tourists. These facilities are also available for the local inhabitants.

The socio-cultural impact of travel on tourists

An area which has received scant research attention is that of how tourists are influenced by their own experiences of foreign cultures. For example, the increase in the number of outbound South African tourists visiting the likes of the United Kingdom, Australia, and Thailand during the late 1990s resulted in lifestyle changes as well as a wider appreciation of foreign cultural activities by the South Africans. Examples of these include changes ranging from clothing fashion styles and culinary tastes to a general broader understanding and appreciation of foreign cultures.

However, certain elements that tourists bring back with them may be less appreciated. Health issues, ranging from sunstroke and skin cancer to stomach upsets, malaria, HIV/Aids, and sexually-transmitted diseases compound the health threats for tourists. The answer to these issues lies in improved education, and an understanding within tourism industry businesses of the need to responsibly inform and educate their customers via brochures, information booklets, websites, and front-line staff.

Another factor which has been overlooked by tourism researchers is that of tourists themselves committing crimes. Tourists commit crimes either against locals or other tourists, or may participate in sex-related activities, drug smuggling, and gambling. Furthermore, tourists, particularly in large groups, are known to display drunken behaviour and other forms of anti-social behaviour. During 'Hermanus matric week', for example, thousands of young South African school-leavers flock to this small Western Cape fishing and tourist resort to participate in partying and underage drinking.

Discussion point

Discuss the socio-cultural impacts that arise from the growing tendency for British and German tourists to buy properties as second homes in South Africa.

Measuring the socio-cultural impact of tourism

Whereas the economic impacts are measurable, the socio-cultural impacts by tourists are the most difficult to quantify and measure. Some effects are obvious, such as the outbreak of diseases and/or infections, while many others, such as changes in social values and the demonstration effect, are difficult to measure. Similarly, those that are easier to identify, such as prostitution, gambling, and increased crime rates are difficult to attribute to tourism rather than other influencing factors (such as the societal issues of unemployment, poverty, and media reporting). This partially explains why these impacts have been regarded as less significant than economic impacts.

Discussion point

In relation to a tourism development in your area, identify and discuss the main types of socio-cultural impacts. Arrange these impacts under the headings of positive and negative.

Research sources used to gather information with respect to socio-cultural impacts include primary and secondary sources (see Table 15.4). *Primary research* involves contact with past, existing, or potential tourists using research methods such as surveys, interviews, observations, and focus groups (group discussions). Surveys, for example, are particularly useful for gaining insight into visitors' and residents' perceptions of tourism's socio-cultural impacts. It is important to obtain a random sample – one that is representative of the population being surveyed, to gauge the accurate impact and the extent of its penetration. The survey should also be administered at different times of the year, to counter the issue of seasonality (as resentment may subside after

the peak season). In addition, it is important to establish whether or not the respondent can make a distinction between a tourist and a member of the community.

There are a range of *secondary research* sources available. These include newspaper articles, crime statistics, notification of infectious diseases data, employment statistics, TV and radio news, and documentary programmes.

Doxey's Irridex model

Numerous theories that seek to measure the socio-cultural impacts of tourism have been proposed. One of the most widely used is Doxey's 'Index of Tourist Irritation' (or, quite simply, '**Irridex**'). Doxey (1975) measured residents' attitudes towards tourism in Canada and the Caribbean, in order to identify the stages that they went through. Doxey's framework shows increasing irritation of residents as the impact of visitor numbers increases (see Table 15.5).

Table 15.4 Data collection sources for assessing socio-cultural impacts of tourism

Indicators	Primary		Secondary data
	Survey	Observation	
Crime rates	✗		✗
Prostitution		✗	✗
Demonstration effects	✗	✗	
Health	✗		✗
Gambling	✗		✗
Social values	✗	✗	✗
Host/tourist hostility	✗		✗

Table 15.5 Doxey's Irridex model

Stage	Characteristics	Symptoms
1	Euphoria	Visitors welcomed, limited formal development
2	Apathy	Visitors taken for granted, contacts become commercial
3	Annoyance	Locals concerned about tourism, efforts made to improve infrastructure
4	Antagonism	Open hostility from locals, attempts to limit damage and tourism flows
5	Resignation	Residents realise that they must adapt to an altered community setting

Source: Doxey, G.V., 1975. 'A causation theory of resident-visitor irritants: methodology and research inferences'. In *Proceedings of the Travel Research Association 6th Annual Conference, San Diego*, pp 195–198. Travel Research association.

Managing the socio-cultural impacts

According to Mason (2003: 82), the key role-players in the management of tourism's socio-cultural impacts include:

- tourists
- the host population
- the tourism industry
- the media
- government agencies (at local, provincial, national, and international level).

The fundamental approach for managing the socio-cultural impacts of tourism in a destination involves focusing on the demand-side: the management of tourists. Tourists are critical in the management of the socio-cultural impacts of tourism, as they are often perceived as the major cause of the problems of tourism. The education of visitors, using interpretation techniques through various verbal and written methods, including books, maps, signs, and tourist guides, is necessary. It is more likely that if the tourist guide is a member of the host community being visited, that guide will show cultural sensitivity towards this community (Mason, 2003: 84).

Initiatives involving the tourism industry include informing the host community of the benefits of tourism, so that they take pride in the destination and 'look after tourists'. A major national initiative to increase awareness of tourism is the Department of Environmental Affairs and Tourism's (DEAT) 'SA Welcome campaign'. Launched in 1999, it aims to sensitise South Africans to the needs of international tourists. The logo for the campaign features a South African flag-draped 'Welcome' character, with arms outstretched in greeting (see Figure 15.5). The core message of the 'Welcome' logo is that 'tourism is everyone's business'. Everyone has a role to play in making South Africa an international destination of note, and improving the tourist's experience.

Figure 15.5 DEAT's SA Welcome campaign logo

The environmental impact of tourism

In the two previous sections, we explored the various ways in which tourism can impact economically and socially on people, both tourists and hosts, in destination regions. In this section we examine tourism's impact upon the environment. There are both positive and negative environmental effects on tourism and associated activities, just as there are with the economic and socio-cultural impacts. In general, the impacts are greater where the environment is more underdeveloped or fragile.

The environment is a powerful resource for tourism, as it plays a key role in attracting tourists to the destination. In view of the inseparable nature of tourism – where tourists have to visit the place of production in order to consume the output – it is inevitable that tourist activity will be associated with environmental impacts. The growth of **mass tourism** in the 1960s, along with an increasing awareness of the impact of humans on the environment, led to a growing realisation that nature is an exhaustible resource. This point was emphasised in the seminal research carried out by Young (1973). Young's study was a prominent turning point in the analysis of tourism's impact on the natural and built environments, as it questioned the validity of uncontrollable tourism development.

Figure 15.6 The concept of the environment

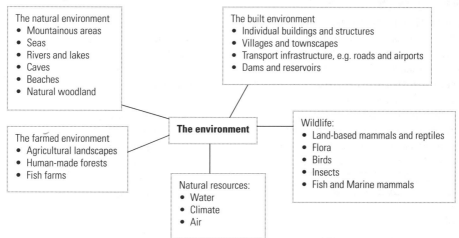

Before examining the impact of tourism on the environment, we must first understand what is meant by the term 'environment'. It is a generic concept, often interpreted as the physical or natural features of a landscape. Swarbrooke (1999), however, identified five main aspects of the environment. These are: the natural environment, wildlife, the farmed environment, the built environment, and natural resources (see Figure 15.6 above).

The main environmental costs of tourism include pollution, erosion of land, litter, traffic congestion, loss of natural habitats, and the depletion of natural resources.

Environmental pollution

One of the most obvious impacts of tourism is pollution. There are three aspects of environmental pollution, namely:

*   *Transport pollution,* including noise pollution, is often amplified in urban areas as a result of increased road and air traffic. Aircraft produce significant amounts of nitrogen oxide during take-off and landings (see Chapter 5 – Managing transport for tourists). Air pollution is also associated with the development of airports for international, domestic, and business tourism. Water travel (used for whale-watching, for example) and water-based sports create water pollution, thus becoming effects of transport pollution.

*   *Architectural pollution,* due to the effect of inappropriate hotel and conference centre development on the natural landscape, as well as other tourist facilities such as car parking, signposting, retail shops, advertising billboards, and toilet facilities.

*   *Visual pollution,* through the design of unsightly tourist structures, in particular high-rise concrete hotels.

Erosion of land

Large increases in visitor numbers can often impact on the environment through land erosion. For example, visitors to national parks such as the Table Mountain National Park have caused the erosion of pathways (see Chapter 4 – Managing visitor attractions – case study). Damage to the land increases when tourists stray off these hardened paths and, in so doing, begin to create new ones. The construction of new facilities in coastal areas can erode sand dunes and beaches. Similarly, the increase in popularity of winter sports holidays has caused large areas of forest to be cleared, to enable the construction of hotels and ski lodges. Beaches are particularly fragile, and can be severely damaged through irresponsible tourism activity such as driving on beaches (see Example box overleaf).

Example Ban on 4x4s driving on beaches

In 2004, DEAT announced a ban on driving on beaches, based on a research study which found that beach-driving had a negative impact on the natural environment of a coastal zone. The study was carried out in the iSimangaliso Wetlands Park (the Greater St. Lucia Wetland Park) in KwaZulu-Natal. Vehicles on beaches, which enable people to visit remote stretches on the coast they would not have been able to on foot, cause a significant disturbance to breeding birds.

Litter

Littering by tourists at destinations and visitor attractions can detract from the aesthetic quality of the environment and harm wildlife. Not only does it change the soil content in terms of nutrients, but litter can also result in animals being attracted into tourist areas. This causes a change in animal feeding habits and diet, as they begin to rely increasingly on the litter as a quick and easy source of food.

Similarly, the disposal of solid waste by cruise liners is a well-documented problem. Until very recently, cruise liners were openly dumping their solid waste into the ocean. Only with great amounts of public pressure and persistent monitoring has this trend been curbed. Although the bigger cruise liners are being carefully monitored, the smaller and less prominent ones are still dumping without action being taken against them, although international environmental agencies are aware of this, and regulations will be put in place and enforced before long.

Traffic congestion

Traffic congestion from cars and tourist coaches is a problem in destination areas that cannot handle large volumes of traffic, such as narrow streets in tourist areas and along scenic routes. At peak periods, traffic congestion can lead to disruption for local road users, damage to roads, the visual intrusion of traffic jams, and an increase in traffic-related accidents.

Loss of natural habitats/wildlife

Tourism development can have a profound effect on ecosystems, often resulting in the loss of the natural habitats of indigenous animal and plant life. In the Florida Keys, USA, for example, a recent study revealed that 57% of the coral reefs showed damage caused by propellers and the grounding of boats. Furthermore, large numbers of visitors can disturb the natural life of animals, and result in the disruption of animal breeding and eating patterns. For example, on safari tours the noise of passengers can place a great deal of stress on the animals being observed.

Depletion of natural resources

Tourism activities can put scarce natural resources, such as water, under pressure. Golf courses and swimming pools require large amounts of water, and often illegally block off streams or take water from reservoirs (Burns & Holden, 1995: 175). Depletion can also be witnessed through deforestation as trees are cleared for land use, fuel, and camp-fires.

Tourism, by contributing to awareness of the need to conserve sensitive landscapes and buildings, can have beneficial impacts. The revenue generated from visitor or guest charges can be used to preserve and maintain threatened visitor sites (see Example box below).

Example Bushmans Kloof's environmental projects

Bushmans Kloof Wilderness Reserve & Retreat is situated approximately 270 kilometres north of Cape Town, on the edge of the Cederberg Wilderness Area. This unique Wilderness Reserve is an ecological oasis situated between the plains of the Great Karoo and the Cederberg Mountains. Over the last 10 000 years, it has been the favoured hunting ground of the San, who once travelled across Africa in search of food and water. Bushmans Kloof is the proud custodian of more than 130 pristine rock art sites, and is widely recognised as 'the world's largest open-air art gallery'.

Bushmans Kloof is actively involved in a number of major environmental projects that have a great deal of impact on the biodiversity of the Cedarberg region. These include the Cape Leopard Trust, set up to conserve the predator's diversity, as well as playing a role in helping to save the Cape mountain zebra from extinction. They have also given their commitment to the Clanwilliam Cedar Tree Project, to guard against the possible extinction of the Clanwilliam Cedar.

Discussion point

Discuss the environmental impacts in relation to a tourism activity in your area. Classify the impacts under the headings 'positive' and 'negative'.

In the next section, we discuss the ways in which the environmental impacts of tourism can be minimised.

Managing the environmental impact of tourism

Carrying capacity, visitor and traffic management and **environmental impact assessments** (EIAs) are the most effective and widely-used tools in relation to helping with the planning and management of environmental impacts.

Carrying capacity

Carrying capacity is the maximum number of people who can use a site without an unacceptable alteration in the physical environment and an unacceptable decline in the quality of the experience gained by visitors (Wall & Mathieson, 2006: 32). It refers to the maximum use of any site without causing negative impacts on the resources, reducing visitor satisfaction, or exerting negative impacts upon the destination. The concept of carrying capacity is important for determining and understanding the impacts of tourism.

O'Reilly (1986) identified four types of carrying capacity:
- *Physical carrying capacity* refers to physical space and the number of people (or the number of vehicles).
- *Environmental carrying capacity* is the extent and degree of tourism impacts upon the physical environment.
- *Psychological carrying capacity*: this is the level of crowding that a visitor is willing to tolerate before he/she decides a particular site is too full, and goes elsewhere.
- *Social carrying capacity*: the reaction of the local community to tourism.

All four carrying capacities are not independent of each other, but it may be possible to exceed the threshold limit of one capacity for a limited amount of time without there necessarily being a harmful effect upon another type of capacity. For example, it is possible that an increase in the number of hikers in a mountain area could lead to increased levels of destruction of flora from trampling, while the satisfaction of the visitors is not diminished.

Visitor and traffic management

Visitor management techniques are used to mitigate the negative environmental impacts of tourism. According to Page and Dowling (2002), there are two types of visitor management technique:
- *hard measures*. Aim to limit access and usage by controlling tourist numbers, using high-regulatory techniques such as charging higher entry prices at peak times, adjusting opening times, managing queueing ,and reducing the number of car park spaces
- *soft measures*. Designed to inform or educate, such as information centres; interpretation, and **codes of conduct**. Essentially, these low-regulatory methods influence visitor behaviour, alter visitor attitudes, and spread the distribution of visits (see Example box).

It should be noted that these techniques tend to be more reactive responses to managing environmental problems, rather than proactive.

Traffic management initiatives include:
- park-and-ride services
- improved public transport
- improved road systems
- designated drop-off points and parking for tourist coaches.

Discussion point

In what situations does a tourism manager decide to use 'hard' and 'soft' measures?

Example TMACC's visitor management techniques

Table Mountain Aerial Cableway Company (TMACC) makes every effort to make visitors feel 'managed', by employing soft and hard measures. They have a code of ethics, and call for visitors to conserve biodiversity and prevent vegetation degradation. Hard measures include signage warning visitors 'not to litter' and 'not to feed the animals'. The carrying capacity of the trails is managed by encouraging hikers to use 'hardened' trails. The area around the viewing deck, where most of the visitors congregate, is heavily controlled, with concrete pathways and handrails. Signage informs visitors what they may and may not do.

www
Browse this website: www.tablemountain.net

Environmental impact assessments (EIAs)

An environmental impact assessment (EIA) is a legal requirement for new tourism developments and land uses. They are carried out by consultants commissioned by developers. EIAs not only evaluate the overall effect that the development will have on the environment, but also identify ways in which negative impacts could be minimised.

Some of the issues that a developer will consider include:
- the costs of the development (during and after construction)
- all of the possible benefits, and who will benefit specifically
- those who may be adversely affected by the development
- whether there is a different way of developing the initiative that would have fewer negative impacts
- how the negative impacts may be minimised.

Sustainable tourism development

The three approaches discussed above focus on visitors or the physical environment. **Sustainable tourism** development aims to address the needs of all role-players in the destination community – locals, the environment, the tourism industry, as well as visitors. This approach aims to maximise the benefits of tourism and minimise the impacts of development on the environment. See Chapter 16 (Managing tourism responsibility) for further discussion on the subject of sustainable tourism development.

Conclusion

This chapter has examined the economic, socio-cultural and environmental impacts associated with tourists and tourism development.

Tourism generates environmental and socio-cultural impacts as well as economic impacts. These impacts, which are mainly concentrated at the destination, may range from economic impacts, such as inflated land value, to more hidden socio-cultural and environmental impacts occurring over a sustained period of time. As yet, there is a dearth of research carried out on the linkages which demonstrate the economic multiplier effect of tourism.

Decision-makers at all levels have to understand the economic, socio-cultural and environmental benefits of tourism. The need for carefully planned and managed tourism in relation to the impacts has become an important issue as international visitor numbers continue to increase. As tourists constantly strive to find new destinations, the need for carefully planned and managed tourism in relation to the impacts has become an important issue.

Review questions

1. What problem do economists have when calculating the economic impact of tourism?

2. Explain why tourism is of interest to politicians trying to alleviate poverty in their region?

3. Explain the key direct and indirect economic impacts of tourism in South Africa.

4. Explain briefly how economists calculate the impact multiplier.

5. What is the association between leakages and linkages?

6. Why would stable and continuous economic growth rates be important to increase tourism?

7. Discuss how tourism can encourage crime at a tourist destination.

Further reading

Bull, A. 1995. *The economics of travel and tourism*, 2nd edition Harlow: Longman.

Fennell, D. A. 2003. *Ecotourism: an introduction*, 2nd edition. New York: Routledge.

Leiper, N. 2004. Tourism management, 3rd edition. Frenchs Forest, New South Wales: Pearson.

Wall, G. & Mathieson, A. 2006. Tourism: change, impacts and opportunities. Harlow, England: Pearson Prentice Hall.

Websites

Statistics on South African tourism: www.southafrica.net

UN-WTO – www.world-tourism.org

SA government statistics www.statssa.org

Fair Trade in Tourism South Africa (FTTSA)

Tourism Concern: www.tourismconcern.org.uk

Green Globe – www.greenglobe21.com

United Nations Environmental Programme – www.unepie.org

References

Economic impacts

Baaijens, S. R., Nijkamp, P. & van Montfort, K. 1997. Explanatory meta-analysis for the comparison and transfer of regional tourist income multipliers. *Regional Studies*, Vol. 32(9), 839–849.

Fletcher, J. E. 1989. Input-output analysis and tourism impact studies. *Annals of Tourism Research*, Vol.16, 514–529.

Goeldner, C. R., McIntosh, R. W. & Brent Ritchie, J. R. 2003. *Tourism: principles, practices, philosophies*, 9th edition. Hoboken New Jersey: John Wiley & Sons.

Raguraman, K. 1997. Estimating the net economic impact of air services. *Annals of Tourism Research,* Vol. 24(3), 658–674.

South African Tourism. 2006. *2005 Annual Tourism Report.* Illovo: South African Tourism Strategic Research Unit.

South African Tourism. 2006. *A Framework/Model to Benchmark* Tourism GDP in South Africa, SA Tourism, Illovo.

Statistics South Africa. 2003. *Tourism Satellite Accounts*, Tshwane: Statistics South Africa.

Thiede, I. 2005. *Measuring the employment impact of international tourism in South Africa*. Unpublished M.Com. University of Cape Town.

TIPS 2004. Quantec Research Unit. *South Africa Standardised Industry Employment* [Online], Available: http://www.tips.easy/data.co.za/tableviewer [2005, February 9].

Tribe, J. 2005. *The economics of recreation, leisure and tourism*, 2nd edition Oxford: Butterworth-Heinemann.

United Nations. 1999. *Handbook of input-output table compilation and analysis*. (Studies in Methods Series F, No. 74, Handbook of National Accounting). New York: Department of Social and National Affairs, Statistics Division.

Williams, S. 1998. *Tourism geography*. London: Routledge.

York, S. 2005. *Eco-tourism can be both a boon and a curse for indigenous peoples*. Institute of Sustainable Living.

Socio-cultural impacts

Brown, F. 1998. *Tourism reassessed: blight or blessing*? London: Butterworth-Heinemann.

Doxey, G. 1975. 'A causation theory of resident-visitor irritants: methodology and research inferences.' In *Proceedings of the Travel Research Association 6th Annual Conference, San Diego*, pp.195–98. Travel Research Association.

George, R. (2003). Tourists' perceptions of safety and security while visiting Cape Town. *Tourism Management,* Vol. 24(5), 575–585.

Greenwood, D. 1989. 'Culture by the pound: an anthropological perspective on tourism as cultural commoditisation'. In V. L. Smith, (Ed.). *Hosts and guests: the anthropology of tourism*, 2nd edition. Philadelphia: University of Pennsylvania, pp. 171–185.

Holloway, J. C. 2006. *The business of tourism*, 7th edition. Harlow: Pearson.

Inskeep, E. 1991. *Tourism planning: an integrated and sustainable development approach*. New York: Van Nostrand Reinhold.

Mason, P. 2003. *Tourism impacts, planning and management*. Amsterdam: Elsevier.

MacCannell, D. 1989. *The tourist: a new theory of the leisure class*, 2nd edition. New York: Schocken Books.

Pearce, D. G. 1989. *Tourism development*. Harlow: London.

Sharpley, R. 1999. *Tourism, tourists and society*, 2nd edition. Huntingdon, Cambridge: ELM Publications.

Smith, V. L. 1992. (Ed.). *Hosts and guests: an anthropology of tourism*. Philadelphia: University of Pennsylvania Press.

Wall, G. & Mathieson, A. 2006. *Tourism: change, impacts, and opportunities*. Harlow: Pearson.

Environmental impacts

Burns, P. & Holden, A. 1995. Tourism: a new perspective. New Jersey: Prentice Hall.

Gunn, C. A. & Var, T. 2002. *Tourism planning*, 4th edition. London: Routledge.

O'Reilly, A. M. 1986. Tourism carrying capacity: concepts and issues. *Tourism Management,* Vol.8(2), 254–258.

Page, S. J. & Dowling, R. 2002. *Ecotourism*. Harlow: Prentice Hall.

Swarbrooke, J. 1999. *Sustainable tourism management*, Wallingford: CABI Publications.

Wall, G. & Mathieson, A. 2006. *Tourism: change, impacts, and opportunities*. Harlow: Pearson.

Young, G. 1973. *Tourism: blessing or blight?* London: Penguin.

ROYAL MAIL SHIP
ST HELENA

Managing the tourist impact on the island of St Helena

Objective

- to discuss the range of economic, social, and environmental pressures that tourism exerts on the island of St Helena

St Helena, for the rest of the world, is known – if known at all – as the place to which Napoleon was exiled by the British, and where he spent the final years of his life. For South Africa, the historical links are richer, as many South Africans would know that Napoleon was not the only person banished there. Prince Dinuzulu, son of the Zulu king, Cetewayo, was exiled there for seven years in 1890 together with some Zulu chiefs, two of whom married island women. During the South African War, some 6 000 Boer prisoners-of-war were imprisoned there. The island has also had its fair share of famous visitors, including Edmund Halley, Captain Cook, and Charles Darwin.

St Helena is one of the remotest islands in the world in any direction. It lies 1 920 kms from the south west coast of Africa, in the middle of the South Atlantic just above the Tropic of Capricorn parallel to the northern Namibian border. Ascension Island lies (1 125 km) north-west of St Helena, making it its nearest neighbour. Tristan da Cunha lies (4260 km) south-west of St Helena. The South American coast is 2 900 kilometres

away, while Cape Town, which is the largest city close to it, is 4 400 kilometres away. No wonder the British sent Napoleon to St Helena. His would have been a very long swim to freedom!

The island was named by the Portuguese Admiral João Da Nova Castella, who discovered it on 21 May 1502, the birthday of St Helen, mother of Emperor Constantine. This small island served for centuries as a port on the way to and from Cape Town, and even today the only way to reach the island is by the Royal Mail Ship, St Helena, which calls at the island a mere 26 times a year. The RMS St Helena, which carries 128 passengers and 1 500 tons of cargo, takes seven days to cruise to the island. The vessel, built with a British government subsidy, provides a lifeline to the island dependencies of St Helena and Ascension, as the former currently has no airport. The British government continues to subsidise the route, experimentally shifting its home port between the UK and South Africa in an effort to lift its appeal. RMS St Helena also calls at Walvis Bay, but is expected to be withdrawn from the route when an airport planned for St Helena is opened around 2012.

The island's population of around 3 880 is known colloquially as the 'Saints'. St Helena has had a number of owners – first the Portuguese, then the Dutch, and finally, from the seventeenth century, the British. St Helena has no political parties, no trade unions, and no crime. With only one town, Jamestown, a very underdeveloped economy and infrastructure, and a dwindling population, St Helena receives more than £13-million (R185m) a year from the British government, making its citizens the most heavily subsidised of the UK dependents. The island has excellent educational facilities, but job creation remains a problem, and many young Saints do contract work on Ascension Island, the Falklands, or in the UK. Others serve aboard the RMS St Helena, which has two crews of 57. St Helena gets all its imports via the mail ship, the only vessel to call at the island regularly.

St Helena has a semi-desert coastline with a tropical interior and a tropical marine climate. It has a wealth of indigenous plants, a dramatic topography, two national parks, as well as important historical buildings dating back to Napoleon's time. It is a real paradise for adventure tourists such as hikers, climbers, fishermen, and scuba divers. St Helena is, however, isolated, which – though a possible selling point for some – can be a disadvantage. The fact that it does not have an airport and is serviced only by a cargo-passenger ship that sails from Cape Town for seven days and nights, and then requires a stay of seven days at the island before departing, is certainly a drawback. Furthermore, it does not have beaches in the classic sense, and most of what the islanders use must be imported.

Nevertheless, with improved accessibility and communication links, it will have good prospects for development of its tourism potential. Needless to say, the cost of constructing an airport will be substantial, given that the planned runway is to be big enough to accommodate long-range Boeing 737-800s and Airbus A320s. This, in itself, calls for a runway of over 2 250 metres in length on what is a small island (122 square kilometres) with very little flat land. The runway is of particular concern to environmentalists, given that the chosen site, Prosperous Bay Plain, is an area of exceptional interest. In addition, the local St Helena Leisure Corporation (Shelco) has come up with a series of proposals, including luxury hotels and a golf course, to entice tourists. Backing Shelco is the international hotel group, Oberoi Hotels and Resorts, which operates a string of luxury sites from Mauritius to Melbourne.

The St Helena administration has welcomed the development project, although it has not found universal acceptance among the Saints, historians, and conservationists. Dr Rebecca Cairns-Wicks, a leading St Helena expert and conservation biologist who lives on the island, is concerned about the environmental impact of the proposed development. She said: 'There are incredibly rare trees and flora on this island. Plants, extinct elsewhere, have survived, and some of the most endangered flora in the world is here'. Dr Cairns-Wicks added: 'There's the false gumwood tree – we're down to the last eight plants in the wild on the island. We have only one surviving variety of land bird, the St Helena Wirebird, and they are down to only about 400'. The Wirebird has drawn birdwatchers from all over the world. A land bird, it flies only when necessary, and its key habitat is right on the flight-path of the new airport.

St Helena's Director of Tourism has also expressed concerns that the development of an airport and an up-market resort could easily lead to the island being swamped by tourists, thereby losing much of its present charm. Not surprisingly, mass tourism is being considered as an avenue of increased economic prosperity. One thing is for certain, St Helena is set to change!

www

www.sainthelena.gov.sh
www.rms-st-helena.com

Case study questions

1. The economic impacts of tourism can be boosted by increasing linkages within the economy. Explain why this might not work very well on the island of St Helena.

2. Leakages are very high, as most goods consumed both by locals and by tourists need

to be imported by ship. Can you think of any projects that the Saints could embark on to try and reduce the amount of imports?

3. Identify the main types of socio-cultural impact of tourism you think the Saints may be facing if they develop tourism to their island.

4. What environmental problems are likely to occur as a result of the construction of an airport on the island?

5. Why do you think the Director of Tourism has reservations about the development of an airport on the island?

Jacob's Ladder and Grand Parade, St Helena

16

Managing tourism responsibly

Nicole Frey

Purpose

The purpose of this chapter is to discuss the key concepts underlying responsible tourism management (RTM), and how this approach can benefit tourism organisations.

Learning outcomes

After reading this chapter, you should be able to:
- explain what is meant by managing tourism responsibly
- demonstrate why it is necessary for tourism companies to adopt sustainable management practices
- recognise the business opportunities that can be achieved by responsible tourism management
- identify the role that tourism plays in addressing national challenges of poverty alleviation, job creation, and inequality
- recognise national and international initiatives that have been introduced to promote ethical and responsible tourism management

- explain what management practices are needed to make tourism more responsible.

Chapter overview

This chapter begins by addressing the global rise in corporate social responsibility (CSR), and describes how this trend has impacted on tourism. The business case for responsible tourism management (RTM) is presented, and the benefits that can accrue to an individual business outlined.

We will then look at the potential of tourism to address the socio-economic challenges in South Africa. The chapter concludes with a discussion on the various national and international initiatives that have been launched to promote the adoption of RTM.

The case study at the end of the chapter provides an example from the tourism industry where responsible management practices have been successfully employed.

Introduction

Responsible tourism management (RTM) is necessary for a sustainable industry, and can be profitable for tourism businesses. Internationally, the pressure on companies to raise their levels of corporate social responsibility (CSR) has increased, and tourism, as one of the largest industries in the world, is not exempt from such global trends. Responsible tourism practices have the potential to bring a host of different benefits to a range of stakeholders. It is therefore necessary that both the private and public sectors recognise how individual and societal objectives can be aligned in order to achieve a representative, sustainable tourism industry. With this in mind, we now turn our attention to what is meant by managing tourism responsibly.

What is meant by managing tourism responsibly?

According to the Responsible Tourism Manual for South Africa (RTMSA, 2002), which was developed for the Department of Environmental Affairs and Tourism (DEAT), the concept underlying RTM is to provide a superior holiday experience for visitors and improve business opportunities for the tourism sector. The objectives of this approach are to increase the socio-economic benefits to local communities, include a broader spectrum of stakeholders in the decision-making process, promote the sustainable use of limited resources, and improve the tourism offering to the consumer (Pender & Sharpley, 2005: 197).

Numerous terms have emerged in recent years that aim to address some of these goals. For the purpose of this chapter we have chosen to use the broader concept of *responsible tourism management (RTM)*, which incorporates most of the underlying principles of the definitions shown in Table 16.1 overleaf.

Discussion point

Discuss the unifying principle which underlies the definitions in Table 16.1.

Reasons for managing tourism responsibly

There are three main reasons why it has become important for the tourism industry to adopt responsible tourism practises. These are as follows:

International trends

Increased pressure from activist groups and individuals such as Greenpeace and Bono (of the band U2) have led to a rise in global CSR awareness. South Africa needs to stay abreast of these international changes if it wants to remain competitive as a country (RTMSA, 2002; King Report II, 2002).

Consumer demand

Consumers in general are demanding more 'responsible' products and transparency from organisations. There has been a marked increase in fair trade products, and research shows clearly that brand equity and loyalty increase with effective CSR. RTM is therefore demand-driven (Goodwin & Francis, 2003).

Increased business opportunities

The tourism industry has seen an international trend away from mass product offerings to more personalised experiences. Respect for local culture and heritage, development of local skills, and increased involvement by the local community in tourism development has led to more authentic and unique experiences which, in turn, enables more stakeholders to participate in the tourism sector.

We will now examine each of these three developments in more detail.

Table 16.1 Definition of sustainable tourism terms

Term	Definition	Author	Emphasis
Responsible Tourism	Responsible tourism aims to provide a better holiday experience for guests and good business opportunities, and better quality of life for surrounding communities through increased socio-economic benefits and improved natural resource management.	Responsible Tourism Manual for South Africa, 2002 (Spenceley, et al., 2002)	1. Develop a **competitive advantage**; 2. Assess, *monitor*, and *disclose* impacts of tourism development; 3. Ensure *involvement* of communities and the establishment of meaningful economic *linkages*; 4. Encourage natural, economic, social, and cultural *diversity*; 5. Promote the *sustainable* use of local resources.
Sustainable tourism	Sustainable tourism means achieving a particular combination of numbers and types of visitors, the cumulative effect of whose activities at a given destination, together with the actions of the servicing businesses, can continue into the foreseeable future without damaging the quality of the environment on which the activities are based.	Middelton, 1998: ix	The responsible management of resources for the use and enjoyment of present and *future* generations. Emphasis is placed on managing the three areas of social, environmental, and financial impacts of tourism.
Ethical Tourism	Ethical tourism is a concept that goes beyond the three principles of sustainability (economic, social and environmental). It recognises that tourists and tourism providers must take some responsibility for their behaviour and attitudes, with each stakeholder group gaining equity in the tourism decision-making process.	Weeden, 2001	Tourists and tourism providers have a moral responsibly for their actions.
Ecotourism	Travelling to relatively undisturbed or uncontaminated natural areas with the specific objective of studying and enjoying the scenery and its fauna and flora, as well as any existing cultural manifestations (both past and present) found in these areas.	Ceballos – Lascurain, 1983, (as cited in Fennell, 2001)	1. Provides for *environmental conservation*, 2. Includes meaningful community participation, 3. Is profitable and can sustain itself.
Cultural/Heritage Tourism	Tourism that respects natural and built environments.	www.planeta.com	Respect for the local natural environment and *local heritage* is emphasised.

Term	Definition	Author	Emphasis
Pro-poor tourism	'Pro-poor' tourism is not a specific tourism product; it is an approach to tourism development and management which ensures that impoverished local communities are able to secure economic benefits from tourism in a fair and sustainable manner.	Ashley, Roe & Goodwin, 2001	Pro-poor tourism may improve the livelihoods of poor people in three main ways: 1. Economic gain through: *employment* and micro-enterprise development; 2. *Infrastructure* gains: roads, water, electricity, telecommunications, waste treatment; 3. *Empowerment* through: engagement in decision-making.
Alternative Tourism	Alternative tourists aim to put as much distance as possible between themselves and mass tourism.	Krippendorf, 1987: 37	Alternative tourism focuses on individualism and having a *unique and authentic* experience by interacting with the local community and environment.

1. International trends

Companies and consumers have realised that unless the planet's finite resources are responsibly managed, they will soon become entirely depleted. The focus has traditionally been on minimising negative environmental impacts of tourism development (see Chapter 15 – Managing the impacts of tourism). Recently, however, social and economic factors such as increased poverty, social inequality, and the eradication of local cultural heritage have been added to the development agenda. The United Nations Millennium Development Goals (MDGs) provide ambitious targets to reduce extreme poverty and hunger. To achieve theses objectives, it is necessary to follow the principles of sustainable development, which are defined below.

Sustainable development

Although specific forums and international organisations had been engaged in the challenges of development that would be sustainable, it was at the 1992 Earth Summit in Rio de Janeiro, and the 2002 World Summit on Sustainable Development (WSSD) in Johannesburg, where world leaders, politicians, and civil society began to seriously discuss the need for **sustainable development**.

Sustainable development advocates a balanced management approach. Present and future generations should be able to benefit from resources. The emphasis, in, tourism lies specifically on minimising and ultimately eliminating the negative impacts of development. These problems include increased inequality in communities, exploitation of natural resources, and high regional leakages. Sustainable development also focuses on maximising long-term positive impacts of development such as creating employment opportunities, increasing the local infrastructure, and preserving the natural and cultural heritage (Spenceley, et al., 2002).

Corporate social responsibility (CSR), Cause Related Marketing (CRM), good corporate governance, corporate citizenship, and corporate social investment (CSI) are terms that have become part of the current management discourse. The increase in terminology and debate indicates that businesses are taking note of consumer pressures for more transparent and ethical business practices. Some of the more common terms are listed throughout this chapter. In a study commissioned by CSR Europe (a non-profit organisation based in Brussels that promotes CSR), 66% of respondents felt that companies should take responsibility for their role in society, and not be solely focused on generating economic profits

(Pender & Sharpley, 2005: 292). In South Africa, 88% of respondents felt that companies should play a greater role in helping the poor and alleviating social problems (UCTUI, 2006). It is important to note, however, that profit generation is an integral part of sustainable development. The emphasis is on creating mutually beneficial (win-win) relationships for all stakeholders, including employees, investors, customers, shareholders, and local communities.

The concepts pertaining to responsibility in the tourism sector need to be viewed in the broader context of the MDGs, as well as the outcomes of both the 1992 Earth Summit in Rio and the 2002 Johannesburg WSSD. These, as with a wide variety of other local, regional and international agreements, are continuing to focus global thinking on the link between rich and poor, the state of the environment and the rights of minorities. These issues are particularly relevant to the tourism sector, and form the foundation of the responsible tourism challenge. Some very important principles emerged out of the WSSD, and are contained in what is referred to as the Jo'burg Memo. These include the following aspects:

- environmental citizen rights
- value in the natural environment
- access to markets and common good
- restructuring financial architecture
- facilitating institutions (Sachs, 2002).

Pro-poor tourism (PPT)

Using tourism as a tool for poverty reduction is often referred to as 'pro-poor' tourism (PPT). PPT should not be seen as a specific type of tourism, but rather as a management approach. It is therefore similar in many ways to RTM. The special characteristics of the tourism sector lend themselves to pro-poor development. These include the labour-intensive nature of tourism, the fact that the product is consumed and produced at the same time, necessitating that people travel to the place of consumption; that tourism by its nature is often situated in more remote areas where economic activity is limited, and plays a pivotal role in stimulating economic growth in least-developed countries (LDCs). PPT pilot studies around the world have highlighted

how important local ownership and control, as well as partnerships with the private sector are in successfully addressing a host of socio-economic challenges (Goodwin & Wilson, 2003).

Responsible management: A strategic tool

In what way all stakeholders can benefit from tourism development is an important question that we have to ask ourselves. CSR stems from philanthropic giving, whereby companies donate a part of their profits to charities or social causes. Previously, little thought was given to how such support could help build brand and company reputation. Szykman's (2004) research findings show that customer perceptions of the company are positively influenced when a company supports a cause that is linked to its core function. In the instance where the link between a socially responsible activity and business operations and objectives is tenuous, consumer scepticism results, potentially harming the firm's reputation (Szykman, 2004). Consequently, CSR has increasingly become part of strategic planning, with companies realising that an inclusive, company-wide approach to responsible management is needed (Pender & Sharpley, 2005: 291).

In the current business climate, it becomes clear that responsible management practices can lead to bottom-line economic gains and can be used to build a strategic advantage (Kotler & Lee, 2005: 8; Porter & Kramer, 2006). We will examine these benefits more closely in the next section.

Triple Bottom Line Accounting Approach

In South Africa, good **corporate governance** was formalised by the 2002 King Report II, which introduced the concept of 'triple bottom line' accounting. This new accounting approach places equal importance on social, environmental and economic performance. Corporate governance is defined as 'the balance between individual and communal goals. The aim is to align as closely as possible the interests of individuals, corporations, and society'.

A fourth 'line' is now emerging within the current global and local CSR thinking. This aspect is not seen as a fourth bottom line, but rather one that supports and holds the three core pillars of the triple bottom line. This fourth aspect is that of governance (see Figure 16.1). What this means is that ethical and responsible governance is the foundation and guiding principle of the other three approaches.

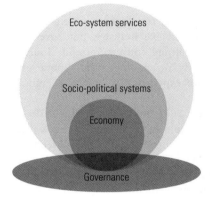

Figure 16.1 CSR approach
(Extract from the Draft National Sustainable Development Framework, 2006)

CSR is also evident in financial markets. A McKinsey & Company survey revealed that more than 84% of investors were willing to pay a premium for the shares of a well-governed company (King Report II, 2002: 14). The emergences of the Financial Times and the London Stock Exchange (FTSE) 4Good index, the Dow Jones Sustainability Group Index, and the Johannesburg Stock Exchange Social Responsibility Index (JSE SRI) provide further evidence of this trend (Porter & Kramer, 2006). These indices are comprised of companies who achieved a certain level of CSR. As a result, organisations are beginning to compete on their social and environmental performances, leading to overall improved management practices. In the next section, we will see how these global trends in business have affected the tourism industry directly.

Discussion point

Consider the definition of CSR in this chapter or in the glossary. Then answer the following questions:

1. Are you aware of any tourism companies that practice CSR?
2. What kinds of activities show their social and environmental commitment?
3. What do you believe to be the motives of companies in supporting certain charities or causes? Do you agree with this objective? Support your argument.

The tourism industry and social responsibility

The tourism industry has been relatively slow to adopt the principles of social responsibility (Tearfund, 2001; Frey, 2007). Tourism, perhaps more than any other industry, has an obvious interest in adopting socially responsible principles, given its high dependency on cultural heritage and the sustained beauty of natural resources.

Lord Marshall, Chairman of British Airways (BA), defines the travel industry as being 'essentially the renting out of short-term lets of other people's environments'. This definition implies that there is a cost associated with making use of a particular environment. This cost should reimburse the host nation for any negative impacts created by the tourist (see Chapter 15 – Managing the impacts of tourism). RTM acknowledges these costs, and tries both to reduce them and to compensate the host nation. Costs are decreased by minimising negative impacts such as labour exploitation and overuse of natural resources. Benefits, on the other hand, are maximised by involving the local community in tourism, and thereby creating income-generating opportunities (Allen & Brennan, 2004: 7).

Furthermore, from a social perspective, the New Partnership for Africa's Development's (NEPAD) Tourism Action Plan (TAP) states that 'tourism is recognised as one of the sectors with the most potential to contribute to the economic regeneration of the continent, particularly through the diversification of African economies' (Rogerson & Visser, 2004: 3). Tourism is arguably the largest industry in the world, and contributes approximately 10,3% to global and 8,2% to local GDP. Moreover, tourism is a highly diverse and labour-intensive sector, providing 1 083 000 South African jobs (7,5% of total employment)[1].

Tourism, therefore, can play an important role in addressing poverty, inequality, and unemployment in the developing world (Rogerson & Visser, 2004: 4). Ibo Island Safaris in Mozambique, as described in the Example box below, illustrates how tourism can have a positive impact on local livelihoods.

Example Ibo Island Safaris Development – Quarimbas Archipelago Mozambique

An estimated 3 000 residents currently live on Ibo Island. Their livelihoods largely depend on a subsistence economy including marine harvesting, minimal agriculture, transport, as well as a very small tourism sector. The current backpacker lodge employs 20 staff. With the development of a proposed up-market lodge, employment is expected to increase to 70. The salaries paid to the 20 staff serve as livelihoods for an average of 20 additional island residents per employee. This implies that the development of a 15-room lodge has the potential to generate livelihoods that could benefit nearly 50% of the entire island population.

Ibo Island Safaris has a local procurement and enterprise development policy in place which greatly reduced regional economic leakages (this differs from most other operators in the region, who fly produce in from South Africa). These policies result in significant creation of revenue for more than 70% of the population.

Livelihoods therefore currently 'earned' from turtle poaching, environmentally marginal fishing practices, biodiversity destruction, and even crime can be greatly reduced and controlled. The additional salaries and income will lead to increased economic activities, enabling the multiplier effect and economic growth.

These benefits will, however, only be realised if the operators apply responsible approaches and actively work to support the emerging local business.

Discussion point

Tourism development is often perceived as a paradoxical term. Discuss this statement with reference to RTM.

2. Consumer demand

Responsible tourism offerings are not only necessary for a sustainable industry, but have also emerged as a strong consumer trend. Tourists are increasingly demanding more unique and authentic travel experiences (Goodwin & Francis, 2003).

Tearfund's 2001 study found that 52% of respondents would be more likely to book their holiday with an operator that had an ethical code of practice in place (Tearfund, 2001). The annual 2002 Association of British Travel Agents (ABTA) survey further indicated that 78% of 'package' tourists felt that the provision of social and environmental information in tour operators' brochures was important to them; their holiday should not harm the environment (87%), and that their visit should benefit the local community (76%)[2].

With the rise of communication systems and the Internet, potential travellers are no longer dependent on travel intermediaries to organise their travel arrangements. Consumers are able to gather information on various holiday destinations, compare offerings, and book all their requirements (for example flights, accommodation, attractions, etc.) online (see Chapter 7 – Managing tourism distribution). One way that destinations can differentiate themselves in this highly competitive industry is through the promotion of local culture and heritage.

Allen & Brennan (2004: 24) note that there has been a rise in the demand for cultural tourism product-offerings. A further benefit can be achieved by placing a value on indigenous heritage. Local heritage is comprised of the traditions, stories, and customs particular to a certain place or people. The RTMSA (2002) notes that communities are not only able to benefit from their unique culture, knowledge, and traditions, but are also given an incentive to safeguard and uphold them. A co-dependent system is consequently formed, making sustainable use of local resources more likely. The challenge for tourism practitioners is to ensure that people living in the immediate surroundings of tourism developments are not exploited, and that local heritage does not become commercialised to the extent that it loses its authenticity. One of the key questions is to understand who, if anyone, actually owns and consequently benefits from tourism related to heritage and culture. Joint decision-making, communication, and the increased involvement of host communities in tourism development are imperative to ensure the sustainability and profitability of these cultural products (Allen & Brennan, 2004: 4). The industry example of 'Wind, Sand, and Stars' tourism highlights how culture is being used to provide employment and safeguard the local heritage (see Example box below).

Example Wind, Sand and Stars

'Wind, Sand, and Stars' in Egypt, trades with local Bedouin families in Sinai and offers expeditions to community projects. The company ensures fair payment to its employees, and subsidises experienced guides to take younger Bedouin tourist guides as their apprentices. In this way, the local community can see that their culture has value, thereby encouraging them to remain in the desert and not seek jobs in the tourist resorts along the costal regions.

---

3. Increased business opportunities

Managing tourism responsibly is based on sound business logic, and has the potential to address some of the socio-economic problems of South Africa.

The South African context

Due to its past, South Africa faces a unique challenge in social development. During apartheid, tourism was 'non-developmental', therefore resulting in a non-representative distribution in tourism ownership. Most historically disadvantaged individuals (HDIs) did not participate in the formal tourism sector, and therefore could not benefit from it economically. Moreover, limited mobility and disposable income precluded most HDIs from travelling themselves. Consequently, there is a lack of support and understanding among South African communities regarding tourism development (Allen & Brennan, 2004: 8). If managed correctly, tourism can lead to job creation, skills development, improved infrastructure, and entrepreneurial opportunities (RTMSA, 2002). South African Tourism's (SA Tourism) recent drive to promote domestic tourism (see Chapter 1) is not only intended to increase tourism numbers, but also aims to educate the South African population about the nature and benefits of tourism. Transformation of the industry has therefore become a key agenda item for DEAT, which has launched several initiatives to bring about this change. The Black Economic Empowerment (BEE) Tourism Charter and Scorecard (2005) recommends how the tourism industry can begin the process of transformation. Tourism will only be able to reach its economic, social, and environmental objectives if a broader base of South Africans is involved in, and has an understanding of, the tourism sector. In order to broaden participation, the tourism industry needs to reflect the demographics of South African society.

A study by Frey (2007) into the responsible management practices of the Cape Town Tourism (CTT) members showed that despite positive attitudes towards RTM, especially small businesses (SMMEs) are finding it difficult to meet the Tourism BEE Charter and Scorecard targets. Only 12.7% of respondents have an HIV/Aids policy and merely 13.7% carry the Fair Trade in Tourism South Africa (FTTSA) trademark. Factors disrupting the linear relaionship between attitude and behaviour include the level of competitiveness in the business environment, the industry sub-sector, business size and the perceived costs of implementing RTM. The findings confirm previous research by van der Merwe & Wöcke, 2007 (2007) and Spenceley (2007) that a majority of South African tourism businesses are not adopting responsible tourism practices despite the evident need and benefits thereof. Frey's (2007) research highlights how important it is to move the industry from a positive attitude to intention to behave responsibility. The channels to implant RTM have to be made simple and accessible.

Businesses will usually not adopt responsible management practices if not forced to do so by legislation (Doane, 2004). The perception is that RTM constitutes an unnecessary cost to the organisation, and thereby contravenes its primary objective of profit maximisation. However, research clearly indicates that responsible management can lead to economic, social, and environmental benefits, including decreased operating costs, stronger brand positioning, increased loyalty, and improved customer satisfaction (Porter & Kramer, 2006; Kotler & Lee, 2005: 9; BEE Tourism Charter and Scorecard, 2005; Allen & Brennan, 2004: 2). Figure 16.2 summarises the various benefits for tourism organisations and destinations of managing tourism responsibly. In the next section we will examine some of these social, environmental, and economic benefits more closely.

The benefits of managing tourism responsibly

Managing tourism responsibly can lead to tangible, directly measurable benefits, and also more indirect advantages. We will now examine some of these business opportunities.

Increased community support

The support of the local community plays a significant role in creating a superior tourism offering. Communities that understand the importance of tourism are more likely to be hospitable and helpful to visitors, and safeguard the natural resources that the tourism offering depends on. Furthermore, by tapping into indigenous knowledge systems, new product-offerings can be developed (Ashley, 2006). Potentially negative factors such as crime and fraud also decrease when the local community has an interest in seeing tourism grow (Spenceley, et al., 2002). The effects of a successful community partnership can be seen in the example of Mbotyi River Lodge:

Figure 16.2 Benefits of managing tourism responsibly

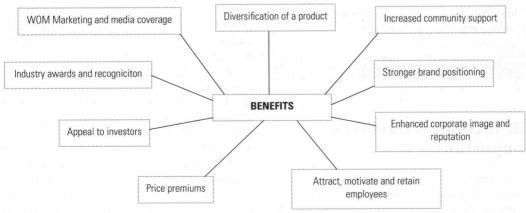

> **Example** Mbotyi River Lodge
>
> In respect of Mbotyi River Lodge, substantial support from the wider community is seen in the fact that there has been a significant decrease in the levels of criminal activity in the area. There has been no burglary at the campsite in the two years since a community partnership was established, and the lodge has had 14 months without any occurrences of theft.

Stronger brand positioning

Research shows that customers are not only demanding, but are also willing to pay premiums for responsible tourism products (Tearfund, 2002). The three main factors that tourists consider when booking a holiday are price, weather, and availability of infrastructure. However, in the case of comparable offerings between tour operators, responsible and ethical factors begin to enter the decision-making process (Pender & Sharpley, 2005: 300). In a highly competitive industry such as tourism, organisations can differentiate themselves by advocating and marketing their responsible management practices, thereby effectively adding an additional layer of value to their existing product offering (Luo & Bhattacharya, 2006).

Enhanced corporate image and reputation

In their research Szykman (2004), Brown, Helland, and Smith (2006) found that companies who promote their socially responsible intentions enjoy a better corporate image in their target markets, provided that their stated objectives are achieved. These companies enjoy a higher level of brand loyalty and brand recognition, and are ultimately more competitive.

Improved employee morale

Fair wages and working conditions are instrumental in recruiting and keeping good staff. Aside from attracting higher-quality employees, productivity and service levels are maximised when employees agree with the company's values and do not feel exploited (Brown, Helland & Smith, 2006).

Price premiums

In a study conducted in the UK, 59% of tourists interviewed stated that they would be willing to pay a premium for a holiday if the tour operator guaranteed that the money was being used for the local environment and community (Tearfund, 2000; 2002). More specifically, the Association of British Travel Agents' (ABTA) survey found that 75% of respondents were willing to pay up to 10% more for an ethical tourism offering. The reasoning behind such behaviour does not lie exclusively with the charitable nature of tourists. Tourists experience a 'feel-good' emotion when they know that their visit is not negatively impacting the host environment. This implies that the premium is paid in recognition of an added benefit and value to the customer, leading to increased satisfaction (Luo & Bhattacharya, 2006).

Appeal to investors

The JSE SRI is comprised of companies who meet a certain level of social responsibility[3]. The index thus provides a comparative measure and creates competition amongst corporates to become more socially active.

In the tourism industry, *Wilderness Safaris* and *Spier Wine Estate* are both clients of the International Finance Corporation (IFC), which places great value on ethical management when granting financing (Ashley *et al.*, 2005). Religious and ethical considerations are also at the core of recent investment funds.

Industry awards and recognition

Awards such as the Responsible Tourism Awards (RTA) and the South African equivalent, the Imvelo Awards, can help promote and market a tourism offering. This industry recognition of responsible management results in positive word-of-mouth (WOM) marketing, advertising, and free publicity. This also serves as a type of third-party recognition, supporting claims made in respect of the responsible approaches by the operators. More information about the RTA can be found in the Example box below.

Example Responsible Tourism Awards (RTA)

The online travel organisation, Responsibletravel.com, initiated the RTAs to recognise companies which were making a positive contribution to the conservation and economic development of communities and the environment they operate in. The awards are widely publicised, and provide tourism organisations with marketing opportunities to showcase their responsible management efforts.

Source: www.responsibletravel.com

Word-of-mouth marketing and media coverage

Tourists who have had a unique holiday experience i.e., interacted with locals, and felt that their visit contributed positively to the local environment, are more likely to spread positive WOM and return for a repeat visit (Trauer & Ryan, 2005). Repeat visitors represent a valuable customer base for the tourism industry due to lower acquisition costs. Moreover, repeat guests are more likely to have already seen the traditional tourism attractions, and will therefore seek out alternative 'off the beaten track' tourism products. This will lead to the expansion of the tourism offering, and can provide smaller local enterprises with business opportunities.

Companies that manage tourism in a sustainable manner have also become newsworthy. This provides free positive publicity for the respective tourism enterprise.

Diversification of product

By involving local communities, South Africa's tourism portfolio can be diversified. Local crafts, festivals, skills, and resources, for example, can be developed to increase the product-offering. Partnerships with local entrepreneurs often lead to new and innovative products. The industry example of Shiluvari Lakeside Lodge shows how

such an approach can be economically profitable (see Example box below).

Example Shiluvari Lakeside Lodge

Shiluvari Lakeside Lodge exposes its guests to the local culture (for example, craft markets and visits to local places of interest), and has made this a pivotal component of its product offering. Occupancy has increased by 25% since 2003. Shiluvari management attributes this growth primarily to the enhanced visitor experience, which has lead to greater customer satisfaction.

Source: Ashley *et al.*, 2005

Discussion point

Consider a tourism organisation you are familiar with:
• Who are the various stakeholders?
• How could its business operations be changed to align with responsible management practices?

This section has looked at the various tangible and intangible benefits that can accrue to businesses which manage tourism responsibly. We will now describe some of the initiatives that have been developed internationally and nationally to promote the adoption of responsible and ethical management practices.

Initiatives to promote RTM

The chapter has, thus far, presented the business case for RTM. The next important question is how such management practices can be enforced. Tourism is a highly diverse sector, operating in many different countries and industries, partly accounting for a lack of legislation controlling it. There are a multitude of different national frameworks, which have not yet been harmonised on a global level, and thus lack proper impact. Numerous national and international initiatives have, however, been launched to encourage the spread and adoption of responsible, ethical, and sustainable tourism management.

We will now examine some of the global and South African initiatives in more detail.

(i) Global Code of Ethics in Tourism

In 1999, the UN-WTO developed a voluntary Global Code of Ethics for Tourism to provide the tourism industry with a common set of guidelines. The code provides a framework to 'promote responsible, sustainable, and universally accessible tourism' (UN-WTO, 1999). It emphasises that in order to reach the objective of developing a sustainable industry, all stakeholders have to participate; be they individual tourism providers, governments, or the tourists themselves. Given that each country has different laws and regulations, the Code was developed to provide guidelines and standards which the industry can voluntarily adopt.

(ii) Tour Operator's Initiative (TOI)

In a show of support for sustainable tourism development, international tour operators developed the Tour Operator's Initiative (TOI) in order to promote corporate citizenship. This initiative is supported by the United Nations World Tourism Organisation (UN-WTO), United Nations Environment Programme (UNEP), and the United Nations Education, Scientific, and Cultural Organisation (UNESCO). The TOI provides indicators to measure the level of responsibility of global tourism suppliers.

(iii) Responsible Tourism Manual for South Africa (RTMSA)

South Africa has been a global leader in promoting RTM. National policy states that tourism development should be 'government-led; private sector-driven, community-based, and labour-conscious' (Spenceley, et al., 2002). This implies that a broad spectrum of people must collaborate to ensure a sustainable tourism industry. The RTMSA was presented to DEAT at the 2002 conference on responsible tourism in Cape Town. Responsible Tourism Guidelines were

developed in 2003 based on the RTMSA. The RTMSA provides advice to tourism businesses on how they can manage their operations more responsibly, whilst acknowledging that companies are primarily profit-driven. Consequently, the recommendations show how management practices can be adapted so that a company's operations remain profitable, whilst taking social and environmental considerations into account.

TOURISM BEE CHARTER
Council

The TBEECC logo

(iv) The BEE Tourism Charter and Scorecard

Although the principles of responsible management might seem desirable at a macro-level, many companies are concerned that they will not benefit by implementing responsible management practices. To encourage the transformation of the tourism industry, DEAT drafted the Tourism BEE Charter and Scorecard in 2005 to advance the overall objectives of the broad-based Black Economic Empowerment Act of 2003. This policy outlines what actions tourism organisations need to take in order to become BEE compliant (Tourism BEE Charter and Scorecard, 2005).

The Charter outlines the areas where organisations can 'score' BEE points; namely: ownership, strategic representation, employment equity, skills development, preferential procurement, enterprise and social development, and industry-specific indicators. We examine the four key objectives of the charter below:

Empowerment

In order for more South Africans to meaningfully participate in the tourism industry, the sector as a whole needs to grow, and a larger proportion of South Africans gain access to direct ownership and control of tourism enterprises. Sharing risks and profits will ultimately lead to true empowerment (ownership and strategic representation).

Human resource development

Inner transformation will take place by accelerating the skills development of black employees in tourism businesses (employment equity and skills development).

Indirect empowerment

The creation of procurement partnerships in communities and in broad-based BEE companies will increase the business opportunities of these enterprises. Tourism organisations are to be recognised for their efforts to support entrepreneurs and local small, medium, and micro enterprises (SMMEs) by purchasing from them, creating market access, and helping to increase operational and financial capacity (preferential procurement and enterprise development).

Social development

The efforts of companies to contribute to the education, health, and other relevant social development issues in the environments in which they operate are to be recognised by the Charter (social development and industry- specific indicators) (Tourism BEE Charter and Scorecard, 2005).

(v) Fair Trade in Tourism South Africa (FTTSA)

Fair Trade in Tourism South Africa (FTTSA) is a non-profit marketing initiative that promotes and publicises fair and responsible business practices by South African tourism establishments. South Africa is a global leader in developing such a certification (Font & Harris, 2004). FTTSA has developed a stringent set of criteria to measure the responsible management of tourism companies. If companies meet these benchmarks, they are awarded the FTTSA trademark[4]. This independent symbol of fairness in the tourism industry serves as a signal to potential tourists and investors regarding the fair operations of the business. The FTTSA trademark has led to positive publicity, product differentiation, and improved consumer attitude for the respective organisations (see Example box below). Companies wishing to

be awarded the FTTSA trademark have to meet the following criteria:

1. *Fair wages and working conditions, fair operations, purchasing, and distribution of benefits.*
   All participants involved in the tourism business should receive an equitable share of the benefits in direct proportion to their contribution in the business. Moreover, stakeholders should be able to participate in tourism development decisions affecting their lives.

2. *Ethical business practices.*
   Products and services delivered to tourists must be of a consistent high quality. Furthermore, business practices must be transparent, allowing access to distribution of ownership, benefits, and profits.

3. *Respect for human rights, culture and the environment.*
   The working conditions must be safe, devoid of gender bias, must not exploit the young, must provide for HIV/AIDS awareness, and safeguard the natural environment. Businesses should strive for sustainable development by increasing knowledge through broader stakeholder participation, reduce leakages by procuring and employing locally, and support HDI entrepreneurs.

FTTSA's logo

www

Browse this website: www.fairtourismsa.org.za

Example Spier Wine Estate

Spier Wine Estate estimates that their FTTSA certification has led to over 52 mentions in print between 2003 and the end of 2004. The value of this coverage was over R300 000.

Source: Ashley *et al.*, 2005

(vi) Heritage Environmental Ratings Programme

The Heritage Environmental Ratings Programme recognises effort by tourism businesses to manage their operations in a more environmentally responsible manner. Members are rated according to their compliance with the certification requirements, which provides them with a marketing platform, especially in overseas markets, where fair trade is becoming an important differentiation criterion. www.heritage.co.za

(vii) Tourism Enterprise Programme (TEP)

TEP is a joint initiative by DEAT and Business Trust (BT) to encourage the growth and development of SMMEs within the tourism sector[6]. It is a policy vehicle by government to bring about the Tourism Action Plan (TAP). TEP helps tourism SMMEs by providing marketing support for events, assisting in business plan development, supporting training, facilitating licensing and certification procedures, and assisting in the tendering process for these businesses to become suppliers.

(viii) Tourism, Hospitality and Sport Education Authority (THETA)

THETA is the Sector Education and Training Authority for the tourism, hospitality, and sports sectors. THETA aims to raise the standards of skills in this sector, and provide guidelines to ensure quality and appropriateness by providing training in skills that are most required by employers in the tourism sector.

**TOURISM, HOSPITALITY & SPORT
EDUCATION & TRAINING AUTHORITY**

THETA's logo

(ix) Tourism Public Private Partnerships (PPP)

In 2004, the National Treasury produced a practical guide to facilitate the formation of partnerships between private enterprises and governmental agencies in the area of nature tourism (for example, private investors collaborating with national parks). Such partnerships have led to job creation, subsequent poverty alleviation, and economic growth. The Kruger Park partnership provides an example of a successful public private partnership (PPP) (see Example box below).

Example Kruger National Park

The partnership between the national conservation agency and private investors in the game lodges in the Kruger National Park has led to R250-million in investments, and the creation of 700 new jobs. The income generated for South African National Parks (SANParks) from this PPP was estimated to constitute R1,6-million in 2004 alone, clearly highlighting the positive impact such initiatives can have.

Source: www.treasury.gov.za

How to manage tourism responsibly

It is evident that managing tourism responsibly makes sound business sense. In the following section we examine what individual businesses and the public sector can do, practically, to achieve the stated benefits of managing tourism responsibly.

Increase local linkages

The potential economic benefits to host countries are considerably compromised by economic leakages (see Chapter 15 – Managing the impacts of tourism). Local linkages and partnerships aim to reduce these **leakages**, increase the multiplier effect, and thereby retain any locally-generated tourism income.

Companies should aim to develop and procure local products, and enter into partnerships with local businesses. The benefits realised in this way include winning local recognition, gaining community support for tourism development, enhanced staff morale, greater customer satisfaction, stronger branding, points on the BEE Tourism Charter and Scorecard, and economic cost savings. For example, businesses can commit to buying agricultural produce from the local community, or allow the community to co-invest in new tourism developments. Such linkages provide communities with an incentive to see tourism grow and prosper (goodwill/buy-in), develop the SMME sector, and support entrepreneurial development. Local linkages can therefore lead to mutually beneficial relationships between tourism businesses and local communities.

There are four main types of local linkages:

1. Procurement from local enterprises: Companies can purchase the goods and services they need from smaller local businesses, instead of using large suppliers. Established organisations can help in training smaller businesses, so that the required quality standards are met.
2. Local employment and wages: Remuneration in the tourism industry has a reputation for being very low. Income from direct employment in the tourism sector is one of the main sources of economic benefit for the local community. Companies should ensure that they pay their staff a competitive living wage. This income will, in turn, most likely be spent directly in the community, leading to a significant multiplier effect, overall upliftment, and growth. Moreover, it is vital that companies commit to training and up-skilling staff (see Chapter 11 – Managing human resources in tourism). If skill levels are increased, new business opportunities and the expansion of the local economy (tourism-based or otherwise) can be realised.
3. Local cultural and heritage products: The country's national tourism organisation (NTO), and South African Tourism's research indicates that South African cultural products are in demand by international tourists. Eighty-five per cent of Americans, 77% of Europeans, and 60% of Asians show interest in exploring South Africa's local heritage (Ashley et al., 2005). Companies can work with communities to see how opportunities stemming from South Africa's cultural diversity can be unlocked. Organising excursions to archaeological sites, supporting a local festival, or developing local culinary experiences can all be used to make a tourism offering unique, and provide guests with authentic experiences.
4. Building local partnerships: Local partnerships differ from stakeholder participation in that partners usually share risks and benefits. Such partnerships ensure that there is a personal incentive to see the business grow and prosper. The Old Gaol Coffee Shop in the Example box below shows the potential success of creating such partnerships.

> **Example** The Old Gaol coffee shop
>
> Jan Harmsgat Country House is a small lodge in Swellendam (Western Cape), where all staff are recruited from the surrounding poor rural areas. The lodge established a partnership with its staff, employing four local women to run the Old Gaol

Coffee Shop. Having gained skills and confidence, the women took a 30% equity stake in the coffee shop in 2004.

Source: Ashley *et al.*, 2005

The various methods to increase RTM that have been discussed in this chapter can be facilitated by government involvement and support.

Producing a written policy on RTM

Tourism businesses should develop a written policy of their responsible and ethical management practices. Such a document can be used as an internal communication tool for employees, as a marketing tool for potential customers and investors, and serves as a guide for stakeholders. Table 16.2 below lists 10 points that should form part of a RTM policy.

Table 16.2 Ten components of a responsible management policy for tourism businesses

Ten components of a RTM policy for tourism businesses

1. *Support local linkages*: Tourism organisations should try to use local suppliers of goods and services where possible, and ensure fair remuneration. Partnerships must be built on mutual respect and profitability.
2. *Clear contract*: Terms and conditions with service providers have to be clear and transparent. It is likely that a significant power imbalance exists between the tourism organisation and the community partners. It is imperative that such power is not exploited, but rather used to build mutually beneficial partnerships.
3. *Social and environmental audits*: It is important to measure the impact of operations both on the natural and the social environments, so that changes can be recommended and successful practices emulated by other businesses.
4. *Culture*: The tourism business should show respect for local culture and heritage when conducting business in and around local communities.
5. *Community partnerships*: Local initiative should be identified, and possibilities for support and training evaluated.

6. *Charitable giving*: A tourism organisation should have a clear policy on charitable giving, and communicate this to staff and customers, integrating the activity throughout business operations.
7. *Monitoring*: All business impacts; social, environmental, and economic should be monitored on a regular and continuing basis to ensure areas of risk and potential improvement are timeously identified.
8. *Code for tourists*: Tourists can be encouraged and educated in how to act more responsibly at a destination by providing information pertaining to appropriate behaviour.
9. *Training*: Staff should be trained on how and why to implement responsible management practices.
10. *Implement policy through the supply chain*: Tourism organisations' policy towards RTM needs to be clear, and communicated openly to service providers. Where it is necessary, training must be provided to facilitate any necessary changes in the supply chain, to achieve responsible management goals.

Source: Tearfund. *Worlds apart: a call to respnsible global tourism.* London. www.tearfund.org (accessed May 2006).

The role of government

Government can also play an active role in facilitating RTM. In a comprehensive report detailing how government can help increase the economic impacts of tourism, Ashley (2006) recommends the following:

- Government should facilitate market access for SMMEs, as well as networking opportunities between various suppliers and potential clients, in order to encourage local procurement.
- Government can help with quality standards and capacity constraints. One of the main challenges facing local procurement is the lack of economies of scale.
- Government can be instrumental in helping producers and clients to sell and buy in bulk by creating wholesale associations and beneficial partnerships.
- Encouraging market demand can also be enhanced by government involvement. Tourists are more likely to purchase local goods and services if information and access are easily available.

- The lack of credit for smaller businesses is a further barrier to entry which government can help overcome. Providing capital for smaller companies lacking a credit history, and who therefore cannot expand their operations, could contribute significantly to the growth of the local economy.
- Finally, government can put mentoring and training opportunities in place, such as the Tourism Funding Programme for Small Businesses (DEAT, 2005), TEP, and THETA. Skills are developed, and more established businesses are able to pass on their knowledge and expertise to newer, up-coming enterprises, helping them meet the high standard required to compete in the market.

All stakeholders stand to benefit from such local linkages. Government benefits by encouraging local economic growth; SMMEs can expand their markets, upgrade their product and develop skills; and local clients often realise cost savings due to the locality of their suppliers and a more distinctive product offering.

Conclusion

This chapter has discussed why managing tourism responsibly is socially, environmentally, and economically beneficial. Research proves that companies which adhere to responsible management practices enjoy higher levels of brand loyalty, customer satisfaction, improved staff morale, stronger community support, and better company reputation.

The South African tourism industry has a pivotal role to play in terms of addressing poverty alleviation, job creation, and inequality. If responsible management practices are adopted, the socio-economic benefits of tourism will be distributed more evenly amongst all South Africans. New business opportunities can be unlocked, entrepreneurial activity encouraged, SMMEs supported, and economic growth ultimately stimulated.

It is imperative that a holistic approach towards tourism development is adopted, whereby the various stakeholders are included in the planning

and benefits of such initiatives. Managing tourism responsibly aims to create mutually beneficial, long-term partnerships.

Notes

1. UN. 2006. *Tourism Satellite Accounting Highlights.* www.wttc.org. (accessed August 2006).
2. ABTA. 2002. *Why Corporate Social Responsibility Makes Sense For Tour Operators: Responding to Consumer Demand.* www.tourismconcern.org.uk (accessed July 2006).
3. JSE. 2003. Johannesburg Stock Exchange Social Responsibility Index (JSE SRI): Background and Selection Criteria. www.jse.co.za (accessed August 2006).
4. www.fairtourismsa.org
5. *Heritage Environmental Ratings Programme.* www.eco-web.com. (accessed October 2006).
6. Tourism Enterprise Programme (TEP). 2006. www.tep.co.za. (accessed September 2006).

Review Questions

1. Write down your own definition of what is meant by 'managing tourism responsibly'.

2. Explain what global trends have lead to the increased demand and supply of responsible tourism practices.

3. In your opinion, what role do tourism companies have in society? Discuss.

4. Why is tourism in South Africa seen to have the opportunity to address a host of socio-economic problems?

Further reading

Department of Economic Affairs and Tourism (DEAT). 2002. *Responsible Tourism Manual for South Africa.* www.info.gov.za

Goodwin, H. & Francis, J. 2003. Ethical and responsible tourism: consumer trends in the UK, *Journal of Vacation Marketing,* Vol. 9(3), 271-284.

Kotler, P. & Lee, N. 2005. *Corporate social responsibility: doing the most good for your company and your cause.* Hoboken, New Jersey: John Wiley .

Websites

DEAT: www.environment.gov.za

Pro-Poor Tourism: www.propoortourism.org.uk

www.theinternationalcentreforresponsibletourism.org

United Nations: www.un.org

References

Allen, G. & Brennan, F. 2004. *Tourism in the new South Africa: social responsibility and the tourist experience.* New York: I. B. Tauris.

Ashley, C. 2006. How can governments boost the local economic impacts of tourism.

Ashley, C., Poultney, C., Haysom, G., Harris, A. & McNab, D. 2005. *The how to?...Guide series: tips and tools for South African tourism companies on local procurement, products and partnerships.* The IFC, dti and DEAT.

Ashley, C., Roe, D & Goodwin, H. 2001. Pro-poor tourism report no. 1 – Pro-poor tourism strategies: making tourism work for the poor, a review of experience. Centre for Responsible Tourism, Overseas Development Institute and International Environment & Development.

Brown, W., Helland, E. & Smith, J. 2006. Corporate Philanthropic Practices: in *Journal of Corporate Finance.* Article in Press, Corrected Proof.

Department of Economic Affairs and Tourism (DEAT). 2002. *Responsible Tourism Manual for South Africa.* www.info.gov.za (accessed August 2006).

Department of Economic Affairs and Tourism (DEAT). 2005. *Tourism BEE Charter and Scorecard.* www.info.gov.za (accessed August 2006).

Department of Economic Affairs and Tourism (DEAT). 2006. *Draft National Sustainable Development Framework Document.* (Unpublished, awaiting approval by Parliament).

Department of Economic Affairs and Tourism (DEAT) & dti. 2005. *Funding Programme for Tourism Businesses Handbook.* www.capegateway.gov.za (accessed February 2007).

Doane, D. 2004. Beyond corporate social responsibility: minnows, mammoths and markets. *Futures,* Vol. 37(2-3), 215–229.

Fennell, D. A. 2001. A Content Analysis of Ecotourism Definitions in *Current Issues in Tourism,* Vol. 4(5), 403–421.

Font, X. & Harris, C. 2004. Rethinking standards from green to sustainable. *Annals of Tourism Research.* Vol. 31(4). 986–1007.

Frey, N. 2007. *The effect of responsible tourism management practices on business performance in an emerging market.* Unpublished MA thesis. The University of Cape Town, Cape Town, South Africa.

Goodwin, H. & Francis, J. 2003. Ethical and responsible tourism: Consumer trends in the UK. *Journal of Vacation Marketing,* Vol. 9(3), 271–284.

Institute of Directors in Southern Africa. 2002. *Executive Summary of King Report on Corporate Governance for South Africa.* www.ecseonline.com (accessed August 2006).

Kotler, P. & Lee, N. 2005. *Corporate Social Responsibility: Doing the most good for your company and your cause.* Hoboken, New Jersey: John Wiley.

Krippendorf, J. 1987. *The Holiday makers: understanding the impact of leisure and travel.* Oxford: Butterworth-Heinemann.

London: Tourism Programme: Overseas Development Institute (ODI) and SNV.

Luo, X. & Bhattacharya, C. 2006. Corporate Social Responsibility, Customer Satisfaction, and Market Value. *Journal of Marketing.* Vol. 70(4), 1–18.

Middleton, V. 1998. *Sustainable tourism: a marketing perspective,* Oxford: Butterworth- Heinemann.

Pender, L. & Sharpley, R. 2005. *The management of tourism.* London: Sage Publications Ltd.

Porter, M. & Kramer, M. 2006. Strategy & Society: the link between competitive advantage and corporate social responsibility. *Harvard Business Review.* Vol. 84(12), 78–92.

Rogerson, M. & Visser, G. 2004. *Tourism and development issues in contemporary South Africa.* Tshwane: Africa Institute of South Africa.

Sachs, W. (Ed.). 2002. *The Joburg memo: fairness in a fragile world - Memorandum for the World Summit on Sustainable Development.* World Summit Papers, Special Edition. Johannesburg: Heinrich Bšll Foundation

Spenceley, A., Relly, P., Keyser, M., Warmeant, P., McKenzie, M., Mataboge, A., Norton, P., Mahlangu, S. & Seif, J. 2002. *Responsible Tourism Manual for South Africa.* Department of Environmental Affairs and Tourism, July 2002.

Szykman, L. 2004. Who are you, and why are you being nice?: Investigating the industry effect on consumer reaction to corporate societal marketing efforts. *Advances in Consumer Research,* Vol. 31(1), 302–315.

Tearfund. 2001. *Tourism: Putting ethics into practice – a report on the responsible business practices of 65 UK-based tour operators.* London. www.tearfund.org (accessed May 2006).

Tearfund. 2002. *Worlds apart: a call to responsible global tourism.* London. www.tearfund.org (accessed May 2006).

Trauer, B. & Ryan, C. 2005, Destination image, romance and place experience: an application of intimacy theory in tourism. *Tourism Management,* Vol. 26(4), 481–491.

University of Cape Town Unilever Institute. 2006. CSR Brand Sustainability project. Cape Town: UCT

United Nations. 2006. *Tourism Satellite Accounting Highlights.* www.wttc.org. (accessed August 2006).

Weeden, C. 2001. Ethical tourism: an opportunity for competitive advantage. *Journal of Vacation Marketing,* Vol. 8(8), 141–153.

Case study
16

Bulungula Backpackers Lodge

Objective

To identify key elements of managing tourism responsibly, and how these practices lead to sustainable development

Over the last few years, the Wild Coast has benefited from the enormous growth of tourism in South Africa – but the benefits have mostly been limited to a handful of backpacker hostels in Coffee Bay and Port St Johns. Serious concerns have been raised in terms of whether tourism has facilitated the distribution and access to these benefits by the local communities.

The Bulungula Lodge comprises a bar, restaurant, and 10 traditional Xhosa rondavels, designed to be both culturally and environmentally appropriate. The ethos of the Lodge is to promote a genuine appreciation for the local community and environment. In keeping with this, the community were encouraged and assisted in starting their own enterprises, such as offering horse-riding, hiring out watersports equipment, providing authentic village accommodation and food, growing and supplying the Lodge's vegetable needs, and offering cultural-history walking tours. The Lodge simultaneously promotes environmental awareness through its use of eco-friendly technologies: compost toilets, water

and energy-efficient showers, and solar-powered electricity. The denuded forest alongside the Lodge is being rehabilitated and additional indigenous trees planted on the Lodge site. Many of these trees are purchased by guests wanting to sequestrate the carbon used in the travel to the Lodge.

The development adheres to all the tourism and environmental guidelines outlined in the Eastern Cape's *2001 Wild Coast Tourism Development Policy*. One of the main principles underlying in the 2000 White Paper for Sustainable Coastal Development is to 'alleviate coastal poverty through pro-active coastal development initiatives that generate sustainable livelihood options'.

This development provides a vital source of income to the Nqileni community, which has no other source of revenue besides state grants and remittances from family members in the cities. The development is therefore aimed at improving not only the economic status of the community, but also provides long-term capacity-building in the tourism sector. Most importantly, this development does not deny the local community access to the resources on which they rely for basic needs. In fact, the project provides members of the community with opportunities to earn regular income from their services to the lodge guests.

One of the key aspects of the Bulungula Backpackers Lodge is that it is owned by both the entrepreneur who developed the lodge, and the community. This shared ownership relationship is one where community leadership plays an active role in the Lodge, and where they participate in decision-making and dividends.

All activities and operations at the Lodge are planned and executed in a manner that will ensure the reduction of the footprint (negative impact) on the environment, as well as any negative social implications on the part of the community.

Resources are managed through the following interventions, innovations and approaches:

- Water supply to the site is sourced from a well situated at the nearby spring. All water runoff and rainwater is harvested. The water is pumped, using a solar-powered pump, into three 10 000-litre tanks. At all times, guests are taught the need for water conservation, so that a target limit of 1 500 litres/day at 100% occupancy is achieved.
- Solar energy is used to power the lighting, music system, and computer. At a later stage, the viability of wind energy will be investigated.
- All solid waste is separated into organic and inorganic components and placed in marked drums. Organic waste is composted, or used to feed local livestock. Inorganic waste is recycled, and removed from the site. Every effort is made to reduce inorganic waste before it reaches the site – unnecessary packaging is left at the supermarket.
- Urine-diversion compost toilets are used. These are designed in such a way that only harmless, odourless compost is generated, which is used to fertilise soil. Grey water (from the kitchen and showers) is piped to a soak-away located on high ground near the football field, away from the wetland.
- Guests are encouraged to arrive at the Lodge by means of public transport, by being offered a discount on the first night of stay. All goods are purchased from locally-owned businesses, ensuring that the revenues generated are retained within the region.

General

The process of establishing Bulungula Backpackers Lodge was one that took considerable time, with challenging community and official negotiations taking place over a period of two years. This process, in a region where other, often illegal, but expeditious processes are the norm, ensured that the lodge was established in a manner that was in accordance with all required legislation, as well as in accordance with the needs and desires of the community.

Potentially, one of the most innovative approaches is the practice of job-sharing where, due to the small number of jobs available, most positions are filled by two staff, each working one week on and one week off. Although this means that the staff earn less, from a community perspective, this allows for greater equity, a fairer distribution of the benefits, and allows community members the opportunity to earn income without this having a negative impact on the traditional obligations they have within the community.

Bulungula Backpackers Lodge broke even in the third year of operation, generating a profit that was distributed per the ownership agreements. The use of the dividend allocated to the community was agreed upon at a mass community meeting, and used to address a number of needs within the broader community.

Case study questions

1. Using a table, list the economic, environmental and social initiatives that the lodge practices.

2. Discuss the key elements of RTM that have been employed by the Lodge.

3. Identify the benefits, as well as the challenges, to the various stakeholders concerning this development. Suggest strategies to build on the potential benefits, and ways to mitigate problems.

4. Visit the Bulungula Backpackers Lodge website, www.bulungula.com. What is the Lodge doing to encourage responsible travel behaviour by its visitors? What else could it do to ensure sustainable development?

17

The future of tourism

Ciné van Zyl

Purpose

This chapter will discuss the future of tourism. It will examine the demographic, political, and technological changes and trends, and their likely impact on tourism businesses.

Learning outcomes

After reading this chapter you should be able to:
- explain tourism growth and the challenges facing tourism businesses
- understand domestic, regional, and international travel patterns and trends
- describe the external factors affecting tourism
- identify key future tourism trends.

Chapter overview

In this chapter, we begin with a discussion on the growth of tourism and the challenges that tourism businesses face in light of various demographic, political, and technological changes. Tourism is constantly evolving, and the uncertainty of the future poses many challenges for planners and managers. Of specific interest are the technological advances and changes – a transformation mainly in the three broad areas of information, transportation, and destinations. The chapter continues by discussing all these external factors that might affect or shape tourism. Finally, it discusses tourism market trends and, more specifically, the radical changes that are shaping the industry and tourists' buying behaviour. These trends should be noted, as they have consequences for the tourism industry and impact on the future decision-making of tourism planners and managers.

The case study at the end of the chapter discusses South Africa's business tourism market, which is set to grow significantly by 2010, and to contribute substantially to the country's booming tourism industry.

Introduction

According to forecasts, the future of tourism is full of promise. International tourism arrivals, domestic and regional travel trends (such as tourism receipts and employment) for most destinations are set to grow. General optimism prevails in the global travel and tourism industry. What is especially important in this chapter, over and above this optimism, is the need to recognise the external forces that might change and challenge a tourism business. An understanding of trends is important, as they provide guidelines as to what is likely to occur in the future, as well as a basis for the planning and marketing of destination and tourism offerings. The impact of external factors that affect tourism must also be considered and monitored when trends are being analysed. Therefore, while you should prepare yourself for an optimistic future, always be alert for unforeseen events, such as terrorist attacks and natural disasters, which affect the industry significantly.

Growth of tourism

Today's tourism industry is the result of many forces operating in the past. The growth and development of tourism have been particularly rapid over the past half-century; as already noted in Chapter 1, and shown below:

- Tourist activity has risen year-on-year since 1950 at an average rate of 7,1%, from 25-million international tourist arrivals in 1950 to 625-million in 1998, growing to 842-million in 2006 (Untied Nations World Tourism Organisation, 2007).
- International tourism receipts grew faster than world trade in the 1980s, and now contribute a higher proportion of the value of world exports than all sectors, except crude petroleum/ petroleum products and motor vehicles/parts/accessories.

These facts seem to indicate that tourism in the first few decades of the 21st century will be a very dynamic sector of the economy, and the future suggests a likely continued growth. For example, international tourist arrivals are forecast to grow to over 1,6-billion in 2020 (UN-WTO, 1997). These volumes represent an annual growth rate of a modest 4,3% in the period 2000 to 2020 (see Table 17.1). The World Travel and Tourism Council's (WTTC) research shows that, globally, 260,4-million people will be employed in jobs generated by tourism by 2011 (WTTC, 1996). At present, it is estimated that around 260-million people work in jobs directly related to the tourism industry, representing approximately 8,3% of total world employment (UN-WTO, 2007).

Table 17.1 Forecasts of international tourist arrivals worldwide and by region, 2000-2020

Tourist arrivals (millions)			
Regions	2000	2010	2020
Europe	390	527	717
East Asia/Pacific	116	231	438
Americas	134	195	284
Africa	27	46	75
Middle East	19	37	69
South Asia	6	11	19
World	692	1047	1602

Source: Tourism 2020 Vision: A new forecast (UN-WTO, 1997)

The strong growth of the tourism industry over the last 50 years is, in part, the result of economic globalisation, including innovations in transport and information and communication technologies (ICT). These factors have made travel cheaper and more accessible. Others leading to tourism's exponential growth include increasing leisure time and disposable income in the leading world tourist-generating markets of North America, Western Europe, and Japan.

One of the key trends in tourism demand is that it will continue to grow globally, as outlined in the UN-WTO's *Tourism 2020 Vision* (1997). However, tourism statistics and forecasts should be interpreted with caution, as definitions might be interpreted differently. Various other tourism statistics are also important for tourism managers in decision-making and future planning.

Regional travel patterns and trends

Statistics on worldwide tourism arrivals should be monitored by all tourism stakeholders, to identify any regional travel patterns and trends (see Example box).

> **Example** Tourism statistics - regional travel patterns
>
> The Internet provides an opportunity for all tourism stakeholders to keep up with the latest world statistics. Among the websites currently available are those of the United Nations World Tourism Organisation (www.world-tourism.org), the World Travel and Tourism Council (www.wttc.org), and South African Tourism (www.southafrica.net).

The following provides a brief summary of global tourism trends and patterns, per region:

Europe

Europe is still the world's number one destination, and continues to dominate the global tourism market in terms of arrivals. Europe's arrivals reached 354,4-million in 2005, accounting for 43% of total world arrivals. France remains the top country in terms of arrivals, totalling 76,1-million in 2005, which is a 2,9% increase over 2004 (SA Tourism, 2006: 7). Europe was disrupted in July 2005 by the London Underground bombings, but a multi-million-pound marketing and public relations campaign by Visit London (London Tourist Board) appeared to mitigate the impact of these attacks.

Furthermore, Europe is the leader in intra-regional travel, as it contains several relatively small countries, and much intra-regional international tourism takes place between neighbouring countries with common land borders. The modes of travel between these counties are mostly ground transportation such as cars, trains, and buses, which are more affordable than travel by air. It is estimated that nearly 80% of all travel in Europe is intra-regional in nature (UN-WTO, 1997: 28). This short-haul travel market is favoured by renewed promotional campaigns to attract nearby markets, improvements in the tourism infrastructure, and the ease of border-crossing between countries in Europe. Recent trends suggest a change in regional growth, in that outbound long-haul travel from Europe is on the increase, and is growing faster than intra-European travel.

A rapid growth in tourist arrivals to the former Eastern European countries is taking place, due to the collapse of the Communist system in these countries. Various Eastern European countries such as Russia have become major tourist generators, as wealthy individuals choose to buy second homes abroad and to holiday in the popular resorts of Eastern Europe. Furthermore, the less affluent Russians and others from Eastern European 'satellite' countries are eager to enjoy their new-found freedom to travel. They visit the Mediterranean resorts mainly, although these experienced declines in tourist numbers during the past few years as the quality of their offerings deteriorated.

Asia and the Pacific

China will become a premier tourist destination and source of tourists in the 21st century.

The growth of travel in East Asia and the Pacific has been exceptional, and a bright future is predicted. Asia and the Pacific received 148-million tourist visits in 2005, a growth of 42% over 2004. China is ranked at number four on the list of top international tourist destinations, with 47,8-million arrivals in 2005 (SA Tourism, 2006: 7). According to the UN-WTO, by 2010 the East Asia/Pacific region will move ahead of the Americas, and will rank second to Europe with 231-million international arrivals (See Table 17.1). Top destinations within the Asian region include Hong Kong, China, and Singapore.

Mainland China has attracted millions of tourists who are interested in its history, heritage, cultural diversity, and natural landscapes, since it opened its doors to tourism in 1978. The growth in tourism can also be attributed to the Chinese government's efforts to promote tourism as well as its removal of restrictions on travel and tourism. Future outbound travel for Asian nations depends on their continued economic growth, which is a major force in world economic performance. China has the potential to generate very many outbound travellers, due to its rapidly expanding economy (30-million outbound travellers in 2005). It is anticipated that, as its economy grows, China will be sending 100-million tourists abroad by 2020; yet this figure still represents less than one in ten of its population.

Australia showed an increase of 17,9% in international arrivals in 2005 (SA Tourism, 2006: 7), and has had a second year of tourism growth for the first time since the Olympic Games. The Pacific Asia Travel Association (PATA) reported in July 2005 that tourists were still, to a certain extent, avoiding the tsunami-hit region (countries most severely hit were Indonesia, Thailand, Sri Lanka, the Maldives, India, and Somalia). Although travel to Thailand increased by more than a million tourists in 2005, UN-WTO recently revised its forecasts, claiming that a full recovery of tourism in tsunami-hit countries was not likely until the winter season 2006/2007.

South Asia

The South Asia region is overshadowed by the size of tourism development in neighbouring East and Southeast Asia. Nevertheless, it has made impressive gains in recent years, although it has started from a smaller base. The region is made up of India, Bangladesh, the Maldives, Pakistan, Sri Lanka, Nepal, Bhutan, Myanmar, Afghanistan, and Iran. The most visited country in this region is India, with nearly four out

of every five international tourists visiting the region choosing India as their ultimate destination (UN-WTO, 1997: 31). Strong growth rates, in the Maldives for beach resorts, and in Nepal for special interest tourism (SIT), is also visible. A growth in European visitors to the region can be attributed to better air transportation access. The prospects for intra-regional tourism growth are strong, while the growth in long-haul, inbound tourism arrivals will be lower. Almost all the countries in the region will benefit from the growth of inbound tourism. Japan is expected to be the top tourist-generating region, as the domestic economy grows and trade increases.

The Americas

Despite events such as '9/11', the Americas experienced 136-million foreign tourist arrivals in 2005. This shows a steady growth for the fourth consecutive year, as arrivals grew by more than 12% over the figures for 2004 (South African Tourism, 2006: 7). The USA continued to be the world's third most popular tourism destination in 2005, with arrivals reaching 49,3-million (South African Tourism, 2006: 7). Canada and Mexico, the largest sources of international arrivals to the USA, accounted for an estimated 55% of the volume in 2005. Brazil received 5,4-million tourists in 2005, while Mexico performed well in the same year, showing an increase of 16,7%. Intra-regional tourism still dominates the Americas.

Any forecast of the outbound tourism potential for the Americas is predicated upon the specific region targeted by tourists. Regions such as the United States and Canada are at a stage where levels of leisure time and income have reached their peak, resulting in a slower growth of outbound tourism for inter-regional travel. The South and Central American nations show the most growth potential for increased outbound travel as economic development and industrial growth escalate there.

Africa and the Middle East

A growth of 7,9% in tourism was experienced in Africa and the Middle East in 2005 – up from 67,7-million in 2004 to 73,1-million in 2005

(SA Tourism, 2006: 7). Kenya attracted 1,7 million tourists over the same period; a 23% increase over 2004 (SA Tourism, 2006: 7). Tourism in Egypt recovered relatively quickly after the July 2005 hotel bombings in Sharm-el-Sheikh (a possible factor for this rapid recovery is that the majority of tourists to Egypt tend to focus on Cairo and the Nile Valley; another is that cheaper package deals might also have contributed to the quicker recovery. Egypt continues to have a strong regional tourism market in North Africa and the Middle East, as most of Egypt's tourists originate from North Africa and the Middle East.

The *Annual Tourism Report* (SA Tourism, 2006: 11) states that foreign tourist arrivals to South Africa surpassed the 8-million mark in 2006 for the first time, closing at 8 395 833. The additional 1 027 091 tourists who arrived in 2006 represented a 13,6% increase over the previous year's figure. This growth rate exceeds the estimated average global growth rate in tourism of 6,1%, and brings the compound average growth rate between the years 2001 and 2006 to 9,2%. The increase in 2006 was strongly driven by arrivals from Africa, as well as from all regions except the Asian region. The biggest growth in tourists during the same period originated from the SADC neighbouring countries of Mozambique, Zimbabwe, Lesotho, and Swaziland, while Botswana and Namibia reported slight declines of 1% and 3% respectively. The growth in the past 12 years was exceptional, with tourism increasing by more than 100% since the year 1994. Thus, South Africa's tourism industry grew rapidly at a rate of 11,8% per year between 1994 and 1998, consolidating its performance between 1998 and 2001 at a rate of 0,3%, and growing by 9,2% from 2001 to 2006 (South African Tourism, 2006: 12).

According to South African Tourism's Strategic Research Unit 2007, 2006 was also an exceptional year, in that the South African economy increased both in volume and value, as the value of the rand stabilised and traded in narrower margins. The Total Foreign Direct Spend (excluding capital expenditure) in 2006 was R49,8-billion, including capital expenditure. Tourism continued to strengthen its status as the 'new gold' of the South African economy; the Total Foreign Direct Spend of R49,8 billion is reported to be R14.3-billion

more than gold exports (SA Tourism, 2007). The tourism sector's contribution to the South African GDP and employment fluctuated both in volume and value, with the number of new jobs created in the economy (direct and indirect) down from 1 024 520 in 2004 to 947 530 in 2006 (SA Tourism, 2007).

A sustained growth of international tourist arrivals to South Africa in the near future is expected, due to the build-up and hosting of the 2010 FIFA World Cup. This huge sporting event should be taken into account by all tourism planners and managers, as it is anticipated that interest in South Africa as a tourist destination will grow pre- and post- the competition, with over 3-million tourists expected to visit the country during the four-week duration.

Discussion point

After reading this section, what, in your opinion, are the reasons why regional travel patterns and trends should be noticed by tourism planners and managers?

External factors that affect or shape tourism

Apart from the regional travel trends discussed, there is recognition in the tourism literature that the future might be influenced by various other factors as well. According to Cooper, *et al.* (2005) these factors can be grouped into two broad considerations, namely:
- external (exogenous) and factors within our control
- factors outside of our control.

These two forces also impact on the tourism experience, and specific tourism processes of change. A number of external factors which have the ability to negatively impact the development of tourism must be considered, in order to acquire a deeper understanding of tourism and to better facilitate tourism planning. Factors with the potential to influence tourism growth include: socio-demographic change, technological developments, political change, sustainability, ethical and environmental issues, global safety, security, and health-related issues. Each of these factors is discussed in the following section.

Changing demographics

Changes in society are a result of a combination of demographic and social change. Demographic changes are easier to forecast, as statisticians can predict or plan for the future. The changing demographic profile of the world's population is an important factor. The following three well-defined groups of travellers will be evident:

- 18- to 34-year-olds, the young market, travelling the most
- 60-year-olds, growth in retiree or mature travellers; often quoted as the senior market
- family market, families with children, and two-income households.

The largest group, the 18- to 34-year-olds, will continue to comprise much of the travelling public, as singles or in groups. Whether travelling alone, with co-workers, or with a group of friends, this age segment will continue to dominate much of the Asian outbound market (UN-WTO, 1997: 34).

An ageing population in most industrial Western societies suggests that travellers will be older and, although healthier and fitter, will require more special attention by tourism businesses suppliers, who need to meet the requirements of these mature travellers. These segments are referred to in marketing by a number of titles, including 'ageing greys', 'goldies', and 'skiers' (Spending our Kids' Inheritance!). In general, tourists in the future will be seeking physical adventure, intellectual enrichment, and culturally rich destinations. Cruises will increase in popularity, in particular for those over 50 years of age. There is a continual increase of outbound travellers aged 45 and over both in Western countries and in Japan. The populations of Western countries are ageing rapidly. Tourism businesses will need to respond creatively to the needs of this market, and provide the exact services required to exceed tourists' expectations.

Families – key tourism markets in the future

The family market is visible; travel will be used to provide quality time for parents and children, resulting in a greater demand for family-oriented attractions, facilities, and accommodation. Family structures, too, will change worldwide, with the numbers of working women, single households, childless couples, and non-traditional families increasing. All have enormous implications for the planning of tourism destinations.

Technological advances and changes

Technology and **virtual reality** (VR) have brought major changes to tourism, and continue to impact on the travel experience and those who use and supply it (see Example box). Technological changes took place mainly in the following three broad areas:

- developments in information
- developments in transport
- developments in destinations.

The Internet provides an opportunity for users to undertake virtual tours of key attractions around the globe; via websites currently available, one can view game at a waterhole in Africa (www.africam.co.za), the Taj Mahal in India (www.taj-mahal.net), and any UNESCO World Heritage site (www.world-heritage-tour.org).

Developments in information

The Internet continues to be a growing booking tool for the travel, tourism, and hospitality industry. Information technology (IT), in particular the Internet, has changed the tourism industry in the last few years. As they become more comfortable, confident, and convinced of Internet security, more travellers are booking and buying travel online. The trend towards late bookings is also on the increase, and the Internet facilitates this tremendously. The use of on-line services such as lastminute.com and expedia.com has increased dramatically (see Chapter 7 – Managing tourism distribution). In China, numerous obstacles to the growth of e-tourism (electronic tourism) have been reported, and the country is lagging behind countries such as the USA, UK, and Germany (Ma, Buhalis & Song, 2003).

The penetration of the Internet and its use as an information resource and for the purchase of tourism offerings will continue to increase. The role of the Internet, including new means of visual presentation, in the tourism industry will increase still further, and prove to be of the utmost importance in the future. The ready availability of tourist information on destinations and offerings, and of increasingly sophisticated search engines to analyse such information, will lend itself to comparison, and thus influence competition more intensely via 'grazing'.

In the future, the Internet will continue to transform the role of **destination marketing organisations** (DMOs), and will create a new role for e-marketing, including the application of customer relationship management (CRM); thereby enabling DMOs to grow their customer databases via their websites.

It will be absolutely necessary for tourism businesses to become technologically advanced. Information and communication technologies (ICT) should be used to allow for better communication between companies and their consumers, however, there are some drawbacks in the use of ICT. One of these is a lack of technology to support tourists while they are on tour. It is difficult for tourists to share their experiences gained during touring. **U-commerce** (ultimate commerce), the transaction of commercial dealings by electronic means rather than through traditional 'paper' channels, is promoted as a more interwoven form of technology to meet the tourists' needs (Watson, *et al.*, 2004: 317) (see Example below).

It had been feared that travel agents would no longer exist because of the rapid diffusion and impact of information technology, but these developments lead to travel agents changing their roles and re-inventing themselves (Poon, 2003b: 21).

The Internet has introduced a significant wave of change, and communication patterns of society have changed. Society has become dependent on e-mail, and interacts with companies via websites. The next wave – introduced through wireless technology – is about to change our lives even more. The increase in transmission capacity of wireless devices lays the foundation for communication unrestricted by physical location. Society can surf the Internet decoupled from landline computers. In addition, society can do it any time, blurring the borderlines of business and private space. In the future, society will experience another wave of change – a world that provides the ultimate form of ubiquitous networks and universal devices; a world that presents an alternative view of space and time (Watson *et al.* 2002). Likewise, society will experience another form of commerce – a form that goes over, above, and beyond traditional commerce, i.e., 'ultimate commerce', or simply 'u-commerce'.

Four constructs form the fundamental dimensions of u-commerce, namely: ubiquity, uniqueness, universality, and unison. *Ubiquity* allows users to access networks from anywhere at any time, and, in turn, to be reachable at any place and any time. *Uniqueness* allows users to be uniquely identified – not only in terms of their identity and associated preferences, but also in terms of their geographical position. *Universality* means mobile devices are universally usable and multi-functional. Currently, for instance, USA cell phones are unlikely to work in Europe, because of different standards and network frequencies, and vice versa. *Unison* covers the idea of integrated data across multiple applications, so that users have a consistent view of their information – irrespective of the device used.

The major difference between U-commerce and other, older, electronic booking methods is the shift from global distribution systems (GDSs) (i.e. Worldspan, Galileo, Sabre, and Amadeus) to the Internet and WWW as a booking medium (expedia.com, hotel.com, priceline.com, ebay.com). Traditionally, the industry has focused on applying technology to support the suppliers of services to tourists (e.g. reservation systems). With the advent of the Internet, some of these systems were extended to customers, for example, many consumers now book their own travel and accommodation arrangements.

Source: Association for Information Systems, 2006

Developments in transport

Air travel is likely to be the larger, more direct, and faster player in the transport sector, particularly with its growing trend towards cooperation, collaboration and mergers. The construction of bigger aircraft, such as the Airbus 380, which seats between 500 and 800 passengers, illustrates the role of technology and expected changes in air travel in the future. Further research into the development of hypersonic flights such as the Scramjet (the name originated from the concept Supersonic Combustion Ramjet) is in progress. Technological developments in other transport fields, such as ferry transportation, passenger rail services, and cars are also taking place.

Space Tourism (ST) is probably one of the most exciting technological developments in the coming years. The Space Tourism Society (www.spacetourismsociety.org) defines the nature of ST as:

- earth orbit and suborbital experiences
- beyond-Earth orbit experiences (to Mars, for example)
- earth-based simulations, tourism, and entertainment-based experiences, such as NASA centres
- cyberspace tourism experiences.

Dennis Tito, an American businessman, became the first tourist in space in 2001. He was followed in 2002 by South African Mark Shuttleworth; by Gregory Olsen, an American, in 2005, and by the first female tourist, Anousheh Ansari, in 2006. These space tourists each paid around US$20-million for the travel experience. Few people are prepared to pay these amounts, and the question remains as to whether this concept will get underway as a viable tourism business activity. A more realistic and promising development is Richard Branson's Virgin Galactic SpaceShipTwo (SS2) which will offer regular sub-orbital flights by 2010. Space tourists will pay around $200,000 per trip.

The increasing availability of low-cost airlines will influence travel flows. An increased preference for mobility and flexibility will stimulate vehicle rentals. The increasing availability of direct links by aeroplane will stimulate demand for international short breaks in cities and regions, to the detriment of rural areas.

Developments in destinations

One key change in terms of technology is the continued growth that occurs globally of artificial environments for tourism and leisure activity. The global theme park industry is a reflection of this trend. This sector has grown US$11-billion a year, with roughly 119 major theme parks spread across the world (Page & Connell, 2006: 522). Some futurists believe that there will be little need to travel away from home in the 21st century. Virtual reality gives tourists artificial worlds to explore, outside normal space and time (Moutinho, 2000: 15).

With the aid of holographs, any environment can be created artificially in the comfort of your home. Activity holidays, such as simulated white water canoe and raft rides on the mighty Zambezi River, can be experienced. The question remains whether this form of entertainment will replace real travel or merely whet the appetite for travel. One thing is for certain: foreign travel can now be experienced by a large group of the population, from the very poor to the severely disabled.

Various forecasters predict underwater leisure as well as more adventurous accommodation, such as plans to build and launch hotels in space by 2015–25 (see Example box).

Technology can be an ally to economic development, but it can also be a threat. New developments can also mean customer loss, job displacement, and unemployment.

Political change

Political changes will continue to have strong effects on tourism. Governments can directly affect the travel patterns of their citizens and visitors, by establishing certain policies and trade relations between countries. As we discussed earlier, the opening up of the Eastern European countries dramatically changed the pattern of travel in Europe, and created new urban tourist destinations. The rapid growth of Prague in the Czech Republic as a tourist destination is such an example. The impact of China – with its population of well over 1-billion, attracts the attention of economists, business, and government policy-makers all over the globe as both an inbound and an outbound tourism market. Changes in political forces can have a significant impact on tourism creating new opportunities for destinations; the post-1994 New South Africa itself serves as a good example. The South African government has identified tourism as a growth industry, and consequently greater emphasis is placed on this sector's future. The government aims to grow arrivals to South Africa to 10 million a year by 2010, create 400 000 new jobs in the industry by 2014, and raising the industry's **gross domestic product** (GDP) contribution from eight to 12% by 2014.

Sustainability, the environment, and ethics

As tourism as an industry reaches maturity in many countries around the world, sustainability becomes a concern among tourists, government, and the tourism industry. A growing debate on sustainability, the interaction of man and nature, and the impact of excessive consumerism and resource consumption exists (see Example box below). Yet implementing strategies and monitoring the effectiveness for sustainable tourism remains a stumbling block, which the tourism industry has to overcome. The issues of global inequalities are illustrated in the patterns of tourism consumption, as international travel still remains an elite activity for the few.

Environmental problems remain important concerns for consumers in spite of their limited understanding of their impact upon them. Without more action at government and public-private sector partnership level, tourism will continue to use and destroy the natural environment. There is a growing concern about sustainability, the protection of the environment, and the preservation of cultural heritage (what with the spread of **sex tourism** and the exploitation of children in prostitution). These concerns are addressed by the agency End Child Prostitution and Trafficking (ECPAT). UN-WTO (1999) has developed practices in tourism.

> **Example** The impact of mass tourism – 2020
>
> The Future of World Travel report found that by 2020 some of the world's top tourist destinations will be damaged by mass tourism and overcrowding:
> * Kathmandu Valley, Nepal could be ruined if the Himalayan ski market booms
> * A boom in visitors to the Dalmatian coastal resorts of Croatia may destroy the last unspoilt Mediterranean coastline
> * The Great Barrier Reef in Australia, which is one of the world's largest marine ecosystems, is at risk from cruise liners
> * Cologne Cathedral, Germany, is at risk of irreparable damage caused by pollution.
>
> Source: *World Travel Report, 2006*

Global security, safety and health

Health issues (such as outbreaks of diseases), natural disasters (such as tsunamis and hurricanes), as well as safety and security concerns are important factors for tourists when making their travel decisions. Health-consciousness will increase still further.

Safety has always been an important prerequisite for attracting international visitors. The threat of international conflicts and wars, increased crime, and terrorism create safety and security problems. Global terrorism, such as the '9/11' event, the Bali bombings in 2002, the suicide bomb attacks in Istanbul in 2003, attacks on the Madrid railway system in 2004, and the London bombings in 2005, has now made the world a much less safe place for international travel. An emerging trend, triggered by the effects of 9/11, is that travellers are seeking destinations closer to home, or within their own country's geographic regions (Poon, 2003b: 11). Travel within a local geographical area has boomed, because of tourists' desire to feel safe and secure.

WTTC's (2002) *Travel and Tourism Security Action Plan* highlights the following four principles to counter the threat of terrorism on global tourism:

- coordination of policy, actions and communications
- measures to ensure a secure operating environment
- measures to deny terrorists freedom of action
- access to, and work with, the best intelligence.

As is likely to continue in the next decade, travellers will be more willing to accept a decrease in their privacy in exchange for improved safety conditions. 'Increasingly, ours is a world of ID checks, surveillance cameras, body scans, and fingerprint databases' (Shenk, 2003: 7). The retina of the eye will become the major identifying feature, rather than the fingerprints used at present. Shenk noted that at Amsterdam's Schiphol airport, frequent fliers can save time with a programme that stores travellers' iris patterns on a card that they can swipe (2003: 17). Surveillance systems will become more common for all future events and tourism attractions. Most countries will move towards globally-standardised electronic national identification cards in place of passports.

Consequently, the majority of tourists will avoid destinations that are perceived to be unsafe. The industry, therefore, should be better prepared in times of crisis to meet tourism demand more flexibly. Aviation safety problems continue to plague many countries, and security at airports will be tightened. Some airlines have also restricted the size, weight and contents of hand luggage, both for safety reasons and to conserve fuel and space.

Discussion point

In light of the importance that international and domestic tourists should feel safe while travelling in South Africa, suggest some tips that could be communicated to these future tourists.

Tourism market trends

The society we live in changes continuously. The world tourism market has gone through a period of dramatic change recently. Nowadays, it is crucial to assess these changes at an early stage, as demand dictates supply. The increasing saturation of the tourism market, and more self-assertive consumers with more disposable income and more leisure time, will determine the profitability of tourism businesses. Increasingly, competition is becoming, and will continue to be, more volatile. It is important to attempt to forecast trends in demand, key questions for travel and tourism suppliers are:

- what will the future hold?
- how will travellers react?
- how will growth occur?

Trends will drive the travel and tourism industry. Trends represent developments and social movements that predict what will happen in the future. It is difficult to attribute new developments in tourism to one trend alone, as they are combinations of **market trends**, in terms of their phase of development and level of importance.

The aim of identifying trends is not to present a definite picture of developments in the future. Essentially, it once again highlights the fact that trends require one to plan for uncertainty. It is said that, as a true trend is impossible to change, planners must anticipate change, and determine a suitable plan of action. The following represents a few of the top tourism trends and developments which are having a significant impact on the tourism industry worldwide, as discussed in various sources (Cook, Yale, & Marqua, 2006; Davidson, 2006; Holloway, 2006; Page & Connell, 2006; Van Zyl, 2005; Poon, 2003b).

1. The radical *changes in the consumer preferences* of travellers can best be illustrated by Poon's (2003a: 130) description of 'Old' and 'New' tourism. Old tourism is the tourism of the 1950s, 1960s, and 1970s characterised by mass, standardised, and rigidly-packaged holidays, hotels, and tourism offerings. New tourism is the tourism of the future, and is characterised by flexibility, segmentation, and a more authentic holiday experience. No longer is sunbathing next to the pool of a luxury 5-star hotel (old traditional market) the primary attraction. Instead, there has been a shift to new kinds of experiences and tourism offerings (Poon, 2003a: 141). The challenge for public- and private-sector tourism planners and the more sophisticated tourist, **special interest tourism** (SIT), has been identified as being able to respond to the specific needs of this target market (Van Zyl, 2005: 5). SIT appeals to the human imagination, and that is something that has no boundaries (Page, 2007: 4). Different types of SIT opportunities are available in the market, as illustrated in Figure 17.1 (also see Example box).

Example Bird-watching as a SIT activity

There are many new types of activities that travellers undertake. Birding, or bird-watching, is regarded as one of the fastest-growing hobbies. To read more about this activity, visit the website: www.birdlife.org.za.

Figure 17.1 Different types of special interest tourism opportunities

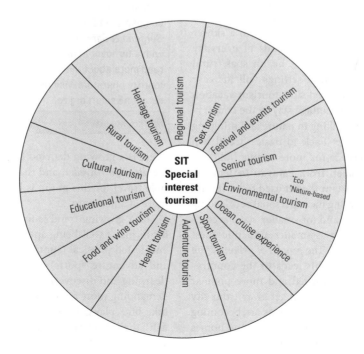

There is a growing mis-match between the offerings and services that suppliers offer, and the needs and expectations of travellers. Destinations need to respond to the needs and demands of the *increasingly experienced traveller*. More investment into human resource development needs to be made.

2. *New tourism destinations*, such as Central and Eastern Europe, the Middle East, and South East Asia (especially China) are rapidly emerging, and represent growing competition for the more established destinations. A demand for new destinations in Eastern Europe, the Americas, and Africa will increase.

3. Growing competition for tourists' time, as the *money-rich* and *time-poor* 21st-century characteristic demands a better balance between work if more priority is given to leisure time and time with friends and family. There is a growing need for *faster, shorter, and more frequent breaks*, and for cheaper business and holiday travel. This trend is driven by busy, stressed-out, and time-poor executives. On this short break, all in one weekend, the drive is for health, wellness, and rejuvenation, and nothing must be left to chance.

4. *Slow tourism* will develop as an important niche segment of the tourism industry, as more and more travellers seek holidays with a slower pace to escape from the demands of everyday life. This trend suggests that health spas, rural countryside, and tranquil settings will increase in popularity. A preferred slow tourism vacation might be a two-week cottage stay in the countryside of the Karoo, walking in nature and mingling with the locals. The 'back to basics' trend will result in a preference for more simple holidays: from hotel to chalet, from caravan to tent. As 'status' is less important than it used to be, leisure behaviour is becoming more personalised, leading to an increased demand for smaller-sized accommodation units, such as smaller authentic guest houses and farm stays. The *process of urbanisation* is likely to continue. This leads to the countryside becoming less crowded and more popular with those visitors seeking to get away from city life. In some countries, these areas are becoming leisure resorts, as the popularity of second homes and 'buy to let' homes for holiday rental grows.

Demand for slower modes of transport, such as rail travel, is likely to increase over the coming years as the environmentally aware and those tired of over-crowded airports cut back on air travel.

5. The future will also see an increase in *medical tourism* – that is, travel to other countries to receive specific treatment or low-cost medical treatment. Tourism suppliers can thus offer packages to cater for the specific needs of these travellers (see Example box below).

Example Medical tourism in South Africa

Foreigners are heading to SA in large numbers to combine a holiday with medical treatment. Generally speaking, the rich and famous all like a bit of 'nip and tuck' for a number of reasons. One of them, the relative anonymity of SA – many medical tourists prefer travelling to SA as a destination for an operation, and taking a short holiday before going under the knife. Afterwards these tourists check into a hotel or guesthouse to recover and recuperate. Mostly these post-operative patients or medical tourists desire privacy, which SA then provides. Medical tourism is currently an R100m-a-year business, with about eight registered medical tourism companies in SA catering for this niche market. *Surgeon & Safari* is a medical tourism company with a turnover of more than R36m a year. To read more about this growing trend and medical tourism operators, visit the following site: www. surgeon&safari.org.za.

Source: George, 2004: 238–249

There is a growing demand to meet the needs of the *disabled traveller*, and the provision of accessible travel for this group is becoming more and more of a necessity.

6. A growing trend is for travellers to search for forms of well-being apart from the old tried-and-tested physical (suntan, strenuous exercises, and adventure sports) and mental stimulation (learning and discovering). Although tourists are demanding more active holidays, (to be active, to hike, bike, play golf, sail, dive, surf, canoe, raft, and fish), they also want to move beyond these physical activities; do something for their well-being

and participate in mind-relaxing activities such as Yoga and Tai Chi. Such activities should also become part of the holiday travel market, as their inclusion could influence decision-making with regard to destinations and offerings. The *demand for seaside holidays* is changing, and affected by the growing fear of skin cancer caused by too much exposure to the sun. As active or activity holidays increase in popularity, the demand for facilities that correspond to this type of holiday will be preferred. The demand for 'wellness' offerings, including spas and fitness centres, will increase. For tourism, this will mean that tourism organisations will increasingly need to include relaxation as one of their offerings.

7. The average *level of education* is increasing. This means that many tourists are undertaking holidays in which the arts, culture, and history play a more important role, resulting in a more educational and spiritual approach to holiday-making. There will be increased demand for specialised offerings relating to the arts, culture, and history in package tours and self-organised holidays.

8. The increase in the *number of independent travellers* who are willing to buy elements of a holiday package and put together a holiday for themselves. Travellers can now book either a flight or accommodation through separate sources, and a 'package' from an entirely different source. The long-term trend will be one where travellers seek *value for money,* rather than one of hunting for bargains. Those resorts offering consistently excellent value will be in demand.

9. The rise in the USA of a *'new upper class'* category of travel consumers will also impact on tourism trends. Travel suppliers will need to cater for these groups in future, who are known as the 'Bourgeois Bohemians' or 'Bobos'. The Bobos' predecessors were the Hippies and the Yuppies. The Hippies emerged during the 1960s. A Hippie is a person whose behaviour, dress, use of drugs, etc., implied a rejection of conventional values and a belief in never-ending youth. The Yuppies (Young Upwardly Mobile Urban Professionals) are now in their 40s and early 50s. They remain deeply competitive and status-conscious, and their lifestyle is based on brands. Also included

among the Bobos are 'Dinkies' ('Double Income, No Kids). These are young couples who have delayed parenthood in order for two-way income-earners to build up financial wealth. The Bobos are urban, well-educated, professionally successful, and extremely materialistic. This group feel driven to expand their cultural horizons through experiences, shopping, and travel.

10. Changes in business, professional, and *conference travel* are expected. Current trends support an increase in business and professional travel. Growing professionalism is needed, as the conference industry is finally recognised as a profession, and educating the next generation of conference managers is necessary. Note should be taken of the changing profile of conference delegates, as more women, older attendees, and multiculturalism are experienced in the industry. WiFi (Wireless Fidelity – a generic term referring to a local wireless network or Internet broadband) connection or cellphone networks should be provided; always *on-line*, and preferably free of charge.

11. *More adventure travel.* A part of the 'Generation X' era (born between 1965 and 1977) wants to experience adventure and undertake extreme activities. Adventure travel is defined as a 'trip or travel with the specific purpose of activity participation to explore a new experience, often involving perceived risk or controlled danger associated with personal challenges, in a natural environment or exotic outdoor setting' (Sung, Morrison, & O'Leary, 1997: 66). Adventure (mountain-biking and snowboarding) and extreme (scuba-diving) sports are typically outdoor or wilderness sports, and go hand-in-hand with ecotourism. Tourism suppliers need to offer packages to cater for this segment. In future, more of the adventure tourist market is likely to consist of GRAMPIES (Greying, Retired, Moneyed, in good Physical and Emotional Health), a term mainly used to describe men (Cook *et al.*, 2006: 407). It is estimated that by 2040 over half of the population in the developed world will be older than 50 years - i.e. more GRAMPIES, thus more adventure tourists (Beedie, 2003: 203). There will also be less distinction between adventure and mainstream tourism. Adventure tourism will become

more approachable and 'do-able' for more people. This gaining popularity trend in adventure tourism activities should be monitored by all tourism stakeholders concerned.

12. More *social conscience travellers* and the antidote to conspicuous consumption, generates positive public relations and ethically sound business practices, such as Fair Trade in Tourism in South Africa (FTTSA) (see Chapter 16 – Managing tourism responsibly and visit FTTSA's website: www.fairtourismsa.org.za). Tourism suppliers, especially hotels and the accommodation sector, should *go green* by instituting waste recycling and water and energy conservation. These measures can both save the earth's resources, and reduce costs.

TO DO

Identify any 10 *tourism market trends* that might impact on the tourism industry, and indicate what travel and tourism suppliers could do to attract this new market segment in the future.

Conclusion

In this chapter the future of tourism has been speculated. It is universally accepted that the tourism industry is a growth industry, with a great deal of potential. The various external factors that might influence the tourism planners, developers, and managers were addressed. In addition, specific market trends impacting on the future of the tourism industry were discussed. These trends have consequences for the tourism industry. It should be apparent to those who study tourism management that it is vital to take note of trends and act upon them. This chapter substantiates the statement 'nothing was ever the same, or will ever be the same'. Successful tourism management is just a question of managing uncertainty and change effectively, and with forethought.

Review questions

1. Is the future of tourism secure?

2. How will society change? Discuss this by referring to demographic and social changes likely to affect tourism.

3. Explain how technology will affect the future of the tourism industry.

4. Identify some key market trends, of which all tourism planners, developers and managers should be aware.

Further reading

Lockwood, A. & Medlik, R. 2002. *Tourism and hospitality in the twenty-first century*. Oxford: Butterworth-Heinemann.

Van Pelt, M. 2005. *Space tourism: adventures in earth orbit and beyond*. New York: Copernicus.

Websites

Africam: www.africam.co.za

Space Adventures www.spaceadventures.com

UNESCO World Heritage sites: www.world-heritage-tour.org

United Nations World Tourism Organisation: www.world-tourism.org

World Travel and Tourism Council: www.wttc.org

References

Association for Information Systems, 2006. *U-Commerce - The Ultimate Commerce*. [Online] Available: http://http://www.isworld.org/ijunglas/u-commerce.htm2006–10–29].

Beedie, P. 2003. Adventure tourism. In S. Hudson (ed.) *Sport and Adventure Tourism*. New York: Haworth Hospitality Press.

Cook, R. A., Yale, L. J. & Marqua, J. J. 2006. *Tourism: the business of travel*, 3rd edition. Upper Saddle River, New Jersey: Prentice Hall.

Cooper, C., Fletcher, J., Fyall, A., Gilbert, D. & Wanhill, S. (Eds.). 2005. *Tourism: principles and practice*, 3rd edition. New York: Longman.

Davidson, R. 2006. *10 top trends in business tourism*. Business Tourism Conference, Sandton Convention Centre: Johannesburg, SA, February.

George, R. 2004. 'Medical tourism: Surgeon and Safari'. In A. Bennett & R. George (Eds.). *South African travel and tourism cases*. Pretoria: Van Schaik.

Holloway, C. J. 2006. *The business of tourism*, 7th edition. Harlow, England: Prentice Hall.

Ma, J., Buhalis, D. & Song, H. 2003. ICTs and Internet adoption in China's tourism industry. *International Journal of Information Management*, Vol.23(6), 451–67.

Moutinho, L. 2000. *Strategic management in tourism*. Wallingford, Oxon: CAB.

Page, S. J. 2007. *Tourism management: managing for change*, 2nd edition. Oxford: Butterworth-Heinemann. London: Thomson.

Poon, A. 1993. *Tourism, technology and competitive strategies*. Oxford: CAB International.

Poon, A. 2003a. 'Competitive strategies for 'a new tourism'. In C. Cooper (Ed.). *Classic reviews in tourism*. Clevedon: Channel View Publications.

Poon, A. 2003b. *The Berlin Report: A new tourism scenario-key future trends*. Bielefeld, Germany: Tourism Intelligence International.

Shenk, D. 2003.'Watching you: The world of high-tech surveillance.' *National Geographic*, Vol. 204(5), 1–29.

South African Tourism. 2006. *Strategic Research Unit, 2005 Annual Tourism Report, 12*. Illovo, Johannesburg: South African Tourism.

South African Tourism. 2007. *Strategic Research Unit, 2006 Performance Report*. Johannesburg: South African Tourism.

Sung, H.H., Morrison, M., & O'Leary, J.T. 1997. Definition of Adventure Travel: Conceptual Framework for Empirical Application from the Providers' Perspective. *Asia Pacific Journal of Tourism Research*, 1(2):47–67.

United Nations World Tourism Organisation, 1997. *International tourism: a global perspective*, 2nd edition. Madrid, Spain: UN-WTO.

United Nations World Tourism Organisation. 1997. *Tourism 2020 vision: a new forecast from the World Tourism Organisation*. Madrid: UN-WTO.

United Nations World Tourism Organisation. 1999. *Global code of ethics for tourism*. Madrid: UN-WTO.

United Nations World Tourism Organisation. 2007. Another record year for world tourism. www.world-tourism.org (accessed February 2007).

Van Zyl, C. 2005. Optimum market-positioning models for South African arts festivals. Unpublished D.Comm. thesis, Tshwane: University of South Africa.

Watson, R., Pitt, L.F., Berthon, P., & Zinkhan, G.M. 2002. U-commerce: expanding the universe of marketing. *European Management Journal*, 22(3), 315–326.

Watson, R., Akselsen, S., Monod, E., & Pitt, L. 2004. The open tourism consortium: laying the foundations for the future of tourism. *Journal of the Academy of marketing Science*, 30(4):329–343.

World Travel and Tourism Council. 1996. *Progress and priorities*, 1996. Brussels: WTTC.

World Travel and Tourism Council. 2002. *Travel and tourism security action plan*. Brussels: World Travel and Tourism Council.

World Travel and Tourism Council and Accenture. 2006. *South Africa travel and tourism climbing to new heights*, 2006. Brussels: World Travel and Tourism Council.

World Travel and Tourism Council. 2006. Blueprint for New Tourism, London: WTTC.

Case study
17

Tourism trends:
South Africa lures
city slickers to bush

Objectives

- to identify a key future trend in the tourism industry of South Africa
- to understand the challenges that tourism managers and planners face
- to act upon the change anticipated.

In the words of Lesley Parker-Jones, they are everywhere. They may not be immediately recognisable as business tourists (individuals, travelling with the purpose of attending a conference, meeting, exhibition, event, or as part of an incentive trip), but you can be sure that they are on the plane with you, and that they will be present when you book into your hotel – or you might even be one of them. The business tourism sector in South Africa has experienced exceptional growth in relation to other tourism segments, although exact figures have still to be compiled. Business tourism, defined at the market of travellers who attend conferences, meeting and exhibitions, is forecast to grow faster than the mainstream tourism industry.

Johannesburg is riding the wave of a tourism boom, and touting *Survivor-* style business meetings to turn it into one of the world's top 10 conference venues by 2010. South Africa has about 1 700 convention venues that are used. South African Tourism also launched its brand

new *Business Unusual* international marketing campaign at road shows in the USA, Europe, and Asia, which offers executives a chance to swap pinstripe suits for shorts in the bush while chalking out strategy or ironing out problems. 'What we're saying is that we can go beyond the usual business conferences and meetings', said Angeline Lue (General Manager of the Business Tourism unit) of South African Tourism. 'You might have in the bush, in a typical *boma* (a round open space in Swahili) environment, a meeting about first-world issues', said Lue, who is in charge of business tourism. 'It might mean bringing in a facilitator who would bring in typical African concepts, such as cattle-herding, stick-fighting, or drum-beating to build up team spirit'.

Breaking into the top 10 by 2010

Lue said that *Business Unusual* drew from South Africa's rich history and multi-cultural tapestry to host conferences modelled on the *bosberaad* (Afrikaans for bush meeting), and *imbizo* (a Zulu gathering where there is no hierarchy, and everyone is free to speak their mind). The concept is part of a concerted effort to turn South Africa into one of the world's top business conference venues by 2010 – the year the country hosts the 2010 FIFA World Cup. 'This year, the global conference and meetings sector is forecast to comprise 10% of the estimated $672bn being generated from travel and tourism activity', the Minister of Environmental Affairs and Tourism, Marthinus van Schalkwyk said recently. Van Schalkwyk said South Africa was currently (2006) rated the world's 31st leading conference destination by the International Congress and Convention Association (ICCA), and 'we have declared our intention to break into the top 10 by 2010'. The top three countries in terms of international meetings hosted in 2006 were the USA, Germany, and the UK.

Supporting jobs

South Africa currently attracts 63% of all conferences held in Africa, helping support 12 000 jobs and contributing R2,6bn annually to the gross domestic product, van Schalkwyk said. South Africa is the top meeting destination in Africa, followed by Egypt and Tunisia. Research by the SA Tourism Business Unit has shown that 37% of delegates return to South Africa within five years, often bringing their families along. The infrastructure is in place for huge international conferences, with centres in eThekwini and Cape Town each having a capacity of 10 000, and another in Johannesburg, which is nearly as large. Major conference centres are also in the pipeline for Polokwane, Tshwane, Bloemfontain, and Port Elizabeth. Soweto also has a number of conference centres that can cater for 1 000 delegates. The country's famed game parks, breathtaking natural beauty and other tourist attractions are also going to be used as bait to reel in business travellers, Lue said. 'Business tourists are, by definition, high spenders', she added. These delegates tend to spend double the amount of money spent by leisure tourists, and stay on average, five to nine days. During a conference they spend on average R1 450 a day, in addition to R916 a day before and after the event. 'Business tourism is a strong driver of growth, because conferencing is year-round, and it can take care of seasonality that we experience in leisure travel'. We are also looking at increasing length of stay and increasing spend by encouraging delegates to bring accompanying persons and to book pre- and post-tours'. Business tourism helps to convert conference delegates to leisure by encouraging repeat visits by WOM

ambassadors. Of the 8,4-million tourists who came to South Africa in 2006, 5% were business tourists, Lue said, adding that the aim was to take the figure of overall total arrivals to 10-million by 2010, of whom one million would be business tourists. South Africa's first ever conference for the business tourism industry hosted on 26 February 2006, addressed the country's international positioning as a destination for hosting major events and incentive travel groups. The conference was aimed at unleashing the potential of business tourism in South Africa.

Reality check

Others are sceptical, however, saying the new game plan fails to take into account the reality on the ground. One of the main stumbling blocks is the widespread fear of insecurity – fuelled by perceptions about unacceptable levels of crime which may deter leisure and business tourists alike from visiting South Africa. Peggy Drodskie, of the Chambers of Commerce and Industry, South Africa, said other impediments included the high price of air travel to come here, and higher accommodation costs compared to exotic Asian destinations such as Bali. 'Also, the service standards need to be improved. They compare poorly with the standards in India, Austria, or Germany, for example', she said.

Spencer Pillai, (general manager, Marketing & Corporate Affairs) of Gallagher Estate Conference & Exhibition Centre, says that the future looks bright for the South African conferencing industry, but the industry needs to work hard in a concerted effort to lift South Africa's profile in the world ICCA rankings.

Case study questions

1. What opportunities does the business tourism market hold for South Africa?
2. Identify the positive and negative characteristics of this market, from the perspective of an events organiser
3. From the knowledge gained throughout this textbook, do you think the targets predicted are realistically set? Motivate your answer.

Glossary

Accelerated and Shared Growth Initiative for South Africa (ASGISA) A government initiative aimed at increasing *economic growth* and reducing poverty. *p206.*

Accommodation Commercial facilities primarily intended to host stayover *tourists* for overnight stays. *p104.*

Accounting A *management* activity of business designed to accumulate, measure, and communicate financial information to various decision-makers. *p225.*

Accounting period Normally one year, the period for which accounts are drawn up. *p225.*

Adventure tourism A type of *niche tourism* involving exploration or travel to unusual, exotic, remote, or unconventional destinations. There is a heavy emphasis on outdoor pursuits, usually encompassing high levels of risk, 'adrenalin rushes', excitement, and personal challenge. *p270, 349.*

Agritourism The provision of touristic activities linked to game, crop and cattle farming, wineries and opportunities on working farms (sometimes called agrotourism or farm-stay tourism). *p190, 270.*

Airports Company South Africa (ACSA) ACSA owns and operates South Africa's main public airports. *p98.*

Alternative tourism A form of tourism that is offered as an alternative to *mass tourism*. Alternative tourism is also known as *new tourism. p270, 319.*

Ancestry tourism Travelling with the aim of learning more about and possibly tracing one's ancestors. This type of *niche tourism* is becoming particularly popular in Africa, which is widely considered to be the birthplace of humankind. *p270.*

Architectural tourism A type of niche tourism, involving exploration of, travel to and visiting architectural destinations such as the Taj Mahal, Gaudi's cathedral in Barcelona, or the Great Wall of China, simply for the sake of viewing them. *p270.*

Association for South African Travel Agents (ASATA) An industry association which represents the interests of South African *tour operators* and *travel agents* (approximately 640 members). *p134, 166, 253.*

Attraction A designated resource which is controlled and managed for the enjoyment, amusement, entertainment, and education of the visiting public. *p59.*

Backpackers Travellers who have a preference for budget *accommodation*, an emphasis on meeting other travellers, an independently organised and flexible travel schedule, longer rather than shorter holidays, and an emphasis on informal and participatory holiday activities. *p270.*

Backpacking South Africa (BSA) A non-profit tourism organisation formed in 1998, which aims to market South Africa globally as a preferred *backpacker* destination. *p166, 277.*

Balance of payments The difference between a country's income from abroad and its expenditure. *p296.*

Basic tourism system An application of a systems approach to tourism, in which tourism is seen as consisting of three geographical components (generating, transit, and destination regions), tourists and a *tourism industry*, embedded within a modifying external environment that includes political, social, physical, and other systems. *p14, 36.*

Benchmarks Performance measures that are used by similar types of tourism businesses to monitor key operations. *p117.*

Black Economic Empowerment (BEE) A process that contributes to the economic transformation of South Africa and brings about significant increases in the numbers of black people who manage, own and control the country's economy, as well as significant decreases in income inequalities. *p129, 327.*

Branding The process of giving an offering a distinctive a name or logo, so that it will become more easily identifiable from its competitors. *p271.*

Break-even analysis Measuring the break-even point (BEP) in order to generate useful insights for management. *p234.*

Budget An organisation's operation plan for a specific period. *p238.*

Budgetary control The use of budget to control the activities of an organisation to ensure that activities are not only effectively performed, but also efficiently executed. *p239.*

Budget tourism A term used to describe mainly young, price-conscious travellers, who carry all their belongings on their backs, use local transport and negotiate for goods and services. *p270.*

Built attractions An attraction (also referred to as human-made attractions) created by people, for example, casinos, convention centres, holiday resorts, aquariums, theme parks and tourist routes and trails (the trails are often made by people, but are linked to *natural attractions* such as whale-watching). *p41, 60, 255.*

Business tourism A trip undertaken with the purpose of attending a conference, meeting, exhibition, event, or as part of an incentive. *p6, 352.*

Call centres Centralised facilities designed and managed to handle large volumes of incoming telephone inquiries, in many cases on a 24/7 basis. *p126.*

Carrying capacity A key concept in environmental impact analysis that relates to the amount of use an environment is capable of sustaining under certain circumstances. *p37, 309.*

Central/computer reservation systems (CRSs) Centralised booking facilities used by hotel groups, *tour operators* and airlines to offer an efficient service to the customer. *p139.*

Chain of distribution The means by which offerings are distributed from principals to consumers, often via *tour operators* and retail *travel agencies. p125.*

Charter services A system of conditions over a finite period that relates to levels of service and frequency of flights in order to secure capacity. *p88, 250.*

Code of conduct Guidelines advising a tourism *stakeholder*, including tourists, on how to behave in an environmentally responsible manner. *p309.*

Collateral materials Printed information about products, services, or organisations, such as fliers, leaflets, brochures, maps, fact sheets, postcards, and posters. *p277.*

Commission Payment made to an agent for selling the offerings of a principal. For example, a *travel agent* is paid commission for selling a tour operator's package holiday. *p137.*

Community-based tourism Tourism in which a significant number of local people are involved in providing services to tourists and the tourism industry, and in which local people have meaningful ownership, power and participation in the various tourism enterprises. *p327.*

Community development The process of economic and social progress involving local community members. *p79.*

Competitive advantage Something that makes a tourism offering stand out as being better than similar offerings. *p318.*

Consortia A combination or group formed in order to undertake a venture that would be beyond the resources of a single individual/company. *p133.*

Consumer behaviour The study of consumer characteristics and processes involved when individuals or groups select, buy, and use products, services, or experiences to satisfy needs and wants. *p267.*

Control The tactical activity carried out to close the gaps between actual performance and daily, weekly, or monthly targets identified by monitoring. *p174, 183.*

Convention & visitor bureau (CVB) An organisation whose mission is to develop tourism to an area by attracting both business and *leisure* tourists. *p159, 167.*

Corporate social responsibility (CSR) Adopting open and transparent business practices that are based on ethical values. It means managing responsibly all aspects of operations for their impact not just on shareholders, but also on employees, communities, and the environment. *p319, 321.*

Corporate governance The balance between economic and social goals and between individual and communal goals…the aim is to align, as nearly as possible, the interests of individuals, corporations, and society. *p321.*

Cost The value of resources sacrificed or foregone in the process of achieving a specific objective. *p226.*

Cost-benefit analysis A method used to determine the relative impact of a development, in which total costs

and total benefits are estimated, and then compared. *p229.*

Courtesy service A transport service for customers provided by an organisation which is not a public transport operator, where the organisation provides its own vehicle, or a vehicle provided by an operator in terms of a contract with that organisation. *p250.*

Cruise tourism Travel which involves a voyage on a ship undertaken wholly for reasons of *leisure* and *recreation. p270, 294.*

Cultural attractions Places or things that are reflective of a particular community, for example, cultural villages, art festivals, museums, and craft markets. *p61, 256.*

Cultural tourism A type of tourism which involves interacting with local host communities and their culture; for example, visiting cultural villages and observing arts and crafts. *p270, 318.*

Customer relationship management (CRM) A system in which a business aims to develop a good relationship with customers, for example, by keeping information about their needs, in order to sell as many offerings as possible to keep customers satisfied. *p281.*

Dark tourism From the Greek 'thanatourism'. This is a term used to describe the tourist fascination with sites associated with death and morbidity, for example, visits to 'dark' sites such as the killing fields of Cambodia, Ground Zero in New York, World War II concentration camps, South African War battlefields, dungeons, and celebrities' death sites. See also *struggle tourism. p270.*

Delict Described as the unreasonable behaviour of a person who acts either intentionally or negligently and thus causes someone to suffer loss or damage. *p257.*

Demographics Factors concerning the characteristics of the population of a country or region, for example, age structure, social class, level of income. *p268, 269.*

Demonstration effect Influencing the behaviour, dress, attitudes or people through demonstration and interaction. *p302.*

Department of Environmental Affairs and Tourism (DEAT) The Ministry of Tourism in South Africa responsible for national *tourism policy*. DEAT has a dual role, in that it is responsible for environment affairs as well as tourism. *p156, 306, 327.*

Destination A place, including a physical or perceived location, consisting of primary and secondary *attractions* and supporting amenities that entice people to visit it. *p15, 37.*

Destination management company (DMC) A local supplier who arranges, manages and/or plans any function or service for an incentive programme, meeting or event. *p126, 140.*

Destination marketing organisation (DMO) An all-encompassing term for either a *convention and visitor bureau* (CVB), a *provincial tourism authority*, *regional tourism organisation*, or a *national tourism organisation. p36, 59, 158, 277, 343.*

Destination mix The resources, facilities and services at a destination that draw tourists to a region. *p63.*

Destination region A geographical area to which tourists travel. *p15, 37*.

Discretionary income The amount of income that remains after household necessities such as food, housing, clothing, education and transport have been purchased. *p19*.

Distribution system The mix of channels used to gain access to, or means by which a tourism offering is made available to potential consumers. *p136*.

Domestic tourism A type of tourism where people take holidays, short breaks, and business trips in their own country. *p5, 18*.

E-commerce The business of buying, selling, marketing, and servicing products over electronic systems, such as the Internet and other computer networks. *p225*.

Economic growth An increase in a per capita output or *gross domestic product* (GDP). *p87*.

Economies of scale A concept which applies when a company is able to spread its costs over mass-produced goods or services. *p135, 231*.

Ecotourism A form of tourism that focuses on environmental and cultural preservation. *p270, 318*.

Educational tourism Travel to a location with the primary purpose of engaging in a learning experience directly related to the location. Also referred to as 'edutourism'. *p270*.

Educational trip *(See familiarisation trip.)*

Enclave tourism When tourists remain in their resort and do not spend money in the local *destination*. The result is that the local destination does not benefit from tourism. *p293*.

Entrepreneur A person who creates a new business in the face of risk and uncertainty, for the purpose of achieving profit and growth. *p190*.

Environmental impact assessment (EIA) A procedure undertaken to assess the likely consequences of tourism projects, so that decisions can be made concerning whether, and in what form, the project should proceed. *p309, 310*.

Ethical tourism Tourism development that adheres to acceptable moral practices and behaviour. *p270, 318*.

Excursionist A tourist who spends less than 24 hours in a destination region. *p3*.

Extreme tourism A type of *niche tourism* involving travel to dangerous places (jungles, mountains, caves, deserts, etc.) or participation in dangerous events. Extreme tourism (also referred to as 'shock tourism') overlaps with extreme sports. *p270*.

Fair Trade in Tourism South Africa (FTTSA) An independent project of the IUCN (World Conservation Union) South Africa, that seeks to facilitate improved access to tourism markets for structurally disadvantaged tourism enterprises. *p165, 328*.

Familiarisation trip A tour which provides *travel agents*, *tour operators*, and other members of the tourism industry with the opportunity to try out facilities and services first-hand, so that they are in the best position to advise clients on their holiday choices. Sometimes called an 'educational trip' or 'fam trip'. *p160, 277*.

Federal Hospitality Association of South Africa (FEDHASA) Sectoral organisation whose 'mission' is to promote and enhance the development and growth of a sustainable South African trading environment. *p165*.

Financial information Information that shows the impacts of management decisions on an organisation's *costs* and *revenues*. *p226*.

Fixed costs The costs of running an organisation that remain unchanged, regardless of whether one has few or many customers. These are costs such as maintenance of buildings, staff costs, building costs, etc. *p69, 228*.

Focus groups An in-depth interview about a topic among 8 to 12 people, with a researcher (called a 'moderator') leading the discussion. *p269*.

Food tourism A form of *niche tourism* in which people primarily visit a destination to experience its food and drink as (also referred to as 'gastronomic', 'gastronomy', or 'culinary tourism'). *p270*.

Fully independent travel (FIT) A form of package holiday (*all-inclusive*), where the majority of services offered at the destination are included in the price prior to departure (e.g. refreshments, *excursions*, amenities, etc.). *p22, 48*.

Galileo A *global distribution system (GDS)* used by South African Airways (SAA) and other major international airlines. *p141*.

Gay tourism A form of *niche tourism* marketed to gay people who are open about their sexual orientation, and who wish to travel to gay travel destinations in order to participate to some extent in the gay life of the destination area. Also referred to as *pink tourism*. *p270*.

Generating region The region (e.g. country, province, city) from which the tourist originates, also referred to as the market or origin region. *p14, 36*.

Geotourism A type of tourism which is concerned with preserving a destination's geographic character, and which includes the entire combination of natural and human attributes that make one place distinct from another. *p35, 270*.

Global distribution systems (GDSs) Worldwide inter-organisation information systems that have been developed by the world's biggest airlines. Examples include Sabre, Worldspan, Amadeus and *Galileo*. *p141*.

Grand Tour A form of early modern tourism that involved a lengthy trip to cities of France and Italy by young British men for purposes of education and culture. *p21*.

Gross domestic product (GDP) A measure of the size and value of a nation's economy, usually expressed as the total value of all goods and services produced during a specified time period, usually one year. *p30, 192, 291*.

Groundhandler An agent which works on behalf of international and South African *tour operators*, *travel agents* and *principals*. *p136*.

Health tourism Travelling to facilities or destinations to obtain healthcare or health-related benefits. *p270*.

Heterogeneous Having different characteristics and needs. *p266*.

Historically disadvantaged individual (HDI) Any person who was disadvantaged by unfair discrimination before the Constitution of the Republic of South Africa came into operation in 1993. *p104*.

Horizontal integration Refers to mergers between organisations at the the the same level in the *distribution chain*. For example, a large hotel group taking over a small independent hotel. *p129*.

Human geography The human activities that shape the face of a location and shared experiences, including the cultural aspects of language, religion, political and social structures. *p35*.

Human resource management (HRM) The function within an organisation that focuses on recruitment of, management of, and providing direction for the people who work in the organisation. *p72, 206*.

Iconic attraction An attraction that is well-known and closely associated with a particular destination, such as the Taj Mahal (Agra, India) or Table Mountain (Cape Town). *p64*.

Image The sum of the beliefs, attitudes and impressions that individuals or groups hold towards offerings, organisations or tourist *destination*. *p59, 271*.

Impacts The effects, which may be either positive of negative, as a result of tourism-related activity. Tourists have at least three kinds of impacts on a destination: economic, sociocultural, and environmental. *p15, 291*.

Inbound tourist An international tourist arriving from another country. *p5*.

Incentive travel A type of *business tourism* concerned with offering holidays as incentives for staff. *p5, 352*.

Inclusive holiday/tour An all-inclusive holiday, sometimes referred to as a package tour or package holiday, which normally consists of the components of *accommodation, transportation,* and other travel services. *p132*.

Infrastructure Items such as airports, roads, railways, communications, and water supply. It includes all those services that need to be in place before development of any kind. *p82*.

Innovation Involves introducing new things, methods or ideas, and has the potential to enhance business procedures, add value, and achieve a *competitive advantage*. *p185*.

Inseparability A characteristic of tourism services: they are produced and consumed at the same time, and cannot be separated from service providers. *p181, 266*.

Intangibility A characteristic of tourism *offerings*, in that a customer cannot actually touch and examine many products before they agree to purchase. *p141, 266*.

Integration The linking (through changes of ownership such as mergers, acquisitions and takeovers) of different stages of the chain of *distribution* to form larger, more powerful organisations. Integration can be *vertical* or *horizontal*. *p128*.

Intermediary Any dealer – a business or person – in the chain of distribution who acts as a link (or 'middleman') between the tourism *principal* and its consumers. *p125, 252*.

International Air Transport Association (IATA) An international trade organisation of airlines that coordinates the air transport industry. *p90, 153*.

International Civil Aviation Organisation (ICAO) An organisation that aims to improve the overall levels of air transport standards across the world. *p89*.

International Congress and Convention Association (ICCA) A network of *suppliers* to the international meeting industry, with over 700 members in 80 countries worldwide. *p6, 353*.

Irridex A theoretical framework proposing that resident attitudes evolve from euphoria to apathy, then irritation (or annoyance), antagonism and finally resignation, as the intensity of tourism development increases within a destination. *p305*.

Itinerary A plan or schedule for visitors to follow. It includes information about dates, times, *accommodation, modes of transport,* and places to be visited. *p135*.

Lead adult price The main adult entrance fee, the full price an adult would pay with no discounts. *p70*.

Leadership The process of directing the behaviour of others toward the accomplishment of the organisation's goals. *p181, 213*.

Leakage The money that does not stay in the area in which tourism occurs, but leaves the local economy. This happens when goods and services are purchased from outside the area, or when foreign owners take their profits out of the area. *p292*.

Leisure A complex issue which most people associate with leisure time or *leisure activities,* choosing to spend their spare time in ways which give them the most satisfaction. *p4*.

Leisure activities Activities performed during one's free time away from work. *p4*.

Life-seeing tourism A type of tourism which provides a purposeful, in-depth experience. *p270*.

Limited-service hotel A small, simple hotel that offers guests no or very few facilities other than sleeping *accommodation*. *p108*.

Literary tourism A type of *cultural tourism* that deals with places and events from fictional texts as well as the lives of their authors. This could include following the route a fictional character charts in a novel, visiting particular settings from a story, or tracking down the haunts of a novelist. This would also include visiting the homes and haunts of other literary authors, such as poets and dramatists. *p270*.

Local tourism organisation (LTO) Local tourism organisations that exist in most municipalities to market tourism in the area. Sometimes LTOs (also called *TICs*) will take bookings on behalf of the destination area. *p164*.

Long-haul destinations Destinations generally considered to be six hours' flying time away, or more. *p46*.

Low-cost airline A company that offers low fares to customers in return for a service with few 'extras'. Examples of low-cost airlines (also known as 'no-frills' or 'budget airlines') in South Africa include kulula. com, 1Time and Mango. *p85*.

Managed attractions Designated permanent resources that are controlled and managed for their own sake, and for the enjoyment, amusement, entertainment, and education of the visiting public. *p59*.

Management The processes of planning, organising, directing and controlling people and other resources to achieve organisational objectives efficiently and effectively. *p173*.

Market The number of people who buy (existing market), or may buy (potential market) an *offering*. *p268*.

Market segmentation The way in which a tourism organisation divides a market into smaller and distinct groups of buyers that share similar needs and characteristics. *p268*.

Market share The percentage of the total market that is held by an organisation or destination, in relation to its main competitors. *p272*.

Market trends The way in which the demand for, and supply of, particular products and services fluctuate over time. *p346*.

Marketing The process of finding out what customers need and want, where they want it, and then providing them with it at a price they are prepared to pay for it and which still enables the provider to make a profit. *p159, 265*.

Marketing mix A combination of different *marketing* activities, namely product, place, price and promotion (also referred to as the 'Four Ps') that are used to accomplish an organisation's objectives and satisfy the needs of *target markets*. *p270*.

Marketing planning The process by which a tourism business attempts to analyse its existing resources and environment, in order to predict the direction it should take in the future. *p281*.

Marketing research The process of gathering and analysing information on existing and potential consumers, and its use for management purposes. *p280*.

Mass tourism The term used to describe the large *multinational* travel and tourism *companies* and popular tourist destinations around the world. *p21, 37, 306*.

Material fact A fact that the insurer takes into account when deciding whether to cover the risk and, if it decides to do so, what the premium and other conditions will be. *p258*.

Medical tourism People travelling to undergo surgical procedures or receive other medical treatment in combination with a holiday. *p270, 348*.

Mode of travel/transport Type of transport used to make a journey between an origin and a destination. *p82*.

Motivation The ability to encourage others to do something willingly. It stimulates interest in something or the achievement of something. *p182, 267*.

Multidisciplinary approach This involves the input of a variety of disciplines, but without any significant interaction or synthesis of these different perspectives. *p12*.

Multi-national company/corporation (MNC) A company that operates across international frontiers, with its headquarters in one country and operating interests in a number of others. *p91, 125, 190, 272*.

Multiplier concept An economic theory that suggests that money spent in a particular area creates jobs, which in turn creates demand for other products and services in the local economy. *p291, 294*.

Mystery customers/guests Researchers who investigate tourism companies through using their services, while pretending to be customers. They usually monitor areas such as the level of customer service and product knowledge. *p117, 119*.

National tourism organisation (NTO) A public sector-funded organisation that promotes travel at a country-destination scale, usually directed towards *inbound tourists. South African Tourism* is the country's NTO, as it is responsible for marketing South Africa internationally. *p7, 59, 298*.

Natural attractions Those features that make up the physical environment, for example the landscape, climate, wildlife, plants, and forests. *p38, 60, 255*.

Nature-based tourism Tourism experiences that have a focus on nature, such as whale-watching, bird-watching, or safaris in South Africa. *p270*.

Niche marketing The process of targeting a small, often specialised section of a larger market, each with clearly defined characteristics. *p269*.

Niche tourism In any market 'niche' is a specific segment, usually with a well-defined product-offering that can be tailored to meet the interests of the customer. In the case of South African tourism, examples might include golf, health tourism, wildlife, or township tours. *p.270*.

Node A point in a network where lines intersect or branch. *p51, 63*.

No-frills airline (See *low-cost airline.*)

Non-government organisation (NGO) An independent organisation which is concerned with meeting a social or environmental need, such as providing housing for the poor, or protecting biodiversity. *p292*.

Non-patrimonial loss Loss that cannot easily be expressed in monetary terms. *p258*.

Observation The process of gathering *market research* information by observing customers and their behaviour. *p280, 305*.

Occupancy rate Ratio comparing the total number of rooms occupied for a given time period to the total number of rooms available for rent. *p114*.

Offering A combination of services that delivers intangible, sensual and psychological benefits, but also some tangible elements. *p11*.

Oligopoly The control of trade in particular offerings by a small group of tourism companies. *p132*.

Organising The process that establishes a structure to guide people towards achieving the business's goals. *p178*.

Outbound tourists International tourists departing from their usual country of residence. *p5*.

Package holiday (See *inclusive holiday/tour.*)

Perishability A feature of tourism product and service – they have limited lives, after which they no longer exist. An airline seat or coach seat for use today cannot be sold tomorrow. *p114, 141, 266*.

Personal selling This involves persuading consumers to buy offerings in a 'face-to-face' encounter, and therefore must be seen as an important promotional tool for the tourism manager. *p278*.

Physical geography The natural features of the planet, such as climate, bodies of water, land masses and resources. *p38.*

Pilgrimage A term for travel undertaken for religious or spiritual purposes. *p20.*

Planning The process of anticipating future events and conditions, and determining courses of action for achieving organisational objectives. *p174, 176.*

Policy A general statement that provides direction for individuals within an organisation. *p148.*

Positioning The *marketing* process of establishing an image for a tourism offering in relation to others in the marketplace. *p270.*

Principal The term given to a company that a travel agency does business with, and whose offerings it sells. For example, if a branch of Pentravel sells a Thompsons Tours holiday, the agent in the deal is Pentravel and the principal is Thompsons Tours. *p126.*

Product life cycle (PLC) A concept which suggests that all offerings follow a series of four stages during their life span, namely: introduction, growth, maturity, and decline. *p65, 271.*

Professional conference organiser (PCO) A company or individual responsible for organising conferences. *p11.*

Property tourism People travelling to holiday destinations to purchase residential property. The property tourism operator who organises the tour may reimburse all or a portion of the cost of the holiday that was taken in order to view the property, on the premise that a property is purchased. *p270.*

Pro-poor tourism Tourism strategies designed to alleviate poverty. *p293, 319, 320.*

Provincial tourism authority (PTA) A public sector-funded body responsible for tourism marketing of the province. *p163.*

Public policy A policy developed by government bodies and officials. *p147.*

Public relations The activities designed to build and maintain mutual understanding between a company and its publics. *p275, 277.*

Rack rate A term which refers to the full, published price at which a hotel room is sold. *p114.*

Recreation The activities that people carry out in their *leisure* time, which may be active or passive, and take place inside or outside the home. *p4.*

Regional geography The components of geography that focuses on regional landscapes, cultures, economies, and political and social systems. *p48.*

Regional tourism organisation (RTO) Public sector-funded organisation that have the function of promoting tourism to their respective regions. For example, Cape Town Tourism is the RTO for the Greater Metropolitan area of Cape Town. *p164.*

Regional Tourism Organisation of Southern Africa (RETOSA) A public and private sector organisation that promotes the *SADC* region as a world-class tourism destination. *p154.*

Resort destinations Communities or areas that contain attractions, entertainment and supporting facilities need to attract and host tourists. *p46.*

Responsible tourism Any form of tourism that operates in such a way that it minimises any negative impacts that it has, and maximises potential positive impacts. *p318.*

Responsible tourism management (RTM) Aims to incorporate social, environmental and economic factors into decision-making in order to create mutually beneficial situations for a broad range of tourism stakeholders. *p292, 317.*

Return on investment (ROI) A measure of management's efficiency, showing the return on all of an organisation's assets. *p109.*

Rural tourism Leisure activities carried out in rural areas, including different types of recreational activities such as *cultural tourism*, *adventure tourism*, guest farms, *backpacking*, horse riding and *agritourism*. *p270.*

SADC (Southern African Development Community) The regional body of Southern African countries that work together to create a Community providing for regional peace, security, and an integrated regional economy. *p154.*

Sales promotions Promotional activities that offer an incentive to induce a desired result from potential customers, travel *intermediaries*, or the sales team. *p278.*

Satellite account A system to help measure the size and impact of sectors that cannot be defined as industries in national accounts. *p295.*

Seasonality Variations in the demand for offerings at different times of the year. *p19, 110.*

Sector Education and Training Authorities (SETAs) Established to ensure that the skill needs for every sector of the South African economy are identified and that training is available to provide for these skill needs. A SETA's main function is to contribute to the raising of skills - to bring skills to the employed, or those wanting to be employed, in their sector. Tourism, Hospitality and Sport Education and Training Authority (THETA) is the SETA for the tourism, hospitality and sport economic sector. *p165.*

Services sector The component of a nation's economy that is made up of tertiary industries. *p266.*

Sex tourism Travelling to a tourist destination with the primary *motivation* of seeking sexual encounters with strangers and sex workers. *p38, 270, 302, 345.*

Shopping tourism A trip which is undertaken to shop for goods that will be used by the tourist him/herself, and will not be re-sold. The goods will be taken back to the tourist's generating country. *p6, 270.*

Skills shortages A lack of adequately skilled individuals in the labour market. *p209, 212.*

Small, medium and micro enterprises (SMMEs) Companies that usually have fewer than 250 employees. *p11, 125, 175, 327.*

Social attractions Attractions where the visitor has an opportunity to see or be part of the way of life of the local population of specific communities. *p61, 257.*

Social tourism The extension of the benefits of holidays to economically marginal groups, such as the unemployed, single-parent families, pensioners, and the handicapped. *p270.*

South African Tourism (SA Tourism) The country's *national tourism organisation* (NTO). Its role is to market the country at an international level. *p161*.

Southern African Association of Tourism Professional (SAATP) An association which aims to represent the collective interests of individuals operating at a professional level within the tourism economy in southern Africa. *p.8*.

South African Tour Operators' Association (SATOA) A representative body for the wholesale *tour operators* in South Africa. *p134*.

Southern African Association for the Conference Industry (SAACI) An association that aims to improve standards of efficiency and professionalism in the conference industry in Southern Africa. *p165*.

Southern African Development Community (SADC) The regional body of Southern African countries that works together to create a community providing for regional peace and security, and an integrated regional economy. *p154*.

Southern African Tourism Services Association (SATSA) A non-profit member-driven association, representing the major tourism role-players including airlines, coach operators, tour operators, accommodation establishments, vehicle-hire companies, *attractions*, *professional conference organisers,* and related *marketing* organisations. *p165, 277, 298*.

Spa A type of resort centred on the use of geothermal waters for health purposes. *p22, 32, 61*.

Special interest tourism (SIT) A tourist trip that is motivated by a particular interest in a *leisure* activity, such as a hobby (birding, hiking, sports, etc.). *p133, 347*.

Sport tourism A tourism activity that has sport as its major theme, for example, people travelling to a sports event such as the FIFA World Cup. *p270*.

Stakeholders Interest groups: these may be the product owners, employees, or even the community in the area. *p62, 275, 277*.

Strategic marketing *Marketing* that takes into account an extensive analysis of external and internal environmental factors for the purpose of identifying *strategies* that are designed to attain specific goals. *p265*.

Strategic planning The process of determining the methods that a tourism organisation will implement in order to meet its objectives. *p176*.

Strategy The methods, techniques and practices that a tourism organisation uses to help achieve its aims and objectives. *p238*.

Strengths, weaknesses, opportunities and threats (SWOT) An analysis used by organisations to access their current marketing situation. *p282, 283, 285*.

Struggle tourism A *niche tourism* market which involves tourists visiting historical sites associated with suffering. See also *dark tourism. p270*.

Suppliers Individuals or organisations that provide offerings in support of a company. In the tourism industry suppliers may include clothing manufacturers, food and beverage companies, and equipment suppliers. *p127*.

Sustainable development In principle, development that meets the needs of present generations, while ensuring that future generations are able to meet their own needs. *p319*.

Sustainable tourism Tourism activities and development that do not endanger the economic, social, cultural, or environmental assets of a destination. *p193, 310, 318*.

System A group of interrelated, interdependent and interacting elements which together form a single functional structure. *p13*.

Target marketing The practice of selecting particular groups or individuals (known as the target market), and using the different components of the marketing mix to encourage them to buy products and services. *p269*.

Timeshare An accommodation option in which a consumer purchases one or more intervals (or weeks) per year in a resort over a long period of time. *p104*.

Tour A tour includes at least two of the following elements: transportation, accommodation, meals, entertainment, attractions, and sightseeing activities. *p132, 260*.

Tour operator An organisation or individual that organises and provides a range of domestic, inbound and outbound packages (or 'inclusive tours'). *p132*.

Tour wholesaler An organisation that puts together a package or *inclusive tour* from the various components of the *tourism industry*, and sells them either directly to the public, or to the public via a *travel agency*. A tour wholesaler is often referred to as a *tour operator. p125, 132*.

Tourism According to the *UN-WTO*, 'The activities of travelling to, and staying in, places outside their usual environment for not more than one consecutive year for *leisure*, business, and other purposes not related to the exercise of an activity remunerated from within the place visited. *p3*.

Tourism and Hospitality Education and Training Authority (THETA) The *Sector Education and Training Authority* (SETA) for the tourism and hospitality industries. *p165, 298, 329*.

Tourism BEE Charter This expresses the commitment of all *stakeholders* in the *tourism industry* to the empowerment and transformation of the industry, and to working collectively to ensure that the opportunities in and benefits of the industry are extended to all. *p327*.

Tourism BEE Charter Council (TBEECC) The Council is appointed by the Minister of *DEAT*, and is expected to execute the Government's policy to promote *Black Economic Empowerment* (BEE) in all sectors of the tourism industry. It is also entrusted with the mandate of driving the implementation of the *Tourism BEE Charter*. p327.

Tourism Business Council of South Africa (TBCSA) The umbrella organisation representing the tourism business sector in South Africa. *p165*.

Tourism Grading Council of South Africa (TGCSA) An industry association responsible for grading tourist accommodation establishments, conference venues and restaurants in South Africa. *p118, 160*.

Tourism industry All the businesses and organisations involved in the delivery of the tourism offering, from travel agents to car rental companies. *p15*.

Tourism management The activity of managing tourism in specific geographical locations for the economic, social and environmental benefit of the recipient business and residential communities. *p3*.

Tourism Marketing South Africa (TOMSA) A trust fund set up by the *TBCSA* to raise funds for the marketing of South Africa internationally. *p162*.

Tourism planning A continual process of research and development decisions to create and sustain tourism in a *region*. *p152*.

Tourism policy A statement of the overall objectives of a tourism organisation and its strategies for achieving these objectives. *p153*.

Tourism satellite account (TSA) A *UN-WTO* economic model which attempts to include all direct and indirect expenditures and their resultant contribution to *GDP*, employment, and capital investment. *p157, 170, 295*.

Tourism system A framework that identifies tourism as being made up of a number of components, often taken to include the *tourist*, the *tourist-generating region*, the *transit-route region*, the *tourist-destination region*, and the *tourism industry*. *p13*.

Tourism transformation strategy (TTS) A *DEAT* government *strategy* aimed at developing black-owned businesses within the tourism industry. *p162*.

Tourist A visitor whose visit to a destination is for at least 24 hours, and whose visit may be for leisure, business, or other purposes. *p5, 14*.

Tourist-generating region The country of origin of *tourists*, as opposed to the *tourist-destination region*. *p14, 36*.

Tourist information centre (TIC) A facility offering information on a range of local *visitor attractions*, events, *transportation,* and *accommodation*. TICs play a very important role in marketing their local areas and providing up-to-date information and a warm welcome to visitors. *p127*.

Transit-route region The places and regions that tourists pass through as they travel from generating to *destination region*. *p14, 36*.

Transportation Businesses involved with the transportation of tourists by air, road, rail, or water. *p15, 82*.

Trade show An event, open exclusively to industry representatives, to discuss and share information. *p70, 276*.

Trading A trip undertaken to shop for goods that will be resold. *p24*.

Travel agent A company or individual that sells a range of travel and related offerings to the public. *p137*.

U-commerce The transaction of commercial dealings by electronic rather than through paper channels. *p343*.

Unique selling point (USP) A particular benefit that one tourism product or service has over another similar product or service. *p163, 270*.

United Nations World Tourism Organisation (UN-WTO) A specialised agency of the United Nations. It has a membership of 144 countries, and promotes the development of responsible, sustainable, and accessible tourism worldwide. *p6, 152, 327*.

Unusual attractions Sites, people, places, and accommodation establishments that are strange or off-beat. *p62*.

Value for money (VFM) Mind estimates that consumers make of a tourism organisation's ability to satisfy their needs and wants. *p7, 273*.

Variable costs Costs which vary as the organisation gains or loses visitors. *p228*.

Variability Describes how a tourism service provision is different each time it is delivered to a consumer. *p266*.

Variance A deviation of actual outcome from the planned outcome. This is the difference between the actual cost/revenue and the budgeted cost/revenue. *p239*.

Vertical integration The process in which organisations at different levels of the *distribution chain* are linked in some way to give a *competitive advantage*. *p129*.

Virtual reality (VR) The presentation of computer-generated, multi-sensory information that allows the user to experience a virtual world. *p342*.

Visiting friends and relatives (VFR) A trip which is undertaken to see, socialise with, or to spend time with relatives and/or friends. The person need not have stayed at the relative's house. The purpose of visit includes weddings and funerals. *p49, 133, 270*.

Visitor attraction A designated resource which is controlled and managed for the enjoyment, amusement, entertainment, and education of the visiting public. *p59, 255*.

Volunteer tourism A trip undertaken which involves tourists who, for various reasons, volunteer in an organised way to undertake holidays that might involve helping or alleviating the material poverty of some groups of society, the restoration of certain environments, or research into aspects of society or environment. *p270*.

Wildlife tourism Tourism undertaken to view and/or encounter wildlife. It can be described as a mix between nature-based tourism, ecotourism, the use of wildlife for consumption, rural tourism and human contact with wildlife. *p.270*.

Wine tourism Visits to vineyards, wineries, wine festivals and wine shows for grape wine tasting and/or experiencing the attributes of a group wine region. *p270*.

Word-of-mouth (WOM) The process of people telling others about products and services. *p66, 266*.

World Heritage Site (WHS) A site that *UNESCO* recognises as being of special historical, cultural or natural importance. *p63, 64*.

Yield management A management system to control costs so as to achieve maximum yield (returns) at minimum outlay, as practised by hotels and *low cost airlines*. *p115*.

World Travel and Tourism Council (WTTC) A forum comprising of 100 of the world's largest tourism businesses. It aims to raise awareness of tourism and its benefits as one the world's largest generators of wealth and jobs. *p3, 153*.

Zoological tourism (see *Wildlife tourism*).

Index

Page references in *italics* indicate figures, illustrations, tables or logos.